PLANT CELLS

Botanical Monographs

Edited by

J. H. BURNETT M.A. D.Phil

Professor of Botany
University of Newcastle upon Tyne

VOLUME EIGHT

PLANT CELLS

PLANT CELLS

F. A. L. CLOWES
M.A. D.Phil.
Lecturer, Botany School
University of Oxford

AND

B. E. JUNIPER
M.A. D.Phil.
Senior Research Officer
Botany School, University of Oxford

Fellow of St Catherine's College
Oxford

BLACKWELL SCIENTIFIC PUBLICATIONS

OXFORD AND EDINBURGH

Printed in Great Britain by
WILLMER BROTHERS LTD. BIRKENHEAD
and bound by
THE KEMP HALL BINDERY, OXFORD

Contents

A*

Preface

Little excuse is necessary for a book on cells. The subject has been completely changed in the last ten years by the use of the electron microscope and the discoveries of molecular biology. Some explanation is perhaps required for writing a book on plant cells rather than on all kinds of cells. Much of what we have to say applies equally to animals as to plants and there is, properly, a tendency towards studying biology instead of botany and zoology. We have chosen to entitle our book *Plant Cells* because we want to restrict the range of cell types described. Any book about cells in general faces the difficulty of having to deal with the enormous range of function and structure in animal cells. Plants are simpler than animals and, apart from our own research interests, confining ourselves largely to plants enables us to write in a more general way about the main features of cells.

However, we have felt no constraint in dealing with the cells of animals and microorganisms where it has suited our purpose. In describing specialization of cells, we have usually restricted ourselves to higher plants in order not to spend too much time on specialization. But again we have used algae and fungi to illustrate points of general interest when these points could not be described from higher plants. Also the topics we write about have been restricted partly by our own interests and partly because some subjects are already well covered in existing books. Thus we have omitted a lot of biochemistry and chromosome morphology. The balance of the book is therefore our personal choice and we hope that many people, even without a botanical training, will be interested in what we have to say. For this reason and also because we realise that not everybody will read the book from the beginning to the end, we provide a glossary and an index. Because of the general plan of the book, there is also a certain amount of repetition where some facts are mentioned to illustrate more than one theme. These passages include further cross references to save space.

Between the writing of this book and receipt of proofs has come the adoption of S I (Système International) units. We have amended the text where necessary to conform with the S I code, but we have not been able to alter the illustrations. The most important changes here are that the micrometre (micron) is now abbreviated to μm instead of μ and the nanometre (millimicron) to nm instead of mμ. Equivalents are given in the glossary under *Units of Length*.

Acknowledgments

We are indebted to many of our colleagues for help in preparing the book.

For reading parts of the manuscript, correcting our errors and giving us ideas:

Mr P.W.Barlow
Dr S.Bradbury
Dr B.S.Cox
Dr K.W.Fuller
Dr C.F.Graham
Dr N.D.Hallam
Mr K.W.Harrap
Dr R.P.C.Johnson
Mr R.Lloyd
Dr M.Lunt
Dr C.C.McCready
Dr W.G.Slater

For the use of micrographs or diagrams:

Dr F.R.Anderson, Dr P.H.Lindenmayer and Dr J.R.Colvin (101)
Dr A.Bajer (93 and 125)
Dr S.Bradbury (28, 29 and 163)
Dr D.E.Bradley (118)
Dr D.Branton (27 and 99)
Mr J.Burgess and Dr D.H.Northcote (86)
Dr J.R.Colvin (101)
Dr L.Diers and Dr F.Schotz (43)
Dr P.Echlin (82)
Prof. K.Esau, Dr V.I.Cheadle and Dr R.H.Gill (149 and 150)
Prof. E.M.Gifford and Dr K.D.Stewart (50)
Dr A.M.Glauert (20)
Mr A.D.Greenwood (33, 44, 45, 52 and 153)
Dr B.E.S.Gunning (42 and 54)
Prof. A.L.Houwink and the late Prof. P.A.Roelofsen (93, 94)
Dr R.P.C.Johnson (143)
Dr R.N.Konar and Prof. H.F.Linskens (145)

Dr B.Landau-Schacher (110)
Dr M.C.Ledbetter (38, 39 and 119)
Prof. W.Liese (115)
Prof. I.Manton and Dr H.Ettl (66)
Dr R.G.Milne (35)
Dr B.Mosse (147 and 148)
Prof. M.J.Nadakavukaren (59)
Dr M.M.K.Nass (162)
Dr D.H.Northcote (26, 105 and 157)
Dr D.H.Northcote and Dr J.D.Pickett-Heaps (84 and 158)
Dr H.Öpik (36 and 89)
Prof. R.D.Preston and Dr E.Frei (77)
Prof. R.D.Preston (113)
Dr W.G.Rosen and Dr S.R.Gawlik (140)
Dr S.Schmid (112)
Dr D.S.Skene (80 and 117)
Dr J.Thompson (138)
Mr C.G.Vosa (128)
Prof. S.W.Wolfe and Dr G. M. Hewitt (129 and 130)
Dr F.B.P.Wooding and Dr D.H.Northcote (151)

For permission to redraw diagrams:
Dr P.R.Burton (40)
Dr L.G.Caro (7)
Prof. J.Heslop-Harrison (155)
Dr R.Krull (107)
Dr D.T.A.Lamport (102 and 103)
Dr R.St.J.Manley (75)
Dr D.H.Northcote (156)
Prof. R.D.Preston (98)

For permission to publish or republish micrographs or diagrams:
The Academic Press Inc (London) Ltd (102 and 103)
Acta Botanica Neerlandica (92, 93 and 94)
The American Journal of Botany (149 and 150)
The Biochemical Journal (158)
The British Medical Bulletin (26)
The Cambridge Instrument Company (82)
The National Research Council of Canada from *The Canadian Journal of Botany* (101)
The Chemstrand Research Centre (101)

Imperial Chemical Industries (*Endeavour*) (98)
The Journal of Cell Biology (129, 130 and 151)
The Journal of Cell Science (20)
The Journal of the Linnaean Society (66)
The Journal of Ultrastructure Research (27 and 99)
Nature (53)
Proceedings of the National Academy of Sciences (162)
Proceedings of the Royal Society (77)
Springer Verlag (*Planta*) (145)
Springer Verlag (*Protoplasma*) (140)
Zeitschrift fur Pflanzenphysiologie (43)

For helping us prepare our own illustrations (those with no acknowl-
edgment in the legends)
Miss H.E.Stewart
Mr P.R.Williams

CHAPTER 1

Techniques in Cell Research

The purpose of this introductory chapter is to enable readers to assess the evidence presented in the rest of the book more readily. It is not to provide an introduction to the use of the techniques themselves, for this is better done in specialist articles where full operational details can be given. So here we shall confine ourselves to the principles of the techniques and appraise their value and limitations in the development of our subject. We devote the greater part of the chapter to electron microscopy because we depend heavily on this technique and because we are far from understanding the conflicting evidence which it presents.

1.1 Light microscopy

The resolving power of the average human eye is about 80μm and most cells have at least two of their dimensions less than this so we cannot see them unaided. Microscopes, both simple and compound, were being used in the early seventeenth century and Leeuwenhoek (1632–1723) was able to see bacteria, unicellular algae and protozoa with them. The foundation of our knowledge of cells occurs with the publication just 300 years ago of the *Micrographia* of Robert Hooke (1635–1703) who used the word 'cell' to describe the compartments that he saw in cork and other plant tissues with the compound microscopes that he had made himself. The dead plant tissues that Hooke saw are specially favourable material for the development of a cell theory because the cell walls are easy to see, but they started the search for the cellular structure, which is the subject of this book, as soon as optical methods improved. Robert Brown (1773–1858) discovered the nucleus and Hugo von Mohl (1805–1872) distinguished between cytoplasm and sap.

The modern light microscope is a development of the compound microscope used by Hooke. Its resolving power has been improved to about $0\cdot3\mu$m and cannot be improved further because of the nature of light. As soon as this was realized people began to think about microscopes which use other waves with shorter wavelengths to improve the

1

resolution. The ultra-violet microscope had a period of popularity for very fine work. Its resolution is $0.15\mu m$, twice as good as that of the light microscope, but it was expensive to make for the small gain in resolution. It had two sets of lenses one of quartz for the u.v. and one of glass to enable the lenses to be focused using light (u.v. forms images invisible to the human eye). No lenses are available for X-rays and so their short wavelength cannot be exploited to produce a high resolution microscope. There are X-ray microscopes available, but these use the equivalent of pin-holes instead of lenses and their resolution is no better than that of a light microscope. Their only value is in utilizing the high penetrating power of X-radiation. Beams of electrons also have wave-like properties and these are used in the currently most popular high resolution microscopes. The lenses for electron beams are electro-magnetic or electrostatic fields. These unfortunately have to be made with small apertures because the method of image formation involves the deliberate exclusion of electrons scattered by heavy atoms and so the practical resolution of 0.5 nm is much poorer than might be expected from the wavelength of the electron beams used, which is around 0.005 nm. Nevertheless the resolution attainable by an electron microscope is better than can be exploited by the present methods of preparing cells and the resurgence of interest in cell structure that has occurred in the last 10 years is almost entirely due to this instrument.

The optical principles of all modern microscopes, light, u.v. and electron, are similar. One lens forms a real image and this is further magnified by a second lens. The magnification can be increased indefinitely by decreasing the focal length of the second lens and by increasing the distance between the two lenses, but the useful magnification is limited by the quality of the first, or objective, lens. It is not magnification that we require in a microscope, but resolution, the ability to see fine detail. Resolution is defined as the distance between two objects which can just be distinguished as separate and this is limited by the diffraction of the waves by which we see the objects. In light microscopy the radius of the innermost black diffraction ring around a point object is

$$\frac{1 \cdot 2\lambda}{2 \sin \theta}$$

(where λ is the wavelength of light and θ is half the angle of the cone of light forming the image) and this is taken to be a measure of the distance apart of two points in the image that can just be resolved. In terms of the cone of light entering the lens from the object

$$\frac{1\cdot2\lambda}{2\sin\theta} = \frac{1\cdot2\lambda M}{2n\sin\phi}$$

(where M is the magnification, n is the refractive index of the medium between object and lens, and ϕ is half the angle of the cone of light entering the lens). This is for two points on the image and, if we divide by M, we obtain the distance apart of two points in the object which can be resolved, i.e.,

$$\text{the resolution, } R = \frac{1\cdot2\lambda}{2n\sin\phi}.$$

The smaller R is the better the microscope. $n\sin\phi$ is called the numerical aperture and this is engraved on most light microscope objectives so that its best resolution may be calculated and used if the microscope and its lamp are set up properly. The relationship between resolution and the wavelength of the rays used will now be clear from the last equation. The design of microscopes and their use is beyond the scope of this book although they must be understood if the instruments are to be used efficiently. Some brief mention of three modifications of light microscopy ought to be made here, however, because they affect the recent results that we shall present on plant cells. The three are phase, interference and polarized light microscopy.

Phase microscopy

Phase and interference microscopes are important to us mainly because they allow us to see living cells better than ordinary microscopes can. The contents of living cells are largely colourless and so we see them indistinctly, usually by differences in reflection. The reflection of light at boundaries of organelles is exploited by dark ground illumination in which a hollow cone of light shines so obliquely on the cell that the direct rays are not accepted by the microscope's objective lens and only the reflected rays reach our eyes. The reflection at the boundaries of organelles is due to the difference between the refractive index of the organelle and that of the surrounding protoplasm. In ordinary (trans-mitted light) microscopy these differences in refractive index lead to differences in the phase of the light rays when they arrive at our eyes—some rays are delayed more than others in passing through the cell. Differences in phase are not perceived by us and so living cells do not display much of their structure. The classical way round this difficulty is to kill the cell and stain its contents differentially and much of what we know of cells comes from the careful use of fixing agents and dyes. But these, of course, alter the cell from its living state and the literature on cytology is full of doubts about whether organelles are real or artefacts (see page 22). Another way around this difficulty is now possible for light microscopy by using phase or interference microscopes. There is unfortunately no way yet of looking at ordinary living cells with electron microscopes as we shall explain.

The phase microscope is a device for converting differences in phase, which we cannot see, into differences in amplitude which we see as shades of grey. This is done by retarding the direct-path light rays through the microscope by say $90°$ or $\lambda/4$ and by reducing their amplitude after they have passed through the cell. The rays diffracted by the cell are unaffected and the rays resultant from the retarded incident rays and the diffracted rays vary in amplitude according to the delays they suffer in passing through the various parts of the cell. To do this we use an ordinary microscope, but arrange for the incident beam to form a pattern, commonly an annulus, which corresponds to a phase-delaying plate of the same pattern placed in the objective lens. The pattern on the plate is raised slightly to delay the direct-path incident rays by $90°$ compared with the diffracted rays which pass through the unraised part of the plate. The pattern on the phase plate is also 'smoked' to reduce the amplitude of the incident rays. Various modifications of these principles exist and the image can often also be improved by the choice of a mounting medium of appropriate refractive index.

With the phase microscope we can watch living cells very clearly by eye or by time-lapse ciné photographs, but we are, of course, still limited by the resolution of light microscopes.

Interference microscopy

The interference microscope is somewhat similar in converting invisible phase differences into visible differences though now of wavelength, not of amplitude, but it has further uses. In it, a wave passing through an object is made to interfere with a wave which has not passed through the same object. The object therefore appears coloured if we use white light and the colour indicates the phase difference between the two waves. The methods used to obtain interference include the use of polarizing screens or spherical mirror condensers to obtain a separation and then recombination of the waves. By the separation of the waves we obtain virtually two objects—the real one and a reference object which is displaced from the real object either vertically or laterally according to the optical design. The advantage of the interference microscope is that it allows quantitative results to be obtained because colours can be distinguished and matched. The phase difference, indicated by colour, is proportional to the concentration of substance in the organelle and to its thickness and so the instrument may be calibrated to measure concentration or mass.

Polarized light

Polarizing microscopes give us information about the arrangement of molecules and, as these instruments were used by biologists long before electron microscopes were made, much of our early knowledge, especially about cell walls, depends on them. The value of using plane-polarized incident light is that it tells us if and how the molecules are orientated, for, if the molecules have a preferred orientation so that the substance has a different pattern of components looked at along one axis compared with another axis, the plane-polarized light will distinguish between the axes of the substance and its refractive index will differ according to the axis in which it is measured (Fig. 1). Such a substance is called anisotropic to distinguish it from substances in which the molecules are orientated in a random fashion or evenly spaced in all directions as in a crystal of sodium chloride. Anisotropic substances are birefringent and when ordinary unpolarized light passes though them it emerges so that it may be resolved into two components whose planes of vibration are at right angles to each other and have different refractive indexes.

Polarizing microscopes employ such a birefringent substance in which one of the component rays is either quenched or refracted out of the way so that the emergent light is polarized in one plane. When a second, similar polarizing substance is placed in the microscope's optical path with its axis at right angles to the first no light will emerge. When a cell with anisotropic organelles is placed between crossed polarizers it in general appears bright against a black background because the plane-polarized light incident upon it is split into two components vibrating at right angles to each other and a component from both of these components will be accepted by the second polarizer now called an analyser. If the cell is rotated in the plane of the microscope stage four positions occur in the 360° at which the birefringent object appears dark. These four positions are those at which the molecules are orientated parallel to the plane of the polarizer and analyser. To ascertain which pair of positions corresponds to the polarizer we put another birefringent plate between polarizer and analyser. This plate is orientated so that its axis is at 45° to the polarizer and the background now becomes coloured instead of black. The colour is due to there being a path difference between the two component rays emerging from the plate because one is slowed down more than the other. If the path difference equals the wavelength of green light the background is red by interference after the analyser has resolved both components into a single plane. The plate commonly used is of selenite or quartz cut thick enough to give a path difference of about 550 nm to produce the red of the first order of Newton's colour scale. Our cell organelle itself would be coloured too if it was thick enough to provide an adequate path difference, but usually cell components are not thick enough and so appear white between crossed polarizers without a selenite plate. But when the selenite plate is inserted the path difference produced by the organelle is added to or subtracted from the 550 nm and the organelle now appears coloured. It will be red like the background in the four extinction positions parallel to the polarizer and analyser. If it is turned clockwise on the stage from one of the extinction positions and the colour of the organelle changes to blue or green (an addition in path difference) the original extinction position had the molecular axis of the organelle parallel to the polarizer. If the colour turns to yellow (a subtraction in path difference) the original extinction position had the molecular axis of the organelle parallel to the analyser. Objects with radially symmetrical molecular arrangements will show a red cross separating two blue quadrants and two yellow quadrants. If the molecules radiate out from a centre of the object as they do in a starch grain the top right-hand and bottom left-hand quadrants are blue (Fig. 1). If the molecules are tangentially arranged, as they are in the pits of cell walls, the top right-hand and bottom left-hand quadrants are yellow under the same microscope. This, of course, is true however we rotate the object, but the colours of the quadrants are reversed if the selenite plate is rotated through 90°.

As well as the anisotropy of static structures such as cell walls and crystals, biologists are often interested in the anisotropy of flow which also produces birefringence. The molecules of protein or aggregates of these may be long and, if they are made to flow as in the streaming of protoplasm, they become orientated all in one direction like logs in a river. Birefringence of flow then shows that orientation occurs as a result of flow and that the particles moving are log-like.

10 μ

B 10 μ

FIG. 1. A: Starch grains under a polarizing microscope. When a Red I plate is placed between polarizer and analyser the top right and bottom left quadrants are blue and the other quadrants are yellow showing that the molecular arrangement is radial.

B: Radial walls of tracheids of *Pinus* under a polarizing microscope showing the bordered pits which have tangentially orientated cellulose microfibrils as shown in Fig. 131.

Intrinsic (or crystalline) birefringence occurs in structures in which the intermolecular or inter-ion bonds are regularly asymmetrical. This is the sort of anisotropy found in most crystals and the birefringence produced by it is independent of the refractive index of the medium surrounding the object. In this it differs from form birefringence, which is caused by the orientation of non-radially symmetrical particles in a medium of different refractive index. Birefringence is called positive if the refractive index is greatest parallel to the axis of the organelle and negative if at right angles to the axis.

Cytochemistry and spectrophotometry

The concentration of certain substances in certain organelles allows recognition of these substances where a specific chemical test is available. The best known reactions of this kind are those that produce coloured compounds and reactions can often be made to be specific by selectively removing other substances in the cell. Thus, in the Feulgen procedure, RNA is removed by acid hydrolysis and only the DNA-containing organelles are coloured red. Such procedures may be made quantitative by measuring the absorption of light by the coloured areas by using a microdensitometer. In this way the amounts of DNA in nuclei may be compared if a tissue is stained in Feulgen. The absorption of ultra-violet light by nucleic acids can also be measured, in this case even in living cells. These techniques are usually employed with parallel studies of tissues treated with pure enzymes so that one can be sure about the identification of the substance measured.

1.2   Electron microscopical techniques and the interpretation of micrographs

The science (or art) of electron microscopy is a very recent development. As far as plant material is concerned, most of the work has been done in the last ten years. Such explosive growth has its drawbacks. The wealth of new techniques, new discoveries and new conflicts may be comprehensible to those working in the subject, but the lack of standardization, the dazzling array of new protoplasmic objects with new and often inconsistent nomenclature, and the extreme difficulty that many people have in thinking afresh in terms of nanometres and microns instead of microns and millimetres results in widespread confusion. The purpose of this section is to introduce the standard techniques in electron microscopy, to demonstrate their uses and limitations in order to give some help in interpreting results.

The first thing we must know about the electron microscope is that the specimen is placed in a high vacuum because an electron beam is stopped by appreciable numbers of atoms. This means that our specimens must be thoroughly dehydrated and therefore dead (with the possible exceptions of some viruses) and they must be prepared so as to withstand the impact of high speed electrons and the consequent heating. All this is a severe restriction on biologists and makes it necessary for us to understand the preparative techniques before we can interpret the images we look at.

The second thing we have to know is that our eyes do not perceive electrons. But photographic emulsions react to electrons in almost the same way as they do to photons and this means that we have to rely on the image made on a photographic plate—the electron micrograph.

The plate that is placed in the electron microscope is developed and produces what would be called a 'negative' in ordinary photography. Now we have to admit that, as yet, there is no standard way of printing micrographs, e.g. blackness in some micrographs (most sections) indicates high density to electrons, deriving from high concentrations of stain, and usually indicates either membranes or masses of polymerized material (Fig. 30). Blackness on other micrographs, most replicas and freeze-etched preparations, where heavy metal shadowing has been used, indicates regions of low electron density, i.e. where metal has not been deposited on a specimen (Fig. 118). This convention is, strictly speaking, a reversal of the image given by sectioned material, but is used with shadowed material to give black or 'normal' shadows which help interpretation (Fig. 79). Negatively stained preparations are usually printed to give black (stained) backgrounds and white objects (Fig. 59). Here the virus, macromolecule or membrane is white, in contrast to their black counterparts in sections.

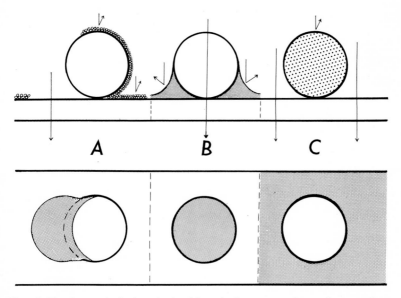

FIG. 2. The three principal methods of introducing contrast in an electron microscope specimen. The top row shows the treatment; the bottom row the result in an electron micrograph. (A) Heavy metal shadowing; the shadow being produced by the absence of metal in the 'lee' of the object. (B) Negative staining; the contrast being produced by embedding the electron translucent object in an electron-dense 'glass'. (C) Positive staining in which electrons are scattered by heavy metals deposited within the object itself. In A a 'positive' is usually made before printing.

The formation of the image in an electron microscope is fundament-ally different from that in a light microscope. In the former, contrast is achieved by *differential electron scattering*, i.e. removal of different numbers of electrons from different parts of the image-forming beam; in the latter, by *differential light absorption* which involves removing different numbers of photons of differing wavelengths from the image-forming beam. Hence material or stains which absorb different parts of the visible spectrum of light to different extents and thus appear variously coloured and dark or light may have no effect whatsoever on the electron beam. The achievement of contrast in the electron micro-scope depends ultimately on the differential incorporation of alien metals into the specimen. Generally heavy metals with atomic weights greater than 96 (molybdenum) are used although manganese (55) is an interesting and useful exception.

There are at the moment three basic techniques for the use of heavy metals, all of which have wide application and capacity for development (Kay, 1965). These are

1   Heavy metal shadowing
2   Tissue (or positive) staining   Fig. 2
3   Negative (or background) staining

In this context 'stain' for the electron microscope means anything possessing electron scattering power, generally, but not exclusively, with affinity for certain chemical groups within the cell. This is obviously different from the meaning of the word 'stain' in light microscopy, but the use of the word is so common as to be beyond reform.

Shadowing

The first metal technique is almost as old as electron microscopy itself, having been devised by Williams and Wyckoff in 1946. Their technique is applicable only to specimens with relief such as surface replicas or freeze-etched surfaces (Figs. 3, 26, 27, 80) or to whole objects, such as viruses, isolated microfibrils or ribosomes (Figs. 35, 77). A heavy metal, such as gold, palladium or platinum, is evaporated, under high vacuum, from a point source, on to the specimen to be examined (Fig. 3). It is deposited on the 'windward' side of the object since the metallic atoms travel only in straight lines, and, in the lee of each object there forms a region free of metal which corresponds to the shape and size of the object. The heavy metal in the deposited area impedes the free passage of electrons, hence more electrons flow through the region lacking the metal coating, than pass through the coated region and, as a result, produce a blacker image on the photographic emulsion (Fig. 118). If the angle of deposition is known it is easy to work out the height of objects by simple trigonometry from the length of the cast shadow. The technique has a number of limitations, which, although unimportant at low magnifications, become progressively more important and limiting as higher resolution is demanded. In the first place, as can be seen from Fig. 3 the deposition from an angle of a coat of metal tends to distort the shape of the object. This is unimportant where, as in the projections

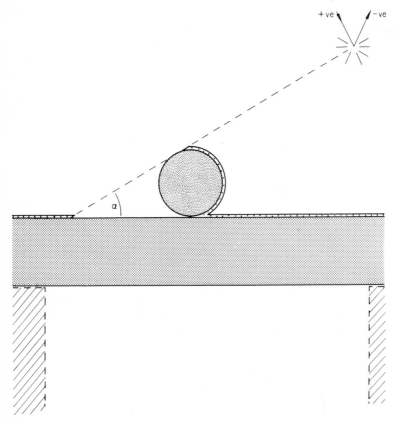

F𝐼G. 3. 'Shadowing' with a heavy metal. A heavy metal such as Au, Pd or Pt is evaporated under a high vacuum from a point source onto the specimen to be examined. The metallic atoms travel only in straight lines and in the 'lee' of the object a region free from metal is left. Through this region electrons flow readily and blacken the photographic plate more extensively than elsewhere on the specimen, hence the appearance of a dark shadow on the micrograph. If α is known it is simple to work out the height of the object from the length of the shadow cast.

from a leaf surface (Fig. 79), the target object is large in relation to the thickness of the metal coating, which is 1–3 nm, but it becomes serious where the object is small, e.g. tobacco mosaic virus, which is only 15 nm in diameter. The second disadvantage of shadow-casting is that all metals deposited in this way tend to form crystals whose sizes vary according to the metal used and the manner in which they are deposited. Metals, such as gold and palladium when alone, may produce crystals as large as 4 nm; alloys give better results producing crystals of about 2·5 nm and the simultaneous platinum/carbon shadowing method developed by Bradley (1965) inhibits crystallization so successfully that the particle size with this technique is probably below 1 nm (Fig. 118).

Positive staining

Tissue, or positive staining, is in some ways analogous to tissue staining for the light microscope in that the stains are incorporated into the tissue from the living or dead state and confer contrast within the object by virtue of the degree to which they combine with specific chemical groups within the cell. In spite of the intense research into electron microscopical techniques over the last twenty years there is still no battery of stains comparable to that available to the light microscopist. Specific stains for specific chemical groups equivalent to leuco basic fuchsin (Feulgen) for DNA, Sudan IV for fats and pyronin and methyl green for RNA-DNA are lacking for the electron microscope and, with few exceptions, the heavy metal stains available for the electron microscope, e.g. osmium tetroxide, potassium permanganate and lead and uranium salts are relatively unspecific or unknown in their action.

It may, in fact, help the electron microscopist very little if a specific stain for protein, for example, is discovered because, at the resolution achievable by the electron microscope, practically all cell components and structures have at least a little protein incorporated in them. Similar difficulties would arise with lipids also.

Progress is, however, being made and Albersheim & Killias (1963) have demonstrated an electron-dense stain specific for the galacturonic acid fraction of pectin, and Holt & Hicks (1961) have been able to localize the enzyme, acid phosphatase, in animal tissue, by taking advantage, through what is known as the Gomori reaction, of the affinity for lead salts of phosphate groups.

Staining may be simultaneous with fixation when potassium permanganate is used or it may take place after fixation when fixatives such as glutaraldehyde are used. These latter have no electron scattering properties, but serve only to rigidify the tissue. Staining may take place before or after the tissue has been embedded by soaking the specimen or its individual sections in solutions of salts of heavy metals.

Table 1 gives all the fixatives and stains in common use for electron microscopy and their particular uses. Formaldehyde has not seen much use in plant tissue and its place has been taken by buffered solutions of glutaraldehyde. This was introduced for electron microscopy in 1963 (Sabatini, Bensch & Barnett) and soon found spectacular application in plant material. Ledbetter & Porter (1963) showed that structures hitherto unknown or unresolved in plant cells, such as microtubules and spindle fibres, were clearly revealed by the use of glutaraldehyde as a fixative in conjunction with osmium as a bulk stain and lead salts as section stains.

Osmium alone, as a staining fixative has not been as successful in plant tissue as it was in the early days of the electron microscope with sections of animal tissue. The preferred fixative for plant material, in spite of its limitations, was, until the introduction of glutaraldehyde, permanganate. This produces excellent fixation and staining of membranes, but fails to fix and may even help to destroy nucleic acids and proteins. It may also cause precipitates of manganese dioxide to form by reaction with sucrose in phloem and vacuoles (Johnson, 1966). Neither does it distinguish the individual carbohydrate components of a plant cell wall. It does, however, have a marked affinity for lignin and the process of lignification can be studied under the electron microscope by using permanganate (Esau, 1965; Wooding & Northcote, 1964 and Esau, Cheadle & Gill, 1966b). Sometimes therefore it is a selective stain and, although it has often been condemned as a destructive fixer and stain it has considerable value provided that its limitations are understood. Osmium is a much less specific stain and, particularly in conjunction with glutaraldehyde fixation, probably reveals a high proportion of the cell contents in a fixed and stained condition. The extensive preservation of the cell (Fig. 119) is often extremely valuable, particularly where fine detail is required, but the very multiplicity of structures preserved means that certain salient features may be obscured. Sometimes, however, osmium may fail to preserve structures such as endoplasmic reticulum (ER) membranes which are known to be present from comparable permanganate staining (Diboll & Larson, 1966) (Fig. 32).

Fixation and staining of higher plant tissue, even with the best combinations of fixatives and staining in the hands of the best operators has never produced such impressive results as those of animal tissues and

TABLE 1

Fixatives and stains for electron microscopy

Fixatives	Contrast-enhancing fixatives	Tissue stains	Section stains
Buffered formaldehyde	OsO_4. Commonly used as 1–2 per cent solution in water, veronal/acetate or cacodylate buffers. Acts as cross-linking agent thereby preserving cell structure.	OsO_4. A general stain for most cell constituents, including proteins, lipids and nucleic acids. Believed to react with the double bonds of unsaturated fats and with proteins at the double bond side groups of tryptophane and histidine.	Phosphotungstic acid. Non-specific general stain, but in animal tissue reacts most strongly with connective tissue.
Buffered glutaraldehyde		$KMnO_4$. Specific for membranes and the lignin of secondary cell walls. May actually destroy some other components such as some proteins and nucleic acids. May preserve membrane structure in sites where this is not preserved by OsO_4, e.g. the ER of root cap cells.	Lead citrate. Non-specific general stain. Reveals microfibrillar structure of the cell wall, when used after glutaraldehyde and osmium probably by reacting with the non-celluosic polysaccharides surrounding the cellulose.
Buffered acrolein	$KMnO_4$. Commonly used as 1–4 per cent solution in water.	Bismuth. Believed to be specific for phosphate groups of nucleic acids.	Uranyl acetate. Enhances the contrast of the nuclear region. May be specific for DNA at acid pH.
		Indium. Enhances the contrast of nucleic acids.	Generally for the greatest possible contrast a section is double stained in uranyl acetate followed by lead citrate, but see Fig. 44.
		Uranyl acetate. A general stain for all cell components and particularly proteins.	
		Hydroxylamine and ferric chloride. Specific for carboxyl groups. Can be used to detect presence of carboxyl-containing polysaccharides in pectin.	
		Ruthenium red. May also be specific for carboxyl groups and thus indicate pectin distribution.	
		Phosphotungstic acid. Used in 10 per cent ethanol. In animal tissue it strongly enhances the contrast of connective tissue.	

the reasons for this are not understood. The slow penetration of fixative and stain through the cell wall was held at one time to be responsible, but the primary cell wall, at least, is now known to be no considerable barrier to penetration and some fundamental difference between plant and animal cells in their affinity for stains must be held responsible.

Uranyl acetate as a tissue stain is now commonly used to add unspecific contrast to glutaraldehyde-osmium-prepared tissue. Bismuth appears to combine with the phosphate of nucleic acids and not with the protein and hence may have some selectivity for all components containing nucleic acids (Albersheim & Killias, 1963). These two authors are also responsible for the introduction of the hydroxylamine-ferric chloride reaction as an electron stain specific for free carboxyl groups in pectic substances.

A stain whose potentialities do not seem to have been exploited by electron microscopists in plant tissue is ruthenium red (ruthenium sesquichloride). Ruthenium's atomic weight of 102 puts it well in the category of electron scatterers. Preliminary results show that it has considerable electron scattering capacity and its supposed specificity for pectin, or, more precisely, carboxyl groups could turn out to be very useful in histochemical tests.

Negative staining

The limitations of the shadow-casting techniques for viruses were soon realized as the resolution of the best electron microscopes improved beyond 2 nm. A positive staining technique in which heavy metals are incorporated into normally electron-transparent particles has had only a very limited success with viruses. A significant advance in virus-preparative procedures was, however, made when it was discovered that electron-transparent particles could be embedded in an electron dense matrix (Horne and Brenner, 1958). The original procedure was to prepare a neutral 2 per cent solution of phosphotungstic acid (PTA), add this to the virus suspension and spray the mixture on to a support film. Droplet patterns of the potassium phosphotungstate (KPT), enclosing or surrounding the virus particles, produce the image shown in Fig. 2B.

The technique is simple and quick in operation: there is very good preservation and high contrast in the electron microscope and only very small volumes of material are necessary. However, the technique is limited to very small particles, viruses, nucleic acid threads and isolated and broken fragments of some cytoplasmic particles such as the cristae

B

of mitochondria. Apart from KPT, a number of other negative stains has come into use, e.g. uranyl acetate and phosphomolybdic acid. Their general pattern of behaviour seems to be identical to that of KPT and it seems that in each case the heavy metal dries more rapidly on the support film than on the biological material and sets like a rigid and structureless 'glass' around the particle (Horne, 1965). The lack of structure within the glass (unlike the crystallinity of the metal within shadowed preparations) and the intimate contact with the specimen are the main reasons for the high level of resolution achieved with this technique.

Preparation of specimens

The achievement of contrast for the electron microscope is of course only half the story and each of the contrast devices described above may be combined in a number of ways with general methods of specimen preparation of which the most common are as follows:
1   Whole specimens, e.g. viruses, or isolated materials such as cellulose microfibrils which are small enough to be transparent to the electron beam without further preparation.
2   Sectioning, of impregnated animal or plant tissue, or of unimpregnated organic or inorganic material.
3   Replicas.
4   Freeze-etching.
5   Dispersal by the Langmuir trough.
6   Scanning.
   Whole specimen electron microscopy is more or less self-explanatory and the only details of particular interest are those which concern the enhancement of contrast on or within the specimen and which we have already considered in the section on the achievement of contrast.

Sectioning

Tissue for sectioning in the electron microscope is usually embedded in resins either of the methyl/butyl methacrylate type or aliphatic-based epikote resins such as 'Araldite' or 'Epon'. These are then polymerized by the addition of accelerators, by heat, or by ultra-violet light or combinations of these three. Only these cross-linked synthetic polymers can withstand cutting down to 50 nm which is the maximum that can be penetrated by the electron beam. A full description of the types of resins available and the techniques used for embedding a wide range of specimens is given by Glauert (1965a). The Araldite/Epon type resins have recently almost completely replaced methacrylate as embedding media since they polymerize evenly in all directions and shrink very little, about 2 per cent, as polymerization proceeds. For these reasons they tend to distort tissue very little and they have the added advantage over methacrylate of being almost completely stable in the electron beam.

Sections for the electron microscope are cut on ultramicrotomes using glass or diamond knives. The bogy of embedding and sectioning artefacts is continually being raised, but it is very difficult to find authenticated instances where sectioning on this scale does introduce distortion. Some materials are difficult to section for the electron microscope, notably storage material such as starch and paramylon and reaction products such as the dense polyphenols produced in plant tissues by wounding or fungal attack, and extreme difficulty has been experienced in the cutting of secondary cell walls (Chapter 5).

The thickness of the section for an electron microscope (50 nm) means that few objects are small enough to lie within a single section; the exceptions are ribosomes at 20 nm, most viruses and a few other objects of small transverse dimensions if suitably orientated, e.g. microfibrils which are 8–30 nm in diameter. This means that common cell components such as mitochondria are cut by the knife in any plane, and considerable difficulty arises in the interpretation of the images revealed. Fig. 4 shows a section through parts of two chloroplasts. As can be seen, only those membranes that are precisely at right angles to the plane of section are seen clearly because only they will reinforce their image through the depth of the section. Any membranes not cut exactly at right angles show progressively more confused and less dense images as the angle away from that parallel to the electron beam is increased. One of the plastids in Fig. 4 shows the very confused and imprecise electron microscopic image of a granum at right angles to the electron beam. Similar difficulties are encountered in recognizing Golgi bodies whose cisternae lie in the plane of the section and therefore at right angles to the electron beam (Fig. 30).

In a good light microscope, the best objective lens has a numerical aperture of about 1·3 when immersed in oil. The depth of field, which is defined in terms of a standard amount of acceptable confusion, is approximately equal to $(1/NA^2)\mu m$. Therefore with the best light microscope objective lenses a depth of field of roughly 0·6 μm is achieved. Electron microscope lenses are very much poorer in relative terms than light microscope lenses because their lenses have to be designed to exclude scattered electrons. The wavelength of the electron

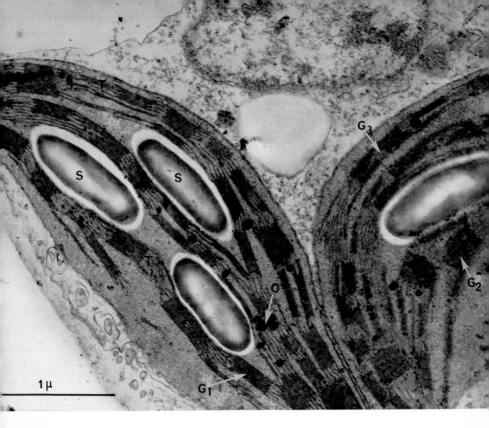

FIG. 4. Electron micrograph of parts of two chloroplasts from a leaf of *Peperomia magnolaeifolia* grown in sunlight. Conspicuous starch grains (S) occur between the thylakoids (T). Granal lamellae, G_1, are cut precisely at right angles to the plane of section, G_2 lie approximately in the plane of the section and G_3 oblique to the plane of section. Osmiophilic globules (O) lie between the thylakoids. (Glut/Os/Pb/U)

beam, which is the ultimate limiting factor in microscopic resolution, ought to allow a resolution some 250 times better than that at present achieved, which is a little better than 1 nm. This relative inefficiency of electron lenses is reflected in the numerical aperture (NA) which, in the objective lens of the AEI EM6B, at the present time one of the most advanced instruments in terms of the design of objective lens, is about 1/200.

The simple relationship between the numerical aperture and the depth of field of a light microscope, as given above, cannot be used for an electron microscope. However, the depth of field of an electron lens can be determined by the following equation

$$D = \frac{2d}{\alpha}$$

(D = depth of field, α = angular aperture of the lens, and d = the resolution. If $\alpha = 5 \times 10^{-3}$ radians and $d = 0.5$ nm, then $D = 0.2$ μm. This means that the depth of field of an electron microscope is much greater than the thickness of the section or other specimen. This is not usually true in light microscopy and necessitates a completely different approach to the interpretation of electron micrographs from that used on light micrographs. It means first of all that the whole depth of the section or replica or whole object, will reinforce or confuse the final image presented to the eye. Hence only if a membrane is cut exactly at right angles by the knife and is thus viewed exactly parallel to the electron beam will a good image be obtained (Fig. 19). It also makes for difficulties in the interpretation of replicas and this brings us to the common and useful technique of replication for the electron microscope.

Replicas

Our third technique concerns those many biological specimens that may be too delicate, too robust, or too electron-dense to be suitable for sectioning. It is, however, possible to get electron microscopic images of the surfaces of such objects by replicating or casting them in a material that is thermostable and of a thickness not too great for the penetrative power of the electron beam. Fig. 5 shows this in diagrammatic form and, as can be seen, such a technique has considerable application in the study of the surface metals, crystals, paints and plastics and, more recently, biological surfaces. A full discussion of replica techniques is given by Bradley (1965). Many materials are now used for replicas; carbon is probably the most widely used and the application of the carbon replica technique to plant surfaces is described by Juniper & Bradley (1958) and a study of plant surfaces using the technique is given by Juniper (1960). Such a technique, resulting in specimens with a high relief, is obviously suited to the exploitation of the metal shadow-casting technique and the final images are often of surprising aesthetic attraction as well as of scientific value (Fig. 118). Nevertheless, as Fig. 78 shows, the image, in spite of its attractiveness and apparent wealth of detail, may not always be what it seems. Consider the image P and the diagram P'. Here the replica has cast the surface of a solid rod and by chance this solid rod lies with its long axis parallel to the electron beam. The vertical sides of the replica of the rod reinforce each other through the depth of the replica and hence show up as regions of high density (white in the micrograph), but the cap over the top of the rod is reinforced by nothing beneath and therefore in contrast gives the false impression that the rod

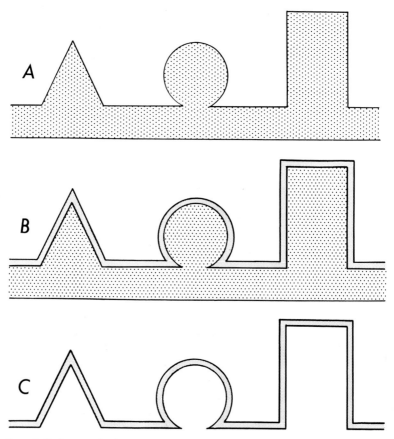

Fɪɢ. 5. Surface replication, The surface to be examined (A) is coated with a thin layer of electron translucent, thermostable material (B). Carbon evaporated under high vacuum is commonly used. The parent material is then etched, washed or peeled away from the replica (C) and this may then be shadowed as in Fig. 3. Note that the evaporated carbon replicates re-entrant angles.

is hollow. Were the depth of focus of an electron microscope not so great, this difficulty might not arise.

The following abbreviations are used in the legends to the micrographs to describe the techniques of preparation.

Glut/Os/Pb/U = Fixed in glutaraldehyde, post-fixed in osmium tetroxide and stained, after sectioning, with lead citrate and uranyl acetate.

Glut/Os/Pb = As above, but omitting the uranyl acetate stain.

Glut/Os/U	= As above, but omitting the lead citrate stain.
Glut/Mn	= Fixed in glutaraldehyde and stained with potassium permanganate.
Mn	= Fixed and stained with potassium permanganate alone.
$LiMnO_4$	= Fixed and stained with lithium permanganate.
Ad/Os/Pb/U	= Fixed in α hydroxy-adipaldehyde, post-fixed in osmium tetroxide and stained, after sectioning, with lead citrate and uranyl acetate.
C/R/Au/Pd	= Carbon replica shadowed with gold and palladium.
Pt/C/R	= A replica using platinum and carbon simultaneously.
St/Au/Pd	= A 'Stereoscan' electron micrograph in which the surface has been shadowed with gold and palladium.
N/S/P	= Whole objects negatively stained with phosphotungstic acid.

Freeze-etching

The fourth, the most recent and perhaps the most difficult technique so far as interpretation is concerned, is freeze-etching. This is again essentially a surface technique, but the surface examined is artificially produced and can be selected at will (Moor, Mühlethaler, Waldner & Frey-Wyssling, 1961, and Moor & Mühlethaler, 1963).

The tissue to be examined is either frozen directly or frozen after incubation for some time in glycerol and water to prevent the formation of ice crystals and frozen too at such a speed, about 10°C per second, that the damage caused by ice-crystals is reduced to a minimum. After freezing in a vacuum the object is mounted in a microtome still in a vacuum and cut (Fig. 6). The surface is then etched by freeze-drying under high vacuum, to a depth into the tissue of a few tens of mμm (Fig. 6). The etched surface is replicated in a manner identical to the preparation of normal platinum/carbon replicas of a surface. The whole operation is carried out at $-100°C$ and at a pressure of $2-3 \times 10^{-6}$ mmHg. The vacuum is then broken, the replica is floated away from the surface of the tissue on water and any organic material that remains on the surface of the replica is washed away with strong oxidizing agents and sulphuric acid. The replica is washed and picked up on a Formvar-coated grid.

The cutting of this frozen tissue should more accurately be described as splintering. The result is that the knife may never come in contact with much of the tissue surface, and the fracture may, in places, penetrate along lines of weakness into the tissue thereby yielding cross-sections, and will commonly follow along membrane surfaces thereby revealing images with a third dimension not possible with conventional sectioning techniques. A freeze-etched, replicated surface is therefore neither a section nor a replica of a complete surface, but an irregular marriage of them both and since the plane of observation of the cell's contents changes all the time, interpretation is difficult (Figs. 26, 27). It is perfectly possible to be looking in one micrograph at a surface, transverse and oblique view of parts of the same organelle. Nor is it always easy to see at first sight where the boundary of one cell or organelle ends and another begins. In spite of these difficulties the technique overcomes the objections to using the powerful fixatives and embedding agents necessary for conventional sections. It now seems, however, that the information derived from the freeze-etching technique has not contradicted, in any major way, information from fixed and stained tissues. This lends support to the view that the basic structure of the cytoplasm is faithfully preserved by such methods and that many of the earlier fears of introducing artefacts are unfounded. Where the freeze-etched picture does differ from the fixed, stained and sectioned picture is in the addition of information. It appears that a few structures, for example the small particles on the outside of vacuoles, on the surface of Golgi cisternae and on the outer surface of the plasmalemma may form a different category of protoplasmic units not so far revealed, or possibly destroyed by normal fixation and staining techniques (Branton & Moor, 1964). The freeze-etching technique also appears to confirm information from techniques of preparation other than fixation and sectioning. The much disputed 'oxysomes', granules on the surface of the cristae of mitochondria, invisible in sectioned preparations and only visible by mitochondrial isolation and negative staining (Chapter 4 and Fig. 59) are revealed by freeze-etching (Chance & Parson, 1963). Although these particular particles appear to be the same size under freeze-etching as under negative staining (c 10 nm), what have been taken to be ribosomes in freeze-etched pictures are 9–14 nm across, whereas the

Fig. 6. Freeze-etching. (A) The specimen is frozen to −190°C. (B) The specimen, at −180°C and under vacuum is cut or fractured with a knife. (C) The cut surface is allowed to sublime ('etching') at a slightly higher temperature (−95 to −100°C), but still under vacuum. (D) The specimen is recooled to −165°C and the etched surface is then coated with a mixture of carbon and platinum. (E) The carbon-platinum replica is then detached from the specimen and mounted on a support grid for examination.

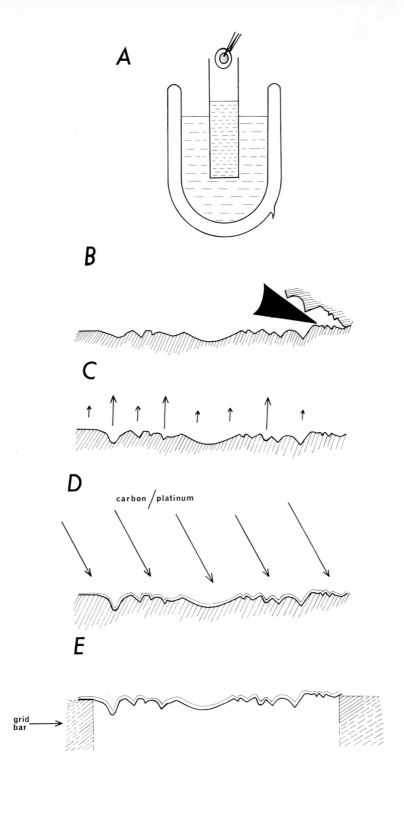

A

B

C

D

carbon / platinum

E

grid
bar

accepted diameters for ribosomes, in fixed and sectioned or shadowed images, are 15–25 nm. But there is some evidence that these are not ribosomes at all, but globular elements of membranes (see page 77).

Langmuir trough spreading methods

Kleinschmidt, Lang, Jacherts & Zahn (1961) developed this ingenious and effective way of releasing and rendering visible in the electron microscope DNA from protoplasts and viruses. Other polymers such as acidic polysaccharides and even whole chromosomes have more recently been studied by variations on the original method. The technique can be used to measure the length of DNA molecules and hence may be used as a guide in determining molecular weights. It has also more recently been used to investigate the extent of single strand breaks in the duplex DNA of coliphage T7, with results that support the ultracentrifugal evidence (Freifelder & Kleinschmidt, 1965). It has been used to determine the length of DNA from *Hemophilus influenzae* (MacHattie, Berns & Thomas, 1965), and the ring structure of mitochondrial DNA (Fig. 162). More recently its use has been extended outside the nucleic acid field to include investigations into whether or not branching is present in the polysaccharide hyaluronic acid (Fessler & Fessler, 1966) and has now been used successfully to study whole chromosomes in meiosis of *Oncopeltus* (Figs. 129, 130), and microtubules and chromosomal fibres from *Triturus* (Gall, 1966).

The principle is very simple. On to a trough containing a solution, sometimes called the substrate, is applied a solution of a basic protein plus the nucleic acid or other polymer which is to be examined. In some cases, e.g. whole chromosomes and microtubules, the protein that is normally present in the living cell is sufficient. The protein spreads as a monolayer on the solution, pulling out as it goes the constituent threads of the polymer until they are evenly distributed across the surface. The protein monolayer plus the polymer is then mounted on grids, the excess liquid of the polymer and protein is removed by a solvent and the remaining film of protein and polymer is then shadowed for the electron microscope usually in all directions on a rotating stage, with platinum or uranium (Figs. 35, 162). The rotation is necessary to ensure that each length of the polymer, which forms a random pattern on the support grid, receives a shadow from every direction. Hence the whole of the polymer's length and not just that portion which was at right angles to a fixed shadow source becomes visible in the electron microscope. Difficulties experienced with the technique are that breakage of the protoplast or virus to release DNA, or mechanical shearing of whole nuclei to release whole chromosomes may damage the long and very fragile molecules or bundles of molecules. The DNA threads may fail to spread with the protein on the solution, remaining in a congested tangle which defies either length or structural determination. Some of these difficulties may be overcome by adjusting the pH of the trough solution and the concentration of the basic protein as a spreader.

These are direct methods for the observation of cell structure and the localization of specific compounds. None of these is, however, dynamic and we must consider two interesting advances in electron microscopy, which enable one to observe and discover not only the localization at any one point in time of a specific compound, but also to follow it through a metabolic sequence in the cell or from cell to cell. These are:
1 Conjugated and non-conjugated heavy metal markers
2 High resolution autoradiography.

Markers

The fluorescent antibody technique enables antigens to be labelled in animal tissue by light microscopy. A fluorescent substance, fluorescein isothyocyanate is covalently linked to an antibody and this conjugated antibody is allowed to react within the cell with the homologous antigen. The conjugated antigen is detected under the light microscope by its fluorescence, in ultra-violet light. This technique was adapted for the electron microscope by conferring on the antibody sufficient electron density to render it visible but without inactivating it. This is achieved by labelling it with ferritin, a crystalline protein containing up to 25 per cent iron. For obvious reasons this technique has so far been limited to animal tissue (Glauert, 1965b) but non-conjugated markers have found some application in plant electron microscopy. Ferritin again has been used in this way as have colloidal gold and saccharated iron oxide, and these electron dense particles have been used too as neutral markers to demonstrate the passage of materials into and through tissue and membranes. Brandt & Pappas (1962) have used such markers to follow the path of pinocytosis in amoebae, and Barton (1964) has followed the uptake of ferritin into plant roots.

These inert markers are in some ways analogous to the use of 'vital' stains in light microscopy in that it is assumed that they have no toxic effect on the plant or animal in the process of their absorption or incorporation and therefore represent faithfully pathways of movement in the living cell, though, of course, the cell is dead when examined under the electron microscope and alive when vital dyes are used under the light microscope.

One of the most powerful tools for the dynamic study of reaction paths under the electron microscope, high resolution autoradiography, has only recently been applied successfully to plant tissue. It does not differ in principle from autoradiography for the light microscope and is described on page 28.

Scanning

A new technique of using an electron beam to scan a specimen, as opposed to the normal transmission electron microscopy has recently been developed (Oatley & Smith, 1955). This gives us a method of examining solid specimens directly, and in many cases is the easiest method to use, particularly if the surface structure is very rough, or has other characteristics that make it impossible to examine directly in other types of microscope or in replica form in a transmission electron microscope. The micrographs produced are similar to those produced by reflection light microscopy, but with a better resolution and, like ordinary electron microscopy, with a greater depth of field (Fig. 82). The resolution of this technique lies midway between that of the light microscope and the electron microscope, and varies depending on the accelerating voltage of the beam used, from 0·2 μm at 3 kV to 20 nm at 20 kV.

The basic principle of a scanning electron microscope is that a beam of electrons, emitted by a heated tungsten filament, is focussed by condenser lenses, into a fine beam which is projected on to the specimen. This beam is made to scan in a raster on the surface by scanning coils in a manner very similar to that of a television set. Electrons reflected to a collector from a specimen are picked up by a scintillator/photomultiplier system and the collected signal is used to produce an image on a cathode-ray tube screen. Specimen preparation is normally very simple. Specimens are stuck on to a stub and are coated with a thin layer of conducting material such as gold/palladium. The conditions under which this metal is deposited are almost identical to those of heavy metal shadow-casting for transmission electron microscopy. Thus it is not possible to examine any very volatile surface, but normal shadow-casting and replica work tells us that thin metal coatings follow very faithfully the original topography and with the resolution possible in the scanning electron microscope, the problems of crystallization of the metal do not apply.

A comparison of the techniques of carbon replication with metal shadowing and scanning electron microscopy on a similar specimen may be made by studying Figs. 78, 79, 80 and Plate 7 from Amelunxen, Morgenroth & Picksak (1967). With the obvious exception of the higher resolution of the former technique there is no significant difference between them.

Image reinforcement

The fine detail of much biological structure lies just beyond the present limits of preparative techniques for the electron microscope. These limits are imposed, however, more by contaminating dirt, minor molecular disarray on the surface of the object, and the finite size of the staining material ('noise'), than by the performance of the instruments themselves or by the contrast of the specimens or their stains. A number of sub-microscopic biological structures possesses either a linear or radial symmetry. The most striking of these are, of course, crystals and viruses, but many others are now being discovered such as microtubules and flagellar components. It is possible to take advantage of these patterns of symmetry to enhance the photographic image. With a radially symmetrical object such as a spherical virus or a transverse section through a microtubule (Fig. 39), the photographic paper is rotated about the axis of symmetry of the object, and an exposure made at a predetermined number (n) of equal sub-divisions of 360°. Each exposure will be $1/n$ times the normal photographic exposure for the material. When the correct value of n has been determined, the fundamental periodicity will be reinforced and the 'noise' eliminated. At all other positions the image will appear confused. In this elegant way Markham, Frey and Hills in 1963 were able to determine the substructure of a number of viruses, and the 'Markham' method has now been widely applied, and in particular has been used to determine the number of sub-units in the transverse section through the different forms of microtubule (Fig. 39).

This brief discussion of techniques for the transmission and scanning electron microscopes will have indicated that there is nothing yet comparable to the phase contrast, interference or polarizing light methods of the light microscope, methods which do not necessarily require the introduction of fixatives or dyes. Every biological image in the electron microscope is dependent on the introduction of metal. Even the freeze-etching technique, which comes closest to the ideal of perfect preservation, depends ultimately on the carbon-platinum shadowing technique to give it sufficient contrast to render its detail visible. The electron microscope, unlike the light microscope, has probably never 'seen' any biological specimen in its living state. For this reason too the best of the modern electron microscopes with resolution of about 0·5 nm are still well ahead of preparative techniques for biological material. It may be possible, however, to use very high voltage microscopes, which are now being developed, to look at living cells. Very little comparative and definitive work has been done on the relative levels of resolutions achieved by the different techniques, but a consensus of opinion from practising electron microscopists is summarized in Table 2 in which the resolving powers are compared. For comparison the best resolution of a light microscope is 300 nm and of a u.v. microscope 150 nm.

TABLE 2

Technique	Best resolution	Working resolution
Gold/palladium shadowing	7·5 nm	8·0–10 nm
Platinum shadowing	5·0 nm	6·0–7·5 nm
Platinum/carbon shadowing	1·8 nm	2·0–2·5 nm
Negative staining	1·0 nm	1·5–20 nm
Sectioning	2·5 nm	3·0–5·0 nm
Freeze-etching with Pt/C shadowing	2·5 nm	3·0–5·0 nm
Scanning electron microscope	10·0 nm	30 nm–200 nm

1.3 Autoradiography

This has been one of the most useful techniques in turning the study of cells from a purely morphological one to one concerned with functions. Although the technique has been known for a long time it is only since the advent of large atomic reactors that radioactive isotopes of biological interest have become freely available. Essentially the technique consists of feeding the plant or animal with some substance containing radioactive atoms and using a photographic emulsion to trace the radioactivity. This can be done on a macroscopic scale to see, for example, where iron taken up through the roots goes to in a plant or on a microscopic scale—the one that concerns us here. Conventional isolation techniques for cell organelles may also be used in conjunction with any method of detecting radioactivity—photographic emulsions, Geiger counters and scintillation counters. Autoradiography has recently been applied successfully even for the electron microscope though its resolution is only about four times better than that produced by ordinary autoradiographs.

The important isotopes in biology are all emitters of β-particles which are electrons ejected from the atomic nucleus. These strike the photographic emulsion which is placed on top of the cell or section and, like ordinary light rays, they activate the crystals of silver halide so that these are reduced to silver grains by development (Fig. 7). The photographic emulsion can be one of two sorts. Either it can produce one silver grain for every few atomic disintegrations or it can record the path of a single β-particle by producing silver grains at intervals along the path. The first type of emulsion is the one most commonly used in autoradiography, but the second also has its uses in localizing small sites of accumulation of emitters of β-particles of high energy. The emulsions

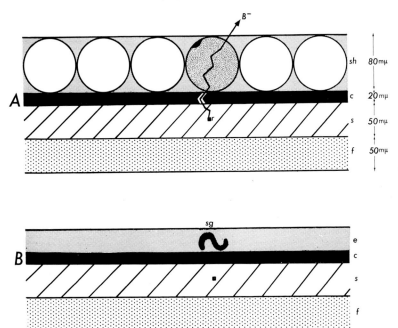

Fig. 7. High resolution autoradiography. (A) The ultra-thin section (s) is mounted on a support film (f) and coated with a thin layer of carbon (c). The monolayer of silver halide grains (sh), in gelatine, is deposited on the top. This sandwich is kept in darkness for several weeks while radioactive atoms (r) within the section give off β-particles that sensitize the silver halide grains above. The sensitized grains are reduced to silver grains (sg) by photographic development; the unsensitized silver halides are washed away by fixation. The whole sandwich (B) is then photographed in the electron microscope (see Fig. 158).

can be solid gelatine films stripped off a plate and laid over the cell or section or they can be applied as liquids and allowed to dry in contact with the specimen. The emulsion is normally kept in contact with the specimen so that we look at the specimen in the microscope with the overlying transparent film containing the silver grains. Under the light microscope the layer of silver grains is slightly out of focus when the specimen is in focus, but in the electron microscope the depth of field is so large that both are seen clearly as if in one plane (Figs. 7, 158). The specimen can be stained either before or after coating with emulsion or examined under a phase microscope. For some purposes the film is removed from the specimen after development once the initial register has been decided on and further films can then be used on the same specimen if its radioactivity has not decayed too much.

The resolution of an autoradiograph depends largely on the thickness of specimen and film and to a lesser extent on the energy of the radio-active source and the mode of development of the photographic film. β-particles emanate from the specimen in all directions. Obliquely travel-ling particles produce silver grains in the film at sites not directly above the place of origin. The further the radiation travels across the specimen and film before hitting a silver halide crystal the greater the lateral dis-placement of the silver grains from the site of radioactivity and the poorer the resolution. Similarly the more energetic the particles on average the greater the spread of silver grains around the source of radioactivity. Of the three isotopes most frequently used in biology, ^{32}P produces β-particles of average energy about ten time greater than ^{14}C and about a hundred times greater than ^{3}H (tritium). ^{3}H will therefore give autoradiographs of very much better resolution than ^{32}P and is the isotope to choose, if possible, for autoradiography at the cellular level. The resolving power is of the order of 1 μm when tritium is used in ordinary autoradiography and about 0·3 μm when used in conjunction with the electron microscope (Salpeter & Bachman, 1964; Glauert, 1965b). At the electron microscope level the ultra-thin prepara-tions used do not limit the resolution; it is the size of the silver grains, which appear worm-like after development (Figs. 7, 158), that restricts resolution to so much above the resolving power of the microscope. Stripping film emulsion has a backing of gelatine containing no silver halides to give it handling strength without making the emulsion so thick that it impairs resolution. In electron microscopy there are now means of producing monolayers of silver halide crystals.

The choice of isotope to be used depends on the chemistry of the object investigated and the availability of suitable compounds as well as on the resolution desired. ^{14}C and ^{3}H can be put into most substances of biological interest but in some positions the isotope is so easily exchanged in the cell that the exercise is valueless. An ideal compound for autoradiography is thymidine because it is incorporated into only one insoluble substance, namely DNA, and its exchange rate is negligible. We shall frequently refer to this substance in its tritiated form. That which is not incorporated into DNA is easily washed out and so autoradiographs show precisely the regions that have synthesized DNA during the exposure of the cell to the precursor. ^{32}P-labelled phosphate, another favourite substance, has several disadvantages besides the high energy of its radiation. It is incorporated into many substances in a cell, some soluble, others insoluble and the exchange rates are often appreciable. Nevertheless these disadvantages can be overcome if it is chemically desirable to use labelled phosphorus. Some of the organic compounds can be removed by washing or by hydrolysis by acids or specific enzymes etc. Specific enzymes are also nearly always used in control autoradiographs to make sure that the substance into which the isotope is incorporated has been identified correctly.

Investigation of the synthesis of substances that are rendered insoluble by cellular processes and are not washed out by water or other liquids used in processing the specimen and emulsion is much easier than investigation of soluble substances. But there are techniques even for these by using freeze-drying and protecting the specimen from the water in the emulsion by interpolating a thin waterproof film, of nylon for example.

It is also possible to investigate the synthesis of two substances simultaneously by making use of the difference in average energies of β-particles from different isotopes. An ^{3}H-labelled precursor of DNA and a ^{14}C-labelled precursor of protein may be fed to a plant for example. Two emulsions are then placed over the sections, one on top of the other. The radiation from the tritium does not penetrate beyond the nearest film, but the radiation from the ^{14}C, which penetrates about 50μm, produces autoradiographs in both films. The low depth of focus of a good light microscope enables us to separate one layer of silver grains from the other.

Autoradiography not only enables us to see where things are synthesized, but also at what rates and along what chemical pathways and how they are transported and broken down. The number of silver grains over each organelle within the resolution of the technique indicates the amount of isotope incorporated either on a comparative basis between one organelle or cell and another or on an absolute basis if the decay of the isotope (half-life), the efficiency of the emulsion in the particular experimental procedure and the duration of exposure are known. Exposures of up to a month are commonly used for isotopes with long half-lives. We try to use as little isotope as possible because of radiation injury to the cell (and expense) and therefore exposures tend to be long, but not so long that chemical fogging approaches the level of autoradiographic blackening. It is always necessary to use a blank control with no radioactivity to enable us to detect spurious images caused, for example, by the chemical reaction of the specimen or traces of fixative with the silver halides.

A particularly important method of using autoradiography is pulse or flash labelling. In this, plants are fed with the radioactive substance for a short time only, e.g. 30 minutes, then they are washed to remove all unincorporated isotope and allowed to live in non-radioactive surroundings for a time before sampling them and preparing autoradiographs. Such a technique enables us to tag certain parts of cells and watch their progress through a mitotic cycle for example. Chapter 7 gives example of this method in determining time parameters of the cell cycle. Northcote & Pickett-Heaps (1966) have also used this technique to chart the progress of tritiated glucose from incorporation into cap cells to its discharge in the form of galactan and arabinan through the peripheral cap cell walls as mucus (see page 250 and Fig, 158).

1.4 Chromatography

With the exception of microscopy, it is hard to think of a more generally useful tool for the biologist than chromatography. When interest shifted from what is seen to what happens the biologists of the nineteenth and early twentieth century sought from the chemists a degree of precision in technique that the chemist was unable to supply. The chemistry of life concerns a mixture of known and unknown substances often in low concentrations; from this mixture each component must be extracted and identified before further progress can be made. The ordinary methods of chemical analysis require large amounts of material which makes them unsuitable for cytological investigations. A new technology which begins to approach what a cytologist requires is chromatography. This, like many well-used scientific terms, no longer means what its inventors intended. Interpreted literally it is the production of a colour scheme or diagram. When the botanist, Tswett, in 1903 passed an organic solvent solution of plant pigments through a glass column packed with finely divided inulin, he observed the formation of sharply defined colour bands or zones. The production of this 'chromatogram' showed that the green pigment of a plant leaf could be broke up into a number of coloured components and that these could be separated from one another by a difference in their ability to be adsorbed upon the inulin.

The adsorbing material must not, of course, be able to react with the mixture of material flowing through it. Neither should the mixture react with the agent effecting its passage through the adsorbent. This agent may be a liquid or a gas, and the adsorbent bed may be a column of material in a tube, after the manner of Tswett's pioneering work, a sheet of paper or a layer on a plate. Two phases are involved in any one system, the stationary, sorptive phase, and the mobile eluting phase. Three kinds of chromatography are recognized which depend ultimately upon differential adsorption, differential partition or differential ion-exchange. Often in any one system more than one of these mechanisms operates; often it is not known how exactly a chromatographic method works, but for convenience we can divide it into these three systems. Adsorption chromatography is usually carried out in columns, using as a solid phase such substances as talc, alumina, magnesium oxide, or charcoal. The last named is frequently used in columns for the separation of organic phosphates. Tswett and the early workers were mostly concerned with pigments and thus observed the formation of coloured zones in the column of the adsorbent, each zone corresponding to a pure pigment. The technique of 'developing' the column with a pure solvent was an important technical step in the fractionation process as the pure zones were seen to separate more and more from each other as development proceeded. The different zones of an adsorption column can either be separated from each other mechanically, and eluted separately, or, as is more commonly done now, the whole column may be washed by a series of solvents with stronger and stronger eluting power.

Partition chromatography depends upon the fact that when a solution of a substance is shaken with an immiscible solvent, the solute distributes itself between the two liquid phases, and when equilibrium is reached the coefficient

$$\frac{\text{concentration in solvent 'A'}}{\text{concentration in solvent 'B'}} = \alpha$$

where α = the partition coefficient.

Paper is commonly used in partition chromatography because it contains a high percentage of cellulose and thus has a great capacity to hold water. The paper acts as a carrier for the stationary aqueous phase of the two-phase solvent system and the developing solvent, usually a non-polar liquid, acts as the mobile phase. The solute is separated into its different components which move along the paper at varying rates, depending upon their different partition coefficients. Silica gel, which also has a very high affinity for water, is now commonly used in columns for the same form of chromatography.

Ion-exchange systems are becoming increasingly important in separation techniques, but they can be used to separate only charged substances such as amino acids and organic acids; they cannot be used, for example, to separate untreated sugars. Columns are normally used and these are packed with a resin that exchanges either cations or anions. Resins that contain acidic or phenolic groups in their structure will exchange cations and those that contain amino groups will exchange anions.

1.5 Centrifugation

The constituent organelles of cells are of different sizes and densities. Moreover the same organelle, at different stages of differentiation of a cell, may change its size and density. Sometimes advantage can be taken of these properties to separate a particular organelle from others in the same cell by centrifugation after separation of the cells and the breaking open of their walls. A centrifuge separates two or more substances, usually particles in suspension which have different densities. The separation of the precipitate and the supernatant is induced by the centrifugal force created within the centrifuge, and the rate of settling of spherical particles can be calculated from Stoke's law.

$$V = \frac{2r^2(D - d)g}{9\eta}$$

where　V = rate of settling in cm/sec.
　　　　r = radius of spherical particles in cm
　　　　D = density of spherical particles
　　　　d = density of suspension medium
　　　　η = viscosity of suspension medium
　　　　g = acceleration due to gravity, 981·188 cm/sec

The settling rate of an object may be increased by:
1　Increasing the size of the particles.
2　Lowering the viscosity of the suspension medium.
3　Lowering the density of the suspension medium.
4　Using forces greater than gravity ($1 \times g$).

The actual g created in a centrifuge is measured as the Relative Centrifugal Force (RCF) and can be obtained from the following formula

$$\text{RCF (in } g) = 1 \cdot 118 \times 10^{-5} \times R \times N^2.$$

where R is the radius of the centrifuge in cm, i.e. the distance from the centre of the shaft to the tip of the centrifuge tube, and N is the number of revolutions per minute of the centrifuge head.

The type of centrifuge needed for any experiment depends upon the RCF value needed. This is determined by the particle size, the sedimentation properties of the particles, i.e. their shape and density, and the speed at which sedimentation is required. Yeast cells in suspension need a minimum of $1,000 \times g$; nuclei sediment in a few minutes at between $1,000$ and $2,000 \times g$, mitochondria need about $12,000 \times g$, but most viruses need between $50,000$ and $200,000 \times g$ to achieve sedimentation in a comparable time.

The centrifuges used for the kind of work described above are called preparative centrifuges. Another instrument is the analytical centrifuge. In this, a specimen is introduced into a cell in the rotor. The cell contains a liquid medium and, under centrifugal force, the specimen moves outwards through the medium. At the boundary between the pure medium and the medium containing the specimen there is a change in refractive index and adsorption of light and some optical device is used to photograph this boundary during centrifugation often using ultra-violet light. If the specimen consists of particles all of the same molecular weight there is a single boundary; if the particles are of two or more significantly different molecular weights there are two or more boundaries, each of which shows up as a peak on the photograph. The position of the peak and its size give information about the rate of sedimentation and the concentration of the substance.

A parameter, which can provide a great deal of information about protein molecules and small particles such as ribosomes or viruses, is the sedimentation coefficient or s. This is calculated from the position of the boundary and is the rate at which a particle sediments through the suspending medium in a field of 1 dyne (or $1/981 \times g$) in centimetres per second. These rates are of course very small, of the order of 10^{-12} cm/sec^{-1}/dyne^{-1}. More commonly used is the Svedberg unit or S which is 1×10^{-13} cm/sec^{-1}/dyne^{-1}, and this unit gives reasonable numbers for the sedimentation coefficient. These for viruses and ribosomes lie mainly in the range 50 S to 200 S. In practice this means that, in a centrifuge rotor whose radius is $6 \cdot 5$ cm rotating at about 30,000 rev/min and developing about 200,000 × g, a small virus sediments about 1 cm in about 30 minutes. From the sedimentation coefficient the molecular weight may be determined.

The centrifuge can give us valuable information about cell particles which is difficult to obtain by other means. Ribosomes for example can be extracted from minced plant or animal tissue and centrifuged selectively. Table 3 gives some idea of the effect of different RCFs in a centrifuge on plant tissue.

Ribosomes are of similar size to small viruses. Like them they contain ribonucleic acid and protein, and may be very difficult to distinguish from them in the electron microscope. However ribosomes require for their stability Mg^{++} ions, and so may be separated from viruses by adding Versene (ethylenediaminetetraacetate) in appropriate amounts. According to the Mg^{++} content, isolated ribosomes can subsequently be divided into two or more centrifuge units (see Table 4, page 110).

TABLE 3

R.C.F.	Time	Precipitate
A few hundred × g	A few minutes	Cell fragments
1,000 − 2,000 × g	A few minutes	Nuclei
3,000 × g	A few minutes	Chloroplasts
12,000 × g	A few minutes	Mitochondria
100,000 × g	30–60 minutes	Ribosomes

Density gradients

Density gradient centrifugation is an ingenious development of the standard technique and was devised by Brakke (1951). The water in the centrifuge tube is replaced by a gradient of densities, often of sucrose solutions of differing concentrations. If suspended particles sediment ideally, i.e. as discrete entities, those of each sedimentation rate move down as a separate zone. Centrifugation may continue until the particles reach density equilibria, and thus the separation achieved depends on particle density only. If centrifugation is stopped earlier a separation is achieved which depends on the rates of sedimentation and may be independent of the density. Theoretically separation according to sedimentation rate will have a greater capacity to separate similar particles, since for two particles to have the same rates of movement through a tube with a density gradient, their densities and their ratios of mass to frictional constant must be the same. In addition to the density gradient, aqueous systems almost certainly have an osmotic pressure gradient and, then, for two particles to sediment simultaneously would be almost impossible. They would have to observe not only the above criteria of similarity, but also must change their degree of hydration at the same rate as the osmotic gradient changes.

1.6 X-ray diffraction

Rays of light are bent at the edge of an opaque body and break up the edge of a beam into a series of light and dark bands, if monochromatic, or coloured bands, if not monochromatic. This is due to interference between the bent or diffracted rays. If the opaque body is patterned as, for example, a grating consisting of opaque bars separated by transparent spaces, the diffraction of a monochromatic beam of light passing through it produces a diffraction pattern of black and white bands that provides information about the dimensions of the pattern of the body if the wavelength of the light is known. This is true only if the wavelength of light (400–700 nm) is of the same sort of order of size as the pattern of the body.

Diffraction phenomena are common to all kinds of electromagnetic waves from radio waves to X-rays and the short wavelength of X-rays (less than 1 nm) has been exploited to give information about the three-dimensional lattice of atoms and molecules within crystals from the diffraction pattern produced on a photographic plate. The interatomic and intermolecular distances of biological material are of the order of 1·0 to 0·1 nm; for example the C–C distance in aliphatic compounds is 0·154 nm and the repeating distance of cellobiose units in cellulose is 1·03 nm (Fig. 72). The wavelength of X-rays produced by accelerating electrons by a potential difference of 50 kV is 0·025 nm. Few of the biological solids are regular enough in their internal patterning to give a diffraction pattern that can be interpreted, but cellulose, DNA and a few crystalline proteins have had their structures revealed in this way. Even so, a protein produces diffraction patterns containing many thousands of spots and these need complex mathematical techniques to analyse. The labour involved in analysis is warranted only for the most important substances.

The X-ray diffraction pattern is recorded on a photographic plate when the specimen that produces the diffraction is illuminated by a narrow beam of X-rays. The diffraction pattern consists of a series of concentric rings or spots or arcs around a centre that marks the position of the direct rays. If the atoms or molecules are not regular in position the pattern is a set of concentric bands. The imperfect arrangement of molecules in cellulose produces rings of arcs. Perfect orientation in crystals produces rings of spots. The distance between the spots and the centre of the pattern indicates the space between the repeating units of the specimen. In some kinds of protein fibres, for example, the spots on the equator of the pattern may indicate the lateral separation of the chains of molecules of the fibre and the spots on the meridian may indicate the distance between the units, in this case, amino acids, of the chain molecules. The interpretation of the diffraction pattern is assisted by inserting heavy marker atoms chemically into the specimen. These may then be identified on the pattern by the greater scattering power.

CHAPTER 2

Dimensions

2.1 Number

An adult man has 6×10^{13} cells. A tree that is many times bigger than a man has a similar number of cells because many of the cells of trees are much larger than human cells. An important difference between animals and plants is that plants, especially big ones, have a large proportion of dead cells. Most of the cells of the wood and many of the cells of the bark of a tree are dead: nevertheless even these dead cells may remain permanently an essential part of the plant body. Plants lose a lot of their cells regularly by the abscission and decay of organs. A deciduous tree with 200,000 leaves may lose 4×10^{12} cells every year at leaf-fall alone. Other organs—fruits, bud-scales, twigs etc. also contribute to the loss of cells above ground. Below ground, most of the roots are ephemeral and decay *in situ*. Animals also lose cells by death: a man loses 1–2 per cent every day in this way and these are mostly replaced equally regularly. Plants replace their lost cells and produce more cells for growth at less frequent intervals because they are influenced much more by the climate than is man. Moreover, plants produce their cells in special, localized regions, the meristems, whereas animals produce cells all over the body, though there are also special cell-forming tissues for some kinds of cells. The localization of cell production in plants is related to their lack of mobility and their method of nutrition which demand a large external surface area. The main meristems of a plant are those at the apices of every root and shoot. In the larger species of dicotyledons and gymnosperms there is also the cambium, a cylindrical sheet of meristematic cells lying between the wood and the bark. Each apical meristem has from 1,000 to 500,000 dividing cells and there can be 15 million root apices in quite small plants and a somewhat smaller number of shoot apices. The cambium of a large tree may have 500 million dividing cells.

The number of cells in a culture or an organ can often be considered to increase exponentially, i.e. according to the compound interest law, $n = n_0 e^{\lambda t}$, where n is the number of cells at time, t; n_0 is the number at the start; λ is a constant and e is the base of natural logarithms, 2·7183. The numbers of bacterial cells in cultures fit closely to this law over part of their growth curve, but there is also a lag phase at the beginning, before the steady state of the logarithmic phase of growth is reached, and a stationary phase at the end when the numbers of cells remains constant. The lag phase is due to the necessity of building up various substances from the medium in which the cells are growing before any increase in cell number becomes apparent. The stationary phase is due to the exhaustion of the medium or inhibition of further multiplication by metabolic products of the cells. This is true of bacteria, but other factors may be implicated in the lag and stationary phases in other kinds of cells. The number of cells in a culture or a growing organ therefore fits a sigmoid curve when plotted against time as does cell size and other aspects of organic growth (Fig. 8). When cell number grows exponentially a plot of the logarithm of cell number against time gives a straight line and over this period the increase is said to be logarithmic.

The extent to which the cells of plant organs increase in number exponentially is disputed. Maksymowych (1959) found that the leaves of *Xanthium* showed an exponential rise in the number of cells during their development up to 116×10^6 for the ninth leaf and 156×10^6 for the thirteenth leaf. Erickson and Sax (1956a), however, found that in roots of *Zea* the increase in cell number was not exponential in early development; nor was the curve of increase symmetrically sigmoid. For many calculations it is convenient to assume that increase in cell number is exponential and this is usually justified when dealing with a part of the meristem that is not losing cells to a non-proliferating state (see Chapter 7). If a whole meristem is considered, increase in number of cells is not exponential because some of the cells stop dividing and the number of dividing cells may remain constant or even diminish.

2.2 Size

Plant cells vary in size from spheres about $0·5\mu m$ in diameter in the smallest blue-green algae to structures easily visible to the naked eye whose resolution lies between 25 and $100\mu m$. The green alga, *Acetabularia*, which is usually regarded as a single cell, consists of a protoplast without septa containing a single nucleus in its vegetative phase and is several centimetres long and a few millimetres across. Even among higher plants there is a considerable range in cell volume—up to about a million fold going from the small cells of apical meristems to the mature cells of some kinds of fruits for example. In root tips the meri-

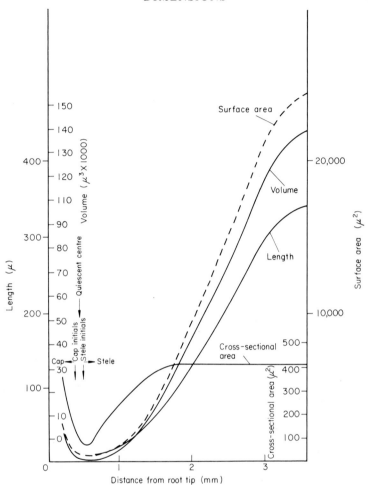

FIG. 8. The dimensions of cells along the axis of a root tip of *Zea*. The root cap extends from 0·4 mm to 0 and the quiescent centre and stele from 0·4 mm upwards.

stematic cells have a volume of about 1,000μm³. Within 3 mm of the meristem these cells increase 130-fold in volume in the central stele and about forty-fold in the cortex (Fig. 8). The fusiform cambial initials of conifers are often 5 mm long and over 1,000,000μm³ in volume and their derivatives in the xylem and phloem may be twenty times this volume. A cotton fibre, one of the longest cells, may be 30 mm long. Animal cells also have a wide range of size. Human small leucocytes are about 3μm across, but the axon of a nerve cell may be 1 metre long. The yolky eggs of birds, which are initially single cells, are huge: when without yolk, animal eggs are still large—100μm in diameter in man. Bacteria range from 0·2 to 5·0μm and viruses from 30 to 250 nm.

Generally it is the cells that are least active metabolically that are the biggest. The size of cells is limited by their surface area-to-volume ratios. Unless special conditions operate, the need of cells for nutrients, respiratory exchange of gases etc, is proportional to their volume, i.e. to the cube of the radius if the cell is spherical. But the ability of a cell to take in nutrients and exchange gases is proportional to its surface area, i.e. to the square of its radius if it is spherical. This is what limits the size of cells as well as the size of organisms and organs. Plant cells have ways of overcoming this limitation (1) by polar growth in which the surface area as well as the volume increases proportionally to the increase in length because the cross-sectional area does not change at all or changes very little and (2) by vacuolation which enables a cell to grow to a considerable size without much increase in the amount of protoplasm. Rate of metabolism is also related to the size of cells. This is seen to best advantage in animals where very active species have smaller cells than less active species.

Concerning the proportion of the increase in cell volume due to increase in transverse dimensions and increase in length Fig. 8 shows for the root apices of *Zea* how the cross-sectional area of the cells along an axial line increases about five-fold in the stele and reaches a plateau at about 1 mm from the stelar initials on the proximal side of the quiescent centre whereas the length of the cells increases over thirty-fold and continues to increase for 2 mm further. The increase in cell volume and surface area that occurs after 1 mm from the stelar initials is due entirely to increase in cell length (Fig. 8). The surface area/volume ratio in these cells varies very little. It is highest at 6·6 in the region of the stelar initials when the cells are at their smallest. After that it falls to 4·0 at 1 mm from the root tip (500μm from the stelar initials) and then rises more or less steadily to 5·7 at 3,600μm from the tip.

Concerning the amount of protoplasm in a cell as it grows, we have some information from analysis of slices of root apices. In a mature plant cell usually less than 5 per cent of the total volume is occupied by protoplasm (Fig. 9). Over 90 per cent of the volume is occupied by the vacuole and another 5 per cent is taken by the cell wall. There are some exceptions to this, notably in the root cap where the mature cells have only small vacuoles (Fig. 10), but these cells never reach the size of the largest cells of the plant as may be seen in Fig. 8. Also some kinds of plant cells acquire up to 90 per cent of their dry weight in the wall. The

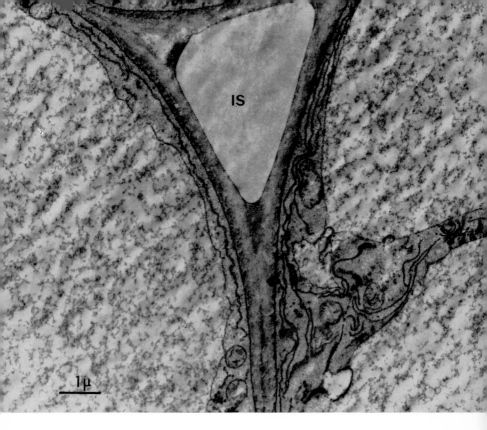

F<small>IG</small>. 9. Electron micrograph of parts of three cortical cells from the elongating zone of the primary zoot of *Zea*. The cells are almost fully vacuolated and intercellular spaces (IS) have already begun to form. (Mn).

average dry weight of root cells varies from 5×10^{-10} g in the region of the initials to about 70×10^{-10} g at 9 mm from the tip in *Pisum* (Brown and Broadbent, 1950). The average cell volume ranges from less than $10,000 \mu m^3$ in the initials to $180,000 \mu m^3$ at 6 mm from the tip in these roots and so the fresh weight is 20–300 times the dry weight. These figures are averages for the whole cross-sectional area of the root and so include all kinds of stelar cells, cortical and epidermal cells and therefore differ from the data in Fig. 8. The protein nitrogen per cell varies from 0.4×10^{-10} g in the initial region to a peak of 3.4×10^{-10} g at 5·2 mm from the tip. Thereafter it falls to about 2.5×10^{-10} g. These figures, which we shall discuss further in connexion with cell growth, show again how the limitations normally imposed by surface/volume relationships are overcome in many kinds of plant cells and enable them to be larger than unvacuolate cells such as the bacteria or some kinds of algae possess.

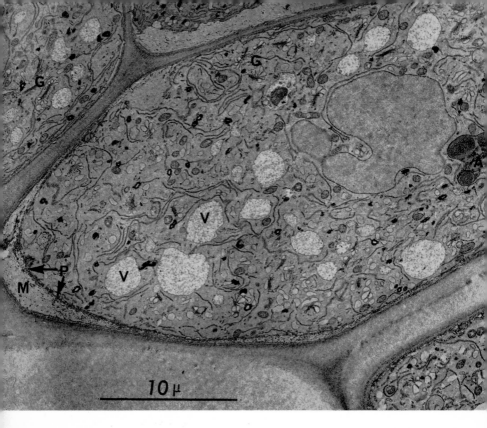

Fɪɢ. 10. Electron mictograph of a mature peripheral root cap cell of *Zea*. Only small vacuoles (V) have so far formed. The ER is distributed apparently at random throughout the cell, the Golgi bodies (G) are budding off hypertrophied vesicles and the material from these vesicles is accumulating between the plasmalemma and the cell wall (M). The plasmalemma itself is highly folded (P). The amyloplasts (A) are apparently shrinking and losing their starch grains. Compare their appearance with those of the central cap cell from the same root in Fig. 30 (Glut/Mn).

Considerations such as these make it convenient to use the mass of protein as the unit in dealing with many physiological measurements. A mature plant cell may have 2×10^{-9} g of protein. If the average molecular weight of protein is 10^6 this indicates that the number of protein molecules of all sorts in a cell is only of the order of 10^9 (Avogadro's Number = 6×10^{23}). The number of protein molecules of any one sort will be much smaller than this, say 10^6. The protoplasm of a mature plant cell is spread 1μm thick or less over the surface of the cell, which we find from Fig. 8 to be about $25,000\mu m^2$. This implies that the molarity of a particular enzyme protein is only about 10^{-7}. The figure for small unvacuolate cells is similar and other molecules in the protoplasm probably are similarly sparse. A concentration as low as this means that there is a strong probability that the molecules will not be uniformly distributed. Thus even before we consider the division of protoplasm into morphologically recognizable organelles we have a basis for heterogeneity in the probability of a molecule being in a particular place at any moment of time. The kinetic problems brought about by the smallness of these numbers are very important and they have, no doubt, considerable morphogenetic consequences that have hardly been tackled except theoretically as, for example, by Turing (1952). He showed how even the simplest system of inter-reacting morphogenetic substances, starting in a homogeneous distribution, would necessarily lead to instability, the setting up of stationary waves and so on, which would give rise to structural patterns such as plants and animals possess.

Some of the factors that affect cell size are concerned with differentiation and are discussed in the section on cell growth (see page 59). Another factor is the nucleus-to-cytoplasm ratio because the surface area of the nucleus limits interchange with the rest of the cell. This is discussed in Chapter 6, but directs our immediate attention to ploidy. Often polyploid cells are larger than diploid cells of comparable tissues. This can be seen most readily in the shoot apices of polyploid chimeras where each discrete layer of the tunica and corpus may comprise cells of different ploidy. Such chimeras are best known from the work of Satina (1959) and Dermen (1945) where polyploidy was induced by treatment of the meristem with colchicine, but similar cytological chimeras do also arise spontaneously. Giant forms of some plants are also due to the cells being large and usually polyploid though other giant races are due to greater cell number than greater cell size and some are due to both. The amount by which cell volume is increased by polyploidy varies enormously. In some polyploid plants whose cells are larger than normal when they are formed the cells revert to normal size after a period either of growth or of reproduction. Changes in the nucleus other than polyploidy can also initiate an increase in cell size. Sometimes the chromosomes themselves become bigger, or extra chromosomes may be acquired and both of these conditions can be accompanied by an increase in cell size. The nucleus is denser than the cytoplasm. It constitutes about 10 per cent of the protein of a cell though only about 2 per cent of the total volume of the protoplasm (Brown, 1960). Why does it not sink in the cytoplasm?

The age of a plant can also affect cell size. This is best known from the studies of tracheid size in coniferous tree trunks where tracheids increase their average dimensions, especially length, with distance from the centre of the trunk up to a maximum at sixty years old in some trees.

On top of this regular change in size there is also a fluctuation imposed by the climate. Average length of tracheids is affected by the number of pseudo-transverse divisions (see Fig. 11 and page 220) that the cambium undergoes in a season to produce new cambial initials. Thus in a good year, when the perimeter of the cambial cylinder has been increased a great deal by pseudo-transverse divisions, the average length of the tracheids produced in that annual ring may be smaller than in a bad year with a smaller increment in the trunk's diameter. Trees belonging to the dicotyledons mostly behave similarly, but are more difficult to investigate because of the wide variety of cells produced by their cambia. Some dicotyledonous trees do not increase the number of cambial initials by pseudo-transverse divisions, but by radial divisions and this kind of division does not affect the length of initials.

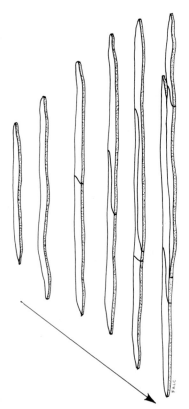

FIG. 11. A fusiform initial of the cambium showing its growth in length and multiplicative division by oblique radial walls to form four new initials.

Another ageing effect, this time in an apical meristem, is seen when the size of cells in leaves at various levels up a stem is examined. Ashby (1950) found a gradient of diminishing cell size in the leaves up a shoot and showed that this was not due to water starvation at the top of the plant as had been previously suggested, but was due to something produced by the young leaves, probably a hormone inhibiting the expansion of the leaves above them. Other instances of diminishing cell size occur in ageing clones of plants. In some, at least, of these, virus infection is the cause and leads to an attenuation of the vigour of the plant.

The relationship between cell size and the size of organs is one that has received quite a lot of attention especially in studying crop production and the effect of auxins on the growth and proliferation of cells. Variation in the size of some fruits is determined by cell size and that of others by cell number. In nature these are both controlled by nutrition, and hence by the number of fruits that survive to maturity, and also by hormonal stimulation and hence, for example, by the number of seeds set per fruit. In commercial practice auxins and gibberellins are sometimes supplied artificially to developing fruits to increase their size, to change the duration of development, or to prevent them being abscissed. Mature plant tissues normally contain intercellular spaces occupied by gas and these can be very extensive especially in plants submerged in water (Figs. 9, 19).

2.3 Shape

The shape of plant cells has intrigued people for a long time partly because of the mathematical content of the subject. As in other topics where biologists have had to use mathematical ideas, a lot of confusion has arisen from incomplete understanding of the mathematics. The problems of form may conveniently be divided into three groups. (1) The shape of unicellular plants and single cells living freely, (2) the shape of cells in multicellular plants where the cells are closely packed and (3) their shape where the cells have spaces between them.

The forces concerned with the shape of cells living freely are surface tension, gravity and other internal and external pressures. A cell that is homogeneous inside, floating in a homogeneous fluid, will tend to become spherical because a sphere is the figure with the minimal surface area/volume ratio. There are spherical plant cells to be found, for example free-living eggs and spores and some of the smallest unicellular algae, but the condition is not all that common. The surfaces of some cells form parts of spheres. This is true of cylindrical cells with free end walls such as we find when a filamentous alga, such as *Prasiola crispa*, breaks into short lengths. Thompson (1942) shows that in such a cell the end walls, if they are similar in construction to the cylindrical wall, form parts of spheres whose radii are twice the radius of the cylinder. The end walls of filamentous algae sometimes bulge outwards in this fashion.

Where a free cell departs from the spherical shape it is due to forces in addition to surface tension acting on the cell at a time when its surface is still plastic. Differences in plasticity between one part of the surface and another lead to more complex shapes and these may be 'set' by

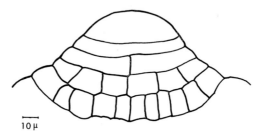

10 μ

FIG. 12. The apex of a thallus of *Dictyota dichotoma* showing the mode of division of the apical cell.

future changes in the surface. So also do directional differences in plasticity and inhomogeneity in the density of the cell contents produce complex shapes. Gravity distorts a plastic sphere unless its force is neutralized by continuous revolution. Catenoids, the solids of revolution formed from catenaries, may arise in this way due to the distortion of a sphere by gravity. In most cases we do not know why free cells take on the complex shapes characteristic of their species, but Thompson (1942) discusses examples of cell shapes on these lines and there is no doubt that they could be explained on purely physical factors if we knew enough about them.

The problem of cell shape as it affects multicellular plants is rather different because the pressures that cells exert on one another become important moulding forces. A cell wall newly formed after mitosis in a multicellular plant tends to meet the existing walls at right angles. This is true in cells with curved sides as well as those with plane sides. Thus the paraboloid apex of some algae divides to cut off an apical cell shaped like a biconvex lens much as in Fig. 12. The new cell wall stays at right angles to the older walls only so long as it is plastic. As soon as it

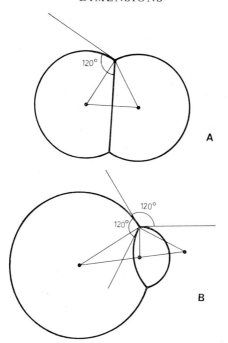

FIG. 13. The division of a sphere into (A) two equal cells and (B) two unequal cells. In A the dividing face is plane, in B the dividing face is part of a sphere bulging into the larger of the two daughter cells.

acquires the same rigidity as the older walls it exerts a force on these causing the walls to meet at an angle of nearer 120° often becoming curved in doing so. Groups of cells that appeared once as files of quadri-laterals in optical section thus become sheets of hexagons. Spherical cells whose walls are still plastic and which divide into equal halves also become transformed so that the dividing wall meets the tangents to the surfaces of the daughter cells at 120° so that the distance separating the centres of the two daughters is equal to their radii (Fig. 13A). In this example the dividing wall is plane. But if the plastic, spherical cell divides into two unequal halves the dividing wall will bulge into the larger of the two daughters because the pressures within the two daughters are inversely proportional to their radii and the partition must, in order to attain equilibrium, exert a pressure equal to the difference between the pressures of the daughters (Fig. 13B). The radius of curvature of the partition equals the product of the two daughter cell radii divided by the difference between them (Fig. 13) and the tangents to all three spherical surfaces again meet at 120°. If the original spherical cell has a rigid wall the initially plastic partition will meet the parent cell wall at right angles. This means that if the cell is divided into equal halves the partition is plane and if it is divided into unequal halves the partition is curved. Similar geometrical principles apply if one or both daughters of a spherical cell divide (Thompson, 1942) and the configurations produced mathematically in Fig. 14 are approached closely in dividing eggs or spores or in groups of bubbles in contact with one another. Thus cells that divide into four by two walls at right angles to each other tend also to acquire 120° angles by the formation of a 'polar furrow' (Fig. 14B) for the same reason that four soap bubbles placed together in one plane do not meet each other at one edge. They slip until only three meet at each of two edges. There are some tissues in which four cells do meet at a point, but where this happens an air space is commonly formed enabling the walls to meet at 120° and, in general, more than four do not meet at a point and more than three do not meet at an edge. Deviations from these geometrical ideals are due to cells not having weightless and perfectly plastic walls.

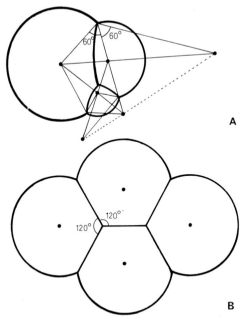

FIG. 14. The division of a sphere into (A) three daughters of unequal size and (B) four daughters of similar size.

Surface tension also leads to the production of isodiametric cells as well as angles of 120°, but this is often upset by the polar growth of plant cells. Also there is a tendency for cells to divide into equal sized daughters, but several interesting exceptions exist to this rule, which is attributed to Sachs. The root hair-forming cells (trichoblasts) and the stomatal guard cells are commonly formed from an unequal division (see page 418). Another of the rules attributed to Sachs states that each new plane of division tends to intersect the preceding one at right angles. This leads to the so-called Errera's law which states that cells tend to divide by walls of minimal area. They do this under conditions of equilateral stress and the most obvious exceptions are free spherical cells and the fusiform initials of the cambium which, when they are producing offspring to the xylem and phloem, divide by the wall of maximal area as does a spherical cell. The cambium is certainly not under equilateral stress, but it is not yet known why the cells divide as they do. Nevertheless considerations such as these help us to explain cell patterns in multicellular organisms on purely mechanical grounds.

Many people, from Stephen Hales 240 years ago onwards, have approached the problem of cell shape by considering what form closely packed objects can take. Hales compressed peas together and concluded that they became dodecahedra. Matzke (1950) believes that it is unlikely that Hales would really have found regular dodecahedra though probably a few of his peas approached this shape. There are two kinds of regular dodecahedra, one with rhombic faces and one with pentagonal faces. Only the rhombic dodecahedra can fill space completely when packed together, however (Fig. 15). Of all space-filling polyhedra with plane sides of similar shape it possesses the minimal surface area/volume ratio. When packed in a space-filling array three faces meet at every edge at 120°. To form rhombic dodecahedra by pressure it is necessary to start with perfect spheres of exactly equal size and uniform consistency and to stack them carefully as cannon balls are stacked. Then if the pressure is applied so that no lateral slip occurs between the spheres rhombic dodecahedra should be formed because each sphere touches twelve others. In practice it is difficult to prevent the figures from slipping and then, and also if the spheres are not stacked, the spheres become predominantly tetrakaidecahedra. Duffy (1951) gives 33 per cent as the number of fourteen-faced figures found when regular lead shot is compressed. Soap bubbles of equal size also produce fourteen-faced figures as the predominant form (36 per cent). The average number of faces is 13·7 and figures with twelve to sixteen faces account for over 99 per cent of the total.

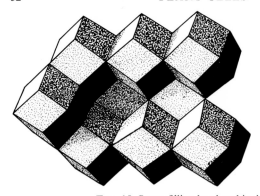

FIG. 15. Space-filling by rhombic dodecahedra.

Fourteen-faced figures are important in discussing cell shape because the orthic tetrakaidecahedron which has eight hexagonal faces and six square faces (Fig. 16) has a smaller surface area/volume ratio than the rhombic dodecahedron and is the only regular fourteen-faced polyhedron with plane faces that fills space. Its faces meet at an edge in threes at 120° and four edges meet at every corner at 109° 28'. The so-called minimal tetrakaidecahedron, which has eight curved hexagonal faces and six quadrilateral faces with curved edges has the minimal surface/volume ratio of any space-filling solid. The change from the rhombic dodecahedron to the tetrakaidecahedron by introducing slip

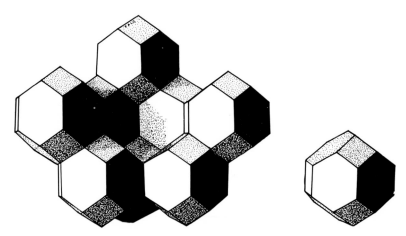

FIG. 16. Space-filling by orthic tetrakaidecahedra.

into the formation of space-filling polyhedra from spheres produces a reduction in surface area of about 0·5 per cent (Lewis, 1943). But the importance of the orthic or the minimal tetrakaidecahedra can be exaggerated since cells rarely approach these ideal figures. As we have seen, even if we start with perfect plastic spheres of equal size and compress them until there are no interstitial spaces, two-thirds of the resulting figures are not even fourteen-faced though fourteen-faced figures constitute the prevalent type in lead shot or bubbles. If we start with spheres of mixed sizes we obtain more irregular polyhedra, though the average number of faces is still near fourteen (Matzke, 1950). Not only do the polyhedra produced by compressing spheres mostly have a number of faces different from fourteen, but, even among the tetrakaidecahedra, few are orthic or minimal. Matzke's soap bubbles, for example, had none with six quadrilateral faces and eight hexagonal faces. The commonest class was that with one quadrilateral, ten pentagonal and two hexagonal faces. Similar polyhedra can be seen in the solid foams made from plastics.

When we come to look at plant cells we find greater irregularity in shape than exists in the compressed spheres of equal size. This is due to the fact that the cells are not of equal size since cell division is not synchronous and does not proceed at equal rates throughout a region; nor does cell growth, which also tends to be polar. Nevertheless the average number of faces among more or less isodiametric cells is usually close to fourteen. Duffy (1951), for example, has shown that, in the root apex of *Lycopersicum* where the cells are compact without intercellular spaces, the average number of faces is 13·85. Polyhedra with from ten to nineteen faces occur, but tetrakaidecahedra predominated taking 25·5 per cent of the total. Polyhedra with thirteen faces accounted for 23 per cent of the total; those with fifteen faces, 14·5 per cent; those with twelve faces 14·2 per cent; and those with sixteen faces, 9·3 per cent. So 86·5 per cent of the cells had twelve to sixteen faces. The commonest polyhedron was that with four quadrilateral faces, four pentagonal faces and six hexagonal faces. This type accounted for 13·5 per cent of the total or 53 per cent of the tetrakaidecahedra. Cells of this type do not necessarily look alike of course. Other common combinations were four quadrilaterals, four pentagons and five hexagons (8·3 per cent); three quadrilaterals, six pentagons and four hexagons (6·5 per cent); four quadrilaterals, four pentagons and four hexagons (6·5 per cent). Only 1·8 per cent had six quadrilaterals and eight hexagons and no other faces like the 'orthoid' tetrakaidecahedra and none of these were regular like the orthic or minimal tetrakaidecahedra. Of the faces of the cells, polygons with three to nine sides were found. Hexagons predominated (36 per cent), pentagons accounted for 33 per cent and quadrilaterals 28 per cent. 70·5 per cent of the cells had none but quadrilateral, pentagonal and hexagonal faces. All the cells had different volumes and none had faces of identical size. There were slight differences between the analyses for different regions of the roots. The work of others shows similar results for closely packed cells though some divergence occurs in tissues with free surfaces and those with non-isodiametric cells. Matzke (1950) found that in the surface layer of the shoot apical meristem of *Elodea* the cells had an average of ten faces and the commonest type was that with four quadrilaterals, four pentagons and two hexagons. Wheeler (1962a, b) found that, in general, pentagons were the commonest kind of face though in some samples hexagons prevailed. Quadrilateral faces were the commonest in tissues with two free faces on opposite sides, i.e. cells of monostromatic sheets. In cells with one free face (epidermises) quadrilaterals sometimes were as frequent as pentagons. The fusiform intials of the cambium also have more faces than we might have expected. Dodd (1948) found that in *Pinus* the cambial cells had from eight to thirty-two faces with an average of eighteen. The average cell has two large tangential faces, six more or less radial faces on each side contacting adjacent fusiform initials and two faces on each radial side contacting ray initials. Wheeler (1955) showed that the special kind of criss-cross division that occurs in monocotyledons with secondary growth in thickness when the primary meristem mantle becomes the secondary thickening meristem leads to a higher than usual number of faces in the meristematic cells —15·4 ±0·3 in *Aloe barbadensis*. Here, triangles and heptagons are formed at the expense of hexagons. Ordinary division also changes the number of faces per cell, of course. For example, in the *Elodea* cells already mentioned, the average number of faces is 11·7 before division and 9·3 afterwards (Matzke, 1950). Division of one cell while reducing the average number of faces in its own progeny, will add faces to adjoining cells.

Four rhombic dodecahedra meet at a point (Fig. 15) and this arrangement is unstable as we have seen. Lewis (1943) has shown how these points become eliminated by pressure and sliding so that a mass of fitting dodecahedra become orthic tetrakaidecahedra if the pressure is applied parallel to the axes. If the pressure is not parallel to the axes, the rhombic dodecahedra are converted into a wide range of polyhedra. Lewis has calculated what these polyhedra will be. There will be 729 different polyhedra with quadrilateral, pentagonal and/or hexagonal and no other faces. The number of faces will vary from twelve to eighteen with an average of fourteen and the commonest class fourteen. The percentages of faces with x sides may be shown to be:

x	12	13	14	15	16	17	18
%	9	26	33	22	8	1·6	0·14

The most frequent class of polyhedron will be that with three quadrilateral faces, six pentagonal faces and four hexagonal faces and these will account for 16 per cent of the total. Only 0·4 per cent of the polyhedra will be orthoid tetrakaidecahedra. The similarity between these calculations and the kinds of cells actually found in plant tissues is sufficiently good, even though the calculations start with solids of equal size, for there to be little doubt about the effect that space-filling has on the shape of cells.

Polar growth of cells and flattening will both lead to departures from polyhedra with minimal surface area. Cell division affects shape, as we have shown, in reducing the average number of faces in the progeny of the dividing cells. But it also leads to an increase in the number of faces in neighbouring cells. Lewis (1943) has calculated that, if a cell plate formed after mitosis meets on average six faces of the cell, the average number of faces per cell will stay at fourteen. If it meets less than six faces, the average number of faces in the tissue will decrease, if more than six, the average will increase. The tendency of plant cells to occur in columns because of the predominantly longitudinal growth and consequent predominantly transverse division also affects the shape.

The shapes of cells that have spaces between them is determined by their arrangement and, in some, by the forces exerted by surrounding cells. In plants it is common for the cells of meristems to be compact, but for the adult tissues to have intercellular spaces which often account for 10 per cent of the volume in parenchyma and may reach 30 per cent of the volume in the mesophyll of leaves and even higher percentages in other aerenchymas. These intercellular spaces arise by the separation of cells as they grow and round off when their meristematic activity is mostly over (Fig. 9). The spaces, which are usually occupied by gas, do not occur in all parts of the plant body. They are commonest in large-celled parenchymatous tissues such as the cortex and pith of stems and roots and in fleshy fruits and are mostly absent from the regions of the vascular system, the periphery of organs and near the endodermis. In the central cortex of roots, for example, the parenchymatous cells become cylinders with elliptical cross-sections, touching neighbouring cells only over restricted areas of their vertical walls. The end walls do not separate from

C*

each other so readily. The reason for the development of air spaces is presumably that the expansion of outer tissues allows for a greater expansion in volume of the inner regions than can be accommodated by the growth of the constituent cells. These become convex and rounded though remaining attached to contiguous cells at some areas, possibly where plasmodesmata are well developed. Where the expansion of the outer tissues is considerably greater than can be matched by the cell growth within, a conspicuous aerenchyma develops with the inner cells becoming stellate by the stretching of the cells which adhere at points of contact. This is what happens in the formation of the spongy mesophyll of leaves according to Avery (1933). In *Nicotiana* the air spaces do not occur until the leaf is about 100 mm long. The cells of the epidermis stop dividing earlier than the other cells of the leaf, but they go on enlarging after the cells of the mesophyll have stopped growing, producing large schizogenous spaces in the spongy layer and small ones in the palisade layer whose cells finish dividing a little later than the spongy cells. The reciprocal pulls exerted by the spongy cells on the epidermis result in the distortion of the epidermal cells to become sinuous especially on the side next to the spongy mesophyll. On the other (upper) side the distortion is reduced by the intervention of the palisade layer.

The amount of stellation produced in cells by the processes described above varies considerably. In some leaves the mesophyll cells have only slightly concave faces, in others stellation is more conspicuous. The best known of the more regular stellate cells are those in the pith of some species of *Juncus* (Fig. 17). In these there are up to about twelve long arms to each cell connected at their ends to other similar cells forming a fairly regular three-dimensional array. Presumably the cells were originally close-packed dodecahedra and they have been stretched to become dodecahedral stars by the outer region of the stem expanding both lengthways and in girth. In other species of *Juncus* with aerenchymatous pith, two dimensional stars with about six arms exist and are presumably formed either from monostromatic sheets of cells originally in hexagonal packing or from blocks of cells that are stretched horizontally, but not vertically.

So far we have considered cell shape as something that is largely determined by forces outside the cell itself—gravity, pressure of surrounding cells and tensions exerted by surrounding cells. But there are also factors inherent in the cell itself that decide its shape. This is obvious when we think of idioblasts, cells of peculiar shape or structure embedded in a tissue of different cells (Fig. 18). But it is also true of ordinary plant cells. Growth of a cell has been considered to be due partially to the

F IG. 17. A: Separated stellate cells from the pith of *Juncus*. (Dark ground illumination.)

B: Stellate cells in pith of *Juncus* seen in transverse section of stem. (See also Fig. 94.)

turgor pressure of the cell forcing the cell wall to yield. The pressure is exerted equally in all directions, but the wall does not yield equally all over except in spherical cells, which, as we have seen, are not all that common even among free-living cells and are rare in multicellular plant bodies. The non-uniform growth of cell walls can be partly explained by external forces as we have seen, but there is much evidence to show that it is also partly due to their anisotropy. The cellulose molecules are ordered in parallel arrays of microfibrils which are arranged usually so that they run round the longitudinal walls almost transversely (see Chapter 5). Experiments by Green (1962) on the large-celled alga, *Nitella*, and the coenocytic alga, *Bryopsis*, show that there is a causal relationship between the orientation of the microfibrils and the direction of stretching of every part of the cell wall. Thus it is likely that the normal polar growth of cells is at least partly due to the restraint exerted by the microfibrils on transverse expansion and this causes the cells to become cylindrical rather than spherical. The cellulose microfibrils are laid down in their correct orientation by the cytoplasm and the mechanism for this is discussed in Chapter 5. Green holds that the cytoplasmic elements responsible for orientation are themselves orientated at right angles to the microfibrils that they produce. This is disputed by most other workers (see Chapter 5), but it is probably true that it is the orientation of the cytoplasmic elements that is upset by agents, such as colchicine and, as a

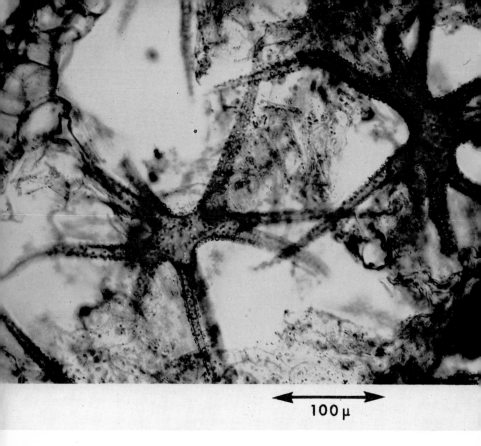

100 μ

FIG. 18. Sclereid idioblasts in a floating leaf of *Nymphaea alba*.

consequence, the parallel arrays of microfibrils are disorganized so interfering with the polar growth of cells. Many plant cells have several layers
of microfibrils sometimes orientated differently in each layer, but the
inner layers are produced mostly after cell growth has ceased and it is
the outer first layer which must influence cell shape the most (Figs. 77,
120).

The actual course of surface growth of a cell involves a complex geometrical study which has rarely been attempted, but which is now becoming worth doing as we acquire more knowledge of the submicroscopic
structure of cells. Green (1965a, b) has used anion exchange resin beads
and other particles placed on the surface of the cells of *Nitella* to watch
their displacement relative to each other as the plant grows. He found
that, in the lenticular apical cells of the main axes, both the meridional
and the latitudinal rates of growth increased towards the tip of the cell
so that the rate of area expansion of the wall was much higher at the summit than at the base. In spite of this, a marker placed on the summit

remained there during the period of observation. This last point is of interest in the study of apical meristems because Soma and Ball (1963) have found considerable flux at the summit of the multicellular shoot apices of higher plants so that the summit cells are continuously being displaced to the flanks and replaced by cells moving up from the flanks. Green's technique also shows that during the early part of the existence of an apical cell in *Nitella* the latitudinal component of growth near the base is greater than the meridional and yet, in the cell cut off from its base, it is the meridional component that is greatest. The surface of the apical cell near the summit grows isotropically. Green considers that the transverse expansion of the apical cell may align the wall fibrils and also the cytoplasmic precursors of wall texture into arrays that subsequently decide the growth rates in different directions of the cells derived from the apical cell.

2.4   Growth

One of the characteristics of living things is their ability to use the resources of their environment to add to their own size. In this they are not unique, but the way in which they do it is. In unicellular organisms the constituent cells grow and then divide into two separated cells. In larger organisms each cell grows and then divides into two cells which remain together. In the most complex organisms with cells of many different kinds there is some restriction on which cells grow and divide and this is developed to its greatest extent in plants and other branching organisms where growth is restricted to special regions especially at the tips of the branches. Thus cell growth and cell division go together and, in plants it is easiest to study cell growth not by watching cells grow, but by examining a growth region in which the cells at different distances from a point represent phases in growth. This is the reason why so many studies of cell growth come from analyses of root tips. As a simplification we may regard a root tip as consisting of (1) an initiating region in which the cells are continuously generating new cells (2) a region in which the cells continue to grow and divide but where growth becomes more prominent than division and so the average cell is larger and (3) a region in which cell growth occurs but no division. These three regions merge into one another and occur at successively remoter points from the tip. The very tip of a root is occupied by a cap with its own initials and this is separated from the initiating region of the rest of the root by a region in which neither growth nor division occur (Fig. 136). It should be noted that the device of using distance from the tip as a substitute for a time axis has its faults because the course of differentiation may change, but it is very convenient and many of the features of growth elucidated by its use have been confirmed by using a real time axis albeit with great labour. The simplicity of the plant system has enabled us to investigate growth phenomena here more fully than in animals.

The general features of cell growth resemble those of other aspects of organic growth like growth of whole organs or multiplication of free-living cells. The growth curve is sigmoid as can be seen in Fig. 8 for length, cross-sectional area, surface area and volume of stelar cells in the roots of *Zea*. The distance over which growth occurs depends upon the width of the root and its vigour and therefore upon the species, the root's position on the plant and its environment. The magnitude of growth in a plant cell is generally higher than in animals partly because so much of the differentiated cell is taken up by the large vacuoles which animal cells lack. Yet the growth of a plant cell is not a simple distension of an elastic sac by the ingress of water. It is true that the water content increases more rapidly than other components, but the dry weight also increases over tenfold in roots of *Pisum* (Brown, Reith & Robinson, 1952) and goes on increasing after the maximal volume is attained. Much of the increase in dry weight can be accounted for in the growth of the cell wall, but the protein also increases to about ten-fold at the maximum and then falls slightly (Brown & Broadbent, 1950). There is a concomitant rise and then a fall in respiration. Brown and his colleagues also provide data on the enzyme content of cells during growth and, for many of them, there is an increase up to the end of the growth period and then a fall, though there are differences between the patterns of activity for different enzymes.

The limits set to the extent of cell size have already been discussed in the section on cell size (see page 45), but it should be mentioned here that they are not determined by a check to the elastic stretch of the wall because turgor pressure does not increase steadily with growth (Brown & Robinson, 1955). The relation between the physical properties of walls and growth is discussed in Chapter 5. The differences found between the sizes of cells in an organ are largely caused by the differences in the relative times of cessation of cell division in the meristem. Thus, in roots, the central stele is the first region within the meristem to stop cell division and consequently contains the largest cells higher up the root, within the mature parts. Central regions generally are the ones with the largest cells in nearly all organs though the reason for this is not known. One theory is that oxygen content is lowest in the centre of the organ and this dictates the early cessation of mitosis, but there is little evidence to substantiate the theory and it could not explain the situation in the cortex of roots. Here it is the middle cells that stop dividing first and become the largest in the mature parts. The inner and outer cortical cells go on dividing for a longer time although one might expect the inner cells to be more deprived of oxygen than the middle ones, which also develop intercellular gas spaces earlier than the inner and outer cortex. The cells of the central stele of the roots shown in Fig. 8 grow over 170-fold from about $800\mu m^3$ to $140,000\mu m^3$ at 3 mm distance from the initials. The epidermal cells of the same root reach a volume of $23,000\mu m^3$ over the same distance starting from the same volume as the stelar initials—an increase of twenty-nine-fold. The inner cortical cells grow forty-five-fold to reach $36,000\mu m^3$. The inner cortex and the epidermis have a much longer lag phase of enlargement than the central stele because their cells continue dividing for a longer time and this restricts the size of their cells over the first millimeter from the initials. Brown and Broadbent (1950) provide figures from macerated root slices for the average volumes of all the different kinds of cells over the cross-sectional area of roots at a range of distances from the tip. For *Pisum* the average volume reaches $180,000\mu m^3$ at 5 mm from the tip starting from $7,000\mu m^3$. Over the same distance the protein-nitrogen per cell increases eleven-fold and then falls off slightly above 5 mm from the tip. The maximum value for protein-nitrogen per cell per unit cell volume occurs at only 1 mm from the tip.

In many investigations of rates of growth of cells it is elongation of the cell rather than changes in volume that have been measured. Much of this work has been done on the root tips of *Vicia faba* by people primarily interested in radiation effects on cells and an example of this work is the very detailed account given by Gray and Scholes (1951). Under their conditions of growth, the rate of elongation of unirradiated roots is $900\mu m$ per hour and the average rate of cell elongation is $6·1\mu m$ per hour. The whole elongation of a cell to its maximal length, $156\mu m$, takes 20 hours. The elongating region of the root extends to 9·7 mm beyond the meristem which occupies only 2·9 mm of the tip and contains a quarter of a million cells. These figures for growth rates are averages for all the cells of the root.

So far, in this section, we have considered cell growth in terms of volume or protoplasmic mass. There remains some consideration of the polarity of cell growth. Some aspects of this we have already mentioned in the section on size (see page 40) because it affects the limitation of cell size imposed by the surface area-to-volume ratio. In stems and roots, cells grow most in the direction of the axis of the organ. In leaves there is no preferred axis of growth in many plants, though the palisade mesophyll usually elongates at right angles to the surface. Sinnott (1944) investigated the relation of cell growth to the shape of gourd fruits in the Cucurbitaceae. In this family the fruits have many different shapes, some are elongated along the axis and, in some, most expansion is perpendicular to the axis giving a disc-shaped organ. Sinnott demonstrated that the shape of the fruit reflects the mitotic axis of the cells. In the elongated gourds the majority of mitotic spindles are orientated parallel to the fruit axis whereas similar numbers of mitotic spindles could be found at all angles from 0 to 90° to the axis in the isodiametric fruits. The spindles themselves do not determine the plane of cell division, for they roll around as may be seen by plotting their orientation between metaphase and telophase or by watching ciné films of mitosis (see page 224). But there is a relation between the orientation of the new wall laid down after mitosis and the direction of cell growth. Growth is normally perpendicular to the new wall. We can think of whatever determines the orientation of the new wall as determining the polarity of growth of the new cells or we can consider the polarity of growth of the old cell as determining the orientation of the new wall. These two ideas are not really alternatives except for simplifying the analysis of a particular morphogenetic situation.

This discussion of the orientation of cell growth and division in relation to the future shape of an organ raises a problem of the cell theory. Should we regard the cell as a unit where morphogenetic factors operate so that we think of the activities of each cell as helping to determine the characters of the plant? Or should we regard the whole mass of the individual plant as the unit? In this case the way it is partitioned into cells is of only secondary importance. As with other enigmas of this sort which acquire an element of mysticism about them, the difficulty is forced on us by our methods of analysis. The problem is slightly different in animals where the mobility of cells often determines the direction of growth in an embryo.

Concerning the polarity of growth and orientation of dividing walls in free-living cells most of our experimental information comes from *Fucus* zygotes. Centrifugation and gradients of light, heat, electrical potential and of various chemical substances are known to affect the direction of growth or the plane of the first division. In many eggs, the point of entry of the sperm cell can determine these. The recent work on freely suspended cultures of somatic plant cells shows the plane of division to be unrelated to the morphological features of the cell and unpredictable, though we shall see (see page 227) that it probably becomes predictable at some time before the onset of mitosis.

Once a cell has divided, its daughters have an obvious physical basis for polarity, for, as R. Brown (1958b) has pointed out, the half-spindles give the daughter cells a gradient of cytoplasmic make up. The end of the daughter cell containing the remnants of the pole of the spindle are different from the end containing the remnants of the equator and the new wall not only in the remnants it contains, but also in the organelles it excludes or attracts. If more divisions occur in the progeny parallel to the original dividing wall, the differences between the ends of the file of cells so produced will be enhanced. This kind of origin of heterogeneity may be responsible for the divergent differentiation of two sister cells such as happens in the epidermis of some roots where one cell becomes a trichoblast and its sister a normal epidermal cell or in leaves where one cell becomes a stomatal mother cell and its sister a normal epidermal cell. The trichoblast is the sister nearest the tip of the root and in monocotyledons the stomatal mother cell is the sister nearest the leaf tip. Avers (1963) has shown that there is a heterogeneous distribution of the endoplasmic reticulum preceding the onset of the unequal division that gives rise to a trichoblast and its sister in *Phleum*.

The relationship between cell growth and division has been studied closely in meristems, especially in roots. Generally what happens is that a cell grows, reaches a critical size, and then divides. It may, of course, turn out to be more useful to think of the process the other way round; the cell divides into two and each daughter is then stimulated to grow. We do not yet know how the relationship between growth and division is controlled. Division is not necessarily accompanied by growth. In many animal and plant embryos little or no growth occurs during the early development, and division leads therefore to a progressive decrease in average cell size. This can, of course, also occur when the organism is growing. The size of cells in shoot apices sometimes shows a progressive diminution with age although the cells are growing. In apical meristems, cell division limits the extent of growth of any one cell, though it does not appear to upset the constancy of growth rates within a cell complex. Thus Sinnott (1939) has shown that logarithmic growth is continued smoothly even when the means of growth changes from cell multiplication to cell enlargement. When division stops, the cells still go on growing and Goodwin and Avers (1956) have shown that the relative elemental growth rate, $\delta(\delta x/\delta t)/\delta x$, reaches a maximum outside the meristem in root tips. This maximum is as high as $1 \cdot 1 \mu m$ per $1 \mu m$ per hour in the epidermis of *Phleum* roots. In *Zea* Erickson & Sax (1956a) have shown that the relative elemental rate of cell formation reaches its maximum of $0 \cdot 16$ per hour at $1 \cdot 25$ mm from the tip in the region where the relative rate of change of mean cell length is still negative. In this plant the relative elemental rate of elongation reaches its maximum at 4 mm. Cells outside the meristem that have gone through the full extent of their growth cycle are not incapable of further division. In plants, though not in animals, all cells retain their potentiality for division so long as they retain their nuclei and cytoplasm, but, in normal development, division becomes less probable as a cell grows and it requires a special stimulus such as wounding or an artificial supply of hormone to stimulate cells into mitosis. When stimulation occurs the cells change their affinity for stains probably by increasing their cytoplasmic RNA content before mitosis occurs. This process, which is called dedifferentiation although the cells do not always revert completely to the condition of cells of typical meristems, is necessary before cells can change the course of their differentiation. It occurs, where lateral root primordia will be formed. The cells in these regions are fully differentiated parenchymatous cells in most kinds of roots, though not in all, and they undergo dedifferentiation and cell division and their progeny organize themselves into a primordium whose cells resemble those of an apical meristems in being isodiametric and non-vacuolate.

It is generally held, though without certainty, that auxins control the growth of cells in plants. It is thought that auxins are produced in the meristem or other young tissue and that they affect the growth, especially the elongation of the cells in the elongating zone. We know that externally supplied auxins, such as IAA and gibberellins, do affect cell growth, but it is still not clear what happens in nature. Externally supplied auxins are usually provided at concentrations much higher than a cell is likely to experience from the plant's own auxin, but we know very little about the distribution of natural auxin on the cellular scale where the knowledge would be useful, because assay methods are inadequate. The position is further complicated because cells at different phases of development re-act differently to IAA and to other growth substances both in growth, which may be promoted or inhibited, and in mitosis. One view is that what matters is not so much the amount of auxin available to the cell, but the balance between several substances. The mode of action of auxin is also unclear, but is discussed further in Chapter 5 because some of the theories implicate its effect on the cell wall.

According to Nitsan and Lang (1966), the synthesis of DNA is necessary for the elongation of some kinds of plant cells though it is not clear why this should be so. But it may explain the action of gibberellin, which promotes DNA synthesis and cell elongation. The case for the necessity of RNA synthesis for cell growth is stronger. Cell enlargement is accompanied by protein synthesis and, when enlargement is accelerated by auxin, protein synthesis is not accelerated to the same extent in all tissues. This suggests that synthesis of a particular protein, present in different amounts in different tissues, limits growth. The fact that actinomycin-D inhibits auxin-induced growth suggests that the action of auxin is on a nucleic acid system controlling the production of some essential protein, i.e. that cell enlargement is controlled through the nuclear synthesis of messenger-RNA (see page 341 and also Noodén & Thimann, 1963; Key & Ingle, 1964).

Another of the problems that concern cell growth in plants is that of the relationship between adjacent cells during growth, for different cells do not grow to the same extents. The problem is particularly a botanical one because of the lack of mobility in plant cells with their rigid walls. Firstly it should be said that most plant cells grow conformably together so that they do not slide in relation to their immediate neighbours, and the plasmodesmata (see page 256), which connect adjacent cells are not sheared. There are exceptions to this rule as we shall see. The conformable growth of tracts of neighbouring cells is called symplastic growth (Priestley, 1930) and it can be seen readily in areas of cells that can be watched while they grow. The epidermal cells of grass roots are commonly used for this purpose, but there is no reason to believe that cells in the interior of organs, which can not be watched, behave differently. In symplastic growth the cell growth is coordinated so that adjacent cells do not become separated even if some are dividing and some are not and the same is true even if some cells are enlarging and some are not. This means that different parts of the same cell wall may have to grow at different rates to accommodate the growth of two or more different cells in contact. How this is arranged except by mutual restraint is not known. Generally cells grow throughout their length, but a few, such as root hairs and certain kinds of sclereids grow only at their tips, at any rate during the later part of their expansion. Waves of growth travelling along cells starting at the basal end have also been reported in grass roots (Sinnott, 1939).

At one time it was thought that all cell growth in plant tissues would result in the slipping of one cell in relation to its neighbours. This theory seemed to be supported by the considerable change in cell pattern of a tract of cells between the beginning and end of a period of growth. Now we can account for this change in cell pattern by the theory of symplastic growth in most cases, but there are a few occasions when this theory cannot explain the change in spatial relationships of cells. These mostly occur where special cells, such as fibres and tracheids, come in contact with other kinds of cells especially in tissue derived from the cambium. In some plants, fibres elongate much more than the other cells derived from the same or similar cambial initials. The fibres may themselves grow symplastically in relation to each other as the other cells do, but there must be some intrusion of the fibres into the other tissues. This kind of growth is therefore called intrusive growth and appears to occur mostly at the tips of the cells. The cells form new contacts where they prize apart other cells by intruding between them. If the growth of the intrusive cell is confined to the very tips there needs to be no shearing of the plasmodesmata between the intrusive cell and its original neighbours though the plasmodesmata of the cells between which the growing cell is intruding are broken by the separation. But if, as is more likely, an appreciable length of the intrusive cell tip performs the intrusive growth the plasmodesmata in its tip will be sheared. The same applies to any pit pairs that exist between the intrusive cell tip and its original neighbours. Secondary pit pairs and plasmodesmata form on the new cell contacts just as, in the red algae, floridean pits are often formed between cells that come to lie next to one another by the accidents of development. It is not clear yet whether the intrusive cell tip slides along the surface of the cells with which it is making new contacts or whether the intrusive cell merely lays down new wall as its tip progresses like a military track-laying vehicle does as it moves over the ground. The difficulty is that the interesting cases are in internal tissues and therefore cannot be watched and so our ideas depend upon evidence that can be interpreted in more than one way.

Intrusive growth of the kind we have described occurs in fibres and tracheids especially and usually both ends of the cell grow. Intrusive growth of the same kind also occurs in the production of new fusiform initials in unstoried cambia. The multiplicative divisions of the cambial cells (i.e. those that increase the number of initials) are nearly transverse in all gymnosperms and most angiosperms and yet the average length of the initials increase with age as a rule. What happens is that the pseudo-transverse division results in two initials where there was one before and that both daughters grow intrusively to reach or exceed the length of the mother and in this process the nearly transverse dividing wall becomes distorted into a very elongated S- or Z-shaped wall, i.e. one that is longitudinal over most of its length (Fig. 11). Dicotyledons with storied cambia undergo multiplicative cambial division by radial walls and growth of the cambium needs only to be symplastic. In unstoried cambia where the wall formed in multiplicative division is tilted it is common to find the direction of tilt to be the same over an area or domain of the cambial sheet. In some trees the domain pattern changes with time. Where it does not change it will lead to a pronounced spiral grain in the wood derived from the cambium for a tilt in one direction will lead to an S-shaped partition wall once intrusive growth is over and a tilt in the other direction will lead to a Z-shaped partition. In recent years several investigations have cleared up this and related problems in wood anatomy concerned with cell growth (e.g. Bannan, 1950, 1960; Hejnowicz, 1961, 1964).

Intrusive growth of a different kind must also occur in the expansion of vessel elements. In some angiosperms the cross-sectional area of the vessel cells expands much more than in other cells of the secondary xylem after initiation from the cambium. This means that the vessel element must have more cells in contact with it at any level at the end of its growth than at the beginning. The transverse expansion of the vessel also deforms many of the surrounding cells and this contributes to the new cell contacts.

CHAPTER 3

Cytoplasm

Physical Properties, Membranes, Ribosomes and Tubules

It is traditional to consider the living matter of cells, the protoplast, in two parts, the nucleus and the cytoplasm. The more we learn about cells the more difficult it becomes to separate these two parts even structurally, for physical connexions exist between cytoplasmic organelles and the nucleus, and some workers now even use the term 'cytoplasm' to include the nucleus. Nevertheless, for the purpose of dividing this book into sections of convenient length, we shall adopt the traditional division and further divide the section on cytoplasm into two chapters, one dealing with general features, membranes, ribosomes and tubules and the other with organelles. These subdivisions are also purely arbitrary, for, as we shall see, the membrane systems cannot properly be considered without the cytoplasmic organelles and the nucleus.

A lot has been learnt about the chemistry of cells from the reactions of fractions of homogenates of tissues. In these techniques the cells are broken open and the various parts are separated by centrifugation often using density gradients. Necessary precautions such as using isotonic solutions of the right pH and right ion concentration are now standard techniques in biochemistry. A glance at a list of enzymes (perhaps 10,000 different kinds) and other substances found in any one cell shows that there must be some means of separating substances one from another to prevent chemical chaos from reigning within the living cell. Many cells, for example, contain diastases capable of breaking down starch, but in normal metabolism this does not occur and phosphorylases are the enzymes that effect the degradation. The localization of chemical reactions is investigated by two main means—(1) the reactions *in vitro* of fractions obtained by treating homogenates so as to separate one part from the rest and (2) cytochemical techniques mostly looking for localization of enzymes and syntheses. By these techniques we now know for example that mitochondria are the sites of oxidative reactions. They contain all the enzymes necessary for the aerobic phase of respiration, the electron transfer system and the system promoting aerobic phosphorylation with the generation of adenosine triphosphate (ATP). They are not always the exclusive sites of the enzymes involved in these systems; for example, some of the enzymes of the Krebs cycle also occur elsewhere in the cell. Similarly we know that the chloroplasts are the sites of the photolysis of water, fixation of carbon dioxide and of the phosphorylases necessary for starch synthesis. The ribosomes are the sites of cytoplasmic protein synthesis and most proteins are enzymatic.

We shall see that not only are certain reaction systems localized in particular organelles, but, even within an organelle, there may be a physical separation of substances that might otherwise react with one another and stop a series of chemical steps in an essential system. The ubiquitous membranes of cells discovered by electron microscopy are probably important in this way.

Enzymes may be localized in time as well as in space. They may be produced only at a particular phase of the cell's development or they may be inactivated at certain times. This kind of localization must be important in differentiation and will be discussed in Chapter 8.

Living plant cells appear under the microscope as transparent objects separated from each other by walls. The walls are often the most conspicuous part of plant cells and it was they that drew Hooke's attention to the cellular nature of organisms and caused the word 'cell' to be used for the units. Animal tissues, without cell walls, are not nearly so conspicuously cellular. Plant cells are, however, not completely isolated from one another. Their cytoplasts are nearly always interconnected by plasmodesmata, protoplasmic strands whose functional significance is still imperfectly known (see Chapter 5). The contents of living plant cells are transparent and mostly colourless. Under the ordinary light microscope we can make out the larger organelles only by the small changes of refractivity at their surfaces. The phase and interference microscopes enable us to see more clearly in living cells those organelles that are above the resolving power of light microscopes, but most of our detailed information comes from killed and stained cells. The only common coloured objects in plant cells are the plastids of certain tissues and the vacuoles of a few species. The organelles that occur in all plant cells are mitochondria, Golgi bodies, nuclei, nucleoli, chromosomes, ribosomes and plastids of various kinds. Ribosomes are well beyond the resolution of the light microscope and so have never been seen in living cells. The other organelles, especially the mitochondria, plastids and Golgi bodies give the cytoplasm a granular appearance in life. Under the electron microscope the cytoplasm also exhibits a granular appearance of a different magnitude. The stuff which surround the cytoplasmic organelles and membranes, the groundplasm or hyaloplasm, contains granules varying in size from 10 nm in diameter downwards to the limit of resolution. This granular appearance varies with the type of fixation and probably is formed by the reaction of the proteins with the fixative. Physical investigations show that the cytoplasmic matrix behaves like a sol or a gel and that one state can turn into another. In the gel state, at any rate, some of the protein must presumably be in a filamentous form, possibly in microtubules, to give the cytoplasm its gel-like properties, but this is not always seen under the electron microscope. It may be deduced from experiments with sieves. The plasmodia of slime molds, which are convenient large sources of protoplasm, can pass freely through sieves with pores larger than about 1μm diameter. If forced through a sieve, though, the plasmodium is killed unless the pores are wider than about 200μm.

3.1 Physical properties

Chemical analysis shows that cytoplasm contains proteins, lipids, nucleic acids and various substances soluble in water. The long molecules of the proteins give cytoplasm most of its peculiar physical properties, though the lipids are important in determining the features of barrier membranes. Many of the physical properties of protoplasm are known from colloid chemistry, but protoplasm cannot properly be treated as an ordinary gel or sol. The experiments with myxomycete plasmodia and sieves mentioned above show this. There must be some framework within the protoplasm that is more gel-like than sol-like therefore, but the framework must be able to break and rejoin to account for the flow and streaming of cytoplasm. Cytoplasm is also thixotropic presumably due to the breaking of bonds between protein molecules by mechanical agitation and their subsequent restitution when agitation stops. Cytoplasm exhibits birefringence of flow, i.e. it appears bright between crossed polarizing filters if it is streaming, but not if it is stationary. This again indicates that the constituent molecules are long chains that become orientated like logs in a river during streaming and thus the refractive index varies according to whether the fluid is looked at across the direction of flow or with the flow. Orientation of fibrils 5 nm across has now been seen under the electron microscope. Cell walls exhibit form birefringence because the cellulose molecules, which are also long chains, are permanently orientated in more or less the same direction.

The viscosity of cytoplasm as measured by the rate of fall of a body through it or the amplitude of Brownian movement is greater than that of water, but less than that of many liquids though it is difficult to give meaningful data here because cytoplasm is a non-Newtonian fluid and its properties are further complicated by the presence of sheets of endoplasmic reticulum. The starch grains that are thought to act as statoliths in some kinds of cells move under the force of gravity at rates some twenty times more slowly in cytoplasm than in water and so, by Stoke's law (see page 34), the viscosity of cytoplasm is about twenty. Values as low as two have also been obtained (R. Brown, 1960). Measurements of cytoplasmic viscosity were made before it was known that there were sheets and tubes of endoplasmic reticulum in the cell and they therefore probably do not mean very much.

Cytoplasm also has a certain amount of elasticity as may be seen if we pull out a piece of protoplasm from a cell with a micromanipulator.

Streaming and other movements

A cell is not a static thing. It grows and develops from one kind of cell into another. Movements are going on within the cell all the time so long as it remains alive. The most conspicuous of these movements is that referred to as streaming of the cytoplasm or cyclosis in which the organelles move in relation to one another in streams. This movement, which can be watched in any living cell, involves the mass movement of whole regions of the cytoplasm not only the particles themselves, for organelles of different sizes move together as if carried in a stream. The regions that move can be quite small. For example it is common to see a strand of cytoplasm traversing a large vacuole in which two streams flow in opposite directions even when the strand is only 1μm across. The streaming is often confined to a small part of the cell at any one time.

Honda, Hongladarom and Wildman (1964) give evidence to show that the cytoplasm of mature cells of higher plants is stratified. Next to the wall there is a cortical gel layer which moves little or not at all. This layer contains the chloroplasts as well as a few mitochondria and spherosomes. Interior to this layer there are at least two layers of mobile endoplasm (kinoplasm). The outer of these contains most of the mitochondria and the inner, which displays faster movement, contains most of the spherosomes.

The nature of this streaming of cytoplasm is still a mystery although many experiments have been done on it. We know that anaerobic conditions and respiratory inhibitors depress the rate of streaming. Raising the temperature over a suitable range and applying ATP or certain auxins accelerate the rate. The rate in plant cells has been measured as up to 19μm per second over several seconds (Mahlberg, 1964).

The orientation of plastids and mitochondria that can be seen in living cells suggests that there may be some other kind of movement within the cytoplasm. Some people think that these organelles are capable of autonomous movement, but it may be that when they move as if not in a stream they are merely moving with the cytoplasm but not so fast as in normal streaming. Honda et al., though, believe that mitochondria and spherosomes can move from one layer to another in the stratified cytoplasm described above. Certain plastids can orientate themselves according to external conditions of light intensity. Thaine (1965) holds that particles move because of physico-chemical interactions between their external surfaces and the surfaces of the endoplasmic reticulum. Each particle then moves autonomously and sometimes in the opposite direction from the flow of fluid endoplasm. At other times the flow is stronger than the forces of particle motivation and the particles are swept along with the fluid and we see this as cytoplasmic streaming. One cannot see the streaming unless particles are carried along with the fluid.

One view about the cause of cytoplasmic streaming is that it is due to transformation within membranes, especially endoplasmic reticulum (ER). Membranes probably ought to be regarded as labile in their molecular structure and Kavanau's view (1963) is that transformations of the molecular structure are propagated longitudinally along cylinders of ER leading to the impelling of the cytoplasmic matrix. In this way elements of ER jet propel themselves by a pulsatile pumping action in which the cytoplasmic matrix within a tube of ER is ejected in the opposite direction. But many other theories exist (see Kamiya, 1960; Wohlfarth-Bottermann, 1964) and the mechanism is still obscure. An interesting observation that may be relevant is that of Nagai and Rebhun (1966) that at the interface between the stationary ectoplasm and the moving endoplasm in *Nitella* there are bundles of filaments. Each bundle contains 50–100 filaments 5 nm across and several microns long orientated parallel to the direction of streaming. Nagai and Rebhun suggest that these filaments are directly involved in generating the motive force for streaming. This supports Hayashi's insistence on the importance of the outer gel layer of the cytoplasm for the generation of the shearing force that he thinks occurs at the boundary between the static gel layer and the motile endoplasm. Hayashi (1964) showed that streaming stops as soon as the outer gel layer is damaged and restarts as soon as the gel reforms.

3.2 Cytoplasmic membranes

Our knowledge of the structure of these depends almost entirely on the electron microscope. It is true that the physical properties of cells led to belief in the barrier membranes of cells before their structure could be seen. Plasmolysis and similar experiments show that there is a membrane of some sort on the outer surface of cells (on the inner side of the wall in plants) and at the margin of water vacuoles. The appearance of cells in mitosis shows that there is a membrane around the nucleus and this disappears or fragments at the end of prophase and reappears around the two daughter nuclei at the end of mitosis. Osmotic phenomena suggest that there must also be a membrane around the plastids and mitochondria. But the rich membrane system of the rest of the cytoplasm was quite unexpected (except in special cases) until it was revealed by electron microscopy. Previously it had been thought that the cytoplasm could be regarded as a liquid or solid in which were suspended the microscopic organelles with specialized chemistry. Electron micrographs of sections show that cells also contain membranes permeating the whole of the ground substance of the cytoplasm (Fig. 10). These membranes appear to form sheets and tubules and are now called endoplasmic reticulum (ER). It is true that the ER can be seen in favourable material in living cells by phase microscopy and had, in fact, been seen in animal cells by impregnation methods sixty years ago, but it is doubtful if its significance would have been realized without the knowledge gained from electron microscopy (Porter and Machado, 1960; Moulé, 1964; Larson, 1965).

The concept of cell membranes arose largely from a consideration of the physical and chemical properties of boundaries of cells and organelles long before we knew anything about their morphology. It was largely based upon the intuition of Danielli and his school working in the 1930's on the physical properties of mixtures of lipids and aqueous fluids. Lipid molecules orientate themselves to form layers in aqueous fluids. The structure of these layers is usually interpreted as a bimolecular leaflet, i.e. two sheets of lipid molecules in biological systems, but other configurations may exist (Fig. 20; Lucy & Glauert, 1964). It is almost certain that it is the lipids of the protoplasm that confer the peculiar permeability properties on cell membranes, though their morphology at the molecular level is still a matter of opinion. Many workers assume that the bimolecular leaflet of lipid is sandwiched between two layers of protein, but it is possible that some membranes consist of a sheet of lipid globules stabilized by protein coats (Sjöstrand, 1963). For some account of these lipids in plant membranes see Benson (1964).

Under the electron microscope all the different kinds of cell membranes exhibit some similar features. In thin sections of fixed material all appear as two dark lines separated by a light line (Figs. 19, 20), but

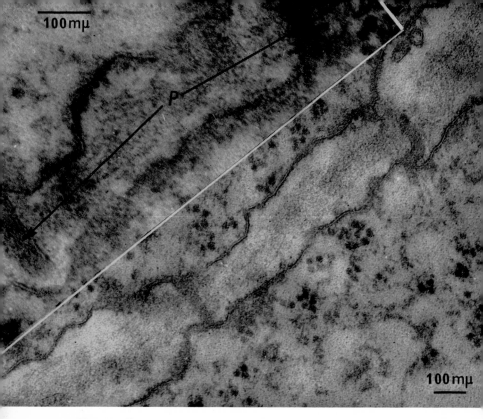

100mμ

100mμ

FIG. 19. Electron micrograph of the plasmalemma on either side of a wall in the elongating zone of *Zea* roots. In places where the membrane is normal to the plane of section the plasmalemma is resolved into the two dark lines separated by a lighter space characteristic of a single unit membrane. Inset at a higher magnification another part of the wall showing the unit membrane lining two plasmodesmatal canals (P). (Glut/Os/Pb/U)

some membranes have this arrangement doubled. Early electron microscopy failed to show the unit membrane as two double lines and a light line and it appeared as a single dark line so that the double membranes looked like what we now see in a single dark line of the earlier work except for dimensions. This has led to some confusion, but we shall use the nomenclature of Robertson (1962, 1964) in which the term 'unit membrane' refers to the triple structure now resolved by the electron microscope in favourable planes of sectioning as two dark lines of about 2 nm width separated by a light line about 3·5 nm wide, the dimensions being those measured after permanganate fixation (Fig. 19). The whole unit membrane thus appears about 7·5 nm wide. The dimensions quoted in the literature vary considerably and this can be due to the uncertainties of measurement at this level with the electron microscope, to differences in fixation and staining and also probably to real differences between different membranes. Yamamoto (1963), for example, gives figures for different membranes within the same cells (*Rana* abdominal sympathetic ganglia) in which there is a variation of 15 per cent. The membranes of the mitochondria, nucleus, Golgi cisternae, and ER fall between 85 and 89 per cent of the width found in the plasmalemma and Golgi vesicles. Sjöstrand (1963) also distinguishes between different unit membranes by their width with the unit membrane of the ER being the thinnest at 5 to 6 nm, that of the Golgi 8 nm and that of the plas-malemma 9 to 10 nm. There is also some work that suggests that some of the membranes are asymmetrical in that one of the dark lines is thicker than the other. This is true of the plasmalemma of rat ureter epithelium where the outer line is twice as thick as the inner and of some other animal cells where the inner dark line is darker and thicker than the outer (Hicks, 1965). Grun (1963) showed this not to be true in *Solanum* root tip cells, but he did find it true of the tonoplast of these cells where the inner dark line, that next to the vacuole, varied from 2·5 to 25·0 nm across while the outer line next to the cytoplasm was only 2·5 nm wide. Perner (1965) holds that the space between the two unit membranes of double-membraned organelles disappears in cells of dormant, air-dried seeds. These kinds of observations naturally lead to questioning of the utility of the unit membrane concept, but it can hardly be expected that membranes performing such varied functions as they presumably do in cells would have identical morphology at this resolution and the better our resolution becomes the greater the likeli-hood of seeing differences, though the important differences are in the nature of the globular enzymic proteins and the electron microscope may never resolve these. Already the unit membranes of the mito-chondria and chloroplasts have been resolved into isodiametric com-ponents, sheets of stalked globules in the cristae of the mitochondria, the oxysomes, and the complex quantasomes in the chlorophyll-bearing lamellae of the plastids (see Chapter 4).

The appearance of the membranes as three lines in sections is pre-sumably due to the reaction of the metal in the fixing agent with the non-lipid components and the polar groups of the lipids on the outside. The fact that, after osmium fixation, the outer line of the plasmalemma is weaker than the inner shows that there is some polarity in the struc-ture of the membrane which therefore differs from the original concept of Danielli.

In view of the recent work done by freeze-etching on membranes some modification of our interpretation of fixed material is needed.

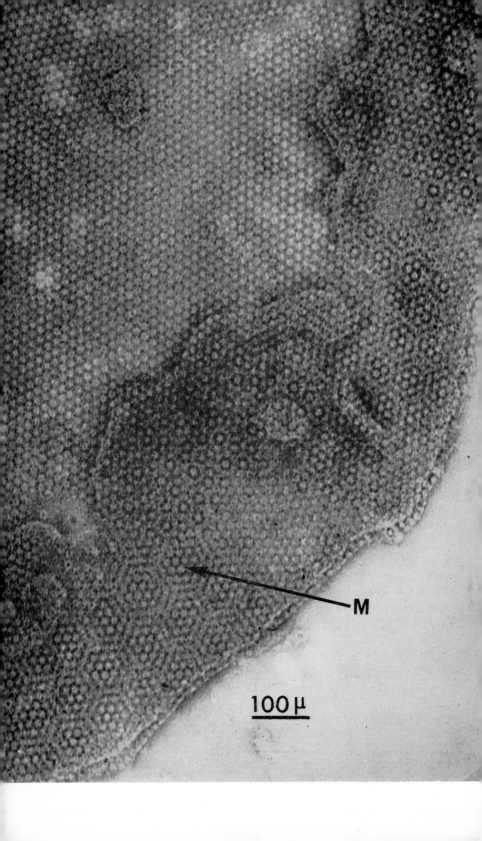

M

100 μ

Mühlethaler, Moor & Szarkowski (1965) have shown that freeze-etched lamellae of chloroplasts, which show the triple layering described above in sections, really consist of a central layer on both sides of which are partially embedded protein particles. The central layer is almost certainly lipid and is 4 nm thick. The particles are 6 nm in diameter and are embedded to a depth of 2 nm so that a particle on one side of the membrane can touch one on the other side and the middle layer is perforate. The total width of this unit membrane is therefore 12 nm. In sections of fixed chloroplasts on the other hand the central layer is 3·5 nm and the two dense lines are each 2 nm giving a total thickness of 7·5 nm to the unit membrane. The discrepancy between the two kinds of observations is probably due to the fixation introducing distortion, for the freeze-etched preparations are likely to be most life-like. Mühlethaler *et al.* regard the two dark lines as being due to the uncoiling of the protein molecules by the disruption by the fixative of the hydrogen and disulphide bridges that maintain the tertiary folded structure of the protein. In this way they think the partially embedded particles become spread out as a thin film on each side of the lipid layer to give the artefact seen in sections. Other membranes of the cell may well be similar in structure. The differences that do occur may be due to differences in the composition, size and closeness of packing of the protein particles making the dark lines thicker or thinner. Branton (1966) agrees with the idea of membranes being constructed partially as a double layer and partially as globular units and thinks that the 8·5 nm particles frequently seen in freeze-etched preparations are not ribosomes as was originally thought, but the globular units revealed by splitting the membranes during the fracture. He also thinks that the extent to which a membrane consists of globular units varies from organelle to organelle. Thus the nuclear membranes in his *Allium* root tips seem to consist almost entirely of a smooth sheet whereas the chloroplast membranes consist almost entirely of globules.

A point that has never been satisfactorily explained is the role of calcium in membrane systems. It is known that calcium is required, but

FIG. 20. Electron micrograph of an isolated and negatively stained membrane from the surface layers of the bacterium *Micrococcus radiodurans*. This membrane is seen in surface view and presents an array of hexagonal units very different superficially from the impression given by sections seen at right angles to the membrane. However some people believe that membranes may exist as alternative forms, the bimolecular leaflet (Fig. 19) and a micellar structure as this figure indicates. Part of the membrane has folded over and gives confusing Moiré patterns (M). (N/S/P)   Micrograph by Dr A. M. Glauert.

what role it plays is not certain. Marinos (1962) showed that calcium deficiency leads to the break up of the nuclear envelope, the plasmalemma and tonoplast.

It will be convenient now to consider the cell membranes in groups; those belonging to the endoplasmic reticulum, plasmalemma and tonoplast, will be described in this chapter and those belonging to the cell organelles, Golgi, plastids, mitochondria and nuclei in later chapters. For, although there are similarities between all the kinds of membranes and there may well be an ontogenetic connexion between some of them, most of our knowledge comes from studying the various kinds separately.

3.3   Plasmalemma

The plasmalemma, which is also called the plasma membrane, cell membrane or ectoplast, is the outer membrane of the cell lying nearest to the cell wall in plants. It is often difficult to separate it from the wall and it is the most difficult membrane to see. In sections it usually appears as a single unit membrane, i.e. two dark lines separated by a light line (Fig. 19). In plants it sometimes appears to be symmetrical in that the two dark lines appear similar in density and thickness. But in some animal cells the inner layer appears darker and sometimes wider (Grun, 1963) and this is true in some plant cells too. Whaley, Mollenhauer & Leech (1960a) describe the outer layer in meristematic plant cells as nearly as dense as the inner layer after permanganate fixation, but not dense after osmium fixation although the inner layer is dense. It has been suggested that the outer line might consist of carbohydrate and the inner of protein separated by phospholipids in the light line (Robertson, 1962).

The outline of the plasmalemma can be smooth or irregular with particles lying in bays between the wall and the membrane. In young fungal cells the plasmalemma adheres closely to the wall, but in old cells it undulates sometimes with quite deep invaginations (Hawker, 1965). The particles lying outside the membrane are called lomasomes and are collections of small tubules. These were originally discovered in fungi, but also occur in algae and higher plants (see p. 194; Fig. 100). Invaginations of the plasmalemma containing small projecting strands of cytoplasm occur in some plant cells (Grun, 1963). Mercer and Rathgeber (1962) noticed that the plasmalemma becomes convoluted during the secretion of nectar by the hair cells of the nectaries of *Abutilon* and the plasmalemma of the carbohydrate-secreting cells of the periphery of the root cap in *Zea* and *Triticum* becomes so tangled as to be scarcely distinguished as a bounding layer at all (Fig. 21).

The plasmalemma is also concerned with the process of pinocytosis in which invaginations of the membrane form vesicles which are pinched off in the cytoplasm. This process, originally noticed in amoebae and macrophages, and now well-established as occurring in the endothelial cells of blood capillaries, accounts for the large scale intake of liquid, but solid particles such as polystyrene granules or ferritin can pass into the cell in pinocytotic vesicles in the same way. The membrane of a vesicle may disappear in its passage through the cytoplasm so that the liquid or solid particle inside is incorporated into the cell or the contents may be handed on to an adjacent cell and the vesicle membrane is then reincorporated into the plasmalemma on the other side of the cell. Pinocytosis appears to be normally a method of supplementing the osmotic turgor pressure in taking water into a cell, but if solids are taken in it is difficult to separate this process from export of material carried out by the Golgi vesicles. As we shall see in Chapter 4, the Golgi

FIG. 21. Electron micrograph of peripheral root cap cells of *Zea*. Golgi-secreted material is accumulating between the plasmalemma and the cell wall (M) and the matrix materials of the extreme outer layer of cells is breaking down releasing the cells from the surface of the root cap. (Glut/Mn)

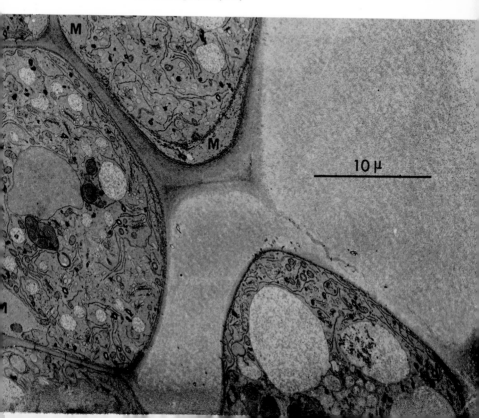

vesicles carry substances to the outside of the cell often to be incorporated into the cell wall or to form some other extra-cellular structure. In doing this the vesicle membrane, which is a single unit membrane like that of pinocytotic vesicles, is incorporated into the plasmalemma. There is thus some interchangeability between the plasmalemma and the Golgi bodies which produce the vesicles and it may even be that the Golgi vesicles are used to extend the surface of a cell or even to form it. The tangled appearance of the plasmalemma in Fig. 21 may be caused by membrane-bound Golgi vesicles being incorporated at a great rate into a membrane that is not expanding. Pinocytotic vesicles and Golgi vesicles are hardly distinguishable under the electron microscope and the direction of movement, of course, has to be guessed. Bradfute, Chapman-Andresen & Jensen (1964) conducted an enquiry into whether pinocytosis ever takes place in higher plants and concluded that there was no evidence for it at all. Using living endosperm cells they showed that what may appear to be pinocytosis can result from degeneration of the cell under observation, from the cell flowing round particles and from the outwards movement of a vacuole. Cocking (1966a), on the other hand, holds that he has good evidence for pinocytosis in isolated protoplasts of higher plants. His observations were on tomato fruits (*Lycopersicum*) whose cells had had their walls removed and which were incubated with tobacco mosaic virus. The virus particles become attached to the plasmalemma especially in small invaginations. They later appear within vesicles inside the cytoplasm, though still attached to the plasmalemma, and finally in vesicles free in the cytoplasm. The obvious conclusion is that the virus enters the protoplast in a pinocytotic vesicle. Cocking (1966a) has also shown that similar isolated protoplasts take up ferritin by a similar method. There seems here to be no reason to confuse a movement outwards from the cytoplasm with pinocytosis, but it is, of course, easy to be sceptical about the relevance of observations on isolated protoplasts for pinocytosis in natural conditions. But a somewhat similar phenomenon has also been described in the infection of nodule cells in the roots of a leguminous plant (Goodchild & Bergerson, 1966). Here the bacterial infection thread enters the host cell by invagination of its plasmalemma. The so-called 'coated vesicles' are also thought possibly to originate as pinocytotic invaginations of the plasmalemma in actively dividing cambial cells (Srivastava, 1966). These vesicles are about 110 nm across and they have an alveolar sculpturing on their 20 nm thick membranes. Smooth-surfaced vesicles found in these cells are also considered to be pinocytotic by Srivastava.

In *Streptomyces* there are curious organelles called mesosomes associated with the plasmalemma. These look like pinocytotic vesicles except that they are often filled with concentric layers of membranes (Chen, 1964). As this organism is similar to the bacteria it may be that the membranes are concerned in respiration.

The plasmalemma is only 7 to 10 nm thick and is therefore not visible under the light microscope, but its existence was postulated from the physical properties of cells before it was seen. There are no morphological pores in the membrane except perhaps where elements of the ER pass through it in plasmodesmata, the protoplasmic connexions between plant cells (see page 256). In sections the plasmalemma appears smooth, but in freeze-etched preparations it appears granular (Figs. 99, 105; Frey-Wyssling & Mühlethaler, 1965). Plasmolysis experiments show that the cell wall allows both water and solutes freely into most kinds of plant cells, but that the cytoplasm then restricts the movement of solutes more than that of water. Water can also be withdrawn freely from the vacuoles and probably from the cytoplasm too. The early arguments for the existence of barrier membranes rested largely on the improbability of the main body of cytoplasm, with its high water content, acting as a barrier to solutes. Thus it was thought that there was a surface layer of cytoplasm that controlled the ingress of substances from outside and the action of various chemical solvents led to the view that lipids played an important role in this barrier.

The theories about the origin of the plasmalemma fall into three groups. One view is that it arises as a purely physical organization, as a surface to the cytoplasm by the accumulation of surface-active lipoproteins. Such a surface might arise on any mixture of appropriate substances by the attraction and repulsion of hydrophilic and hydrophobic molecules. In support of this is the rapidity with which plasmalemmas are formed after cutting amoebae and after the extension of pseudopodia. The dispersion of the membranes around pinocytotic vesicles has also been considered as evidence for this view though some such vesicles survive passage through the cytoplasm. Another view is that the plasmalemma is an independent organelle autonomous in its growth and perhaps also in reproduction. A third view is that the plasmalemma is formed from the membranes bounding Golgi vesicles. There is some evidence (see page 183) that the membranes of Golgi vesicles which are transported to the exterior of the cell are incorporated into the existing plasmalemma. It may also be that the new plasmalemma formed after mitosis is made entirely or in part from the swarms of vesicles that congregate at the region of the cell plate. In cells whose walls arise late after a free-nuclear stage (some endosperms) the plasmalemma cannot be formed from the Golgi vesicles for these are absent from such cells according to Buttrose (1963). Probably all three views are right for some cells in some circumstances.

3.4   Vacuoles and tonoplasts

Water vacuoles are prominent features of differentiated plant cells though not of animal cells. Plant cells, not fully differentiated, often contain numerous small vacuoles, but these constitute a small proportion of the volume of the cell. As the cell grows the vacuoles also grow and they coalesce to form a single vacuole which may occupy over 90 per cent of the volume of the cell and may have thin strands of cytoplasm traversing it. Marinos (1963) holds that vacuoles grow by the dilation of protrusions of the membrane around them. The growth of animal cells is not accompanied by conspicuous enlargement of their vacuoles, but by a greater increase in the amount of protoplasm than occurs in plants. The cell sap, as the contents of a vacuole are called, contains many kinds of substances dissolved in the water or in a colloidal state; even fat droplets have been reported. Probably any soluble compound produced by cells can exist in the vacuole, but some substances, like tannins and anthocyanins, occur mostly in vacuoles and sometimes give the cell sap quite a high viscosity and cause the tissue to be coloured. Substances may also accumulate in vacuoles beyond saturation point or may reach saturation point by the withdrawal of water to form crystals. It is probable that the crystals found in cells are always surrounded by a unit membrane and, if this is so, it suggests that they must always be made in vacuoles or plastids (see page 145). Apart from water, vacuoles contain substances that cannot be otherwise removed from the cell and therefore the tonoplast acts as an excretory organ. Vacuoles may also serve as stores for reserve substances, especially sugars.

Two common fallacies exist about vacuoles in plant cells. One is that meristematic cells never have large vacuoles and the other is that root cap cells do. The first, no doubt, arose because apical meristems have cells with no large vacuoles, though, even here, mitosis may be seen also in vacuolated cells. The cambium is an example of a meristem whose cells are highly vacuolated. The second fallacy, about cap cells, is due to the poor fixation of cytoplasm usually employed for light microscopy because most people interested in root tips want to see only the chromosomes. When adequate cytoplasmic fixatives are used, the root cap cells are seen to remain 'unvacuolate', i.e. with only minute vacuoles, until they are sloughed off on the periphery of the root tip (Figs. 10, 30). Root cap cells are peculiar in this respect.

The tonoplast is the name given to the unit membrane surrounding a vacuole. (The same word is also used for the protoplasmic envelope around vacuoles removed from cells by certain procedures, but this is much thicker than a unit membrane and the two structures ought to be given different names.) As was the case with the plasmalemma, the existence of a tonoplast was demonstrated before it could be seen. Some solutes penetrate into the cytoplasm more quickly than into the vacuole and accumulate there before going into the vacuole thus suggesting a barrier membrane. After a cell has been plasmolyzed by losing water from the vacuole to the surrounding hypertonic solution the tonoplast has a reduced surface area and, in this condition, can be handled and removed from the cell presumably with some of the rest of the cytoplasm sticking to it. In liquid this 'tonoplast' becomes spherical and, because it retains its differentially permeable properties, its vacuole can swell and shrink osmotically. Tonoplasts are especially rich in lipids and it is these that presumably give the membranes their differential permeability. The tonoplast is impermeable to some substances that are let in by the plasmalemma and differential permeability is maintained far longer by the tonoplast than by the plasmalemma when a cell is placed in certain dyes.

Under the electron microscope the tonoplast shows the usual single unit membrane arrangement of two dark lines separated by a light line. After osmium fixation the inner dark line, the one next to the vacuole, appears finer than the outer according to Frey-Wyssling & Mühlethaler (1965) though Grun (1963) reports the opposite (see page 75). It is possible that these differences in density or thickness are artefacts of the kind reported by Griffiths & Audus (1964) caused by the direction of penetration of the fixative.

The origin of vacuoles is still not properly understood and there are two ways of looking at the subject. One is to consider the physical forces involved and the other is to regard the vacuole as an organelle capable of growth and perhaps even of reproduction. Both views are useful. A vacuole may be regarded as arising by the attraction of water molecules to a region of the cytoplasm. When this happens they push apart the hydrophobic molecules in the neighbourhood and these then form a boundary to the vacuole. Coalescence of vacuoles may then be explained as due to the mutual attraction of like molecules and repulsion of unlike molecules when two vacuoles touch one another. Electron

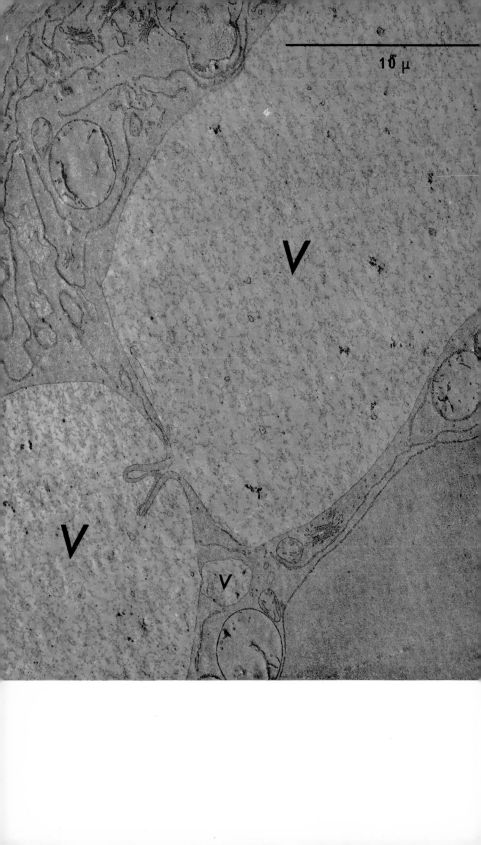

micrographs often show finger-like penetrations of one vacuole into another (Fig. 22). Splitting of vacuoles could be brought about by movement in the cytoplasm. Frey-Wyssling & Mühlethaler (1965) regard the large vacuoles of plants as being caused by the lack of sufficient nitrogen compounds to produce enough protein to fill the space of a growing cell. It is interesting in this connexion that the very rapidly dividing cap initials of the roots of Zea have more conspicuous vacuoles than their non-meristematic derivatives or the cells of the quiescent centre next to them (Fig. 23). Animals, which take in more nitrogen, do not suffer this fate. But large vacuoles do confer an advantage on plant bodies in giving them a great deal of rigidity that would otherwise have to be provided by mechanical tissue. One has only to compare a wilted plant with a turgid one to realize this. It is true that aquatic higher plants, which do not need this rigidity, also have large vacuoles, but many algae do not have large vacuoles.

When regarded as an organelle, the vacuole is sometimes thought of as originating as the small spherical bodies with dense contents seen in electron micrographs of meristematic cells and sometimes as arising from the separation of the two unit membranes of part of the ER. It is possible that the ER gives rise to vacuoles as it may do to other cytoplasmic organelles, but the stages between ER and an unmistakable tonoplast are not certain and Manton (1962) has demonstrated how easy it can be for electron micrographs to mislead us into thinking there is continuity between ER and vacuoles. Nevertheless Bowes (1965) holds that vacuoles arise in meristematic cells by the accumulation of material in localized regions of the ER giving an appearance such as occurs in Fig. 24. In non-meristematic cells he thinks vacuoles also arise from degenerating organelles and by the breakdown of the nucleus and cytoplasmic ground substance. Larson (1965) believes that, in germinating pollen of Parkinsonia, ER cisternae swell and incorporate more ER to become vacuoles whereas, in other species, the prevacuolar bodies mentioned above give rise to the vacuoles possibly with some incorporation of ER as they enlarge. Whaley, Kephart & Mollenhauer (1964) regard the small spherical bodies with dense contents as the precursors of vacuoles in meristematic cells. They lose their affinity for the metal of the fixative and become irregular in shape. They reproduce by fragmentation and coalesce to form clearly recognizable vacuoles. The

FIG. 22. Electron micrograph of part of a cortical cell from the primary root of Vicia. Vacuolation of the cell is starting and a number of small vacuoles (V) are coalescing by projecting fingers into each other. (Mn)

tonoplast of one vacuole grows by acquiring that of another vacuole and also possibly by active growth. Though it is perhaps more realistic to think of the vacuole as expanding and thus causing the existing tonoplast to acquire and organize lipid and protein molecules as it comes across these in pushing the cytoplasm away. Another of the difficulties about understanding the electron microscope picture is that it is impossible to distinguish between small vacuoles and the vesicles produced by pinocytosis or by the Golgi bodies. Marinos (1963), indeed, holds that vacuoles arise by enlargement of the entire space in a single Golgi cisterna and his electron micrographs of shoot tip cells of *Hordeum* certainly show membrane-bound spaces lying against Golgi bodies as if an outer cisterna has swollen. Also Pickett-Heaps (1967a) has demonstrated that vesicles probably derived from Golgi discharge into vacuoles of stomatal guard cells and hair cells of *Triticum*. Intensive study on some suitable material is needed to clear up the uncertainties existing today. A particular difficulty occurs in the sieve tube elements of the phloem and in latex cells where there is apparently no tonoplast surrounding what would otherwise be called a vacuole. It may be that the centre of these cells should not be considered as a vacuole but merely as rather watery cytoplasm. Sieve tubes and laticifers are discussed in Chapter 9.

Contractile vacuoles, such as exist in some unicellular algae without proper cell walls as well as in animals, present special problems for the understanding of water relations. They expand, sometimes by the rapid ingress of water from feeder canals, and then contract by expelling the liquid outside the cell. It is not known whether the ingress of water is due to some active secretion or whether it is purely osmotic. Nor is it known whether water is expelled by an active contraction of the membrane or whether it is due to a build-up of the hydrostatic pressure in the cytoplasm forcing the vacuolar liquid out at a weak spot. Bennet-Clark (1959) favours the latter view. Contractile vacuoles are also mentioned in connexion with the Golgi (p. 190).

The whole problem of water relations of ordinary plant cells is very

Fɪɢ. 23. Electron micrograph mosaic of meristematic cells of the root cap of *Zea*. The cap junction (CJ) marks the boundary between the quiescent centre and the cap initials. The cap initial cells (CI) have a number of small vacuoles, these slowly disappear as the cells cease dividing and mature. The cells of the quiescent centre (see Fig. 51) have no vacuoles. The proplastids of the cap initials rapidly accumulate starch as the cells mature and at the same time the ER, which appears fragmentary and dispersed in the cap initials, comes to lie parallel to the walls in the central cap cells. (Mn)

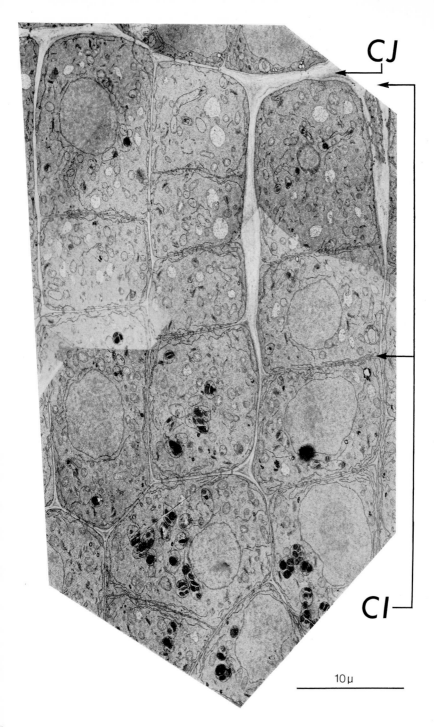

CJ

CI

10 μ

D*

complex and still imperfectly understood. Water exists in the vacuole, the protoplast and also in the wall. The protoplast can expand and contract as water goes in and out. The wall is also elastic and normally under a high tension. These properties and differential permeability to other substances make realistic mathematical models difficult to erect. But the subject is so important to an appreciation of the earth's water balance that a great deal of work is done on it and this cannot be treated adequately in this book. The reviews of Bennet-Clark (1959) and Dainty (1963) will serve to introduce the subject.

3.5 Endoplasmic reticulum

The ER appears in sections as lines of double unit membranes permeating the cytoplasm. Its existence was unsuspected until the advent of adequate methods for electron microscopy became available, though now we know that it is possible to see ER even in living cells under phase microscopy (Porter & Machado, 1960; Moulé, 1964; Thaine, 1965) and the fibrillar bodies seen by Neméc (1901) in gravitationally stimulated cells are probably masses of ER (Griffiths & Audus, 1964). ER occurs in all plant and animal cells except in mammalian erythrocytes. These do not contain nuclei and this may be significant, for the ER is often connected to the nuclear envelope, frequently surrounds it and may be generated from it. ER may also be absent from cells of bacteria and blue-green algae which lack a membrane-bounded nucleus.

A complete three-dimensional picture of the ER has never been made, but freeze-etched preparations show it as extensive fenestrated sheets in root-tip cells (Figs. 25, 26, 27; Branton & Moor, 1964). From the appearance in sections it has also been described as forming canals and vesicles. In meristematic cells Whaley, Mollenhauer & Leech (1960a) think of it as forming flat sac-like elements of considerable depth, but as forming tubules at the periphery of the cells. One of the results of giving a plant a photoinductive cycle to promote flowering is to change the distribution of the ER in the summit cells of the shoot apex (Gifford & Stewart, 1965). In the vegetative condition the ER appears sparse and confined to the periphery of the cell, but within three hours of giving an inductive cycle to *Chenopodium* it becomes distributed throughout the cytoplasm. In root tips it appears sparse in the cells of the quiescent centre and in the meristematic cells and well developed in the expanding cells both of the elongation zone of the root and of the cap. But we have shown that the area of ER increases more or less proportionally with the volume of the cell in the root cap (Fig. 53) and we estimate there to be

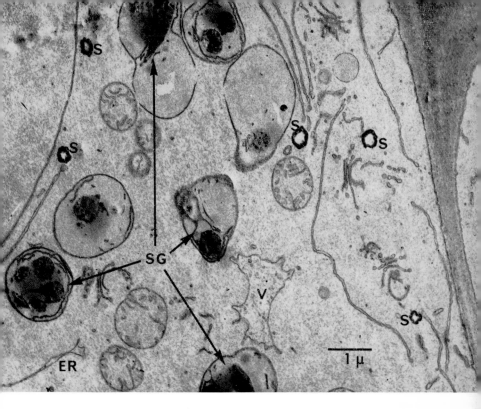

FIG. 24. Electron micrograph of a central root cap cell of *Zea*. The starch grains (SG) are beginning to grow within the amyloplasts. Spherosomes (S) are scattered throughout the cell. The contents of the small vacuole (V) are barely distinguishable from the rest of the cytoplasm. The fragment of ER indicated shows what may be the first stage in the development of a vacuole. (Mn)

about $400\mu m^2$ of it in the dividing cells and up to $10,000\mu m^2$ in the fully differentiating cells of the cap (Clowes & Juniper, 1964; Juniper & Clowes, 1965). In the meristematic cells, the profiles of ER are short and irregularly dispersed, whereas, in the mature cells, the profiles are longer and often arranged parallel to the walls and nuclear envelope even in non-vacuolate cells and it is this more regular arrangement and also, in the root cap, the capacity to accumulate in parts of cells under a gravitational stimulus (see page 447), that gives the impression of a higher density of ER. In the cells on the periphery of the root cap the profiles form irregular rings and loops as they sometimes do when cells are subjected to various stresses or injury (Figs. 21, 65). There appears to be a progressive breakdown of the ER as other cells of the root differentiate (Whaley, Mollenhauer & Leech, 1960a), but breakdown is not the inevitable fate of the ER in fully differentiated cells. In some fruit tissues the ER forms a membrane around compartments of cytoplasm which become separated from each other as ripening takes place (Cocking & Gregory, 1963) and, in the resin canal cells of *Pinus* and the companion cells of *Acer*, the ER closely surrounds individual plastids (Wooding & Northcote, 1965a, b). Mercer & Rathgeber (1962) show that the ER proliferates in anaerobic conditions and forms continuous folded sheets. Whaley, Kephart & Mollenhauer (1964) show that lowering the oxygen tension or adding carbon dioxide or monoxide, cyanide or colchicine or irradiating with gamma rays leads to a great increase in ER even within a few seconds of treatment. Perez del Cerro (1961) reports that ribonuclease also induces the ER to proliferate and we have found that cutting a root down the middle produces a 1·7-fold increase in the area of ER per unit volume of cytoplasm within a few seconds. Stacks of ER profiles occur normally in pollen according to Larson (1965) who interprets them as stores in these cells.

FIG. 25. Three-dimensional representation of parts of two plant cells. Compare it with the electron micrograph (Fig. 34) from which it was drawn. The ER forms much-branched, fenestrated sheets throughout the cells and passes from one cell to another via the plasmodesmata. Sections through mitochondria (M), plastids (P) and Golgi bodies (G) are shown and both surface and transverse views of the nuclear membrane (NM). Compare this picture also with Fig. 27, a freeze-etched preparation of a similar plant cell.

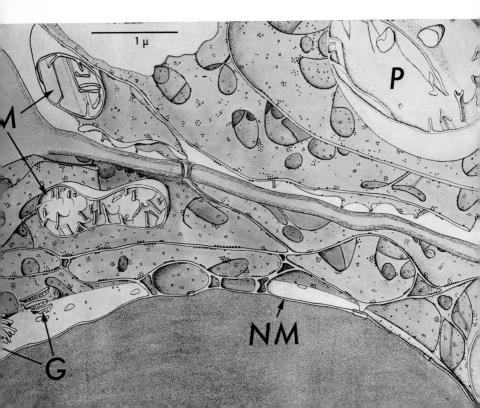

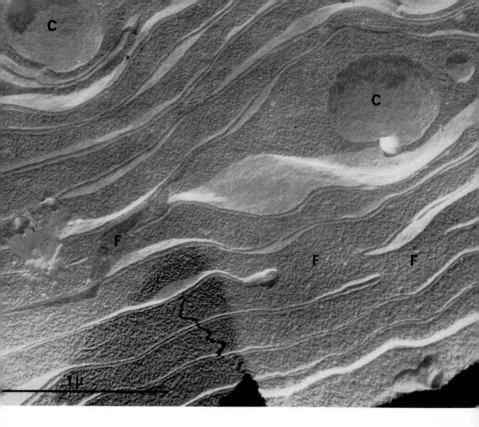

FIG. 26. Electron micrograph of a replica of a frozen and etched wheat (*Triticum*) root tip cell. Sheets of ER have been fractured and exposed both in transverse and surface view. Fenestrations in the ER are visible (F) and there are also casts of two unidentified cytoplasmic organelles (C). Compare this figure with the artistic interpretation of ER in Fig. 25.   Micrograph by Dr D. H. Northcote.

When first seen in thin sections, the ER appeared as two dark lines 8 nm thick separated by a light line 15–20 nm thick. Subsequent work has shown that each of the dark lines may be resolved as two dark lines separated by a light line, and so, in the nomenclature of Robertson, the ER consists of two unit membranes (see page 74) which are separated by a space of variable width. The membranes are continuous at the ends of profiles so there are no free edges. Frey-Wyssling (1964) regards the space between the unit membranes as a watery fluid which he calls the enchylema. This space can widen to form vesicles. The whole ER system is hollow and the internal spaces are possibly continuous throughout the cell. Each sheet of ER seen in freeze-etched preparations or in oblique sections should be treated as a flattened bladder which is connected internally with all the other ER bladders and also with the nuclear

FIG. 27. Elcetron micrograph of a freeze-etched preparation of an *Allium* root tip cell. The nucleus (left) shows a large number of nuclear pores (NP). Beside it a mitochondrion (M) has broken in half and shows its internal structure. Surface views and profiles of the fenestrated ER indicated can be seen throughout the cytoplasm. The surface of a vacuole can be seen (V) and both concave and convex surfaces of spherosomes (S).   Micrograph by Dr D. Branton.

envelope. The nuclear envelope is also a double unit membrane and its lumen (the perinuclear space) openly communicates with the enchylema of the ER (Figs. 25, 27). The outer of the two unit membranes of the nuclear envelope projects into the cytoplasm as the ER. But sometimes, where there is a pore in the nuclear envelope, both of its unit membranes run off into the cytoplasm to constitute ER. The nuclear envelope and the ER are therefore part of the same system and we see one of the difficulties of having to separate organelles in order to describe them.

Some parts of the ER are covered by ribosomes, spherical organelles of about 20 nm diameter, on the outer surfaces, i.e. on the cytoplasm side, not the enchylema side. These ribosomes also occur unattached to ER in the cytoplasm. They also occur inside other organelles. ER coated with ribosomes is termed 'rough-surfaced' and ER without ribosomes is called 'smooth-surfaced'. Some cells, such as pancreas exocrine cells and most plant cells, have only rough-surfaced ER, others, such as liver cells, have both rough- and smooth-surfaced ER and some cells such as steroid-secreting cells and the tips of pollen tubes have no ribosomes on the ER at all. The rough-surfaced ER of plant cells is sparse compared with the typical animal secretory cells and the ribosomes seem to be less regularly spaced on plant ER membranes than on animal membranes. Some ER membranes studied by Wooding and Northcote (1965b) surrounding the plastids of resin secreting canal cells of *Pinus* are coated with ribosomes only on the cytoplasmic face and are smooth where they face the plastid. Cytoplasm with rough-surfaced ER is sometimes referred to as ergastoplasm and regions of cytoplasm rich in rough-surfaced ER have a strong affinity for basic dyes such as toluidine blue because of the presence of the RNA-rich ribosomes. In the pancreas rough-surfaced ER occupies most of the cytoplasm (Fig. 28). Ribosomes are the sites of protein synthesis in the cytoplasm and so secretory cells are rich in them. A few years ago one of the fractions obtained from centrifuging broken up cells was called the microsome fraction because it consisted of small particles. This fraction is now believed to consist of fragments of ER with its attached ribosomes. The ribosomes can now be separated from the membranes and contain most of the RNA content whereas the membranes contain most of the protein and phospholipid, though Dashek and Rosen (1966) have shown that labelled uridine is incorporated into the cytoplasm of the tips of pollen tubes and that both the label and the smooth-surfaced ER disappear after RNA-ase treatment. This appears to be good evidence for the existence of RNA in the ER membranes of this material and is supported by the finding that the ribosomes of a microsomal fraction of *Glycine* do not account for the whole of the RNA content (Chrispeels *et al.*, 1966). In plants, both rough- and smooth-surfaced ER occur, sometimes in the same cell and therefore probably continuous with one another (Porter, 1961). Buvat (1963) holds that most of the ER near the cell wall is rough-surfaced whereas that in the rest of the cytoplasm is smooth. Rough-surfaced ER is conspicuous in the hyphal tips of the haustoria of the angiospermous parasite, *Cuscuta* (Bonneville & Voeller, 1963), but protein secreting plant cells are not consistently rich in ergastoplasm as animal cells are.

In animals, so far as we know, the smooth-surfaced ER is always tubular (Fig. 29) whereas rough-surfaced ER is always sheet-like. However, in plants, although the rough ER is invariably sheet-like, the smooth ER can be either sheet-like or tubular. For example, the smooth

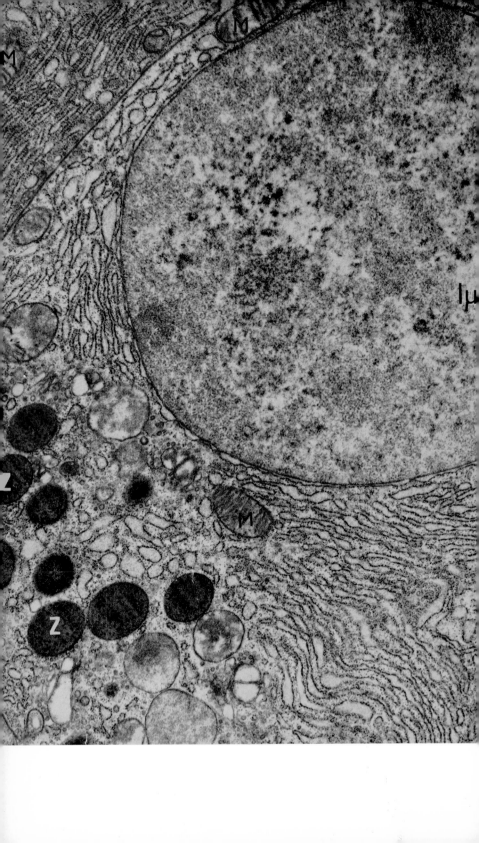

ER of the pollen tube tips already mentioned is tubular and there are reports of tangled skeins of tubular, smooth ER at the poles of the mitotic spindles. Cambial initials are said by Srivastava & O'Brien (1966a, b) to have smooth, sheet-like ER in winter which they think may turn into rough ER in summer. Also, in plants smooth ER areas lie side by side with rough areas of the same ER sheet (Bouck, 1963). Some cells, such as the companion cells of phloem and resin canal cells have asymmetrical ER where one side is rough and the other is smooth. In animals, on the other hand, no conversion of smooth to rough or vice versa occurs. No ER sheets or tubes have both rough and smooth areas and no asymmetrical ER is known to exist although the outer side of the nuclear envelope does bear ribosomes in animals though this is rare in plants. In general, the type of ER possessed by animal cells may be predicted from the function of the cell. This is not true of plants.

It is quite common to see in differentiated cells, though not in meristematic cells, profiles of ER lying parallel to the cell walls and also to the nuclear surface (Fig. 30). Stacks of 'annulate' lamellae occur parallel to the nuclear envelope of many animal cells. These observations suggest that ER is generated from the nuclear envelope like ticker tape and is concerned perhaps largely with wall synthesis in plants though this possible origin does not necessarily imply that it carries information like ticker tape from the nucleus about synthesis of walls or anything else.

In specialized cells the ER may be modified in appearance. Jensen (1963) found that in some cells in the developing fruit of cotton the ER was expanded at intervals to form spheres and that in the egg cell and embryo there were tubules between the cisternae. These modifications are probably related to the peculiar nutritional requirements of the egg and its derivative cells. Shortage of oxygen seems to lead to the formation of concentric rings of ER in parts of the cytoplasm which consequently stain heavily with basic dyes (Frey-Wyssling & Mühlethaler, 1965). In some kinds of cells the ER consists wholly of flat cisternae and in other kinds it forms mostly tubules, but the significance of this is not understood (Esau, 1963). Sometimes when the ER forms large vesicles this may be correlated with senescence of the protoplasm as in sieve tubes and vessel elements (Esau, 1963; Buvat, 1963). Where this occurs the ER system is clearly no longer a continuous system.

So far, our only information about the function of the ER comes

FIG. 28. Electron micrograph of a pancreatic cell of a mouse showing the conspicuous and profuse rough-surfaced ER; zymogen granules, Z; mitochondrion M. (Os/Pb/U)   Micrograph by Dr S. Bradbury.

from the study of its distribution and structure. Ribosomes are concerned with protein synthesis. They are the sites at which the amino acids are assembled into polypeptide chains. As rough-surfaced ER appears to be associated especially with secretory cells it may be that production of protein for export requires the membranes for movement either of the finished protein or of the raw materials or for organizing the ribosomes. In the pancreas of the guinea pig the zymogen granules are found within the space enclosed by the ER unit membranes and so here the product of synthesis is separated from the sites of synthesis, the ribosomes, by a membrane (Porter, 1961). The internal space of the ER, the enchylema, probably allows movement of substances throughout the cytoplasm and nuclear envelope without them becoming free in the cytoplasm or nuclear matrix. Also the large surface area of the ER may allow for some pattern in the distribution of enzymes. There is some evidence too that the ER may prevent the passage to the wall of Golgi vesicles and that it is orientated parallel to the direction of cytoplasmic streaming (Thaine, 1965). If the function of the rough-surfaced ER is mainly protein synthesis, what does smooth-surfaced ER do? Porter (1961) points out that lipid secreting cells always have smooth ER as do cells secreting steroid hormones (Fig. 29). It also seems to be concerned with the detoxication of animal cells and their carbohydrate metabolism. Microsomes from steroid secreting cells can produce the enzymes for hormone synthesis in the presence of RNA-ase at concentrations sufficient to inhibit synthesis of other proteins. But, in plants, smooth-surfaced ER has been found in any quantity only in pollen tube tips (Rosen & Gawlik, 1966a). In secretory cells the Golgi bodies are known also to be concerned with the secretion (see Chapter 4) and it may be that the ER transports substances to the Golgi to be prepared for movement to the surface of the cell in the vesicles.

Thus, apart from its possible role in protein synthesis in secretory cells, the most likely function of the ER is as an intracellular circulatory system. The translocation of sugars, amino acids and ATP to sites of usage or storage suggests itself from the morphology of the system. Because of its relation to the myofibrils of striated muscle, Porter (1961) suggests that it may conduct intracellular impulses. In many electron micrographs of plant walls it appears as if the ER passes through the wall from one cytoplast to another. Unfortunately the minute anatomy

FIG. 29. Electron micrographs of cell from adrenal cortex of rat showing in A smooth-surfaced, tubular ER and in B mitochondria with tubular cristae. (Ad/Os/ Pb/U)   Micrographs by Dr S. Bradbury.

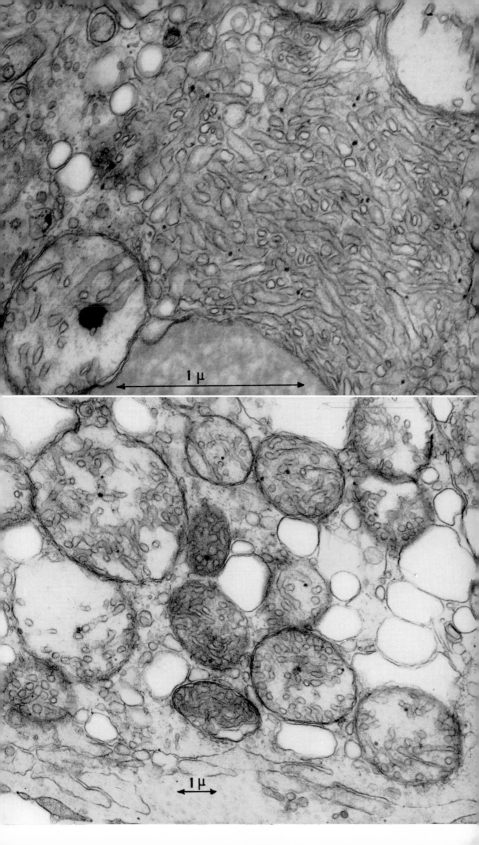

of such places seems never to be quite good enough to see exactly how this occurs. Is there a tube of cytoplasm in which a tube of ER runs or is it merely that a part of the ER has been caught in the cell plate at an early stage of wall formation (Fig. 25, 31, 32)? Porter & Machado (1960) report no ER tubules in plasmodesmata, though other workers disagree. The nature of plasmodesmata is discussed in Chapter 5, but there is the possibility that the ER allows movement of substances between cells within the enchylema of ER tubules running through the plasmodesmata.

The sieve tubes of the phloem, which conduct organic substances over large distances in plants, are said to have a cytoplasm rich in ER arranged parallel to the long axis and, according to Frey-Wyssling &

FIG. 30. Electron micrograph of central root cap cells of the primary root of *Zea*. Taken from the same root and prepared in the same way as in Figs. 10 and 21. The ER of the central cap cells unlike that of the peripheral cap cells is predominantly either parallel to the cell walls or parallel to the nuclear membrane. Compare this distribution with Figs. 10 and 21 in which the ER is apparently randomly dispersed. The amyloplasts (A) are almost filled with large and densely staining starch grains. Compare these with the amyloplasts in Figs. 10 and 21. The Golgi bodies are relatively small (see Fig. 64) and are producing small vesicles. The Golgi bodies (G) are in the plane of the section. Large numbers of plasmodesmata cross the transverse walls (TS), but very few cross the longitudinal walls (L). (See Fig. 124). (Glut/Mn)

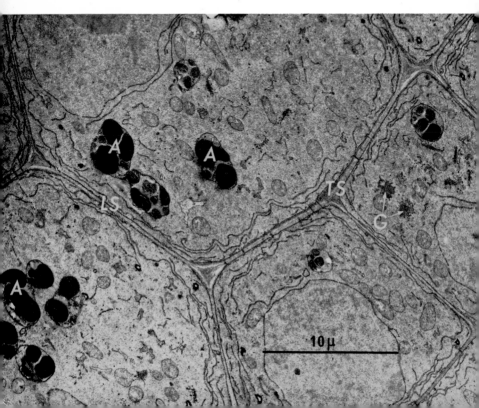

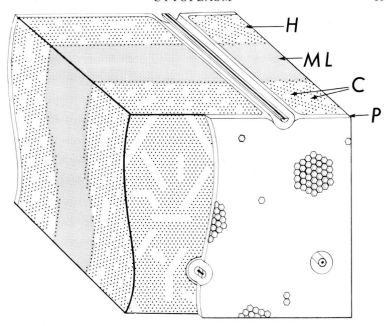

F IG. 31. Three-dimensional representation of a primary cell wall. The plasmalemma
(P) lines the plasmodesma (see Fig. 20 A). On the surface of the plasmalemma are
numbers of small granules c. 8·5 nm in diameter (see Fig. 105), believed to be
associated with wall formation. The middle lamella (ML) is clearly demarcated from
the primary wall on either side, by the absence of cellulose microfibrils (C) embedded
in hemicellulose (H).

Mühlethaler (1965), bunches of ER tubules pass through the sieve plate
pores (but see page 412). Wooding & Northcote (1965) noticed an
association between the ER and the plastids in phloem cells. There is a
transitory sheathing of the plastids in the sieve tubes and a permanent
one in the companion cells and also in resin canal cells. These plastids
have little internal differentiation and Wooding & Northcote think that
the ER serves for the transport of sucrose to be stored in them in the
companion cells. The association in resin canal cells also suggests that
the ER and plastids are here the synthetic units for the terpenes of the
resin.

Another function suggested by association is one in wall synthesis.
ER profiles are often found lying close to and parallel with walls,
especially recently formed walls (Fig. 30). Hepler & Newcombe (1964)
also draw attention to an association with secondary wall formation.
Porter & Machado (1960) note that more ER per unit volume occurs in

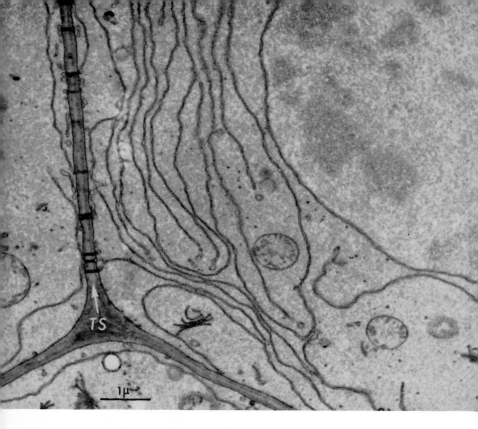

F IG. 32. Electron micrograph of a central root cap cell of the primary root of *Zea*. The accumulation of ER at one end of the cell has been brought about by gravitational disturbances. A number of connections is made between the ER and plasmodesmata through the transverse wall (TS) (see Fig. 106). (Mn)

the epidermal cells than in cortical or stelar cells and this they also relate to the higher rate of wall synthesis in the epidermal cells.

The ER gives the impression of being flexible in the cell, able to move both with the cytoplasmic matrix and also freely within the cytoplasm. Bouck (1963) showed that excised pea roots subjected to centrifugal forces of around 20,000 × g for a day has rough-surfaced ER that is slow to stratify, but quick to reorientate afterwards. Griffiths & Audus (1964) showed that the amyloplasts of statocyte cells in the root cap of *Vicia* displace the ER to the upper halves of cells when the root receives a twenty-minute geotropic stimulation by turning it to lie horizontally. But they regard this movement as due to displacement by the heavy amyloplasts which sediment to the lower side of the cell. Other organelles were similarly displaced by the amyloplasts falling to the lower side and did not appear to move otherwise in the gravitational field. Just how the movements in the statocytes affect the growth of the root, carried out by the elongating zone often several millimetres away from the cap, is not known. It may be that the ER itself is concerned rather than the amyloplasts, for it may act as a valve presenting a variable barrier to the movement of growth hormones in the cell.

On the origin of the ER and its relation to other membranes in the cell there is much controversy. There is little doubt about the connexion with the nuclear envelope already mentioned. This is seen in most electron micrographs (Figs. 33, 34). Buttrose (1963) for example, regards the ER as arising from sac-like proliferations of the outer unit membrane of the nuclear envelope. Blebs from the inner unit membrane give rise to cytoplasmic ground substance in his material, wheat (*Triticum*) endosperm. As is well known, the nuclear envelope ceases to exist or fragments at the beginning of mitosis and a new one is formed around the daughter nuclei at the end of mitosis. Frey-Wyssling (1964) holds that the nuclear envelope does not disappear at prophase, but breaks down into short fragments of ER and similarly, at telophase, the envelopes of the daughter nuclei are reconstituted from the existing ER. In yeasts, Lindegren (1962) believes that ER is extruded from the nuclear vacuole through a special 'assembler' which produces a ribbon which folds up in the cytoplasm. The investigations of Bell & Mühlethaler (1962) on fern eggs led them to believe that, as the egg cell matures, the nuclear envelope evaginates into the cytoplasm as a membrane system from which plastids and mitochondria as well as ER were formed. The organelles could therefore be regarded as initially part of the nuclear envelope—ER systems which later become detached. Other workers do not accept this interpretation either on the grounds that the developments of undisputed plastids and mitochondria from the ER has never been shown or because fern eggs are peculiar cells and what occurs in them may not occur elsewhere. There is substance in both these arguments, for (1) the electron micrographs published by Bell & Mühlethaler show only vesicles, which do not resemble either plastids or mitochondria, attached to the ER. The fate of these vesicles is not certain. It may be that they do become detached and then differentiate into plastids or mitochondria and, in any case, it is probably unrealistic to expect them to differentiate into either kind of organelle when still attached. (2) The fern egg does have many characters not found in other cells and its key position in development probably makes this a necessity. But occasional observations on other cells do support the view that the other membrane systems of cells can be linked with the ER either onto-genetically or secondarily for some special purpose.

Some electron microscopists (e.g. Larson, 1965) have reported continuity between the ER and the plasmalemma. Frey-Wyssling (1964) regards this as unlikely because it would mean that there was an open connexion between the perinuclear space and the outside of the cell. Larson's material was the pollen of *Hippeastrum* and it may be that this has an unusual structure but there is good evidence that striated muscle has such connexions. Belief in a tubular network communicating with extracellular space was based on A. F. Huxley's work on the inward conduction of excitation and appropriate apertures have now been seen (e.g. Rayns, Simpson & Bertaud, 1967). As we have seen (see page 79), the plasmalemma can give rise to vesicles in pinocytosis, though perhaps not commonly in plants, and the Golgi vesicles can probably be incorporated into plasmalemma. Therefore some workers would have us believe in two discrete membrane systems, one linking the plasmalemma and Golgi and the other linking the nuclear envelope, ER, mitochondria, plastids and spherosomes, the organelles being budded off the ER or directly off the nuclear envelope. The position of the Golgi is equivocal in such a dual system. Whaley, Mollenhauer & Leech (1960a) hold that there is at least a periodic association between the Golgi and the ER. A difference in the appearance of the membranes of the Golgi bodies and those of the Golgi vesicles has already been noted (see page 75). Formation of organelles from the ER or nuclear envelope may be something that occurs only in special cells, for, as we shall see in Chapter 4, possibly all the organelles can reproduce themselves once formed.

ER is certainly present in meristematic cells. It does not all have to be produced from the nuclear envelope except possibly in certain exceptional cases. It appears relatively simple though we have shown that its appearance is deceptive. Whaley, Kephart & Mollenhauer (1964) suggest that the very rapid increase in the ER that occurs after some experimental treatments shows that there is a quick transfer from molecular units already present in the cytoplasm to lamellae, though their observations do not necessarily imply that ER is created *de novo* in the cytoplasmic matrix. Thaine (1965), though, claims that he has seen undifferentiated regions of the cytoplasm being transformed into ER in living cells. ER segments may be trapped by the cell plate as it forms after mitosis. At anaphase the ER invades the spindle from the cytoplasm

FIG. 33. Electron micrograph of part of a cell from a *Spinacia* leaf. The nuclear membrane with pores (P) is joined to the rough-surfaced ER (J). The cell also contains mitochondria (M) and a developing chloroplast (C). (Glut/Os/Pb/U)

Micrograph by Mr A. D. Greenwood.

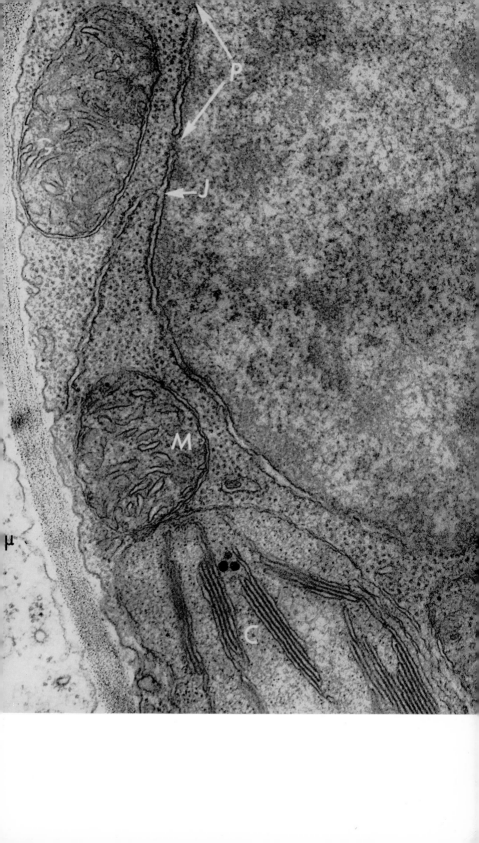

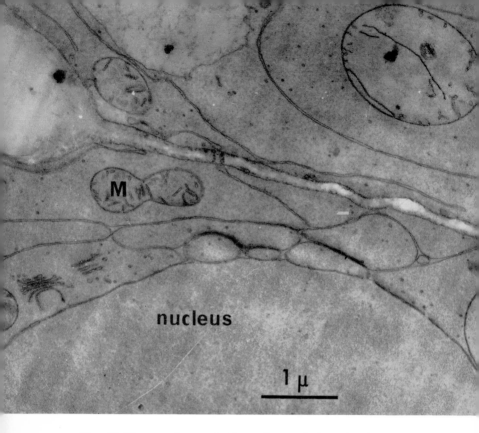

M

nucleus

1 μ

FIG. 34. Electron micrograph of part of two cells from the elongating zone of the primary root of *Vicia*. Note the continuity between the nuclear membrane, ER and plasmodesmata. The dumb-bell-shaped mitochondrion (M) may have been in the process of dividing. (Mn)

around it and, according to Porter (1961), it forms a lattice of tubules at the spindle equator in which what are supposed to be pectin vesicles appear and fuse together. Newcomb (1963) also regards the cell plate or phragmoplast as ER which has changed from a lamellar form to a tubular form making a lattice in which pectin-rich vesicles arise possibly by the lysis of the spindle matrix. Other views on cell wall initiation are discussed in Chapter 5.

3.6   Ribosomes

These are very small particles that are believed to be the centres of protein synthesis in cells (Figs. 35, 36). They began their history 25 years ago as part of the so-called microsomal fraction obtained by breaking cells open and centrifuging the contents in steps at successively higher speeds to remove the larger particles. This microsomal fraction contained small particles first noted in plants by Robinson & Brown (1953) plus debris now known to be mainly fragments of the endoplasmic reticulum. Nowadays techniques for removing the phospholipid membranes of the ER by deoxycholate are used and these free the particles from the ER. These free ribosomes retain their integrity and can synthesize protein *in vitro*. When adequate techniques for looking at cells under the electron microscope materialized small particles of similar size to those of the microsomal fraction (20 nm) were found in the cytoplasm and especially on the ER. These particles were called Palade granules, but it was quickly realized that they were the same as the microsomal particles. As they are rich in RNA, we now call them ribosomes both in the cell and in the centrifuge. (The term microsome was formerly also used for the much larger particles now called spherosomes, see page 190.) The high percentage of RNA in ribosomes gives cytoplasm strongly basophilic properties when they are present in large numbers.

To the biochemist a ribosome is a ribonucleoprotein particle in the size range 20–100 Svedberg units. To the cytologist ribosomes are osmiophilic particles of about 15–25 nm diameter. They are not seen in cells fixed in permanganate, but are well preserved by fixation in osmium tetroxide (cf. Figs. 30 and 33). Particles of a similar size are not seen on the ER membranes of cells after freeze-etching and replication (Branton & Moor, 1964). They are, of course, well below the resolution of a light microscope.

FIG. 35. Electron micrograph of isolated and shadowed ribosomes. These ribosomes were extracted from *Nicotiana* leaves and rotationally shadowed. The ribosomes have remained together in groups (polysomes) and appear to lie along a common axis.   Micrograph by Dr R. G. Milne.

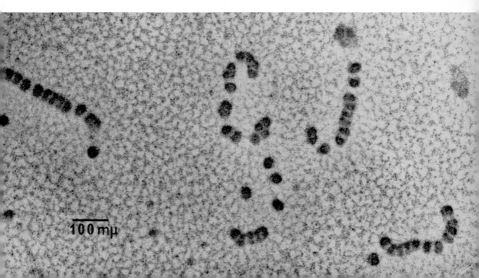

100 mµ

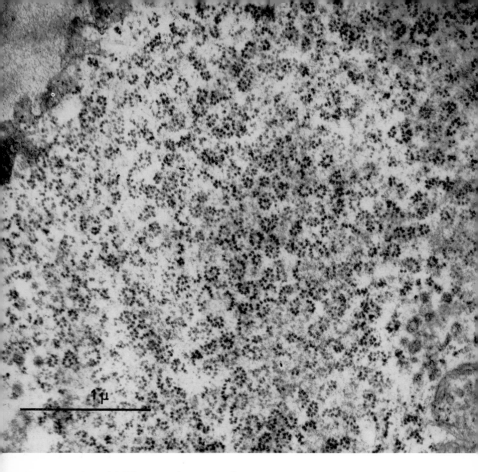

FIG. 36. Electron micrograph of polysomes in a cell of a cotyledon of *Vicia*. (Glut/Osm/Pb/U)   Micrograph by Dr H. Öpik

Occurrence and origin

Ribosomes occur in all cells, animal, plant or bacterial as far as we know. They appear free in the cytoplasm or else attached to the ER. Others appear to associate with the nuclear membrane and possibly other organelles as well, although association with the nuclear membrane is rare in plants but common in animals. In plants, the meristematic and undifferentiated cells contain ribosomes free in the cytoplasm and not on the ER to any great extent. In differentiated cells, attachment to the ER is more common, but free ribosomes also exist. Setterfield (1961) reports that, in *Avena* coleoptiles, the number of free ribosomes per cell remains more or less constant throughout the period of cell elongation and then declines sharply when growth stops.

Few attached ribosomes occur in growing cells in this material, but there is a significant increase during the maturation of the cells. ER studded with ribosomes is termed rough-surfaced and that free of particles is termed smooth-surfaced. The significance of attachment to the ER is still not known though it has been suggested that ribosomes attached to the ER are more active in protein synthesis than free ribosomes. In bacteria, yeasts and other fungi they are solely free (Fig. 37). In animal secretory cells that export protein, such as pancreatic exocrine, the ER is conspicuously rough-surfaced (Fig. 28). Not many plant cells are known to secrete proteins and those that do, such as some of the glandular cells of the insectivorous plants, do not have large amounts of conspicuously rough-surfaced ER. On sheets of ER lying at the outside of a plant cell sometimes the side next to the plasmalemma is smooth while the other side is rough. This occurs in the phloem at the sieve plates (Pickett-Heaps & Northcote, 1966). It also occurs in the ER-

FIG. 37. Electron micrograph of a *Rickettsia* pathogenic to a saturnid moth *Samia cynthia* x *ricini*. No membrane-bounded structures are found within the rickettsian and the only structures that can be seen, in common with higher organisms, are the ribosomes and the unit membrane surrounding the whole organism. The function of the rickettsian's protruding fingers is unknown. (Glut/Osm/Pb/U)

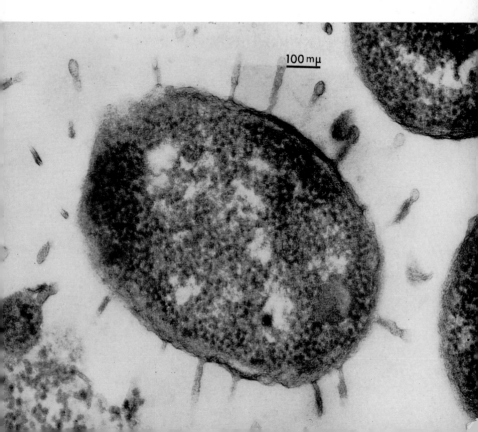

sheathed plastids of companion cells and the glands of *Pinguicula*. One view about the attachment to the ER is that the ER may assist in the translocation of the protein made on the ribosomes. The circumstantial evidence of correlation of attachment with protein secretion makes this view plausible, but it has also been suggested that the ribosomes merely stick to the surface of the ER as the ER develops in the cell or during the preparation of the cell for the electron microscope. On the other hand, some studies have suggested that the particles are partially embedded in the ER membranes. The fact that most of the ribosomes are free in meristematic cells indicates that attachment to the ER occurs after their formation and there is some evidence that detachment from the ER occurs in ageing cells and may also be a seasonal phenomenon (see page 398). Sometimes the ribosomes appear to be grouped into clusters with the appearance of rosettes or spirals or circles. In plants these clusters are mostly seen free in the cytoplasm (Falk, 1961; Clowes & Juniper, 1964), but they also occur attached to the ER in the later stages of differentiation of cambial derivatives (Cronshaw, 1965) and of maturing cotyledon cells of *Phaseolus* (Öpik, 1965) (Figs. 36, 89). It is possible that the clusters are groups of ribosomes attached to a thread of messenger RNA, for, in some preparations, a fibre about 1 nm across and destroyed by ribonuclease treatment can be seen connecting all the particles of the cluster. Under the electron microscope ribosomes often appear to consist of a large and a small unit, and Öpik has noticed that, where the groups of ribosomes form, the axis of symmetry of each ribosome is often normal to the path of the spiral (Figs. 35, 36). Such clusters are called polysomes, polyribosomes or ergosomes and will be discussed later (see page 113) in connexion with protein synthesis. Echlin (1965) has found helical threads with ribosomes attached in a staggered manner in pollen mother cells. Such threads were absent in the tapetum of the same stamens where the ribosomes are always attached to the ER. Rough-surfaced ER does not occur in the pollen mother cells.

Ribosomes also occur in nuclei, plastids and mitochondria (Tso, 1962). Murakami (1963) demonstrated them in the chloroplasts of *Spinacia* where RNA had already been found and also in the spherosomes, but could not find them in the mitochondria of the same cells. Morton and Raison (1963) found them in the proteinoplasts of the endosperm of *Triticum*. Nougarède & Pilet (1964) report that the degradation of protein in vacuoles at the onset of germination of *Triticum* seeds is accompanied by an increase in ribosomes. Öpik, on the other hand, reports that mitochondrial ribosomes disappear during germination in the cotyledons of *Phaseolus*. It looks as if the ribosome is the unit of protein production in most parts of cells.

About half a million ribosomes are present in a cell. In the bacterium, *Escherichia coli*, there are 6,000 per cell which has a volume of $1\mu m^3$. Rabbit reticulocytes contain 100,000 in about $100\mu m^3$ and they constitute about 0·5 per cent of the cell volume. In yeast there are 500,000 in $120\mu m^3$. In terms of molarity this gives us a figure of 1×10^{-5} to $2 \times 10^{-6} M$ (Ts'o, 1962).

On the origin of ribosomes very few facts exist. Chipchase & Birnstiel (1963) believe that the structural RNA of the cytoplasmic ribosomes comes from the nucleus and that autoradiography implicates the nucleolus especially in its origin. There are ribosomes in the nucleolus and it has been shown by the complementarity proved by hybridization with denatured DNA that the nucleolar RNA is identical in base sequence with the RNA of the cytoplasmic ribosomes. Such information once caused people to think that ribosomes might be made in the nucleoli and that they then migrated into the cytoplasm carrying the genetic instructions from the nucleus. But it is widely believed that another form of RNA that carries the nuclear instructions and some, at least of the nuclear ribosomes stay there and probably synthesize nuclear protein. The nucleolar RNA could still be the precursor of ribosomal RNA, however, even if the nucleolus is not the site of cytoplasmic ribosome production. But Chipchase & Birnstiel (1963) have shown that only a minority of the ribosomal RNA cistrons in seedlings of *Pisum* occur in nucleolar DNA. Most of them occur in the chromatin of the nucleus outside the nucleolus and so they think that most, if not all, of the ribosomal RNA is synthesized by the non-nucleolar regions of the chromatin and then transferred to the nucleolus possibly for final assembly into ribosomes. If ribosomes are not made in the nucleolus they could multiply themselves in the cytoplasm or they could be organized *de novo*. The simplest hypothesis is still that they are made in the nucleolus and migrate into the cytoplasm (see page 344) and there now seems to be, at least in animals, good electron microscopical evidence for this (Painter & Biesele, 1966).

Structure

Under the electron microscope at high resolution ribosomes appear roughly spherical or occasionally made up of two parts, and of the same order of size as the simpler plant viruses. They consist of about equal quantities of protein and RNA though they do not change either in size or number when treated with RNA-ase according to Perez-del-Cerro (1961). Freeze-etched preparations of cells of *Allium cepa* have demonstrated particles of 9–14 nm diameter especially on the surfaces of vacuoles, ER and Golgi bodies. Branton & Moor (1964) point out that these may be ribosomes although higher plant ribosomes fall in the 15–25 nm size range in ordinary preparations. It is difficult to reconcile the types of preparations, for the freeze-etched ones show no particles in the expected size range. It could be that osmium tetroxide, which is used to fix cells for sections to show ribosomes, swells the particles or it may be that cutting the frozen preparations splinters the ribosomes into their subunits. But Branton (1966) suggests that these particles are not ribosomes at all, but the globular units of which all membranes are made in part, revealed by splitting the membrane down the middle in the fracturing of the frozen cell.

The substructure of ribosomes is known best for *E. coli*. Here, after breaking open the cells and centrifuging, there are found four different stable forms of sedimentation coefficients 100S, 70S, 50S, and 30S. The form that is obtained after centrifugation depends on the concentration of free magnesium in the suspension (Table 4). Removal of the magnesium splits the 70S ribosomes into two components. Huxley & Zubay (1960) have shown that the 70S particle consists of a 30S particle joined to a 50S particle. Two 70S particles go to form the 100S dimers by apposition of the exposed faces of the 30S subunits. When 50S particles are present in a medium in which 100S particles would be stable they also form dimers of 81S by the apposition of the same faces that are

TABLE 4

Characteristics of ribosomes

Source	Sedimentation constant	Sedimentation constant of the RNA of each subunit
Animal cytoplasm	80S	29S 18S or 30S 18S (Stutz & Noll, 1967)
Plant cytoplasm	80S	25S 18S (Loening & Ingle, 1967) 25S 17S (Stutz & Noll, 1967)
Chloroplasts	67S 70S	22S 16S (Noll, 1967) 23S 16S (Loening & Ingle, 1967)
Mitochondria	73S	23S 17S (Küntzel & Noll, 1967)
Bacteria	67–72S	23S 16S (Taylor & Storck, 1964; Loening & Ingle, 1967)

apposed to the 30S particles in the 70S particles. The 70S particles show a clear cleft between the two subunits.

The 50S subunits, when on their own, measure 14–16 nm in diameter and, when united in a 70S particle they measure 16×13 nm. So it is concluded that the subunit is dome-shaped and is attached by its flat end. The 30S subunits appear 16–18 nm long and 7 nm wide when combined and 15–18 nm across when free. This suggests a disc-shaped structure though when free they show various forms, triangles, trapezia or polygons. They never appear as regular polyhedra as the small viruses do. Watson (1963) estimates the molecular weights to be $5 \cdot 5 \times 10^5$ for the 30S subunit and $1 \cdot 1 \times 10^6$ for the 50S subunit and considers both to contain only one RNA chain molecule. He thinks of the basic protein as structural rather than catalytic though ribosomes do possess enzymes.

Animals and plants (including fungi but excluding blue-green algae) have 80S ribosomes consisting of a 40S subunit joined to a 60S subunit. (Table 2). This is true of the ordinary ribosomes of the cytoplasm, but plastids and possibly mitochondria as well as bacteria and blue-green algae contain 70S ribosomes. Two 80S units can form a dimer of 120S. In *Pisum*, ribosomes have a molecular weight of 4 to $4 \cdot 5 \times 10^6$ and, in shadowed preparations, they appear to be oblate spheroids of 25 nm diameter and 16 nm high (Ts'o, 1962). The 60S particles of *Pisum* can also associate together to form a heavy dimer and can be dissociated into one 40S and two 26S subunits. Bayley (1964) considers the 60S and 40S units to be discs of diameter equal to that of the whole ribosome (29–25 nm) and 8–9 nm thick and that the 26S subunits are rod-shaped particles $21–25 \times 9$ nm existing in pairs parallel to each other. He believes the rod-shaped particles are sandwiched between two 40S units in the whole ribosome and that, when the ribosome cleaves, it forms a 40S unit plus two rods and a free 40S unit, or two 50S units consisting of one disc plus one rod. No cleavage furrow corresponding with that reported by Huxley and Zubay (1960) for *E. coli* has been found in *Pisum* and Bayley thinks this is likely to be due to the junction between the two discs having a protein coat around the RNA. However, cleavage furrows are seen in some higher plant preparations.

Protein synthesis

The connexion between ribosomes and protein synthesis could be said to start with the observations of Brachet and Casperson that active protein synthesis always seems to accompany richness of RNA in the

E

cells. A full account of this most important branch of biology would be out of place in this book and has been given in many reviews and modern text books. But a brief treatment is useful here in connexion with the role of ribosomes and our future discussion of the mitotic cycle, differentiation and cell heredity.

Protein synthesis is one of the most important functions of a cell to understand because not only is it responsible for the cell's ability to grow and multiply, but any theory about it has to account for the production of many different kinds of cells within the same organism as well as for the differences between organisms. Most biologists now believe that most, if not all protein synthesis takes place on the ribosomes. Isolated ribosomes can synthesize protein *in vitro*. The sort of protein produced must be specified by the nucleus because we know that nuclei of different genetic make-up are responsible for the differences between individual organisms. Briefly the current view is that the DNA of the nucleus carries the instructions for protein synthesis as a code written as the sequence of the four bases, adenine, guanine, cytosine and thymine, along the length of the DNA molecule. The simplest theory, which is attracting increasing experimental proof, is that a sequence of three bases specifies one amino acid along the protein chain. There are twenty different amino acids in proteins and proteins differ from each other in the arrangement and number of these amino acids. A triplet code with codons of three nucleic acid bases is adequate (giving sixty-four combinations) for the specification of twenty amino acids; in fact there is evidence that the code is degenerate in the sense that more than one codon can specify one amino acid (see page 342). Experiments *in vitro* have now decoded the whole system of amino acid specification (Table 8). The DNA base sequence does not determine the protein species directly because the DNA is in the nucleus and proteins are mostly made in the cytoplasm on the ribosomes. The most popular current theory is that the coded information of the DNA is transferred to an RNA molecule which acts as a messenger from the nucleus to the ribosomes.

There are at least three kinds of RNA in a cell. The ribosomal RNA accounts for 75–85 per cent of the total and is combined with protein. It has a molecular weight of around one million. It differs from other RNA's in having few of the uncommon bases such as ribosyluracil (Ts'o, 1962). The RNA that is thought to carry the coded instructions of the nucleus, messenger RNA, bears the base arrangement complementary to that of the DNA. Its most easily determined feature is that it has a rapid turnover and is short-lived, in microorganisms at least. Not much is known about it in higher plants and animals and some workers question its existence. It is thought that each chain would consist of several hundred nucleotides and that it would require a molecular weight of about 600,000 to code for a protein of molecular weight 70,000. The third kind of RNA is called transfer—or soluble RNA. It has a much lower molecular weight—about 24,000, and less than about 80 nucleotides. Its role is to combine selectively with amino acid—adenylate enzyme complexes so that the amino acid is transferred to the terminal adenylic acid group of the t-RNA chain. In this process adenosine monophosphate and the enzyme are released and become available for rephosphorylation by ATP. There is at least one kind of t-RNA for each of the twenty amino acids and each molecule carries its attached amino acid to a ribosome for assembly into a protein chain. The t-RNA molecule is a single chain, but is apparently folded in the middle to give a double helix. At one end is a guanosine residue and at the other there is a cytosine-cytosine-adenine series which carries the amino acid. At the point where the molecule is folded it is thought that there are three nucleotides which are not paired with others along the chain and that these three form a key which fits at the appropriate place along the m-RNA molecule. Adenine of one molecule is attracted to uracil on the other, and cytosine to guanine, just as in DNA synthesis except that, in RNA, uracil replaces thymine.

DNA	—	DNA	—	m-RNA	—	t-RNA
A	—	T	—	A	—	U
G	—	C	—	G	—	C
T	—	A	—	U	—	A
C	—	G	—	C	—	G
	DNA		mRNA		m–t	
	synthesis		*synthesis*		*keying*	

Transfer and ribosomal RNA's each have their own distinct base composition differing from that of DNA and there is apparently little species-specificity shown by the plants so far investigated. But m-RNA must be species specific and also phase-specific because different proteins are made at different times in the differentiation of a cell.

The role of the ribosomes in protein synthesis is not fully understood yet. It is assumed by many that m-RNA is coded by DNA and migrates from the nucleus to the cytoplasm and there joins with several ribosomes. The filament sometimes seen under the electron microscope connecting one ribosome with possibly others to form a polysome may be the m-RNA molecule. The t-RNA with its amino acid also moves to a ribosome. The problems are (1) why cannot it just attach itself to the m-RNA molecule without a ribosome being present and (2) why does the ribosome need RNA itself? It may be that the ribosomes are needed to hold the m-RNA molecule ready to receive the t-RNA molecules, for their own RNA appears not to participate in protein synthesis at all. It is probably inert because of its bonding to protein, but one cannot help feeling that it must have some role possibly in linking with the t-RNA. The functional unit is a group of ribosomes— the polysome or ergosome and the number of ribosomes in the unit may be related to the length of the protein molecule to be produced. Or it may be that a long m-RNA molecule can code for a whole sequence of protein molecules needed for example for a reaction that requires several enzymes. Haemoglobin synthesis appears to need five ribosomes though some polysomes with four or six units also occur (Rich, 1963; Warner et al., 1963). The ribosomes are, in this example, separated by 5–15 nm and the total length of the polysome is 150 nm. The nucleotides on the m-RNA molecule are 0·34 nm apart and so, assuming a codon of three nucleotides specifies one amino acid, such a polysome could synthesize a protein chain of about 150 amino acid units. In *Pisum* the clusters of ribosomes assumed to be polysomes have the individual particles much closer together, actually touching or no more than 2–3 nm apart (Bayley, 1964). Polysomes of between fifty and seventy ribosomes have been seen in cells infected with poliovirus and these presumably synthesize virus protein, for the normal polysomes of the cell disappear. Polysomes of up to eleven ribosomes occur in *E. coli* and of thirty to forty in HeLa cells (human cancer cells in culture). Helical formations of about thirty ribosomes and up to 500 nm long can occur in cotyledonary storage tissue of *Phaseolus* and these may also be polysomes (Öpik, 1966). These are initially free in the cytoplasm, but appear to attach themselves to the ER during the germination of the seed, for the helices disappear from the cytoplasm and spirals of ribosomes appear on the ER. The m-RNA chain therefore acquires a number of t-RNA molecules attached to it by the key codons. Each t-RNA molecule has an amino attached to one end and these are in the sequence ordered by the m-RNA. The amino acids join together to form the protein specified originally by the DNA of the gene and then separate from the t-RNA. The ribosomes are believed to travel along the m-RNA molecule from one end to the other while the protein chain is being linked up and then they fall off. Other ribosomes attach themselves at the front end so that the chain always has a number of ribosomes travelling along it. In haemoglobin we know that the molecule is started at the $-NH_2$ end and finished off at the $-COOH$ end.

Most recent theories have assumed that the m-RNA migrates from the nucleus to the cytoplasm and there collects the complement of ribosomes to form the working unit of protein synthesis, the polysome. A rather different interpretation is provided by Bach & Johnson (1966) from their work on HeLa cells. They produce evidence from the timing of certain labelling phenomena to support the view that the polysomal aggregates of ribosomes and m-RNA are formed actually in the nucleus or on the nuclear surface and move from it into the cytoplasm while associated with the endoplasmic reticulum that comes off the nuclear envelope. The polysomes then free themselves from the ER. It is true that, in many plant cells which are expanding very rapidly and presumably manufacturing large quantities of ER and m-RNA, profiles of ER are frequently seen close to the surface of the nuclear membrane (Fig. 30). This is most conspicuous in non-vacuolate cells whose nuclei are small in relation to the cell volume, for here there are two major sites for the ER—(1) close to the cell wall and (2) close to the nuclear envelope.

Nearly all the facts on which the theory of protein synthesis is based come from work on microorganisms especially *E. coli* and its infecting phages. The most questioned part of the theory applied to higher organisms concerns the identity of m-RNA. The basic fact here is that cells fed with radioactive uracil, a precursor of RNA, have the label incorporated into the nucleolus straight away and a little time later the label appears in the cytoplasm. Logically we are not justified in jumping to the conclusion that the label moves from nucleus to cytoplasm in an RNA molecule, but this is perhaps the most attractive hypothesis with a lot of circumstantial evidence to support it. The theory is discussed further in Chapters 6 and 8.

The existence of DNA in organelles other than the nucleus makes it likely that organelles such as plastids and mitochondria can make their proteins to their own specifications using their own ribosomes. Kirk (1963, 1964) has, for example, demonstrated with almost complete certainty the existence of both DNA and RNA-polymerase in chloroplasts. Moreover the DNA has a different base composition from that of the nucleus. In *Euglena*, Brawerman (1962) infers the existence of ribosomes containing RNA of different base composition from those of the rest of the cytoplasm in the chloroplasts. These plastid ribosomes appear only during the formation of chloroplasts induced by illuminating a previously dark-grown culture and so they probably play a role in the synthesis of plastid protein. It is not known whether the ribosomes associated with the chloroplasts induced by light in *Euglena* are actually assembled within the chloroplasts themselves. Nor, for that matter, is it known where ordinary cytoplasmic ribosomes are assembled as the evidence for implicating the nucleus is still rather tenuous. But Morton & Raison (1963) demonstrated that actinomycin-D does not inhibit the incorporation of amino acids into storage proteins in the proteinoplasts of the endosperm of wheat and so here synthesis of storage proteins is probably not dependent on DNA-linked synthesis. We further comment on the role of ribosomes when we come to consider the functions of nuclei in Chapter 6.

3.7 Microtubules and fibrils

Although she did not in fact use the term, microtubules in plant cells were first reported by Manton (1957) in *Sphagnum* and *Pteridium aquilinum*. She commented that these tubules seem likely to be connected intimately with the overall shape of the cell. Ledbetter & Porter (1963), using glutaraldehyde, a more gentle and less destructive fixative than had previously been available, revealed the presence of similar structures in the root tips of a number of higher plants (Figs. 38, 39). More or less simultaneously with this discovery it began to be realized that microtubules, as they now came to be called, were ubiquitous in both the plant and animal kingdoms. They are found in protozoa including amoebae and in a wide range of animals where distribution has been reviewed by Slauterback (1963), and, subsequently to Ledbetter & Porter's work, in a wide range of plant tissues (Hepler & Newcomb, 1964; Pickett-Heaps & Northcote, 1966a and b). As we shall see, however, we are not justified in considering microtubules from plants and animals as anything more than superficially similar since they may differ both in their fine structure and in their response to fixation (see page 120). It was also soon realized that these microtubules are very similar to the spindle fibres, which had been studied in animal tissue under the electron microscope for some time, but which, with the assistance of better fixatives, now became visible in plant material (Manton, 1964a and b; Pickett-Heaps & Northcote, 1966a). There are also similarities between microtubules and the fibrils of flagella (Fig. 40).

The microtubules in the cytoplasm are tubes between 23 and 27 nm in diameter and of an undetermined length (Fig. 38). Some have been traced for several microns, but no ends ever appear to have been seen. In longitudinal sections they appear as two parallel lines with each line being about 7 nm thick and the central space about 10 nm. In transverse

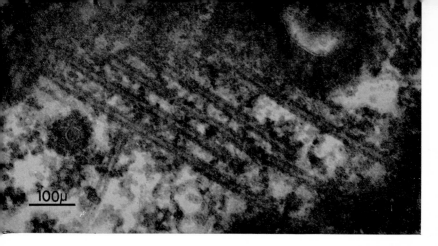

FIG. 38. Electron micrograph of microtubules from a meristematic cell of a root tip of *Juniperus*. (Glut/Osm/Pb/U)   Micrograph by Dr M. C. Ledbetter.

sections this 7 nm-thick wall can be seen to be made up of a number of subunits and an extensive examination of a number of such sections of microtubules in several angiosperms and gymnosperms suggest that the number of sub-units per circle is thirteen (Ledbetter & Porter, 1964), (Fig. 39). The centre-to-centre spacing of these subunits is about 4·5 nm and they are believed, in plants, to lie in rows parallel to the long axis of

FIG. 39. Electron micrograph of six microtubules from a meristematic cell of a root tip of *Juniperus*. These microtubules are seen in transverse section and show clearly that the wall is made up of a number of more or less spherical sub-units. In *Juniperus* roots the number of sub-units is believed to be 13. See Fig. 40. (Glut/Os/Pb/U)
          Micrograph by Dr M. C. Ledbetter.

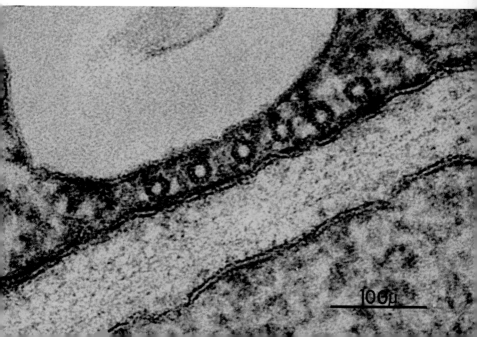

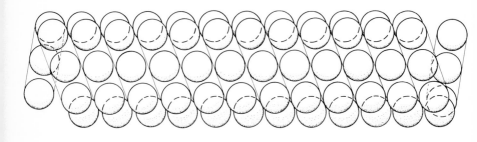

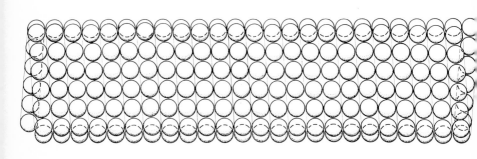

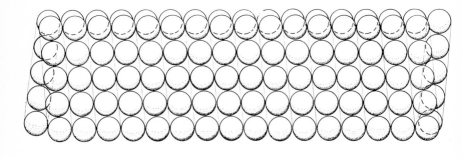

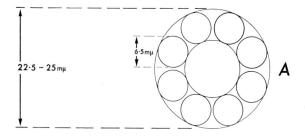

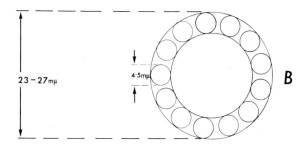

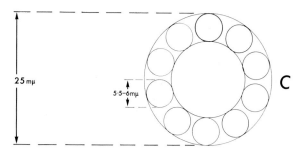

FIG. 40. The structure of microtubules and flagellar fibrils. Suggested interpretations of the dimensions and distribution of the sub-units of microtubules in (A) lung-fluke sperm with eight sub-units (Burton, 1966); (B) in higher plants, e.g. *Juniperus* and *Euphorbia* (Ledbetter, 1965) and some animals, e.g. nucleated erythrocytes of *Triturus* with thirteen sub-units (Gall, 1966) and (C) for comparison, the flagellar fibrils in rat sperm tails with ten sub-units (Pease, 1963).

E*

the microtubule (Fig. 40). This number of subunits is a feature of some, but by no means all, animal microtubules (Gall, 1966). In some recent work on microtubules of lung-fluke (*Haematoloechus medioplexus*) sperm from the lungs of *Rana pipiens*, there appear to be about eight subunits in a complete unit, each having a centre-to-centre spacing of about 6·5 nm (Burton, 1966). Longitudinal sections of microtubules and, more recently, preparations spread whole on support films suggests that they are normally straight and, where they do bend, they form circles of large radius. The general impression given is that they are straight, rigid and relatively brittle rods, where they do break they do so abruptly with no sign of thinning near the fracture (Gall, 1966).

In interphase cells the microtubules are generally found lying parallel to one another, just inside the plasmalemma, but not closer to it than 17·5–20 nm. They also remain separated from one another and do not approach closer than 35 nm (Ledbetter & Porter, 1963). Although they are most numerous just within the plasmalemma, they are not confined to this part of the cell cortex and they have been found up to 1μ into the cell. A more detailed examination of their distribution in differentiating cells and their possible roles in cell differentiation will be found on pp. 441–6.

In dividing plant cells, as in animals, microtubules similar in dimensions to those already described are found in the spindle zone, but appear to be absent from the periphery of these cells. These microtubules are slightly smaller than those in the periphery of non-dividing cells, they generally seem to be about 15–20 nm in diameter, but appear to have the same fine structure. The spindle microtubules of animals and plants, although similar in their dimensions and distribution appear to differ in their response to fixation methods. Spindle microtubules are visible in cells in mitosis of animals after OsO_4 fixation (Fig. 157; Roth & Daniels, 1962). However, they are not preserved in higher plants except by fixation with glutaraldehyde and subsequent fixation and staining with OsO_4 (Ledbetter & Porter, 1963).

Gall (1966) has also pointed out that cytoplasmic microtubules may differ quite markedly from the chromosomal fibres. He has isolated them both together from the nucleated erythrocytes of *Triturus*, spread them using the Langmuir trough methods, and then negatively stained them side by side on an electron microscope support film. The cytoplasmic microtubules, as we have seen, give the impression of being straight, rigid relatively brittle rods whereas the chromosomal fibres often follow tortuous paths and may sometimes be pulled out into thinner strands (Fig. 83).

The spindle microtubules or chromosomal fibres are orientated normal to the cell plate. Prior to prophase, microtubules are found mainly outside, but usually very close to the surface of the unbroken nuclear envelope (Fig. 125). As the nuclear envelope starts to disintegrate microtubules begin to penetrate into the chromosomal region. Some of the microtubules are found to run right through the spindle zone in anaphase, from one polar region to the other; others, those on the outside, appear to curve slightly to follow the shape of the spindle. Some of the microtubules appear to connect with chromosomes and, in a few cases, an attachment of microtubules on two sides of a chromosomal mass has been seen (Pickett-Heaps & Northcote, 1966a). At the polar region the microtubules become a cone-shaped umbrella, but never terminate at any organelle. At anaphase the microtubules are seen to connect the chromosomes to the nearest spindle pole only.

In or just prior to division of the nucleus, as we have pointed out, microtubules are not normally found in the periphery of the cell. The exception to this is a band of perhaps 150 microtubules, three to four deep and spread over about $2\cdot5\mu m$, close to the wall and far removed from the spindle zone (Pickett-Heaps & Northcote, 1966b). They appear as an equatorial band around the nucleus prior to the onset of mitosis (Fig. 151). At the moment there seems to be no evidence to indicate whether these microtubules are the wall microtubules of Ledbetter and Porter, condensed and reorientated, or whether they are formed de novo. As the nucleus goes into prophase there is a marked decrease in their numbers and an increase in the number of microtubules in the spindle zone. It is interesting that neither the preprophase band of microtubules nor the spindle microtubules appear in cells treated with colchicine (Pickett-Heaps, 1967). Also, in embryoids grown from cultured cells of Daucus, microtubules were only rarely observed by Halperin & Jensen (1967) in the presence of auxin, but they occur in all other cells. This band of preprophase microtubules appears to predict the site at which the cell plate will join the wall of the mother cell both in symmetrically and asymmetrically dividing cells. Thus the future plane of division can be predicted by the position of these particular microtubules before mitosis starts (Pickett-Heaps & Northcote, 1966b), but probably by the positioning of the nucleus rather than by a direct effect on the position of the cell plate. The role of the microtubules is discussed in connexion with wall synthesis and spindles on page 246 and page 441. In the cytoplasm they seem to be concerned with orientating the formation of long molecules possibly by channeling the Golgi vesicles.

CHAPTER 4

Cytoplasmic Organelles

Some of the cytoplasmic organelles of plant cells are listed in Table 5 with their numbers per cell and dimensions. Many other organelles of unidentified function are still being found in electron micrographs and the nomenclature has become confused. Cytosomes or microbodies, for example, which are names given to organelles with a single boundary membrane, were formerly called phragmosomes on the apparently mistaken assumption that they were concerned with the cell plate after mitosis (Mollenhauer, Morré & Kelley, 1966). There are also other organelles possessed by lower plants which are not possessed by higher plants. These include eye-spots, contractile vacuoles, pyrenoids, cnidocysts, trichocysts and kinetophores. These are mentioned briefly. In addition there are flagella or cilia which occur in motile cells up to the gymnosperms, but not the angiosperms, and are confined in the higher plants to the male gametes. The relationship between the organelles, all of which except the ribosomes have membranes around them, and the other membrane systems of the cell has already been discussed in Chapter 3. We shall also discuss the role of organelles in cell heredity in Chapter 10.

The simplest of present-day organisms, the bacteria and blue-green algae, lack most of the organelles found in other plants and animals. They perform all the important functions of other cells—respiration, photosynthesis, protein synthesis, etc.—without the specialized organelles—mitochondria, chloroplasts, nuclei—that are concerned elsewhere. The system evolved by the higher plants and animals of segregating the complex organizations of enzymes into membrane-bound compartments is presumably more efficient or allows more sophisticated structures to be built. Some very small cells have one organelle of each sort. This is true of the flagellate *Chromulina* with one nucleus, one plastid, one mitochondrion, one Golgi area and one fat body (Manton, 1959).

The ontogenetic origin of organelles is still largely uncertain. We have discussed this partly in relation to other membranes in Chapter 3 and we shall discuss the problems of self-reproduction in this chapter. Phylogenetic origin is even more uncertain and the speculation on the nature of plastids and mitochondria is reported in this chapter.

TABLE 5

Plant cell organelles

	Size	Number per cell
Nuclei	10–20μm	1
Plastids	5 × 2μm	20
Mitochondria	1μm	700
Spherosomes	1μm	300
Golgi bodies	2 × 0·5μm	400
Ribosomes	25 nm	500,000
Enzyme molecules	2 nm	500,000,000? (10,000 different kinds)

4.1 Plastids

The term 'plastid' includes several different sorts of cytoplasmic organelles having a developmental relationship to each other. All except the early developmental stages, called proplastids, are well within the resolving power of the light microscope and they are often the most conspicuous objects in living plant cells because of their pigmented or highly refractive contents. They do not occur at all in animal cells. Although the proplastids of embryonic and meristematic cells are often too small to be distinguished under the light microscope, their presence had been deduced from the hereditary characteristics of plastids. They can be seen under the electron microscope and are the precursors of probably all the kinds of plastids in higher plants (Fig. 23).

Mature plastids may be classified according to their contents into (1) chloroplasts—those containing the green pigments of chlorophyll, which is sometimes masked by other pigments, (2) chromoplasts—those containing only non-photosynthetic pigments, (3) amyloplasts—those occupied by starch grains, (4) proteinoplasts and (5) elaioplasts—those containing protein crystals and fat respectively. Some people prefer to separate those chloroplasts whose colour is not green from those that are green. Such non-green, chlorophyll-containing plastids occur in some of the algae, for example, the phaeoplasts of the brown algae. Some people regard the chloroplasts as a special class of chromoplast and indeed chloroplasts often degenerate into non-photosynthetic chromoplasts. We are here concerned mainly with higher plants and chloroplasts will be treated separately from non-photosynthetic plastids because of their importance and differences in structure. But it is sometimes useful just to divide plastids into two big groups, chromoplasts and leucoplasts, according to whether they contain any pigment or none.

A. *Chloroplasts*

These occur in the cells of the green parts of plants. In some, but not all plants, they can be induced by light in organs such as roots or tubers which are usually not illuminated in nature. Even in leaves they are not always present in all the cells. Notably they are lacking or scarce in the epidermal cells of some species. In such plants, chloroplasts may occur in the guard cells and their metabolism may be concerned with the operation of the stomata though this cannot be universally so because some species, notably grasses lack properly developed chloroplasts in the guard cells (Brown & Johnson, 1962). Numbers per cell as high as 200 have been reported and generally the palisade cells of leaf mesophyll contain the most. Among angiosperms 15–50 was the range found by Ueda & Wada (1964) in leaf mesophyll compared with 4–35 in the epidermis. Pteridophytes have similar numbers in epidermal and mesophyll cells. Those algae with small numbers of chloroplasts per cell usually maintain this number constant by coordination of plastid division with mitosis. In higher plants the number per cell can vary with the tissue and with environmental conditions and need not be constant even for similar cells in similar situations. Bartels (1964) found the mean number per cell to be 11·7 for stomatal guard cells and 11·8 for ordinary epidermal cells in *Epilobium* whereas the palisade cells of the same plant contain from 15 to 75 per cell. The epidermal cells of some species are said to have no chloroplasts though sister cells that are not in the epidermis have a full complement. The supply of nitrogenous fertilizers can affect the number of chloroplasts per cell. Some evidence suggests that when the number increases, the size of the plastids decreases and that polyploid cells have bigger chloroplasts than diploid cells, but we have very little idea about what influences the number of plastids in different kinds of cells. In leaves, it has been estimated that there are about 400,000 chloroplasts per square millimetre, mostly in the palisade mesophyll, and so there may be 10^{14} chloroplasts in a tree.

In higher plants the chloroplasts are ellipsoidal or shaped like a biconvex or plano-convex lens about 5μm in diameter and 2–3μm thick (Fig. 4). In *Acetabularia* there is an endogenous circadian rhythm in the shape of the chloroplasts correlated with photosynthetic activity (Driessche, 1966). In leaf mesophyll, chloroplasts are usually seen lying in the cytoplasm with the broad side parallel to the cell wall. Sometimes they move with the streaming of the cytoplasm and some people believe they are also capable of independent movement. It is not known how this latter movement is brought about though amoeboid chloroplasts have been described as abnormalities as, for example, in *Antirrhinum* where cells with both normal and amoeboid plastids were seen by Maly and Wild (1956). Some of the algae have large, elaborately shaped chloroplasts. This is especially true of the *Conjugales* in the green algae where *Spirogyra* has one or more ribbon-like chloroplasts and some of the desmids have complexly fluted chloroplasts in an axile position. Most of the large algae have plastids similar in external appearance to those of higher plants though their internal structure is quite different.

Chemical composition
Good preparations of isolated chloroplasts may be obtained after breaking open the cells in a blender and there is a great deal of chemical information about them. Of the dry matter, about 50 per cent is protein, 35 per cent lipids and 7 per cent pigments. The pigments in higher plants are the chlorophylls a and b and the carotenoids, carotene and xanthophyll. These are the pigments that enable the plant to photosynthesize. The chlorophyll molecule has a hydrophylic porphyrin end and a lipophilic hydrocarbon end and is combined with protein as the similar haem molecule is in the haemoglobin of blood.

Starch grains sometimes occur within chloroplasts (Figs. 4, 56). They probably are only temporary reserves in the higher plants and they are said to grow in the light and shrink in the dark. The special starch-containing amyloplasts are described on page 140. Many algae and the peculiar bryophyte, *Anthoceros*, have special regions of the chloroplast called pyrenoids and these are probably the sites of starch deposition (see page 139).

DNA
Do chloroplasts possess nucleic acids? The question is of particular importance because plastids are self-replicating organelles and it would be interesting to know if the replication is controlled in the same way as it is in the nucleus. Until recently the chemical analyses that demonstrated the presence of small amounts of nucleic acids could be criticized on the grounds that the chloroplast preparations could have been contaminated by other cell fractions. But we now know that plastid DNA

differs from nuclear DNA chemically and this eliminated the contamination hypothesis. Tewari & Wildman (1966), for example, have shown that the chloroplasts of *Nicotiana* leaves contain a DNA of different density and of different melting temperature from the nuclear DNA. It contains no 5-methylcytosine, which the nuclear DNA has, and it has a guanine-cytosine content of 43 per cent compared with one of 40 per cent in the nuclei. As much as 9 per cent of the tobacco leaf DNA consists of this plastid DNA which amounts to $4 \cdot 7 \times 10^{-15}$g of DNA per chloroplast. Its molecular weight is about 4×10^7. Determinations of plastid DNA in other plants also yields values usually between 10^{-15} and 10^{-14}g. per plastid.

Similarly autoradiographs of cells fed with tritiated thymidine (thymine deoxyriboside, which is incorporated into DNA) and other nucleic acid precursors did not at first help us much, for, although silver grains were usually found in the autoradiographic film above the chloroplasts, their numbers were often, but not always, very small, similar to the background count except in some algae, and they could have been due to chance radiation or to chemical fogging. The perfection of techniques for making autoradiographs for the electron microscope has more or less resolved this problem now and there is little doubt that both plastids and mitochondria do incorporate thymidine. Bernier & Jensen (1966) showed, for example, that in the shoot apices of *Sinapis* 51 per cent of the cytoplasmic label occurred over these organelles though they occupied a smaller fraction of the area of the sections. Moreover, serial sections showed labelling of one organelle in several sections thus precluding chance effects.

There has been, however, some doubt about whether the labelling of chloroplasts by tritiated thymidine means that DNA is present or not. Thus Lima-de-Faria & Moses (1965) found that the leaves of *Zea* showed heavy labelling of the chloroplasts after feeding with tritiated thymidine—92·3 silver grains per plastid and seven to eight times the density in adjacent regions of the cytoplasm. But they also found that neither DNA-ase nor RNA-ase removed the label appreciably, while trypsin removed 21 per cent and hot trichloracetic acid removed 27 per cent. They concluded from this that thymidine is incorporated into something other than DNA, probably protein or something associated with protein. Their experiment, of course, does not demonstrate that DNA is not present in chloroplasts, but it makes it necessary for us to be careful about the interpretation of incorporation experiments and not to assume that all thymidine incorporation implies the synthesis of DNA without checking. The demonstration by Muckenthaler &

Mahowald (1966) that the labelling of mitochondria of egg cells of *Drosophila* after feeding with tritiated thymidine could be prevented by DNA-ase digestion only after protease treatment is taken to indicate that the mitochondrial DNA is protected by the precipitation of protein around it during the fixation of the cells. The nucleus is not similarly protected. These results may thus necessitate a reinterpretation of the work of Lima-de-Faria and Moses on chloroplasts because chloroplasts may behave like mitochondria when fixed.

In algae several experiments have shown that some species incorporate thymidine into chloroplasts, but not at all into the nuclei (Stocking & Gifford, 1959; Steffensen & Sheridan, 1965). This is taken by Steffensen and Sheridan to indicate that the enzyme, thymidine-kinase, may be absent from the coding sequence of nuclear DNA but present in chloroplast DNA.

Bell & Mühlethaler (1964a), using autoradiographs of tritiated thymidine-fed gametophytes of the fern, *Pteridium aquilinum*, have shown that in somatic cells, although most of the DNA is in the nucleus, some occurs in the chloroplasts and possibly also in the mitochondria. But, in the egg cells, most of the DNA occurs in the cytoplasm and, of this, most is in the proplastids and mitochondria. The egg cell is in a special position as regards syntheses because it is the precursor of the whole fern plant and so its chemistry could be expected to differ quantitatively from that of the somatic cells.

Another piece of evidence that is relevant here is that Ris & Plaut (1962) and Gunning (1965a) have found that there are areas within higher plant chloroplasts that contain DNA fibrils and which appear very similar to the nucleoplasm of bacteria and blue-green algae. In these lower organisms there is no membrane-bound nucleus, but the DNA exists in the nucleoplasmic areas as fibrils. Some, but not all, chloroplasts have areas that react positively to the common tests for DNA—Feulgen and acridine orange fluorescence.

There has been considerable interest in whether the plastid DNA is similar to nuclear DNA in view of the semi-autonomous status of the plastids. The unicellular flagellate *Euglena*, has been used extensively for this investigation. Cytoplasmic nucleoprotein had been shown to exist and to be responsible for chloroplast replication in this organism. Moreover two different kinds of DNA were found, both of them double stranded. (The evidence for double strandedness rests largely on the base ratios obeying the Watson-Crick base pairing law that adenine content should equal thymine content and cytosine should equal guanine. Also there is an increase in optical density at 260 nm wavelength when double stranded DNA is heated and the double helices separate.) Edelman, Cowan, Epstein & Schiff (1964) have shown that one of the DNA's occurs in the plastids and that this has an entirely different base composition from the other, which is present in larger amounts (97 per cent) and presumably in the nucleus. Edelman *et al.* reckon that each chloroplast in *Euglena* has 12×10^{-16}g of DNA, i.e. about two and a half million nucleotide units and about the same amount as a bacterial cell possesses. We also know that in the uninucleate alga, *Acetabularia*, which has 10^{-16}g of DNA per plastid (Gibor & Granick, 1964), the chloroplasts go on multiplying even when the nucleus is removed (Shephard, 1965). In this plant, then, the plastid DNA can presumably replicate itself in the absence of nuclear DNA.

In higher plants Kirk (1963) has demonstrated DNA to the extent of 0·15 per cent of the dry weight in highly purified preparations of chloroplasts of *Vicia*. This DNA has an adenine-to-guanine ratio of 1·67 compared with one of 1·54 for the nuclear DNA.

Steffensen & Sheridan (1965) have shown that the brown marine algae, *Dictyota* and *Padina*, not only have DNA in their chloroplasts, but that there appears to be a limited DNA-synthetic period just before the fission of the plastids analogous to the S period in the mitotic cycle of animals and plants (see Chapter 7). This was determined by the incorporation of tritiated thymidine and, in these particular algae, the nuclei do not take in thymidine even when dividing. If this discovery of DNA synthesis is confirmed it will be an important step towards acceptance of the self-reproduction and semi-autonomous state of plastids.

RNA

Concerning RNA, perhaps the most valuable evidence is that ribosomes (see Fig. 42) occur in chloroplasts. In *Avena*, organelles looking like ribosomes but about two thirds of the size of normal ribosomes occur in the stroma of the plastids and they often occur in groups which suggest polysomes (Gunning, 1965a). Extracted ribosomes from *Nicotiana* fall into two size categories according to whether they come from chloroplasts or the cytoplasm. The chloroplasts have 70S ribosomes of 27×21 nm and the cytoplasmic ribosomes are 80S and 29×22 nm (Miller, Karlson, Boardman, 1966). The two categories show also other differences in morphology and the plastid ribosomes are very like those of bacteria. It is interesting in view of the old theory that plastids are symbiotic blue-green algae in evolutionary origin that the ribosomes are also smaller than normal in this group of plants and also in the bacteria (Table 2). If the ribosomes are grouped as polysomes it implies perhaps the presence of messenger-RNA within the plastids and we know that net protein synthesis occurs in plastids. We also know now that DNA-dependent RNA synthesis occurs in plastids. Kirk (1964) has demonstrated with almost complete certainty the existence of RNA-polymerase in chloroplasts of higher plants. Brawerman (1962) has shown that ribosomes with RNA of nucleotide composition different from nuclear RNA appear in chloroplasts when a culture of *Euglena* grown in the dark is transferred to light. These ribosomes probably are concerned with the synthesis of the proteins of the plastids as they grow in the light. Eisenstadt & Brawerman (1964) have also shown that the ribosomes of *Euglena* chloroplasts are smaller and possess lower sedimentation constants, as well as containing RNA of base composition different from cytoplasmic ribosomes.

Bové & Raacke (1959) found large amounts of amino acid-activating enzymes in isolated chloroplasts of *Spinacia* and they regard these as probably endogenous to the plastids and not adsorbed on their surfaces partly because the plastid enzymes have a pattern of activation different from that of the rest of the cytoplasm. These enzymes are the ones concerned in the formation of the amino acid-AMP-enzyme complexes

FIG. 41. Chloroplasts of an *Antirrhinum* leaf showing grana under a light microscope.

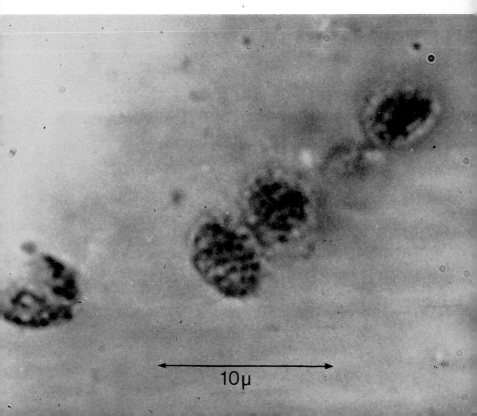

before attachment to transfer-RNA of the amino acid in the process preceding the linkage of the amino acids to form proteins on the ribosomes. Thus almost all the necessities for protein synthesis are known to exist in the plastids.

Structure

Before the advent of the electron microscope all that could be seen of the chloroplasts was that they were green (or some other colour in the algae) and that those of higher plants contained a number of darker discs called grana (Fig. 41). We now know that all the chlorophyll of a plant (except for the blue-green algae) resides in its plastids and that they have a complex internal structure suited to their complex chemical role.

Each plastid is surrounded by two unit membranes both of which, in good, potassium permanganate-fixed preparations, can be resolved into two electron-dense layers. Each unit membrane is 5 nm thick and its component dense layers are each 2 nm thick and separated by a 1 nm space. The space between the two unit membranes is 2–3 nm thick. The plastid envelope is semipermeable and is similar in appearance to the mitochondrial envelope though one of the effects of infection of plants by tobacco mosaic virus is the rupture of the chloroplast envelope whereas mitochondrial and nuclear envelopes remain intact (Weintraub & Ragetli, 1964). In certain species of algae (in the Chrysophyceae and Cryptophyceae) the chloroplast has an extra double membrane, continuous with the outer membrane of the nucleus, surrounding its own double membrane. In some, the starch is formed outside the chloroplast but inside this outer membrane (Gibbs, 1962). In higher plants, too, plastids are sometimes found closely sheathed by endoplasmic reticulum. Wooding & Northcote (1965b) believe this condition may be concerned with the transfer of substances to the exterior of a cell as for example in the conduction of resin or its precursors from the epithelial cells to the resin ducts in *Pinus* or in the conduction of carbohydrate away from phloem companion cells (see page 407).

Within the chloroplast envelope there is ground substance or stroma traversed by a complicated system of lamellae whose morphology varies from species to species and according to environmental conditions. In the stroma there are also ribosomes, osmiophilic globules and

FIG. 42. Electron micrograph of a greening plastid from a leaf of *Avena*. The plastid contains a prolamellar body (P), a stromacentre (S) and chloroplast ribosomes (PR). Note that these ribosomes appear smaller than the cytoplasmic ribosomes (CR) in the same section. (Glut/Os/Pb/U)   Micrograph by Dr B. E. S. Gunning.

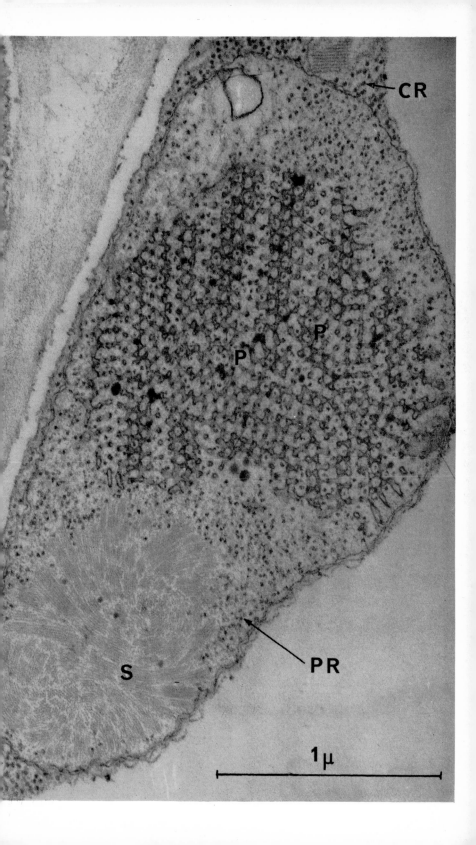

starch grains (Fig. 4). Gunning (1965a) has also reported one (or rarely two) aggregations of fibrils, which he calls the 'stromacentres', in some, but not all, species that he has fixed by the glutaraldehyde-osmium tetroxide technique (Fig. 42). This stromacentre is about 1μm across and the fibrils about 8 nm in diameter. The same fixation procedure also displays the area resembling the nucleoplasm of bacteria and blue-green algae already referred to on page 127. Some of the algae also have pyrenoids and eyespots in the stroma.

The osmiophilic globules referred to above vary from 10 to 500 nm in diameter. The smaller ones being characteristic of young chloroplasts and the larger ones, which are often less osmiophilic, of older chloroplasts. Similar structures occur in other kinds of plastids (see page 143). In chloroplasts they occur often in large numbers. Greenwood, Leech & Williams (1963) have isolated a suspension of globules from chloroplasts of *Vicia faba* and believe that they contain plastoquinones, which are also important components of the lamellae, and two galactolipids along with other lipids. They do not contain β-carotene or chlorophyll. It appears that the globules are merely deposits of lipids playing no special role in the development of the lamellae, for they increase in size while the lamellae are being formed.

The lamellae within the chloroplast are like the double membranes of the envelope in appearance in cross sections. Under some conditions of fixation each unit membrane can be resolved into two electron-dense layers separated by a 1 nm space as in the envelope (Figs. 44 A, B). They are stacked parallel to each other. This laminated structure seen under the electron microscope gives a negative uniaxial form birefringence to the chloroplast in the living state. The lamellae form a system of flattened sacs called thylakoids by Menke (1960a). Some of the thylakoids extend through the whole plastid, others are quite small. These small thylakoids are more or less circular discs and they occur one above the other like piles of pennies. It is a pile that constitutes a granum seen under the light microscope (Fig. 45). A pile of 10–100 thylakoids each separated by a 2 nm inter-thylakoid space would be 150 nm–$1\cdot5\mu$m in thickness and the granum so formed is from $0\cdot3$ to 2μm in diameter. Grana vary in number per plastid and in size. In leaf mesophyll 40–60 per chloroplast are found in many plants, but smaller numbers and

FIG. 43. Electron micrograph of a young chloroplast (P) and a mitochondrion (M) from a developing leaf of *Oenothera*. Note the close association between the surface of the mitochondrion and plastid. The small arrows point to cristae of the mitochondrion which Diers and Schötz (1965) have shown by serial sections to form complex shapes. (Mn)   Micrograph by Dr L. Diers and Dr F. Schötz.

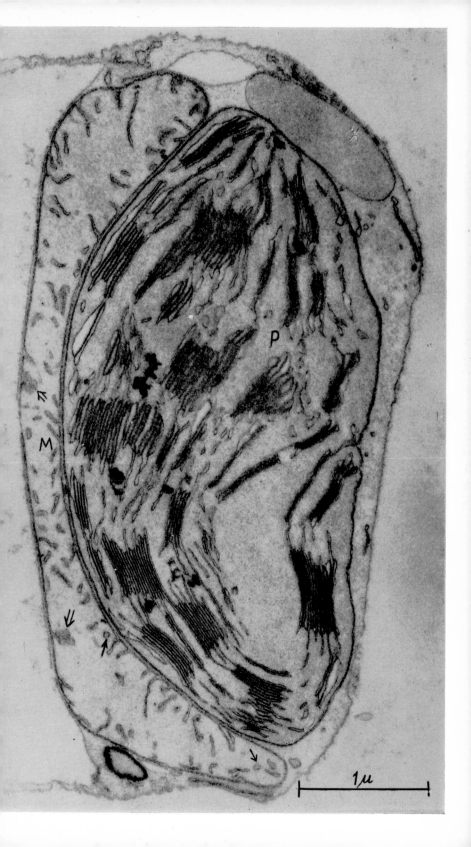

even none can be found in other cells. Some people hold that chlorophyll occurs only in the grana and those plastids with few or no grana are pale green or colourless. In some mutant chloroplasts with no lamellae at all, chlorophyll can occur in the early life of a plant, but it later disappears. According to Schoetz (1956), some such plants cannot assimilate carbon dioxide even in the green stage. Among the algae, green plastids also exist without grana, even in normal individuals. According to Granick (1961), the grana are smaller in sungrown plants, smaller in the palisade than in the spongy mesophyll and smaller in the summer than in the winter.

The lamellae traverse most of the width of the chloroplast, but it is only in limited regions that they form the small thylakoids of the grana. The lamellae in between the small thylakoids are called stroma lamellae. They appear less electron dense and thinner. The reason for this according to Menke (1960b) is that the lamellae of two adjacent double membranes are seen in section as one thick lamella so that the grana lamellae appear twice as thick or dense as the stroma lamellae. It has been rather difficult to investigate the relation between the small thylakoids and the stroma lamellae because of the great depth of focus of the electron microscope. In sections cut parallel to the plane of the lamellae many lamellae are seen at once, but an interpretation of the structure has gradually emerged. The stroma lamellae are continuous with the granal thylakoids of different grana. But in sections cut at right angles to the lamellae it can be seen that pairs of stroma lamellae also link several successive granal thylakoids in the same granum. As well as this, there are spaces in the stroma between grana where no lamellae are seen in sections. The interpretation of these facts by Heslop-Harrison (1963) and Wehrmeyer (1964) is that the stroma thylakoids are perforate and that the granal thylakoids are tongues of the lamellar system attached to the stroma lamellae by fairly small arcs of their circumference (Fig. 46). One lamella, by perforation, can produce several tongues lying one above the other like a three-dimensional fret. These constitute part of the pile of small thylakoids that go to form a granum. The stroma lamellae are also linked to one another in a similar manner in the middle of the lamellae as well as at their outer margins. The whole lamellar structure thus forms a single complex, membrane-bound cavity, the cavity between the unit membranes of the double membrane system. The stroma lamellae are often seen to be at a small angle to the grana lamellae presumably because the latter project from the stroma lamellae stiffly (Heslop-Harrison, 1963). Where they lie parallel to each other the neck attaching the grana thylakoid to the stroma thylakoid is bent

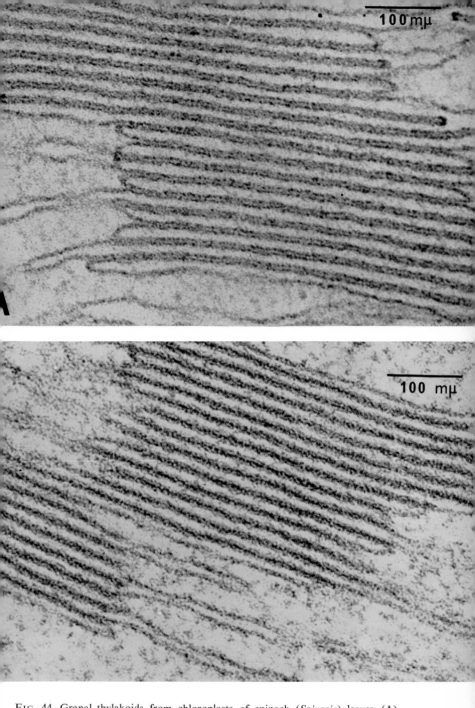

Fig. 44. Granal thylakoids from chloroplasts of spinach (*Spinacia*) leaves. (A) the section was stained with lead citrate alone. (B) an adjacent section from the same block which was stained with uranyl acetate and lead citrate. With lead citrate staining alone there is a gap between paired membranes of the granal region. With uranyl acetate staining as well the gap is filled by additional darkly staining material. (Glut/Os/Pb/ or U)   Micrograph by Mr A. D. Greenwood

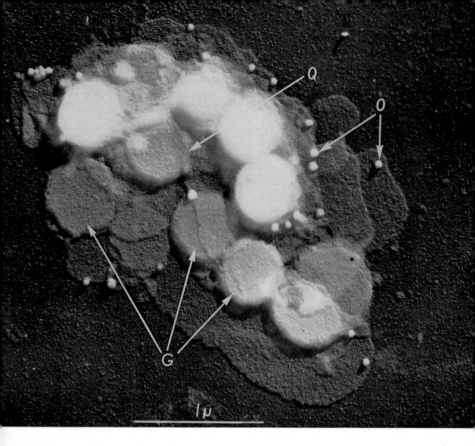

Fɪɢ. 45. Electron micrograph of a shadowed fragment of a *Vicia* leaf chloroplast. Compare the appearance of the grana (G) in this type of micrograph with those of a section such as in Figs. 4 and 43. On the surface of the granal lamellae can be seen small particles (Q) which may be identical to those seen in freeze-etched preparations. Osmiophilic globules (O) are also present, but note their absence from $KMnO_4$ fixed preparations in Fig. 43.   Micrograph by Mr A. D. Greenwood.

slightly. Other investigators have thought that there are several discrete thylakoid systems in each plastid instead of a single one.

How this complex structure develops will be described on page 153 where the relationship between proplastids and all the different kinds of plastids is discussed. Its relevance to the photosynthetic functions of the chloroplast is still not clear, but some speculation is permissible. The reactions of photosynthesis may be conveniently grouped into four:— (1) The absorption of photons by the pigments and the transfer of their energy to ADP to form ATP. (2) The photolysis of water into hydrogen and oxygen with the transfer of the proton to NADP to form $NADPH_2$. The oxygen is liberated. (3) The addition of carbon dioxide to ribulose diphosphate, a sugar with five carbon atoms, to form a C_6 compound which splits into two molecules of phosphoglyceric acid. (4) The conversion of phosphoglyceric acid to trioses, which polymerize to give hexose, and the regeneration of ribulose.

It has been demonstrated by experiments on isolated plastids that the chloroplasts contain all the photosynthetic pigments, the electron transport systems and the enzymes for carbon dioxide fixation. Because most of the chlorophyll occurs in the grana we may conclude that photolysis of water occurs there yielding $NADPH_2$, ATP and oxygen. The reducing and oxidizing potentials would presumably have to be separated and Sager (1959) thinks that the thylakoid membrane may form an energy barrier with the reducing potential generated in photolysis migrating to the stroma (outer) side. The dark reactions, the fixation of carbon dioxide and the subsequent stages of the Calvin cycle up to starch may then occur in the stroma. Park & Pon (1961, 1963) hold that chlorophyll occurs uniformly in the lamellae and that the grana contain more chlorophyll than the stroma lamellae merely because the grana constitute the largest part of the thylakoid system. They regard the

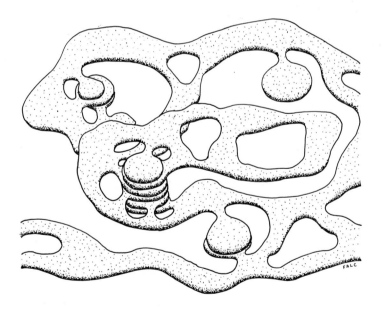

FIG. 46. A representation of the thylakoid system of a chloroplast of a higher plant based upon the work of Heslop-Harrison (1963) and Wehrmeyer (1964). Compare with Fig. 4.

lamellae as being the sites of the light reactions and the associated electron transport pathways; the stroma as containing the enzymes needed for carbon dioxide fixation. On the evidence provided by fractionation after sonic rupture of the plastids, Park and Pon support the view that lamellae should be regarded as a pair of unit membranes attached to small particles. These particles appear as oblate spheroids 20 nm across (Fig. 45). They were considered to hold most of the carboxydismutase activity and to be packed on both sides of the unit membrane so that they would have to overlap each other to allow for the separation of the unit membranes observed in sections. The combination of a piece of unit membrane with a particle was called a quantasome, but the same word is now also used for the particles even when the lamellae are considered to be made of the particles and not to be separate from them.

Park (1965) regards the thylakoids as being subdivided into quantasomes which have now been shown to exist in a variety of arrays from random to paracrystalline. Each quantasome is $18 \times 15 \times 10$ nm with a molecular weight of 2,000,000 and containing 230 chlorophyll molecules. The quantasomes themselves can be further subdivided into four units spaced on 9 nm centres. Weier, Engelbrecht, Harrison & Risley (1965) have also reported subunits of this size. The quantasome may be analogous to the electron transport particles of mitochondria. Both contain cytochromes, copper and iron. The quantasome may be the morphological unit for the light reactions of photosynthesis but there are variations in the fine morphology of chloroplasts with growth conditions. As we have pointed out in Chapter 3, the interpretation of the unit membranes generally accepted until now will probably have to be modified in view of the discoveries made by freeze-etching and other methods which are more likely to yield a life-like picture than fixation and sectioning. Mühlethaler, Moor & Szarkowski (1965) have given convincing evidence that the lamellae of chloroplasts consist of a lipid film on both sides of which are partially embedded protein particles. These particles, 6 nm in diameter, are grouped into fours on the outer side of the thylakoid, but apparently not grouped on the inner side. The relationship between this structure revealed by freeze-etching and the quantasomes seen in the preparations of Park is not clear yet, but both views are probably nearer the truth than the layered arrangement seen in sections of fixed cells. Mühlethaler et al. regard the layering as due to the spreading of a thin protein film over the lipid layer after the fixing agents have destroyed the tertiary folded structure of the protein of the particles. Nevertheless it is probably still useful to retain the unit membrane concept at least until we see how far the discoveries made on chloroplasts are confirmed for other cell membranes.

The role of the carotenoids in chloroplasts is not fully understood. They are not essential for any photosynthetic steps, but may be used in the transfer of energy to chlorophyll. Although it looks as if the chloroplasts have all the apparatus necessary for photosynthesis an interesting corrective to this point of view is supplied by the experiment of Schweiger & Schweiger (1965) on *Acetabularia*. This green alga has a single nucleus at its base and the plant can be cut in two and the nucleus-containing part can be grafted on to an anucleate part of another plant. Schweiger and Schweiger grew two plants in long day conditions in opposite phase to each other. After fourteen days the nuclei were exchanged by grafting and the hybrid plants were put in constant illumination. They found that the evolution of oxygen changed its periodicity to that which the new nucleus formerly possessed. Another experiment had the bottom half of the plant kept in the opposite illumination phase from the top half of the same plant for fourteen days. When the whole plant was then subjected to constant illumination oxygen evolution became periodic, exhibiting the phase of the nucleate half.

Algal chloroplasts

Although this book is concerned with higher plants it is worth while comparing their chloroplasts with those of the algae. The main difference seen by the electron microscope is the absence of grana. The lamellae appear uniform in electron density and thickness. The lamellar structure appears to be an essential part of the photosynthetic apparatus and occurs even in the blue-green algae and photosynthetic bacteria, which have no discrete plastids with envelopes and likewise no nuclear envelope (Ris & Singh, 1961; Wildon & Mercer, 1963). Indeed a lamellar structure consisting of stacks of flat vesicles is also present in the rods of the retina of eyes, cells that are also concerned with the reception of light energy. The chloroplasts (phaeoplasts) of the brown algae have coarse lamellae extending the whole length of each plastid. Each lamella consists of four double membranes. In the blue-green algae and photosynthetic bacteria the lamellae may be single or double membranes. In some unicellular algae the lamellae disappear when the organisms are cultured in the dark and they reappear in the light. The substructure of the lamellae seems to be similar to that of higher plants (Weier, Bisalputra & Harrison, 1966).

Information about pyrenoids is confused. Typically these appear under the light microscope as bright regions of the chloroplasts and they seem to be associated with starch synthesis. They are found in many algae and have also been reported in the bryophyte, *Anthoceros* and the pteridophyte, *Selaginella* though they may have been confused with grana. They do not occur in higher plants. It is sometimes said that pyrenoids and grana are mutually exclusive. *Anthoceros*, which has pyrenoids is said not to have grana for example. There seems to be no clear physiological reason for their being mutually exclusive and *Chlamydomonas* has both according to Paolillo (1962). Pyrenoids usually lack both pigments and lamellae, but some have been reported with lamellar stacks which are not interrupted by the formation of starch grains around them. There are tubules to be seen in some but not all pyrenoids under the electron microscope and these may be involved in the conduction of carbohydrates etc. to the sites of starch formation around the pyrenoid. The starch deposit may then grow sufficiently to envelop the surrounding lamellae of the chloroplast to give the appearance of a pyrenoid containing lamellae. The pyrenoids of some algae seem to accumulate lipids instead of starch. When a plastid with a single pyrenoid divides the cleavage occurs so that the pyrenoid is also divided into two (Manton, 1959). Some algal chloroplasts have more than one pyrenoid.

B. *Amyloplasts*

These are plastids filled with starch (Fig. 30). This substance accumulates in plastids of almost any degree of differentiation and hardly ever accumulates except in plastids. Small starch grains are formed within chloroplasts, often before the lamellar system has developed. Amyloplasts have specialized as organelles for the accumulation of starch in storage cells in the non-green parts of plants. Some amyloplasts begin life as chloroplasts, but typical amyloplasts are never coloured. Those of *Pellionia* are exceptional in always being green although few lamellae and no grana are produced (Badenhuizen, 1963, 1964). In other plants there are amyloplasts which turn green when exposed to light. In *Iris* tubers such plastids form grana from vesicles as in chloroplasts (Badenhuizen, 1964). Quite often the starch grains may distend the plastid envelope and it is then difficult to see that the grain is within a plastid, but probably most starch grains that appear naked are enclosed within a plastid envelope or have lost it at a late stage of development. The membrane around each starch grain arises from invagination of the inner membrane of the plastid envelope and the whole is enclosed within the envelope (Cronshaw & Wardrop, 1964). Many of the organelles referred to as leucoplasts are probably amyloplasts or stages inter-mediate between them and proplastids. Caporali (1959) showed that two sorts of plastid develop from the proplastids in the roots of *Lens*. One sort enlarges and gains starch-bearing vesicles early in develop-ment: the other remains relatively small with no starch-bearing vesicles until much later in development. In the dormant meristems of potato tubers the plastids are regarded as multifunctional by Marinos (1967), being able to accumulate starch, phytoferritin, lipids, nucleic acids or proteins in readiness for sprouting.

The number of starch grains within an amyloplast varies with the species and the tissue. In the pollen of *Zea*, for example, only one grain occurs (Larson, 1965), but in the root cap of *Zea* several grains per amyloplast are found (Fig. 30). In other plants up to forty are known to occur. The starch grains within amyloplasts are usually layered though, in some kinds, the grains have to be treated before this can be seen. The concentric shells are due to fluctuations in substrates or enzymes prob-ably arising in cereals from the alternation of night and day because grains formed under continuous light and at constant temperature lack the stratification. In underground tubers, however, endogenous rhythms seem to be reponsible. The difference between the shells and the amorphous layers in between them appears to be in water content alone. The shape of the grain is independent of the shape of the plastid and is probably determined by the chemistry of formation.

Starch consists of two kinds of molecules, amylopectin and amylose. These both consist of glucose units joined by α 1:4 linkages. (Cellulose also consists of glucose units, but these are β-linked) (see page 206). Amylose is probably unbranched to give a spiral chain of 300–1,000 units, but amylopectin also has 1:6 linkages to produce a branched molecule which is less soluble than amylose and forms a more viscous solution (Fig. 47). Polarized light studies show that the chain molecules

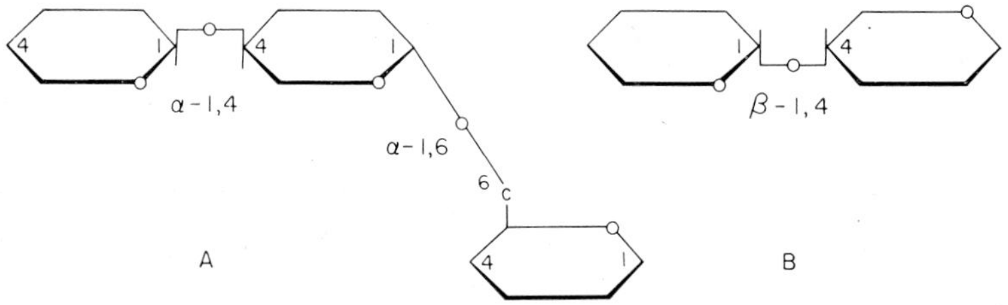

FIG. 47. (A) $\alpha - 1,4$ link and $\alpha - 1,6$ link such as is found in amylopectin. (B) $\beta - 1,4$ link such as is found in cellulose.

are arranged in an orderly array radially within the grain (Fig. 1), but the full molecular architecture is still not known. There are differences in the proportions of amylose and amylopectin and in the method of packing in the paracrystalline form so that every species of plant has a differently shaped starch grain (Badenhuizen, 1963).

The enzymes concerned in starch formation within the amyloplasts are thought to be phosphorylase and the Q-enzyme which is concerned with branching. Possibly these act with an enzyme using uridine diphosphoglucose (UDPG) as a glucose donor. Some cereals have in their endosperm a so-called waxy starch which looks and feels different from ordinary starch and stains red with iodine, not blue. The waxy starches consist mainly of amylopectin though some of the waxy grains have a little amylose in their centres. It is probable that, in all starch grains, amylose is formed first and this can be transformed by the Q-enzyme to amylopectin. In ordinary starch, crystallization occurs before the branching of the molecules is complete, whereas it occurs after most of the amylose has been transformed to amylopectin in the waxy starch (Badenhuizen, 1963). Our knowledge of starch formation is far from complete, however, and the molecular structure of the grains probably varies with factors such as the amount of water available, the amount of fatty acids, salts, phosphate and phospholipids present within the plastid, the type of primer used, and the kind of complexing with proteins.

Amyloplasts are common in storage organs of plants and they form the main item in most people's carbohydrate nutrition. They also often occur in endodermal cells and in root cap cells where they may behave as statoliths. They are heavy (specific gravity 1·6 or more) and sediment to the lower side of the cells whichever way the root is orientated and it may be that their action on the plasmalemma or their displacement of other cytoplasmic organelles leads to the geotropic responses of root elongation (Griffiths & Audus, 1964) though nothing is known about the nature of the stimulation (see pages 266, 447).

C. *Non-photosynthetic chromoplasts*

The colour of plants is due either to the plastids in the cytoplasm or soluble substances in the vacuoles of the surface cells. Yellow and reds are commonly produced by chromoplasts and blue and purples are usually due to the vacuolar sap. It is possible to have both kinds of colouring in the same plant. Probably the most interesting example of this is the graft chimera, *Cytisus adami*. The brownish petals of this plant have an epidermis with a purple sap derived from *Cytisus purpureus* and a mesophyll with yellow chromoplasts derived from *Laburnum vulgare*. So far as we know the only function of chromoplasts is to produce coloured tissues which have mostly been selected for roles in attracting animals.

Chromoplasts are formed either from chloroplasts or amyloplasts or from plastids intermediate in appearance between proplastids and either of these two and the process can be watched as petals, fruits, carrots, etc change colour. Fats and carotenoids accumulate within the plastid as droplets and the lamellae are distorted and sometimes destroyed by their accumulation (Figs. 48, 49). The plastid may even rupture and release the droplets into the cytoplasm. In the petals of *Ranunculus repens* the osmiophilic globules eventually fill the whole of the chromoplast (Frey-Wyssling & Kreutzer, 1958). In the carrot (*Daucus*) and in red fruits of

FIG. 48. Electron micrograph of a chromoplast from a red fruit of the red pepper, *Capsicum annuum*. The original lamellae of this modified chloroplast have been replaced by fibres of carotene and large numbers of osmiophilic globules varying in size from 10 nm to 100 nm. (Glut/Os/Pb/U)

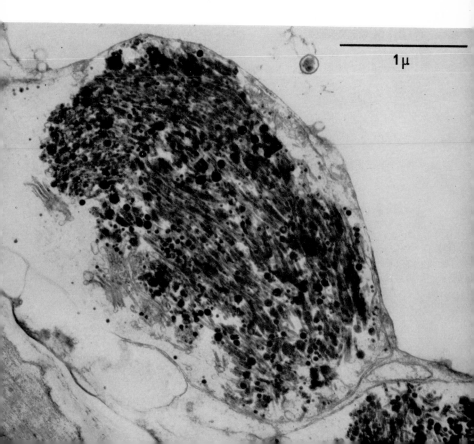

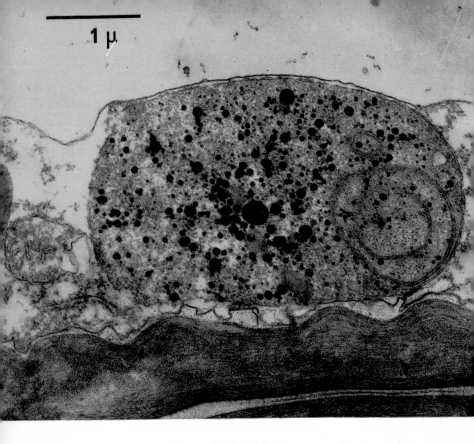

FIG. 49. Electron micrograph of a 'white' chromoplast from the fruit of a mutant form of *Capsicum annuum*. Lamellae are almost completely absent but there are numerous and very variable osmiophilic globules. (Glut/Os/Pb/U)

Capsicum, carotenoids crystallize within the plastid. In the latter species, where the chromoplasts are formed from chloroplasts, parallel protein and carotenoid molecules form fibrils within the stroma and the stroma lamellae become disorganized in the pale green stage of development. When the fruit turns yellow the grana lamellae also disappear and in the final red stage the fibrils lying almost parallel to each other fill the whole chromoplast and give it its narrow spindle-shape (Steffen & Walter, 1958) (Fig. 48). In the skin of Valencia oranges (*Citrus*) the chromoplasts are formed in the usual way by the breakdown of the internal membranes, the formation of osmiophilic granules and the synthesis of carotenoids. But, during ripening, the inner membrane of the plastid envelope continues to invaginate and this is thought by Thomson (1966) to be associated with the synthesis of chlorophyll, which continues in these plastids. Comparable changes can also occur in chloroplasts in plants deficient of certain minerals (Thomson, Weier & Drever, 1964).

Some red eyespots or stigmata possessed by motile algal cells may also be regarded as specialized chromoplasts. They are thought by some people to be organs for the perception of light because of their structure and the fact that they occur in organisms that move phototactically, but their functioning remains obscure. In other algae (e.g. *Chlamydomonas*) the eyespot occurs within a chloroplast as a plate of pigment-containing vesicles lying near the surface of the plastid. Eyespots are often closely associated with cilia and a similar combination occurs in the retinal rods of the eyes of higher animals and it has been suggested that the two organs are homologous (Frey-Wyssling & Mühlethaler, 1965). The red pigment of the eyespot is a carotenoid.

D. *Proteinoplasts and aleurone grains*

Proteinoplasts or proteoplasts are leucoplasts with protein crystals in them. Not much is known about them except that they have poorly developed thylakoids which never form grana (Heinrich, 1966). Nor is much known about their relation to the protein crystals such as aleurone grains which lie free of membranes in the cytoplasm. Protein bodies with a single membrane around them have been reported by Öpik (1966) in cotyledons of *Phaseolus*. They are closely associated with rough-surfaced ER and helices of free ribosomes. Morton & Raison (1963) report proteinoplasts containing ribosomes in the endosperm of *Triticum* and it is interesting that actinomycin-D apparently does not inhibit the incorporation of amino acids into their proteins. This suggests that synthesis of storage protein is not dependent on DNA-linked synthesis of messenger-RNA as is thought to be the case for synthesis of other kinds of cell protein. Newcomb (1967) reports that the protein is always deposited within membrane-bounded sacs inside the plastid. Chloroplasts are also rich in protein and may contain over half the protein in a leaf, but proteinoplasts are presumably reserves of stored protein like aleurone grains, which are thought to arise in vacuoles rather than plastids. Aleurone grains can be irregular, amorphous masses or they can have crystalline zones within them.

E. *Elaioplasts*

These are plastids filled with oil and, at least in some cells, are probably derived from the breakdown of chloroplasts. Oil droplets, like protein crystals, also occur free in the cytoplasm especially in rapidly metabolizing cells. Elaioplasts can easily be confused also with spherosomes (see page 190) which have a single unit membrane around them and the relation between the two kinds of organelles needs further investigation (Walek-Czernecka & Kwiatkowska, 1961).

F. *Multifunctional plastids*

The plastids of dormant tuber buds of potato (*Solanum*) are capable of accumulating a number of substances (Marinos, 1967). In them are found starch grains, phytoferritin as 8 nm granules, lipid droplets usually in clusters, nucleic acids and also proteins which are enclosed in a double-membrane-bounded body as are the protein crystals in proteinoplasts. The membranes are somehow derived from the inner envelope. These inclusions tend to disappear when sprouting begins. Marinos believes that, under certain physiological conditions such as dormancy, plastids in meristems are potentially multifunctional organelles. They are capable of a range of biochemical tasks which result in the accumulation and storage of a variety of materials which can be used when sprouting begins. In certain shoot apices the proplastids contain large, densely staining, membrane-bound inclusions which are apparently transferred to vacuoles. Gifford suggests that this is how polyphenols are synthesized and accumulated in vacuoles (Fig. 50).

G. *Proplastids and the development of plastids*

In the lower plants chloroplasts can readily be seen to divide in meristematic cells. Moreover, in *Euglena*, if a cell loses its chloroplasts, its progeny never regain them. In such cells, chloroplasts are therefore never created *de novo*, but arise from the division of existing mature chloroplasts. In the higher plants the situation is different, for, although there is no reason to believe in *de novo* creation of chloroplasts, chloroplasts normally do not occur in the cells of meristems or embryos. Breeding experiments however lead to the postulation of plastid precursors in the dividing cells and these, called proplastids, can be seen in electron micrographs (Fig. 51). They divide to keep pace with cell division and in apices whose mitoses are partially synchronous the number of plastids per cell reaches a maximum at the same time as the number of mitoses reaches its maximum (Schröder, 1962).

In the higher plants there is, indeed, some evidence that mature plastids, even chloroplasts, do divide (Fig. 52). The method of division

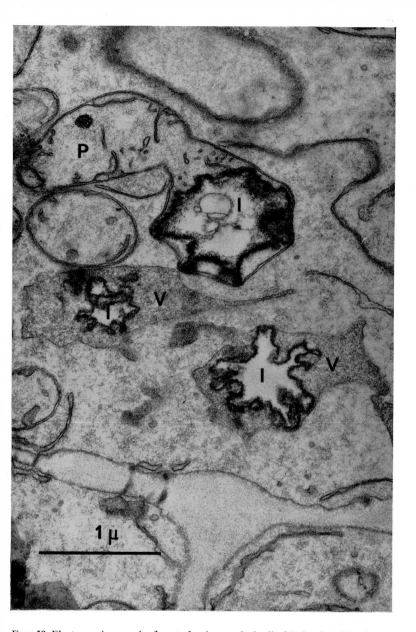

Fig. 50. Electron micrograph of part of a shoot apical cell of *Kalanchoë*. Membrane-bound inclusions (I) in the plastids (P) are believed to contain lipids and phenolics. It is thought that these inclusions are formed by the enlargement of a particular type of tubular plastid membrane and are then transferred to vacuoles (V). (Mn)
Micrograph by Prof. E. M. Gifford.

is thought to be by a constriction to form a dumb-bell-shaped organelle and the subsequent fusion of the inner and outer membranes. The appearance of dumb-bell-shaped plastids in sections is not, by itself, good evidence that the plastids are about to divide because the dumb-bell shape could arise from sectioning organelles of several forms. However, the finding by Yotsuyanagi & Guerrier (1965) that the dumb-bell shape in *Allium* was accompanied by the presence of two DNA-containing regions, one in each half, gives weight to the view that this configuration does indeed precede fission in both proplastids and mito-chondria. Also Gifford & Stewart (1965) have reported circumstances in which it is reasonable to assume that the dumb-bell shape is associated with plastid multiplication at the summit of a shoot apex. In the vegeta-tive condition the summit cells of the apex contain few dumb-bell-shaped plastids though the cells on the flanks of the meristem, which are assumed to have a higher rate of division and growth, have large pro-portions of them. When the plant studied (*Chenopodium*) is given a few photoinductive cycles to promote flowering the proportion of dumb-bells increases in the summit cells presumably as a prelude to the enhanced rate of growth and mitosis that precedes flower formation.

A special type of fission has been noted in the moss, *Splachnum*, by

FIG. 51. Electron micrograph of a group of cells from the quiescent centre of the tip of a primary root of *Zea* (see Fig. 136). These cells have relatively thick walls, fragmentary ER, poorly developed mitochondria (M) and plastids (P) and small Golgi bodies (G) with very few vesicles around them. Note the 'quilted' appearance of the cell walls with plasmodesmata and the round white spherosomes.

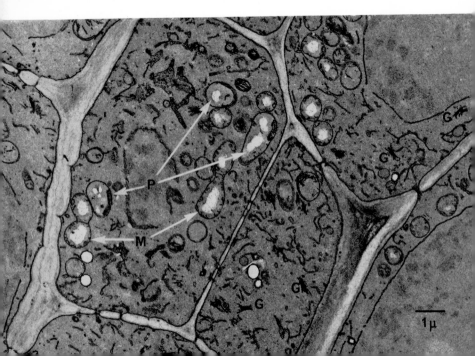

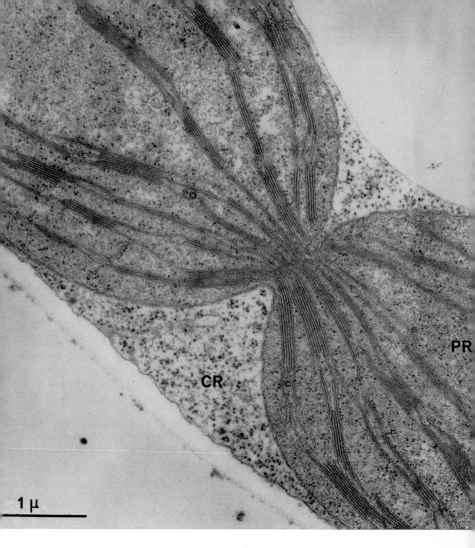

PR

CR

1 μ

FIG. 52. Electron micrograph of a 'dividing' chloroplast from a *Spinacia* leaf. Similar images of 'dividing' chloroplasts have been seen in *Vicia*, *Kalanchoë* and *Pisum* leaves, but it is not known how the lamellae of the chloroplasts separate. Note the difference in size between the cytoplasmic ribosomes (CR) and the plastid ribosomes (PR). (Glut/Os/Pb/U)   Micrograph by Mr A. D. Greenwood.

Maltzahn and Mühlethaler (1962). In dedifferentiating cells of this plant the plastids and mitochondria produce little buds which are thought to be cut off and grow into normal sized organelles thus enabling a rapid increase in numbers. Another possible method of division is that described by Gantt & Arnott (1963) for the gametophyte of *Matteuccia*, by Schötz and Senser (1964) for *Oenothera*, and by Diers (1966) for

Sphaerocarpus in which the inner membrane of the envelope invaginates in a circle all round the periphery and eventually meets in the middle dividing the chloroplast into two halves. The invagination does not appear to interfere with the lamellae and how it operates and how, if at all, the two halves separate are not known. It must be admitted that the evidence for division of mature plastids in angiosperms is rather thin and it is possibly a rare occurrence.

Higher plants do not have mature plastids in their meristematic cells: they have proplastids and, with some exceptions, the lower plants, for which the evidence for mature plastid division is good, do not. One of the exceptions is *Lomentaria* and probably also other red algae with a complex body. Here the cells of the apical region contain proplastids with no lamellae (Bouck, 1962). (The word, proplastid, is, however, used sometimes to include the chloroplasts of algae grown in the dark which are structurally different from the chloroplasts of etiolated higher plants (Kirk & Tilney-Bassett, 1967)). It is not possible to be sure about the occurrence of proplastids because the organelles to which we ascribe the functions of proplastids may possibly give rise to mitochondria as well. At an intermediate stage of development they are very similar to mitochondria in appearance under the electron microscope and are indistinguishable under the light microscope. It only becomes possible to distinguish proplastids with certainty after the alignment of the vesicles into lamellae when the organelle is bigger than 1μm. But there exist in the cytoplasm organelles as small as 20 nm in diameter with a double membrane around the outside. These minute organelles are sometimes called initials to distinguish them from the proplastids that contain vesicles aligned parallel to the envelope. All stages from these up to organelles about 1μm across with the beginnings of vesicles or cristae exist. There are no criteria for distinguishing these as proplastids or precursors of mitochondria. They have a double membrane around the outside and the inner layer invaginates to form tubes or sacs called cristae (cristae mitochondriales) in the mitochondria and vesicles in the proplastids. It has therefore been suggested that mitochondria and proplastids are interconvertible, but this view has become less attractive in recent years since better preparations for electron microscopy enable one to distinguish early stages of mitochondrial development in the youngest cells in nearly all cases. Moreover the view can hardly be maintained in *Euglena*, which can go on respiring after the irreversible loss of its chloroplasts. A phylogenetic relationship between the two organelles is a possible working hypothesis even if there is no onto-genetic connexion.

In the belief that the photoreceptor for phototropic growth is probably a carotenoid Thimann and Curry (1961) have put forward the view
that it is the proplastids at the tips of shoots that initiate the phototropic
response of growth towards a unilateral source of light. Carotenoids are
most likely to occur in plastids and green plastids can move within a cell
in relation to light. So Thimann and Curry suppose that the proplastids, for example in the tips of *Avena* coleoptiles, migrate to the wall
opposite the source of light and somehow enhance the transport of
auxin through that wall to cause the shoot to grow faster on the side
away from the light. If this is confirmed there would be an interesting
functional link between the carotenoid-containing proplastids of the
shoot and the starch-containing plastids of both root and shoot, for
these have long been considered to initiate the growth response to
gravity by behaving as statoliths.

Some of the bryophytes and pteridophytes occupy an intermediate
position between the lower plants whose plastid precursors are usually
full-sized plastids and the higher plants whose plastid precursors are the
minute, simple proplastids. The proplastids in the apical cells of some
bryophytes are $1\cdot5$–$2\cdot0\mu$m across and contain 3–5 grana whereas the
chloroplasts of mature cells are about 7μm across and contain 60–80
grana. *Isoetes*, according to Paolillo (1962), has usually one proplastid
per cell in its meristems. This organelle is similar in the leaves, roots and
shoots. It differs from the proplastids of angiosperms in being large—
8–10μm in diameter and 1μm thick. It is disc-shaped with a deeply staining
rim and a weakly staining centre. It divides before mitosis after becoming elongated and the two daughters move to opposite poles of the
spindle. Eventually it gives rise to more than one plastid per cell and the
mode of maturation into chloroplasts or leucoplasts is similar to that of
the smaller angiosperm proplastids (Granick, 1961; Paolillo, 1962). The
proplastids of the egg cells of the fern, *Pteridium* are also large and they
are amoeboid according to Bell & Mühlethaler (1964b) who believe, but
have not proved, that they are generated from the nuclear envelope in
this particular kind of cell (see page 459). The proplastids of angiosperms are also sometimes described as amoeboid.

In angiosperm meristems the number of recognizable proplastids per
cell appears to be about twenty; that excludes the small organelles that
could be precursors either of plastids or of mitochondria. In the initial
cells of the root cap of *Zea*, for example, there are twenty to thirty
recognizable proplastids per cell. About this number of amyloplasts is
also found in the mature, non-meristematic cells of the cap (Fig. 53). In
the intermediate, dividing cells the number is slightly lower. It looks

F*

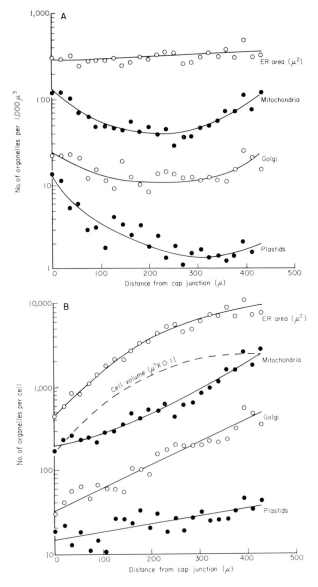

FIG. 53. Average numbers of organelles and areas of endoplasmic reticulum (A) per unit volume of cytoplasm and (B) per cell (log scales) at various levels along the lengths of the root cap of *Zea*. The cap junction is where the cap joins the rest of the root. The meristematic cells of the cap lie near the cap junction and the tip of the root is 440μm from the junction. (From Juniper and Clowes, 1965.)

therefore as if cell division, for a short time, outstrips proplastid division, but eventually the proplastids catch up. An interesting point is that these plastids do not go on increasing in number per cell to keep up with the increasing size of the cells whereas the numbers of mitochondria and Golgi do increase with cell size (Juniper and Clowes, 1966). These amyloplast precursors go on dividing until they are about half their final size, about $1\cdot5\mu m$ long. Sizes of recognizable proplastids within the range 400–900 nm are common though Mühlethaler & Frey-Wyssling (1959) and others consider organelles as small as 20 nm as proplastids.

In the large uninucleate alga, *Acetabularia*, the number of chloroplasts doubles every 8–9 days in the light (Shephard, 1965). During cell differentiation the proplastids, which are colourless or pale yellow, grow. They initially consist of a simple double membrane containing a granular stroma. When they are about $0\cdot5–1\mu m$ in diameter the inner of the envelope unit membranes invaginates into the stroma. At first these invaginations look very like the cristae of the mitochondria, but they come to lie parallel to the surface of the proplastid instead of standing at right angles to it. Then they align themselves in planes to form flat, sac-like lamellae, the thylakoids. It is not clear at what stage, if at all, the invaginations of the inner membrane of the envelope separate from the envelope to form vesicles. Hodge, McLean & Mercer (1956) have suggested that all lamellar systems, those of the cytoplasm as well as those within the plastids, arise in this way by the budding off and subsequent fusion of small vesicles. In chloroplasts the discovery of the fenestration of the thylakoids makes it desirable to be careful about the interpretation of sections, for it may be that discrete vesicles never exist. A single section will not distinguish between a group of vesicles and a single fenestrated and branching thylakoid. What happens after the initiation of lamellae in the formation of mature plastids depends upon the kind of plastid, on whether the plant is grown wholly in the dark or with light periods and, to some extent, on the species.

Let us consider the chloroplasts first. In the dark the vesicles aggregate into tubes with a regular spacing. These tubes then fuse to produce one or more prolamellar bodies. These are probably the small granules seen under the light microscope and which fluoresce red in the plastids of etiolated plants. In etiolated *Avena* leaves, Gunning (1965b) has found one, two or three prolamellar bodies per chloroplast. They consist of a three-dimensional cubic lattice of tubules of about 21 nm diameter (Fig. 54). The tubules are fused together at each point where three meet. The plastid stroma permeates the lattice and Gunning reports one ribosome-like particle to each cube of stroma bounded by eight tubule

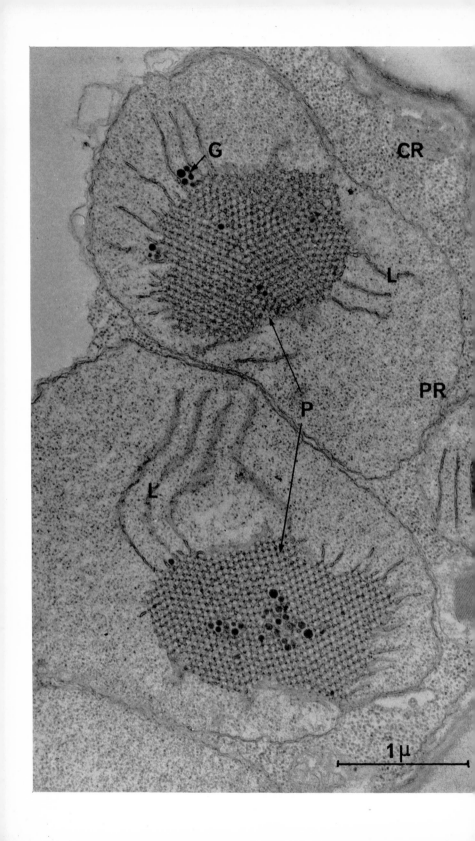

junctions. In some plants as little as two minutes of light is sufficient to disperse the prolamellar body which then is replaced by vesicles which become aligned into layers or sometimes into concentric shells (Boardman & Anderson, 1964). These concentric rings also appear in plants grown in low light intensities (Eilam & Klein, 1962) and also at high light intensities at low temperatures (Klein, 1960). When a plant is transferred to suitable conditions the rings disappear and the plastid develops normally. Chlorophyll is not normally formed in the dark, but the precursor, protochlorophyll occurs and, on the evidence of fluorescence, Boardman & Anderson think that the prolamellar body is the site of chlorophyll synthesis in the early stages of greening. But similar bodies have been seen in the sieve elements of *Dioscorea* free in the cytoplasm (Behnke, 1966). We also have to explain why some plants turn green in the dark whereas most do not. Because of the similarity of the action spectra, Virgin, Kahn & Wettstein (1963) think that the conversion of protochlorophyll to chlorophyll is connected with the conversion of the prolamellar tubes into vesicles. This has a low energy requirement whereas the next step of alignment has a very high energy requirement. The vesicles that emerge from the prolamellar body after illumination appear to fuse to form the disc membranes that aggregate into grana. It is with grana formation that the main phase of chlorophyll synthesis is associated. Xanthophyll formation can proceed in the dark but carotene formation seems to be light-dependent.

Chloroplasts from plants grown in the dark are called etioplasts by Kirk & Tilney-Bassett (1967). When the plant is grown in normal light conditions no prolamellar body of the sort found in etiolated plants is formed, but some workers believe that there is always some focus for lamella formation in proplastids and that this divides at the division of the proplastid. The flattened vesicles formed from the inner membrane of the plastid envelope grow and align themselves in planes and branch to form the discs that later become the grana thylakoids. These discs become more numerous and form piles one above the other that will constitute the grana. It is not known why the thylakoids fenestrate to form the discs attached by a short neck to the stroma thylakoids or why the discs come to lie one above the other. A different mechanism for the proliferation of discs has been described by Menke (1960a). This

Fig. 54. Electron micrograph of two greening plastids from an *Avena* leaf. Prolamellar bodies (P) and rudimentary lamellae (L) can be seen along with osmiophilic granules (G). CR, cytoplasmic ribosomes; PR, plastid ribosomes. (Glut/Os/Pb/U)
Micrograph by Dr B. E. S. Gunning

assumes that the double membrane invaginates from a region on the circumference of the disc. Schötz (1965) holds that multiplication of the discs may also occur by a budding process. It is not known whether all the vesicles that align and fuse are derived from the envelope's inner membrane or whether new ones bud off from existing vesicles. But alignment into planes and formation of piles of discs requires light. The enlargement of proplastids was said to require light in dicotyledons though not in monocotyledons (Granick, 1961), but this is not generally true (Virgin, Kahn & Wettstein, 1963). As they become larger, the plastids assume a more constant and definite shape.

A particularly interesting investigation is that of Brawerman (1962) on *Euglena*. This shows that plastid ribosomes appear during the formation of the chloroplasts which occurs when a culture, normally grown in the dark, is transferred to light. Moreover, as Brawerman infers that these ribosomes contain an RNA of base composition different from that of the ordinary cytoplasmic ribosomes, he holds that they probably play a role in the synthesis of plastid proteins.

Starch grains appear at a fairly early stage in the development of chloroplasts, before the completion of the lamellar system and before the division phase of the proplastids is over. Presumably the glucose units are acquired from some other part of the plant and the enzyme system necessary for starch synthesis must be present before the chlorophyll.

Development of amyloplasts from proplastids initially follows the same course of invagination of the inner membrane of the plastid envelope. The lamellae so formed become quite long, though not orientated, and the starch grains are formed within pockets of the lamellae. As the grains grow, the lamellae become less obvious (Larson, 1965). There must be some important organizational difference between the proplastids that produce chloroplasts and those that produce amyloplasts. It is not just that chloroplasts are produced in light and amyloplasts in dark, for, although both acquire starch grains, the proplastids that produce amyloplasts never acquire a prolamellar body as chloroplast precursors do in the dark. According to Granick (1961), amyloplasts are capable of becoming chloroplasts and, as we have already noted, proplastids may acquire starch grains before developing the full lamellar organization of mature chloroplasts.

The development of other sorts of plastids is from chloroplasts, or amyloplasts or the stages intermediate between them and proplastids. Nonphotosynthetic chromoplasts can, for example, be derived from chloroplasts, either mature or partially developed, or from leucoplasts (Fig. 55).

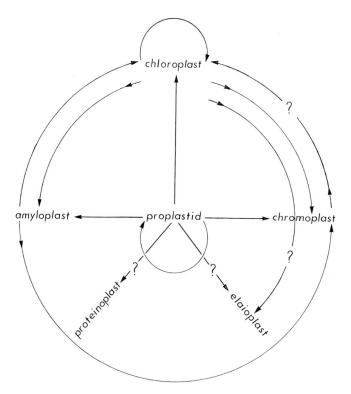

FIG. 55. The interrelationships of plastids. Only proplastids and mature chloroplasts are known to divide.

H. *Control of development*

Chloroplasts that fail to develop fully in a tract of cells cause an easily visible change in the appearance of the plant and so their development has been much investigated. Failure to take the normal course of maturation can be due to purely physiological or to genetic reasons. The best known example of the former is the foliar epidermis of many species of plants where chloroplasts are absent or fewer in number or poorly developed. In some species the guard cells behave differently from the other cells of the epidermis in the number and development of the chloroplasts. In many plants the epidermis is the only tissue derived from the outermost layer of the shoot meristem, but it is not a genetic difference that causes the plastids to behave differently from those in the inner tissues, for if the epidermis is induced to divide periclinally to produce a multiple layer of cells the inner cells develop chloroplasts in the normal way. This happens in the variegated chimera of *Pelargonium zonale* known as 'Freak of Nature' (Fig. 159B). Here the epidermis proliferates on the margin of the leaves producing green tissue, but the epidermis over the central part of the leaf does not have enough chlorophyll to mask the genetically white mesophyll. The situation in some chimeras is more complex and still not perfectly understood (Clowes, 1961; Tilney-Bassett, 1963). In some plants there is an indication of competing genetical and physiological control of chloroplast development. This is shown in the so-called bleaching effect in variegated leaves. Thielke (1955) pointed out that, in a variegated *Hemerocallis*, the epidermis showed sectoring into strips whose guard cells were green when overlying green mesophyll, but not green when overlying yellow mesophyll. Yet the epidermis ought to be homogeneously green genetically. The failure of the guard cells to become green in the yellow strips is presumably due to some influence of the yellow cells underneath, but why the ordinary epidermal cells behave differently from the guard cells in respect of their chloroplasts is not known. It is not only a matter of the failure of pigments to appear for, according to Badenhuizen (1963), epidermal plastids have phosphorylase, but do not normally produce starch and as we have seen above starch can be formed in normal green plastids before they become green. A similar problem arises when we consider cells that, after differentiation, dedifferentiate and become meristematic. Are the plastids of the new cells derived from the mature plastids of the original differentiated cell or do some proplastids remain undeveloped and provide for such contingencies?

We know from experimental breeding that the development of plastids is controlled by the nucleus, the plastids themselves and the cytoplasm. A large number of mutations, many of them induced artificially by radiation, has been studied. The inheritance of plastid characters is discussed in Chapter 10, but the development of mutants can usefully be described here along with normal light and dark development.

Mutant chloroplasts can show arrest of development at the vesicle stage or lamellae may be formed but not grana or development may be

FIG. 56. A: Electron micrograph of a normal chloroplast from the green central region of the same leaf as Fig. 56B. The thylakoids almost entirely fill the stroma of the plastid and a heavy accumulation of starch has taken place. (Glut/Os/Pb/U)

B: Electron micrograph of a defective chloroplast from the white margin of a leaf of *Pelargonium zonale*, c.v. Frank Headley. Note that although this leaf was growing in sunlight no starch has accumulated, there are sparse and disorganized lamellae, but a number of osmiophilic granules are present. (Glut/Os/Pb/U)

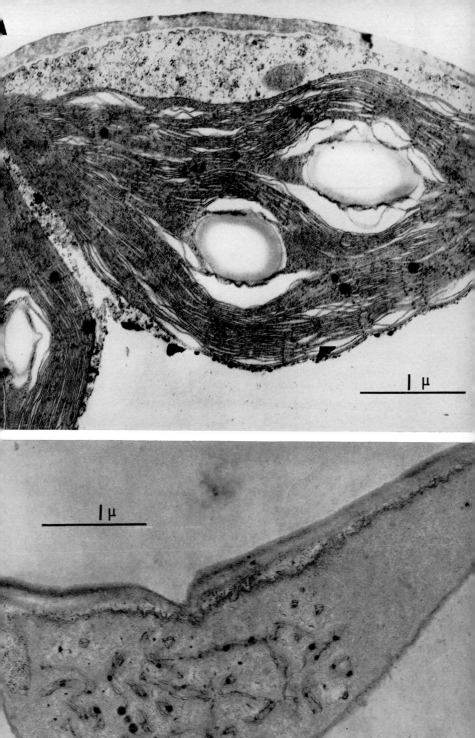

'albina', block the early development of the proplastids either prevent-ing the accumulation of the vesicles derived from the inner membrane of the envelope or causing them to accumulate in a prolamellar body as normal plastids do in the dark. 'Albina' plastids grow and may reach the size of normal chloroplasts and chlorophyll synthesis goes on (Wettstein, 1961). Several gene mutants of the 'Xantha' type produce yellow tissue. In some of these, protochlorophyll is not formed although lamellar discs are present; in others chlorophyll and carotenoids are formed but completely abnormal (Fig. 56). Some gene mutations, known as in droplets, not in lamellae; in yet others normal amounts of carotenoids are formed, but a reduced amount of chlorophyll appears (Granick, 1961). The class of nuclear mutants that produce pale green tissue and known as 'viridis' suffer from some interference with later stages of plastid development. The number of lamellar discs is often smaller than normal. A group of 'lutescens' gene mutants produces green seedlings, but, in later life, the thylakoids swell and destroy the normal arrange-ment causing the plant to become yellow (Wettstein, 1961). There is also a 'virescens' mutant in *Hordeum* in which the plastids are deficient of chlorophyll and carotenoids in the young plant but gain normal levels later on (Maclachlan & Zalik, 1963). Several mutants of *Oenothera* cause destruction of the normal chloroplasts produced in early life and the degree of destruction is varied, some stopping at a yellow-green stage, others going on to produce white tissue. High temperatures and low light intensities can slow down or stop some of these changes. Two interesting gene-dependent or gene-induced mutations of unknown nature in *Hordeum* have been investigated by Wettstein (1961). In one of these ('striata-3') the yellow sectors of the leaves contain plastids with double membranes in concentric rings. In the other ('variegated') the white sectors of the leaves contain 'albina' plastids. But both also contain abnormal mitochondria which are irregular in shape and size and contain cristae that are greatly extended presenting a wavy appear-ance in sections.

Some mutant plants can develop normal chloroplasts when specific amino acids are supplied. Chemical investigations of the type commonly done on microorganisms can now be carried out therefore on the forma-tion of plastids. It has also been possible to combine different plastid defects in the same plant and effect a kind of intercellular complementa-tion leading to normal plastid production (see page 466).

Thus it is likely that many of the plastid mutants are due to a blockage of the normal pathway of development, but, once blocked, further changes may occur to give the plastid an appearance different from the normal developmental stages of plastids. Many of the mutations are lethal to plants containing no other plastids, but chimeras often survive, the non-green parts presumably obtaining nutrients from the green parts. It is also sometimes possible to maintain a wholly white or yellow plant artificially by feeding it with sugar.

More is known about plastids than any other cytoplasmic organelle in plants and a detailed review especially concerned with the bio-chemical and genetical aspects has now been published by Kirk & Tilney-Bassett (1967).

4.2 Mitochondria

Mitochondria are small organelles found in the cytoplasm of plants and animals. They are concerned with respiration and convert the energy released by oxidation either to the bond energy of ATP or to osmotic work in moving solutes across their membranes. They probably occur in all kinds of aerobic cells. The only organisms without them are the bacteria and blue-green algae and these may have regions of the proto-plast with similar function and structure (mesosomes) just as they have nuclear regions not delimited by a membrane. Yeasts have mito-chondria in aerobic culture, but not in anaerobic conditions where the cytoplasmic membrane system is of unusual construction and takes over the functions of mitochondria. The name 'mitochondrion' is due to Benda and means a thread-like grain. These organelles were known by other names previously and, even now, some authors refer to the mito-chondria of plants as chondriosomes.

Form and size

They can be cylindrical or spherical particles, saucer-shaped or of variable shape. If cylindrical, they are commonly about 3μm long; if spherical, they are commonly from $0\cdot5$ to $1\cdot5\mu$m in diameter, i.e. they are of the same dimensions as a whole bacterial cell and easily visible under the light microscope provided adequate techniques are used to colour them. They can be seen in living cells with phase microscopy though often they are hardly distinguishable from Golgi bodies and other particles of similar size unless they have a special shape or site in the cell. For some cytologists they used to be defined by their *intra-vitam* staining with the dye, Janus Green B. This acquisition of a blue colour, which occurs only in aerobic conditions, is due to the presence of cyto-chrome oxidase which prevents the reduction of the dye by reduced flavoproteins present in the cell. After staining, the mitochondria fade in anaerobic conditions as, for example, after some time under a cover glass.

Their form and size varies with the genetic make up, the age and metabolic state of the cell. Cronshaw & Wardrop (1964) found that in a secondary xylem for example they were 0.6μm in diameter in the ray cells but only 0.35–0.5μm in the tracheids. Yotsuyanagi (1962) and others have described characteristically modified mitochondria produced by cytoplasmic mutations and causing changes in the chemistry of cells. Shape can also change rapidly as one watches them under a phase microscope

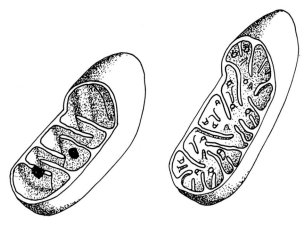

FIG. 57. Mitochondria with baffle-like cristae and villus-like cristae. See also Figs. 29B and 58.

and there is some evidence that they can move autonomously (Frederic, 1952). They can almost certainly divide and fuse together. In degenerating cytoplasm of pollen they and the plastids swell, fuse and rupture (Larson, 1965). Like plastids, they are surrounded by an envelope consisting of two unit membranes and the inner one invaginates to form projections, the cristae, into the fluid matrix. The term 'cristae mitochondriales' was used by Palade originally for invaginations that are now known to be flat structures like baffles interdigitating from all round the inner surface of the mitochondrion. It was subsequently found that some organisms have mitochondria with tubular invaginations of the inner membrane and some people prefer to call these 'microvilli' or 'tubules' and reserve the term 'cristae' for the flat indentations. Whether the cristae are flat or tubular is not always revealed by single electron micrographs and we shall use the term to refer to both kinds of invaginations of the inner membrane in the mitochondria (Figs. 29, 33, 34, 57). Mitochondria in which the cristae are not yet fully developed look somewhat like young plastids (Fig. 51). In individual cases it may be difficult to decide into which category an organelle should be placed, but this difficulty is not so acute now as earlier workers found it. It becomes very much easier to make this distinction after the invaginations of the unit membrane, the cristae or thylakoids are well developed. These invaginations mostly run transversely in the mitochondria and are frequently seen to be connected to the inner of the bounding membranes. They mostly run longitudinally in the plastids in which connections to the bounding membranes are not so frequently seen.

It is assumed now that the organelles with double membranes, but without invaginations that are sometimes found in young cells are precursors of plastids. Where cells of different ages are available for comparison as in plant meristems we can see that there is an increase in the surface area of the cristae with age (Clowes & Juniper, 1964). This can be also seen at the onset of germination in plant embryos (Nougarède & Pilet, 1964). The shape of the cristae of the mitochondria probably requires further systematic investigation. Manton (1961) holds that they are tubular in the Phaeophyceae, Chrysophyceae and Xanthophyceae among the algae, and in some Protozoa, but flat in the Chlorophyceae and the higher animals and plants. Hoffman & Grigg (1958) believe that they are usually tubular and several other people have reported them as being tubular in the higher plants. The use of serial sections by Diers & Schötz (1965) has brought to light very complex forms in the cristae of leaf cells in *Oenothera*. Some of these are like branched pitchers attached to the inner membrane of the envelope. Cristae with narrow stalks attaching them to the inner membrane of the envelope have also been seen in liver (Daems & Wisse, 1966). The flat baffle-like cristae are said to occur in cells with high rates of respiration in animals.

It is quite easy to remove mitochondria from cells and make preparations of them fairly free from other cell components by centrifugation procedures and so we know quite a lot about their chemical composition. Of their dry weight, most is protein, 65–70 per cent in some estimations, and 25–30 per cent is phospholipid. The reason why mitochondria are not seen after ordinary fixation techniques for the light microscope is that fat solvents, such as alcohol, destroy them unless they

have been rendered insoluble by the fixation. There is also some RNA
and traces of DNA which we shall discuss further (see page 171).

Number

Each cell of an animal or plant usually has a lot of mitochondria. It has
been estimated, for instance, that rat liver as 500–1,400 per cell. Sea
urchin egg cells have 14,000 and the large amoeba, *Chaos chaos*, has half
a million. Animal sperm cells have as few as twenty. In plants we have
found from about 100 to 3,000 in root cap cells of *Zea*. The meristematic
cells have the smallest numbers in this tissue and the organelles increase
in number as the cytoplasmic volume increases though not in a parallel
fashion (see Fig. 53). In the liverwort, *Sphaerocarpus*, Diers (1966) found
that the numbers of mitochondria in the egg cell increased from 250–400
to 800–1,300 during maturation. This three- or four-fold increase
accompanied a similar increase in the volume of the egg and in the
number of plastids. In the rat liver, mitochondria constitute about 19
per cent of the cell volume (22 per cent of the cytoplasmic volume) and
15–23 per cent of the total nitrogen of the cell (Lehninger, 1964). The
flagellate alga, *Micromonas*, has a single mitochondrion and the sperm
cell of *Fucus* is said to have only four.

Function

Mitochondria are found often near sites of mechanical work in cells.
This is especially well seen in unicellular organisms with few mitochondria where, for example, a mitochondrion is often associated with
a flagellum (Fig. 58). Cells with high rates of respiration usually have
many mitochondria. This is true for example of the nectar-secreting
cells of *Abutilon* flowers (Mercer & Rathgeber, 1962).

Isolated mitochondria are a favourite material for biochemical investigations and from these we know that they contain organized
assemblies of the respiratory enzymes responsible for ATP formation
and for osmotic work. They require fatty acids, pyruvic acid or amino
acids, ADP and phosphate to produce ATP. Glycolysis occurs in the
cytoplasm, but the mitochondria are exclusively the sites of succinic,
D-β-hydroxybutyric, lactic, malic and isocitric dehydrogenases (Walker
& Seligman, 1963), and it is thought that the enzymes of the Krebs cycle
and of fatty acid oxidation are attached to the surface of the cristae.

has pointed out that the structure of mitochondria can vary with nutrition as well as with the position of the organelles in the body of the plant. The form as well as the number of the cristae themselves can vary with the tissue. They are fenestrated sheets in blowfly flight muscle, but are branched, finger-like processes in neurons (Lehninger, 1964). In general, plant mitochondria are not so complex as animal mitochondria.

The problem of what happens in organisms that can grow in either aerobic or anaerobic conditions is important for the understanding of mitochondria. In the yeasts, *Torulopsis utilis* and *Saccharomyces cerevisiae*, there are mitochondria in aerobic cultures as there are in purely aerobic yeasts. In anaerobic culture they have no mitochondria and no cytochromes, but they have a new membrane system which contains two primary dehydrogenases of the terminal respiratory chain which, in aerobic culture, are located exclusively in the mitochondria (Linnane, Vitols & Nowland, 1962). Aerating an anaerobic culture leads to the lining up of the special membranes to form a parallel array which subsequently fuses and folds in to form primitive mitochondria with a few cristae. At the same time cytochromes are synthesized. Yotsuyanagi (1966) has drawn attention to an interesting phenomenon in strains of the yeast, *Saccharomyces cerevisiae*, in which both unit membranes of the mitochondria invaginate to form a ball of concentric membranes when the respiratory enzymes are heavily inhibited genetically. These balls, which look like myelin figures in section, are always associated with a DNA region and Yotsuyanagi thinks they are analogous with the mesosomes of bacterial cells already mentioned on page 81.

One of the important features of mitochondria is the large surfaces that they provide in the cell. For example a liver cell having 1,000 mitochondria $3 \cdot 5 \mu$m long $\times$ $1 \cdot 0 \mu$m diameter has a total area on the outer surface of the mitochondria of $13,000 \mu m^2$, i.e. four times the external surface area of the cell itself. It has been calculated that such mitochondria provide a further $16,000 \mu m^2$ of surface on the cristae, this in a cell whose mitochondria are not particularly rich in cristae (Lehninger, 1964).

The mitochondrial envelope is semipermeable but Brierley & Green (1965) believe that the outer membrane has different permeability properties from the inner membrane. Each of these membranes is considered to be a unit membrane of the usual multiple structure (see page 73) though we shall see later that there may have to be modifications of the unit membrane theory. Brierley and Green have shown that ADP, phosphate etc. can penetrate the outer membranes rapidly by passive diffusion and also can pass out and so this membrane does not confer the osmotic properties on the organelle. They hold that energy is required to move ions through the inner membrane to the matrix and that it is this membrane therefore that is the differentially permeable layer. Passive diffusion through the outer membranes leads into the possibly fluid space between the membranes, which is continuous with the interior of the cristae. This is probably the importance of the degree of development of the cristae in cell differentiation. There is some evidence that the outer unit membrane is not continuous, for large molecules can pass through it into the perimitochondrial space, the space between the outer and inner membranes. In freeze-etched preparations minute cracks may also be seen on the outer surface (Frey-Wyssling & Mühlethaler, 1965).

Much work has been done on the swelling of mitochondria under experimental conditions. For a discussion of this in relation to plant tissue see the paper of Longo & Arrigoni (1964).

Fine structure

Let us now consider the structure of mitochondria in greater detail, for considerable effort has been put into this problem in view of the biochemical importance of relating structure to activity at the molecular level. After osmium tetroxide fixations the envelope of the mitochondrion appears as two dense lines each about 5 nm thick separated by a lucid layer about 8·5 nm across. After potassium permanganate fixation each of the dense layers may be resolved into two dark bands 2·5 nm thick separated by a light band of similar thickness. The lucid layer now appears about 10 nm thick so that the total thickness of the envelope is 25 nm. The envelope appears to consist therefore of two unit membranes similar to the other membrane systems of the cell (see page 73) separated by a perimitochondrial space. Sjöstrand (1963) has seen the membranes of mitochondria looking like sheets of globules of 5 nm diameter and other recent work has demonstrated the granular nature of the membranes. Stoeckenius (1963) found spheres 8·5 nm across attached by stalks 4–5 nm long to the membrane of the cristae and probably also to the inner membrane of the envelope with which the cristae membranes are continuous. These pedicellate spheres, which

FIG. 59. A and B: Medium and high-powered electron micrographs of isolated and negatively-stained cristae from mitochondria of blended *Ricinus* seeds. The amoeba-like structures in Fig. 59A are believed to be cristae of the mitochondria irregularly expanded due to the osmotic shock following blending. Evenly distributed around their edges are knob-like particles which, at high magnification B, are seen to consist of a stalk and a head. (N/S/P)

Micrograph by Prof M. J. Nadakavukaren

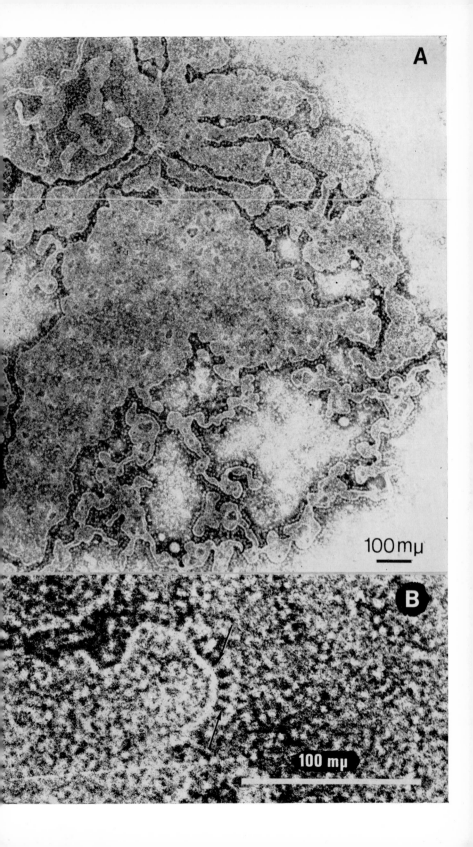

A

100mμ

B

100 mμ

have also been reported by Nadakavukaren (1964) in the endosperm of *Ricinus*, are not seen in sectioned cells, but in negatively stained, unfixed mitochondria and it is assumed that they are destroyed by normal fixation (Fig. 59). Fernandez-Moran, Oda, Blair & Green (1964) calculate that there are between 10,000 and 100,000 of these elementary particles in each mitochondrion. Green (1964) supposes that there are also particles on the outer surface of the outer unit membrane, but these were not reported by Stoekenius or Nadakavukaren. They are however present in freeze-etched preparations. When the mitochondrial membranes are disrupted preparations of particles of similar size to the pedicellate spheres, but without the stalks, are found. These are the elementary particles and each has a molecular weight of about two million and contains a complete electron transfer system for oxidation of succinate or $NADH_2$ by molecular oxygen (Green & Fleischer, 1963). It may be that all membranes are made up of globular units such as these in mitochondria (Fernandez-Moran, Oda, Blair & Green, 1964) or it is possible that there is a distinction between unit membranes such as Robertson (1964) describes and granular membranes. This last is what Weier, Engelbrecht, Harrison & Risley (1965) suggest, for they report that chloroplast membranes are made up of spherical units in both the lamellae and the envelope whereas the plasma membranes in the same preparation appear as continuous sheets such as we imagined the lamellae to be at one time. However there is also some evidence that the particles seen in some preparations are artefacts. Thus Sjöstrand, Cedergren & Karlsson (1964) hold that what appears to be a membrane standing on an edge with particles protruding from it is most likely a myelin-figure transformation of lipoprotein where the particles could be either lipid or protein sweated out of the lipoprotein membrane.

There must be differences between the kinds of membranes found in cells because they must bear different assemblies of enzymes and the resolving power of the electron microscope must show these differences when adequate techniques of preparation become available. D. E. Green (1964) envisages particles on the outer surface of the mitochondrion doing the oxidations that supply electrons and catalyse syntheses with the help of ATP while the stalked particles on the matrix side of the inner and cristae membranes do the electron transfers leading to the production of ATP. The stalked particles (oxysomes) may be concerned with electron transfer and oxidative phosphorylation and proton transfer, the oxidation-reduction of $NADH_2$, may occur in the perimitochondrial space, the region between the outer and inner unit membranes according to Frey-Wyssling (1964). Some sort of spatial separation of the chemistry must occur as in photosynthesis and the oxysomes are probably analogous with the quantasomes of chloroplasts (see page 138).

The matrix of mitochondria, the substance into which the cristae project from the envelope, has also received some attention recently. It is thought to consist of proteins and lipids, the protein being probably soluble. Within this matrix there are in many mitochondria particles of 25 mμ diameter of high electron density and usually referred to as ribosomes. They account for part, at least, of the RNA found in mitochondria which amounts to from 0·5 to 6 per cent of the dry weight. The ribosomes that have been definitely identified in Neurospora mitochondria have sedimentation coefficients of 73S (Küntzel-Noll, 1967). In some animal mitochondria there are granules that accumulate divalent cations and thus regulate the ionic concentration of the cytoplasm (Peachey, 1964). In the immature mitochondria of young cells of Zea root tips there is also a zone of low electron density containing filaments (Chrispeels, Vatter & Hanson, 1966). These filaments are probably DNA fibrils such as have been reported from mitochondria from a wide variety of plants and animals (Nass, Nass & Afzelius, 1965), bacterial nucleoplasm (see page 329) and some plastids. These filaments were not found in the fully differentiated cells of Zea, but have been reported in such cells in lower plants. The fibrillar core to the mitochondrial matrix has now been shown to consist of DNA in the slime mould, Didymium (Schuster, 1965) and DNA has been recognized in a wide range of mitochondria and its significance in cytoplasmic organelles is also discussed in Chapter 10. It has for some time been expected that nucleic acids would be found in mitochondria because of the genetical evidence. Mitochondrial, like plastid, mutations occur as a result of extranuclear changes and many of these have been brought about by ultra-violet light, which is absorbed strongly by nucleic acids, and by dyes that affect nucleic acids. There appears to be less DNA however in the mitochondria than in the plastids and this accounts for the difficulty of identifying it chemically (Gibor & Granick, 1964). Mitochondrial DNA, like plastid DNA, differs in base composition from nuclear DNA (Rabinowitz, Sinclair, De Salle, Haselkorn & Swift, 1965). It differs also in metabolism and structure. Nass (1966) has shown that in mouse fibroblasts the mitochondrial DNA, which is double stranded, consists of a circular thread whereas nuclear DNA is linear. This is reminiscent of the DNA of some viruses, which can be circular during part of the viral replication cycle, and of some phages whose DNA is usually linear, but can become ring-

shaped (Fig. 162). Nass holds that there are from two to six ring molecules of DNA of molecular weight 10×10^6 bound to the membranes
at one or more sites in each mitochondrion.

Heterogeneity

Avers & King (1960) have produced evidence for some degree of
chemical heterogeneity in a population of mitochondria. They used four
histochemical tests on the mitochondria of root tips of four species of
grass. Using Janus Green B, which demonstrates cytochrome oxidase,
they found 85–95 mitochondria per cell and the Nadi reaction for
cytochrome oxidase gave a similar figure. However, tests for acid phosphatase indicated that there were slightly more particles per cell (98–
108) with this enzyme and tests for succinic dehydrogenase indicated
that there were only 42–58 particles per cell on average with a positive
reaction. Also some cells were totally devoid of succinic dehydrogenase-
containing particles. Avers and King interpret these results as showing
that these cells have about 90 mitochondria per cell, but that only a
fraction of them have active succinic dehydrogenase in them. The
slightly higher figure for acid phosphatase-containing organelles may
be due to the presence of this enzyme in other organelles as well as
mitochondria. We should, however, point out that plant cells normally
contain about 700 mitochondria. Some other organelles are the same
size as mitochondria and carry other hydrolases as well as acid phosphatase. As well as the chemical heterogeneity among mitochondria
there is also cytological heterogeneity, for among the festucoid grasses,
which have special root hair-forming cells, there are more organelles
with any of the three enzymes than in the sister cells that do not form
hairs. There is also structural heterogeneity in some unicells, e.g.
Euglena, where the mitochondrion associated with the base of the
flagellum is of different shape from the other mitochondria of the cell
(Fig. 57).

Origin

About the origin, replication and early development of mitochondria
we know even less than we do about plastids. At cell division the mitochondria are distributed passively to the two daughter cells and there is
then an increase in the number of mitochondria as the daughter cells
grow. In root cap cells of *Zea* the meristematic initials each have about

200 mitochondria. As the cells grow and mature this number increases (Fig. 53), though at first it does not quite keep up with the increase in volume of cytoplasm, but by the end of cell growth the number per unit volume reaches the level at which it started in the initials and each cell has 2,000–3,000 (Juniper & Clowes, 1965). How the increase in number that must occur in dividing cells comes about is not known. There is some evidence for believing that the mitochondria can divide (Fig. 34). Their dumb-bell shape under the electron microscope often suggests that division was about to occur, but this is hardly good enough without more direct evidence though the finding by Yotsuyanagi & Guerrier (1965) that each half of the dumb-bell contains a group of DNA fibrils makes fission a most attractive hypothesis. Mitochondria appear able to fuse together and this sometimes precedes division of the fused mass (Lehninger, 1964). Maltzahn & Mühlethaler (1962) have commented on the appearance of budding in both plastids and mitochondria in dedifferentiating cells of the moss, *Splachnum*. This appears to be a special kind of fission enabling a rapid increase in the number of these organelles.

Various other methods of forming new mitochondria have been suggested. The nucleus, Golgi bodies, ribosomes, endoplasmic reticulum, plasma membrane and other organelles have from time to time been said to give rise to mitochondria. Some people believe that mitochondria and plastids have a common origin in ontogeny as well as in evolution. The spherical organelles of about 50 nm diameter that are usually called proplastids in plants have been interpreted as common precursors of both mitochondria and plastids. It is possible that both of these organelles could arise by invagination of the inner membrane of the envelope, but this view is losing ground in the face of new techniques and greater experience. These enable one to distinguish between the two at earlier and earlier stages of development. Also it is becoming increasingly obvious that both mitochondria and plastids enjoy a high degree of autonomy and possess their own DNA and RNA. It seems likely that they will be proved to be independent of each other.

Hoffman & Grigg (1958) hold that fission of existing mitochondria is probably not common in the meristematic cells of animals and plants. They hold that mitochondria usually are generated from the nuclear membrane by the invagination of the inner unit membrane into the nucleus and the subsequent extrusion of the organelle into the cytoplasm. Their main evidence for this is the frequent finding of invaginations of the nuclear envelope and of mitochondria attached to it. Although they think this is the usual mode of formation, they suggest that, in cells with too much cytoplasm for the nucleus to be able to cope with the demand for mitochondria, the plasma membrane can also form mitochondria by invagination.

In fern egg cells Bell & Mühlethaler (1964b) believe that mitochondria are produced from the nuclear envelope as they believe plastids are produced. Firstly the mitochondria degenerate and this process starts in the mother cell of the egg and ventral canal cell. The mitochondria start by being larger than those of somatic cells and they contain opaque granules. When the egg cell is formed the mitochondria appear swollen and contain few cristae. Within one to two hours they become small vacuoles whose contents are deposited on the surface of the egg. Within a further one to two hours the nucleus evaginates and the cytoplasm becomes filled with mitochondria of normal appearance. Bell and Mühlethaler hold that it is the outer unit membrane of the nuclear envelope that evaginates into the cytoplasm, forms a hooded structure and so produces both the outer and inner membranes of the mitochondrion. When free in the cytoplasm they are often umbo-shaped or cup-shaped and therefore appear as rings or dumb-bells in sections. From the relatively heavy cytoplasmic autoradiograph formed after feeding with tritiated thymidine Bell & Mühlethaler (1964a) hold that the mitochondria and plastids contain more DNA in the egg cell than at any other stage in the life history of the fern. (Cytoplasmic labelling by tritiated thymidine unassociated with organelles is also characteristic of many kinds of egg cells and has been interpreted as 'storage' DNA.) The fact that they find autoradiograph also over mitochondria of somatic cells implies that the mitochondria synthesize DNA themselves, though the incorporation of tritiated thymidine into cytoplasmic organelles does not always necessarily imply DNA synthesis as it does in nuclei, which have a negligible turn over. But the work of Parsons (1965) on *Tetrahymena* suggests that thymidine incorporation into mitochondria does represent synthesis and that this occurs throughout the mitotic cycle even when the nucleus is not in its DNA-synthetic stage. The fact that some workers have shown that the mitochondrial label is not removed by DNA-ase digestion is also not proof that the thymidine is not incorporated into DNA. Muckenthaler & Mahowald (1966) found this failure to remove cytoplasmic label in the egg cells of *Drosophila* though DNA-ase did remove the nuclear label. But they also found that pretreatment with protease enables DNA-ase to remove the cytoplasmic label also. They interpret this result as probably due to the precipitation of protein around the mitochondrial DNA during fixation of the cells (rather than to the DNA being bound *in vivo* to a protein) in such a way that the DNA-ase cannot act on the DNA moiety. The fern egg seems to be peculiar in its production of mitochondria from nuclei, at any rate, on such a vast scale. Other workers (e.g. Jensen, 1965; Diers, 1966) have failed to find any comparable transformation of the nuclear membrane in the eggs of other plants or even any degeneration and elimination of the original mitochondria and it has to be admitted that, even for fern eggs, the postulated transformation of the nuclear evaginations into mitochondria has still to be proved. If the theory of Bell and Mühlethaler is true there is a mechanism for the elimination of any genetic mutations that have arisen in the extra-nuclear DNA in the previous generation. The next generation starts with a completely new set of mitochondria and plastids whose DNA is presumably coded by the nucleus.

The experiments of Luck (1963a, b) throw a different light on the formation of mitochondria in the fungus, *Neurospora*. Luck had a choline-requiring mutant and fed it with tritium and ^{14}C-labelled choline and transferred it to an unlabelled medium. Choline is incorporated into the lecithin of mitochondrial membranes. In autoradiographs the radioactivity was found to be randomly distributed in the mitochondria through three mass-doubling cycles (360 minutes in cultures at the logarithmic phase of growth). At the end of each cycle the average count was half of the original and so the replication of the mitochondria is non-conservative (Fig. 131). Therefore the mitochondria are not formed *de novo* and also not from other structural precursors (other membranes or particles). *De novo* formation would show conservative type labelling where the production of labelled mitochondria would decrease as a logarithmic function of time and the average grain count per labelled mitochondrion would remain the same. Formation from structural precursors would require non-random labelling. A similar result was obtained by Parsons (1965) for the amoeba, *Tetrahymena*, in an experiment in which the mitochondrial DNA was labelled with tritiated thymidine. Greenawalt & Hall (1964) have however suggested that in the *Neurospora* experiments it would be more useful to look for the generation of mitochondria from precursor structures in the conidia rather than in logarithmically growing cells and they believe they have evidence for this kind of origin in conidia.

Frederic (1952), who used phase microscopy to watch mitochondria in living chick embryo cells in culture, showed that at the onset of cell division the mitochondria decreased in numbers. He believed that the organelles break up into pieces too small to see and that new mito-

G

chondria were formed from these after mitosis. Such a view would also be consistent with the type of labelling of mitochondrial populations found by Luck and by Parsons.

In the lower green plants the evidence is again in favour of self-replication. The pigmented flagellates, *Chromulina* and *Micromonas* have a single mitochondrion per cell and this divides to keep pace with mitosis (Manton, 1959a, 1961b). Also in *Anthoceros* and *Chrysochromulina* the mitochondria grow to form a cluster which Manton thinks will then separate. The evidence about replication from genetical studies is not nearly so good as it is for plastids, but we know of examples of maternal inheritance of defects in the cytochrome system in *Neurospora* and this is likely to be due to the maternal supply of mitochondria though it does not rule out other structural precursors carried over with the cytoplasm and the factor of inheritance need not necessarily be a particle at all.

Thus there is good though not conclusive evidence for the production of new mitochondria from (1) their growth and subsequent fission (2) the multiplication of subunits made from the breaking up of existing mitochondria and there is less good evidence for (3) from nuclear evaginations. Only in the unicells with a single mitochondrion are we certain of the method of reproduction and it may be that all these methods do actually happen in different cells or in different circumstances. There is some evidence for a cytoplasmic factor in their inheritance, probably borne in the mitochondria themselves. We may assume that their DNA serves a genetic function and probably it has a distinctive base composition different from that of nuclear DNA as has the chloroplast DNA (see page 125). A role in protein synthesis is perhaps less certain though we know that isolated mitochondria can incorporate labelled amino acids into some of the mitochondrial proteins, though not others and they possess a DNA-dependent RNA polymerase and amino acid activating enzymes (Haldar, Freeman & Work, 1966).

As with plastids and unicellular algae and ribosomes and viruses some people have been struck by the resemblance between mitochondria and bacteria. This is sufficiently close for it to have been suggested that mitochondria have evolved from parasitic bacteria which have allowed the symbiotic association to become more efficient and therefore bigger. The respiratory enzymes of bacteria are located in the protoplast membrane (Lehninger, 1964) and there are no organelles equivalent to the mitochondria of higher organisms because of the scale of the cell.

4.3 Golgi bodies

Occurrence

These organelles were originally described by Golgi in 1898 from Purkinje cells of the cerebellum of an owl. They appeared as a net-like region of cytoplasm around the nucleus capable of reducing silver nitrate after certain fixation procedures. The name 'Golgi apparatus' came to be applied to organelles of different appearance that reduced silver nitrate or osmium tetroxide in other kinds of cells and considerable controversy raged over the question whether or not these organelles were similar in anything but their reducing properties or whether they existed at all in living cells or were artefacts of fixation. The second point was to some extent cleared up by the use of phase microscopy for bodies regarded by some workers as parts of the Golgi apparatus can be seen in many kinds of living cells. Although most kinds of animal cells, from vertebrates to protozoans, have regions of cytoplasm that reduce silver nitrate or osmium tetroxide, such organelles had never been demonstrated in plant cells except in a few algae (Buvat, 1963) and botanists never became much concerned about the identity and functions of the Golgi apparatus.

The electron microscope put an end to this phase of plant cytology for, as soon as adequate techniques for preparing plant cells for electron microscopy became available, organelles similar in appearance to those identified as Golgi components in vertebrate cells were found (Buvat, 1957). It is still not clear exactly why Golgi bodies cannot be recognized under the light microscope in fixed higher plant cells, for they are within its resolving power so far as size is concerned and the bigger ones found in algae may be recognized in living cells by phase microscopy.

In both animals and plants there is now good evidence that Golgi are concerned with carbohydrate secretion, but the chemical make-up of the secretory products differs in different organisms and they appear to have been adapted for a considerable range of functions. Golgi have not been found in bacteria or blue-green algae even under the electron microscope (Buvat, 1963), but, so far as we know they occur in all other groups of plants and in all kinds of cells, except mature sieve tubes (Northcote & Wooding, 1966). Other possible exceptions are the sperm cells of bryophytes and pteridophytes (Manton, 1961). In some fungi ordinary Golgi bodies have been found, but in others they may be represented by loose aggregations of tubules (Hawker, 1965). When they were first found in plant cells some people preferred to call them dictyosomes because they were identified by their structure only as being similar to individual components of the Golgi seen in certain animal cells, but they are now usually called Golgi apparatus or Golgi bodies. Some people hold that the dictyosomes occur in groups and that the whole group ought to be called a Golgi apparatus, but it is not yet clear what type of association, if any, exists between the dictyosomes. Mollenhauer & Morré (1966) consider that a plant cell may have one or several Golgi apparatuses each consisting of many dictyosomes and tubular interconnexions between dictyosomes have occasionally been reported, but we do not know how significant these are. In animal cells the dictyosomes may fuse together to form a large Golgi apparatus at some point in the cell's life cycle. There is little point here in going further into the classical Golgi controversy as it hardly concerns plants: for reviews see Baker (1957) and Picken (1960).

Structure

In plant cells the Golgi bodies or dictyosomes are always scattered through the cytoplasm and not localized as a 'complex' or 'apparatus' near the nucleus as they are in many animal cells. Though, where there is only a single Golgi body in a cell as happens in some flagellate plant cells, it usually lies near the nucleus and the bases of the flagella (Manton, 1961). They move in the cytoplasm, but differently from the mitochondria and spherosomes which travel more rapidly in a stream (Mollenhauer & Morré, 1966). They appear in sections as stacks of flat sacs or cisternae (Fig. 60). There are usually four to seven cisternae in each Golgi, each $1-3\mu$m in diameter and the stack is about $0\cdot5\mu$m high. The number of cisternae in a Golgi may be much higher than this, up to twenty in certain plant cells and in animals. The cisternae are separated one from another by a space of relatively constant height—$11\cdot5$ nm in some estimations. This suggests that there is some intercisternal spacing structure and Cunningham, Morré & Mollenhauer (1966) believe they have identified this as groups of parallel fibres which lie between adjacent cisternae and may project beyond the cisternal edge. They apparently do not touch the cisternae though. The fibre bundles are separated from each other by about 10 nm. Further evidence for the existence of some spacing structure is that whole dictyosomes may with care be isolated: they do not separate into the component cisternae. The flat cisternae appear swollen around the rim after some fixation procedures and there are often vesicles attached to it or situated as if they had been budded off from the rim. Vesicles of the same size also occur elsewhere

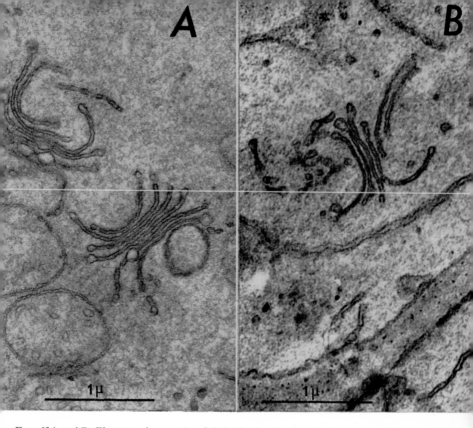

FIG. 60A and B: Electron micrographs of Golgi bodies from central root cap cells of primary root of *Zea*. A and B show vesicles close to and connected with the edges of the cisternae. A shows a number of dilations in or near the centre of the cisternae and both A and B show what may be a stage in Golgi division by separation of the cisternae (see Fig. 62). (Mn)

in the cytoplasm and, in some cells, there is reason to believe that they are produced in large quantities from the rims of the Golgi cisternae and travel in the cytoplasm. In meristematic cells of *Anthoceros* Manton (1960) has observed tubules arising from the edge of the cisternae rather than vesicles. These tubules anastomose and form reticulate frills around the Golgi apparatus. This kind of structure has also been seen in cells from the stem of *Allium cepa* by Cunningham, Morré & Mollenhauer (1966). These workers obtained Golgi from broken cells and enriched their preparations by sucrose gradients. They found the cisternae to be highly fenestrate at the periphery. There is a compact central region less than 1μm across from which tubules project for more than 1μm all round the cisternae. The central region is the part of the cisternae seen in ordinary sections under the electron microscope. The tubules anastomose to form a frilly network and the whole cisterna looks like a disc of

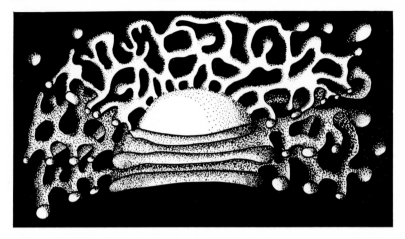

FɪG. 61. Reconstruction of a Golgi-body cut across its diameter showing the fenestrated outer region giving off vesicles.

lace over 3μm in diameter (Fig. 61). The tubules are 20–40 nm across and
there are vesicles of two kinds attached to them. One kind is nearly
spherical, uniformly 50 nm in diameter and with a rough surface which
stains well. The other kind is flattened, round or oblong looked at from
on top, of variable size (20–80 nm in diameter), with a smooth surface
and low affinity for stain and accumulates phosphotungstic acid in the
centres. The rough-surfaced vesicles occur at the ends of the tubules or
attached by a stalk to the periphery of the tubular net. The smooth
vesicles are attached directly to the sides of the tubules or interposed
between two segments of a tubule usually within the net. The rough
surfaced vesicles predominate on the small cisternae while large
cisternae carry both types.

   Each cisterna consists of a unit membrane enclosing a space and
there are no ribosomes associated with either the membrane or the
space. The unit membrane when suitably fixed shows the usual triple
layered structure (Sjöstrand, 1963). When isolated by centrifugation
procedures, animal Golgi have been shown to have little RNA, but
much alkaline phosphatase and lipid (Buvat, 1963).

Origin

In plant cells that do not vacuolate we have shown that the number of
Golgi bodies keeps pace with the size of the cells as these grow and
divide (Fig. 53). Gifford & Stewart (1965) have also shown that the

Golgi increase in number per cell in the summit cells of a shoot apex when the plant is given a few photoinductive cycles to promote flowering. This induction leads to a higher rate of cell division at the summit and the proliferation of the Golgi is presumably related to this though it may be associated with the induction itself. It is not clear how multiplication occurs. In plant cells Buvat (1963) has pointed out that the Golgi often lie side by side, with the cisternae of one organelle exactly in line with those of another, thus giving the impression that they have been derived from a single Golgi by division (Fig. 62). But Buvat also suggests that they may arise *de novo* in the phragmoplasts of dividing cells. Cronshaw & Wardrop (1964) have shown that in vacuolated xylem cells of *Pinus*, where the tonoplast and plasmalemma are very close together, the cisternae become separated rather than lying in stacks. This suggests another possible means of multiplication as well as showing that, if there is a structural connexion between the cisternae, it cannot be very strong (Fig. 62).

Several investigations have suggested that there is an age difference between one face of the dictyosome and the other—that there is a forming face and a maturing face. Cunningham, Morré & Mollenhauer (1966) believe that the cisternae of maturing faces are compressed, while those of forming faces are often swollen and that cisternae are continuously being separated from the dictyosome at the maturing face and continuously being formed from the opposite face. Amelunxen & Gronau (1966) think that the wide cisternae may be derived from endoplasmic reticulum and that the compressed cisternae on the opposite face give rise to vacuoles in the leaves of *Acorus*. The idea of a difference in maturity between the cisternae of a dictyosome seems to be confirmed by an observation of Bainton & Farquhar (1966) on the polymorphonuclear leucocytes. It seems that two kinds of granules are produced by the Golgi of these cells. One, which is called azurophil, of about 80 nm diameter is produced only at the progranulocyte stage of the cell and from the cisterna on the concave face of the dictyosome. The other, called 'specific', and about 50 nm across is formed during the myelocyte stage from the cisterna at the convex face.

Function

We have little direct information about the chemical activities of the Golgi because differential centrifugation has so far not been so successful in making pure preparations available for biochemical investigation as it has done for mitochondria or ribosomes. However there is much

CISTERNAL DIVISION
lower plants ?

CISTERNAL SEPARATION
higher plants ?

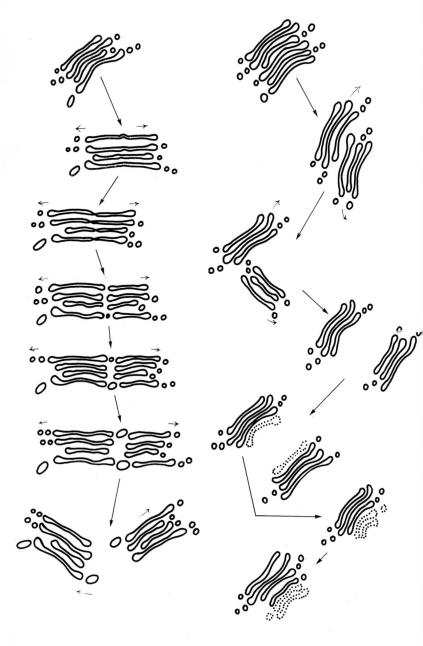

indirect evidence from both animals and plants that the Golgi are concerned with secretion and, particularly in plants, with the formation of
cell walls and extracellular structures. In the outer root cap cells of *Zea*,
for example, hypertrophied Golgi bodies produce large vesicles which
move through the cytoplasm, pass through the plasmalemma and may
displace it from the cell wall (Mollenhauer, Whaley & Leech, 1961;
Mollenhauer & Whaley, 1963) (Fig. 10, 63). When this secretory function is over the Golgi revert to the same appearance as they had in the
quiescent cells of the root (Whaley, Mollenhauer & Kephart, 1962)
(Figs. 64, 65).

The most elegant demonstration of the role of Golgi in polysaccharide transport is that of Northcote & Pickett-Heaps (1966) in the
root cap cells of *Triticum*. They looked at autoradiographs prepared for
the electron microscope of roots fed with tritium-labelled glucose for
various periods and showed that the glucose is converted into galactose,
galacturonic acid, arabinose etc. in the Golgi bodies and that these are
transported, probably as insoluble pectic substances, in the Golgi
vesicles to the plasmalemma where the labelled substance is incorporated into the cell wall and the slime around these cells. Some of the
glucose is also used in starch and cellulose synthesis in the amyloplasts
and wall, but the Golgi are not concerned with these processes.

In pollen grains the cytoplasm associated with the generative and
vegetative nuclei is different in appearance and staining reactions. One
of the differences is that the vegetative nucleus is associated with more
Golgi which have more cisternae and produce more vesicles than the
generative nucleus. Larson (1963) believes that this difference is correlated with the role of the vegetative nucleus in synthesizing wall material
for the pollen tube. This belief tends to be confirmed by the work of
Rosen, Gawlick, Dashek & Siegesmund (1964) and Dashek & Rosen
(1966) who showed that in *Lilium* pollen tubes growth is confined to the
apical 3–5 microns which contain Golgi vesicles and some smaller
vesicles of unknown origin but no other organelles. The Golgi vesicles
are probably the sites of the later stages of pectin synthesis before the
final polymerization in the newly formed wall itself.

The role of the Golgi has been further studied by Larson (1965) in the
pollen of several species. In resting pollen grains the Golgi each have
5–7 cisternae and they produce small vesicles. These are 42·5 nm across

FIG. 62. Two methods by which Golgi reproduction may take place. By cisternal
separation (see Fig. 60) followed by the replication of new cisternae. By cisterna
subdivision, followed by the extension of each individual cisterna.

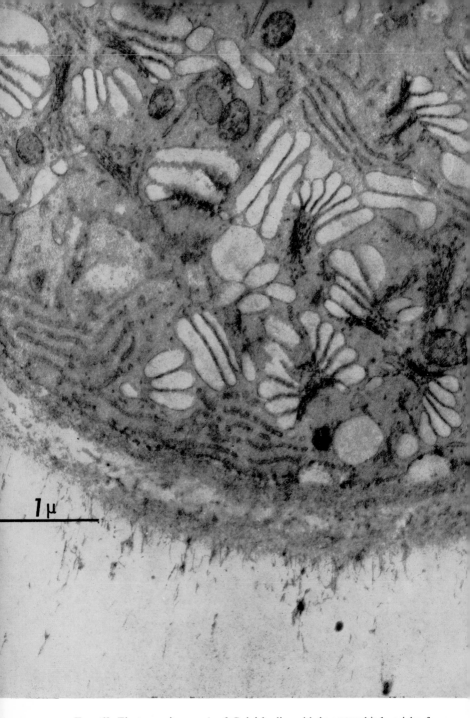

FIG. 63. Electron micrograph of Golgi bodies with hypertrophied vesicles from a peripheral cap cell of the primary root of *Zea*. These large electron-translucent vesicles are believed to contain pectin and hemicellulose; they pass to the plasma-lemma, coalesce with it and discharge their contents into the wall. In these cells much of the contents of these vesicles finds its way into the mucus surrounding the root cap (see Fig. 146). (Glut/Mn)

and similar unattached vesicles are found distributed throughout the cytoplasm. On germination of the pollen there is a dramatic change in the Golgi. Within 18 minutes of placing in the culture solution the production of small vesicles stops and is replaced by the production of large vesicles about 150 nm across. These vesicles later appear free in the cytoplasm where they may fuse one with another to become up to 500 nm in diameter. Larson believes that these vesicles are produced on one face of the Golgi apparatus often by a whole cisterna being converted into a row of vesicles so that the number of cisternae may be reduced to one or two in some parts of the pollen tube. The large vesicles move in the cytoplasm and, when they reach the plasma membrane, their contents are secreted to the outside and are incorporated into the pollen tube wall. They accumulate especially in the tip of the tube and their membranes may here be incorporated into the expanding plasmalemma. What happens to their membranes when they deposit their contents into the wall of the non-growing part of the tube and in the pollen grain itself is not known. A similar conversion from small vesicle production to large vesicle production occurs in root caps (see page 183).

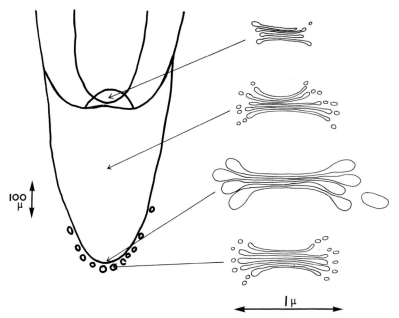

FIG. 64. The appearance of Golgi bodies (drawn to the same scale) in different parts of a section of a root tip of *Zea*. See Figs. 51, 60, 63 and 65.

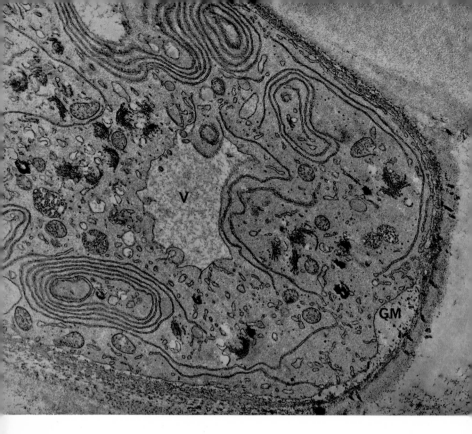

FIG. 65. Electron micrograph of a detached cell from the margin of the root cap of *Zea*. The cell is beginning to vacuolate (V). The ER, unlike that of the central cap cells, is distributed in loops and whorls throughout the cell, and the Golgi bodies have reverted to a non-hypertrophied state. Plasmodesmata which once crossed the transverse wall of two contiguous cells now jut out into space. A little Golgi-derived material (GM) still remains between the plasmalemma and the cell wall and the mucus and the remains of the dissolved cell walls can be seen as a granular material (M) around the cell. (Glut/Mn)

The Golgi are also believed to be concerned in the secretion of substances by some of the glandular cells of insectivorous plants (Schnepf, 1961a, b).

Another similar piece of evidence comes from the haustoria of the parasitic flowering plant, *Cuscuta campestris*. The hyphal tips of these haustoria contain very large Golgi bodies absent in other cells of the parasite though ordinary Golgi are present in all the cells. Bonneville & Voeller (1963) think that these enlarged Golgi are probably the source of enzymes used for breaking down and absorbing the walls and protoplasm of the host plant cells.

In dividing cells there is also evidence that the Golgi may be concerned with wall formation. Whaley & Mollenhauer (1963) have shown that in mechanically injured cells the Golgi are stimulated to produce more vesicles and they believe that the vesicles fuse to form the cell plate at the end of mitosis. Juniper (1962) believes that some at least of the Golgi vesicles fuse in chains parallel to the axis of the mitotic spindle to form the cytoplasmic connexions between sister cells (Fig. 85). There certainly seems to be a concentration of Golgi around the spindle at the end of mitosis and the number of vesicles budded off from the cisternae also appears to increase then.

In the root hairs of *Raphanus* Bonnett & Newcomb (1966) believe that both proteins and carbohydrates are first accumulated in the Golgi cisternae and then segregated in the large, smooth-surfaced vesicles that are released from the cisternae. From these vesicles arise by evagination small vesicles with chambered coats. These are thought to take the proteins and transport them to the surface of the root hair for use in wall synthesis while the smooth vesicles move the carbohydrates to the region of wall extension at the tip of the hair.

Thus there is much circumstantial evidence that the Golgi are concerned with secretion and that in plants they are especially associated with the formation of cell walls and extra-cellular substances. It looks as if they may have taken on roles in carbohydrate metabolism during evolution and, if this is right, it may explain why the cytochemical techniques that display the Golgi for light microscopy in animals fail to do so in plants. Not all secretion by plant cells is performed by the Golgi however. There is some evidence that the transfer of some substances is carried out by the endoplasmic reticulum. This appears to be true of resin or its precursors in the resin canals of *Pinus* and possibly also of carbohydrate from phloem companion cells (Wooding & Northcote, 1965b, c). There is also the possibility that the ER and the Golgi are together concerned with secretion. Many secretory cells have the ER well developed and it may be that enzymes are first transported to the Golgi by the ER either through direct connexions or the use of travelling vesicles cut off from the ER. The Golgi may then use these enzymes and perhaps other substances transported in the same way to make the secreted substance which is finally moved to some other site by the Golgi vesicles.

One of the most interesting discoveries made with the electron microscope is that by Manton and her colleagues of the origin of scales in the Golgi vesicles of some flagellate algae. In *Mesostigma* (Manton & Ettl, 1965) there are three different kinds of scales on the surface of the cell. There are elaborate, basket-shaped scales covering the whole of the external surface of the cell except for the flagellar pits. These scales are 0·6 × 0·5μm and consist of a meshwork with pegs that project inwards into the basket. Beneath these scales there are several layers of plate-like scales 0·3 × 0·2μm. The third type is much smaller, 0·03μm wide, and plate-like. These occur underneath the big plate-like scales and also over the surface of the flagella where they are imbricated and form a close-packed mosaic.

All these kinds of scales are found also within the cell inside vesicles that are clearly derived from the Golgi bodies and Manton's interpretation is that they are prefabricated by the Golgi and transported in the vesicles to the outside of the cell, probably in the flagellar depression, from where they must be spread over the appropriate position on the surface of the cell (Fig. 66). It seems that the different kinds of scale are made in different vesicles, but the vesicles may later coalesce after fabrication is complete. Several different flagellate algae have now been investigated and shown to have scales of similar origin. It has now been found that in *Chrysochromulina chiton* the major sugar components of the scales are ribose and galactose and that the form of the scales can be changed by altering the composition of the nutrient solution (Green & Jennings, 1967).

Similarly the non-cellulose wall or theca of *Platymonas* is made up of stellate particles which are made inside Golgi vesicles and are transported to the surface. After the division of a cell the new theca is formed by the coalescence of the particles on the surfaces of the daughter cells inside the mother cell theca. Coalescence starts near the pyrenoid and Manton & Park (1965) think that an enzyme causing the sticking of the particles together may be synthesized or liberated at the pyrenoid and secreted to the surface.

The Golgi of diatoms, which occur in pairs with ER membranes connecting them, are also believed to be concerned in the formation of the silica deposition vesicles which lay down the scales of the cell surface (Drum, 1966).

FIG. 66. Electron micrograph of the alga, *Mesostigma viride*. The Golgi body (or bodies) (G) of this alga are responsible for the production in vesicles (V) of the three types of scale found on the alga's surface. Scales of the different types are not normally found together in the same vesicle until their manufacture is quite complete, after which adjacent vesicles grow, coalesce and lose contact with the Golgi cisternae. The vesicles with their scales then migrate to some part of the plasmalemma, coalesce with it and in a manner as yet unknown pass through it and allow the scales to join those on the outside. (Glut/Os/Pb/U)

Micrograph by Prof I. Manton and Dr H. Ettl.

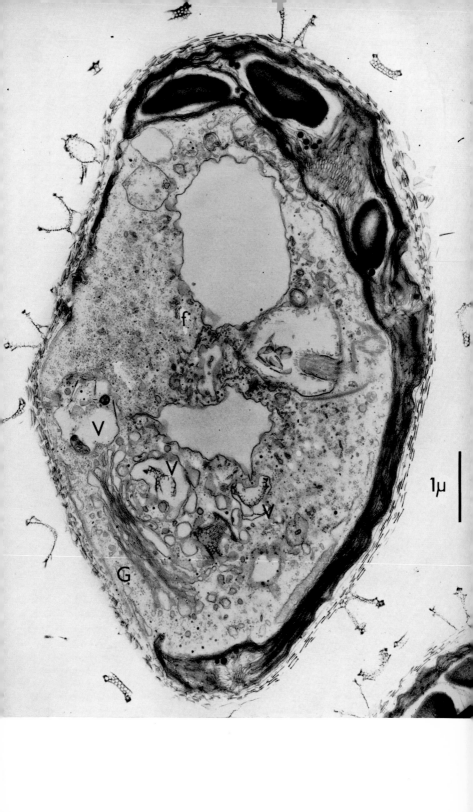

An interesting role for the Golgi has appeared from the work of Schnepf & Koch (1966a, b) on the anomalous alga, *Glaucocystis* and on *Vacuolaria*. Both algae secrete water. In *Glaucocystis* spores the Golgi, which surround the nucleus, consist of 15–20 cisternae. They are probably formed on the outer side while the inner ones swell and form a row of vesicles which swell into vacuoles. The vacuoles discharge their watery contents by bursting and their membranes are incorporated into the plasmalemma. *Vacuolaria* has contractile vacuoles which are formed from the fusion of swollen cisternae formed from the outer face of the Golgi. The whole Golgi complex consists of about fifty interconnected dictyosomes whose cisternae lie parallel to the nuclear envelope and separated from it by a fenestrated sheet of ER. Schnepf and Koch hold that it takes only thirty minutes to discharge a volume of water equal to the cell's volume in this way.

4.4 Spherosomes

Spherosomes are spherical organelles between 0·5 and 1·0μm in diameter occurring abundantly in nearly all plant cells. Attention was drawn to them in the early days of light microscopy because they shine conspicuously under dark-ground illumination whereas the other cytoplasmic organelles of similar size do not. This property is presumably due to a bigger difference in refractive index between the organelle and the cytoplasmic matrix. They have a high affinity for fat-soluble dyes and the oil content accounts for their refractivity.

These are the objects originally called microsomes by Hanstein nearly ninety years ago, but only with the advent of the electron microscope has it been possible to be certain of not confusing them with mitochondria or proplastids (Fig. 51). They have a single unit membrane around them and a fine granular appearance inside which indicates that there is protein as well as oil in the stroma. Murakami (1963) found ribosomes in those of *Spinacia* and acid phosphatase has been detected in them in the bulb scale cells of *Allium*, the classical material for spherosomes. Wooding & Northcote (1965) have found clusters of small spherosomes, 0·1–0·2μm in diameter in the phloem companion cells of *Acer*. Other kinds of cells of the same plant contain spherosomes, but not in clusters and some of them have large inclusions within the organelles after glutaraldehyde fixation.

One view about their formation is that they develop by the accumulation of oil at the end of a strand of endoplasmic reticulum which then becomes cut off by a constriction to form the vesicle which grows. If this is so, they resemble in origin the vacuoles of some kinds of cells. Bowes (1965) regards spherosomes and vacuoles as being organelles of the same kind which have diverged in their late development. Very little is known about their role in the cell's economy except that their presence indicates lipid synthesis and even less is known about their occurrence in cells. It is generally assumed that they are not simply oil droplets in the cytoplasm because they leave a protein ghost when oil is extracted and they do not coalesce when they bump into each other as they often do in their rapid motion in living cells (Sorokin & Sorokin, 1966). But it is not clear if they are the same as elaioplasts or if there is a developmental relationship between the two kinds of organelles (see page 145). Frey-Wyssling, Grieshaber & Mühlethaler (1963) believe that spherosomes may persist in the cell or they may become oil droplets by the gradual replacement of the granular stroma by oil. Such oil droplets found in cytoplasm have a unit membrane around them and presumably are formed from some membrane-bound organelle because artificial mixtures of oil and gelatine produce droplets of oil surrounded by a single dark line under the electron microscope and not the triple structure of a unit membrane.

4.5 Lysosomes

Lysosomes are enzyme-containing organelles similar in appearance under the electron microscope to spherosomes. They are about $0·4\mu$m across and have a single unit membrane on the outside and a dense granular stroma which sometimes contains a large vacuole. In differential centrifugation procedures they occur in the fraction intermediate between the mitochondria and ribosomes. They are best known from animals where they perform important functions in certain kinds of cells especially phagocytes, but there is some evidence for their existence in plant cells.

They are regarded as devices for separating hydrolytic enzymes from the rest of the cytoplasm where the enzymes would cause the autolysis of the cell if they were discharged into the protoplasm. 'Suicide bags' is a name that is appropriate for this function.

All the enzymes so far identified in lyosomes have a low pH optimum (de Duve, 1963). They contain large amounts of acid phosphatase and this property has been used in attempts to identify them in root tips of *Vicia faba* (Gahan & Maple, 1966). Acid phosphatase content is probably a bad way of identifying lysosomes because other organelles, which contain none of the hydrolytic enzymes, do contain acid phosphatase.

Lamport & Northcote (1960a) found that at least 80 per cent of the acid phosphatase of cultured tissue exists in cell walls and Dauwalder, Kephart & Whaley (1966) came to the conclusion that lysosomes do not exist in roots of *Zea*. They found concentrations of acid phosphatase activity, but these were associated with some Golgi bodies, though not those from either the root cap cells that are about to slough off and die or from the cells that undergo differentiation and breakdown to form xylem and these are the cells where one might expect to find lytic activity.

Several hydrolytic enzymes, a ribonuclease, a deoxy-ribonuclease, protease, a β-glucuronidase and a β-galactosidase also occur in lysosomes and their rupture leads to the disintegration of proteins, nucleic acids, carbohydrates, etc. Without rupture of the membrane, the enzymes exhibit no activity and this provides an answer to the question that has puzzled biologists for a long time—how are hydrolases controlled within cells?

Lysosomes are polymorphic in animals, adapted for many different functions and consequently many different names are given to them. A particularly interesting investigation is that of Allison & Paton (1965) on human embryo lung cells in culture. These cells were given photosensitizing dyes such as neutral red and acridine orange which are taken up by the lysosomes. The cells were then cultured in dye-free medium in the dark. Illumination leads to damage of the lysosome membrane and the consequent release of the enzymes which cause death of the cell or chromosome aberrations. The cells are not damaged unless they have taken up dye into the lysosomes. The action of these photosensitizing dyes in causing cell damage in light had been known before, but had previously been considered to be direct rather than through the bursting of the lysosomes which accumulate the dyes. Allison and Paton think that the lysosomes' enzymes probably break both strands of the DNA double helix at the same time in producing chromosome aberrations rather than one at a time as pancreatic DNA-ase does.

In some animal cells lysosomes are concerned with phagocytosis and pinocytosis. When foreign bodies are engulfed by cells lysosomes appear in the cytoplasm, acquire a positive phosphatase reaction and digest the foreign material within themselves, often leaving an undigested residue inside. The organelles can, in some cells, then be passed out of the cell, but in others they stay in the cell and it is conjectured that the accumulation of these bodies may give rise to other ageing phenomena. A lysosome can also digest a part of its own cell, a mitochondrion or a piece of ER, for example. This sometimes occurs in starvation and is perhaps a method of feeding on itself without doing permanent damage to the cell. This sort of autophagy also occurs when an organ becomes redundant as in the metamorphosis of a frog tadpole. Proteolytic enzymes in lysosomes are responsible for the loss of the tail. There is also evidence that the work of the osteoclasts in remodelling bone is due to the discharge of the contents of lysosomes outside the cell and the subsequent feeding on the disintegrated particles of bone by the osteoclasts. Vitamin A is supposed to activate the lysosomes and this is perhaps why excess of this substance causes spontaneous bone fractures. Certain steroids such as cortisone may stabilize the lysosome membrane and this may account for their reduction of inflammation. It has also been suggested that colchicine may behave in the same way and this, perhaps, is why it can alleviate gout in man, for part of the discomfort of this disease may be due to the release of lysosomal enzymes by the polymorphonuclear leucocytes when they attack the crystals of sodium monourate (Rajan, 1966). In some congenital diseases of man where an enzyme is missing from the proper complement the substrate of the enzyme is stored in lysosomes. For a review of the work of animal lysosomes see Novikoff (1961) and De Duve & Wattiaux (1966): very little is known yet about these organelles in plants probably because plants do not present the same problems to their cells as animals do. In some plant cells workers have found it impossible to distinguish between lysosomes and spherosomes (Jensen, 1965). There has been some speculation about the phylogenetic and ontogenetic origins of lysosomes. They are present in all kinds of animal cells, but absent from bacteria as with other membrane-bound organelles. Bacterial hydrolases are often secreted outside the cell or else located at the cell surface and perhaps in this way the cell is protected from their actions. The large size of other cells makes this an impossible solution for them. Lysosomes structurally resemble Golgi vesicles and pinocytosis vesicles and one view of their origin in a cell is that they are vesicles of this kind, derived either from the Golgi body or from the plasmalemma, and acquiring their hydrolases from the endoplasmic reticulum. It may also be that they can be budded off directly from the ER.

There is no doubt that there are many situations in plants where degradation of organelles or other structures does take place as part of the normal processes of differentiation, e.g. the breakdown of the cross walls of xylem vessels, the degradation of the whole cytoplasmic contents of laticifers and the senescence of tissues. Some of these phenomena will be discussed further in connexion with specialized cells and the breakdown of plant cells and tissues. Some of these processes must be due to hydrolytic enzymes released exactly at the right point in time to achieve a particular catabolic process, and there is some evidence for the existence in plants of any bodies comparable to the lysosomes in animals.

4.6   Lomasomes

These are organelles found in the periphery of the cytoplasm associated with cell walls. They occur in fungi, algae and in higher plants. In *Chara* and *Nitella* they consist of a single unit membrane, 7·5 nm thick, continuous with the plasmalemma containing a system of interconnecting tubules with dense contents (Barton, 1965; Crawley, 1965). These resemble the bodies originally called lomasomes in the fungi and they are thought to be concerned with wall synthesis. Some cells of higher plants also display tubules in or near the wall. These may be seen, as in cotyledonary storage tissue of *Phaseolus*, even when no wall synthesis is taking place and so, if they are concerned with building walls, they must persist afterwards in this tissue (Öpik, 1966). In most higher plant cells organelles similar to those of *Chara* and *Nitella* had not been found until recently with the advent of glutaraldehyde fixation. Esau, Cheadle & Gill (1966) have shown that the plasmalemma—wall interface varies in appearance in higher plants with the fixative. It is smooth after permanganate, undulate after osmium and very irregular after glutaraldehyde and contains pockets protruding into cytoplasm. These pockets bear aggregations of tubules, which are circular in cross section and there seems to be little doubt that they should be equated with the lomasomes first found in fungi. (Fig. 100).

Arrigoni & Rossi (1963) have demonstrated that these lomasomes most likely are concerned with wall expansion, for, in *Avena* coleoptiles that are illuminated enough to inhibit growth by 8 per cent, the number of lomasomes per cell falls. The relation between the tubules of the lomasomes and the microtubules found in the peripheral cytoplasm of plant cells is not clear, but both appear to be concerned with wall formation (see Chapter 5).

4.7   Flagella

Although not possessed by flowering plant cells at all, flagella or cilia, are worth a brief mention here because of their general biological interest. The highest plant in which they occur is the gymnosperm tree, *Ginkgo*, where the male gametes have hundreds of cilia. The male gametes of the bryophytes, pteridophytes and cycads have two or more and many kinds of motile cells in the algae and fungi have one or more though flagella are not here the only means of making cells move. The red and blue-green algae and flowering plants are notable for the complete absence of flagella. Many kinds of animal cells, not only motile ones, possess flagella or cilia even in the highest groups. The distinction between flagella and cilia is an arbitrary one. Where the organelle is short (5–10μm) and occurs in large numbers it is called a cilium; where it is long (up to 150μm) and occurs singly or in small numbers it is called a flagellum. Undulipodia is a collective name favoured by Frey-Wyssling & Mühlethaler (1965). In plants they are usually long and occur in small numbers per cell and even, as in the cycads and *Ginkgo*, where they might fit the definition of cilia, they look different from the regular arrays found in ciliates or in the ciliated epithelial cells of animals.

One of the most interesting facts that has emerged from electron microscopy is the similarity of construction in all kinds of flagella and cilia except for those of the bacteria. They consist of a cylindrical membrane sheath containing a ring of nine peripheral fibres and two axial fibres (Fig. 67). This is true of the sperm tails of animals and the flagella and cilia of all plants and animals with very few exceptions, which are slight modifications of this pattern. For example, the single forward-directed flagellum of the male gamete of the marine diatom, *Lithodesmium*, has the nine peripheral fibres, but no axial ones (Manton & Stosch, 1966). The 9 + 2 pattern can often be seen in whole mounts of flagella because the fibres fray and the two axial ones appear thinner than the

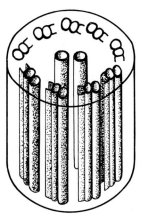

FIG. 67. Part of a flagellum showing the arrangement of the two single, axial fibres and nine double peripheral fibres within the sheath.

nine peripherals. The arrangement of the fibres can, of course, be seen only in sections through the flagella. The total diameter of the flagellum or cilium cylinder is only about 200 nm and so they are not resolved easily by the light microscope though experts knew enough about them for the classification of the algae to be partly based on their numbers, position and relative lengths. Even the fraying into strands had been seen before the advent of the electron microscope. The classification of a few species of algae has had to be revised in the light of electron microscopic studies.

The flagellum sheath is continuous with the cell membrane, but the fibres run into the cytoplasm and there constitute a body called variously the basal granule, centriole, kinetosome or blepharoplast. The basal granules vary from species to species but essentially they consist of the bases of the nine peripheral fibres since the two central fibres usually stop short of the base. They appear, surprisingly, to be related to the centrioles in animal cells, which are concerned with mitosis (see page 474), but it is not clear yet what the relationship is. Perhaps the centriole acts as an organizer for the formation of the flagellar fibres as it is said to do in the formation of the spindle fibres (see page 316). There is often also a spatial relationship with the nucleus and sometimes fibres from the basal granule converge near the nuclear envelope. In some flagellates, a mitochondrion lies close to the flagellar base and presumably supplies it with ATP for its mechanical work (Fig. 58). In ciliated cells, the cilia are in regular arrays and so are the basal granules.

The fibres themselves are tubular and, according to Pease (1963), each consists of probably ten beaded filaments. The two axial fibres are simple and placed so that the plane connecting them is perpendicular to the plane of ciliary movement. They are circular in cross section, 20 nm in diameter and their centres are 30 nm apart. There is a possibility that they are surrounded by a central common sheath or helical fibre on their own. Electron micrographs sometimes give indications of such a structure, but not always. Similarly there are possibly nine additional fibres running longitudinally between the central two and the peripheral nine. These, if they exist, are much finer than the others. The nine peripheral fibres are double, like two of the central ones lying side by side in the tangential plane and slightly squashed together, so that the width in the radial plane of the flagellum is slightly greater than half the width in the tangential plane, about 18×30 nm. Some micrographs show that one of each pair of subfibres has two tangentially directed arms. Some people hold that these all face one way; others are not so sure about this. The subfibre with the arms is slightly nearer the centre of the flagellum than its partner so that each pair is at an angle of 5–10° to the tangent (Fawcett, 1961). In the basal granules the peripheral fibres are triple instead of double. Some micrographs suggest that there are radial filaments crossing from the axial fibres to each of the nine peripherals and thickenings in the middle of these filaments may be the objects that have also been interpreted as the nine additional longitudinal fine fibres already mentioned. At the tip of the flagellum the peripheral fibres become single and the tapering of the flagellum is said to be due to the axial two being longer than the peripheral nine and the peripheral nine being of unequal extent, but, in some plants, the axial two stop before the peripherals. In addition to all this structure, mammalian sperm tails have helical fibres wound around the outside of the nine peripheral fibres, inside the flagellar membrane. Some algal flagella bear scales on the surface. These are prefabricated in the Golgi vesicles and moved to the cell surface (see page 187).

In motile plant cells there are two kinds of flagella sometimes both represented on the same cell. One is a smooth structure and the other bears hairs along its length. Some fungal zoospores, for example, have a backwards-directed flagellum of the simple or whiplash type and a forwards-directed flagellum of the hairy or tinsel type (*Flimmergeissel*). Others have a single posterior whiplash flagellum (Hawker, 1965). Similarly in the algae, the motile cells of the Phaeophyta and Xanthophyta often have a smooth (acronematic) flagellum trailing and an anterior hairy (pleuronematic) flagellum. The two anterior flagella of the Chlorophyta are smooth. The hairs or mastigonemes on the tinsel flagella are commonly in two rows on opposite sides and often in tufts of two or three. It is not yet known if the hairs are just surface projections or whether they are connected internally to the fibres (Fawcett, 1961). Bradley (1965, 1966) believes that the hairs penetrate the flagellar membrane and that they are tube-like with the basal part rigid and the rest flexible. Filaments may be seen coming from the end of the tube-like body of the mastigonemes in the Chrysophyceae. Some flagella also have spines attached to one of the peripheral fibres. *Himanthalia*, for example, has a spine about three-quarters of the way along the flagellum where the mastigonemes end. In sperm cells, such spines may be the means by which the motile cell attaches itself to the egg cell.

Modified flagella also occur in the algae. In *Chrysochromulina* and some other flagellates there is an organ called a haptonema as well as a flagellum. The haptonema is superficially like a flagellum, but has a swollen tip and can be coiled. It is thinner than a flagellum and probably serves as an anchor for the cell. Internally it differs from a flagellum in having three concentric membranes enclosing a ring of six or seven fibres. In some Protozoa the flagella may fuse to form cirri or undulating membranes and even the rods and cones of the retina are considered to be modified flagella. In the dinoflagellates there are two flagella, one is backwards-directed and of normal construction, the other undulates usually in an equatorial groove and is abnormal. The equatorial flagellum is ribbon-like and one edge of the ribbon consists of a sheath with hairs and the usual 9 + 2 fibres. This is joined to a band whose outer edge of the ribbon contains a striated strand shorter than the other edge so that the flagellum looks like a spiral staircase (Leadbeater & Dodge, 1967).

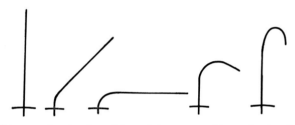

FIG. 68. Diagram showing from left to right one possible mode of making a beat stroke and recovering from it in a flagellum.

A lot of work has been done on the mode of action of flagella and cilia, but the fundamentals of this still eludes us. One theory is that the matrix of the organelle is stiff and that the nine peripheral fibres are contractile. The bending of the flagellum is then supposed to be due to an impulse which is conducted axially along the two central fibres and also laterally from one peripheral to its two neighbours causing the shortening of one peripheral then its two neighbours, then their far neighbours and so on right round the flagellum. The contraction is followed by relaxation so that the bend at one point is followed by straightening at that point and bending further along the flagellum away from the basal granule (Fig. 68). The initial kink will cause the motive stroke of the flagellum and the subsequent relaxation and bending further along will produce the recovery stroke. This kind of mechanism presupposes that the fibres run straight and not helically and could well account for the movement of cilia, which is rhythmic due to the conduction of the impulse for the action from cilium to cilium in waves. The metachronal waves move ciliates bodily through the water and move mucus along sheets of ciliated epithelium. The behaviour in flagellates must differ somewhat because some have anteriorly-directed flagella, some posteriorly-directed and some both. Dinoflagellates have one ribbon-like flagellum that remains in an equatorial groove around the cell and merely undulates, but in doing so it appears to produce most of the forward thrust of the cell possibly by pushing against one of the flanges of the groove. The second flagellum trails in a longitudinal, or sulcal, groove and beats in a planar wave possibly responsible for the spiral path of the swimming cell (Norris, 1966).

Some interest has been aroused in the origin of flagella and the inheritance of their precursors. When flagellates fuse in syngamy or become non-motile some of them lose their flagella and the progeny gain new ones somehow. This new formation of flagella must also occur in multicellular plants and animals that produce flagellate gametes or zoospores. This process has been followed in some detail in *Marsilea*, a fern whose sperm cells have over a hundred long flagella, and in *Zamia*, a cycad whose sperm cell has about 20,000 flagella, by Mizukami & Gall (1966). In *Marsilea* two blepharoplasts appear in the cytoplasm of the cells within the antheridium during the stages leading to the formation of the sperm cells. It is not clear, how these blepharoplasts arise. They are spheres originally $0\cdot3\mu$m in diameter and solid. They grow to about $0\cdot8\mu$m and become hollow spheres containing 100–150 closely packed tubules arranged over the surface of the sphere. The tubules are $0\cdot1\mu$m in diameter and $0\cdot07\mu$m long and show differentiation into nine subunits at their periphery. The blepharoplasts move to the spindle poles at least at the last division in sperm cell formation and there they play some role in organizing the mitotic apparatus. In performing this they are called centrioles or centrosomes (Fig. 163). (There is considerable confusion over nomenclature here.) After the last cell division the blepharoplast breaks up into a cluster of its component tubules also called centrioles individually. These arrange themselves near the nucleus and then migrate to the cell surface where they become the blepharoplasts or basal bodies of the flagella because the flagella grow out from them. The centrioles show the typical cartwheel structure of basal bodies in having nine triplet fibres around the periphery as well as a hub-like structure bearing spokes radiating towards the fibres. The arrangement in *Zamia* is essentially similar though the blepharoplasts are conspicuous organelles up to 27μm in diameter. A similar organization takes place in spermatogenesis in snails. It is generally supposed that blepharoplasts arise from pre-existing centrioles either by breaking the centriole into a large number of blepharoplasts as described above or simply by one or both centrioles migrating to the surface of the cell and there organizing the development of the flagellum. However, there are some flagellates whose precursor cells appear to have neither centrioles nor blepharoplasts. This is true of *Naegleria*, which transforms from an amoeba to a flagellate (Dingle & Fulton, 1966).

4.8 Crystals

Inorganic crystals, mostly of calcium oxalate or silica, are fairly common in plant cells and are probably deposited as waste products. Animals can usually excrete such inorganic substances. Calcium oxalate has several crystalline forms and multiple units of these also occur. Raphide is the name given to a bundle of needle-like crystals and druse is the name given to collections of crystals that radiate from a centre (Fig. 69). Somewhat similar are cystoliths (Fig. 70). These are outgrowths from the cell wall that are impregnated with calcium carbonate. Silica often occurs in grasses where it impregnates cell walls, but sometimes also forms bodies within the cell of the amorphous, opal type.

Crystals and similar inclusions occur in some plants in ordinary cells, in others in certain tissues only and in others only in special cells called crystal idioblasts. They appear often to be formed in the vacuoles, but the plastids of the crystal-containing cell seem to play some part in crystal formation (Mollenhauer & Larson, 1966).

Fig. 69. Druses in cortical cells of the stem of *Hedera helix*. Polarizing microscope.

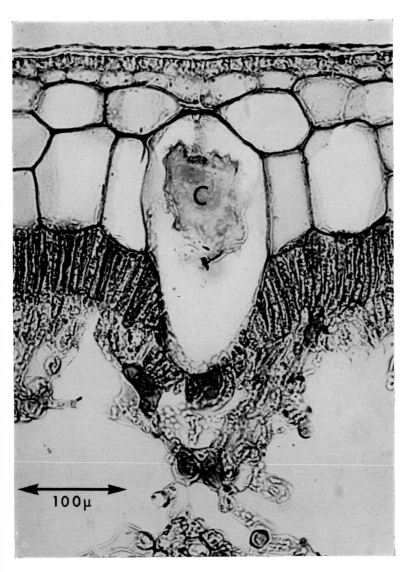

FIG. 70. A cystolith (C) in a cell of the leaf of *Ficus elastica*. The main mass of the cystolith is suspended by a stalk from the upper wall of the enlarged hypodermal idioblast.

4.9   Cnidocysts and trichocysts

These are ejectile organelles found in some dinoflagellates (*Polykrikos* and *Neuratodinium*). They are similar to the well-known nematocysts of coelenterates, but their function in dinoflagellates is unknown (Norris, 1966). Smaller ejectile bodies occur in other dinoflagellates, some emitting a mucous substance and some emitting a fibril. These and the similar organelles in ciliates are called trichocysts.

CHAPTER 5

Walls and Surfaces

The structure of the plant cell wall must be studied and understood in terms of its three main roles. It acts firstly as a semi-rigid envelope, providing most of both the compressional and tensile strength of the cell and of the plant body as a whole. Secondly it must expand and deform as the cell grows and differentiates and thirdly it must provide both a passage for materials for cell growth and sites for enzymic activity. None of these roles can be discussed in isolation since each interacts with and is dependent upon the others. Since the wall is usually the only part of the cell that survives death it was once thought of as a rigid, inert envelope, but it is now known not to be a dead structure, but one with activities of its own. Thus the mature cell wall provides some, but not a complete, record of successive, differing depositions of materials derived from the cytoplasm. It cannot, of course, indicate where subtraction of material has taken place.

5.1   Constituents

The great bulk of plants (the only known exceptions are a small order of algae, the *Codiales*) possesses walls in which a microfibrillar framework is embedded in a gel-like matrix. The framework in higher plants is invariably cellulose, but in the fungi it is sometimes chitin and in some algae it is β, 1–4 linked xylan.

In higher plants the cell wall may, by selective cleaning with different solvents, be fractionated into the following major chemical groups in this order (Northcote, 1963):—

1. Lignin.   2. Pectic substances.
3. Hemicelluloses.   4. Cellulose.

Other less common but no less important constituents are fats, waxes, tannins, pigments, terpenoids, proteins, gums and mucilages. Certain cell walls may be formed entirely of callose (see page 216) and those of pollen grains are of a unique polymer, sporopollenin. A list of the principal cell wall chemical components is given in Table 6.

TABLE 6
The principal chemical constituents of the components of higher plant cell walls

Pectins	D-galacturonic acid Methyl esters of D–galacturonic acid L–arabinose D–galactose L–rhamnose	Suberin	Hydroxy-docosanoic acid Di- and tri-hydroxy-decanoic acid Friedelin Pentacyclic triterpene with a keto group in the 3-position
Cellulose	D–glucose ($\beta-1, 4$ linked chains)	Cutin	Mono-, di- and tri-hydroxy-octa- decanoic acid Dihydroxy-hexadecanoic acid
Hemicelluloses	D–galactose D–glucuronic acid D–glucose D–mannose L–arabinose D–xylose	Waxes	Esters of higher aliphatic acids and higher aliphatic or cyclic alcohols Ursolic acid Paraffin hydrocarbons Higher ketones
Lignin	p–hydroxycinnamyl alcohol Coniferyl alcohol Sinapyl alcohol	Tannin	Flavan–3–ol Flavan–3, 4–diol
		Callose	D–glucose ($\beta-1, 3$ linked chains)

1   *Lignin*

Lignin, one of the most important secondary wall constituents, acts as a waterproof cement and thus makes physically possible the development of fibres, vascular tissue and thus most of the advanced morphological features of higher plants. Lignin is in fact, after cellulose, the most abundant plant polymer. It is a polymer of various derivatives of phenyl propane, namely p-coumaryl, coniferyl and sinapyl alcohols (S. Brown, 1964).

These alcohols can cross-link with the neighbouring di-phenolic units in a number of ways, and the structural strength of lignin is probably a result of the complex reticulate pattern of heterogeneous linkages. In this way lignin is similar to other branched plant polymers such as cutin and suberin. Lignin shows a pronounced maximum absorption at 282 nm, so that the degree of lignification can be assessed and quantitatively measured in the UV microscope using the 280 nm line of a mercury lamp.

2   *Pectic substances*

The pectic substances are amorphous, plastic and highly hydrophilic substances. They have no apparent structure even under the electron microscope. They consist of polymers of D-galacturonic acid, L-arabinose, D-galactose and L-rhamnose. The fact that they are highly plastic and hydrophilic renders them invaluable in maintaining the high degree of hydration and flexibility of young cell walls. It has been suggested that they act in some way in controlling the plasticity of the wall and this possibility will be discussed later in the chapter. Pectin is exploited in making jam and confectionery, in pharmaceuticals and cosmetics and as a general emulsifying agent (Kertesz, 1951).

3 Hemicelluloses

The cellulose microfibrils are embedded in a matrix of polymerized sugars other than glucose. These are amorphous or para-crystalline and consist of linear or branched polymers of, amongst other sugars, D-xylose, L-arabinose and D-mannose (Table 6).

In addition to these sugars there are also the polyuronide hemicelluloses of which D-glucuronic and D-galacturonic acid are most commonly found. As Table 6 demonstrates, the distinction between the hemicelluloses and the pectins is not absolutely one of chemical constituents, but rather of physical properties, mainly solubility, which depends on their degree of methylation, cross-linkage and the extent to which different sugars are joined in the same molecule (Northcote, 1963).

There is evidence that some of the matrix substances (e.g. the xylan chains) lie parallel to the microfibrils, i.e. are at least partly para-crystalline (Fig. 76B) and not wholly amorphous. Chemical bonding between the microfibrils and the surrounding matrix may account partly for the impurity of the cellulose fraction and would indeed be of considerable structural value. This makes the common analogy between the wall and reinforced concrete not so apposite.

4 Cellulose

Cellulose is the framework material; the hemicelluloses and pectic substances, since they are laid down in conjunction with or in sequence with cellulose, are often called the matrix materials. The rest, with the exception of callose, can be called the encrusting substances since they are laid down on or into existing cell walls.

Cellulose, the most important constituent of the cell wall, forms the structural framework around which all the other substances lie. It consists mainly of linear chains of β-D-glucose. A-cellulose, the fraction of the whole cell wall left after delignification and extraction of hemi-celluloses and pectic substances, consists largely, but not entirely of β-1,4 linked glucose. The glucose normally forms a ring structure in which an oxygen bridge links carbon atoms numbers one and five (Fig. 71). The molecule is shown below. The ring is at right angles to the plane of the paper, the thin bonds lie behind and the thick bonds lie

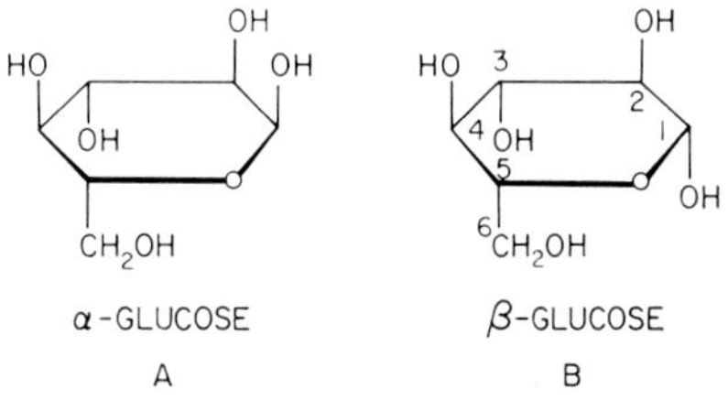

α-GLUCOSE

A

β-GLUCOSE

B

Fig. 71. Glucose. This molecule forms a ring structure in which an oxygen bridge links carbon atoms numbers one and five. The ring is at right angles to the plane of the paper, the thin bonds lie behind and the thick in front. α-glucose (A) differs from β glucose (B) only in the position of OH group on carbon 1.

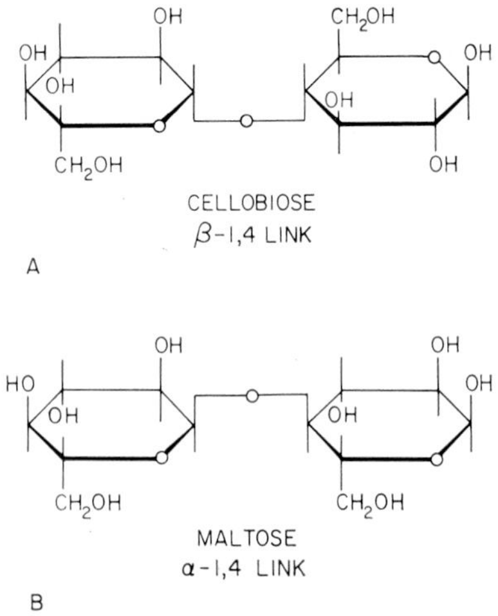

CELLOBIOSE

β-1,4 LINK

A

MALTOSE

α-1,4 LINK

B

Fig. 72A: The cellobiose molecule. Each glucose unit is rotated through 180° with respect to the preceding unit via the β-1,4 link. Cellobiose is the basic repeating unit of cellulose though cellulose is, however, synthesized by the addition of single glucose units.

B: The maltose molecule. Although made up of the same sub-units as cellobiose and linked through the same carbon atoms (1,4), maltose is stereochemically different from cellobiose in that all the glucose units face the same way.

in front. When two such heterocyclic molecules condense with the loss of a molecule of water the disaccharide, cellobiose, is formed. This compound is stereochemically different from the compound maltose, a disaccharide produced by the hydrolysis of starch (Fig. 72). Further polymerization of glucose units results in long chains of molecules and, although there seems to be a good deal of dispute over the matter due most probably to different sources of material, the average number of units may lie between 3,000 and 10,000 thus giving molecular lengths of between 1·5 and 5·0 microns. In addition to the straight C-1 to C-4 linkage shown in Fig. 71, additional bonds (hydrogen bonds) occur between the hydroxyl groups of C-3 and the ring oxygen of the next residue. This capacity to make numerous linkages with neighbouring chains is one of the fundamental distinctions between the two polymers of glucose, cellulose and starch. The α-1,4 link of starch results in a coiled molecule, a slow helix of six glucose molecules per revolution, making in effect a cylinder in which most of the OH groups potentially capable of forming linkages project into empty spaces, whereas the hydroxyl groups of C-atoms, 2,3 and 6 in cellulose, are free to form bonds with neighbouring chains (Figs. 73, 74). It is also believed that

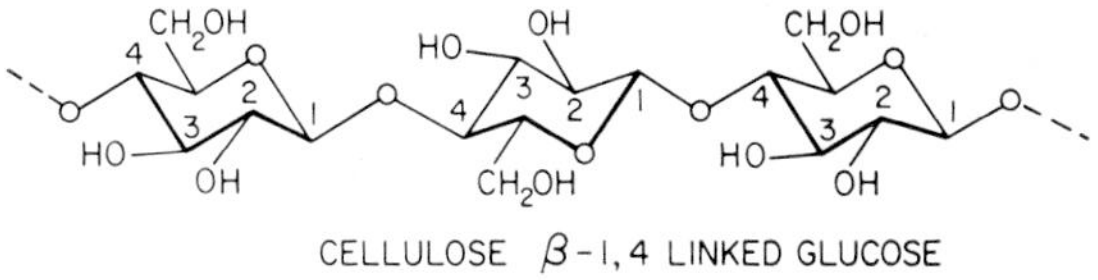

CELLULOSE β-1,4 LINKED GLUCOSE

FIG. 73. Part of a cellulose molecule. The glucose units are drawn in the 'chair' configuration. All the OH groups stick outwards, are available for hydrogen bonding with other molecules and, due to the β-type link, are equally distributed on either side (see Fig. 74).

the chains of β-1,4 linked glucan are generally arranged strictly parallel to one another and are regularly spaced in a crystal lattice, which provides opportunities for cross-linkage between adjacent molecules (Figs. 75, 76A). The chains in the crystal diagram are drawn straight whereas, in accordance with Fig. 73, they should be kinked. The repeating period along the b fibre axis of 1·03 nm, found by X-ray diffraction analysis, is identical with the length of a cellobiose molecule, thus confirming the polymerized cellobiosic nature of the cellulose molecule.

The β-1,4 link is extremely rigid and the individual molecules must, as Roelofsen (1959) has described them, behave like strips of rubber, but strips of rubber with a strong attraction, through the weaker but

H

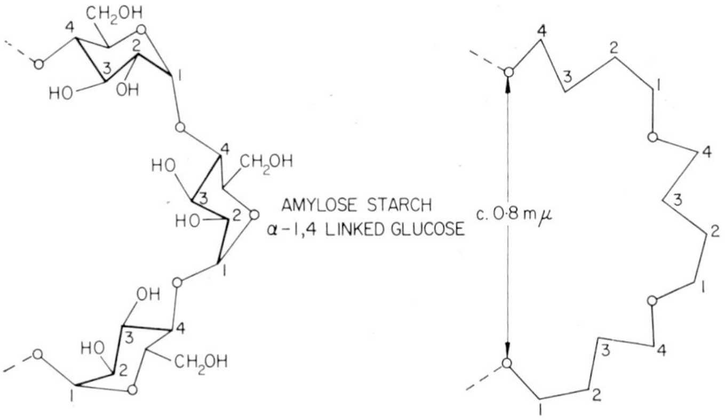

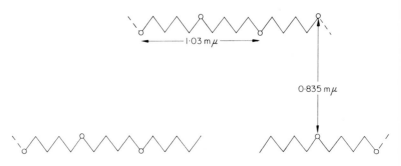

FIG. 74. Part of an amylose starch molecule. The $\alpha - 1,4$ link results in a helical molecule in which all the OH groups stick inwards into space and are not available for hydrogen bonding with other molecules. The right hand diagram gives the approximate dimensions of the amylose helix.

FIG. 75. Cellulose molecules showing the lengths of each cellobiose unit (the repeating period along the molecule) and the distance between each molecule in a crystal of cellulose.

numerous hydrogen bonds, for all the other strips of rubber in the polymer. The mechanical strength of cellulose is a severe hindrance to making thin sections. Page & Sargent (1965) have pointed out that it is almost impossible to cut, as opposed to shattering, these compact molecules of cellulose. This fact is of inestimable value to a tree, but is an awkward obstacle to the study of the fine structure of secondarily thickened tissues.

Up to 100 glucan chains are thought to group together to form long thin crystallites (sometimes termed micelles or elementary fibrils). The

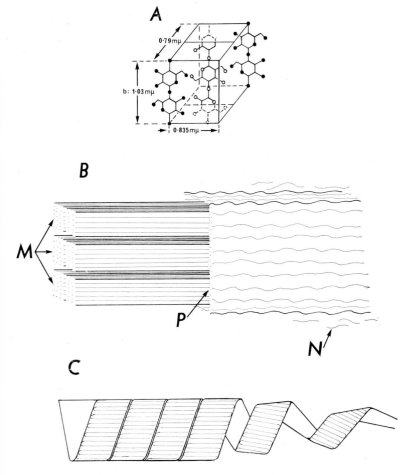

FIG. 76A: The crystal lattice of cellulose showing the distribution of the individual glucose molecules. The chains of glucose units should be drawn kinked as in Fig. 73, but for the sake of simplicity are shown straight.

B: A microfibril, made up of several totally crystalline sub-units, the micelles (M), between and around which lie less regularly arranged glucose chains, the para-crystalline region (P). Linkages may also be made between the outside of the micro-fibril and non-cellulose polysaccharides (N).

C: Another way in which the chains of glucose units may be arranged in the microfibril. According to Manley (1964) a helix 3·5 nm wide is the basic unit and this helix is made up of cellulose molecules running almost at right angles to the 'tape' when unwound, but parallel to its axis when in the helical form.

micelle is about 5 nm wide, although the widths reported vary according to the source of the cellulose. There is some evidence that these crystallites are shaped like rulers (Fig. 76B). They, in their turn, are organized in groups of up to twenty to form microfibrils which are 8–30 nm in diameter, and are probably flattish ribbons having one dimension up to four times greater than the other (Preston & Kuyper, 1951). These may, in their turn, be aggregated to form macrofibrils up to $0·5\mu$m in diameter and some 1,500 of these may form a fibre such as a cotton hair cell over 300μm in diameter. Amongst this hierarchy of aggregation, from the morphological point of view, the microfibril of Fig. 76B is undoubtedly the basic structural unit.

The conventional view of microfibrillar architecture is shown diagrammatically in Fig. 76B, but, as Manley (1964) has pointed out, this reconstruction may not be the only possible one. Using phosphotungstic acid as a negative stain to render the microfibrils visible in the electron microscope instead of the more usual heavy metal shadowing, he has shown that the microfibril has a beaded appearance and, from this and some other evidence, he has suggested that its actual structure is a helix as shown in Fig. 76C. This is not inconsistent with the X-ray evidence of glucose molecules parallel to the microfibrillar axis since they may be arranged as in Fig. 76C at an angle to the coiled constituent band.

Cellulose microfibrils occupy a relatively small volume of the fresh wall, as little as 10 per cent in some tissues according to Roelofsen (1965), and this must mean that the microfibrils are relatively widely spaced, for, on the average, one microfibril is separated from the next by at least four times its own diameter, e.g. 50–100 nm. Such a spacing means that the electron micrographs of shadowed microfibrils (Fig. 77) in macerated cell walls give a very misleading impression of cell wall construction since they resemble a linen-like textile and not, as is more likely, reinforced concrete in having widely spaced rods.

FIG. 77A: Electron micrograph of the microfibrils in a cell wall. The alga, *Chaetomorpha*, has been treated to remove all the cytoplasmic and matrix materials of the cell wall leaving only the cellulose which has then been shadowed. The individual microfibrils are somewhat closer together than they would be in the intact wall because of the removal of the matrix. They show the near orthogonal pattern of deposition (see Fig. 98) and interweaving common to many cell walls.

B: Microfibrils from *Chaetomorpha*. Granular material on the plasmalemma surface of the wall, through which a number of the microfibrils run, may be concerned with cellulose synthesis (see Fig. 98).

Micrographs by Dr E. Frei and Prof R. D. Preston.

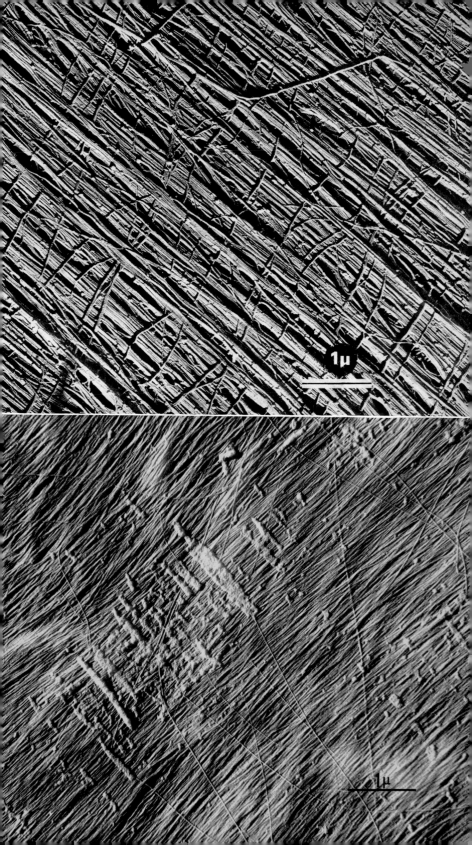

5 *Fatty constituents*

The most important fatty constituents of cell walls are cutin, suberin and waxes. Cutin is, like lignin, a cross-linked polymer, but this time the monomers are mono-, di-, and tri-hydroxyoctadecanoic acids, and di-hydroxyhexadecanoic acid (Baker & Martin, 1963). These are esterified to a varying extent to form the tough, chemically resistant, varnish-like layer over the epidermal walls of all the aerial parts of a plant and some other cell surfaces too.

Suberin, which occurs in association with cellulose in cork cells, is again comprised of long-chain hydroxy fatty acids very similar to those of cutin (the distinction may be one solely of position not of constituents) of which the most important are hydroxy-docosanoic acid, di-hydroxyoctadecanoic acid, tri-hydroxyoctadecanoic acid (the same as the cutin component) and friedelin, a tri-terpene with the formula $C_{30}H_{50}O$. Suberin differs slightly in its chemical properties from cutin, being much more readily saponified by alkali, but, like cutin, it is highly resistant to enzymic attack, hence the resistance of cork stoppers to decay even though kept in damp cellars for generations. There is also some evidence that suberin, surrounding the lignin of secondary cell walls, may help to preserve it from decay and thus maintain the structural strength of the timber (Roelofsen, 1959).

6 *Waxes*

Waxes, which are a heterogeneous assembly of compounds are associated with suberin and cutin and may be embedded within the cuticular layers or suberin layers of the plant or secreted on to the surface of aerial parts of the plants including those of fruits and seeds. They consist of mixtures of esters of higher aliphatic acids and higher aliphatic or cyclic alcohols, long-chain paraffins, ketones and acids. It was thought at one time that the paraffin hydrocarbons, secondary alcohols and ketones exclusively possessed odd numbers of C-atoms. N-nonacosane comprises about 90 per cent of the paraffins of apple fruit wax (Fernandes *et al.*, 1964), but Mazliak (1963) has shown that all the paraffins from C-15 to C-33 are present as well. In addition to these compounds, there are frequently present both saturated and unsaturated fatty acids, cyclic acids such as ursolic acid, which is a derivative of a tri-terpene and is now known to be a common constituent of apple fruit wax (Mazliak, 1963), and some tri-terpene-ketones themselves such as cerin and friedelin. Friedelin is a constituent of suberin.

The glaucousness or bloom of many leaves, stems, fruits and petals is due to crystalline patterns of wax formed on the surface (Figs. 78, 79,

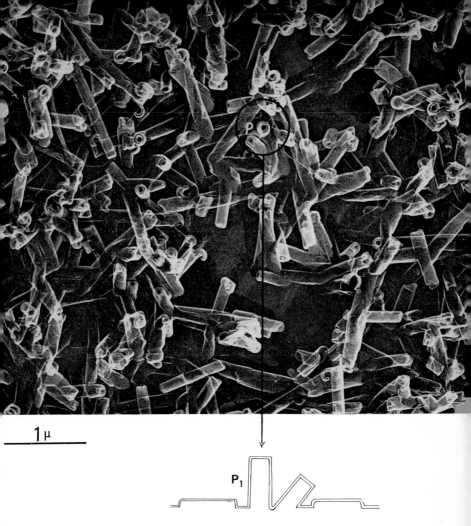

1μ

P_1

FIG. 78. Shadowed carbon replica of the adaxial leaf surface of *Tulipa* sp. As the attached drawing shows, the effect of replication is to suggest that what are probably solid rods (P) look like hollow tubes (P_1). (C/R/Au/Pd)

80). It appears that, in general, the paraffins and occasionally some of the acid components of the wax are responsible for the crystalline patterns formed, whereas the esters contribute to the general greasiness as in some varieties of apples. Both help to inhibit water loss.

7 Tannins

The tannins are a heterogeneous collection of polyhydroxyphenolic compounds. They may be divided into two main groups. Firstly the hydrolysable tannins which yield on hydrolysis carbohydrates, usually glucose, and phenolic acids (e.g. gallic acids). These may be further sub-divided into the gallotannins in which gallic acid is the main phenolic compound produced by hydrolysis and the ellagitannins which yield ellagic acid as well as gallic acid on hydrolysis. Secondly the condensed or non-hydrolysable tannins, which contain little or no carbohydrate, are made up of flavan-3-ol and flavan-3,4-ol, as amorphous polymers. They are found commonly in leaves, but are present also in xylem and phloem, periderm of stems and roots, testas of many seeds, and bacterial galls. Small quantities are present in all cells. Apart from their capacity to convert animal skins to leather, they may confer resistance to virus infection (Cadman, 1960) and fungal attack and render oak leaves pro-gressively less palatable to leaf-eating insects as the season progresses (Feeney, 1967). They account for the bitter taste of some fruits, tea and beer.

FIG. 79. Electron micrograph of a replica of a *Pisum* leaf surface. This replica is from the adaxial surface of the leaf, the inset shows the abaxial surface with a different crystalline pattern of waxes. The guard cells around the stomata have fewer wax projections. (C/R/Au/Pd)

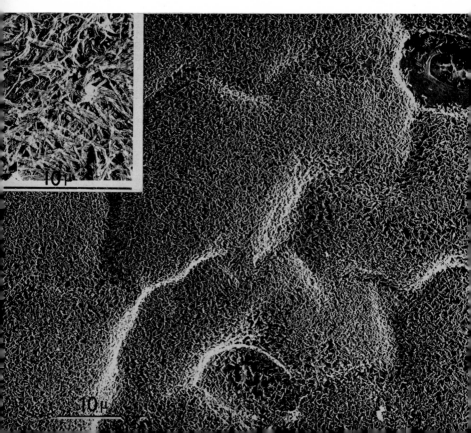

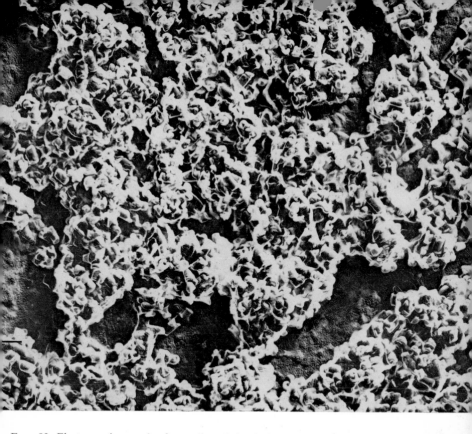

FIG. 80. Electron micrograph of a replica of the fruit surface of Victoria plum (*Prunus domestica*). (C/R/Au/Pd)   Micrograph by Dr D. S. Skene

8   *Proteins*

Proteins, commonly but not always containing the rare amino acid hydroxyproline, are now known to be constituents of the cell walls of both higher and lower plants. It is not yet known for certain what structural role they play. It is possible that they act as bridging agents in controlling cell wall plasticity and some speculative, but interesting suggestions will be given later in this chapter and in the sections on cell growth and differentiation.

9   *Gums and mucilages*

Gums and mucilages should also be included in the constituents of cell walls in so far as they frequently seem to be breakdown products of a cell wall or occasionally of cell contents. The breakdown of cell walls will be discussed later in this chapter. Decaying walls are frequently

H*

found on the outer layers of many plants and seeds (Mühlethaler, 1950) and one mucilage which has been examined from the root tips of *Zea* (Juniper & Roberts, 1966) consists, on hydrolysis, of xylose, arabinose, glucose, galactose and small quantities of uronides. This mucilage is visible in the electron microscope as a fine granular matrix (Fig. 65). It may be derived from the breakdown of the walls of peripheral cells and also from the secretory activity of the Golgi bodies (see page 250). Gums, which are commonly the reaction products of cells to insect or fungal attack or to wounding, do not differ fundamentally from most of the mucilages above in that they are mainly complex polysaccharides. Suspensions of *Acer* cells in culture produce a mixture of polysaccharides with a composition very similar to the pectin and hemicellulose fractions of the cell wall. This mucilage is excreted into the medium in amounts proportional to the cell mass in the log phase of growth (Becker, Albersheim & Hui, 1963).

10   *Callose*

A special substance, callose, is rarely a structural constituent of normal plant cells, but is found in association with primary and secondary walls. This polysaccharide is nothing like so widespread or abundant as cellulose. It is remarkable in the great rapidity with which it may be formed and destroyed within cells. It is commonly deposited in cells in homogeneous masses and frequently for only brief periods, as a temporary plug. After injury in a stem cortex it is rapidly formed in the pits, blocking the connexion between undamaged tissues and damaged and potentially necrotic tissues. In fact, one of the problems that has bedevilled research into the fine structure of phloem cells is the speed with which callose may be formed in the sieve plates (Eschrich, 1963; Northcote & Wooding, 1966) and many wrong conclusions have been drawn as a result of lack of appreciation of this fact. Evert & Derr (1964) have also shown that callose is present in inactive sieve elements, but probably not in normal active sieve tubes.

Another plugging action of callose, not the result of wounding but a natural phenomenon, occurs in pollen tubes as they grow through the stylar tissue. The pollen tube forms callose plugs behind it as it proceeds and there appears to be little net increase in pollen tube protoplasm.

Callose is an unbranched β-1,3-linked glucan, it is not birefringent, shows no structure under the electron microscope and the X-ray diffraction diagrams faintly indicate a structure with a periodicity of 1·5 nm (Fig. 81). A clue to the mode of formation of callose is given by the

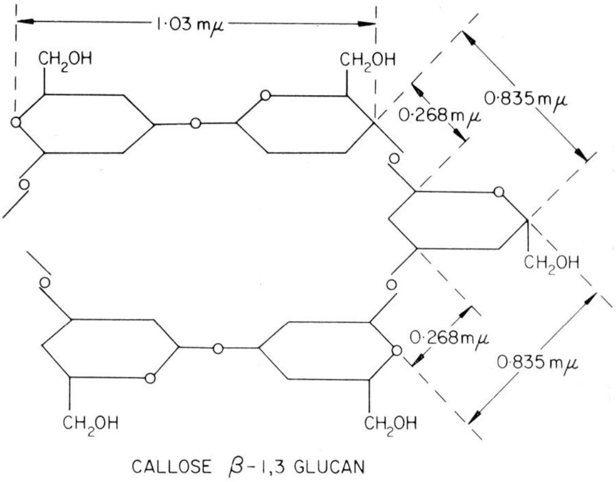

CALLOSE β-1,3 GLUCAN

FIG. 81. The molecule of callose. The irregular distribution of the glucose molecules in space ensures that callose has no crystalline structure and appears homogeneous.

normal formation of callose in pollen grains. We know already that the Golgi bodies in many cells are associated with the accumulation of precursors of hemicelluloses and pectins (Northcote & Pickett-Heaps, 1966; Dashek & Rosen, 1966). In immature pollen grains the Golgi bodies are certainly very active in producing vesicles and the cells are filled with vesicles (Heslop-Harrison, 1966). Eschrich (1962) has shown that some of these vesicles give indications of bearing phosphate-containing carbohydrate precursors by giving an electron-dense precipitate with lead acetate. Similar precipitates are found embedded in the callose layer itself. However, Northcote & Wooding (1966) associate callose formation in sieve tubes with the ER and not with the Golgi.

11   *Sporopollenin*

The last of the structural materials is sporopollenin whose chemistry has only recently been elucidated (Shaw & Yeadon, 1966). It is not a homogeneous material, but appears to be an intimate mixture of cellulose and xylan, with a high proportion of lipid and an as yet unidentified lignin-like material. This forms the outermost cell wall layer of pollen grains and the spores of pteridophytes and is a polymer even more resistant to the attack of microorganisms than cutin and suberin. This degree of resistance is interesting and is invaluable to archaeologists, who employ preserved pollen grains as quantitative and qualitative markers of previous floras and of agricultural activity (Fig. 82).

These then are the organic compounds of the plant cell wall. We must not forget though that virtually all walls are completely saturated with water and that many of the properties of walls stem from this inorganic constituent.

5.2   Organization

The various substances described above combine physically and chemically with one another in the construction of the higher plant cell

FIG. 82. Scanning electron micrograph or *Salix* pollen grains. The scanning electron microscope with its great depth of focus is able to resolve the surface detail in many planes. (St/Au/Pd)   Micrograph by Dr P. Echlin and the Cambridge Instrument Company.

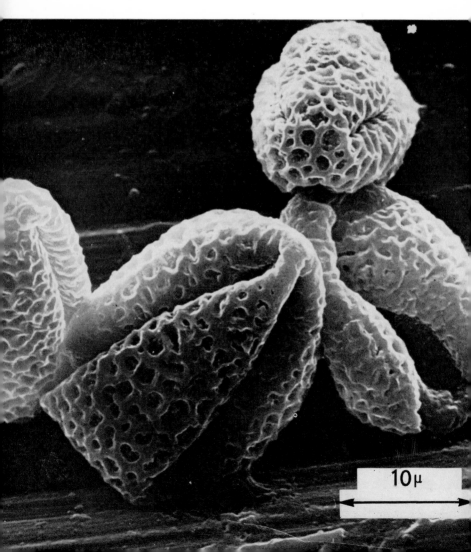

10μ

wall and their separation and identification is often a complex process. The pattern of distribution, their concentrations and proportions and individual degrees of polymerization often change through each successive stage of the wall's existence. Variations in relationships between wall components may give variation in structural properties and so the analogy of reinforced concrete should not be pressed too far. They may also enable growth to occur to differing extents in different directions and in different parts of the wall and differential deposition of other components to occur. The nature of most such relationships is not known although some involving the pectic substances and proteins have been hinted at previously. The carboxyl groups of pectic substances may react through ionic bridges and ester bonds; it is possible too, but unproven, that pectic substances are distributed throughout the cell wall and act as key bonding agents with the hemicelluloses. The common occurrence of insoluble protopectin and the presence of arabinans and galactans (see Table 4) amongst the pectic preparations suggest that pectic substances are intimately associated with other components of the matrix. It is also thought that proteins may play a part as bridging agents. It may well be that flexible and adaptable interactions between components of this sort form the basis for extensibility of the cell wall under natural conditions and under the influence of externally applied growth-regulating compounds. The branched structure of many hemicelluloses increases their chance of interacting with themselves or with other structural substances, and it may no longer be useful to think of a precise distinction between say the cellulose microfibril and the surrounding matrix. It may be better to imagine a progression from a highly crystalline through a para-crystalline to an amorphous state (Fig. 76B).

5.3 Primary wall

We can divide the processes of wall formation into those that result in cell division, those that control the deposition and the composition of the primary cell wall, those that result in cell enlargement and those that determine the final structure of the secondary and tertiary cell wall. The primary wall means here that part of the wall formed while the cell is expanding.

The initiation of a wall begins with the division of a protoplast into two daughter protoplasts. The division of the nucleus and the division of the cytoplasm are not necessarily either synchronous or immediately sequential events. Fig. 83 shows nuclear division in endosperm that is not succeeded by wall formation. In endosperm, the phragmoplast or precursor of the cell wall may be formed between sister or non-sister nuclei, and either immediately after mitosis or some time later. The phragmoplast appears, *under the light microscope*, as a dense cytoplasmic region which develops between the daughter nuclei of a mitotic division. Through this region, extending towards the daughter chromosomes, run some fibres. Just what these fibres correspond to under the electron microscope remains to be found. The continuous spindle fibres of the light microscope (Bajer, 1965 and Bajer & Allen, 1966) cannot possibly be the microtubules of the electron microscopist (Ledbetter & Porter, 1963, 1964) since these latter are 20 nm in diameter, show no sign of fasciation and could not possibly be resolved by the light microscope even under the most fortunate conditions. A possible explanation of this paradox is that microtubules form diffraction haloes.

When the phragmoplast develops at the end of a normal mitotic division it may come from the remnants of the mitotic spindle, but, when it occurs between non-sister interphase nuclei, it must originate from other components of the cytoplasm.

However, wall formation generally starts by the formation of a phragmoplast in the equatorial plane of a fibrous spindle which extends between the two daughter nuclei (Figs. 83, 84). The first visible manifestation of a cell wall is called the *cell plate*. This begins to form within the phragmoplast. As the cell plate solidifies within the spindle zone, the phragmoplast disappears from the centre, but persists at the periphery until the plate appears here too (Fig. 84). Generally the cell plate progresses across the equatorial plane until it reaches the existing side walls. In the long cambial initials of gymnosperms, after starting almost transversely it comes to lie longitudinally by differential growth of the longitudinal walls. Moreover in stomatal guard mother cells the cell plate begins to form at right angles to the original spindle axis, but the edges of the cell plate curl round eventually to join the same wall (Fig. 144) (see page 418). Before mitosis takes place in a vacuolate cell a special layer of cytoplasm comes to occupy the plane along which the phragmoplast and the cell plate will subsequently form. This cytoplasmic layer was named the phragmosome by Sinnott & Bloch (1941). Under the light microscope the phragmosome may be visible around the

Fig. 83. Electron micrograph of a phragmoplast which is forming between nuclei of the endosperm of *Haemanthus katherinae*. Golgi bodies do not seem to be involved in the formation of endosperm cross walls (see page 224). There are, however, large numbers of ribosomes some grouped into polysomes and a heavy concentration of microtubules. The width of the phragmoplast as seen under the light microscope is given by the two arrows. (Glut/Os/Pb/U)   Micrograph by Dr A. Bajer.

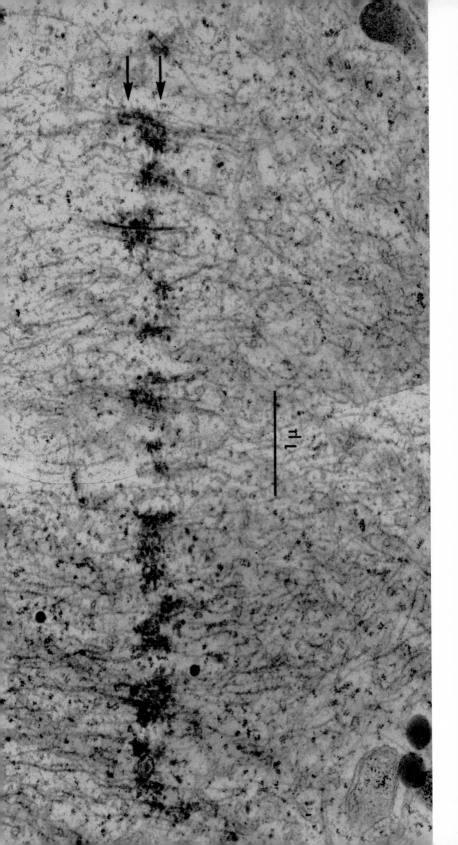

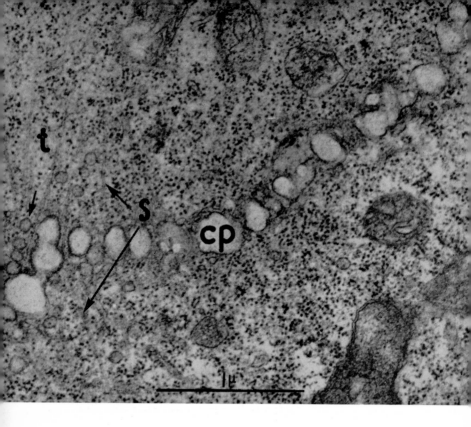

FIG. 84. Electron micrograph of a cell plate forming in a young leaf of wheat. (*Triticum*). This micrograph represents a later stage in cell plate formation than that shown in Fig. 85. It is thought that a number of the small Golgi-derived vesicles fuse to form the larger vesicles (cp) and these finally coalesce to create the cell plate itself. The cell plate is developing towards the left of the picture. On the extreme left a number of microtubules (t) appear to be 'guiding' small Golgi vesicles into position (arrow). These microtubules are relatively straight, whereas those already embedded in the wall have become sinuous (s) and there is no sign of microtubules at all in the older section of the wall to the right. (Glut/Osm/Pb/U)

Micrograph by Dr J. D. Pickett-Heaps and Dr D. H. Northcote

FIG. 85. Electron micrograph of a cell plate in the root tip of barley (*Hordeum*). At the very earliest stage of cell plate formation Golgi vesicles cluster between the daughter nuclei. Some align themselves in short chains along the spindle axis, possibly orientated by the microtubules (see Fig. 84 arrow). These short chains initially extend well beyond the thickness of the cell plate which is indicated by the two parallel lines. There are indications (arrow) that some of these vesicles may fuse to form threads and it is suggested that some of these threads may be the precursors of the plasmodesmata. (Mn)

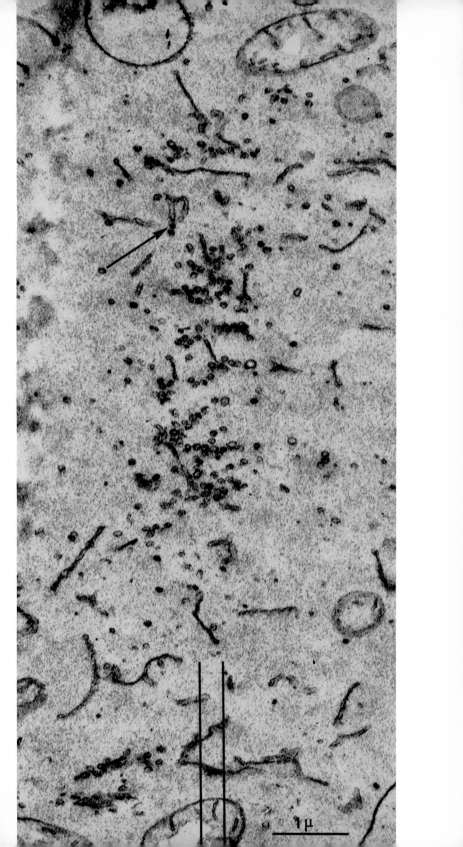

1 μ

nucleus or spindle both before and during mitosis, but apart from the very recent observations of Pickett-Heaps & Northcote (1966), which concern only the very periphery of the cell (see Fig. 86), there is, as yet, no structure seen under the electron microscope to correspond with the phragmosome (in this sense) prior to mitosis. Porter & Caulfield (1958) and Porter & Machado (1960) use the word phragmosome in a different sense to describe membrane bounded bodies, supposedly carriers of enzymes, that are assumed to play a part in cell plate formation in *Allium* root tips. Manton (1961) was able to confirm their existence in *Anthoceros*, but not necessarily their involvement in cell plate formation. However they were not noticed at all by Whaley & Mollenhauer (1963) or Juniper (1963). It is now believed that *Allium* root tips are peculiar in this respect, for these bodies have not been observed in most other tissues (Mollenhauer, Morré & Kelley, 1966).

Under the electron microscope we see that cell plate formation is initiated by the concentration and coagulation of a large number of 100 nm vesicles (Figs. 85, 87) which are now generally believed to be derived from the Golgi bodies (Whaley & Mollenhauer, 1963; Juniper, 1963; Frey-Wyssling, Lopez-Saez & Mühlethaler, 1964; Esau, 1965; Whaley, Dauwalder & Kephart, 1966). These concentrate initially around and between the spindle fibres (Fig. 84) and it should be noticed how very similar these spindle fibres are to the microtubules now known to be of common occurrence around the periphery of plant cells (see page 246). Pickett-Heaps & Northcote (1966b, c) have noticed that the plane of division of a cell may often be predicted prior to mitosis by the occurrence at the periphery of the cytoplasm of a ring of many micro-tubules the site of which is subsequently reached by the growing cell (Fig. 86). Just what the role of these microtubules is in the formation of the cell plate or whether their appearance there is just a coincidence is not yet known. But it is interesting to note that Sinnott (1944) demon-strated that the mitotic spindle in the developing fruits of the Cucur-bitaceae appears to swing during mitosis as if something outside itself was controlling its final orientation. It may be that the spindle axis is not initially determined, but has later to be positioned so that its equa-torial plane lines up with the ring of microtubules. Porter and Machado's micrographs of cell division in *Allium* root tips show that the ER invades the cell plate region as sheet-like structures frayed out at the ends to give tubules and vesicles. The ER, however, in the pictures published by Whaley & Mollenhauer (1963) and by Juniper (1963) does not appear to play so intimate a part in this initial process. There is no doubt that the Golgi bodies in meristematic cells are frequently found around the perimeter of the cell plate and appear to be secreting vesicles identical in size and staining reaction to those lying within the cell plate area. The recent work of Northcote & Pickett-Heaps (1965) lends weight to this assumption (see page 250) for it demonstrates that the Golgi vesicles of certain other cells can be shown to contain polysaccharides or their precursors of the pectin and hemicellulose type. These compounds, transported by the Golgi vesicles (Whaley & Mollenhauer, 1963) could be the initial constituents of the cell plate, but it should be pointed out that, as yet, in spite of several statements to the contrary, there is no direct evidence that the vesicles around cell plates do contain pectic substance or their precursors. In fact, even the evidence that the cell plate is composed of pectin is based on an erroneous assumption about the absolute specificity of ruthenium red for pectic substances. Ruthenium red does stain the cell plate, but it is specific only for carboxyl groups and, although pectic substances do contain carboxyl groups, they contain substances without them and carboxyl groups are found elsewhere than in pectic substances. So all one can say is that

FIG. 86. Electron micrograph of a preprophase band of microtubules from a root of *Phleum*. This group of microtubules marks the line where the cell plate will join the wall of the mother cell. (Glut/Os/Pb/U)

Micrograph by Mr J. Burgess and Dr D. H. Northcote.

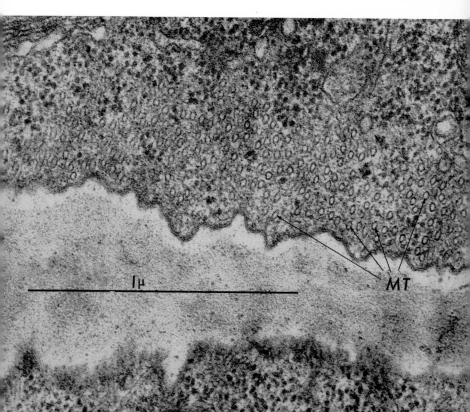

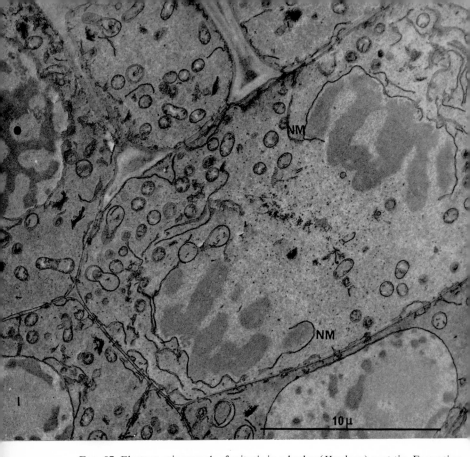

FIG. 87. Electron micrograph of mitosis in a barley (*Hordeum*) root tip. Formation of the cell plate is initiated by the clustering together, between the daughter nuclei, of large numbers of Golgi-derived vesicles. Most other organelles including the ER seem to be excluded from this region at telophase. The formation of the two new nuclear membranes is not yet complete. Fragments of the new nuclear membranes (NM) coat the exposed surfaces of the telophase chromatids. Interphase nuclei (I) with their electron-dense chromosomes are present in the other cells. (Mn)

ruthenium red demonstrates a high concentration of carboxyl groups in the cell plate. With these reservations it can be stated that coagulating vesicles do form the cell plate and are derived from the Golgi bodies.

Plasmodesmata, cytoplasmic connexions between cells, are commonly, if not exclusively, formed on the cell plate as well. There is a number of theories as to how this may occur. Porter & Machado (1960) believe that segments of the ER may become trapped within the congealing cell wall (of *Allium* root tip) and that these form the plasmodesmata. If Porter and Machado are correct, one must assume that some gross modification of the ER takes place as it is trapped, since it is generally agreed that plasmodesmata are smooth hollow threads

(Juniper, 1963; Lopez-Saez, Gimenez-Martin & Risueno, 1966). Juniper believes that the plasmodesmata are formed by the linear linking of a number of vesicles, possibly derived from the Golgi, since these vesicles are seen to align themselves along the spindle axis (Figs. 84, 85). The Golgi vesicles are membrane-bounded, and probably contribute to the membrane at which their contents are incorporated. Therefore *a priori* it seems likely that a membrane-bounded pore of a diameter exactly equal to that of the Golgi vesicles could be formed by them. A linear arrangement of vesicles similar to that observed by Juniper (1963), but not specifically connected by the authors (Esau & Gill, 1965) with plasmodesmatal formation, was noticed along a phragmoplast fibril during cell division in the procambium of *Beta*. The chance of seeing such a phenomenon must, because of the speed of cytokinesis, be very small indeed (the cell plate according to Bajer (1965) grows at an average rate of $0.5\mu m$ per minute) and this may account for the sparsity of observations of this sort. An account of the development, structure, distribution and possible role of plasmodesmata will be found on page 256.

The flow of Golgi vesicles on to the cell plate to initiate the cell wall can be explained on the assumption that the retreating daughter nuclei leave between them a 'cytoplasmic vacuum'. This 'vacuum' is filled by cytoplasmic matrix and those particles able to move most rapidly in to the area. Their presence is indicated by the movement observed by Bajer in ciné films of cytokinesis. What mechanism then directs these vesicles into a disc about $0.25\mu m$ thick within and around the internuclear fibrils? There is some evidence that the initial concentration of the cell plate vesicles in the equatorial plane occurs only where phragmoplast fibrils are present (Esau & Gill, 1965; Fig. 84). We must add to this Northcote's observation that the point where the cell plate will finally reach the cell wall is usually marked by an equatorial ring of microtubules before prophase, and we have already noted the resemblance of microtubules (Fig. 89) to phragmoplast fibrils (Fig. 84). Bajer has put forward a suggestion to account for the orientation of the vesicles or granules which appear in his ciné-micrographic studies of cell plate formation. These vesicles, which cannot be identified with the Golgi vesicles since the size difference has to be accounted for, accumulate strictly on one plane and fuse in a continuous plate. This phenomenon, according to Bajer, would be achieved by 'the pulling action of the fibrils on the droplets in two opposite directions in the same manner as the traction fibres of the chromosomes pull at the kinetochores (centromeres) and bring them to the level of the metaphase plate'. No sign of any fibres attached to Golgi vesicles has ever been seen. Bajer is also of the opinion that the light microscopic evidence suggests that the phragmoplast fibrils are not anchored anywhere at their ends. The fibrils are kept in extension by 'transport activity' operating along the sides of these fibrils from the equator to the poles. This mechanism would continue to keep the fibrils extended in a polar direction even when they move transversely within the phragmoplast. These ideas are consistent with the most recent observations on the microtubules that pass through the cell plate. These microtubules remain parallel to one another during cell plate formation, move outwards as plate formation proceeds and do not, in plants, appear to have any anchorage at either end.

Nothing very much seems to be known about the formation of the two plasmalemmas of the cell plate, but we assume that the Golgi vesicles, which are themselves bounded by a membrane similar to that of the plasmalemma and which are known to contribute to the growth of the plasmalemma by a process of reverse pinocytosis (see page 250) may well be one, if not the sole contributor to these membranes.

Another feature of cell plate formation should not be overlooked. There is indirect evidence that protein is present in the middle lamella (Ginzburg, 1958). Lamport & Northcote (1960) have shown that primary cell walls are enzymically active and carry, for example, 80 per cent of the phosphatase activity of the cell. So we must assume that protein as well as carbohydrate incorporation is a feature of cell wall formation probably from its inception. Where this protein comes from or where it is situated is not known, but, as we shall see, the Golgi bodies are beginning to be implicated in plant cells with protein as well as carbohydrate aggregation.

Growth of the primary wall

Growth of the cell wall may now be divided into growth in area and growth in thickness. How do cells expand? The turgor of the vacuole is widely believed to be the driving force of cell expansion (Green, 1962). This belief is based on the capacity of solutions hypertonically insufficient to cause plasmolysis to inhibit cell expansion. Nevertheless root cap cells, which are for all practical purposes non-vacuolate during the phase of expansion, succeed in increasing their volume fifteen-fold without the formation of a large vacuole (Juniper & Clowes, 1965). Perhaps cytoplasmic turgor rather than vacuolar turgor is responsible here. The pressure within a cell is the same in all directions, but plant cells do not usually expand equally in all directions; therefore the directions of growth must be a function partly of the pressures of the surrounding tissue and partly of the anisotropic resistance of the cell wall to expansion. In any cylinder under internal pressure the tension within its walls is anisotropic too since the transverse stress is twice that of the longitudinal stress parallel to the cylinder axis. This explains why an iron rainwater pipe always cracks along its length when ice forms within it.

5.4 Primary wall thickening

Theories of deposition

Increase in thickness of a plant cell wall occurs by the deposition of material layer on layer. This is known as appositional growth (Fig. 88A).

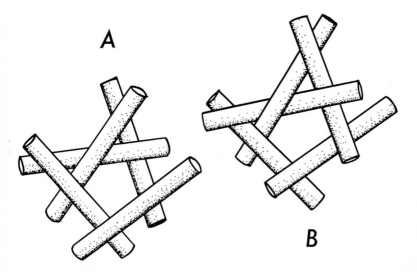

FIG. 88. Appositional and intussusceptional growth. (A) Microfibrils deposited upon a wall. (B) microfibrils inserted into an already existing structure. It is often difficult to decide from a macerated cell wall preparation which process has taken place.

It is the most obvious way for it to happen and it is generally agreed to make the major contribution, but there may also be intussusceptional growth, the insertion of new particles into a pre-existing structure (Fig. 88B). Whether cellulose microfibrils insert themselves is a matter for dispute (Roelofsen, 1959), but Beer & Setterfield (1958) seem to have provided very good evidence that, at least in collenchymatous cells, they

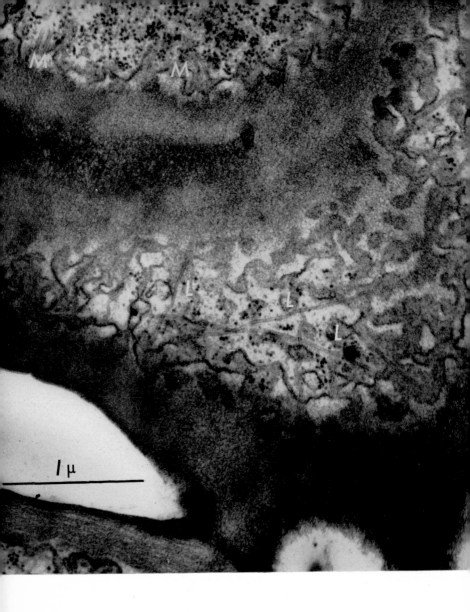

FIG. 89. Electron micrograph of a ripening bean (*Phaseolus vulgaris*) cotyledon. This section has glanced through the common wall of two cells just exposing the cytoplasm of the lower cell and cutting more deeply into the cell above. In the lower cell numerous microtubules run between the growing lobes (L) of the young cell wall. In the upper cell, in which the section has passed more deeply in the cytoplasm, the microtubules (M) are seen only in oblique view at the edge. The ribosomes, which lie deeper in the cell behind the microtubules, are clearly seen. (Glut/Os/Pb/U)

Micrograph by Dr H. Öpik.

can. Synthesis at the tip and interweaving of fibrils certainly are most easily explained by the hypothesis. Moreover Setterfield & Bailey (1958) have shown by tritium autoradiography that label is incorporated into the cellulose and non-cellulosic fractions throughout the thickness of the cell wall, though with some preponderance in the inner layers. There seems to be no dispute about the view that structural materials other than cellulose, e.g. lignin and cutin, may be incorporated by intussusception into existing wall. The incorporation of an as yet unidentified material (Figs. 30, 90) into the expanding cell walls of the root caps of *Zea* and *Hordeum* (Juniper & Roberts, 1966), appears from the staining

FIG. 90. Electron micrograph of central root cap cell walls of *Zea* (see Fig. 136). At maturity these walls appear to be impregnated with a material which stains with $KMnO_4$ and which forms a recticulum throughout the wall. This reticulum is lost as the cap cells reach the periphery and it may be that this is some protective compound preventing the breakdown of the walls of the central cells until they reach the margin. The existence of a similar material has been suggested by O'Brien and Thimann (1967) in the longitudinal walls of tracheary elements. (Glut/Mn)

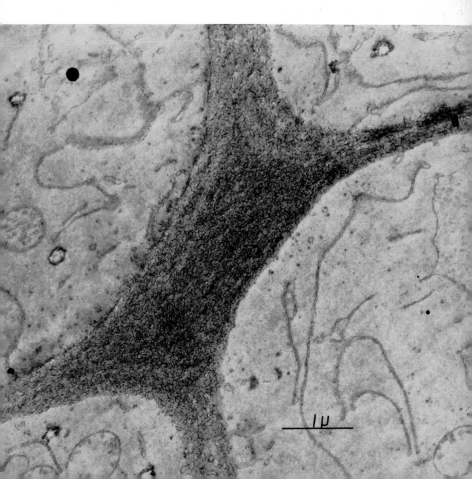

reaction under the electron microscope to take place from the region of middle lamella outwards. Also Northcote & Pickett-Heaps (1965) have shown that Golgi-derived hemicelluloses and pectins may be moved across the cytoplasm of root cap and cells, through the plasmalemma, even through the cell wall and into the mucus surrounding the root tip (see page 250). In addition, the middle lamella, although it is the first formed and most deeply embedded of cell wall constituents, is maintained in width despite growth in area (Roelofsen, 1965). It is easier to think of movements of soluble compounds in the wall if we remember that all primary walls and most secondary walls are bathed in water, that water is a major constituent and may comprise over 90 per cent of the total weight. The cellulose and matrix materials are no more than the fabric of a sponge around and between which the water penetrates.

Let us for the moment, however, concentrate on the deposition of the microfibrillar (cellulose) network of the primary cell wall, although bearing in mind that this probably is intimately connected with the formation of the rest of the wall components. Theories to explain the deposition of the microfibrillar network in cell walls during growth are numerous. Those in most common use are:

1. Mosaic growth
2. Protoplasmic polar or bipolar tip growth
3. Islands of synthesis
4. Multinet growth

The mosaic growth pattern of microfibrillar deposition was suggested by Frey-Wyssling & Stecher (1951) who noticed in macerated cell wall preparations open areas traversed by relatively few microfibrils. Some of these were assumed to be pits or potential pits, but some were thought to be regions of the wall penetrated briefly by the cytoplasm and, into these, new microfibrils would be woven. In the meantime new open areas would appear elsewhere and so the cycle would proceed and produce a changing mosaic. This theory seems now no longer to be widely held and it is probable that all the areas seen by Frey-Wyssling and Stecher were primary pit-fields. Moreover the mosaic growth theory lacks conviction since it is unable to explain how considerable extension of a wall could take place even when no new material is deposited as appears to happen.

Our second theory originates from Mühlethaler (1950), who, noting the interwoven texture of growing primary cell walls, assumed that this texture would be too intricate to allow the sliding and mutual reorientation necessary for growth to occur. He noticed too that near the tips of parenchymatous cells of *Zea* and *Avena* coleoptiles the walls appear thinner and the microfibrils so few that the tips seem almost open. He therefore proposed that growth takes place by the protrusion of the protoplast through the sparse microfibrils at the end of the cell and that growth did not, in fact, consist of an intercalation of new material into an existing framework but in the addition of new zones at the tips. To distinguish this hypothetical growth process from the observed growth at the tips of cotton hairs in which new microfibrils are deposited behind the advancing front of cytoplasm, this is best called protoplasmic tip growth. Contrary to Mühlethaler's original idea it can be said first of all that even thickened cell walls may be stretched up to one and a half times their own length without rupturing (Bonner, 1936) so that microfibrils, however deeply embedded and entangled can reorientate themselves to adjust to an imposed extension. There seems to be no reason therefore to suppose that a cell could not stretch in growth. Secondly, autoradiographic experiments on tissue similar to that investigated by Mühlethaler have shown that label is incorporated into the cellulose fraction over the whole length of the cell (Beer & Setterfield, 1958 and Setterfield & Bailey, 1957). Wardrop (1956) found that ^{14}C-glucose incorporation and distribution was inconsistent with the idea of tip growth at least as far as sub-epidermal parenchyma was concerned. Firstly there was no evidence of concentration of ^{14}C near the tips. Secondly there was no indication that the pit fields were islands of synthesis either. Thirdly Wardrop noticed that in *Avena* coleoptiles the microfibrils on the outer surface become progressively disorientated from the transverse direction in cells increasing in length, not what one would expect on a universal tip growth hypothesis. Fourthly Wardrop also noted in *Avena* coleoptiles that extension of the parenchymatous cells resulted in the separation of the pit fields and this could occur only if the cells expand throughout their length. From this we must assume that the concept of protoplasmic tip growth is not a normal phenomenon in parenchymatous cells. It does, however, occur, as we shall see, in certain cells such as root hairs and pollen tubes.

Islands of synthesis, a hypothesis somewhat similar but on a finer scale to the mosaic growth theory of Frey-Wyssling was put forward by Preston & Kuyper in 1951. They noticed, on the inner surface of the wall of vesicles of *Valonia*, granular cytoplasmic aggregates about 1–3μm across. The individual granules were approximately 50 nm across and were intimately associated with randomly orientated microfibrils. These aggregates were thought to be synthetic centres and the authors subsequently found similar aggregates in the supernatant of homogenized cambium. Provided that one assumes that the islands of synthesis are frequent enough (to be compatible with the overall distribution of synthesis observed in labelling experiments), and distributed all over the cell wall (to be compatible with the overall redistribution of microfibrils observed) this theory is consistent with all the evidence so far accumulated on cell wall growth. We shall have more to say on Preston's hypothesis of wall growth when discussing methods by which microfibrils could be orientated within the cell wall.

The multinet growth theory, the theory of most universal application in plant cell growth, we owe to Roelofsen & Houwink (1953). This theory is based on observations firstly on the growing hairs of *Gossypium*, later on those of *Ceiba* and *Asclepias*, the staminal hairs of *Tradescantia*,

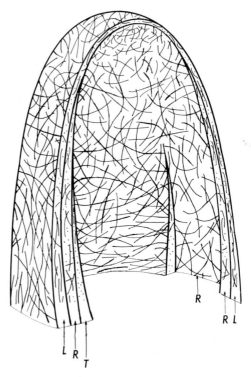

FIG. 91. The deposition of microfibrils in a cotton hair (*Gossypium*). Growth occurs over the whole of the hair. Random deposition at the tip is replaced by predominantly transverse deposition (T) just behind the apex. As growth proceeds each microfibril will shift outwards and, regardless of its original angle of deposition, will become criss-crossly (R) and finally axially (L) orientated.

and in the protruding parts of the stellate cells of the pith of *Juncus* leaves. In these cells the primary wall shows, as a rule on the outside, a loose network of microfibrils with a more or less distinct axial orientation, whereas, on the inside, there occurs a denser texture of microfibrils with a predominantly transverse orientation (Figs. 91, 92). The supposition is that at least the major part of new building materials, cellulose as well as non-cellulose fractions, is deposited against the inside of the wall. In tubular cells the new cellulose microfibrils are always orientated either transversely or in a low pitch helix. As cell growth proceeds these microfibrils are gradually reorientated towards a more or less longitudinal direction at the same time as new microfibrils are deposited transversely within. The old microfibrils as well as being orientated

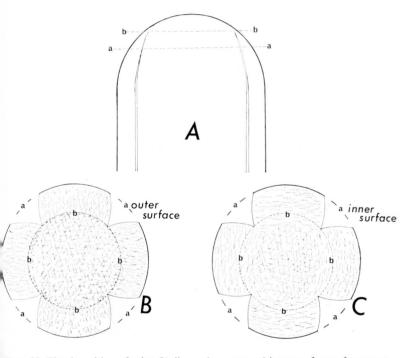

FIG. 92. The deposition of microfibrils on the outer and inner surfaces of a cotton hair tip (*Gossypium*). (A) a longitudinal section through a cotton hair tip, line b–b is the level at which transverse deposition of microfibrils begins on the inner face, line a–a an arbitrary level determining the boundaries of Figs. B and C. (B) microfibrillar orientation on the outer surface; random deposition grading off into an axial distribution. (C) Microfibrillar orientation on the inner surface; a somewhat smaller area of random deposition grading off into axial deposition.

Redrawn from Roelofsen (1965).

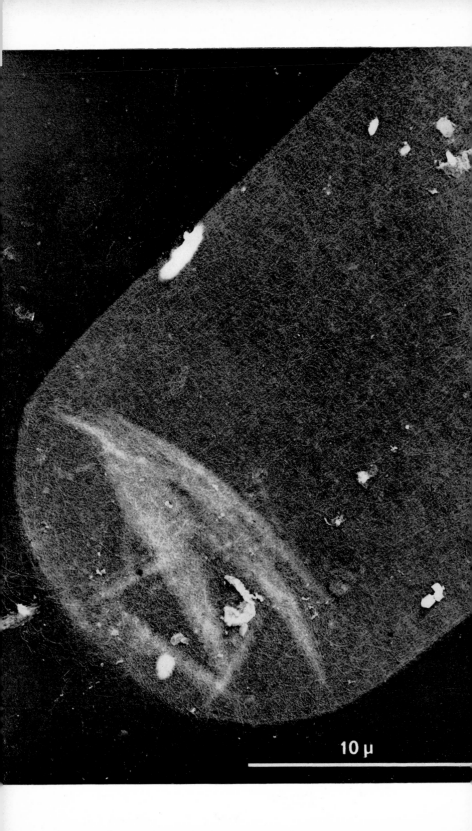

10 μ

progressively in a longitudinal direction will, of course, be straightened at their ends, and splayed out.

Thus the oldest microfibrils, intussusception excepted, should on this theory always be on the outside and the youngest on the inside, and as the construction of this wall may be compared with multilayered fishing nets with no knots, the type of growth and deposition which produces such a structure was called 'multi-net growth'. As Houwink & Roelofsen (1954) so well expressed it 'we may compare the latter with a tangle of fresh filiform algae spread on a glass plate. The algal threads, though frequently intertwined, will freely slip past one another. The tangle can be extended at will and the threads will become oriented accordingly'. The only objection one could possibly make to this piece of imagery is that the microfibrils, unlike the algae, would not be in contact with one another, but probably up to four times their diameter apart. The outcome of the multinet theory in dynamic terms is illustrated diagrammatically in Fig. 91 and in Fig. 92 and it should be emphasized that Fig. 91 does not imply a precise boundary between zones, but, since it is generally believed that growth and deposition are continuous the zones merge imperceptibly into one another.

These differences of inner and outer wall microfibril orientation on which the theory is based were also noticed by Wardrop (1956) in both *Avena* coleoptile sub-epidermal parenchyma and in *Allium* parenchyma. The obvious test of the multi-net theory is that the orientation of the outermost microfibrils should reflect the extent and direction of the growth of the cell.

Since the *Gossypium* cotton hair has now become one of the classical objects of biological study, it may be worth while looking at it closely (Fig. 93). Fig. 91 shows a three-dimensional diagram of the tip of a cotton hair. The tip shows the random orientation of microfibrils both on the outer and inner surfaces; in this respect it is similar to those structures such as root hairs and pollen tubes which grow only at the tip (see page 400). Immediately below the hemisphere of the tip, about 1μm below the randomly orientated area, the outermost microfibrils

FIG. 93. Electron micrograph of the tip of a cotton hair (*Gossypium*). This is a macerated wall and all the matrix materials have been removed to show the cellulose microfibrils more clearly. At the extreme tip the microfibrils are completely random, but, as growth proceeds, those on the outside become progressively reorientated into a more or less axial distribution. Compare this micrograph with the three-dimensional reconstruction of a cotton hair tip in Fig. 91 in which all three layers of the wall of elongating zone are shown. Micrograph by Prof A. L. Houwink and Prof. P. A. Roelofsen.

FIG. 94. Electron micrograph of the wall of an arm of a stellate cell of a *Juncus effusus* stem. The arms grow along their entire length as the cell becomes stellate (see Figs. 17, 18) and are therefore similar to cotton hairs. While growing they deposit microfibrils transversely on the inner face of the wall (T). On shifting outwards these fibrils become random and finally axially orientated (A). A similar situation is seen at the base of Fig. 91 where the transverse depositional zone extends outwards through a random layer to the axial layer on the outside.

Micrograph by Prof A. L. Houwink and
Prof P. A. Roelofsen.

appear to be axially orientated. This is unlikely to have been achieved by the synthesis of new axial microfibrils on top (or outside) of the old layer of randomly orientated ones, but it is evidently due to re-alignment in growth. The microfibrils that are deposited on the inner surface of the hemisphere just below its summit are initially more or less transversely orientated. Due to stretching of the outer layers as growth proceeds, these microfibrils will have been separated and reorientated within the wall into a more or less axial direction in the same manner as those laid down at the tip. A similar situation is found in the stellate hairs of *Juncus* leaves (Fig. 94).

It does not seem to matter whether or not the initial reticulate pattern of microfibrillar deposition is disturbed. For example, in coleoptile segments in which growth is disturbed by colchicine, but in which wall deposition continues, it is found that the final distribution of the outer microfibrils is consistent with the multi-net theory's predictions from the pattern of growth.

The multi-net hypothesis, although applicable to many cells cannot account for all the diversity of primary wall structure. The problem of corner thickening, such as occurs in much collenchyma and which at first sight is incompatible with the multi-net idea has naturally received considerable attention (Roelofsen, 1965). This is an instance where extensive strip thickening takes place before growth has finished. 'Thickened primaries' is the name that Majumdar & Preston (1941) have given such cells. Wardrop & Cronshaw (1958) think that, during elongation, microfibrils initially present on the cell faces could be pulled into longitudinal corner thickenings. This is, however, contrary to the findings of Setterfield & Bailey (1958) who showed by autoradiography that wall material could be incorporated in the corner thickenings of collenchyma cells right through the thickness of the wall as well as on the inside. Wardrop & Cronshaw (1958) suggest that preferential thickening may be expected since the corners of cells are not penetrated by plasmodesmata so that microfibrillar synthesis could proceed unchecked compared with the contact faces of the cells where plasmodesmata and pit fields are present. There is no doubt that in some cases wall deposition is restricted around the plasmodesmata (Clowes & Juniper, 1964) and that, in the cortical cells of *Vicia faba* (Fig. 95), the walls against intercellular spaces where there are no plasmodesmata are thicker than those against other cell walls where plasmodesmata penetrate. Roelofsen (1959) has suggested that there is a tendency for the cell wall material to migrate away from the faces of cell contact just as liquid in a soap bubble film under pressure tends to migrate away from the contact area. This model, however, would not explain why restriction of thickening takes place even in meristematic cells between which there are no intercellular spaces and in which one would suppose pressures were more or less equally distributed.

Fig. 96 shows diagrammatically the pattern of growth of a collenchymatous cell. Very young collenchymatous cells do not differ much from parenchymatous cells. The walls appear not to be birefringent under crossed polarizing plates and Roelofsen's interpretation of this is that the inner layers of the wall (see Fig. 120 for comparison) made up of transversely orientated fibrils are compensated for by the axially orientated outer layers of the wall, hence the absence of birefringence.

I

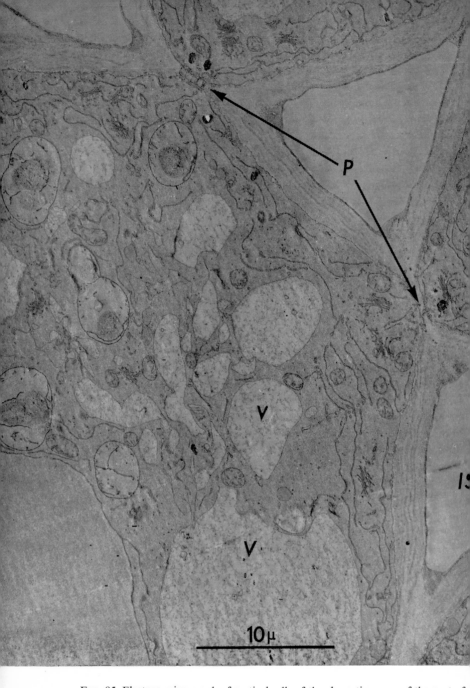

FIG. 95. Electron micrograph of cortical cells of the elongating zone of the root of *Vicia*. The cells are beginning to vacuolate (V), intercellular spaces (IS) have already formed between the cells and the plasmodesmata (P) are confined to small areas of the wall. The wall areas traversed by plasmodesmata are thinner than those bordering onto inter-cellular spaces. The ER is parallel to these thicker areas of wall, but is excluded from, or lies at right angles to the thinner areas of the wall crossed by plasmodesmata. (Mn)

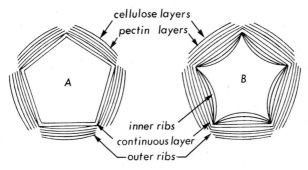

FIG. 96. The distribution of cellulose and pectin layers in collenchyma. A. The cellulose and pectin layers lie outside the original continuous layer; B. the cellulose and pectin layers are found both inside and outside a continuous layer.

However, the walls become birefringent as a result of more axially orientated microfibrils appearing at the surface. In 'type A' collenchymatous cells in Figure 96 all the thickening ribs lie outside a continuous layer in which the microfibrils are transversely orientated. This pattern was observed by Roelofsen in mature tissue of *Apium* petioles which are resting stages for growth in the next season for this biennial plant. In the 'type B' collenchyma, cell ribs also occur within the continuous layer and these have an axial orientation of the microfibrils.

At least in the later stages of collenchyma thickening, the pattern suggests that microfibrillar synthesis is distributed in patches not uniformly as the multi-net hypothesis suggests. However, very little is known about the development of collenchyma yet.

There are also several instances (apart from root hair cells and pollen tubes, to which attention has already been drawn) in which localized growth does take place. Böhmer (1958) studied growth of the cell walls in *Avena* by autoradiography. He showed that localized growth does not take place in either the epidermal or sub-epidermal parenchyma, but, in the primary xylem elements, there does appear to be more radioactivity towards the tips which seems to indicate that increased synthesis takes place there at least.

In summarizing the many and diverse sources of information on growth and the deposition of wall material the following statements seem to be generally true. (1) New material is continually added to the wall as it grows *in area* since, in most cases in spite of great increase in primary surface area, no appreciable overall decrease in thickness is noted. Possible exceptions to this are staminal hairs of *Tradescantia* and root hairs. Whether surface growth takes place uniformly is still open to discussion. (2) The constituent wall layers (Fig. 31) frequently remain constant in thickness and are not apparently diluted by rapid extension growth, hence some form of selective reinforcement of each layer throughout the wall must be taking place. (3) Most autoradiographic studies seem to indicate deposition not only uniformly over the surface of the cell, but throughout the thickness of the wall as well.

Nevertheless one should interpret all these results with care since they may indicate only turnover and not additional synthesis in spite of the fact that they agree with other lines of evidence. Moreover, as already pointed out, the resolution of light microscope autoradiography is rarely better than 2–3μm and therefore barely adequate for the job.

Microfibril synthesis

It was commonly assumed at one time that wall formation had to take place at a cytoplasm-wall interface. Mühlethaler (1961) has reviewed the literature on this and draws attention to a number of situations, mainly in the slime moulds, where microfibrillar synthesis may occur at a distance from the protoplast. Perhaps the most spectacular of these examples of extra-cellular formation of cellulose microfibrils is that achieved by *Acetobacter xylinum* (Ben-Hayyim & Ohad, 1965) although this cannot in any sense by termed a wall. A wall polymer with a micro-fibrillar texture (although probably not cellulose) and showing evidence of orientation, has been shown by Bednar & Juniper (1964) to form outside existing hyphal cell walls (Fig. 97) in the fungal hyphal layer of lichens and to cement the individual hyphae into a coherent, rubbery layer.

The microfibrils of any one wall layer frequently interweave (Fig. 77A). This also suggests that they are not produced solely at a cytoplasm-wall interface and, further, that they are not formed by the end-to-end joining of preformed chains. This is also strongly suggested by *Acetobacter*'s synthesis of cellulose in which cellulose is formed by whole cells in the 'prefibrous' form and may pass through 'Millipore' filters of 0·45μm pore diameter (Ben-Hayyim & Ohad, 1965). In each example the synthesis of cellulose by the addition of monomer units to the end of an existing chain already *in situ* seems to be the most satisfactory explanation.

Preston (1965) has suggested from electron microscopical evidence that microfibrils lying in two or even three directions are synthesized simultaneously and goes on further to suggest that this would require a synthesizing and orientating mechanism at least three microfibrils thick.

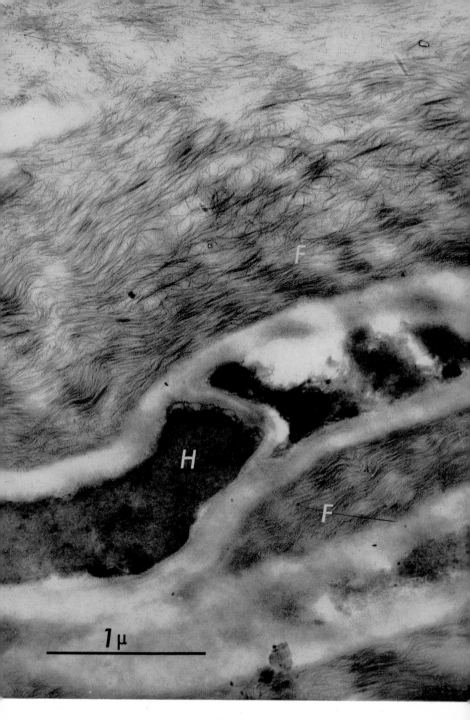

FIG. 97. Electron micrograph through the fungal zone of the lichen, *Xanthoria parietina*. Initially the fungal hyphae (H) are separated from one another, but as the lichen matures the hyphae appear to manufacture some fibrous material (F) or its precursor, excrete it through their walls and deposit it between themselves and the neighbouring hyphae thus gelling together the whole of the structure. (Glut/Os/Pb/U)

Allowing for normal microfibrillar spacing this could mean an active zone at least $0\cdot5\mu$m deep.

When the organization of the cytoplasm-wall interface is disturbed, as on plasmolysis, prior to sporulation or under the influence of colchicine and other drugs, the ability to synthesize cellulose is generally retained, but the capacity to orientate microfibrils is commonly lost, for in most cases the microfibrils are produced with random orientation. This suggests that much cellulose orientation is controlled in some way by the cytoplasm in spite of the evidence for extracellular synthesis and orientation.

Another interesting observation for which there does not yet seem to be any adequate explanation has been made by Setterfield (1961). If a young bean (*Vicia faba*) stem is grown horizontally in a glass tube to prevent it from exhibiting the normal geotropic response, the cortical cells on the lower side expand radially and retain their existing wall thickness whilst those on the upper side stay the same size but grow thicker walls. Moreover, on the lower side the microfibrils continue to be deposited in a transverse direction with respect to the cell whilst those on the upper side deposit longitudinal microfibrils. This pattern of behaviour is reversible and is an indication of how readily microfibrillar orientation can be disturbed by the environment.

A microfibril synthetic system must have the ability (1) to produce microfibrils by end synthesis, i.e. by addition of nomomer units (GDP-glucose) to the end of an existing cellulose molecule if need be, at some distance from the cytoplasm, (2) to extend over the whole surface of a cell and (3) to be capable of producing microfibrils in three directions in the same plane either separately or simultaneously, but in no other direction (Fig. 77A).

Preston (1964) has produced a model which he supports by electron microscopic evidence from the inner face of a plasmolysed cell of *Chaetomorpha* to fit most the above desiderata (Figs. 77B, 98). Each granule in the figure represents an enzyme complex which, coupled with a microfibril end as a starter, would join glucan residues until the microfibril end comes in contact with the next granule which would then take over and so synthesis would continue. The packing of granules is such that it would restrict the direction of growth of the microfibrils and constrain them to two directions at right angles to one another with occasional departures along the diagonals to these directions. Preston is, however, at pains to point out that no facts support this model except for the observations on *Chaetomorpha*, which is an alga, and possibly the fine structure revealed by the freeze etching technique

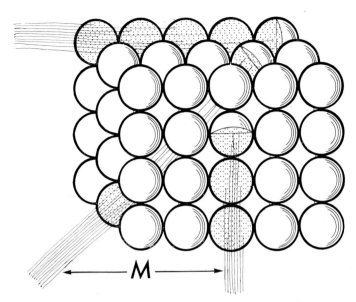

FIG. 98. Preston's hypothetical structure that may be responsible for the synthesis of the cellulose in the cell wall. The globules represent enzyme complexes which add glucose units to the existing cellulose microfibril (M). The three layers of globules allow for interweaving and the spatial arrangement of the globules allows for synthesis to take place in three different directions, but no other. (See Figs. 77A & B).   Redrawn from Preston (1964).

(Moor & Mühlethaler, 1963) (Figs. 99, 105). But the structures seen in freeze-etched preparations are of a completely different order of size from those proposed by Preston (see page 260).

Crawley (1965) and Barton (1965) have drawn attention to membrane-bounded bodies adpressed to the walls of *Chara* and *Nitella*, these appear to be structurally similar to the lomasomes of some fungi already mentioned in Chapter 4 (Fig. 100). (Hendy, 1966.) It has been suggested that these may be connected with wall synthesis. Comparable organelles have only recently been seen in higher plants and there seems little value at the moment in relating these to Preston's hypothetical granules. Possible mechanisms for orientating cell wall fibres were discussed before Preston's theory. Alignment has been attributed to cytoplasmic streaming (van Iterson, 1937), to the stretching of the cell wall under turgor pressure (Roelofsen, 1959), to the influence of proteins of a spindle fibre nature said to exist in the outer cytoplasm of plant cells (Green, 1962) and to microtubules aligned parallel to the microfibrillar orientation within the wall (Ledbetter, 1965).

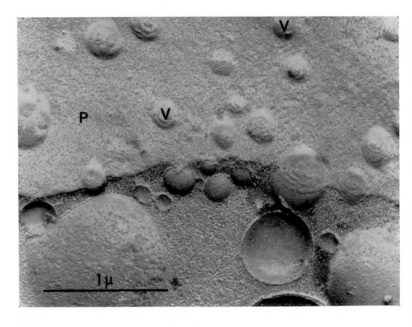

FIG. 99. Electron micrograph of a replica of a frozen and etched root cap cell of *Allium cepa*. Vesicles (V), probably derived from the Golgi bodies, are passing through the plasmalemma (P) towards the cell wall. Numerous small particles can be seen covering the outer surface of the plasmalemma. In the lower half of the picture an area of cross-fractured cytoplasm can be seen.

Micrograph by Dr D. Branton.

Green's hypothesis was based on long cytoplasmic elements which were supposed to have many of the properties of spindle fibres. It was supported by the observed anisotropy of the outer region of the cytoplasm of certain plant cells. The fibres to which the anisotropy was thought to be due were supposed to organize microfibril synthesis *perpendicular* to their long axis. The orientation of these cytoplasmic elements was thought to be influenced by strain and their lateral bonding was assumed to be broken by colchicine hence the disorganization, but not the cessation, of microfibrillar formation produced by this drug. It was conceded at the time that such a mechanism could not account for microfibrillar textures in secondary cell walls or in algae with layers of microfibrils at different angles.

Filamentous structures, the microtubules, similar to those envisaged by Green have turned up all right in both animals and plants. These are discussed in Chapter 3. Where they are associated with wall synthesis

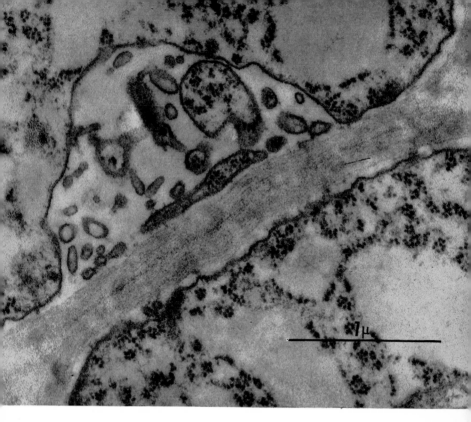

FIG. 100. Electron micrograph of a structure similar to a lomasome from the elongating zone of the primary root tip of *Zea*. The plasmalemma of the cell wall is extended to surround an irregular vesiculate structure in which membrane-bounded pockets of an unidentified substance occur. Embayments of the cytoplasm into the lomasome can be recognized by their possession of ribosomes. (Glut/Os/Pb/U)

their orientation parallels the orientation of the microfibrils. This is, of course, contrary to Green's hypothesis in which the cytoplasmic fibres were supposed to bring about synthesis perpendicular to themselves.

We can now review the other theories that have been put forward to account for the orientation of cellulose microfibrils. The oldest hypothesis, that of protoplasmic streaming, must clearly be abandoned as a universal explanation. There is no doubt, as Crüger in 1855 and more recently Sinnott & Bloch (1945) showed, that, in a number of instances mainly of spiral thickening in vessels, paths of protoplasmic streaming are followed by the deposition of bands of secondary wall material. However, in growing cells no streaming parallel to the initial cellulose orientation has ever been observed and, in *Tradescantia* and *Trianea* hairs, and probably cotton hairs, it is in a direction almost at right angles to the microfibrils (Roelofsen, 1965). It should also be noted here that

I*

Nagai & Rebhun (1966) have found in the streaming region of *Nitella* cells, fine filaments 5 nm in diameter and in bundles of 50–100, parallel to the direction of the streaming. The microtubules on the other hand, although numerous in these cells are isolated from the protoplasmic streaming region by the chloroplast layer and are not parallel to the streaming direction. These very fine filaments found by Nagai and Rebhun are similar to the 7 nm filaments found by Wohlfarth-Botterman (1964) parallel to the direction of protoplasmic streaming in *Amoeba* and are therefore presumably not connected with wall building at all. Similar filaments 5–7 nm in diameter and grouped into bunches $0 \cdot 1$–$0 \cdot 2 \mu$m wide have also been found in *Avena* coleoptiles (O'Brien & Thimann, 1966). These too lie parallel to the direction of cytoplasmic streaming. The microtubules in these cells are also at right angles to the filaments. Mitochondria are found close to or touching these fine filaments and O'Brien and Thimann suggest that they are connected with cytoplasmic streaming.

Van Iterson's theory supposes that the predominantly transverse stress in tubular cells during elongation was responsible for the initial deposition of microfibrils in a transverse direction. The theory fails to account for walls with alternating lamellae of crossed fibrils and, as Green (1962) demonstrated, if all stress and strain are eliminated by constraining *Nitella* cells in a tight jacket, deposition of transverse wall lamellae still continues. Nor does it account for the change in deposition in Setterfield's horizontal bean. What is more, if colchicine, which inhibits orientated microfibril deposition, is added and subsequently removed, the jacketed cells of *Nitella* still revert to transverse microfibril deposition thus proving also that no template action of the existing wall microfibrils influences subsequent deposition.

The microtubules are perhaps the strongest contenders at the moment for the role of cellulose alignment (Figs. 89, 149). Amongst other attractions, they occur in both primary and secondary tissue, and as we now know, they are disorganized by colchicine which upsets spindle fibres and microfibril orientation in the wall (Pickett-Heaps, 1967b). Microtubules have been found aligned along the bands of secondary thickening and colchicine, apart from its other effects is known to prevent the development of secondary thickening in *Sphagnum* leaves (Bünning, 1957). However, enthusiasm for this latest contender should be modified by the knowledge of their absence in pollen tubes, which have perfectly normally orientated cellulose microfibrils (see page 400), and of their absence from the rapid growth phase of *Cladophora* (Goodman, unpub.). They are also not concerned with the extra-cellular production of microfibrils in *Acetobacter* or of microfibrillar material in the lichen *Xanthoria parietina*. Moreover Setterfield and Bailey contend that cellulose synthesis can take place at some distance from a cytoplasm wall interface. The widely accepted view that intussusception can contribute to growth in thickness in primary walls tends to weaken Ledbetter and Porter's idea that the microtubules might act as primers for microfibrillar synthesis.

There seem to be few clues to the method by which cellulose microfibrils, or their precursors, find their way through the plasmalemma and align themselves into the cell wall. It is difficult to know what significance to attach to the intriguing presence of contorted tubules of size similar to microtubules and microfibrils between the plasmalemma and cell wall of differentiating xylem (see Plate 12 of Cronshaw & Bouck, 1965). In spite of their dimensions, it is difficult to believe that these are cellulose microfibrils, and Cronshaw and Bouck believe that they are microtubules. But, if they are, why are they so irregular in shape and how are they transferred through the plasmalemma?

A very interesting series of experiments was reported by Colvin (1965). In these, drops of a 1 per cent solution of polypropylene in orthoxylene at 130°C were dispersed on the surface of glycerol at 165°C. The resulting films were cooled slowly before mounting and shadowing with metal (Fig. 101). The films are composed of 'microfibrils' of indefinite length and of widths very similar to those of cellulose (15 to 30 nm); they may aggregate to form bundles of two or more threads, but their most striking feature is the orthogonal orientation of the microfibrils and their interweaving to form a coherent layer. This interweaving can be the result only of the penetration of a microfibril under construction into a group of previously formed and aligned threads. In addition, the films have ruptures (Fig. 101B) which strongly resemble the simple pits of plant cell walls even to the bundles of microfibrils crossing the opening, the distribution of microfibrils around the periphery, and the apparently torn microfibrils. This micrograph should be compared with a real pit (Fig. 113).

We must therefore accept that non-living systems are capable both of end synthesis and orthogonal orientation.

Deposition of matrix

If the mechanism whereby microfibrils in primary cell walls are produced and orientated remains in doubt, what then of the production and deposition of the other components of the cell wall, the hemi-

celluloses, the pectins, lignin and the rest? There is plenty of evidence to
implicate the Golgi in the formation of the cell plate, of the pollen tube
wall and the root hair tip. There is still no high resolution autoradiography comparable to that achieved by Northcote (see below) to give
the contents of Golgi vesicles entering walls of expanding cells a
definite chemical character although there is a number of confident
statements in the literature to the effect that they contain pectin. It seems
likely that they do contain at least a high proportion of pectin, but, in
spite of the work of Albersheim & Killias (see page 15), there is no
unequivocal method of identifying pectin histochemically under either
the light or the electron microscope.

A great deal of attention has been paid, since their initial discovery
by Mollenhauer and his colleagues, to the Golgi of the peripheral root
cap cells of *Zea mays* (1961). These cells have in fact ceased growing, but
do not thicken their walls. Northcote & Pickett-Heaps (1966) have now
demonstrated that the Golgi of these cells incorporate tritiated glucose
and transfer the label to their vesicles. The vesicles move to and
coalesce with the plasmalemma and then transfer the label to the mucus
that surrounds the root tip (Fig. 158). The majority of material in which
the label has been found has been identified as the polysaccharides,
galactan and arabinan. Both of the sugars, galactose and arabinose,
have been found as constituents of the mucus surrounding the root tips
of normally growing roots (Juniper & Roberts, 1966). We may therefore say with some confidence that these particular Golgi secrete
polysaccharides which, after a brief sojourn in the cell walls, contribute
to the mucus. These Golgi and their associated vehicles look very different from the Golgi of meristematic or elongating cells (Figs. 60, 63, 64).
This may mean that they, at different times, perform different chemical
functions. There are instances of such a switch in role in animal cells,
but, as Juniper and Roberts have pointed out, under normal conditions
Golgi are likely to be substrate-limited. However, in these peripheral

FIG. 101A: Electron micrograph of polypropylene 'microfibrils'. These fibrils were
formed by dissolving polypropylene in hot orthoxylene and allowing them to
disperse and crystallize on the surface of hot glycerol. The film of fibrils was then
allowed to cool, mounted and shadowed like an ordinary macerated cell wall preparation. Their shape and dimensions are identical to those of cellulose microfibrils and
they orientate themselves into a nearly orthogonal pattern. Compare Fig. 77.

B: 'Microfibrils' produced as in A spontaneously develop sparse areas in the film
very similar to pit fields in plant cell walls (compare with Fig. 113).

Micrographs by Dr R. R. Anderson and
Dr P. H. Lindenmeyer from Colvin (1965).

cap cells, their food supply is suddenly enriched by the breakdown of the amyloplasts and the release of the carbohydrates they contain (Fig. 21). This could explain the hypertrophy of the Golgi and their vesicles. It is possible that the Golgi of meristematic and other enlarging cells are equivalent, in everything but size to the Golgi of the peripheral root cap cells. If so, they contribute to the pectin and hemicellulose fraction of the cell wall generally. There is no method of distinguishing under the electron microscope between the hemicellulose and pectin supplied by the Golgi to the cell wall and, since the chemical distinctions between these two components are somewhat blurred (they have common constituents) the Golgi probably do contribute to either or both. If, however, the Golgi do contribute to the matrix of the wall as a whole, one must then suggest a hypothesis to explain the preponderance of pectin in the middle lamella and primary cell wall and its progressive phasing out and replacement by hemicellulose as wall development proceeds (Thornber & Northcote, 1961). (Table 4).

The impression may have been given that the successive deposition of a number of polymers on to and into the cell wall results in a dense structure through which only small molecules such as water or salts in solution could pass. This may not be the case. An extensive and interconnecting transport system of 20–40 nm holes has been discovered in the leaves of *Helxine* (Gaff, Chambers & Markus, 1964). Gold sol particles 4 nm in diameter were shown in the electron microscope to move from the xylem along definite channels within the walls to the epidermal cells. The role of this intramural capillary system is not known but if it is of general occurrence the results seem to suggest that the movement of water and substances in solution and suspension through the walls may not be as random as was originally thought.

Extension

We have now examined the structural components of the primary cell wall and the processes by which they may be formed and deposited. We know that the cellulose framework is often so firmly bound to the hemicellulose matrix that it is extremely difficult to achieve a complete separation of the two. How, then, does growth take place with the concomitant re-arrangement of the cellulose skeleton and presumably of the non-crystalline fraction as well.

There is considerable evidence to suggest that structural polysaccharides are broken down by enzymes of endogenous origin (Esau, 1953). Matchett & Nance's ^{14}C incorporation experiments are consistent with this view (1962). Their data may be interpreted as indicating that extension of the primary wall is accompanied by increases in the rates of breakdown and resynthesis of the structural network of the wall and they suggest that the plasticity of the cell wall is in part a function of the rate at which wall constituents are degraded. The turnover of ^{14}C is certainly increased when test tissues are supplied with growth promoting levels of IAA (Ordin, Cleland & Bonner, 1955) and decreased by growth inhibiting levels of mannitol and galactose. However, a relatively long period of time is necessary for this degradation process to accelerate (as shown by ^{14}C) whereas accelerated growth rate in response to auxin, as we shall show later, requires a very short time indeed. Plasticization of the cell wall follows almost immediately after the application of auxin and whatever significance Matchett and Nance's results have for the later stages of wall synthesis it seems unlikely that resynthesis of structural components is directly involved. What other components, then, within the cell wall can be implicated in the rapid changes in plasticity observed. Tupper-Carey & Priestley (1924) were the first to demonstrate that primary cell walls contain protein and later workers have found that the bulk of one particular amino acid, hydroxyproline, lies within the cell wall. Ginzburg (1958) has also put forward evidence for a protein component in the middle lamella of plant cells and was able to show that the proteolytic enzyme, pepsin, separates cell from cell without seriously damaging the cells themselves.

It was Preston in 1961 who pointed out that the proline and hydroxyproline portion of wall protein is immune to the metabolic processes of the plant, locked up as it is away from enzymes of the cytoplasm. He put forward the suggestion that the wall protein may be associated with the varying plasticity of the developing cell wall.

It seems to be generally agreed that cellulose itself, in the form of microfibrils, is almost inextensible. Therefore we must look to connexions between the microfibrils and between the microfibrils and the matrix for plasticity of the cell wall. As long ago as 1935 Bonner suggested labile cross-linkages between the cellulose microfibrils, but so little was known of the general structure of cell walls that the matter rested until Bennet-Clark suggested in 1956 that plasticity of cell walls might be raised when the carboxyl groups of the pectin fractions were methylated, and that low plasticity would result from low methylation and extensive calcium bridging. However, it could not be proved that auxin or growth promoting substances affects the amount of cell wall methyl ester, but later Cleland (1963) was able to show in coleoptiles that the early effects of auxin on cell wall methylation were independent of cell elongation. It does not look, then, as if a methylated-pectin to calcium-pectate shift is a serious contender for the control of cell extension, but we should not ignore some interesting experiments by Klein & Ginzburg (1960). They studied the effect of ethylene-diamine tetraacetic acid (EDTA) on the plasticity of the cell wall. EDTA is a strong chelating agent and one might expect that it would remove cations from the cell wall. Klein and Ginsburg were able to show that EDTA loosens the cell walls. They also claimed that 'cellulose fibrils' can be made visible under the electron microscope in sections stained with uranyl salts. When EDTA-treated roots are stained with heavy metals prior to fixation they do not show these spread 'cellulose fibrils'. Since EDTA is unlikely to act directly on the cellulose it is most likely to act on the intercellulose material in achieving the loosening of fibrils within the walls. The fact that chelation of metals by EDTA not only loosens the cellulose fibrils, but also brings about the separation of the cells, suggests that the cellulose network may be bound by the same cement that binds the cells. This material, they claim, must be distributed *throughout* the wall since their electron micrographs do not indicate any specific localization of cell cementing substances. They also point out that, when a uranyl salt was used as a source of substitute wall-cementing cations, it was found mainly in the inner part of the cell wall, where Setterfield & Bailey (1958) have shown the greatest concentration of cellulose fibrils to lie. Thus a substance, which is able to bind metal ions occurs in the cellulose layers and not in the middle lamella. The binding material may consist of pectins or proteins, both of which have a strong capacity for binding cations, and it may well be that this hypothetical binding material may be the site of action of IAA, which is known to have chelating properties.

A very low concentration of IAA applied to root hairs enhances elongation significantly within a few minutes of application and this seems to hint that cell expansion is, at least initially, mediated through a change in the quality of the cell wall rather than through alterations in the relative amounts of cell wall substances available for building. Bearing in mind Klein and Ginzburg's work we should look now at the most popular hypothesis of the moment.

There seems little doubt that protein, generally containing hydroxyproline, is found in significant quantities in many higher plant cell walls (Lamport, 1965). Hydroxyproline is otherwise a rare component of proteins; collagen is one of the very few other proteins known to contain this amino acid. In higher plants, hydroxyproline has been found in every wall except that of pollen tubes. These contain a protein with proline, but not hydroxyproline. Lamport puts forward evidence that covalent bonds exist between the carbohydrates of the wall and the protein for it is difficult to separate protein from wall. Also cellulase removes about 70 per cent of the wall leaving a wall-shaped structure containing 80-90 per cent of the protein originally present. The carbohydrate-protein complex left contains arabinose and galactose in the ratio of about 3:1 and this may indicate the presence of a galacto-arabinan. Furthermore Ginzburg (1961) has shown that heat pretreatment of pea root tips above 60°C brings about an enhancement of the effect of EDTA and this can be interpreted as due to heat destroying the protein-cementing complex. There is also good evidence presented by Lamport for the presence of the sulphur-containing amino acids, cystine and cysteine, in this protein complex. These were detected both by direct analysis and the rapid incorporation of ^{35}S into the wall protein of sulphur-starved cells of *Acer*.

On the present admittedly somewhat thin evidence, Lamport has drawn up a hypothetical scheme for the existence of a hydroxyproline-rich wall protein complex, which he calls 'extensin'. He suggests that it acts structurally by forming labile S-S bridges between the carbohydrate-protein complex as in Fig. 102. He suggests that auxin may intervene in this system in a way summarized in Fig. 103 since auxin is known to increase the respiration rate in a system in which phosphorylation is limiting; thus auxin may affect this phosphorylation process. This in turn would provide reducing power via $NADPH_2$ to convert the di-sulphide bridges to sulphydryl bonds. Ascorbic acid is known to be present in walls (Butt, 1959). This may complete the control mechanism cycle by forming dehydro-ascorbic (or monodehydroascorbic acid) which could reoxidize the non-acting sulphydryl groups of the 'extensin' back to the bridging disulphide.

Thompson & Preston (1967) consider that little significance should be attached to the absence of hydroxyproline from the proteins of *Nitella* cell walls since cystine is certainly present. The quantity of cystine-containing protein is also high enough to qualify it for a role in lower plants such as is suggested for it in higher plants. Free hydroxy-proline is known to inhibit the growth of both animals and plants, and Holleman (1967) believes that hydroxyproline is incorporated into the proteins of the cell wall and, as a result, renders them inert. The proline ⇌ hydroxyproline equilibrium may then determine whether or not a wall is allowed to extend and whether or not the S-S bonds of Lamport's 'extensin' system are permitted to function.

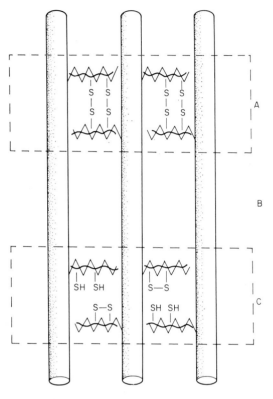

FIG. 102. 'Extensin' in a primary cell wall. Lengths of the microfibrils, according to Lamport (1965), are protected from enzyme attack by their intimate association with proteins and galacto-arabinan (A and C). Other lengths (B) are unprotected and susceptible to cellulase attack. In the lengths A and C the galacto-arabinan complexes are represented by the thin zig-zag lines and the proteins by the thick wavy lines. In section A, S–S bonds between proteins connected to different galacto-arabinan complexes tie the 'knots' between different microfibrils. In length C, reduction of the S–S bonds, or formation of S–S bonds in a protein will loosen the 'knots'. For an explanation of a possible way in which such a hypothetical system might operate see Fig. 103.   Redrawn from Lamport (1965)

5.5   Plasmodesmata

Plasmodesmata are protoplasmic threads connecting cells through both primary and secondary walls. Since we believe that most of them if not all are formed in the primary wall stage, they are described here, although they persist and play a number of important roles in secondary walls (see page 269).

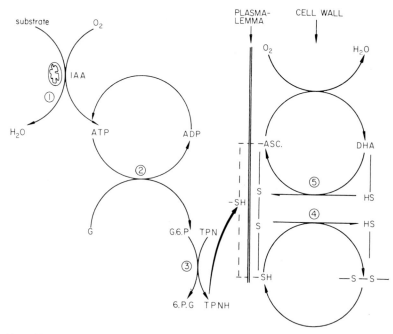

FIG. 103. Hypothetical scheme for wall extension. The possible sequence of metabolic events which may lead to an increase in the reductive cleavage of 'extensin' S–S bridges (see Fig. 102). Stage 1. IAA increases the ATP level, supposedly by acting as a coupling factor for mitochondrial phosphorylation. 2. The increase in ATP level leads to an increase in glucose 6-phosphate. 3. This in its turn increases the substrate available for glucose 6-phosphate dehydrogenase thereby leading to an increase in the level of $NADPH_2$. 4. This leads on to a general increase in the level of reduced sulphydryl compounds, one or more of which may reductively cleave 'extensin' bridges. 5. Ascorbic acid oxidase may complete the control mechanism cycle by generating dehydroascorbic (or monodehydroascorbic) acid which would re-oxidise the SH groups of 'extensin' back to S–S bridges.

Redrawn from Lamport (1965).

The study of plasmodesmata, pit fields and pits is bedevilled by the fact that information from the electron and light microscopes has not yet been reconciled. Plasmodesmata are readily recognizable under the electron microscope and something is known about their formation, structure and distribution (Figs. 104, 105, 106, 108). Because of their width, initially about 20 nm, these structures ought to be invisible in the light microscope. Yet plasmodesmata can be seen under a light microscope. It may be that there are two kinds of plasmodesmata and this could account for the disparity between the counts of plasmodesmata made under the light and electron microscopes (Newcomb, 1963). There seems to be a case for distinguishing the two by nomenclature. Most plasmodesmata seen under the electron microscope appear to be about 25 nm in diameter, at least in the early stages of their development. In one group of specialized cells, the salt-secreting gland of *Tamarix* and probably other salt-secreting species as well, the transfusion area between the collecting cells and the inner secretory cells is crossed by plasmodesmata 80 nm in diameter (Thomson & Liu, 1967). More will be said about these cells and the distribution and role of their plasmodesmata in Chapter 9.

Under the electron microscope thin hollow threads, frequently connected to the ER membrane, run through channels in the cell wall which are lined with plasmalemma (Kollman & Schumacher, 1962; Lopez-Saez, *et al* 1966; Robards, 1968). (Figs. 19, 32, 109.) A few tissues, for example those in culture and endosperms which form walls after a free-nuclear stage, do not, at least in the early stages, seem to have plasmodesmata, and it is interesting that endosperm walls do not seem to be formed by Golgi activity as other walls are (Buttrose, 1963).

Several authors have calculated from electron micrographs the number of plasmodesmata running from cell to cell. Ziegler & Ruck (1967) find between 5,000 and 6,000 per $100\mu m^2$, Heslop-Harrison (1966b) 700, Strugger (1957) between 600 and 700, Juniper 450, and Krull (1960) between 60 and 240. These figures, although somewhat disparate and taken from a variety of tissues, mean that even the smallest meristematic cell of $15\mu m$ cube must be joined to its neighbours by between 1,000 and 100,000 threads.

As cells expand the number of plasmodesmata per unit area of wall must fall if post-cytokinetic formation of plasmodesmata does not take place. Juniper has shown the number of plasmodesmata across the transverse walls of the developing cells of the cap of *Zea* falls from $450/100\mu m^2$ in the meristematic cells to $81/100\mu m^2$ in the peripheral cells (Fig. 106). These figures are consistent with the dilution of the number of plasmodesmata per unit area solely by cell wall expansion and suggest that no secondary formation of plasmodesmata occurs *in this tissue* provided that none are lost. We have found no unequivocal evidence for the secondary formation of whole plasmodesmata of this type, but light microscopists have frequently reported that plasmodesmata are reformed after sliding growth (Livingstone, 1964). They are also said to occur across graft junctions (Hume, 1913) and between the

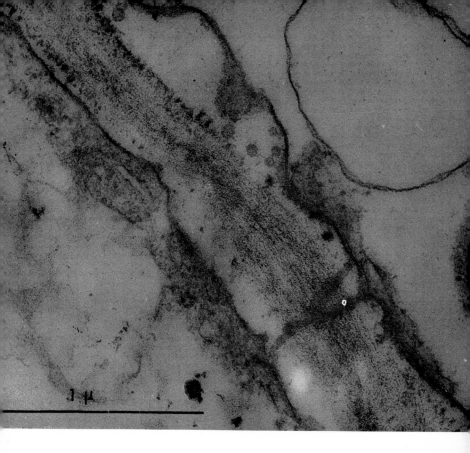

FIG. 104. Electron micrograph of a wall in the secretory zone of a pitcher of *Nepenthes*. Note the branched plasmodesma. (Glut/Os/Pb/U)

cells of parasitic plants and their hosts (Esau, 1948a and b; Bennett, 1944). No plasmodesmata are found across the boundary between the nucellus cells and the megagametophyte of *Zea mays* (Diboll & Larson, 1966) nor across endosperm walls (Buttrose, 1963) nor between sporogenous cells and tapetum.

Secondary penetration of the wall by plasmodesmata is perhaps not the only way in which the dilution of their numbers by extension growth may be circumvented. It is possible that existing plasmodesmata may divide along their length, and Krull (1960) shows a number of electron micrographs of plasmodesmata with multiple branchings which she claims arise from simple plasmodesmata (Fig. 107). This is a possible mechanism for increasing the number of plasmodesmata, but it does not explain why some branched plasmodesmata are branched strictly only on one side, as in the companion cell-sieve tube junction. In the cap cells of *Zea* no such branching has ever been seen. The increase in area

FIG. 105. Electron micrograph of a replica of a frozen and etched plasmalemma from a pea (*Pisum*) root tip. Note the granules on the surface of the plasmalemma and the indentations of a pit field in the centre of the micrograph. A pit field in section can be seen in Fig. 108.

Micrograph by Dr D. H. Northcote.

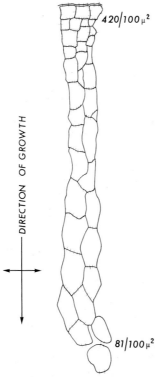

$420/100\,\mu^2$

DIRECTION OF GROWTH

$81/100\,\mu^2$

FIG. 106. The distribution of plasmodesmata in the root cap of *Zea*. The files of cells in the diagram run from the cap junction (top) to the extreme apical tip of the cap (bottom). Plasmodesmata are formed solely at cell divisions in the first two or three cells; divisions take place in all planes, but predominantly transversely. Thereafter the number of plasmodesmata per unit area depends on the extent of growth of the wall. Since growth is predominantly longitudinal the number of plasmodesmata per unit area on the longitudinal walls soon falls to a very low level, whereas significant numbers of plasmodesmata remain across the transverse walls even where the cells loosen from the extreme root tip. The number of plasmodesmata seen in an electron micrograph is indicated by lines across the walls. The figures are the numbers calculated per unit area. (See Figs. 30, 32 and 65.)

of the longitudinal walls of these cells ensures that, although a few plasmodesmata are visible in the longitudinal walls of the meristematic cells, almost none are visible in the longitudinal walls of the mature peripheral cap cells (Fig. 124). This pattern of distribution, if transport of materials occurs through plasmodesmata, would readily allow longitudinal flow, but obstruct, except in the meristematic cells, lateral flow.

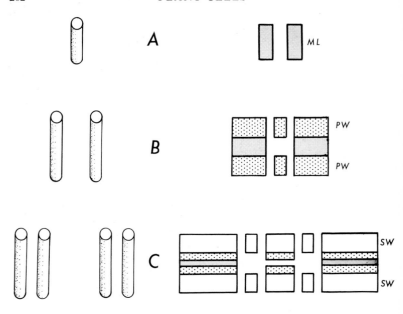

FIG. 107. A possible mechanism for the formation of plasmodesmata. (A) a single plasmodesma traverses the middle lamella (ML). (B) This plasmodesma divides longitudinally as wall extension proceeds and lengthens to compensate for the increasing thickness of the primary wall (PW). 'Mittelknoten' form in the region of the middle lamella between the two plasmodesmata. (C) Further sub-division and extension of the plasmodesmata continue; 'Mittelknoten' now occur both on the site of the middle lamella and part of the primary cell wall.

Redrawn from Krull (1960).

The simple pattern of growth of cells may, on this basis, determine the subsequent transport directions of a tissue. Branched plasmodesmata have been seen by Northcote & Wooding (1966) in the developing sieve elements of *Acer pseudoplatanus*, by Krull (1960) in the parenchyma of *Viscum album*, by Roelofsen (1965) in the phloem parenchyma of *Cucurbita*, by Esau (1963) in the phloem of the root of *Vitis* and by Juniper in the pitchers of *Nepenthes* (Fig. 104).

Most plasmodesmata under the electron microscope are more or less straight tubes, but some of the plasmodesmata in the parenchyma of *Viscum album* have expanded central regions, in the part lying within the primary wall. These are called 'Mittelknoten' by Krull, a term first used by others to describe the swollen central regions of some plasmodesmata under the light microscope.

Perhaps the most bizarre plasmodesmata are those joining companion

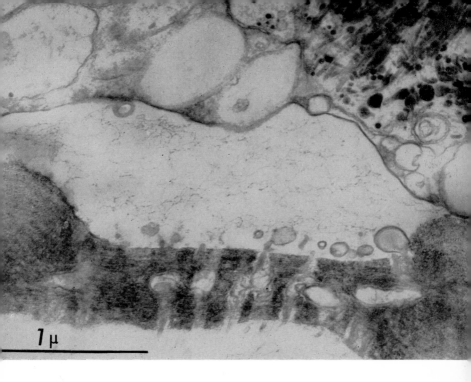

7 μ

Fɪɢ. 108. Electron micrograph of a primary pit field in the wall of a red fruit of *Capsicum annuum*. Threads S appear to pass through the plasmodesmata and deposition of material onto the wall has been severely restricted around the group of plasmodesmata. Under these conditions of fixation the fibrous structure of the cell wall shows up clearly. (Glut/Os/Pb/U)

cells to sieve tubes. These have between eight and twenty-seven individual threads on the companion cell side linking up in the centre of the wall to a single tube which runs to the sieve tube (Fig. 142). There is a suggestion, too, that this plasmodesmatal complex may be encrusted by callose as in sieve plate pores.

Plasmodesmata persist in the cell walls until, as in the cap cells of *Zea* and *Triticum*, the cells reach the periphery of the cap, separation of sister cells takes place and the plasmodesmata are left sticking out into the mucus surrounding the root tip (Fig. 65). An unresolved problem is the fact that some mature cells lack plasmodesmata although they have them in their juvenile stages. In pollen, for example, they disappear at leptotene (Heslop-Harrison, 1964, 1966).

What is the relationship between the plasmodesmata seen by electron microscopists and having diameters of approximately 25 nm, what we could call the 'microplasmodesmata', and the plasmodesmata described by light microscopists which are $0\cdot2\mu$m across, the 'macroplasmodesmata'? There seems to be a tendency for bunches of the plasmodesmata to remain in close continuity, i.e. for wall expansion to be restricted between the members of the bunch and so a bunch could be seen as a unit in the light microscope. Or the threads may fuse to form a larger unit. Such a fusion may have taken place in the expanding cortical cells of the root tip of *Vicia*, in the fruit wall of *Capsicum* shown in Figs. 95 and 108 and in the micrographs of Evert, Murmanis & Sachs (1966). Microplasmodesmata are scattered and not bunched in fungi (Hawker, Gooday & Bracker, 1966). This may explain why they are not seen at all under the light microscope. We should not however overlook some observations made by Frey-Wyssling & Müller (1957). Using macerated cell wall preparations and observing the distribution of the microfibrils of the cell walls of growing stems of *Cucurbita*, they noticed that, although no spaces between the microfibrils are initially present some soon develop. These are between $0·1$ and $0·2\mu$m across and their circumferences are formed by tangentially placed microfibrils. Some of these are subsequently blocked by further deposition of microfibrils. These areas are quite obviously not normal microplasmodesmata. It is interesting that they are very much closer to the size of plasmodesmata seen under the light microscope, but obviously do not develop from or have any connexion with microplasmodesmata. They may not in fact be plasmodesmata at all.

Counts of macroplasmodesmata under the light microscope are very different from those of microplasmodesmata. Livingstone (1935) studying the outer cortex of the stems of *Nicotiana*, found 21–24 threads per 100μm^2 uniformly distributed in the transverse walls and 7–9 threads per 100μm^2 arranged in groups in the side walls. Krull (1960) whose observations we have already quoted states that counts of plasmodesmata under the electron microscope are about ten times greater than those of the same cells under the light microscope. The problem is not yet resolved. It may be caused by diffraction haloes (see p. 220).

We have shown that the number of plasmodesmata per unit area of wall surface varies with the degree of extension that particular area of wall has undergone. What has also recently been discovered is that the structure of plasmodesmata may vary from one wall to another of the same cell (Wark, 1965; and Wark & Chambers, 1965) (Fig. 142). The companion cell of the phloem forms complex multiple plasmodesmatal connexions to the sieve tube, but makes ordinary connexions with the phloem parenchyma on the other sides; the phloem parenchyma makes ordinary plasmodesmatal connexions between sister cells and with the companion cells, but as far as can be seen, no connexions at all with the sieve tubes. Thus the sieve tubes are connected solely to the companion cells, and since as we have seen, the multiple connexions occur only on the companion cell side, some method of plasmodesmatal development other than that postulated by Krull must be responsible for the branching. Companion cells do not grow at different rates from the sieve elements therefore an enhanced growth in area around the plasmodesmata on the companion cell side, coupled with sliding growth to relieve the tension that would be set up seems very unlikely. The sequence of events that precedes the development of the branched plasmodesmata is described in the section on phloem differentiation on page 403.

Primary pit fields

Primary pit fields, to the light microscopist, are regions in which primary cell wall growth in area and in thickness is restricted in the area of a group of plasmodesmata (Fig. 108). The primary wall is continuous across the pit field area, but, because thickening has continued around it but not over it, the area is deeply depressed and, in sections where large numbers of pit fields are present, the wall may present a beaded appearance. This restriction of thickening is well known to the electron microscopist and is a feature of many cell walls, but not those of root cap cells (compare Figs. 32, 51). Since the individual threads of the pit-field are well within the resolution of the light microscope we could speculate that these are aggregations or bunches of plasmodesmata. Primary pit fields, even during the most rapid phase of growth, do not increase in number or significantly in size, although they may become widely separated from one another. Apparently, the microfibrils in the plasmodesmatal region cohere so strongly they do not slip past one another. Thus the pit fields are not islands of synthesis as was once thought, but are in fact islands of quiescence.

Function of plasmodesmata

What function do plasmodesmata and pit fields serve? There is no doubt that the plasmodesmata make frequent connexions with the ER. The sheets of ER often connect the reforming nuclear membrane to the plasmodesmatal threads sometimes before cell division is complete (Fig. 109). It has been claimed that such ER connexions would permit the transport between cells of food material and stimuli. There seems to be little evidence for this convenient hypothesis. If they do transport

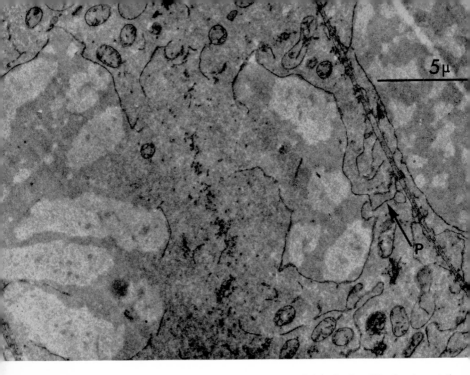

5μ

P

Fig. 109. Electron micrograph of a dividing cell in a barley (*Hordeum*) root tip. At telophase of mitosis the two new nuclear membranes are almost complete. At P a segment of ER links a plasmodesma to the new nuclear membrane. (Mn)

materials, one must assume that they do so selectively since plasmodesmata are seen between cells of different kinds. Tannin-free cells are connected to cells loaded with tannin in the parenchyma cells of *Vitis* phloem (Esau, 1963). Pulling off the root cap of grasses, which breaks the plasmodesmatal connexions across the thick cell wall of the cap junction and replacing it totally prevents the transfer of the stimulus of gravity perceived in the cap (Juniper, Groves, Landau-Schacher & Audus, 1966; Fig. 110). On the other hand cut and replaced root tips can continue to transmit the stimulus (Keeble, Nelson & Snow, 1929).

However, there are no plasmodesmata through the walls dividing the guard cells of the stomata of grasses from their subsidiary cells (Brown & Johnson, 1962), and there must be a considerable traffic in materials across this membrane. But it may well be that so thin a wall, only 100–150 nm in thickness, is no barrier to the transfer of material.

According to Behnke (1965) there is sufficient space in the lumen of a plasmodesma to enable viruses to migrate from one parenchymatous cell to another. This does not, as he admits, prove that viruses migrate through plasmodesmata. Esau, Cronshaw & Hoefert (1967) in an electron microscope study have shown that sugar beet yellow (SBY) virus

can be seen in plasmodesmata connecting sieve elements and parenchyma and in the plasmodesmata connecting parenchyma cells as well
as in the pores of the sieve plates. They believe that they arrive there
passively by mass flow, but they think it possible that the virus infection
may modify the plasmodesmatal structure, since the lining to these
channels does not seem to be visible when the virus particles are actually
inside. SBY virus is 10 nm in diameter and the channel down the
plasmodesma in Fig. 19 is 16–17 nm in diameter. There is thus adequate
room for a virus of this size to pass. Whatever the contribution of
plasmodesmata may be, viruses migrate very slowly from cell to cell and
move rapidly only in xylem or phloem elements.

Kassanis, Tinsley & Quak (1958) found that tobacco mosaic virus
(TMV) moved from cell to cell in tissue cultures in which they found no
plasmodesmata, at about 1 mm per week, approximately the same rate
as it moves through cells of leaf parenchyma. Although this does not
rule out plasmodesmata as a route for TMV transmission, it does
suggest that there are other paths by which they can travel. Singh &
Hildebrandt (1966) have shown that relatively massive TMV inclusion
bodies, in the form of large crystals, several microns long and up to 1μm
wide, can move slowly from cell to cell of *Nicotiana* callus tissue. These
crystalline inclusion bodies are so large that they cannot possibly be
using plasmodesmatal pathways and, moreover, these crystals seem also
to be able to pass through the nuclear membrane.

If the evidence for viral transport via plasmodesmata is limited the
evidence for the exploitation of plasmodesmata in fungal attack is even
less. No use is made of plasmodesmata by the penetrating hyphae in a
number of fungal saprophytes of *Pinus* and *Betula* (Corbett, 1965)
probably because the hyphae are too large. Some hyphae do, however,
use pits to penetrate from cell to cell (Schmid and Liese, 1964). Although we cannot at the moment assign any role to the plasmodesmata
with any confidence, it may be significant that the most complex plasmodesmata, i.e. those with multiple branchings, are found between cells
that are most active metabolically, e.g. phloem sieve tube and companion cells and around the secretory cells of the pitcher of *Nepenthes*.

Ectodesmata

We have seen that some plasmodesmata may, by the removal of sister
cells, reach the margins of tissue and lead outside the plant (Fig. 65).
Where structures similar to plasmodesmata terminate in outer walls of
epidermal cells they are called ectodesmata (Franke, 1961 and 1964a).

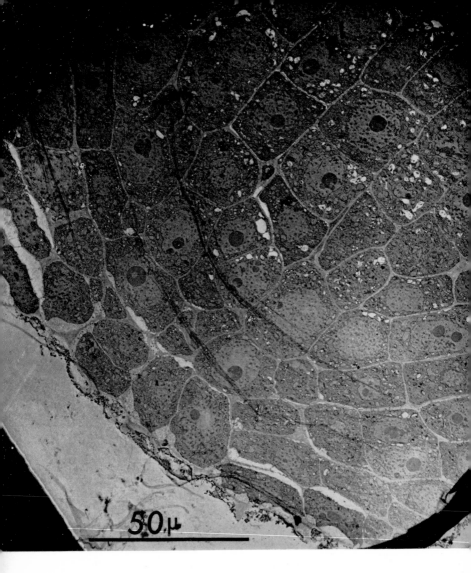

50μ

FIG. 110. Electron micrograph of a decapped *Zea* root tip. The root cap has been pulled away, the breakage occurs through the wall of the cap initial cells (see Figs. 23, 136) and not through the thick wall of the cap junction which remains intact. (LiMnO4)   Micrograph by Dr B. Landau-Schachar.

Unlike the peripheral plasmodesmata of root cap cells, these ecto-desmata do not extend all the way to the outer surface of the leaf, but are apparently always covered by the cuticle. Franke believed at one time that ectodesmata were protoplasmic connexions of a special type. It now appears that they may, in fact, be non-cytoplasmic pores below the cuticle filled with some material having reducing properties and so giving a strong reaction with the fixatives used to demonstrate them (Franke, 1964a and b and 1967). Franke has suggested that the contents may be ascorbic acid. They are probably not protoplasmic structures, but this does not rule out a possible function in the absorption of solutions applied to leaves. The fact that there is a diurnal rhythm in morphology and numbers makes them of interest regardless of their identification and function.

Obviously differing from ectodesmata yet not strictly identical to normal microplasmodesmata are the strands that pass through the exine and intine of developing microspores. In position they are somewhat analogous to ectodesmata, since this pollen wall is somewhat similar to an epidermal cell wall, but they are a good deal smaller than ecto-desmata and very similar in size to microplasmodesmata. They are sometimes seen to branch (see Fig. 15 of Rowley, Mühlethaler and Frey-Wyssling, 1959). As the pollen grain matures, it seems that these strands disappear from the intine (Heslop-Harrison, 1964). Rowley et al. suggest that they are present only during active growth and that the pollen grain becomes more or less autonomous prior to being shed from the anther. Nothing seems to be known of their origin.

5.6 Pits

The transition between primary pit fields and pits is almost as poorly documented as that between plasmodesmata and pit fields. The distin-guishing feature of a pit is that the secondary wall is completely absent in the area of the pit (Fig. 111). Pits are usually formed over pit fields, sometimes more than one to a pit field, but they may also arise over primary wall areas that possessed no pit fields, and conversely some pit fields are subsequently completely covered by secondary wall layers.

Microplasmodesmata can be seen in electron micrograph sections of some angiospermous pits crossing the pit membrane which is basically the middle lamella, proving that at least some pits are derived from sites traversed by microplasmodesmata in the original middle lamella (Machado & Schmid, 1964; Schmid, 1965). In other tissues microplasmo-desmata persist and are never associated with pit fields and pits. They even endure, retaining and presumably elongating their structure as wall thickening proceeds even in such heavily thickened cells as the sclereids of pears (*Pyrus communis*) (Bain, 1961, Plates 4/2 and 5/1).

Pits are often but not always symmetrical (Figs. 111, 114). Sometimes, as in a pit between a vessel and a parenchymatous cell the pit membrane develops an additional layer over the middle lamella on the still living parenchymatous side when the vessel dies. In angiosperms the primary wall forming the pit membrane is normally left without modification, and is not lignified (Bamber, 1961). But in conifers a torus, a thickened central region (Fig. 113) occurs on the pit membrane which is reinforced by radial strands which are formed by the fusing together of extra microfibrils (Fig. 112) (Frey-Wyssling, Bosshard & Mühlethaler, 1956). The torus is thought to be a sandwich of the middle lamella between two equal layers of primary wall thickenings. There is some dispute about whether the torus is lignified or not, because, although it is not stained by the normal lignin dyes, Sachs (1963) showed by selective cleaning of the carbohydrate content of cell walls in *Pinus taeda* that a considerable lignin-like residue remains. It is possible that lignification varies from species to species. Although the middle lamella and primary wall normally contain the highest proportion of lignin, usually lignification requires the presence of a secondary cell wall which never seems to

FIG. 111. Electron micrograph of a pit between cortical cells of the root of pea (*Pisum*). (Glut/Os/P/U)

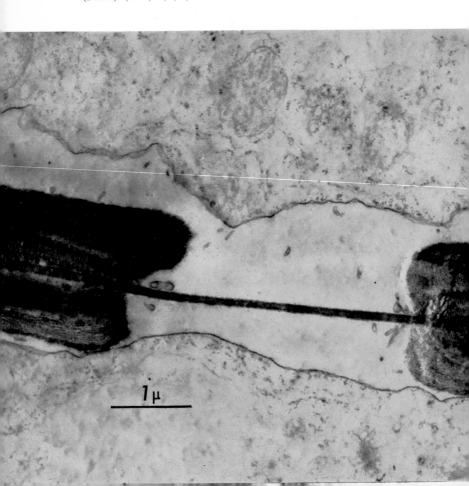

1 μ

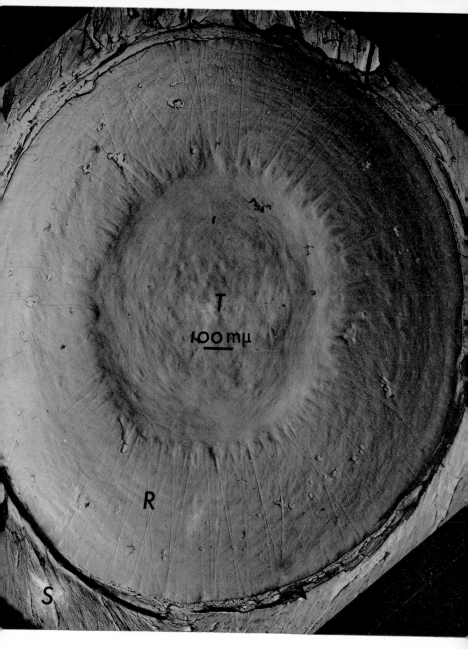

Fig. 112. Electron micrograph of a carbon replica of a spruce (*Picea*) pit. In a pit membrane the primary wall is completely unobscured by secondary wall (S). In gymnosperms a thickened central region of the pit membrane, the torus (T) develops and the membrane is reinforced by radial strands (R) thought to be formed by the fusing together of extra microfibrils.　　　　Micrograph by Dr R. Schmid.

K

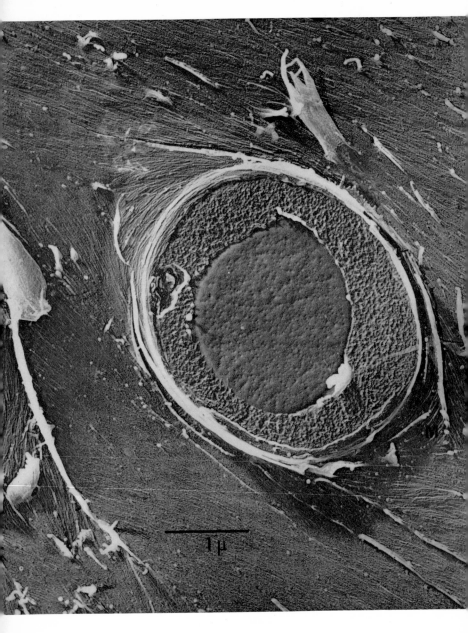

FIG. 113. Electron micrograph of a carbon replica of a Douglas fir (*Pseudotsuga*) pit. Compare the distribution of the microfibrils (M) around the pit with those in Fig. 101B and see also Fig. 1B.

Micrograph by Prof R. D. Preston.

be present in the torus. The pit membrane of angiosperms is probably complete, but the pit membrane of gymnosperms is penetrated by a number of small apertures about $0\cdot3\mu$m in diameter which allow the free passage of colloidal markers from one tracheid to another (Cronshaw, 1960; Frey-Wyssling *et al.*, 1956).

In the pits of the vessels of some dicotyledons, complicated extension of the pit border into ramifying outgrowths giving the pit a sieve-like appearance have been described by Côté & Day (1963) and Schmid (1965) (Fig. 114). These vestures, which are normally symmetrical, but

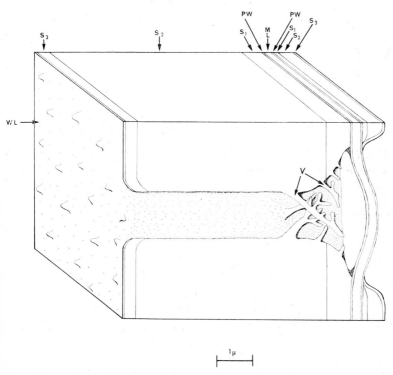

FIG. 114. A bordered pit showing the unequal development of the wall on either side of the pit membrane made up of a middle lamella (ML) and primary wall (PW). The S_1, S_2 and S_3 layers, particularly S_2, are often unequally deposited. This diagram also shows the protuberances of the warty layer (WL) (See Fig. 115) and the vestures (V) which are the protuberant outgrowths of the chamber of the pit.

may be features of only the bordered side of a single bordered pit, appear to be outgrowths of one or more of the layers of the secondary wall— the S_1, the S_2, or S_3 (see page 285) depending on the disposition of these layers at the pit border (Fig. 114). The surface of these vestures is often highly warty and resembles the warty layer over the S_3 of some conifer tracheids (Fig. 115). (Wardrop, Ingle & Davies, 1963.)

In some plants xylem parenchyma cells protrude through the pits into vessels presumably because the pit is a weak area of the wall which gives when pressures differ on the two sides. These protrusions are called tyloses and they may completely block the lumen of a vessel.

5.7   Cytomictic channels

Neither plasmodesmata nor pits normally provide large areas of cytoplasm continuous between one cell and another. Large continuities between non-vacuolate cells are, however, known. They were probably first seen by Gates (1911) who observed them between the microsporocytes of *Oenothera*. Heslop-Harrison (1964 and 1966) and Weiling (1965) have studied these cytomictic channels or plasma canals under the electron microscope and, although there seems to be no direct

FIG. 115. Electron micrograph of the warty layer from a vessel of *Fagus sylvatica*. (See Fig. 120 for its relationship to the other cell layers.)

Micrograph by Prof W. Liese.

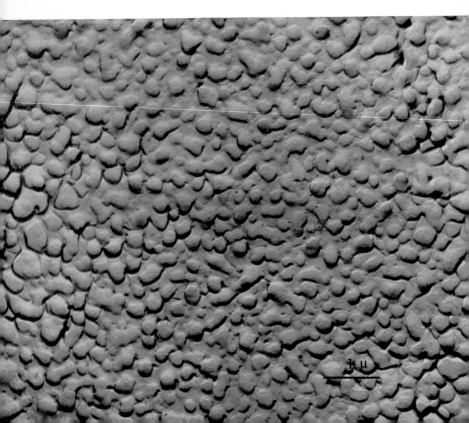

evidence to indicate that they originate from plasmodesmata, Heslop-Harrison does not exclude the possibility. Weiling, however, observed, that the plasma canals are present at the same time as plasmodesmata. One kind of these cytomictic channels is formed during prophase in the normal development of the male archesporium of angiosperms and may comprise almost 25 per cent of the surface area of the interface. There seems little doubt that these intracellular channels, which are up to $1 \cdot 5 \mu m$ across, are not fixation artefacts; but it is possible that the movement of nuclear material through them seen by Gates and confirmed by Heslop-Harrison and Weiling is brought about by damaging neighbouring cells, for archesporial tissue is notoriously susceptible to damage. Whatever the meaning of the apparent transfer of nuclear material, there seems no doubt that these huge cytomictic channels can, during the pre-meiotic period and the prophase of meiosis, provide a means of transfer of materials between the meiocytes, a transfer which is halted abruptly at the close of meiosis by the formation of the apparently impermeable callose wall of the tetrad. Weiling points out that in many ways these canals are more similar to sieve pores than to plasmodesmata and perhaps they should be thought of as analogous to them. Chamberlain (1937) noticed what must be similar continuities around the growing unfertilized egg cells of cycads. Initially the pits between the egg cell and the jacket cells are closed by a thin membrane, the middle lamella, but finally the growing egg cell becomes so turgid that it breaks through, leaving the egg cell in complete continuity with the jacket cells. It looks as if these channels have evolved in relation to the special problems of the nutrition of developing reproductive cells.

Holes in the walls between guard cells are described on page 417.

5.8   Plant surfaces

Where the surfaces of plant cells come into direct contact with the air a number of characteristic changes takes place, the most striking of which is the accumulation of several different substances between the wall and the air, known collectively as the cuticle. All the aerial parts of a plant in contact with the environment possess such a cuticle at least in some form and, from the time that a leaf or other structure is no more than a minute primordium in the apical meristem, it is covered by the rudiments of the cuticular membrane in the form of a very thin, but continuous and pliable layer. Although each of the constituent layers of the cuticle grade into one another, it is convenient to consider them separately. The cellulose cell wall on the outer face of each epidermal cell, usually has very little in the way of secondary thickening in a normal mesophytic leaf. In xerophytic plants there may be some secondary thickening and even some lignification. Outside the cellulose wall, grading both into the cellulose and beyond into the cuticular layer is commonly but not invariably found a layer of pectic material (Fig. 116). This is

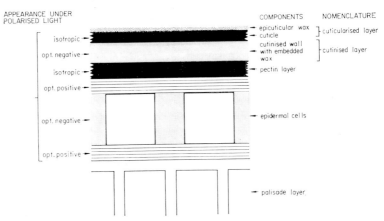

FIG. 116. The components, nomenclature and appearance under polarized light of the cuticle.
By using a selenite plate giving the 1st order red colour of the
Newton scale ▤ is blue and
▥ is orange (or vice versa)
▬ is red like the background.

often continuous with the middle lamella of the anticlinical walls of the epidermal cells. It is difficult at first sight to understand where this often relatively thick layer of pectin comes from. It is improbable that it represents the remains of the middle lamella laid down at the end of the last mitotic division, since the outer surface of the epidermal cells are not formed from a cell plate and have never been part of a wall common to two cells. The development of this pectin layer from the primordial to the mature state has not been followed, so that we do not know for certain whether pectin is deposited before or after the cell stops growing. Either way, addition to this layer must take place through the existing wall. There are examples of massive deposition of pectins in other tissues, both during extension and after growth has ceased. Majumdar & Preston (1941) have shown that alternate layers of cellulose and pectin are laid down, predominantly during extension growth, in the development of the collenchyma cells of *Heracleum*. It is not known where the pectin comes from or what controls the deposition of the alternating layers and a study of the activity of the Golgi bodies and the distribution of the microtubules on the lines of the work done by Wooding & North-cote (1964) would be interesting in this tissue. Deposition of pectic materials in cells which have ceased to grow is reported by Carlquist (1956). Here warts of pectic material intrude into the intercellular spaces of collenchyma cells of some *Compositae*. Their intrusion takes place after the collenchyma cells have attained their mature shape and hence after the walls have ceased to thicken since collenchyma has no secondary walls. The accumulation of materials other than pectins between the cellulose wall and the cuticle is also well established. Oil, sugars and amino acids accumulate in large quantities here in the outermost cells of the stigmas of *Petunia* (Konar & Linskens, 1966a and b) (Fig. 145). This accumulation finally becomes so great as to force the cuticle off in flakes.

There is no difficulty then in understanding how augmentation of this pectin layer could take place. In addition cellulose microfibrils occur outside this pectic layer. The amount of cellulose decreases as the surface is approached and it is embedded in an increasing quantity of cutin waxes.

Figure 116 shows the distribution and the terminology (according to Esau) of the layers of the cuticle. Where the walls themselves are impregnated with cutin, they are said to be cutinized; where the cuticle occurs as a discrete layer, the surface is said to be cuticularized. The cuticle, varying in thickness, covers not only the apical meristem as we have already noted, but also the stomatal cells and the sub-stomatal cavities. It has also been found on the free surfaces of the mesophyll cells and the inner walls of the epidermis where these bound internal air spaces and also in salt glands (see page 423). Thus beyond the pectin layer above the cellulose cell wall there is usually a progressively decreasing amount of cellulose with an increasing concentration of cutin, commonly culminating in a pure layer of cutin on the outer surface. Frequently in the cutinized layer are found deposits of wax. There is some evidence that the wax is orientated either in the form of rodlets or plates since birefringence of the cutinized layer just below the pure cuticle, disappears after long extraction with fat solvents (Meyer, 1938). Moreover the birefringence of the cutinized layer is of opposite sign to that of the cellulose layer and is therefore unlikely to be due to the cellulose of the cutinized layer (Fig. 116). More waxes, in a crystalline form may be found on the surface of the cuticle itself. In spite of considerable work on the extraction of these and the intracuticular waxes it is not known whether they differ from one another chemically. Some of these epicuticular waxes form obvious crystalline patterns, the 'blooms'

1μ

FIG. 117. Electron micrograph of a replica of an apple fruit surface (*Malus sylvestris*). This replica is from the surface of a Cox's Orange Pippin. Unlike the other leaf and fruit surfaces this is greasy and does not possess a waxy bloom. The surface is revealed as covered with rather irregular and flat waxy plates with no very small regular crystalline projections to scatter light from the surface and create the visible bloom. (C/R/Au/Pd)   Micrograph by Dr D. S. Skene.

of many leaf, fruit and seed surfaces and these are important to plants in reducing the wettability of surfaces. Other wax mixtures fail to crystallize and, as in many apple fruit surfaces, form an oily layer above the cuticle (Fig. 117). These also reduce wettability though not so much as a blanket of wax crystals (Fig. 118). Waxes are not the only materials that may be deposited outside the cuticle. Ursolic acid ($C_{29}H_{46}(OH)(COOH)$), proteins, sugars, oils and flavonoids can all be moved to the plant surface through the cuticle of unspecialized cells as well as through specialized organs such as hydathodes, nectaries, glands and stigmas.

The wall shows a progressive change from the relatively hydrophilic layers of cellulose and pectin, through the neutral or slightly hydrophobic cutinized layers to the highly hydrophobic wax layers. There are exceptions to this generalization. The existence of cellulose beyond the pectin layer indicates that cellulose synthesis, in all probability, continues at a distance from the cytoplasm and beyond the pectin layer. It is through these carbohydrate layers that the esters of the cutin, and the paraffins, alcohols, acids and esters of the waxy layers must pass as the cuticle develops. It is interesting to speculate that the plastids of epidermal cells of many species, containing little chlorophyll and therefore not being major sites of photosynthesis, may be involved in cuticle synthesis.

Many suggestions have been put forward to explain the appearance of all the different layers on the leaf surface. At various times pits, ectodesmata and sub-microscopic canals have been suggested as passages of transport for the cutin and waxes. Neither pits nor ectodesmata extend into the cuticular layers, and it is now known that ectodesmata are not cytoplasmic connexions in the usual sense, but regions of reducing power, and therefore would be unlikely to act as a means of outward transport. Submicroscopic canals, which appear to lie under each wax crystal, have been suggested as the means by which the epicuticular wax reaches the leaf's surface (Hall, 1967). Every form of wax projection that has been examined with surface replicas has a pore or pores at its base. Hall has not, however, so far demonstrated that these canals run right through the cuticular layers. Moreover the independent movements of certain wax components on to a surface to form 'blooms' has been demonstrated by Bisson, Vansell and Dye (1940) in blocks of bees' wax in which one cannot imagine organized channels existing. Here one must assume that certain of the more volatile of the wax components are able to move independently on to the surface and to crystallize there in a form very similar to the waxes seen on leaf surfaces. Also there seems to be no reason why the cell wall and the cuticular layers above it, bathed

K*

as they are in water, should not act as a means of separating out organic compounds on a small scale. Even over the very short distance involved, a few microns, these layers would be able to achieve some separation of the mixture of substances that flow up through them. Partial or complete separations could be expressed anatomically as the different layers of cuticularization and cutinization and the patterns of crystallization on the plant's surfaces. The pits observed by Hall below the individual crystals may well be not continuous canals, but just superficial modifications of the cuticle brought about by the deposition of crystals which may modify the environment of the cuticle.

Certain regions of the leaf surface show interesting modifications of this cuticular pattern. For example the waxy layers over the guard cells are commonly either completely absent or very much reduced both in thickness and the degree of crystallinity (Fig. 79). Upper and lower sides of the same leaf may differ not only in the thickness of the cuticle as has been known for a long while, but also in the patterns of crystallization of the epicuticular waxes (Fig. 79). A similar surface development, although using very different chemical constituents, occurs in the development of the pollen grain coat (Fig. 82).

Pollen grain surfaces

The surfaces of pollen grains and some other spores are organized into a remarkable and complicated series of layers, which have been described by an unnecessarily complex terminology. The following subdivisions only will be used. The whole pollen grain wall is called sporoderm and this is divided into an inner part, intine, and an outer part the exine. The intine is composed of carbohydrates, including callose, cellulose and possibly pectin and the exine is composed of the very complex polymer of lipid, lignin and carbohydrate called sporopollenin (see page 217). The inner and outer layers of the exine are joined by systems of hollow funnels and pillars, the complexity of which almost defy description. All the cavities within the layers of the exine appear to be occupied by cytoplasm which is continuous with that of the tapetal cells. As in the cuticle of higher plants the exine comprises several layers having different chemical properties (Larson, 1964).

Where do these extraordinary, complex structures of the exine and intine develop; are they derived from within the pollen grain itself or from the tapetal cells, which act as nurse cells, or both, and what controls the manner of their deposition? The evidence so far available suggests that there may be contributions from both sides of the young micro-

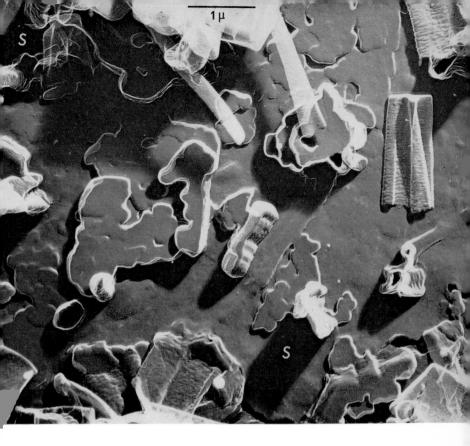

FIG. 118. Electron micrograph of a replica of a cabbage (*Brassica*) leaf surface. This replica was made by depositing simultaneously carbon and platinum onto the adaxial surface of the leaf. The carbon forms the body of the replica and is, as Fig. 5 indicates, capable of replicating re-entrant angles, the platinum forms the shadows (S) and is prevented from crystallizing by the presence of the carbon. The absence of metal crystals raises the resolving power of the replica. (Pt/C/R)

Micrograph by Dr D. E. Bradley.

spore membrane, but the control is almost entirely the responsibility of the pollen grain itself. Several people have shown that, in the early development of the pollen grains of a number of plants, the cytoplasm of the young tapetal cells contains large numbers of densely staining bodies, the so-called Ubisch bodies or 'spheroids' (Rowley, Mühlethaler & Frey-Wyssling, 1959; Heslop-Harrison, 1962). They are often concentrated against the plasmalemma of the tapetal cells and, at a later stage on the outside of their walls (Fig. 119). They resemble the bumps of the sculptured surface of the mature pollen grains, and they respond in the same manner to a number of chemical tests. They are variable in

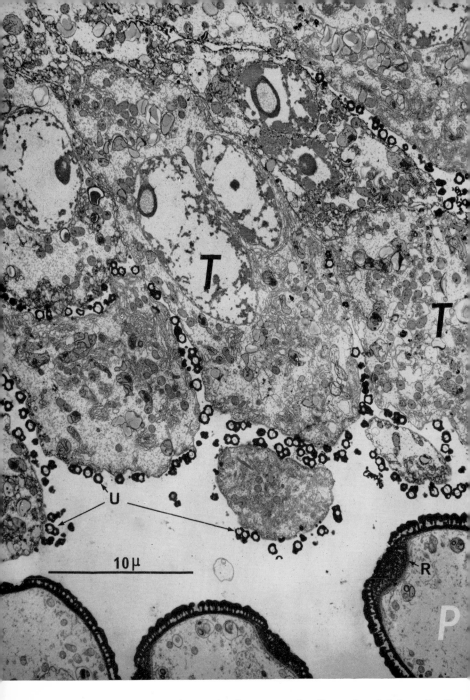

FIG. 119. Electron micrograph of tapetum and pollen grains of *Saintpaulia*. The Ubisch bodies (U) have just been discharged from the tapetal cells (T). Material similar in staining properties to these bodies has already begun to form the exine of the pollen grains (P). Poral regions of the pollen grains (R) where the exine is interrupted (see Fig. 155) are shown. (Glut/Os/Pb/U)

Micrograph by Dr M. C. Ledbetter.

form and characteristic of the species like the exine. They can be seen to grow in the tapetal cells as pollen grain development proceeds.

The Ubisch bodies are associated in the tapetal cells with membrane-bounded organelles which are lost at some stage. In *Cannabis sativa*, according to Heslop-Harrison, they migrate to the plasmalemma of the tapetal cells as a cup, convex surface foremost, whereas in *Silene*, the particles seem to be presented at the plasmalemma in a random orientation. The exine of the pollen grains at a later stage appears to consist partly of Ubisch bodies, but there is no evidence yet to show that it acquires them from the tapetal cells, which break down and are said to supply the pollen with other substances, though this is the most attractive hypothesis. If it is true, it still has to be shown how they migrate to the exine. Heslop-Harrison noticed that exine formation is not markedly affected if the pollen grains are sterile in *Silene*. Even though the protoplast breaks up early on, exine is formed. Heslop-Harrison puts this fact forward as evidence for the role of the tapetum in the formation of exine by its supply of Ubisch bodies.

There is, however, evidence to suggest that part, at least, of the sporoderm formation is under the control of the microspore protoplast. If the exine-forming substrate is located in the somatic cells it looks as though some of the direction of the deposition of this exine is the responsibility of the ER of the microspores. In the pollen of *Silene pendula*, long before the special spore mother cell wall has broken down to release the individual microspores, profiles of the ER begin to align themselves parallel to and very close to the plasmalemma of the young microspore (Heslop-Harrison, 1963a and b). Thus, in these places, a triple membrane separates the pollen protoplasts from the mother cell wall. Heavy deposition of the layers of the exine begins to take place between, but not opposite the regions where the ER lies against the plasmalemma. Thus the ER is opposite what become the thinnest regions of the wall (Fig. 155). The ER seen against the plasmalemma is, at least at some period of time, an extension of the nuclear membrane and thus could be a mechanism of direct nuclear control. There are several reports of stacks of lamellae of unit membrane dimensions, on which sporopollenin accumulates to form part of the exine including the buttressing layers of the germinal apertures (Rowley & Southworth, 1967). These buttressing layers may grow up to 0·3 and 0·4μm in thickness, but they retain the lamellation of the original unit membranes within them until maturity. Unit membranes occur associated with the Ubisch bodies, which may at first lie at a distance from the surface of the microspore in the tapetal cells. Thus sporopollenin formation is asso-

ciated with unit membranes both in Ubisch bodies and in the inner part
of the exine. The subsequent directing of the sporopollenin depends on
the distribution of the ER in the microspore protoplast if Heslop-
Harrison's theories apply.

The intine of the pollen grain apparently contains cellulose throughout and callose and pectins as well if the ruthenium red test is valid. The
intine appears to be both directed into position and formed from within
the pollen grain, but the way in which this is brought about is not yet
known (Larson, 1964).

5.9   Secondary walls

We have considered the components of primary walls, their incorporation and effect on growth and now we must consider the rather different
problem of the formation of secondary and so-called tertiary cell walls.
These are formed after cell expansion has stopped and so what is
deposited stays in the same place until the death of the cell and often
beyond that.

Chemical composition

Pectin is a component only of the younger stages of the primary wall
and the carbohydrate matrix of secondary walls is exclusively hemicellulose.

At some time in the transition from primary wall thickening to
secondary wall thickening the contents of the Golgi vesicles which are
feeding the wall may change from predominantly galactan, galacturonic
acid and arabinan to xylan and galactomannan. Just exactly when or
how this switch takes place is unknown. Moreover, at the same time,
the proportion of cellulose to matrix material continues to rise. It is
generally agreed that, in secondary walls, most if not all increase in
wall thickness takes place by apposition of additional skeletal and
matrix material and not by its intussusception (Fig. 88). The encrusting
substances, lignin, cutin, suberin and waxes, may indeed move into the
cell wall and, some of these are synthesized within the protoplast and
passed through the plasmalemma and the existing wall to be deposited
outside.

Callose, whose structures and properties have already been discussed,
cannot be described as a normal encrusting substance, but will be mentioned in this discussion of secondary wall material because of the frequency with which it is encountered in damaged or senescent tissue.

Structure

The secondary walls, particularly of fibres and tracheids, show both microscopic and sub-microscopic layering. The microscopic layers are commonly known as the S_1 (outer), S_2 (middle) and S_3 (inner) (Fig. 120). The S_3 layer, the last to be formed, is sometimes called the tertiary wall, but this term suggests some fundamental difference in deposition, which is unnecessary and confusing and, following Bailey's example (1957), we shall use the S terminology. The S_3 layer is usually thinner than either the S_1 or S_2 and may be absent altogether.

The S_1 layer normally consists of four submicroscopic lamellae, alternate ones having microfibrils in opposed helices (Fig. 120). The S_2 layer, the middle of the secondary wall consists of numerous lamellae in which the orientation of the microfibrils is at only a small angle to the long axis of the cell. There seems to be a tendency for the microfibrils of this very thick and conspicuous wall layer to be aggregated into macrofibrils or sheaves (Wardrop, 1964). This much lamellated layer is also the site of deposition of a lot of the lignin of the secondary wall. The S_3 layer is always poorly developed in contrast to the S_2 layers and, where present, the orientation of the microfibrils of its few lamellae approaches a slow helix along the length of the cell. The microfibrils of the S_3 are often joined in small bundles and these small bundles cross over one another (Liese, 1963). There is evidence too that the S_3 layer may differ chemically in some way from S_1 and S_2, since it has been shows that the effect of the fungal attack of *Chaetomium globosum* on *Pinus sylvestris* is to destroy the secondary wall except for the S_3 layer which is left intact (Corbett, 1965).

Sometimes the slow spiral microfibrillar structure of the S_3 layer is visible in replicas of untreated surfaces, but sometimes the surface, i.e. the inner surface of the wall, is covered by a thin film (Liese & Ledbetter, 1963). This is non-cellulosic, is easily removed, and shows, in some species, a pattern of large or small lumps, the largest of which are visible in the light microscope (Fig. 115). This warty structure is found in gymnosperms as well as in the dicotyledons and may be the *post-mortem* remnants of the cytoplasm (Wardrop & Davies, 1962) or may be the remains of the trabeculae described by Wark (1965).

5.10   Reaction wood

There are exceptions to the general pattern of microfibrillar deposition in secondary walls described above. One of these is the distortion of

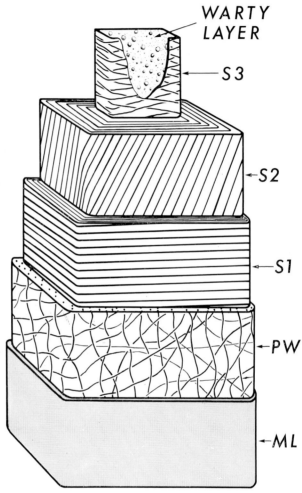

FIG. 120. The layers of the primary and secondary cell. The middle lamella (ML) is the first layer to be deposited and contains no cellulose. On top of this while the wall is still extending is deposited the primary wall, in which the microfibrils are randomly orientated. After extension has ceased the S_1 layer microfibrils are deposited at a large angle to the axis of the cell. There are usually four distinct layers in the S_1. In each successive layer the direction of the helix of deposition is reversed. The greatest thickness of the wall is usually provided by the S_2 layers in which the microfibrils are deposited at a small angle to the cell's axis. There is often a large number of layers in the S_2. In each successive layer the direction of the helix of deposition is also reversed. The S_3 usually makes only a small contribution to the wall's thickness and may sometimes be absent altogether. The microfibrils, as in S_1, are deposited at a large angle to the cell's axis. Just before or at the death of the cell a warty layer, containing no cellulose, is deposited onto the S_3.

microfibrillar deposition which takes place when the tissue is not vertical. The term 'reaction wood' is used for this abnormal wood of horizontal branches, the trunks of leaning trees and occasionally in roots. In such a situation in branches and trunks the upper surface is in tension and the lower in compression and the effects on the fine structure of the secondary wall are often profound. Frequently, but by no means always, a difference is found between the reaction wood of coniferous and angiospermous timber. Höster & Liese (1966) in their comprehensive survey of the distribution of reaction wood found that only 50 per cent of the investigated species exhibit reaction tissue in their stems, 25 per cent in their roots and that the distinction commonly held to exist between conifers and angiosperms can be maintained only in general. In many conifers, as Fig. 121B shows, the pith is nearer the upper side of the branch and the abnormal tissue is on the lower side, i.e. the compression side, whereas in many angiosperms the pith is

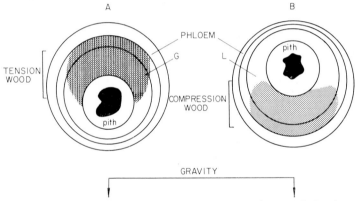

FIG. 121. Reaction wood in transverse section. (A) tension wood showing the acentric pith, the asymmetric development of the phloem and the distribution of the gelatinous layer (G). (B) compression wood showing the acentric pith, the asymmetric development of the phloem and (L) the area of compression wood in which the tracheids have a very much higher proportion of lignin to cellulose than in normal wood.

nearer the lower side and the abnormal wood is the tension side. Compression wood in conifers is readily recognized; it is reddish, the annual growth rings are generally wider than those of the opposite side of the stem and, within the growth ring, there is little distinction between early and late tracheids (White, 1965).

Tracheids of compression wood are shorter than those of normal wood probably as a result of the extra number of anticlinal divisions which take place in the vascular cambium (White, 1965). Preston (1948) has shown that the orientation of the micellar spiral of the S_2 layer, the most prominent layer of the secondary wall, is related to the tracheid length by the equation $\cot \theta = 1 + bL$, where L = tracheid length; θ = micellar angle, i.e. the angle between the pitch of the micelles and the longitudinal axis of the tracheids and a and b are constants. As the average length of normal tracheids increases in successive growth rings, so the micellar angle decreases (or the micellar spiral steepens), but in the short tracheids of the compression wood, the micellar angle is abnormally small and the S_3 layer is generally absent (Wardrop & Dadswell, 1950). Wardrop and Dadswell also found that compression wood tracheids contain more lignin and less cellulose than comparable tracheids from normal wood. From the economic point of view compression wood may be disastrous: it has been known to cause failure in structural timbers. It is heavier and more brittle than the normal wood, due presumably to the different proportion of lignin and cellulose and perhaps to the reduction in length of the tracheid elements. Longitudinal shrinkage is severe.

Tension wood, the reaction wood of many angiosperms, in contrast to compression wood, is found on the upper side of a non-vertical branch (Fig. 121A). Like the gymnosperm reaction wood, it is usually spotted by the presence of eccentrically placed pith, but generally it is more difficult to recognize this phenomenon than in compression wood. Anatomically, tension wood shows a more compact structure than normal wood, the vessels are smaller in size, there is a larger proportion of fibres, but most striking of all is the presence in the fresh wood of the 'gelatinous' inner layer or G layer to many of the fibres. In transverse section, the fibres surrounding the vessels are conspicuously different because the innermost part of the wall is unlignified and appears gelatinous (Wardrop & Dadswell, 1955). Sometimes these gelatinous fibres occur in small patches or wide bands depending on the severity of the strain. Fig. 122 shows the structure of a normal wood fibre and a gelatinous fibre. The G-layer, unlike the S_1–S_3 layers, which may or may not be present outside the G-layer, is composed almost entirely of cellulose and is never lignified. Like compression wood, the presence of tension wood in angiosperms is not appreciated by those concerned with the economic uses of timber. As in compression wood, shrinkage is abnormally high and although it has a high tensile strength, due presumably to the abnormal number of axially orientated cellulose microfibrils, nevertheless its other properties are so different from those of normal wood as to make it undesirable or even dangerous in structural timbers.

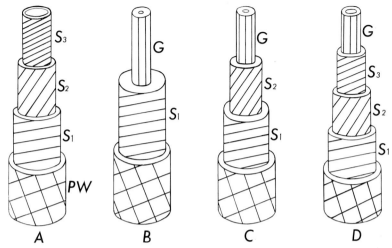

FIG. 122. The orientation of microfibrils in reaction wood. (A) the normal orientation in the primary wall (PW), the S_1, S_2 and S_3 layers. (B–D) the different patterns of disturbance of microfibrillar orientation that can occur in the 'gelatinous' fibres of tension wood. The gelatinous appearance is brought about by the total absence of lignin. Only cellulose is present in which the microfibrils are axially orientated (G). They may replace the S_1 and S_2, the S_2 and S_3 (B), the S_3 only (C) or form an additional layer inside the S_3 (D). Where S layers are present, they are lignified in the usual way.

The impression may have been given that the phenomenon of reaction wood is restricted to the xylem of angiosperms and gymnosperms. However, Liese & Höster (1966) noticed that in the secondary phloem of some gymnosperms an anomalous structure in the wall of some of the fibres was visible. They showed with light and electron microscopy that in the phloem of both roots and branches, the phloem fibres have a gelatinous layer similar to that of the tension wood fibres of angiosperms. However unlike normal asymmetrical reaction wood these gelatinous fibres of the secondary phloem are distributed all around the stems and branches.

Reaction wood is, of course, a product of the re-arrangement of microfibrillar deposition in secondary walls, and so it is worth recalling Setterfield's observations on horizontally grown *Vicia* stems in which microfibrils are deposited axially in the primary walls instead of transversely, in the cells on the upper side (see page 244).

In spite of technological importance of the secondary wall, providing as it does the raw material of wood, paper, board, some textiles and plastics, straw and cork, it must be admitted that almost nothing is known about the way in which the cellulose microfibrils are deposited in this part of the wall. Nor do we know the way in which the deposition of hemicellulose and lignin is coordinated with cellulose deposition. A possible line of attack in investigating this problem would be a study of the conditions, already mentioned, in which the deposition of cellulose microfibrils, both in primary and secondary cell walls, is disturbed, either by reorientating the tissue or by applying certain drugs (Pickett-Heaps, 1966). Tissue cultures may well prove valuable too in studying this coordination.

Another puzzling feature about cellulose is that, in spite of its antiquity, only a few bacteria, fungi and arthropods possess the enzyme, cellulase, in any quantity. It is rarely found in higher plants though it has been implicated in leaf abscission and is absent from the stomachs of herbivorous vertebrates, which depend on symbiotic, cellulose-hydrolysing bacteria.

5.11   Lignification

Less is known about the chemistry of lignin and the process and control of lignification than any other major wall constituent. Lignin may form up to 30 per cent of the wall by weight. It is found in pteridophytes and seed plants, and its emergence in geological time is, in fact, correlated with the development of aerial forms of plant life, as these demand greater strength from their structural tissues. This late development is true of phenyl propanoid derivatives generally including flavonoids, which appear about the same geological time.

X-ray diffraction pictures of wood before and after lignification show very little change. This suggests that little, if any, upset of the crystalline structure of cellulose has taken place (Wardrop & Bland, 1959). However, there is a slight increase in the size of the cellulose micelles, which, according to the above authors, may show that there is an increase in the crystalline phase of the micelles at the expense of the para-crystalline phase that is known to surround it (Fig. 76B). It is therefore suggested that it is possible for the lignin to penetrate into the paracrystalline, but not the fully crystalline phase of the micelles. There is no doubt, however, that lignin can penetrate between the individual microfibrils. An example of this close association occurs in jute (*Corchorus*) fibres where small amounts of lignin prevent the complete mercerization of the cellulose with NaOH. The close association between lignin and cellulose can be demonstrated another way. Lignin from the middle lamella and primary wall cleaned with H_2SO_4 is nearly homogeneous. The proportion of microfibrils to matrix materials in primary wall is low. The lignin from secondary wall, on the other hand, is penetrated by numerous pores 20–30 nm thick; presumably the cellulose microfibrils that previously occupied these pores swelled slightly before dissolution (Wardrop & Bland, 1959).

Lignification is often said to be most common in the middle lamella. This statement needs qualification. In primary xylem, lignification is restricted mainly to the bands of thickening. This is made dramatically clear in figures 149 and 150. It scarcely extends to the primary wall at all. In secondary xylem liquification also occurs in the middle lamella because there is rather more space in the loose-textured, pectin-rich primary wall than in the more dense tissues of the secondary wall or because lignin, which is believed to link covalently with matrix polysaccharides does so more effectively to uronic acid polymers than to the preponderant cellulose of the secondary wall. The distribution of lignin in a cell wall is by no means always symmetrical as is suggested by Ruch & Hengartner (1960). Fortunately lignin reacts strongly with $KMnO_4$ and therefore is readily resolved in the electron microscope. As Fig. 149 shows, in the two adjacent xylem vessels of *Beta* lignification begins in isolated areas. As Fig. 150 shows, at maturity the whole of the spiral thickening is totally lignified, but the primary and secondary wall regions between the bands of thickening remain unlignified. Where a vessel is bordered by a parenchymatous cell, lignification does not extend beyond the middle lamella region on the parenchyma side at least until the total degeneration of the cytoplasm (Wooding & Northcote, 1964). This refers only to primary xylem. In secondary wood, i.e. that produced by the cambium, lignification seems to begin in the cell corners in the primary wall and then to spread rapidly outwards and into the middle lamella. In *Picea abies* up to 90 per cent of the lignin is present in the middle lamella and primary wall and only 10 per cent or so in the secondary wall and, of the middle lamella and primary wall, over 70 per cent can be lignin, with 14 per cent pentosans and only 4 per cent cellulose. A detailed review of the early work on the distribution of lignin in walls is given by Wardrop & Bland (1959).

Where does the lignin come from? Does it or its precursors arise in the meristematic tissue and diffuse centripetally into the differentiating cells, or do they arise in the cells themselves when and where they are needed. The evidence on this point is conflicting. Potential lignin precursors such as coniferin and syringin do occur in the cambial zones. If labelled coniferyl alcohol is fed into the cambial zone, it can be shown to be incorporated into the lignin of the mature wood. However, under these very artificial situations even the normally unlignified cells of the phloem can be made to lignify. We can therefore speculate that lignin precursors can move centripetally from the meristematic cells to potential sites of lignification, but this does not explain the highly localized pattern of lignification that often takes place, for example, the lignification of corners in secondary wood, of small groups of cells the 'stone cells' of pears, and the very limited lignification of the thickening of primary wood vessels and tracheids. We must presume that these areas are already 'programmed' for lignin polymerization whether the precursors are derived from outside or inside the cell to be lignified. Although it is impossible to say how lignin is organized in the cell, or where its precursors are synthesized we can say with some confidence that the Golgi bodies, which have been implicated in almost every other phase of wall building, probably have no part in this at all. Lignification means that phenolic compounds intimately penetrate the non-crystalline and probably to a certain extent the microfibrillar structure of the plant cell wall. As will be seen on pages 295 and 297, phenols in certain situations may act as enzyme inhibitors. Wardrop and Bland have put forward the hypothesis that lignification is not only a means of stiffening and strengthening the wall, but it forms part of a mechanism of controlling growth in the differentiating cell by combining with those constituents of the cell wall whose metabolism is governed by substances such as auxin.

Lignin, at least under certain conditions has, like suberin and cutin, the most surprising resistance to decay. Probably again its high polyphenol content is such an active and polyvalent enzyme inhibitor. Many virulently cellulolytic micro-organisms are unable to destroy wood because of the intimate nature of the association between the lignin polymers and the wood polysaccharides, both cellulosic and non-cellulosic. Lignin apparently acts here as a physical barrier preventing polysaccharide-breaking enzymes of a wide range of organisms from getting at a sufficient number of glycosidic bonds in the polysaccharides to achieve a significant degree of hydrolysis. Thus all wood-destroying micro-organisms must possess enzymes that can destroy lignin as well as the wood polysaccharides, or at least dissociate the lignin from the polysaccharides they attack.

It is a measure of this capacity to resist decay, i.e. enzyme attack by micro-organisms that fossil lignin can be extracted by the same chemical treatments used to extract contemporary lignin and it seems that, under reducing conditions, which are ideal for fossilization, bacterial or fungal attack of lignin is reduced to a minimum so that the lignin is preserved at the expense of the cellulose, hemicellulose and pectin constituents (Barghoorn, 1964).

Because of its abundance (after cellulose, it is the most common plant polymer), lignin is an economic embarrassment. The pulp and paper industries have been conspicuously unsuccessful in finding profitable outlets for the vast quantities of waste lignin derived from paper making.

5.12   Breakdown of cell walls

For the most part, the breakdown of cells and tissues as an integral part of a sequence of differentiation is not so important in plants as it is in animals. Plant cells grow and die and their walls persist in death as structural units. There are, however, a few instances where selective breakdown by changes in the cell walls is extremely important. In some (e.g. pollen mother cells, phloem, zygotes and laticifers) the breakdown of the whole or part of a wall results in the fusion of still living protoplasts. In some (e.g. ripening fruits, epithelial cells of the scutellum, root cap cells and stigmatic surfaces) the breakdown is restricted to certain components of the wall so that cells simply separate from one another, or the cuticle, as in the stigmatic surface, is separated from the wall. In others (e.g. in the eruption of endogenous buds or roots or in the penetration of the haustoria of parasitic plants such as *Cuscuta*) cortical cells must be crushed to allow the new organ to emerge. Very little seems to be known about the way in which these eruptions come about. In the rest, e.g. xylem vessels, the total or partial breakdown of an end wall at the same time as the death of the protoplasm results in the fusion of two or more dead cells.

Breakdown between living cells

The creation of a sieve pore is apparently brought about by the dissolution of the non-cellulose fraction of the cell wall, in this case the middle lamella region around the plasmodesmata (see page 407). The plasmodesmata or perhaps the traces of ER through them, appear to swell in this region, degrading the middle lamella while the callose at the surface of the wall is eroded away at the same time until fully pierced sieve pores are produced (Northcote & Wooding, 1966).

Cytomictic channels between cells that are also very much alive develop during prophase of meiosis in the normal development of pollen of angiosperms (see page 274). It is not clear here whether it is the cellulose, or the non-cellulose fraction of the cell wall which first breaks down, nor for certain whether the site of each cytomictic channel is marked by the prior existence of a plasmodesma. Nevertheless the plasmalemma forms smoothly along the walls of each channel and the impression is given of the controlled penetration of a primary wall very similar to that of sieve pore formation.

Another example of cytoplasmic fusion which is very similar to that observed in phloem cells and pollen mother cells is that occurring between the pairs of guard cells of grasses (Brown & Johnson, 1962). At the ends of the guard cell pair the wall is incomplete and the protoplasts are apparently confluent. These passages are much larger than microplasmodesmata. The early stages of the process do not seem to have been observed and so it may be that the wall is never completed rather than it being broken down afterwards.

The only breakdown of zygote fusion walls which seems to have been studied is in *Phycomyces blakesleeanus* and the ascomycete yeast, *Hansenula wingei* (Sassen, 1964 and 1965). Sassen claims here that not only are the matrix materials destroyed, but also the skeletons. An enzyme capable of breaking down chitin is presumed to occur in both the zygotes and mycelium of these fungi. Why this particular enzyme is inoperative except at syngamy Sassen explains by assuming that it is unmasked by some substance that diffuses from one gametangium to the other, possibly an unmasking protein. It should however be pointed out that the evidence for a chitinous skeleton in *Hansenula* is not complete (see Roelofsen, 1959).

Sassen has also studied the breakdown of the walls of articulated laticifers of higher plants. Breakage here starts at the centre of the transverse wall, the edges of the hole curl back and the breakdown extends towards the periphery. On either side of the transverse wall, where breakdown is taking place, large numbers of electron dense bodies are seen between the plasmalemma and the degenerating wall (Sassen, 1965, Plates 24–27). Sassen suggests that these dense bodies play a part in the breakdown of the wall, but it seems just as likely that they are breakdown products themselves.

The softening of fruits

The rapid physiological softening of fruits, of which pears (*Pyrus communis*), medlars (*Mespilus germanica*), persimmon (*Diospyros kaki*) and tomatoes (*Lycopersicum esculentum*) are some of the best known and most striking examples, is practically a complete mystery. Roelofsen

(1954), after an extensive study of the ripening of *Mespilus germanica*, came to the conclusion that there was no evidence for the presence of any enzyme which could be responsible for the wall degradation. This mystery may be explained by the observation made earlier that enzyme inhibitors can mask the presence of an enzyme. For example, a specific inhibitor of pectinase (probably a polygalacturonase inhibitor, but not yet chemically identified) has been isolated from *Pyrus communis* (Weurman, 1953). More recent work has shown that a polygalacturonase can be detected in *Lycopersicum* and *Persea* fruits, but this can only be detected over a very brief period (McCready, McComb & Jansen, 1955). As McCready and his coworkers point out, all pectin-containing plants may well have enzymes present that can hydrolyse polygalacturonides to their constituent units. But, due to the action of suppressors, these may be detectable only at brief periods of differentiation.

Leaf abscission

This is one of the few cases in which cellulases appear to be concerned in the modification of cell walls. Horton & Osborne (1967) have shown that cellulase activity rises in the abscission zone as a response to senescence of the distal tissue of the leaf of *Phaseolus*.

Other examples of cell separation

A number of other tissues suffer a partial breakdown of the wall, without necessarily bringing about the death of the individual cells. The release of mucus from the root cap cells of *Zea mays* which may aid the passage of the root tip through the soil appears to come about by partial dissolution of the non-crystalline fraction of the walls of the peripheral cells (Juniper & Roberts, 1966). It looks as though the cellulose skeleton in the peripheral cells remains *in situ* (Figs. 65 and 123). The central cap cells may be protected from premature breakdown not by lignin, which chemical tests show is not present, but perhaps by some other inhibitory substance similar to that observed by O'Brien & Thimann (1967) in the middle lamella and primary walls of tracheary elements (Fig. 90). The epithelial cells of the scutellum of barley (*Hordeum sativum*) separate from one another, apparently by the breakdown of the middle lamella, and then grow on independently (Nieuwdorp & Buys, 1964). A secretion which brings about the loosening of the cuticle above the epidermal cells of the stigmas of *Petunia hybrida* has been studied by Konar & Linskens (1966). The secretion comprises fatty acids, amino

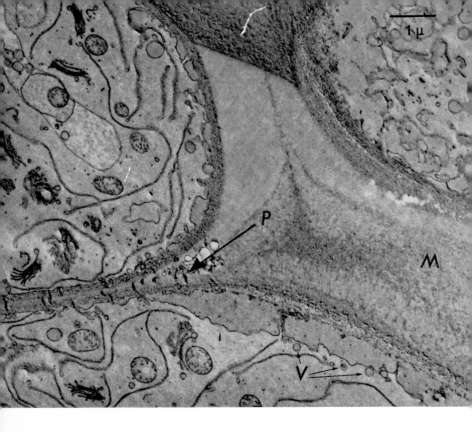

F IG. 123. Electron micrograph of the extreme tip of the root cap of *Zea*. Some of the components of the cell walls are beginning to break down and are being released as mucus (M). Plasmodesmata are being torn apart (P). The cells are still discharging Golgi-derived wall material. A few Golgi vesicles (V) can be seen about to coalesce with the plasmalemma and the material already accumulated between it and the wall. (Glut/Mn)

acids and sugars; it passes in the form of droplets through the epidermal cells and the stigmatic papillae and accumulates between the wall and cuticle (Fig. 145). The cuticle breaks up into flakes and some of the epidermal cells become loose. The principal function of this retsecion, apart from loosening the cuticle and epidermal cells thus facilitating the passage of the pollen tube, seems to act as a liquid cuticle to check transpiration and as a liquid trap to retain pollen grains.

Breakdown between dead cells

In young vessels undergoing secondary thickening those parts of the end wall due to be penetrated are not covered by any secondary deposition (Esau & Hewitt, 1940). The end walls, before they break down, are penetrated by more plasmodesmata per unit area than the side walls. This we should expect from the origin of plasmodesmata discussed on page 226. The organelles in these cells do not appear to be any different in structure or numbers from those of meristematic cells except that the endoplasmic reticulum comes preferentially to lie parallel and close to those walls that are about to break down. It may be that here the ER is behaving, as in phloem cells and pollen grains, as a barrier to the normal movement of Golgi material to the wall (Fig. 155). As the cytoplasmic organelles begin to degenerate, the deposition of secondary material on the longitudinal walls ceases and the vacuole and cytoplasm become indistinguishable. The fragmentary cytoplasm may persist for a while between the thickenings of the longitudinal wall. The transverse walls now begin to swell, but this is probably due to hydrolysis rather than the addition of new material. Gaps appear in the transverse wall, part dissolves and part seems to fall into the developing vessel (Sassen, 1965). Sassen believes that this breakdown affects both the matrix and skeletal materials, but O'Brien & Thimann (1967) believes that this breakdown may involve only the matrix materials (Fig. 153). The persistent cellulose, which forms an insignificant fraction of these transverse walls, may then be swept away rather than succumbing to a cellulase. This leaves us with the problem of why the enzymes that attack the end walls do not attack the side walls. The thickening bands are protected by ilgnification as are the persistent bars of the end walls in those species that have multiple perforations. It may be that other protective substances are also involved—possibly polyphenols which we have noted elsewhere as being able to suppress enzyme activity.

CHAPTER 6

Nuclei

That nuclei are present in all cells was recognized by Robert Brown as long ago as 1831. Some exceptions have since been found notably in the mature red blood cells of mammals and in mature sieve tube elements in higher plants, but, even here, the early stages of both these cells possess nuclei. As with other organelles, the bacteria and blue-green algae are peculiar in having no easily recognizable nuclei with a bounding membrane, but the electron microscope has revealed discrete regions of nucleoplasm with some of the morphological features of ordinary nuclei and breeding experiments have revealed the functional equivalent of chromosomes at any rate in some bacteria. Generally there is a single nucleus in each cell, but exceptions exist here too especially among the algae and fungi where the protoplasmic unit may contain from two to many thousands of nuclei and in some cases it is impossible to think of cells at all. Among animals there are sometimes more nuclei than one, two occasionally in liver cells, a large number more regularly in osteoclasts. Cells with two nuclei occur in plants as a result of certain accidents such as exposure to cold or as a result of certain chemical treatments such as with 8-ethoxy-caffein (Clowes & Stewart, 1967; Howard & Dewey, 1960).

The nucleus has been studied more intensively than any other part of the cell and for many people 'cytology' has come to mean the study of the nucleus and especially of its chromosomes. Study of nuclei started early owing to the lucky chance that nuclei and cytoplasm stain differently. Even in the early days of biology it was realized that the nucleus was the important part of the cell in sexual reproduction because sperm cells could be seen to consist almost entirely of nucleus and yet they seem to contribute as much to the offspring as the very much larger egg cell. As well as this, it was known that cells deprived of their nuclei do not survive for long and so it was assumed that the nucleus exercised control over the life of the cell. The more sophisticated investigations of modern biology have somewhat modified our views on the role of the nucleus, but have not diminished our view of its importance in reproduction and control. So much has been written about the nucleus in relation to genetics that we can give here only a brief summary of the work. The complexities of chromosome behaviour in relation to inheritance are covered in many books (e.g. Darlington, 1958, 1965; Lewis & John, 1963) and are left out of our treatment in favour of some of the modern work on structure and physiology of nuclei. We shall also assume that we need not describe mitosis or meiosis though we give the nomenclature concerning these processes, in so far as it is used here, in the glossary.

6.1 Nuclei in interphase

Nuclei go through cycles in dividing cells. During part of the cycle they exist as discrete organelles with an envelope, but, in preparation for cell division, chemical changes take place in the chromosomes and the envelope disappears allowing the complex movements of the chromosomes to take place free in the protoplasm. These complex movements of mitosis enable halves of each chromosome to go to each of the two daughter cells. The existence of this cycle, called the cell cycle or mitotic cycle, has been known for a long time because the chromosomes are not easily seen except during mitosis, but we now know a great deal more about it and it is the subject of the next chapter. The part of the cycle during which the chromosomes are not easily visible after ordinary staining techniques for the light microscope is called interphase or 'resting phase' to distinguish it from the part of the cycle when the chromosomes are visibly active. Actually, as we shall see, the chromosomes are not at rest during interphase at all and the period is sometimes called the metabolic phase, but, to save confusion, we shall retain interphase as the name for this part of the cycle. In sexually reproducing organisms the diploid germ line cells undergo meiosis, a process more complex than mitosis, in which the homologous chromosomes come together, divide once and separate to four different haploid cells. In animals this takes place in the formation of gametes; in the higher plants, which all have two separate generations, it takes place in the formation of the spores that grow into the haploid, gamete-bearing generation. The meiotic cycle differs from the mitotic cycle even in the interphase part of it, but we shall note some of these differences in Chapter 7.

The interphase nucleus, if spherical, is about 10μm in diameter; larger in some species, smaller in others. In meristematic plant cells it may occupy up to three quarters of the volume of the cell, but usually it is smaller relatively to the cell than this (Fig. 124). There are sometimes quite regular differences in nuclear shape in the tissues of a multi-cellular organism. The elongated dividing cells of the vascular cambium have spindle-shaped nuclei; polymorph leucocytes are named for their differences in nuclear shape; the silk spinning cells of insect larvae have branched nuclei; the cotyledonary storage cells of germinating seeds of *Phaseolus* have nuclei of irregular outline (Öpik, 1965); in the desmid, *Micrasterias*, the nuclear surface appears to be pulled out into strands extending into the cytoplasm (Waddington, 1963); in pollen cells the vegetative nucleus is highly lobed and the generative nucleus is spindle shaped (Larson, 1965). In *Tradescantia* the generative nucleus is pencil-shaped, 3μm in diameter and 80μm long whereas the microspore nucleus is spherical and about 12μm in diameter (Evans & Sparrow, 1961). Even cells whose nuclei appear round under the light microscope often display conspicuous lobes under the electron microscope. It has been suggested that an irregular outline denotes intense activity between nucleus and cytoplasm by increasing the boundary area through which things could pass and there is good evidence that interphase nuclei can alter their shape.

The size of nuclei varies both with the species and with the kind of cell that contains them. Sparrow & Evans (1961) give the following average volumes for root tip nuclei:—

Lilium henryi	$1,100\mu$m^3
Tradescantia paludosa	640
Allium cepa	570
Vicia faba	490
Zea mays	280
Glycine max	150

They believe that there is a correlation between the size of the nuclei and their DNA content and this appears to be true from their data where comparable cells are considered (see page 310). Polyploid nuclei are bigger than diploids. For example Sparrow & Evans give $2,525\mu$m^3 as the nuclear volume of a tetraploid variety of *Lilium longiflorum* and $1,660\mu$m^3 for a diploid variety. Tissue-dependent variations in nuclear size are most conspicuous in reproductive cells. The nuclei of egg

FIG. 124. Electron micrographs of two cells from the root cap of *Zea* showing the difference between a meristematic cell (A) and a fully differentiated cap cell (B) in nucleus/cytoplasm ratio. Note that the nucleus in the differentiated cell is lobed and only the transverse walls are crossed by plasmodesmata. (Glut/Mn)

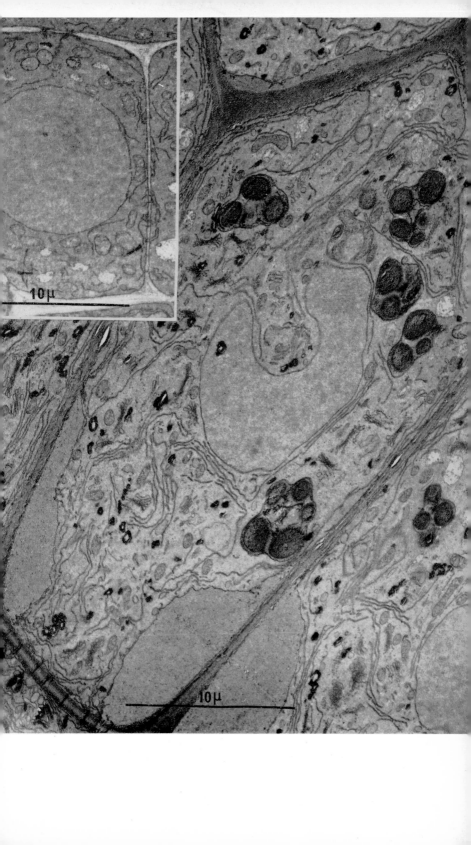

10μ

10μ

cells often increase their volumes many thousand-fold during their development. Nevertheless one generally accepts that nucleus-cytoplasm volume ratios remain constant and it has been suggested that changes in this ratio may be the immediate stimulation for cell division. After a cell is newly formed it usually grows and, in doing so, alters the balance between nuclear and cytoplasmic mass and synthesis and this may lead to chromosome replication and the start of another cycle.

Within a single organ, nuclear volume increases with age of the cells. Thus Lyndon (1963) demonstrated that in root tips of *Pisum* the nuclear volume increases between two and three-fold with distance from the apex, but dry mass does not. DNA content per nucleus increases with age, but this is offset by a decrease in nuclear RNA. The nuclei of some cells also exhibit a circadian rhythm in size and this can give considerable variations in dimensions. The significance of inherent diurnal flux in size is not yet understood.

In living cells all we can see of the nucleus is the envelope, a few blobs and one or more nucleoli. The chief additions to these are the lampbrush chromosomes which may be seen in the oocytes of certain animals and the polytene chromosomes of some insect tissues. The chromosomes of dinoflagellates also remain visible through interphase by staying in a condensed state. If a cell is killed and stained the interior of the nucleus outside the nucleolus can be divided into two regions, the relatively unstained nucleolar sap and the chromatin threads and blobs which is how the chromosomes appear in interphase. Chromatin and chromosomes are so called because of their affinity for basic dyes which is due largely to the phosphoric acid in the DNA that they possess. As the nucleus approaches mitosis the chromatin threads (chromonemata) become the chromosomes which can sometimes already be seen to be double along their length. The blobs are heterochromatic pieces of chromosomes or even whole chromosomes that stain differently (heteropycnotic) from the rest (see page 324). This difference in staining later disappears and reappears. The lampbrush chromosomes and giant polytene chromosomes already mentioned are permanently visible and so the nuclei containing them are considered to be in prophase in the latter and meiotic metaphase in the former. The interesting features of the lampbrush chromosomes are the loops that come from the chromomeres. They vary in size up to 300μm long and are thought to denote metabolic activity in their region of the chromosome. The giant polytene chromosomes which are replicated to over a thousand times the normal width and are about 250 times the normal length of metaphase chromosomes display their chromomeres as bands and these also change in appearance with time denoting activity as puffs or Balbiani rings (see page 316).

6.2   Nuclear envelope

This is a lamellar vesicle made from a pair of unit membranes such as we have described in Chapter 3. Each of the two components can easily be seen to be a triple structure when adequately fixed for the electron microscope, though Koehler (1962) reports that in the yeast, *Saccharomyces*, there appears to be only a single membrane when the culture is starved of nitrogen, but two when growing in logarithmic phase. Evaginations either of both unit membranes or of the outer one alone occur and appear as double or single loops in sections (Peveling, 1961). The nuclear envelope separates the interior from the cytoplasm and presumably controls the medium around the chromosomes. It possesses round pores originally noted by Callan & Tomlin (1950) and which are now known to be holes in both unit membranes where the inner joins the outer. These are seen well in freeze-etched preparations (Figs. 27, 125) and they form a pattern. There are seven to twelve of them per square micron in root tip cells of *Allium* (Branton & Moor, 1964). But the isolated envelopes prepared by Franke (1966) from the same material have 35–65 per square micron. The outer membrane is at many places continuous with pieces of membrane which lie in the cytoplasm—the endoplasmic reticulum (Fig. 33). It is regarded as significant that cells without nuclei are also devoid of ER. The pores have diameters of 20–200 nm, but Branton & Moor's (1964) freeze-etched preparations of *Allium* root tips show that all the pores in an individual nucleus are of about the same size in the range 80–200 nm and so the size may be related to nuclear volume. Their significance is not yet clear. They are not necessarily openings into the nuclear interior and, in tangential sections, sometimes appear to have dense centres (Peveling, 1961). Whaley, Mollenhauer & Leech (1960a) also report that the ground substance in the pores is different from both the cytoplasmic and the nuclear ground substances and therefore they hold that there is no continuity between the cytoplasm and the interior of the nucleus. Waddington (1963) has suggested that the pores in the nuclear envelope of the desmid, *Micrasterias*, are really solid cylinders which become detached to form granules in the cytoplasm. Undoubtedly many substances, such as RNA, pass between the nucleus and the cytoplasm, but how they do this is not known. Some proteins appear not to cross the envelope. Wiener, Spiro & Loewenstein (1965)

L

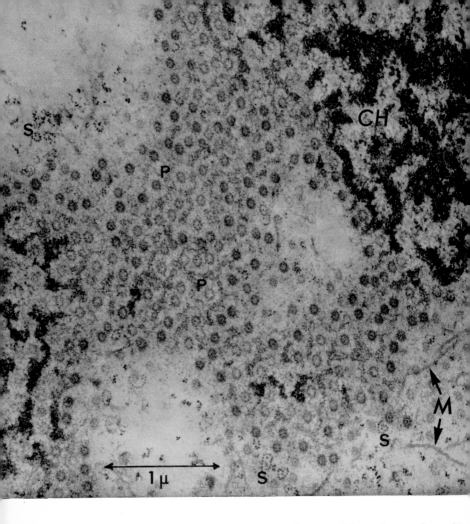

FIG. 125. Section tangential to a nucleus showing part of the nuclear envelope with its pores (P) in a prophase cell of *Haemanthus katherinae* endosperm. Note the microtubules (M) and the polysomes (S) in the cytoplasm around the nucleus and the chromosomes (H). (Glut/Os/Pb/U)   Micrograph by Prof A. Bajer.

consider that the pores in the nuclear envelope in nuclei that are known to be relatively permeable, for example the oocytes of amphibians, are of similar size and structure to those in impermeable nuclei such as occur in gland cells in insect larvae. The total pore area in the latter kind of cell is 25–26 per cent of the area of the envelope and yet they do not seem to allow anything approaching free communication with the outside. Yasuzumi & Tsubo (1966) have shown that in some mouse brain cells ATP-ase may be confined to the nuclear envelope especially its pores. They consider therefore that the nuclear pores are not only concerned with high permeability but also with energy supply to the nucleus by the conversion of ATP to ADP.

The annulus of the pores appears to consist of globular units with a centre-to-centre spacing of 30 nm and of 6–15 nm diameter (Franke, 1966). Markham's rotation method of image intensification (Chapter 1) gives eight as the usual number of these globules. In the centre of the pore there are also one, two or three granules (or possibly tubules, Fig. 125), (Yoo & Bailey, 1967). Sonic vibration disrupts the nuclear membrane, but leaves the pores substantially intact suggesting that these are structural entities and not merely holes in the envelope. The problem of nuclear pores becomes important when we discuss the synthesis of RNA and the construction of ribosomes (page 344), for it would suit several hypotheses if it could be shown that whole ribosomes pass from the nucleus into the cytoplasm. Some measure of support for this view comes from Bach & Johnson's (1966) work on HeLa cells (see page 115).

As well as the round pores, there have been several reports of larger discontinuities in the nuclear envelope (Whaley, Mollenhauer & Leech, 1960b; Esau, 1963), but the significance of these is not known at all. It may be that the pores enlarge after the cell is injured and, certainly, injury to the envelope usually seems to lead to the collapse of the nucleus.

Another means of communication between the nucleus and cytoplasm is through the ER. We have already said that the nuclear envelope and ER are continuous so that there may be a free passage from the 10–30 nm space between the unit membranes of the nucleus (the perinuclear space) and the enchylema of the ER. Moreover there is some evidence to show that the nuclear envelope actually produces ER during interphase and also, at prophase, it may form stores of it by folding to produce the lamellar stacks that are sometimes seen. It may be composed of ER when it is formed at the end of mitosis or meiosis and some ER is trapped within the nucleus when the envelope is formed. At one time it may have been thought that the nucleus gave its commands to the cytoplasm through the ribosomes borne on the ER peeling off the nuclear envelope. But now the intermediate carrier of the nuclear commands is widely believed to be a messenger-RNA rather than the ribosomal RNA and we have to look for another explanation of why the ribosomes carry RNA at all.

Breakdown and re-formation of nuclear membrane

Mitochondria become closely associated with the envelope in prophase of meiosis in animals and cluster round regions of degenerating membrane with their own membranes apparently fused to it (Barer, Joseph & Meek, 1960). No such intimate association of the mitochondria with the nuclear membrane at prophase has been seen in plants. At the end of prophase the nuclear membrane breaks down. It fragments into flattened cisternae of variable size and into roundish membrane-bounded vesicles (Lafontaine & Chouinard, 1963). It is not clear whether all the pieces of broken nuclear membrane break down further into vesicles or whether some remain as cisternae. Even though the nuclear membrane differs from the ER in having no ribosomes attached to its surface, these fragments of membrane are nevertheless difficult to distinguish from isolated cisternae of the ER in the congested and disturbed cytoplasm of a dividing cell. At the end of mitosis the two new nuclear envelopes begin to form around the poles of the telophase figure (Fig. 87). The re-forming envelope consists of membrane-bounded vesicles and flattened cisternae of varying lengths which fuse together. It is not at all clear whether these cisternae and vesicles are from the original nuclear membrane that persists through the whole of mitosis, or whether they are pieces formed *de novo* or whether they are pieces of the ER of the mother cell. It is not unreasonable to assume that they are derived from the original membrane and have been thrust to the poles by the repulsion of the two daughter sets of chromosomes. This re-formation of the nuclear membranes both at the poles of the telophase figure and later around the lagging ends of the telophase chromosomes always occurs near the surface of the chromosomes (Fig. 87). As the telophase chromosomes begin to withdraw into a compact body it seems that this action brings together the isolated areas of nuclear membrane and allows them to fuse into a single unit.

6.3   Nuclear fusion

The electron microscope has elucidated the process of nuclear fusion, which, in higher plants, usually occurs only in the formation of the zygote, in the fusion of the two polar nuclei in the embryo sac and in the fusion of the resulting diploid nucleus with a male nucleus to form the triploid endosperm. In *Gossypium*, according to Jensen (1964), the two nuclei approach but do not touch at first. Elements of endoplasmic reticulum attached to the envelopes of the two nuclei fuse together at several places across the intervening cytoplasm. These elements shorten and first the outer unit membranes and then the inner unit membranes of the envelope fuse. This process forms bridges in between which there is cytoplasm with various organelles. The nuclear bridges enlarge and push the cytoplasm out of the way as they do so, leaving no organelles entrapped. Fusion of the polar nuclei takes 36 hours in *Gossypium*. In some organisms, however, fusions of this kind do not occur in fertilization. The gametic nuclei remain unjoined until the first mitosis and then the chromosomes line up on a common mitotic spindle. Occasionally, as in the tetraploid species, *Rudbeckia speciosa*, the male nucleus never fuses with the female, but it does divide to produce a chimerical embryo. The endosperm nucleus, on the other hand, requires fusion before it will develop further (Battaglia, 1947).

6.4   Nuclear material

The ground substance of the nucleus appears granular under the electron microscope like the ground substance of the cytoplasm, but it has a different electron density. The chromosomes within the interphase nucleus are denser than the ground substance and resemble, in both thickness and density, the chromosomes in mitosis (Fig. 87). In this they appear to differ from chromosomes in preparations stained for light microscopy which are difficult to see well until the onset of the prophase.

DNA

That nuclei contain DNA and that this is the stuff of which genes are made will be known to anyone with any interest at all in biology. The proportion of the nucleus that is DNA varies a lot. For example, in fish sperm 60 per cent of the nucleus is DNA; in calf liver only 16 per cent is DNA and in many eggs only a minute fraction of the nucleus consists of DNA. Nuclei that have a relatively small amount of DNA are poorly stained by the Feulgen procedure or not stained at all. The DNA fraction is low in cells such as eggs because nuclei need to transmit other substances to the next generation. In other cells the DNA content is low because this is a constant feature of all the cells of the particular organism. In somatic cells, typical analyses of nuclei give 80 per cent of dry weight as protein, 10 per cent as DNA,

3 per cent as lipid and 2–3 per cent as RNA. There is a kind of protein that is nearly always associated with the DNA of the chromosomes. This is called histone and generally the amounts of both histone and DNA per nucleus are constant for a species whereas non-histone proteins and the RNA are variable. This last is generally true of all tissues of the body, even sperm cells and eggs, for the differences in the proportions of nuclei occupied by DNA are due to the huge variations in substances other than DNA and histone. Where there are differences in amounts of DNA per nucleus within a species, this is due to two processes. In meristematic cells the DNA and histone have to double their mass in preparation for mitosis and so some nuclei contain twice as much DNA as others. For DNA, this mass doubling occurs during a specific part of interphase, but, although this is so, the period over which it occurs is often about half the mitotic cycle and so intermediate amounts of DNA may be found between the normal level and twice this value. The relative amounts of DNA per nucleus are expressed as 'C values'. A haploid gamete of any species is said to have the 1C amount of DNA. A normal diploid cell prior to DNA synthesis has the 2C amount and a diploid cell after DNA synthesis, just before the next mitosis has the 4C amount of DNA. The second reason for a somatic nucleus having other than the standard 2C amount of DNA is that DNA synthesis does not always stop after mitosis has ceased to occur. Polyploid and polytene nuclei are formed in this way by the processes of endopolyploidy or endoreduplication (page 320). Polyploid cells are very common in plants. Sometimes nearly all the cells away from the meristems become polyploid; sometimes only cells of a particular tissue become polyploid. The best known examples of polytene nuclei are those of the salivary glands of dipteran insects whose chromosomes become so large that they can be used for locating genes if the genetics of the species is known well enough. Polyteny occurs in some plants in the embryo sac—the synergids and antipodal nuclei, in endosperm and in the suspensor cells of embryos. The degree of chromosome replication is not so high as in dipteran cells. Stange (1965) reviews the occurrence of these giant chromosomes and the maximum duplication she reports is $4,096n$ in the suspensor of *Phaseolus* compared with up to $16,000n$ in Diptera. The plant chromosomes lengthen up to only seventeen times compared with a hundred-fold increase in Diptera and the banding is never so distinct. Special kinds of multiple chromosomes occur in some plants and often the polytene unit appears much more like a loose bundle of chromosomes. In *Dicentra*'s antipodal cells, for example, there are

bundles of about eight units held together near the centre but splayed out at the ends. But the repetition of the units makes their structure clearer by the formation of bands even where they are splayed out (Hasitschka-Jenschke, 1959). The control of DNA levels plays an important morphogenetic role in multicellular plants and animals and will be discussed further in Chapters 7 and 8.

The DNA of nuclei is very stable. The turnover is negligible in non-dividing cells and this is why the use of isotopes to label nuclei has been so successful. Isotopes incorporated into DNA are lost at a very low rate even from meristematic cells and thymidine, which is the DNA precursor used most frequently nowadays, is incorporated into nuclear DNA only prior to mitosis, endopolyploidy or endoreduplication. Some doubt has, however, been cast on the fate of thymidine in certain cells. Pelc & La Cour (1959) reported intensive incorporation of tritiated thymidine in non-meristematic cells of *Vicia* root tips that are thought to be preparing neither for polyploidy nor polyteny. They suggested that this may indicate that some metabolic exchange takes place or, less likely, that there can be enrichment of the DNA with thymidine. Other evidence for the existence of metabolically labile DNA has been found in cells that are differentiating, but not in cells that are meristematic. Sampson & Davies (1966) showed that maturing cells of the root of *Vicia* incorporate tritiated thymidine to a greater extent than mitotic cells and that they lose the label during a chase except for a few cells which are assumed to be polyploid. A chase does not remove label from cells in the meristem. Another example of a metabolically active DNA coming to light is that of *Hordeum* roots whose cell division has been inhibited by cationic aluminium (Sampson, Clarkson & Davies, 1965). Here DNA synthesis continues even after cell division has stopped and the DNA synthesized is of unusual base composition, is metabolically labile and part of it exists as a hybrid with the DNA of high molecular weight, which is thought to be the genetic DNA. The assumption of most workers, though, is still that incorporation of thymidine is a true indication of net DNA synthesis and that exchange may safely be neglected in meristematic cells and perhaps even elsewhere.

The amount of DNA per nucleus varies considerably with the species. Table 7 gives some figures for plants and microorganisms. For comparison, human diploid cells have 7·3 pg. All or most of the nuclear DNA resides in the chromosomes and, in the flowering plant species in Table 7 the average amount per chromosome varies from 5·0 pg in *Tradescantia* with twelve chromosomes to 0·16 pg in *Glycine* with forty chromosomes. Sparrow & Evans (1961) regard the DNA

TABLE 7
Amount of DNA per nucleus ($\mu\mu g$)

Trillium erectum	120	(Bonner 1965)
Lilium henryi	100	(Sparrow and Evans, 1961)
Tradescantia paludosa	59	(Sparrow and Evans, 1961)
Tradescantia paludosa	52	(Bonner, 1965)
Allium cepa	40	(Bonner, 1965)
Allium cepa	54	(Sparrow and Evans, 1961)
Vicia faba	38	(Sparrow and Evans, 1961)
Vicia faba	18	(Bonner, 1965)
Pisum sativum	10	(Bonner, 1965)
Zea mays (diploid)	5	(Bonner, 1965)
Glycine max	6	(Sparrow and Evans, 1961)
Neurospora (haploid)	0·04	(Bonner, 1965)
Yeast (naploid)	0·02	(Bonner, 1965)
Escherichia coli	0·005	(Bonner, 1965)

content per nucleus and per chromosome as being related to the sensitivity of the species to ionizing radiations. The more DNA the more radiosensitive the organism is. We do not understand yet why there should be such wide variations; why there should be so much in the monocotyledons for example.

Some determinations show that the amount of DNA can be reduced by as much as 20 per cent by subjecting the plant to cold, but it may be that the cold merely changes the state of the DNA rather than its real mass.

Chromatin, the material of the chromosomes, as prepared by biochemists from embryos of *Pisum* has a DNA content of 36·5 per cent; histone, 37·5 per cent; RNA, 9·6 per cent; and non-histone protein, 10·4 per cent (Bonner, 1965).

At one time it was thought that all the DNA resided in the nucleus, but as we have shown in Chapter 4, we now know that both plastids and mitochondria also contain DNA though the total amount in the cytoplasm is usually small compared with that in the nucleus. The best known Feulgen-positive organelle is the kinetoplast of trypanosomes. this has a DNA-containing region and a mitochondrial region and divides at the same time as the nucleus. In plants, DNA derived from nurse cells is also found in the cytoplasm especially of reproductive cells as in stamens, but these are exceptional and Moss & Heslop-Harrison (1967) have found, for example, that more DNA is released by the tapetum (the nurse cells in stamens) than should be needed for the developing spores. Plastids have around 10^{-16}g of DNA each (*Acetabularia* and *Euglena*) and mitochondria have less than plastids. Nevertheless in a few kinds of cells, especially in the algae, the cytoplasmic label equals or even exceeds the nuclear label when tritiated thymidine has been supplied. Chayen, however, believes that, even in ordinary cells where the normal techniques of cytochemistry and labelling demonstrate a vast preponderance of DNA in the nucleus, the DNA is really in the cytoplasm in living cells and only appears in the nucleus on special occasions or after injury (Chayen, 1960; Chayen & Denby, 1960). He believes that it is injury in normal procedures that produces the normal cytochemical picture of DNA concentrated in the nucleus and that his methods produce more life-like images. Few people accept Chayen's theory and a possible reason for the discrepancy between his results and others is that he uses pectinase to separate his cells before examination. This may produce artefacts more serious than normal techniques do though we do not know why it should do so.

The usual test for DNA cytologically is the Feulgen reaction. In this, Schiff's reagent (N sulphinic acid of p-fuchsinleucosulphonic acid), which is colourless, combines with the aldehyde groups provided by the splitting of the purine-sugar bonds by mild hydrolysis of the cells to form a magenta colour by restoring the quinoid group of the basic fuchsin from which the Schiff's reagent is made. The mild hydrolysis with N/1 hydrochloric acid also removes most of the RNA. It has never been explained why some nuclei are Feulgen-negative or why, for example, nucleoli, if they contain 17 per cent of the nuclear DNA as McLeish (1964) claims, are Feulgen-negative. These difficulties leave us with some doubts about the results obtained with microdensitometers which use the Feulgen reaction to compare DNA content in different nuclei, but nevertheless most cytologists accept such results as sufficiently reliable.

Proteins

The proteins of the nucleus, which constitute the bulk of the dry weight, fall into two groups. Those that are attached by salt-like linkages to the DNA are basic and simple and, of these the simplest, which occur in fish sperm, are called protamines while those of somatic and other cells are called histones. These constitute about 10 per cent of the nuclear dry matter. The other group of proteins is usually referred to as a non-histone protein and constitutes the bulk of the nuclear dry matter and about 70 per cent of the nuclear protein. The non-histone protein con-stitutes the whole of the nuclear sap protein, but only about half of the chromosomal protein. It includes ribosomal protein. The histones have become important recently because of the view that they control the

L*

expression of the genes. It has become clear that different kinds of cells within one organism carry the same genes and so differentiation must be due to differences in carrying out the genetic instructions. An attractive hypothesis is that differentiation is caused by a system that masks some of the genes in some situations or at some times of development. This masking role has been suggested for the histones and will be referred to later (page 387). Other roles that have been suggested for histones are a structural one in organizing the chromatin and one affecting the stability of the cell membranes. Hancock & Ryser (1967), for example, think there is evidence to implicate histones, which are dispersed at mitosis and not conserved as DNA is, in the breakdown of the nuclear envelope at prophase.

The histones are proteins of molecular weight about 12,000 with a high content of basic amino acids (Bonner, 1965). About one in every four of the amino acids is arginine or lysine. The cationic groups of the histone bind to the anionic phosphate residues of the DNA, forming 'nucleohistone'. There are several histones with different amino acids complements in the chromatin of each species and they are not so inert as DNA is: there is a slow turnover of histones in the cell. The protamines, which are known chemically mostly from fish sperm have a molecular weight of about 2,000 and are especially rich in arginine. In sperm cells generally, the nucleus consists largely of protamines or histones combined with DNA. There is comparatively little non-histone protein presumably because the sperm is metabolically inactive. In other nuclei, enzymes are active especially in nucleic acid metabolism, DNA-polymerase synthesizing DNA, RNA-polymerase synthesizing RNA. There are other enzymes too playing a part in nucleic acid metabolism and a few concerned with energy requirements though the important respiratory enzymes, such as cytochrome oxidase and succinic dehydrogenase, are absent.

Several electron microscopists have noticed that there is sometimes a close association between mitochondria and the nuclear membrane and have assumed that this occurs for the easy transfer of ATP to the nucleus. In the root of *Chlorophytum*, Mota (1963), for example, found invaginations of the nuclear membrane containing mitochondria in them though outside the nuclear envelope.

6.5 Nucleolus

Nucleoli are still something of a mystery. They are comparatively large organelles and nobody knows for certain what they do. Somatic cells normally have one in each nucleus for each set of chromosomes. This is because they usually form or coalesce at a definite region, called the nucleolar organizer, of one particular chromosome in the haploid set. They can coalesce and therefore a diploid cell, which could have two nucleoli per nucleus often has only a single one. In the root tips of *Vicia faba* for example, most nuclei have a single nucleolus of 6μm diameter, but a few nuclei have two smaller nucleoli which sometimes stick to one another without fusing. In *Zea* there is only one per cell even if the nucleus has many chromosomes bearing a nucleolar organizer (Mirsky & Osawa, 1961). Some animal oocytes are exceptional in having many nucleoli; some animals (e.g. *Cricotopus*) have none. In some organisms lacking organizers and centromeres, the number of nucleoli formed varies with the tissue (Darlington, 1947). The synergids of the embryo sac of *Gossypium* have one or more micronucleoli about one tenth of the size of the single nucleolus (Jensen, 1965).

Nucleoli are present normally only at interphase. They disappear at late prophase by the time the nuclear envelope goes and reappear at telophase. But in panicoid grasses all the root tips contain a proportion of cells with nucleoli persistent into metaphase or later (Brown & Emery, 1957). When persistent, they are not incorporated into the daughter nuclei after telophase. At telophase the new nucleoli are formed in contact with each nucleolar organizer. The new material used appears to come from the resumption of synthesis by the chromosomes, from fibrils and granules arranged in threads in the spaces between the chromosomes (Lafontaine & Chouinard, 1963). The role of the nucleolar organizer in assembling the nucleoli is still not clear. In most plants and animals the organelles are associated with a particular chromosome at a particular region. The chromatin at this region can lie around the nucleolus as in mammals or in the centre of the nucleolus as in chironomids. But in irradiated cells micronuclei, which are formed from pieces of chromosomes left out of the daughter nuclei at telophase, occasionally have a nucleolus even when it is known that both nucleolar organizers lie within the main nucleus (Mirsky & Osawa, 1961). Normally a nucleolus is formed in a micronucleus only when a nucleolar organizer occurs in the micronucleus. After treatment with maleic hydrazide both the main nucleus and the micronuclei also produce nucleolus-like bodies even when a nucleolar organizer is lacking (Scott & Evans, 1964).

There is no membrane around the nucleolus although the organelle appears so well defined under the light microscope. Some cytologists have remarked on a perinucleolar halo free of chromosomes, but others have failed to find this (Lafontaine & Chouinard, 1963). Some methods of preparation show the nucleolus to be homogeneous, but specialized techniques (e.g. silver impregnation or Feulgen, methylene blue and an orange filter or detergents) can separate two parts which, under the electron microscope, show different constructions. In *Vicia faba* one part, called the nucleolonema, appears filamentous inside with closely packed convoluted fibres and 15 nm granules of irregular shape. The other part, the *pars amorpha*, also contains tightly packed convoluted fibrils of 6-10 nm diameter, but without the granules (Chouinard, 1966). Both fibrils and granules contain RNA. There are also vacuole-like structures of two types. The nucleolonema contains largish vacuoles with loosely scattered fibrils and 15 nm granules. The *pars amorpha* contains small vacuoles of fibrillar material only. At the onset of mitosis these vacuole-like structures disappear and the nucleolus acquires an irregular outline with projections extending between the chromosomes. The fibrils and granules seen under the electron microscope disperse throughout the nucleus and, after the nuclear membrane has gone, they mix with similar structures in the spindle that forms them.

In several other plants La Cour (1966) has shown that the detergent, 'Tween 80', reveals nucleolonemata even in unfixed cells under the phase microscope. In some of his nucleoli the nucleolonemata are long filaments in skeins filling the whole of the organelle. In triploid endosperm cells, three or six nucleolonemal threads occur in each nucleus: in diploid cells, two or four occur. This and other observations make La Cour suggest that the nucleolonemata are not simple filaments, but are loops coming from the nucleolar chromosomes. This view supports the belief that the nucleolus is a manifestation of gene activity like lampbrush chromosome loops or puffs on polytene chromosomes.

There is a mutant of the toad, *Xenopus*, which when homozygous, has no nucleoli and which does not synthesize ribosomes. It also does not have the 15-30 nm granules normally found in the nucleoli of these animals (Jones, 1956). Instead of nucleoli the homozygous mutants have two or more masses of fine granular material with 4-10 nm fibrils resembling the central part of normal nucleoli. It looks as if the nucleolar particles share the same synthetic path as the ribosomes although they are smaller than ordinary ribosomes. This supposition becomes important to us when we come to think about the function of the nucleolus (see page 343). Bernhard (see Perry, 1966) using high resolution autoradiography has shown that incorporation into RNA occurs first into the fibrillar and later into the granular components.

Most nucleoli are Feulgen-negative and do not incorporate measurable amounts of thymidine as seen under the light microscope (Fig. 126).

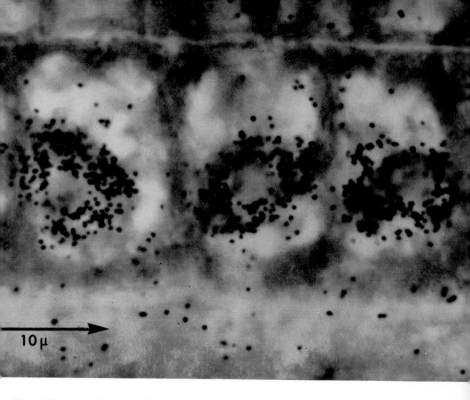

10 μ

FIG. 126. Autoradiograph of 6μ section of root tip of *Sinapis alba* (same root as in Fig. 137) fed with tritiated thymidine for 48 hours and showing three cells with silver grains over the chromatin but not over the nucleolus.

In some species they are stained by the Feulgen procedure. More sophisticated techniques however show chromatin-like regions inside the nucleolus and separate from the chromatin of the nucleolar organizer and the use of DNA-ase indicates that these do contain DNA. Moreover McLeish (1964) has shown that isolated nucleoli of *Vicia* and *Zea* contain as much as 17 per cent of DNA. Jacob (1966) considers this DNA may be primer necessary for RNA synthesis. Nucleoli contain large amounts of RNA and protein and one of the early observations which supported the view that RNA was concerned with protein synthesis was that nucleoli are large in the cells of embryonic tissues that are growing and that they increase in volume when cells become meristematic in both plants and animals. In the root tips of *Zea* for example the cells of the rapidly dividing regions have nucleoli about three times the size of those in the quiescent centre where rates of growth and division are very low (Clowes, 1956). In *Plantago* the difference is twelve-fold (Hyde, 1967). Also nucleoli are especially large in animals in rapidly growing malignant cells and in protein exporting cells such as those of silk glands.

Nucleoli may thus be regarded as similar to the loops of lampbrush chromosomes or to the puffs on giant polytene chromosomes, i.e. as a manifestation of activity of a gene, in this case, the nucleolar organizer. This could be valid even if, as many observations seem to show, the nucleolar substance is collected from the products of all parts of all the chromosomes and not only from the region of the nucleolar organizer. In this connexion it is interesting to note that Stevens & Swift (1966) have shown the puffs of salivary gland chromosomes to contain granules of 40-50nm diameter which are released into the nucleoplasm and then appear to penetrate the pores of the nuclear membrane as rods of 20nm diameter. Stevens & Swift believe that these granules are possibly made of messenger RNA bound to protein and produced by the chromosome at puffing to convey information to the cytoplasm.

We discuss the role of the nucleolus further in the section, 6.10, on the control of protein synthesis.

6.6   Centrioles and Spindles

Centriole is the name given to the bodies concerned with the siting of the mitotic spindle poles. Most animals and those plants with flagella have a pair of them which, at the onset of mitosis, lie just outside the nuclear envelope, except in ciliate protozoans where they and the mitotic spindle occur within the nuclear envelope. They are similar to the basal granules of flagella described on page 196 in having nine fibrils and in replicating themselves, but the exact relationship between the two organelles is not clear yet. The centromeres of the chromosomes at prophase are often arranged near the centrioles. The two centrioles separate before the nuclear envelope disappears and later they appear at the two poles of the spindle. In some cells the centrioles polarize a radiating system of fibres, the aster, which later forms caps to the spindle poles. They also form the terminal point of the microtubules of the spindle in animals, but they are obviously not necessary for spindle formation because most plants lack them. They influence the shape of the spindle since this has pointed poles in cells with centrioles but truncated poles in cells without them making the spindle look barrel-shaped. Endoplasmic reticulum concentrates at the poles of the spindles even as early as prophase before the spindle appears and may be related to the astral rays of animals. In higher plants we have heard that this ER is smooth-surfaced and tubular and forms tightly bunched masses closely associated with the ends of the microtubules of the spindle. The function of this tubular ER is not known. From the spindle poles the ER proliferates and, in some plants, invades the spindle reaching the equator by anaphase (Porter & Machado, 1960).

Most of our detailed knowledge of spindles comes from sea-urchin eggs from which the whole mitotic apparatus—spindle and chromosomes—may be isolated and in which mitosis can be synchronized by artificial insemination. The spindle is made of protein with some RNA and shows birefringence indicating the polarization of the protein. Birefringence of plant spindles requires refined polarizing microscopes to see. Ordinary polarization techniques are not adequate. Birefringence actually appears outside the nuclear envelope before the spindle is seen according to some observers, but is strongest at the region of the centromeres when fully formed. The centromeres may themselves help to organize the molecules of the spindle therefore. Pickett-Heaps & Northcote's (1966c) electron microscopical studies show that microtubules run down outside the nucleus at prophase (Fig. 125). These microtubules are assumed to be spindle fibres, but arise outside the poles, penetrate the disintegrating nuclear envelope and some run right through to the opposite pole. Others are attached to the chromosomes sometimes, but not always, at special regions. Spindle fibres are discussed further in the section on microtubules (see page 116). The concept of spindle fibres involves us in some difficulties because the term has obviously been applied to different images. In fixed cells seen under the light microscope the fibres may be fascicles of microtubules while in living cells under a phase or polarizing microscope the fibres seen may be single microtubules plus their diffraction halos. Bajer (1961), investigating with a polarizing microscope and ciné photography the endosperm of plants, talks of the bodily movement of the fibre towards the spindle pole at anaphase. Thus here the fibre does not reach the spindle pole at metaphase, but moves towards it. In animals the spindle fibres do apparently extend all the way from the equator to the pole all the time. Centromeres at first associate with the spindle at any point and it is not until later that they move to the equator. At anaphase the centromeres split and move towards the poles at a speed of about 1 micron per minute and stop when they have covered about two thirds of the distance from equator to pole. The part of the spindle between the two groups of centromeres then elongates allowing the two chromosome groups to separate further. The mechanism of movement of the chromosomes on the spindle is not known, but the presence of swarms of mitochondria which encircle the spindle at metaphase suggests an energy-consuming process. The spindle fibres attached to the chromosomes shorten, the spindle itself lengthens and, in some cells, the fibre itself moves polewards, but we have little idea how these movements occur. Inoué (1964) holds that the fibres attached to the chromosomes shorten by the removal of material and that the continuous fibres could acquire more material and so lengthen to resist the compressive force exerted on the spindle by the chromosome fibres.

The orientation of mitotic spindles has been studied for its morpho-genetic effect. Sinnott (1944) showed that the prevalent mitotic axis controls the shape of cucurbit fruits which can be sausage-shaped, spherical or squat. He plotted the orientation of the mitotic axis against numbers of cells and found that the pattern of orientation changed from metaphase to telophase. This suggested that the spindle could swing round like a three-dimensional compass needle obeying some command that decided what the future shape of the fruit was to be. Negbi, Baldev & Lang (1964), on the other hand, found no evidence for a shift in spindle orientation during mitosis in the shoot apex of those plants where mitotic activity and orientation relate to whether the stem bolts or produces a rosette plant with short internodes. They consider that spindle orientation, like mitotic activity, depends on separate factors produced by the leaves. Northcote (1966) has shown that spindle orientation is not the primary determinant of mitotic orientation however. He found that a band of microtubules runs round the cell wall before prophase and this band marks the position at which the cell plate will join the wall of the parent cell unless the nucleus is later displaced. In other words, this band of microtubules predetermines the plane of division probably by positioning the nucleus. If Sinnott's theory is right the spindle may adjust its equator to lie on the already determined plane of division. Avers (1963) has shown, in grass root apices, where the epidermal cells undergo asym-metrical divisions to produce hair-bearing (trichoblast) cells and ordinary cells, mitosis is preceded by displacement of the interphase nucleus to the distal side of the cell and the distal daughter becomes the small trichoblast and the proximal daughter the larger ordinary cell. This again suggests polarization of the cytoplasm before the interphase nucleus settles itself, perhaps across a gradient. Similar examples of asymmetrical divisions occur in guard cell formation. In vacuolated cells that divide, a 'phragmosome' is formed from cytoplasmic strands across the vacuole and supports the nucleus. Here again the plane of division is determined before spindle orientation, for the phragmosome gives the position of the future dividing wall.

What happens at the spindle equator after mitosis is described in Chapter 5 in its treatment of wall formation. The orientation of the wall is very important in determining tissue patterns. For example in cambia when the cells divide 'pseudotransversely' to increase the number of cambial initials (Fig. 11) there are whole sectors where the tilt of the dividing wall is in one direction to give either 'S'—or 'Z'—shaped walls but the pattern changes in time preventing the building of pronounced spiral grain in the wood (Hejnowicz, 1964).

6.7   Other nuclear inclusions

The electron microscope has revealed several other organelles within interphase nuclei. Most of these seem not to be of universal occurrence. One is a honeycomb-like structure found in the apical cells of *Pisum* and in some other plant and animal nuclei (Hyde, 1965). The whole structure is about 250 nm across and appears to consist of elongated 'cells' about 25 nm apart, centre to centre. It is constructed of fibres like the chromatin, but more densely packed.

The ribosome-like particles found in nucleoli may come here, for these may not be ribosomes in the usual sense. They are about 15 nm across and therefore slightly smaller than cytoplasmic ribosomes, but they do contain RNA. Other particles about 30 nm across also occur in the chromatin of some cells with a clear halo around them. Other smaller particles about 10 nm across occur in clusters in some nuclei. The significance of these nuclear inclusions is not known.

6.8   Chromosomes

The chromosomes are the most intensively studied parts of living organisms. This is partly due to appreciation of their importance as the carriers of the vast majority of the factors of inheritance and partly due to the extremely profitable co-operation between two different disciplines, cytology and genetics. The result of this is that much of what we know about the structure of chromosomes comes indirectly, from breeding experiments where the use of arithmetic has opened up the study of otherwise unattainable detail.

Number

As a rough generalization we may say that the number of chromosomes per cell is a constant for the species. In most animals two sets of chromosomes occur in each nucleus, one set derived from the father and the other from the mother. The gametes bear one set each, the haploid number, and the diploid number is restored at fusion. The haploid number is obtained at meiosis which occurs in gametogenesis.

In the higher plants there are two generations, one, haploid bearing the gametes and the other diploid bearing the spores. Meiosis occurs in spore production and spores grow into the gamete-bearing generation. In flowering plants the gamete-bearing generation lives separately from the diploid, spore-bearing generation only in the male (pollen grains) and so we loosely think of plants as being diploid and refer to them as male if they bear the sort of spores that grow into male gametophytes. The sporophytes of most flowering plants, however, bear both kinds of spores, those that grow into both male and female gametophytes, and chromosomal sex-determination is uncommon, Haploid examples of the phase that is normally diploid occur in both animals and higher plants. Meiosis and sexual reproduction is then irregular. The number of chromosomes in a haploid set varies from one (in the nematode, *Ascaris megalocephala*) to hundreds in some ferns.

The constancy of the chromosome number is merely a convenient fiction, for, although it is true usually of the regular meristems, the differentiated tissues are often polyploid. We do not realize this as a rule because these cells rarely come into division and display their chromosomes to be counted. We can induce them to do so however by hormonal treatment. For example Torrey (1961) found that kinetin specifically triggers mitosis in the endopolyploid cells of mature root tissue of *Pisum*. In some plants a particular level of ploidy, or poly-somaty, is specific to a tissue, for example trichoblasts in roots of *Hydrocharis*, nodules in leguminous plants, the root cortex of *Spinacia*, the root cap of *Bryonia* (see Clowes, 1961a). In other plants polyploidy is more haphazard and seems to result from the failure to stop DNA synthesis after mitosis has stopped. This may lead to polyteny as well as to polyploidy. Polyteny comes from the chromosomes reproducing themselves over and over again without separating the products into chromatids. Polyteny can reach high levels. Polyploidy arises similarly, but the strands become separate chromatids. The mechanism for this, endomitosis, is hidden because it all occurs in the interphase condition without a spindle. Polyploid and polysomic nuclei are usually in-distinguishable from polytene ones and occasionally both phenomena occur in the same cell. Both may be distinguished from diploid nuclei if one has a microdensitometer to estimate the DNA content. Polyploidy and polyteny may be devices to maintain the nucleus-to-cytoplasm ratio in expanding cells without bothering with mitosis and cell division with their demand for spindle proteins, walls, etc., but perhaps more likely they are merely signs of breakdown of control in cells at the end of their reproductive phase when selection is not so stern. In some cells they are useful because polyploid and polytene cells synthesize DNA faster than diploid cells and so can be used as reservoirs of DNA when a sudden demand occurs. This is perhaps what happens in the tapetum of pollen sacs and other nurse tissues when these break down and provide the reproducing cells with DNA for their mitoses. When the course of differentiation changes and polyploid cells are called upon to divide, somatic reduction division may occur both in nature and under experimental treatments, but normally there seems to be a mechanism to prevent important cells from going polyploid. The germ line must be held diploid (or haploid in plants with considerable haploid phases) and this is done probably by holding the cell at G_1 somehow (see page 361). In plants this is done in the apical meristem of the shoot probably under hormonal control, but, even in roots, which are not usually concerned with holding a germ line, there is a region, the quiescent centre, which is held in G_1 and, when the cells of the rest of the apex are injured, it supplies the cells to form a new meristem (Clowes, 1965a). When the germ line fails to remain diploid, diploid or polyploid gametes result and these may give rise to wholly polyploid plants of the next generation. Wholly polyploid plants also occur when meiosis is irregular often after interspecific crossing. The genetical and evolutionary significance of polyploidy is important and most of the work on it concerns plants. Studying meiosis often reveals the past history of a species because of the pairing of homologous chromosomes in prophase.

Apart from polyploidy, there are other reasons why the chromosome number is not strictly constant. Errors (nondisjunction) occur in mitosis and meiosis resulting in one daughter nucleus collecting both homologous chromosomes and the other daughter neither. When an individual inherits an extra chromosome in this way it is called a trisomic; when it lacks one chromosome it is called a monosomic. Such abnormalities have become of medical interest recently. Mongolism (Down's syndrome) in man, for example, results from a particular trisomy. Other chromosome abnormalities occur in some kinds of tumours both in plants and in animals.

Some plants and animals regularly have what are called supernumerary or B chromosomes. These are generally smaller than the others and sometimes considered to be genetically inert because individuals with none or many appear to differ in no important respects. Some are heterochromatic, some wholly euchromatic and some a mixture (see page 323). Their centromeres often fail to divide properly and this results in non-disjunction which, in some plants, is arranged so that the germ line is always supplied with the supernumeraries and some-times so that somatic cells are deprived of them. All this suggests some selective advantage that is not dose-dependent. Spindle abnormalities in *Hymenocallis* result in root tip cells having from 23 to 83 chromo-somes and pollen mother cells from 69 to 86 (Snoad, 1955). Here it looks as if roots tolerate unbalanced numbers better than stamens.

Chromosome size also varies and not only with polyteny, for the DNA content may remain constant. Variations in size have not in the past attracted so much attention as variations in number.

Gross structure

Traditionally we study chromosomes at metaphase or anaphase when they have attained their greatest contraction and can be seen most easily under the light microscope. They stain with basic dyes and absorb ultra-violet light at 260 nm intensely. They may also be seen in living cells under phase and interference microscopes so that ciné photography is possible. At these stages of mitosis in ordinary somatic cells the chromosomes are cylinders and can be from $0·2$ to 50μm long and from $0·2$ to 2μm across according to the species. The genus *Trillium* has some of the largest known chromosomes in ordinary somatic cells. Away from metaphase and anaphase chromosomes become longer and thinner due to the partial unwinding of the spirals which constitute the chromosome. They reach maximal length in interphase and then may display a relic of the spiral. The lampbrush chromosomes in oocytes of amphibia may reach up to 800μm long. These are in the extended state and are very thin—20–40 nm in places. The shape of the chromosomes is also affected by the position of the centromere along the length of the chromosome because the chromosome bends at this point when it is attached to the spindle if the centromere is not near the end. The centromere appears as a constriction in mitosis and it is the point of association with the spindle which appears to drag the chromosome by the centromere at anaphase to the two poles. Thus a chromosome with a centromere near the middle of its length is bent and trails two arms of equal or unequal length at anaphase. When the centromere is near one end (telocentric) the chromosome appears as a more or less straight rod. There is probably always a short arm in telocentric chromosomes.

Centromere

Under the light microscope we can see four distinctive parts to the chromosomes—centromeres, euchromatin, heterochromatin and nucleolar organizers. The centromere is also known as the primary constriction, or kinetochore, and is responsible for the movements of the chromosomes at anaphase. It is a constriction because it remains in the extended state when the rest of the chromosome thickens by internal coiling at the onset of mitosis. Some chromosomes have a single centromere, others are di- or polycentric, and in some organisms, e.g. *Luzula*, the centromere is diffuse and not localized in discrete regions of the chromosome. This is inferred from the behaviour of the chromosomes under chronic irradiation for example when fragments broken by the radiation collect in the daughter nuclei at the end of mitosis rather than stay outside as happens to acentric fragments in species with single centromeres (Evans & Pond, 1964). The position of the centromere is characteristic of a particular chromosome in every nucleus of a species. In fact chromosomes are identified largely from the position of their centromeres. It was once thought that the centromere divided at the onset of anaphase to allow the two chromatids, which are already separate from each other, to part, each with its own centromere derived from the parent. But the centromere is now known to be divided before this.

At pachytene of the meiotic prophase, when fine details of the chromosome structure are usually described, the centromere may in some chromosomes be seen to possess fibrils and chromomeres, the bead-like objects that also occur elsewhere along the chromosomes. In especially favourable material and after certain treatments these fibrils and chromomeres may also be seen at the mitotic metaphase. Although the centromere as a whole usually appears pale in stained chromosomes, the fibrils and chromomeres in it do stain intensely with Feulgen so that one may assume that DNA is present, at any rate in those centromeres that show this sub-structure (Lima-de-Faria, 1956). The chromomeres, which give the bead-like appearance to pachytene chromosomes, give a banded appearance to the giant polytene chromosomes. They vary in size along the length of the chromosome and give a characteristic structure to each chromosome of the complement. This enables inversions, deletions and other anomalies of chromosomes to be seen in the tissues that possess polytene chromosomes. Under the electron microscope the chromomeres are seen to contain strands folded back and forth.

Euchromatin and Heterochromatin

Euchromatin is the name given to the material which forms the bulk of the chromosomes and includes most of the active genes. It shows a cycle of condensation at mitosis and unravelling at interphase.

Other parts of the chromosome that differ from euchromatin in their coiling or condensation cycle are called heterochromatic and they differ from the euchromatic parts in several ways. Heterochromatin remains condensed in interphase like a piece of metaphase chromosome when the rest of the chromosome, the euchromatin, uncoils. The heterochromatic segments of the chromosome or agglomerations of such blocks appear as spots in the interphase nucleus and are called chromocentres. Near the onset of mitosis the heterochromatic segments uncoil briefly and then recondense before the euchromatin does so. In mitosis the heterochromatin stains differently from the euchromatin— either more strongly or less strongly (positive or negative hetero- pyknosis). It synthesizes DNA at a different time from the euchromatin. In some species the heterochromatic segments of chromosomes fail to stain at metaphase after a period in the cold. This property is not yet fully understood. Sometimes division is defective in these segments and the daughter chromatids remain tied together to form chromatid bridges. Sometimes there is a failure to spiralize so that the hetero- chromatic segment remains as an uncoiled thread at metaphase. These effects of cold are often considered to be due to a shortage or even a loss of DNA (Darlington, 1940, 1947; Barber & Callan, 1941). In an experiment on *Trillium*, Haque (1963) showed that when roots were grown in tritiated thymidine for 16 hours at 22°C, then without tritium for 24 hours and then transferred to 1°C for five days the metaphase chromosomes were labelled in the euchromatic segments, but not in the heterochromatic segments. Thus the low temperature may have caused a loss of DNA selectively from the heterochromatin and this experiment was thought to confirm the view originally put forward by Darlington. But this and other labelling experiments on chromosomes can be interpreted differently and the subject still awaits full elucidation. The chromomeres in the heterochromatic blocks, which are visible only in polytene chromosomes, are smaller than in euchromatin. The cyclic changes in the chromosomes occur sometimes out of phase in the heterochromatin compared with the euchromatin. The observed differences have also been interpreted as meaning that the DNA is more labile in heterochromatin and that it is not 'discharged' at interphase like that of the euchromatin. The packing of the fine fibrils seen under the electron microscope is also different in the two regions.

The heterochromatin is often localized in small blocks along the length of a chromosome especially next to the centromere, near the nucleolar organizer and at the ends of the chromosomes, but sometimes nearly all of a chromosome is heterochromatic compared with the other chromosomes. This is frequently so in the sex chromosomes and supernumerary chromosomes. Some chromosomes are too small for us to determine whether they are eu- or heterochromatic or both. The heterochromatic sex chromosomes in some animals behave in an odd way at interphase. In females one only of the X chromosomes is heterochromatic. In man, for example, a heterochromatic blob from one of the X chromosomes is readily seen in interphase nuclei near the periphery, but much more frequently in females than in males thus enabling the genetic sex to be determined in somatic interphase cells. This condensed region, the Barr body, is said to be inactive genetically in normal females and to be due to the heterochromatization of either the maternal or the paternal X chromosome in any cells of the body. This means that a tissue can be heterogeneous in respect of the activity of the genes of the X chromosome if the individual is heterozygous for them. The genetical evidence for this theory, which is due mainly to Lyon, has, however, been questioned (Grüneberg, 1967). Where extra X chromosomes occur, as in polysomics, they are heterochromatized and are condensed as Barr bodies. Heterochromatic segments may not appear in the earliest stages of development of the organism and sometimes, at later stages, they appear only in certain tissues. In the giant polytene chromosomes of the salivary glands of *Drosophila* the heterochromatin near the centromeres of all the chromosomes is fused together at a chromocentre which includes the whole of the wholly heterochromatic Y chromosome.

Few genes have been mapped in heterochromatic segments but they are not completely inert genetically. The genes that do occur, however, may lie on bits of euchromatin undetected in the heterochromatin and it could be that the DNA base sequences in heterochromatin are unreadable because they are nonsense or because they are 'silenced' or repressed. There is very little crossing over and what there is may be of an unusual type. Correlated with this is the fact that chiasmata are seldom seen in the heterochromatin regions, but this could be due to slipping rather than non-formation. Somatic, or mitotic, crossing over, on the other hand, seems to occur more frequently than might be expected in the heterochromatic segments leading to somatic patchiness in the organism (S. W. Brown, 1966). In some mammals the heterochromatic X chromosome in females is missing. The heterochromatic Y chromosome in males has disappeared entirely in the course of evolution in some species. The fact that the sex chromatin occurs in defined positions in the interphase nucleus suggests that all the chromatin may be fixed in position and Mirsky & Osawa (1961) suggest that this may be the significance of the rotation of the nucleus, to expose all the cytoplasm to all the chromosomes.

We do not know so much about the sex chromosomes of plants partly because so few higher plants are dioecious. There is, apart from this, still a lot we do not understand about heterochromatin. Its chemical nature, for example, is hardly known. But what we do know suggests that it plays an important part in evolution of chromosomes and genetic systems and especially, perhaps, in the suppression of gene action during differentiation by its inability to synthesize RNA. It should, perhaps, be regarded as a transient state open to all regions of the chromosomes.

Nucleolar organizer

There are constrictions in some metaphase chromosomes at which the chromosome does not bend as it does at the centromere. These are called secondary constrictions and some of these, not morphologically distinct from others, are the nucleolar organizers, the sites at which the nucleolus is secreted or collected at the end of mitosis. Commonly one chromosome in each haploid set has a nucleolar organizer which is constant in position. Some organisms do not have nucleolar organizers although they usually have nucleoli, which may then be formed at the ends of chromosomes or at the centromeres. When maleic hydrazide is used to produce micronuclei from acentric chromosomal fragments, nucleoli can arise in both the main nucleus and the micronucleus even in the absence of a nucleolar organizer (Scott & Evans, 1964). The micronuclei can also synthesize DNA provided they do not become pycnotic (intensely staining and degenerate) before DNA synthesis occurs in the main nucleus. Thus the nucleolar organizer is not essential for DNA synthesis, but normal mitotic condensation seems to depend upon having a proper nucleolus formed at a true nucleolar organizer.

Satellites

In some chromosomes a secondary constriction occurs near the end and the body separated from the rest of the chromosome by this delicate filament is called a satellite.

Spirals and fine structure

In some stages of the nuclear cycle and also after some experimental treatments the chromosomes can be seen to consist of coils. It is these coils that partly account for the shortening and thickening of the chromosomes as the nucleus enters mitosis from interphase. In meiosis we see in a few species two coils, a major one with 10 to 30 gyres and a minor one at the limits of resolution of the light microscope with a large number of gyres. In mitosis we usually see only the major coil, which appears at the end of prophase. The image we see is complicated by the fact that the chromosomes may also be seen to exist as a number of parallel threads, two, four or more according to the stage and the species yet the chromatids obviously separate from each other at anaphase without becoming tangled. The chromatids, when they appear at prophase of mitosis, are largely coiled around each other like a two-strand electrical flex. This relational coiling is called plectonemic and the chromatids cannot move apart without their ends revolving (Fig. 127). The major coiling seen in meiosis appears, however, to be paranemic; that is the chromatids are separable by lateral movement alone like a pair of bedsprings (Fig. 128). The chromatids are also internally coiled and the shortening and thickening that we see from prophase to anaphase is at least partially due to this kind of coiling. By internal coiling we imply that it arises from the internal arrangement of the molecules and involves no rotation to the ends, for it occurs in ring chromosomes as well as linear ones. Darlington & Vosa (1963) have shown, by using a telocentric chromosome, that left- and right-handed coiling is equally frequent in the cells of *Tradescantia*. This means that coiling must be renewed at every cell cycle otherwise all cells would inherit the coiling of the zygote. Darlington and Vosa also found that in other chromosomes with a centromere away from the ends the coiling in one arm is more like y to be the opposite of that in the other arm. The combinations LL:LR:RR are 1:7:1. There is no bias across a chiasma.

The main reason why electron microscopy has revealed so little about the chromosomes so far is that the thin sections (about 50 nm) cut through the various spirals so that it is difficult to see how the chromosome areas link up to form a three-dimensional image (Figs. 33, 87). Bopp-Hassenkamp (1958) showed that the chromosomes were made up of subfibrils 2–3 nm across. These coil to build elementary fibrils of about 10 nm diameter and the elementary fibrils themselves coil to produce structures 35–80 nm in diameter. In pachytene of meiosis these themselves coil to produce a fourth order spiral. Ris (1962) regards the 10 nm fibrils as being made up of two 4 nm macromolecules held by histone bridges and linked end to end by nonhistone protein. This suggests that the 10 nm fibrils are made of two DNA double helices with their associated histone. The doubleness of the 10 nm

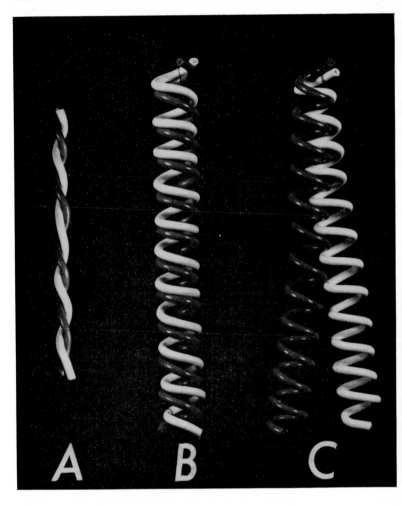

F<small>IG</small>. 127. Plectonemic (A and B) and paranemic (C) coils.

fibrils can sometimes be made out after impregnation with uranyl acetate or after the histone has been removed artificially or in nuclei with protamine instead of histone. Protamine may be wound around the DNA instead of forming bridges as histone is thought to do (Ris, 1963). Another view is that the 10 nm fibrils consist of a protein matrix with a fine filamentous core. The granular appearance of the chromosomes in sections under the electron microscope (Fig. 125) is due to the elementary fibrils being cut in random planes. Fibrils of the same kind can also be seen in whole mounts of the giant polytene chromosomes of dipteran salivary glands. Rae (1966) counted 400–450 fibrils in *Drosophila* and this fits sufficiently well with estimates that these chromosomes are reduplicated commonly to the 512 class of polyteny. The fibrils are extended longitudinally between the bands that occur on the chromosomes while they are condensed within the bands. Rae's work supports the view that these giant chromosomes are cables of chromosome units each of one double helix of DNA extending the whole length of the chromosome. Elementary fibrils of the same kind about 2·5 nm across occur in the nucleoplasm of bacteria and blue-green algae: in fact the fibrils identify this region of the protoplasm as being equivalent to the membrane-bound nucleus of higher organisms,

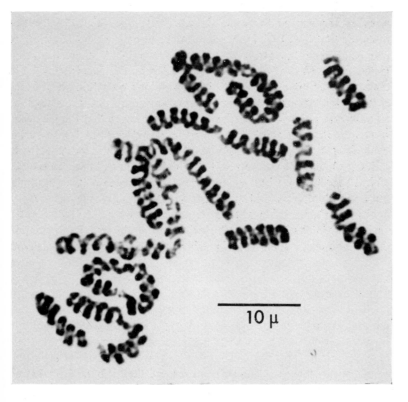

FIG. 128. Chromosomes at first metaphase of meiosis in *Tradescantia virginiana* treated with ammonia to show spirals.   Photograph by Mr C. G. Vosa.

for they are removed by DNA-ase. There seems to be no histone associated with the DNA in bacteria and blue-green algae. This is true also of *Amphidinium*, which, like other dinoflagellates, contains chromosome-like objects made up of 2·5 nm fibrils at all parts of the mitotic cycle (Ris, 1963; Grell & Schwalbach, 1965). (Dinoflagellates have nuclear envelopes like higher organisms.) The DNA of plastids and mitochondria probably also exists as 2·5 nm fibrils.

Chromosomes are said to acquire RNA and phospholipid during prophase and release it at anaphase and it has been suggested that this causes the coiling that we see in mitosis, but the evidence is merely circumstantial.

Many thin sections through chromosomes show what is generally interpreted as an axial complex made up of fibres about 7 nm across and each subdivided into two fibrils (Painter, 1964; Guénin, 1965). This axial structure is made of protein and around it lies the DNA attached at places and forming the coils mentioned above. A popular theory is that the DNA is thus tightly coiled only when the genes are inactive. When the genes are activated the DNA uncoils so that messenger-RNA can be made. If the DNA gene complex is attached to the axial structure at two points it forms a loop containing RNA such as we see in the lampbrush chromosomes of amphibians. If it is attached at only one point it forms the hair-like processes that may be seen at meiosis in other species. The production of loops and processes is equivalent to the 'puffing' of the giant polytene chromosomes of insect salivary glands. The puffs are of RNA and protein and occur at specific loci at specific times in the developmental sequence of the cell. Some but not all biologists hold that the genes at the puffing regions are now active and they subside when gene activity is over. The larger puffs, also called Balbiani rings, may be loci supplying the genetic information for the non-enzymatic proteins produced by the salivary glands. Plants do not have anything exactly equivalent to lampbrush chromosomes, but there is no reason to believe that this implies a fundamental difference and the fuzziness seen around chromosomes in meiotic prophase may correspond to puffing. It is just that amphibians and dipterans provide very favourable chromosomes for investigation and in recent years we have learnt much about gene activity from them (e.g. Beermann, 1961). In other organisms we have not yet been able to relate the 10 nm nucleohistone fibrils and their subunits to what we see under the light microscope.

There are many lines of evidence to suggest that chromosomes are multistranded like rope. Some of this evidence comes from studies on replication (page 335), some from irradiation experiments and some from direct observation. However, there are difficulties in reconciling a multistrand hypothesis with the genetical and cytological complexities that it would involve and some people hope to find each chromatid a single strand. The multiplicity of fibrils that we see under the electron microscope would then have to be explained as due to coiling and folding of the single strand. The best evidence for this view comes from the lampbrush chromosomes where we could interpret observations as consistent with an axis of a folded strand thrown into loops at various points along it. It may be that this sort of structure also occurs in the more usual kind of chromosome, and that it is merely obscured by great condensation. The investigation of Wolfe & Hewitt (1966) on the chromosomes of the insect, *Oncopeltus*, shows 25 nm fibrils aggregating into strands as the nucleus enters leptotene (Figs. 129, 130). At first the fibrils show no apparent order in the preparation made on a Langmuir trough. Then more of them form the parallel aggregates and less of them appear disordered. When a strand first becomes recognizable at leptotene there are at least twelve fibrils in it. The number of fibrils in a strand increases between zygotene and diakinesis probably by parallel folding. By metaphase the apparent multistrandedness disappears as the chromosomes coil. The sex chromosomes at leptotene appear like these metaphase chromosomes. It is not possible yet to say if the strandedness that appears at leptotene is true multistrandedness or whether it is due to folding as in the later stages of prophase.

A simple analysis reveals that a chromosome must have many times its own length of DNA. A single small chromosome may contain 0.5×10^{-12}g of DNA and so it must contain about 150 mm of DNA double helix which is packed into the chromosome perhaps 0.5μm long when fully coiled at metaphase and perhaps 500μm long when uncoiled at interphase.

The evidence presented in the next section (6.9) from autoradiography of tritiated thymidine-fed nuclei hardly helps to distinguish between the unineme and the polyneme hypotheses because there is so much disagreement over the results. But Peacock (1963) holds that isolabelling (labelling of homologous regions of both chromatids) at the X_2 division (the second division after treatment) is good evidence for multistrandedness. One difficulty over multistrandedness concerns how a mutation is brought about, but there is at least one hypothesis which shows how a mutation in one strand could spread to the others (Holliday, 1964).

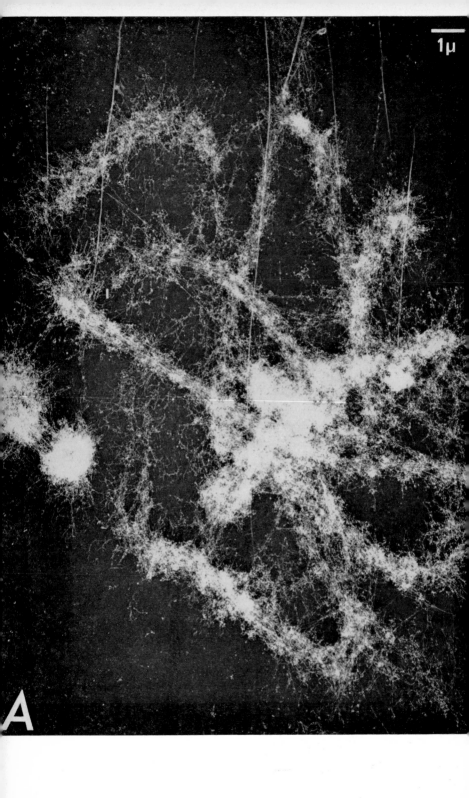

1μ

A

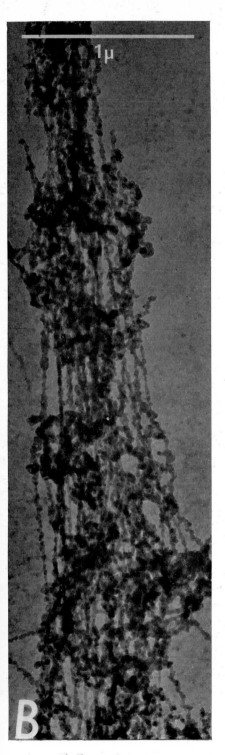

Fig. 129. Electron micrograph of meiotic chromosomes of *Oncopeltus fasciatus* spread by the Langmuir trough method.

A: (with reversed contrast) from zygotene nucleus showing the 25 nm fibres of the synapsed chromosomes.

B: Part of an unsynapsed chromosome at higher magnification.

By courtesy of Prof S. W. Wolfe from Wolfe & Hewitt (1966). Reprinted by permission of the Rockefeller University Press from *J. Cell Biol.* **31** (No. 1), 31–42 (1966).

Synaptinemal complex

At the prophase of meiosis the chromosomes of homologous pairs move towards each other, touch and then lie closely appressed to one another. The force producing this synapsis has long been a problem to cytologists and still is. Only two chromosomes form the united structure and only homologous chromosomes come together. The electron microscope has revealed a peculiar structure, the synaptinemal complex, lying between the paired chromosomes. This consists of three parallel ribbons extending the whole length of the chromosomes. The two lateral components are ribbons 20×100 nm in cross section and consist of densely packed filaments. The medial structure lying between the two lateral ribbons is a complex of parallel rods orientated between the lateral ribbons, but not apparently connecting them (Roth, 1966). Roth regards the outer sides of the lateral ribbons as belonging to the chromatin of the chromosomes.

We do not know yet what role the synaptinemal complex plays in synapsis or how it originates.

6.9 DNA replication and chromosome replication

The Watson-Crick model for DNA structure will be familiar to readers. The essential features of the model are (1) that each molecule consists of two long polynucleotide chains of opposite polarity forming helices around an imaginary common axis (some phages have single stranded DNA). The two chains have a backbone of sugar (deoxyribose) molecules joined to each other through phosphate groups (phosphodiester links). Attached to each sugar molecule is a base, either one of the pyrimidine bases, cytosine (C) or thymine (T) or one of the purine bases, adenine (A) or guanine (G). The proportions of these bases are interesting, for $A = T$ and $C = G$ so that $A + G = C + T$, but $A + T$ varies in relation to $C + G$. The two chains are held together through the specific pairing through hydrogen bonds of $A - T$, $C - G$, $T - A$ and $G - C$. This pairing is required because the distance between the sugar of one strand and the sugar of the other is constant ($1 \cdot 1$ nm) and two hydrogen bonds are required for the $A - T$ link and three for $C - G$ and also for other stereochemical reasons. Because of the specific pairing of bases one helical strand must be complementary to its partner in the arrangement of bases along its length. There are some additional complications, such as the possession of rare nucleotides such as 5-methylcytidylic acid but we need not go into them here.

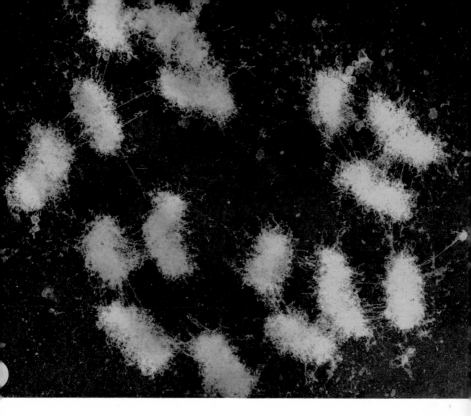

FIG. 130. Mitotic metaphase chromosomes of *Oncopeltus* prepared by the Langmuir trough method. The chromosomes are coiled, but the 25 nm fibrils are still visible. Micrograph by Prof S. L. Wolfe from Wolfe and Hewitt (1966). Reprinted by permission of the Rockefeller University Press from *J. Cell Biol.* **31** (No. 1), 31–42 (1966).

The method suggested for DNA replication is that the two helical strands unwind perhaps from one end and each then acts as a template for the formation of a new strand. The newly synthesized strand is complementary to its template, i.e. similar to the previous partner of the template. This method of replication is called semi-conservative because half of each molecule of DNA consists of an old strand and half of a new strand (Fig. 131). Once formed, a strand is potentially immortal. The enzyme concerned with DNA synthesis is called DNA polymerase and we may imagine it moving along the template strand knitting in the appropriate nucleotides (the monomer of phosphate + sugar + base).

The replication of chromosomes and its relation to the replication of DNA will now be discussed. The assumed semiconservative nature of both processes suggests a relationship, but we are far from clear what it is.

M

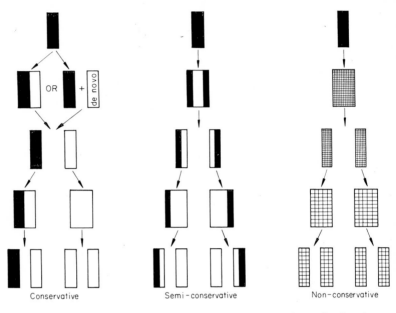

Conservative   Semi-conservative   Non-conservative

FIG. 131. Conservative, semi-conservative and non-conservative replication shown diagrammatically through two mass-doubling cycles. The similar result of *de novo* synthesis of an organelle and conservative replication is indicated at the first mass doubling stage. In non-conservative replication, synthesis need not necessarily be symmetrical as shown.

The use of radioactive precursors of DNA, especially tritiated thymidine, has given us a valuable tool in investigating chromosome replication. This is a particularly important subject because of its bearing on the role of the nucleus in heredity and differentiation. It had been known for a long time, of course, that chromosomes replicated themselves by longitudinal fission and that mitosis must have evolved as a mechanism for ensuring that all cells of the body have the same genetic make-up. The problem to be solved therefore was the exact mechanism of replication and its relation to the DNA molecules.

As a starting point we may take the work of Taylor on plant cells (Taylor, Woods & Hughes, 1957; Taylor, 1958, 1961). His technique was to supply the plant with tritiated thymidine to label the newly formed DNA and then to supply colchicine. The use of the colchicine has become a point of controversy. Its purpose was to contract the chromosomes and spread the sister chromatids, which normally lie parallel to one another so that it could be seen clearly which chromatids were labelled and which were not. The resolution of the autoradio-graphs is, as is explained on page 30, only just adequate for the job if plants with large chromosomes are used and the colchicine technique improves the discrimination. As well as this, colchicine inhibits spindle function and blocks metaphase for a while until the nuclei restitute to an interphase condition with twice the original number of chromo-somes. At the first mitosis after labelling (X_1) in the presence of colchicine all the chromosomes are labelled uniformly along their length. If the colchicine is supplied for a longer time (e.g. 34 hours) some of the tetraploid nuclei come into the second mitosis (X_2) and are again arrested for a time at metaphase. In these, which must have undergone one duplication in the absence of labelled thymidine, one of the chromatids is labelled and its sister is unlabelled. If a third mitosis (X_3) is reached in the presence of colchicine the octoploid metaphases show half the chromosomes completely unlabelled, i.e. with both chromatids unlabelled. In the other half of the chromosomes one chromatid was labelled and its sister was not.

The conclusion that is drawn from these results is that the chromo-some in interphase already has two components although these are invisible after normal cytological procedures. Each of these two com-ponents synthesize DNA in the thymidine incorporating tritium atoms as they do so. This explains why both sister chromatids at the following X_1 mitosis are equally labelled if we assume that one component goes to each chromatid (Fig. 132). The components separate at restitution to different chromosomes which now contain one (original) unlabelled component and one labelled component. In the absence of tritium now both these components add a new unlabelled unit alongside. When the cell passes through the X_2 mitosis half the chromosomes will be labelled in one of the two components and the other half will be wholly unlabelled. This theory implies that duplication of the chromosome occurs after DNA synthesis or perhaps during it.

All this is very reminiscent of the Watson-Crick model for the replication of DNA molecules. In this each helical strand of the DNA acts as a template for the formation of another helical strand of complementary structure. But in the Taylor experiments we face a different order of magnitude and it is still not clear what is the relation of DNA replication to chromosome replication or even how the DNA is arranged in the chromosome. Several models have been suggested to fit the facts. Molecular weights of the order of 10 million have been found in many preparations of DNA and this corresponds to a length of about 5μm but this is a very small fraction of the amount of DNA in

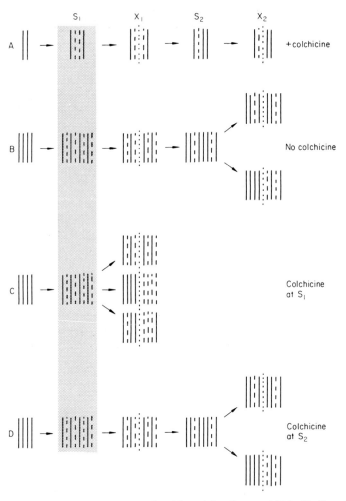

Fig. 132. Diagram to show the Taylor (A) and La Cour and Pelc (B, C and D) interpretations of chromosome replication. S₁ is the DNA-synthetic period in tritiated thymidine. S₂ is the next S period in the absence of tritiated thymidine. X₁ and X₂ are the first and second metaphases after labelling.

most chromosomes. (It may be though, that molecular weights are always determined on broken molecules.) Put in another way, the DNA of a chromosome extends to a length of the order of metres. How is it arranged? Any model has to fit the genetic information especially the fine scale work on microorganisms, the facts on chromosome breakage by radiation and chemicals, on mutations and recombinations as well as what we know about replication and fine structure. Freese's model (1958) has many DNA double helices joined end to end by connecting units perhaps of protein. Each strand is joined to a connecting unit at one end only, leaving the strand free to rotate. The unit at the other end of the DNA molecule is connected to the parallel helix. The whole of this long chain of double helices is then coiled and supercoiled and the connecting units themselves may be linked by weak bonds to give the whole structure extra rigidity. This model is attractive in its simplicity, but, of course, many other possible models could fit the same facts.

Taylor's investigations on *Crepis capillaris* with tritiated thymidine suggest that DNA synthesis starts at the two ends of a chromosome and proceeds towards the centromere (Taylor, 1958). In other plants there are other starting points. Wimber (1961), though, has interpreted his autoradiographs of *Tradescantia* as showing that DNA synthesis is at first general along the length of the chromosome, but that the ends continue to synthesize right to the end of the S period after the rest has stopped. Other examples of asynchrony also have been reported. Some chromosomes have segments that regularly synthesize DNA later than the rest and some cells have whole chromosomes that are later than the others in synthesis. Even homologous chromosomes are not always synchronous in DNA synthesis in some organisms (e.g. man—Lima-de-Faria, 1962). These observations naturally made people look to see if there was a difference between euchromatin and heterochromatin in this respect, but the evidence is conflicting. Some workers think that heterochromatin has a later S period than euchromatin; others think that it is position along the chromosome that matters rather than whether the segment is eu- or heterochromatic (e.g. Pelc & La Cour, 1959).

Darlington & Haque (1966) have shown in *Secale cereale* that the early S period labelling usually occurs throughout the chromosomes. In mid S, labelling is variable both within a single nucleus and between different nuclei, but by late S labelling is localized at the ends which are both heterochromatic in the A chromosomes. Homologous chromosomes sometimes follow the same labelling pattern, but sometimes differ from each other, possibly because they occupy different positions within the nucleus during incorporation of the thymidine. In B chromosomes, which are heterochromatic, DNA synthesis is later than in the A chromosomes. Thus the problem is much more complex than was thought at first and awaits investigation at higher resolution.

La Cour & Pelc (1958) have criticized Taylor's interpretation of chromosome replication on the grounds that the colchicine used in preparing the cells upsets the mechanism of synthesis or the subsequent distribution of the DNA to the daughter chromatids. They found that when no colchicine was used both the sister chromatids were usually labelled at both 24 hours and 48 hours, covering both the X_1 and the X_2 mitoses, but that at X_2 12 per cent of cells showed some chromosomes with both sister chromatids labelled and others with only one sister labelled. If colchicine is present at the first and second syntheses, i.e. during the supply of tritiated thymidine and at the following synthesis without tritium, both the X_1 and the X_2 metaphases had some chromosomes labelled along both chromatids and some along only one of them. La Cour and Pelc surmount these difficulties by assuming the chromosome has at least four rather than two components as in Taylor's hypothesis and that the colchicine influences the segregation of old and new components possibly by affecting the centromere. The two theories are compared in Fig. 132. Unfortunately some other possibilities occur occasionally. These included labelled and unlabelled chromosomes occurring in the same cell at both X_1 and X_2 and chromosomes with only one arm labelled. On top of this there is the possibility of somatic crossing over, sister chromatid and other kinds of exchanges and there are technical difficulties which affect our interpretation of autoradiographs especially those using tritium whose β-rays are so soft that a kink in a chromosome in a plane other than the plane of the slide or a more than usually thick region of cytoplasm between chromosome and emulsion could cause the β-particles to fail to reach the photographic emulsion over a part or whole chromosome or chromatid. It is also possible that the components do not have the replication properties of DNA. Colchicine may also affect the kind of replication that occurs as well as or instead of affecting the segregation of components though Peacock (1963) has shown that colchicine does not affect DNA replication or segregation or the prospects for sister chromatid exchange in *Vicia*.

Attempts to use very high-resolution autoradiography in nuclei have now been made. Bernier & Jensen (1966), using tritiated thymidine for the electron microscope in the shoot apex of *Sinapis*, report three types of labelled nuclei. In one, all the label was in the dispersed euchromatin; in another, all was in the condensed heterochromatin and the third had label in both. This confirms ideas of difference in the position of the S period in the mitotic cycle for different regions of chromosomes at any rate for this meristem. It may not be like this in all species.

6.10 Control of protein synthesis

We may divide the functions of the nucleus into two— (1) the replication of the DNA and the chromosomes and (2) the control of protein synthesis. The first is responsible for ensuring that all cells of the body receive the same genetic information and that this is passed on from one generation to the next in reproduction. The second is concerned with the instructions to the cell about how it should behave, for the proteins are mainly enzymes and it has long been known that the nucleus is necessary for continued protein synthesis.

We now believe that the basis for genetic information is the sequence of bases along the DNA molecules. The number of possible combinations of the four bases is vastly more than the number of living things. The molecular weight of plant DNA is about 10 million when isolated. This indicates a molecule 15,000 base pairs long and some people believe such lengths to be fragments. If there are 15,000 bases to a DNA strand the number of combinations is $4^{15,000}$. The way in which the nuclear commands are given is in specifying the production of particular proteins, most of which are enzymes. Most people accept that a sequence of three bases along the DNA strand specifies one amino acid in the protein. This is done indirectly through the intermediary RNA. RNA has a primary structure similar to DNA though the sugar is ribose and not deoxyribose and, in place of thymine, there is uracil (U). The RNA molecule is made in the presence of RNA polymerase on a DNA template (transcription) as in DNA synthesis except that A specifies U rather than T (see page 334). As an example, the codons UUU and UUC in the RNA specify phenylalanine and UGU and UGC specify cysteine in the protein being synthesized. The whole genetic code in terms of the twenty amino acids that go to make proteins has now been worked out (Table 8). How this was done is described in modern textbooks of biology. As we have noted the code is 'degenerate' in the sense that more than one of the 64 possible codons can specify one amino acid.

In vitro both of the DNA strands of a molecule are transcribed, but *in vivo* only one apparently because the RNA produced in a cell is not base-complementary to itself. A does not equal U and G does not equal C (Bonner, 1965). This means that the RNA cannot be wholly double stranded like DNA and is most likely to be single-stranded. As we have said in the section on ribosomes, there are possibly three different kinds of RNA—messenger, transfer and ribosomal, but all are formed by transcription of DNA. It is however the messenger

TABLE 8

RNA codons for the 20 amino acids of proteins (Data from Crick, 1966). Other amino acids occur rarely in proteins and these may be coded for by one of the codons below and changed chemically afterwards.

Alanine	GCU GCC GCA GCG
Arginine	CGC CGA CGG CGU AGA AGG
Aspartic acid	GAU GAC
Asparagine	AAU AAC
Cysteine	UGU UGC
Glutamic acid	GAA GAG
Glutamine	CAA CAG
Glycine	GGU GGC GGA GGG
Histidine	CAU CAC
Isoleucine	AUU AUC AUA
Leucine	UUA UUG CUU CUC CUA CUG
Lysine	AAA AAG
Methionine	AUG
Phenylalanine	UUU UUC
Proline	CCU CCC CCA CCG
Serine	UCU UCC UCA UCG AGU AGC
Threonine	ACU ACC ACA ACG
Tryptophan	UGG
Tyrosine	UAU UAC
Valine	GUU GUC GUA GUG

RNA that specifies protein structure according to the code. The most elegant demonstration of the existence of m-RNA comes from phage-infected bacteria. Most biologists accept its role in the cells of plants and animals, but it has to be admitted that there is also a case for scepticism. This has been pressed by Harris (1965) on the grounds that there are quantitative anomalies in the observations of the movement of RNA from the nucleus to the cytoplasm. The m-RNA of micro-organisms has a decay time of the order of minutes, but this must be much longer in the higher organisms that have been looked at because protein synthesis goes on for some time after the removal of the nucleus. However, it may be that enucleation affects protein synthesis in ways other than the removal of the messenger and commands could also emanate from the cytoplasmic DNA of other organelles. Another point is that protein synthesis continues after treatment with actinomycin-D, which is always regarded as an inhibitor of DNA-dependent RNA synthesis and which should therefore stop production of m-RNA. RNA synthesis becomes reduced during mitosis though it continues at a low level, but protein synthesis is reduced considerably only in some cases. In others there is no reduction at all (Mitchison, 1966). This difference may indicate different levels of stability in m-RNA in different cells and in different conditions. It does appear to be true that doubling the amount of DNA in a cell (prior to mitosis) does double the rate of total protein synthesis, but this may not be all that significant, for synthesis of specific proteins has a periodic nature like the transcription from particular genes.

The original observation that appeared to add weight to the messenger theory for higher organisms was autoradiographic. A labelled RNA precursor (e.g. ^{3}H-cytidine) is fed for a short time. At first all the label appears in the nucleus. Then after about thirty minutes there is some in both nucleus and cytoplasm. If the cell is fed for a short time with the labelled precursor then transferred to unlabelled medium the chromatin of the nucleus loses its label to the nucleolus, then all the label appears in the cytoplasm. This was interpreted as showing that RNA is synthesized in the nucleus and exported to the cytoplasm as the messenger theory requires. But all that is actually observed is that the labelled atoms, in this case tritium, shift from the nucleus to the cytoplasm. They could be transferred in some substance other than new RNA molecules. They may be incorporated by turnover into the terminal groups of transfer-RNA for example or precursor pools may exist in more than one compartment of the cell. However many biologist are confident that RNA does move from the nucleus to the cytoplasm. Some must stay, as in the nuclear ribosomes, and some of this could be broken down. We do not know how much though or what sort of RNA. RNA synthesis can occur in the cytoplasm as happens for example in *Acetabularia,* but generally the amount so formed is small compared with that formed in the nucleus though again enucleation may alter the cell's metabolism. An interesting question is whether RNA synthesized in the cytoplasm is primed by DNA or RNA. As we have seen, there is cytoplasmic DNA associated with plastids and mitochondria, but there is evidence to suggest that this would code for a different sort of RNA from the hypothetical nuclear messenger.

This brings us to the role of the nucleolus. It seems probable that this organelle is the site, though perhaps not the only one, of the assembly of ribosomal RNA though probably not its synthesis. As we have said in Chapter 4, it was not at first clear why ribosomes are made of RNA at all and the idea of nucleolar assembly of ribosomes is important because we know so little about what the nucleolus does. An interesting observation in this connexion is that of Brown & Gurdon (1964) on a mutant of the toad, *Xenopus*, which has no nucleoli or nucleolar organizers. This animal does not produce ribosomal RNA subunits,

M*

but it does produce DNA, transfer RNA and probably also messenger RNA. It has a pattern of histone synthesis different from normal toads (Berlowitz & Birnstiel, 1967). Thus the nucleolus has no direct concern with t-RNA or m-RNA. Similarly there are reports (Perry, 1966) that in early stages of embryos there are sometimes no nucleoli present in the nuclei and, when this is so, there is no synthesis of ribosomal RNA. There are presumably enough maternal ribosomes for the needs of the embryo. Moreover nuclei from late embryo stages, when transplanted to unfertilized eggs, lose their nucleoli in the new milieu and no further synthesis of ribosomal RNA occurs until the embryo reaches the later stage. This can be taken as evidence for cytoplasmic control over the expression of the ribosome-producing genetic mechanism. Other experiments of the pulse-chase type suggests that the nucleolus has only a limited capacity for RNA synthesis and that the chromatin is the major site of synthesis of RNA which must therefore include the ribosomal RNA. High resolution autoradiography, after feeding with RNA precursors and giving a chase with unlabelled medium, shows that the label appears first in the chromatin then in the nucleolus and finally in the cytoplasm. Specific genes may be responsible for the ribosomal RNA structure as in bacteria and perhaps the nucleolar organizer ought to be regarded as the ribosomal RNA gene.

Ribosomal protein is probably made in the nucleus, but, if it is made in the nucleolus, which ribosomes are concerned? There are ribosomes in the nucleus and they have been used to assemble amino acids when isolated. We know that other proteins are synthesized in the nucleus, but we do not know if nuclear ribosomes differ from cytoplasmic ones as they could do even if both were made within the nucleus. Protein could also be made in the cytoplasm and transferred to the nucleus. This is known to happen in an amoeba where a stable protein is reported to shuttle to and fro from cytoplasm to nucleus spending most time in the nucleus although made in the cytoplasm (Goldstein, 1958).

Bonner (1965) regards the nucleolus as the principle site of nuclear protein synthesis including that of histones. We know that histone synthesis is inhibited by puromycin, a specific inhibitor of protein synthesis at the ribosomes, and also by actinomycin-D, a specific inhibitor of DNA-dependent RNA synthesis. Thus histones are made by the same mechanism as cytoplasmic proteins, i.e. at ribosomes with instructions coming from messenger-RNA. So presumably there are functional ribosomes in the nucleolus and probably the bulk of protein synthesis that goes on there is concerned with the assembly of ribosomes though the RNA for them appears to come from the chromatin outside. This biochemical idea of the nucleolus must be a considerable simplification. We should also have to consider what happens when the nucleolus is not present, in mitosis, and the relation of the chromosomes to the nucleolus when it is being formed at the end of mitosis.

There is some evidence to show that the information for RNA synthesis occurs in the nucleolar organizer and Perry (1966) reports that ribosome formation starts with the synthesis in the nucleolus of large (45S) precursor units. These are broken down to 18S components, which pass into the cytoplasm rapidly, and to 30–35S components, which stay longer in the nucleolus though they eventually are reduced to 28S and exported to the cytoplasm too. According to Perry, there is still some doubt whether there is any protein synthesis in the nucleolus *in vivo* although the *in vitro* experiments support this view. So the problem of ribosomal protein synthesis remains.

There is also a problem arising from the presence of DNA in nucleoli. McLeish (1964), working on isolated nucleoli of *Vicia* found that 17 per cent of the total DNA and 40 per cent of the nuclear RNA resided in the nucleoli. Is this DNA concerned in RNA synthesis or is it merely part of the chromosome trapped in the nucleolus after separation from the nucleolar organizer? 17 per cent seems to be more than we might have expected if the latter explanation is the only one operating. It has been calculated that a fibroblast, for example, produces some 200 ribosomes per second. This must account for 25 per cent of the total production of macromolecules in a cell. If all these are made in the nucleus and this also makes the DNA and some fraction of the nonribosomal protein, the nucleus's share of synthesis is a large fraction of the cell's total synthesis. Certainly we ought to regard the nucleus as an organ of synthesis and we may wonder, like Mitchison (1966), why cells have any cytoplasm at all.

The role of the histones has recently become the subject of great activity. The theory advanced by Bonner and his colleagues (see Bonner, 1966) is that it is the histones that control the expression of genes. It would clearly be very convenient if there was a mechanism that allowed genes to operate only some of the time and only in some of the cells, for in the course of differentiation of a cell different syntheses are required at different times and different cells also require different syntheses. We may regard it as proven that all cells of a plant carry all the genetical information needed to make every kind of cell. The fact that single cells taken from fully differentiated tissues may multiply and produce whole, normal plants bearing every kind of cell found in that species shows that the process of differentiation does not involve the loss of any of the genetic information originally acquired from the zygote nucleus. Production of whole plants from single somatic cells occurs in nature in a few species and the cell cultures of Steward and others have extended the application of this idea of genetic totipotency. Nuclear transplantation in animal embryos provides a similar, though limited, proof.

Bonner holds that DNA complexed with histone does not support DNA-dependent RNA synthesis. As this is the first step in carrying out the command of a gene to synthesize an enzyme, the histone obviously plays a key role in repressing genes or making them unavailable for transcription. He believes that, in specialized plant cells, only 5–20 per cent of the genomal DNA is available for transcription. Presumably different kinds of cells have different genes available for transcription at any one time and the genes that are operating may vary with time in one cell. This is the key problem of differentiation which is discussed further in Chapter 8. It should be stated here though that not everyone agrees that the evidence for the role of histones is so good as to make the theory unassailable. But the theory does provide a basis to work on which was previously available only for microorganisms through the Jacob and Monod model (see page 385). Not only is there scepticism about the role of histones, but also about the importance of the control of transcription (see Chapter 8).

The nucleus therefore contains the apparatus for controlling the production of new cells and for specifying what kind of cells they will be. It is itself a major site of synthesis in the cell. The extent to which it is in complete control and the way in which each nucleus is itself controlled by the overall commands of the organism are discussed in other chapters.

CHAPTER 7

The Cell Cycle

As we explained in Chapter 6, the obvious alternation of condensed chromosomes and an interphase nucleus led to the idea of a cell cycle or mitotic cycle in dividing cells. A cell goes through a series of events, one of which is mitosis. Then the cell itself divides into two and the daughter cells pass through a similar series of events. A cell cycle is the period between one event and the similar event in the next cell generation. In recent years this idea has been elaborated as more and more has been found out about the synthetic processes that go on in a cell and we are now able to consider more clearly the control of mitotic cycles. This problem of control is of more than academic interest because it concerns practical problems such as cancer and the yield of crop plants. In a cancerous growth, cells divide faster than is needed for the maintenance of normal tissue size. The biological problem here is not so much why cancer cells behave in this way as why ordinary cells do not. What controls the growth and division of ordinary cells so that the body maintains an equilibrium in all the different parts? In complex bodies this is a complex problem because some cells, such as the blood-forming cells, have to divide very fast to maintain health and some cells, such as nerve cells, do not divide at all. Loss of control of division leads to the formation of tumours if the cancerous cells are localized and to leukaemias and similar diseases if the cells are mobile as the blood cells are. The treatment of cancer, apart from surgery, consists of trying to reduce the rate of growth and mitosis. This may be done either by killing the cells that have lost normal control with radiation and with mitotic poisons or by regulating their growth through the hormone supply. Removing the pituitary may cure breast cancer, for example. None of these methods are ideal because they inevitably damage healthy tissues as well as cancerous ones. They are the best available to us now merely because we do not yet understand the basic control of cell cycles. Much of what we do know about cell cycles in plants is due to interest in cancer, for there are many advantages in using plants, especially root tips, in fundamental research of this kind.

7.1 Duration

Until recently much of the work on cell cycles was concerned with determining their lengths and the duration of the process of mitosis within
the cycle. In simple plants and cell cultures the rate of mitosis may be
measured by direct means. In multicellular systems it is usually impossible to determine the duration of the cycle (or the rate of mitosis) by
direct observation and various methods of obtaining average rates have
been devised. One of the simplest is that of Brown & Rickless (1949)
and this involves macerating samples of the meristematic tissue before
and after a period of growth and counting the cells. This is a good
method for plant meristems, but it is hard to decide which cells are
meristematic and which are not. Brown & Rickless decided to use vacuolation as the criterion for the non-meristematic state and, although
there are objections to this, they obtained results similar to other workers employing different techniques. In *Cucurbita*, excised root tips gave
an average value for the duration of a whole cycle (T) of between 7 and
13 hours, depending on the temperature, in the best cultures.

Gray & Scholes (1951) investigated effects of irradiation on roots by a
method which involves a geometrical analysis of cell dimensions in sections and the measurement of the rate of elongation of the root. It is
assumed for the purposes of the method that all mitoses contribute to
the lengthening of the root and this assumption must introduce some
error because some contribute to the widening of the root.

Better methods of measuring rates of mitosis involve the use of labelling and of the mitotic poisons. The first labelling method was due to
Howard & Pelc (1953) who discovered that the synthesis of DNA occurs
over a limited period in the middle of interphase. The method depends
on the stability of DNA in the nuclei. It is assumed to be synthesized
only in preparation for mitosis and to have a negligible turnover rate.
Both these assumptions are valid enough in plant meristems though
perhaps not elsewhere (see page 308). The method involves feeding the
root with a radioactive precursor of DNA for various periods and preparing autoradiographs of sections or squashes. The original precursor
used was ^{32}P-labelled phosphate so that RNA, into which the phosphate is also incorporated, has to be removed. Later, ^{14}C-labelled adenine, which is also a precursor of both DNA and RNA, was used because
^{14}C produces β-particles of lower energy than ^{32}P and therefore gives
better autoradiographs. Nowadays tritium-labelled thymidine is used.
The percentages of cells with labelled nuclei after the various periods of
feeding are calculated and the time from the start of feeding to the point

at which the percentage reaches 100 or becomes constant provides a rough estimate of T (Fig. 133). A disadvantage of the method is that it can be used usefully only to measure fairly high rates of mitosis. Low rates involve feeding the cells for a long time with the radioactive substance and this causes radiation damage (Clowes, 1961b).

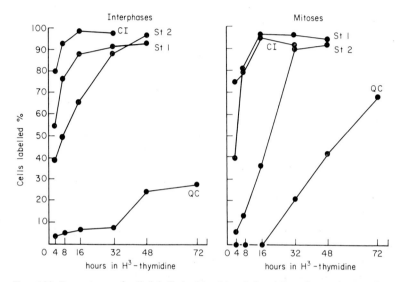

FIG. 133. Percentages of cells labelled with tritiated thymidine after various periods in four regions of the root meristem of *Zea*. QC = quiescent centre, CI = cap initials, St_1 = stele just above quiescent centre, St_2 = stele 200μm from quiescent centre. Data from Clowes (1961b).

Pulse labelling with a DNA precursor provides an equally simple way of measuring average rates of mitosis and has the advantage of providing additional information about the phases of the mitotic cycle. As it is for these that the method is usually used, we shall describe it later on page 355. Pulse labelling suffers the same disadvantage as continuous labelling for tissues with low rates of mitosis because each labelled nucleus carries a source of β-particles.

Low rates of mitosis are inherently more difficult to measure accurately than high rates, but the use of the metaphase accumulation method allows an estimate to be made. Metaphase accumulation is in many ways the most satisfactory way of measuring rates of mitosis in plant tissues. The technique as often used now is that of Evans, Neary & Tonkinson (1957) and consists essentially of providing the tissue with colchicine over a period of time. The tissue is sampled during the colchicine treatment and the fraction of cells in metaphase is counted. Colchicine is a mitotic poison that prevents the formation of a spindle, but it does not, at the concentration used (0·05 per cent), inhibit the progress of the mitotic cycle until metaphase is reached. Then the cycle is arrested for a time before the doubled number of chromosomes returns to an interphase condition in an undivided nucleus (restitution). The accumulation rate has to be determined before any of the nuclei restitute and after spindles that have already been formed have a chance to inter- fere with the counting. For this reason accumulation between about 2 and 8 hours after the onset of colchicine treatment can be used for root tips. Metaphase accumulation over such a period $(t) = e^{\lambda s_2} \cdot \lambda (1 + t/2\lambda)$ where λ is a constant of the exponential growth equation (see page 39), s_2 is the interval between arrival at metaphase and arrival at the follow- ing interphase when the mitotic cycle is not blocked by colchicine. $e^{\lambda s_2} - 1 = $ the fraction of all cells between metaphase and telophase inclusive in untreated roots. From the two equations the constant, λ, is calculated and the duration of a complete cycle, $T, = (\log_e 2)/\lambda$. The increase in the number of cells is assumed to be exponential and, in this simplified version, all the cells are assumed to be meristematic, but a modification may be inserted if they are not.

   Other ways of using colchicine and other substances that arrest the mitotic cycle have been used for measuring the rate of mitosis. The rate at which cells become polyploid after colchicine treatment provides an estimate, though a slightly different one from metaphase accumulation (Van't Hof, 1965).

   The methods that involve measurements of periods of time short in relation to a mitotic cycle assume that division is asynchronous. A difficulty arises in some plant meristems where cell division is partially synchronous. This is true of many shoot apices growing in normal con- ditions of fluctuating light and temperature and some root apices also show partial synchrony. An extra difficulty arises if the phase of partial synchrony is different for different regions of a meristem. This is true of roots of *Sinapis* (Clowes, 1962). Normally in meristems the difficulty is avoided by growing the plants in uniform conditions so that all except inherent rhythms are eliminated, but, of course, this is not the natural environment of the plant. Where cells are completely synchronous in division there is no difficulty in measuring T. Complete synchrony occurs in nature in some endosperms and anthers and in cultures after various synchronizing agents have been used. Treatments that stop the mitotic cycle for a while at a particular phase allow subsequent divisions to be synchronized at least partially. Changes in temperature, chemicals

such as colchicine or 5-amino uracil or hydroxyurea, or the sudden
supply of sperm to egg cells have all been used to induce synchrony,
for it is obviously useful for many investigations to have supplies of
cells all at the same stage of their mitotic cycles.

In higher plants the apical meristems of roots have average rates of
cell division of about once a day. Shoot apices usually have slower rates
of division than roots. Rates of once in seven days have been measured,
but there are variations with environmental conditions and the phase
of the plant. There are also periods of dormancy, when division is
absent or very slow, alternating with periods of great mitotic activity in
both roots and shoots. Away from the apical meristem, the rate of
mitosis drops to zero except in the cambia of plants with secondary
thickening. Within the apical meristems themselves there are wide
variations in rates of mitosis to fit in with the geometry of the apex.
These have been determined only in root meristems so far where durations of the cell cycle vary in *Zea* from 14 hours in the cells giving rise
to the cap to 174 hours in the quiescent centre at the pole of the stele
and cortex (Clowes, 1965) (Fig. 134). Similar variations occur in roots

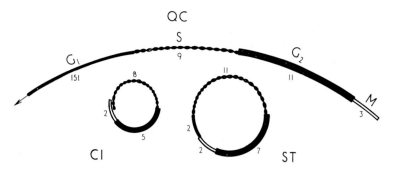

FIG. 134. Mitotic cycles in three regions of the root apical meristem of *Zea* drawn
to the same scale. QC = quiescent centre, CI = cap initials, ST = stele just above
quiescent centre. The figures are the durations, to the nearest hour, of the four phases
of the cycle G_1, S, G_2 and M. Note that in the cap initials S starts before the end of
M and so G_1 is eliminated. Data from Clowes (1965a).

of other plants. The control of rates of mitosis must be important in
maintaining the organization of multicellular bodies not only within
meristems themselves, where the constituent cells have to grow and
divide in harmony with one another to produce a complex pattern
of cells, but also in the body as a whole where the activities of many
cell proliferation compartments must be coordinated to give a proper

balance between the various organs. In a plant the amount of root tissue is related to the amount of shoot tissue and therefore, when growth occurs, meristematic activity in shoots must be coordinated with meristematic activity in roots. The coordination is not simple because the demands are different at different stages of development. They differ in a seedling from those at maturity and coordination is probably brought about by hormones and nutrition. In higher animal bodies coordination must be even more complex than in plants.

7.2 Duration of mitosis

Of greater interest than the duration of the mitotic cycle is the lengths of the various phases. The process of mitosis itself usually takes up a small fraction of the mitotic cycle. The length of this process (M) may easily be calculated if the duration of the cycle (T) is known, for the proportion of cells in mitosis in a tissue (the mitotic index) is related to M/T provided mitosis is not synchronous. If the total number of meristematic cells remains constant, i.e. when as many cells are removed from the meristem as are formed, the mitotic index = M/T. When the cells increase exponentially the mitotic index $\simeq$ (M/T) . $\log_e 2$ if λ M is relatively short where λ is the characteristic constant of the exponential growth equation, $N = N_0 e^{\lambda t}$ (Hoffman, 1949). Table 9 gives values for M and T calculated for regions of a root tip. At ordinary temperatures mitosis lasts a few hours in plant meristems and it lengthens with

TABLE 9

Duration of the mitotic cycle (T), of mitosis (M) and of DNA synthesis (S) in four regions of the root meristem of Zea mays. (Data from Clowes, 1961b; 1965a).

Method of determination	Continuous labelling with ^{3}H thymidine			Metaphase accumulation			Pulse labelling with ^{3}H– thymidine		
	T	M	S	T	M	S	T	M	S
Cap initials	12	2	10	12	3	—	14	2	8
Quiescent centre	—	—	7	174	5	—	—	—	9
Stele just above quiescent centre	25	5	12	28	4	—	22	2	11
Stele 200μm from quiescent centre	40	11	9	29	7	—	23	4	9

decreasing temperature over a biological range. Evans and Savage (1959), for example, showed that in root tips of *Vicia faba* M increases from 1·9 hours at 25°C to 3·1 at 19°C to 6·3 at 10°C and to 14·8 hours at 3°C. T also rises from 22·9 to 26·2 to 64·2 to 260 hours over the same temperature steps. A point that these figures, as well as the figures in Table 9, show is that mitosis occupies a variable fraction of the cell cycle and it is for this reason that the mitotic index itself can give no indication of the rate of mitosis. Although this has been pointed out many times, there are still people who think that the presence of many cells in mitosis indicates a high rate of mitosis.

If M is known, it is easy to find the duration of each of the phases of mitosis, for this is proportional to the number of cells found in a phase compared with the total number in mitosis. (If thin sections are used care must be taken to see that telophases are not over-represented.) In the cap initials of *Zea*, for example, if mitosis lasts 2 hours, prophase occupies about 50 minutes, metaphase 35 minutes, anaphase 20 minutes and telophase 15 minutes. The lengths of prophase and telophase vary from observer to observer because different people differ in recognizing what they consider to be the onset of prophase and the end of telophase. But it is common to find estimates where prophase takes up more of mitosis than any other phase. In root tips of *Vicia faba* at 19°C prophase occupies 90 minutes compared with about 30 minutes for each of the other three phases (Gray & Scholes, 1951). In *Pisum* roots at 20°C prophase lasts 78 minutes, metaphase 14 minutes, anaphase 4 minutes and telophase 13 minutes (R. Brown, 1951). When mitosis is prolonged it is usually prophase or telophase which accounts for most of the prolongation, for when mitosis lasts only a short time the various phases are more or less equal in length.

7.3   The DNA cycle

It has been realized for some time that DNA synthesis takes place in interphase and not in mitosis (Swift, 1950), but the discovery by Howard & Pelc (1951a, b, c, 1953) of a method for determining precisely the position of DNA synthesis in the cell cycle has opened up a profitable new field in investigation of cell cycles. Howard and Pelc originally used ^{32}P-labelled phosphate to label the DNA of root tips and counted the percentage of labelled interphases and labelled mitoses after various periods of feeding with the phosphate. The percentage of labelled interphases reaches a high plateau at about 30 hours and this was judged to be the average length of the mitotic cycle (T). The proportion of cells which synthesize DNA during a short period of feeding was taken to be the proportion of the cell cycle occupied by DNA synthesis (S). This proportion was 16 per cent after 2 hours and, after making an allowance for a possible delay in labelling, Howard and Pelc assigned 6 hours to S. The percentage of labelled mitoses rises sharply after 10 hours. This period of 10 hours (less 2 hours for uptake assessed by Howard and Pelc) is the period that must have been spent by nuclei after their incorporation of ^{32}P in interphase and before the onset of mitosis. This period is called G_2. The graph of percentages of labelled interphases shows a rise up to 10 hours coinciding with the steep rise of labelled mitoses. There is then a plateau of four hours before the percentage of labelled interphases rises again. The length of this plateau was taken to be the duration of mitosis (M) which may also be obtained from the mitotic index as described above. S, M and G_2 when added together come to 18 hours and the difference between this and T gives a period called G_1 which the nuclei spend after the end of mitosis and before the onset of the following DNA-synthetic period.

Figure 133 gives the results obtained in a similar experiment on the root tips of *Zea mays*, but, instead of using phosphate, tritiated thymidine is the label and, instead of using squashes of whole meristems sections have been used so that more homogeneous regions of the meristem could be investigated. The estimates for T and M from this continuous labelling method are given in Table 9. If we use the percentage of labelled interphases at 4 hours to determine S we obtain values of 9·6 hours for the cap initials, 7·0 hours for the quiescent centre, 12 hours for the stele just above the quiescent centre and 9·2 hours for the stele 200μm from the quiescent centre. These values agree well with those obtained by pulse labelling. Estimates for G_2 may also be obtained from labelled mitoses in Fig. 133 and hence G_1 by subtraction. There are several objections to this method of calculating the length of the phases of the cycle and pulse labelling is now used instead.

The methods of determining the time parameters of the mitotic cycle from continuous labelling and pulse labelling assume that the population of cells is asynchronous. As we shall point out later (see page 378), most biological systems develop rhythms and this includes mitosis in a meristematic compartment. In most systems the degree of synchrony reached is only partial, but this upsets the basis for calculation of time parameters of the cell cycle. It is important, therefore, when methods such as we have described are used, to choose material that is either asynchronous naturally or to vary the environmental regime until it is asynchronous. Another limitation of the methods is that it is assumed

that incorporation of the label into DNA indicates net synthesis and that DNA synthesis occurs only in preparation for mitosis. In some systems these assumptions are not valid because some cells possess a non-stable, metabolic DNA, some cells become polyploid or polytene and some cells mature or cease to divide after DNA synthesis. In plant meristems we can usually neglect metabolic DNA, polyploidy and polyteny, for these occur outside the meristems, but this is not always true. D'Amato & Avanzi (1965) have shown that in the root apices of the fern, *Marsilea*, the tetrahedral apical cell, which until now has been considered to be an active part of the meristem, is in fact meristematic only in the root primordia. It later ceases to divide and the incorporation of DNA precursors into its nucleus occurs in raising the DNA content to the 8C level. Most of the investigations of the cessation of division show that cells rest in G_1 and therefore fulfil the condition necessary for valid calculations, but resting at G_2 is also known in both plants and animals and so some caution is required.

The methods for measuring the time parameters of the cell cycle also all assume that S is a homogeneous period whereas, as we have shown in Chapter 6, DNA synthesis can occur at different times in different chromosomes and even at different times in different parts of the same chromosome. So long as it is realized that the S period may contain sub-periods of synthesis within it, the simplification is legitimate. But we ought to stress that the methods could conceal any DNA synthesis that goes on at a low rate outside the S period and so S as measured by continuous labelling or pulse labelling refers only to the major phase of DNA synthesis.

Nowadays the method used for preference to determine the phases of the mitotic cycle is to pulse-label with tritiated thymidine (Quastler & Sherman, 1959). In this, the organ is supplied with the labelled precursor of DNA for a short time which is usually about 30 minutes for root tips. The organ is then washed and allowed to grow in unlabelled medium. Samples are taken at intervals over a period of two mitotic cycles and autoradiographs are made. The percentages of mitoses labelled are then plotted against time from labelling as in Fig. 135. We know that DNA is synthesized over a limited part of interphase and so there is a period during which none of the labelled cells reaches mitosis. This period in an ideal system would be the length of G_2, but in practice the curve does not ascend vertically because the cells sampled vary in the duration of their cell cycles. Therefore we usually measure the time from the origin to the point at which half the mitoses are labelled and this equals $G_2 + \frac{1}{2}M$. The phases of mitosis are sometimes plotted separately instead of together and, instead of making a decision about whether each mitosis is labelled or not, the ratio of the number of silver grains per mitotic nucleus to the number of grains per cell at any phase is plotted as the ordinate (Howard & Dewey, 1960). The labelled mitoses that go to make up the initial rise in percentage are those that were near the end of S during the short pulse. As time progresses along the x axis of the graph (Fig. 135) we find cells that were in

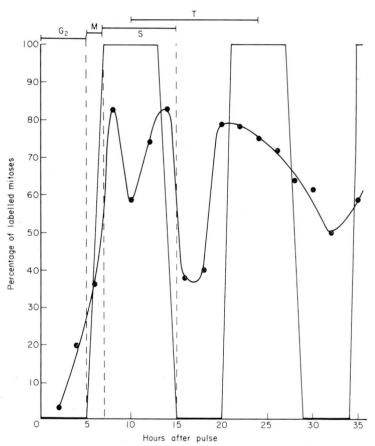

FIG. 135. Pulse labelling of the root cap initials of *Zea* with tritiated thymidine. Percentages of labelled mitoses found at various periods after removal from the radioactive solution. Thick line, data from Clowes (1965a); thin line ideal curve showing how the phases of the cycle are measured and calculated. T, total duration of cycle = 14 hours, G_2 = 5 hours, M = 2 hours, S = 8 hours and G_1 (by subtraction) = minus 1 hour.

the middle of S forming the peak in the curve. During the passage of time the labelled cells pass through mitosis into the following interphase and so become excluded from our percentages and there comes a time when more cells are lost from our curve than are gained by the addition of cells that were at the beginning of S coming into mitosis. Ideally the curve would then drop vertically to zero, but in practice tails off to some low value. The width of the peak at the 50 per cent level is therefore taken as the duration of S, i.e. going from left to right, the time between the point at which cells at the end of S enter mitosis and the point at which cells at the beginning of S enter mitosis.

After the percentage of labelled mitoses falls at the end of the first peak it rises again and forms a second peak as nuclei whose parents were labelled come into mitosis, i.e. the second mitosis after labelling. The distance between the two peaks provides a value for T. In practice the second peak is not so high or clear as the first because irregularities in the cycles damp the oscillation, but the distance between the two leading edges may then be taken to be the same as the distance between the peaks. T may also be calculated by dividing the duration of S by the fraction of all cells labelled immediately after feeding. This provides only an approximate estimate, but can be useful where T is very long and a second peak is not reached during the sampling period. For example, in the work on the quiescent centre of root tips of *Zea* given in Table 10 it would have been laborious to continue sampling over 200 hours in order to obtain a second peak of labelled mitoses. The value given for T, 174 hours, was actually obtained by metaphase accumulation in another experiment on similarly grown roots, but, had this not been available, a good estimate of T (167 hours) could have been found from the measured value of S and the fact that 4·8 per cent of cells in the quiescent centre were labelled immediately after the pulse labelling. M may be calculated from the mitotic index now that T is known and G_1 is obtained by subtraction.

Quastler and Sherman's original results concerned mouse intestinal epithelium, but the method was quickly applied to root tips and figures are given in Table 10. At first the interest was in averages for whole meristems and squashes were used for the autoradiographs. But, if sections are used, the meristem may be divided into regions and there is the additional interest in obtaining data about the organization of meristems and how variations in T are brought about. From the data on *Zea mays* in Table 10 and Fig. 134 it can be seen that prolongation of the cycle is due to lengthening G_1 and that the other phases vary very little. This is not necessarily always what happens, for there is

TABLE 10

Duration in hours of the phases of the mitotic cycle determined by pulse labelling with ^{3}H-thymidine.

		G_1	S	G_2	M	T	
Tradescantia whole root tips		4	11	3	3	20	Wimber (1960)
Tradescantia whole root tips 21°C		1	11	3	3	17	Wimber and Quastler (1963). Double labelling
Tradescantia whole root tips	30°C	2	10	2	2	16	Wimber (1966a)
	21°C	6	11	3	2	21	Wimber (1966a)
	13°C	15	23	8	5	51	Wimber (1966a)
Vicia whole root tips		2	4	8	2	18	Howard & Dewey (1960) see text
Zea root tips							
Quiescent centre		151	9	11	3	174	Clowes (1965a)
Cap initials		−1	8	5	2	14	Clowes (1965a)
Stele just above QC		2	11	7	2	22	Clowes (1965a)
Stele 200μm from QC		4	9	6	4	23	Clowes (1965a)

some evidence that cells can also be held at G_2. Gelfant (1962, 1963a, b), for example, thinks this is true of some of the cells in mouse ear epidermis, but other workers are critical of the data here (Radley, 1965). Mitosis is not a necessary consequence of G_2, for Patau & Das (1959) have shown that, in pith cultures of tobacco (*Nicotiana*), nuclei with the 4C amount of DNA can react to hormone treatments in one of two ways. They can enter a diploid mitosis or they can enter another S phase and then proceed towards a tetraploid mitosis. Nor is DNA synthesis a necessary prerequisite for mitosis, for a cell may lower the level of its DNA by undergoing mitosis without DNA synthesis. This happens in some plant tumours. Tumours may be induced by bacteria such as *Agrobacterium tumefaciens* and *A. rubi* or by bacteria-free extracts from other tumours (see page 394). The cells of the host plant are stimulated to divide and produce the tumour as in the crown gall disease and this leads to an increase in the number of nuclei with high DNA content. Rasch, Swift & Klein (1959) have shown that in tumours produced by *A. rubi* on *Vicia faba* the cells can undergo a reduction in C value from 16 to 2 by successive mitotic cycles in which no DNA synthesis occurs. This process could occur elsewhere in plants and enable cells to proliferate quickly.

An interesting feature of some of the pulse labelling curves is that a dip is sometimes seen in the first peak. Howard & Dewey (1960, 1961) think that this is due to labelling being non-uniform during the DNA-synthetic period. We have seen in Chapter 6 that there is some reason to believe that DNA may replicate at different parts of the S period in different parts of chromosomes in some species and so this dip may not always be present even in tissue that is homogeneous for the cycles of its constituent cells.

Wimber (1966) has used pulse labelling to find the effect of temperature on the phases of the cell cycle. His results are summarized in Table 10. It will be seen that again the variation in the duration of the cycle is mainly due to variation in G_1, but there is some variation in the other phases especially at the lowest temperature. This agrees with other work on plants and on animals in showing a considerable change below 20°C. Between 30°C and 21°C T increases to 130 per cent, G_1 increases to 240 per cent, S to 114 per cent, G_2 to 104 per cent and M not at all. It is for this reason that change in temperature leads to partial synchronization of meristems since one phase is lengthened much more than the others. Changes in temperature ought also to change the radiosensitivity of dividing cells because different phases of the mitotic cycle are differently sensitive. This is discussed later on page 378. In mammalian cells, which live at a constant temperature, S is usually very stable in duration at 6 to 8 hours and G_2 is commonly 40–60 minutes, though different values are found in some kinds of cells. G_1, as in plant cells, shows wide variations up to several months. Certain cells of mammalian embryos have much shorter cycles than the cells of adults.

The pulse labelling technique consists essentially of marking the population of cells at two points, at S by labelling and at M. An extension of this idea is to mark the cells in S at two different times and watch the progress of both marked sets into mitosis. This has been done by Wimber & Quastler (1963) by giving a pulse of tritiated thymidine followed after various intervals by a pulse of ^{14}C-labelled thymidine. The meristems were then fixed immediately and a double film autoradiograph prepared from squashes. As we have described in Chapter 1, the radiation from tritium produces silver grains only in the film touching the cells whereas the radiation from ^{14}C produces silver grains at any level up to about 50 μm. So cells labelled only with tritium show the silver grains all in one plane over the nucleus and cells labelled with ^{14}C show silver grains in all planes of the autoradiographic emulsion. Cells containing both ^{14}C and ^{3}H cannot be distinguished from those containing ^{14}C alone. In this method the ratio of cells labelled with tritium only to those labelled with ^{14}C equals the ratio of the period between the two labels to S. Wimber and Quastler think this provides a better estimate of S than the width of the peak of labelled mitoses because more cells may be used in the calculation. Varying the interval between the labelling processes provides estimates for G_1 and G_2. The results obtained for *Tradescantia* root tips are given in Table 10. A point that became apparent in Wimber and Quastler's work is that using thymidine solutions of relatively high activity (4 μCi/ml) for only 30 minutes disturbs the cell cycle by causing a delay of between one and two hours in G_2 and a delay of several hours in the following G_1. Another double marking technique involves the simultaneous treatment of a meristem with a DNA precursor and colchicine and scoring metaphases, polyploid mitoses and labelled nuclei (Van't Hof & Ying, 1964).

The values for T and its subdivisions obtained by all these labelling techniques are averages for the whole of the tissue examined. There is some reason to believe that, even in tissues that are more homogeneous than whole plant meristems, these averages are made up of cells with widely differing cell cycles. In fact, if we wish to emphasize the diurnal rhythms of organisms, it would be possible to hold that all meristematic cells divide once in 24 hours or a multiple or submultiple of 24 hours and that the values we actually measure are made up of various proportions of cells dividing thus. An example of the evidence for differences in cell cycles comes from Howard & Dewey's (1960) work on root tips of *Vicia faba*. Their pulse labelling method, in which the ratio of grains per mitotic cell to grains per cell is plotted against time after labelling, gives a value of 4 hours for S and 8 hours for G_2. But they also used 8-ethoxy-caffeine (EOC) on another batch of roots and followed this treatment by feeding with tritiated thymidine for one hour. EOC inhibits the formation of a wall between the two daughter nuclei of a mitosis and so the presence of a binucleate cell indicates that the cell has passed through mitosis during the EOC treatment. They found that the percentage of labelled binucleate cells rose from zero at 3·5 hours to a peak of 75 per cent at 14 hours. This means that G_1 must vary from about 3 to 13 hours and that S must be much longer than the four hours determined by normal pulse labelling (Table 8). It is possible that the roots treated with EOC synthesize DNA more slowly than normal roots, but it is also possible that Howard and Dewey's results with EOC are bringing to light a population of cells other than the one whose time parameters are measured by pulse labelling and which do not divide a second time within the part of the meristem investigated. This might account for the discrepancy between the value of 18 hours for T measured between the two pulse label peaks and the values of between 24 and 30 hours measured in other ways. We know that root tips of *Vicia faba* contain regions whose average cell cycles last from 26 hours in the stele to 290 hours in the quiescent centre at 19°C (Clowes & Hall, 1962), but even these figures are averages which could be made up of differing cycle lengths.

7.4 Variation in G_1

An interesting feature of the work on root meristems of *Zea* shown in Table 10 is that G_1 in the cap initials turns out to be minus one hour. This implies that DNA synthesis starts during the previous mitosis in these cells, which have the shortest cell cycles in the meristem (Fig. 134). The method used to measure G_1 is subject to all the errors that occur in measuring T, S, G_2 and M and so not much reliance could be placed on the value of -1 hour. However, if roots are fixed immediately after pulse-labelling with tritiated thymidine, some, though not all, of the telophases are labelled in the cap initials, but not in the stele (Clowes, 1967). It is unlikely that a cell could pass from S through G_2 and M to reach telophase in the labelling period of 30 minutes and, in any case, if cells did this, there would be labelled prophases, metaphases and anaphases, which do not exist after brief exposures to thymidine. This therefore confirms that S can overlap M in these rapidly dividing cells as is shown in Fig. 13.4

This is not the only tissue in which DNA synthesis does not occur in the middle of interphase. In some bacteria and yeast cultures S occupies almost all of the mitotic cycle. In the cell cycle prior to meiosis, S, which can last for several days as in the microspores of *Lilium* and *Tradescantia*, occurs at various periods up to prophase and even into leptotene in some species, but is completed before the end of prophase in all. Synthesis of DNA in early interphase has also been established in several instances. It occurs just after meiosis in the pollen of *Tulbaghia* (Taylor, 1957). G_1 is reduced in ascites tumour cells in mice where S takes 11 hours, M 5 hours, and G_2 2 hours out of the total cycle time of 18 hours. This sort of cycle does not occur in normal cells nor in other kinds of tumours nor even in cells in culture (Baserga, 1963). Changes in the position of S were also discovered by Taylor & McMaster (1954) in the pollen of *Lilium longiflorum*. Here DNA synthesis occurs at the preleptotene stage in the microsporocytes, at late interphase preceding the division of the microspore and during early and mid interphase preceding division of the generative nucleus. All the synthetic periods last several days in this material. Other cells in which S occurs after little or no G_1 period include synchronously dividing cultures of the yeast, *Schizosaccharomyces pombe* (Bostock, Donachie, Masters & Mitchison, 1966), a strain of aneuploid lymphoblastic leukemia cells of mouse grown either *in vitro* or as ascites *in vivo* (Defendi & Manson, 1961), and the slime mould, *Physarum polycephalum*, in which the nuclei of the plasmodium divide synchronously every 10–12 hours (Sachsenmaier & Rusch, 1964). In the latter example, S lasts three hours immediately after telophase, but there is a low level of incorporation of tritiated thymidine throughout G_2 though it is not known whether or not this indicates net synthesis of DNA.

Particular attention has been paid to cases where DNA synthesis is thought to occur during mitosis because of the interest in the molecular events in relation to chromosome duplication and the state of condensation of the chromosomes. DNA synthesis is, of course, not the same as chromosome duplication although the two are normally related. The number of separate DNA double helices in a chromosome is, as we have seen in Chapter 6, a matter of controversy still and sufficient cases are known in which DNA synthesis occurs without replication of chromosomes and in which replication of chromosomes occurs without DNA synthesis (somatic reduction division) for us still to be unsure about the relationship. Interest in the condensation state of the chromsome, i.e. whether its nucleoprotein is coiled or unravelled, occurs because it is generally assumed that, in order to synthesize DNA, it is necessary to separate the two strands of the helix so that a new strand may be fashioned on the template of each of the other two. This may be more difficult to envisage if the DNA molecules are super-coiled in a condensed chromosome such as exists during mitosis.

Some of the earlier workers assumed that DNA synthesis normally occurs during mitosis and this may have coloured their interpretation of the results of investigations. One of the first photometric experiments on this subject was that of Pasteels and Lison (1950) on the glands of Lieberkühn in adult rats and they concluded that S begins during anaphase to telophase and continues into interphase. This result has been criticized on technical grounds. Similarly Gaulden's (1956) work on the neuroblasts of grasshopper embryos with ^{14}C-labelled thymidine which indicated that uptake starts at mid-telophase and continues into early prophase with maxima at late telophase and interphase, can also be reinterpreted according to Taylor (1957) because cytologists disagree about the definition in practice of interphase. However, there are now a few results that indicate that DNA synthesis can occur as precociously as telophase as in the root cap initials of *Zea* and these seem to be associated with rapid rates of division as in the *Zea* example. Thus in the early development of sea-urchin eggs, where T is less than 2 hours at 15°C, the first synthesis after fusion lasts 13 minutes and begins at the first quarter of telophase and the second S period, slightly longer, starts at the same phase and ends in interphase. At 5°C S is lengthened to 27 minutes and begins at mid-telophase (Hinegardner, Rao & Feldman, 1964). We know of no substantiated cases in which S starts earlier than telophase and this may be significant because telophase marks the beginning of chromosome uncoiling.

The relation of S to nuclear fusion of gametes is interesting. In the sea-urchin studied by Hinegardner *et al.* S occurs at or near to fusion, but in *Echinarachnius*, another echinoderm, DNA synthesis takes place in the male and female nuclei independently, beginning 15–20 minutes after fertilization, but before fusion (Simmel & Karnofsky, 1961). So here the major part of S occurs in the haploid nuclei in preparation for a diploid mitosis.

The duration of S has been related to the amount of DNA in the nucleus. Cells with much DNA tend to have extended S phases in general, but there are many examples where the duration of S must be governed by other factors as well. Thus in both haploid and diploid embryos of *Xenopus*, a toad, the lengths of S and the other three phases of the nuclear cycle are similar in spite of the difference in DNA content and therefore the ratio of DNA synthesis must vary by a factor of two (Graham, 1966a). Van't Hof (1966) has also shown in *Pisum* that, although the total cycle time, T, is shorter for colchicine-induced tetraploid cells than for diploid cells of the same tissue, S is similar and so presumably proceeds at twice the rate in the tetraploid nuclei. There are also plants and animals that show differences in S in different proliferating tissues although the cells are similar in DNA content. Another interesting point that emerges from Graham's (1966b) work on *Xenopus* is that when G_1 nuclei are introduced artificially into an egg they all synthesize DNA and undergo mitosis in perfect synchrony with the original egg nucleus even when put into the yolky part of the cytoplasm. This is also true of most naturally occurring multinucleate cells such as the slime moulds but it is not universally true of cells with more than one nucleus. It looks as if the nucleus does not have much autonomy in the timing of DNA synthesis and that it is the cytoplasm that controls this process in the cells of early embryos.

7.5 Biochemical events during the cell cycle

The information gained about cell cycles from labelling DNA has been confirmed and extended by microphotometric measurements and grain counting in autoradiographs. In root tips of *Vicia faba*, Woodard, Rasch & Swift (1961) showed that DNA is synthesized during interphase by measuring the absorption of Feulgen-stained nuclei. Their results on grain counts demonstrated a peak of synthesis at mid-interphase and a minor peak just before prophase. This minor peak coincides with synthesis in some special regions of the chromosomes such as are discussed on page 324 and is obscured by the usual pulse labelling data. Woodard *et al.* were able to correlate the DNA cycle with other events in the cell cycle by using staining reactions and labelled precursors of RNA and protein. Thus azure-B was used as an indicator of RNA, fast green at pH 2·0 for total protein and at pH 8·1 for histone; adenine and uridine incorporation into RNA and phenylalanine incorporation into protein were measured by counting silver grains in autoradiographs. The fast green data for histone followed the same course as the Feulgen data. This means that histone is doubled in preparation for mitosis at the same time as DNA is doubled. RNA, on the other hand, accumulates during telophase, early interphase, late interphase and prophase in both cytoplasm and nucleolus and is lost during the rest of mitosis. Total proteins increase in chromosomes and in nucleoli most during telophase and early interphase and late interphase and prophase, least during mid-interphase and suffer a loss during the rest of mitosis. These results fit in with the expectation that histone and DNA should be synthesized together. The major increase in nuclear volume takes place during early and late interphase according to Taylor (1961) corresponding to the times when protein and RNA are produced, though Sisken (1959) thought that nuclei grow in interphase and then, when they reach a certain volume, they synthesize DNA with little or no further increase in size. Cell mass cannot be the only factor to influence the onset of S since haploid and diploid embryos of the toad, *Xenopus*, have similar cycles though the cells differ in size (Graham, 1966a). Perry (1966) holds that nucleolar synthesis of RNA goes on throughout telophase, except possibly for a brief intermission in early S, and into prophase of both mitosis and meiosis Mittermayer, Braun & Rusch (1967) have shown that the RNA needed for mitosis is formed $1-1\frac{1}{2}$ cycles prior to the mitosis in the slime mould, *Physarum*. A lot of data has been amassed recently on the timing of RNA and protein synthesis in relation to DNA synthesis.

Most of it comes from animal cells especially those whose culture allows easier investigation and, to some extent, the results may not be typical. In HeLa cells, for example, the polysomes are broken down during mitosis and this probably explains the reduction in protein production at M (Scharff & Robbins, 1966). Another complication is that S is not a homogeneous phase because, as we have shown, DNA synthesis may be timed differently in different parts of a chromosome and so RNA synthesis could probably be occurring at one phase and DNA synthesis at another at the same time. The same could apply to protein synthesis and here there is the additional complication that messenger-RNA is long-lived in higher organisms and so there can be a delay between transcription and translocation. These considerations could account for the somewhat confusing picture presented in the literature.

Several people have worked on the timing of the synthesis of specific enzymes in relation to the cell cycle in order to understand better the control mechanisms of protein synthesis. Synchronous cell cultures are the easiest systems for these investigations and consequently there is little information available from higher plants. In the yeast, *Schizosaccharomyces pombe* there is a stepwise synthesis of aspartate transcarbamylase in synchronous cultures, but an unstepped exponential increase in asynchronous cultures (Bostock, Donachie, Masters & Mitchison, 1966). Ornithine transcarbamylase has a similar step-wise synthesis in synchronous cultures, though its synthesis occurs slightly earlier in the cell cycle than that of the previous enzyme. Other enzymes, sucrase, maltase and alkaline phosphatase increase continuously throughout the cell cycle even in synchronous cultures. In other yeasts all enzymes show stepwise production and in bacteria both stepwise and continuous increases have been reported. The main interest of this work is the light it sheds on gene activity. Periodic synthesis could result from a feed-back regulation of the kind we discuss in the next chapter. Continuous synthesis could result from feed-back repression only if there was periodic transcription of several genes.

Thus the mitotic cycle consists of very many events each of them separately controlled in the sense that they can be stopped and started independently, but all of them integrated. Each phase of the cycle serves as a trigger for the next. The balance between nucleus and cytoplasm shifts during the cycle and each relational level leads to a new one. On top of this self-regulating machinery there are imposed commands from the body of the organism as a whole which control the cell cycles so that they react to the genetical and environmental demands in a predictable fashion.

7.6   Sensitivity to radiation

As one of the uses to which ionizing radiations are put is the control of mitotic cycles in cancer, there has been considerable work on this subject. In root tips, growth is reduced to a fraction of the normal rate and depends upon the dose and the sensitivity of the plant. (Generally species with more DNA or bigger chromosomes are more susceptible to radiation damage than others except that polyploids are usually less susceptible than diploids.) This reduction in growth is due entirely to the influence of the irradiation on the meristem as may be seen from experiments in which the tip or the rest of the root is shielded. Growth reaches a minimum value at a few days after the irradiation if an acute dose is given and then returns to normal. Sometimes low doses actually stimulate growth, but this is usually said to be due to suppression of lateral root primordia though low doses can stimulate growth of dormant roots (Van't Hof & Sparrow, 1965). The regrowth of the root after a severe dose of radiation is due to regeneration of a virtually new meristem from the quiescent centre, for this region is less susceptible to damage than the rest of the meristem (Fig. 136). This may be seen by giving an acute dose of X-rays followed by a labelling dose of tritiated thymidine. In normal roots, feeding with the DNA precursor over one or two days labels most of the cells of the meristem, but does not label the cells of the quiescent centre because, as we have seen, these are held at G_1 and proceed through S less frequently than the cells round about (Fig. 137). After irradiation the position is reversed, for now the cells that were originally dividing actively stop synthesizing DNA and dividing whereas the cells of the quiescent centre proceed through S to mitosis and produce from their progeny a new meristem organized like the previous one. This behaviour may also be seen if the durations of the mitotic cycles are measured at intervals after irradiation (Table 11). After acute doses the new meristem recovers a more normal organization by acquiring a quiescent centre. This happens 9 days after receiving 1,800 rads in *Zea* and 14 days after receiving 360 rads in *Vicia*.

In the irradiated meristems discussed above there are two effects on the mitotic cycle. The irradiation or its consequences may so damage the chromosomes that the cell is no longer able to synthesize and grow. When this happens the cell can either differentiate more or less normally without further growth and division or it may die and be crushed by the growth of surrounding cells. This accounts, however, for only part of the reduction of growth of an irradiated root and occurs usually after the cell has gone through its first post-irradiation division, for it is in mitosis that much of the damage to chromosomes becomes apparent by the loss of acentric fragments and the translocation of fragments to other chromosomes. The other effect of radiation is a direct one on the cycle itself. Usually what happens is that the cycle is prolonged and this contributes to the reduction of growth of the organ. But some workers believe that the average length of T is prolonged only by reducing the number of cycling cells and not at all by altering the length of T in the cells that continue cycling. There is some evidence, however, that radia-

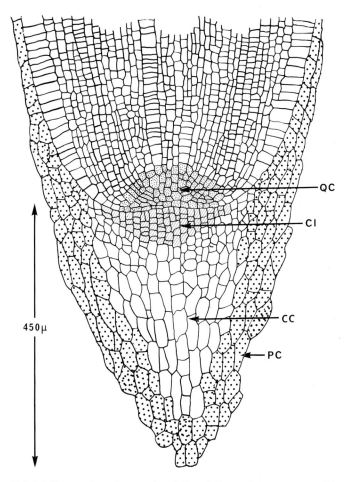

450μ

FIG. 136. Median section of root tip of *Zea*. QC = quiescent centre; CI = cap initials; PC = peripheral cap cells; CC = central cap cells.

N

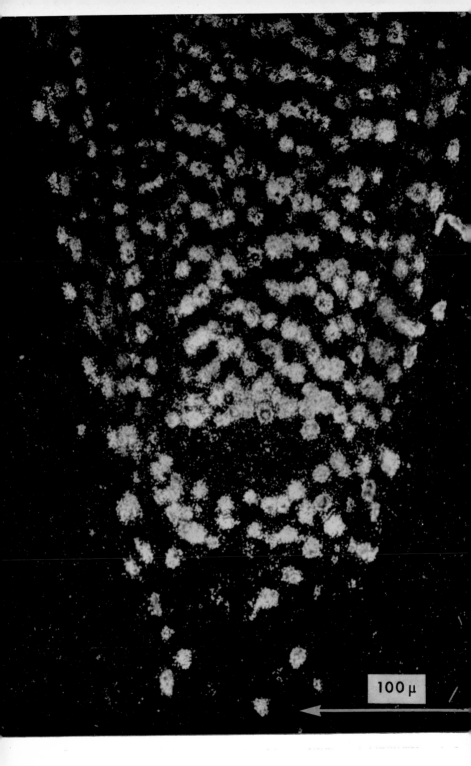

100 µ

TABLE 11

Duration of the mitotic cycle in hours after acute X-irradiation and chronic gamma irradiation. (Data from Clowes, 1963; Clowes & Hall, 1962, 1966.) The regions of the root meristems scored are the cap initials (CI), quiescent centre (QC) stele just above the quiescent centre (ST_1) and stele 200μm from quiescent centre (ST_2).

	Dose	CI	QC	ST_1	ST_2
Zea mays	3 days after 1800 rads acute	134	62	137	54
	6	149	64	86	91
	9	56	234	56	103
	2, 44 rads/hr for 7 days	209	144	48	47
	7·57	99	176	40	58
	12.60	299	178	45	41
	16·51	3580	132	53	73
Vicia faba	3 days after 360 rads acute	95	65	95	40
	7	55	38	55	38
	10	51	46	58	39
	14	74	162	41	35
	0·59 rads/hr for 14 days	45	106	25	29
	1·14	71	77	31	28
	2·28	99	64	45	37

tion may actually stimulate the mitotic cycle under some circumstances, but this is not understood yet.

The sensitivity of a cell to irradiation varies with the phase of the cycle at which the dose is given and differs according to how the sensitivity is assessed and also, to some extent, on the kind of cell. If measured in terms of chromosome breakage, G_2 seems often to be more sensitive than G_1 (Sax & Swanson, 1941; Read, 1959) and metaphase and late prophase seem to be the most sensitive part of the cycle, but only if chromosome damage is measured at the second post-irradiation mitosis (Sparrow, 1951; Davidson, 1958). It is possible to distinguish between a break in a chromatid and breaks in a whole chromosome and, if duplication of the chromosomes occurs during DNA synthesis, obviously a G_1 nucleus should suffer chromosome breaks and a G_2 nucleus should suffer chromatid breaks because the ionization event that causes the break affects the unit in which it occurs. The fact that a G_2 nucleus has twice the amount of chromatin as a G_1 nucleus means

FIG. 137. Autoradiograph of root tip section of *Sinapis* photographed by dark ground illumination. The silver grains (white dots) are clustered over the nuclei that have synthesized DNA during the 48 hours in which tritiated thymidine was supplied to the plant. Note the quiescent centre in which no nuclei have been labelled.

that it presents a target of twice the size to the radiation. This view appears to be confirmed by an experiment of Van't Hof & Sparrow (1965) in which the radiosensitivity of dormant and actively growing roots of *Tradescantia* was compared. The dormant roots have an average nuclear volume of 491 μm^3 and the 2C amount of DNA whereas the active roots have nuclei of 733 μm^3 and are between 2 and 4C. The dose of X-rays required to reduce the growth of the roots to 37 per cent of normal was 305 Roentgens in the dormant roots and 184 R in the active roots. On the assumptions that, for every Roentgen, 1·77 ionizations occur per μm^3 of wet tissue and that for every ion pair 32·5 electronvolts are deposited in tissue, Van't Hof and Sparrow calculated that the energy absorbed per nucleus at the 37 per cent dose was nearly the same in both sets of roots—8611 KeV in the dormant and 7759 KeV in the active meristems. This may be one reason why G_2 is more sensitive than G_1. Another reason is that G_2 nuclei have less time to repair chromosome damage than G_1 nuclei before mitosis occurs to stir up the chromosomes. Chromosomes and chromatids that are broken often rejoin and confer little damage on the nucleus in the end, but if they move, as they do in mitosis, the chance of them joining with the right fragments becomes remote. Healing a break may take time and so the longer time there is before the chromosome moves the greater the chance of rejoining and the less the effect on the integrity of the nucleus. Little is known yet about what breakage and rejoining involves in molecular terms.

If sensitivity is measured as delay to the mitotic cycle, G_1 appears to be more sensitive than G_2 (Neary, Evans & Tonkinson, 1959). Thus when micronuclei are counted at intervals after severe irradiation of a root meristem there are two peaks, one at about 4 days and the other at about 8 days. Micronuclei are produced from acentric fragments of chromosomes that are left out of the daughter nuclei at the end of mitosis (Fig. 138). To be formed at all, the chromosome (or chromatid) must be broken and the nucleus must have undergone mitosis. The peak of micronuclei at 4 days is probably due to the cells that were in G_2 at the time of irradiation and the peak of 8 days is probably due to the cells that were in G_1 at irradiation being delayed greatly in reaching their first post-irradiation mitosis (Clowes, 1963, 1964). These two peaks appear clearly only if fairly homogeneous regions of the meristem are scored individually. They do not occur where whole root tips are scored.

Differences in radiosensitivity at different phases of the cell cycle are coupled with differences in the cell cycles themselves to give variation

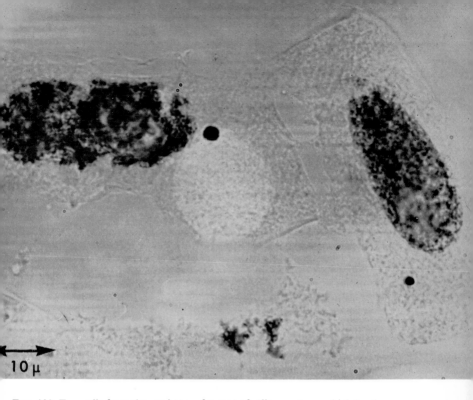

10 μ

FIG. 138. Two cells from the meristem of a root of *Allium sativum* which has been exposed to an acute dose of 140 rads of X-rays. Note the micronucleus present at the side of the main nucleus of each cell. It has been formed by an acentric fragment of a chromosome being left out of the nuclear envelope after mitosis. This has occurred between irradiation, when the chromosome was broken, and the time of fixing the cell (48 hours). Courtesy of Dr J. Thompson.

in the reaction of the tissues of the body to radiations. This has been demonstrated most clearly in root tips which obey the law of Bergonié and Tribondeau (1906) because of it. This law merely states the empirical fact that cells with high rates of mitosis and a long mitotic future are more sensitive to radiation than cells with a low rate of mitosis and little genetic potential. Bergonié and Tribondeau put forward this law to explain the success of radiotherapy in the treatment of cancer, for it was considered that tumour cells differed from healthy cells in having a higher rate of mitosis. Some workers believe that the law is either not true or is unnecessary. There are several well-known exceptions to the law, for example, the small leucocytes which are very sensitive and yet have a low rate of mitosis (Bond, 1959). Moreover organisms do recover from moderate doses of radiation presumably by the division of the cells of the meristematic compartments. Nevertheless there are enough kinds of cells exhibiting obedience to the law to make some explanation desirable. The popular explanation of differences of sensitivity is that cells that divide fast reach mitosis quicker after irradiation than cells that divide slowly and so display their radiation-induced damage as impairment of their reproductive potential (Lajtha, 1961). This is true, for the molecular event that breaks a chromosome may not affect the cell greatly so long as the chromosome remains within the nucleus. The break may even be repaired. But, when mitosis sets in, chromosome fragments without centromeres are often left (to form micronuclei) outside the daughter nuclei which consequently contain an unbalanced gene complement. This does not apply to those members of the Cyperaceae and Juncaceae with diffuse centromeres because most fragments are collected on the spindle at mitosis. Thus Evans & Pond (1964) have shown that the ratio of micronuclei to metaphase fragments is 1 to 5 in *Vicia faba*, which has single centromeres, whereas the ratio is 1 to 518 in *Luzula*, which has diffuse centromeres.

The manifestation of chromosome damage after mitosis may well account for some of the observed effects of radiation and an animal often dies of the effect of depleting a tissue of its rapidly dividing cells before more slowly dividing cells have a chance to display their chromosome damage. But, as we have seen in root tips, rapid division often is correlated with the elimination or reduction of the least sensitive phase of the cell cycle, G_1, which is also the one that would allow most time for chromosome repair. So that, in this situation, there is a real difference in radiosensitivity between fast and slowly dividing cells. It is difficult to investigate this point in animals because it is difficult to trace over a period of time cells which are mobile and replaceable as animal cells are. But if Gelfant's theory about separate G_1 and G_2 populations of cells (see page 358) is true, it could affect the appreciation of what is likely to happen after irradiation.

Another point that concerns radiation and cell cycles is the difference between acute and chronic doses. Many people have considered that what is significant here is the total accumulated dose to the cell. Thus in a population of dividing cells such as a root meristem when a dose of X-rays is given acutely all the cells receive the same dose. But if the radiation is continuous the total dose received by a cell is the dose rate multiplied by the duration of the cell cycle (T) and so it varies with the rate of mitosis. This way of considering chronic radiation seems to be valuable in assessing injury. Thus Van't Hof & Sparrow (1963) found a linear relationship between damage and dose per mitotic cycle in root tips of *Pisum* up to about 450R per cycle. In their experiment

T was reckoned as the time taken to produce 1 per cent of dividing tetraploid nuclei after colchicine treatment and averages for the whole meristem were used. Variation in T was obtained by changing the temperature and the radiation itself was considered not to affect T during the three days of irradiation so long as the dose was below 450 R per cycle. Van't Hof and Sparrow also consider that temperature itself is not important in affecting the amount of damage done to the cells here measured as the percentage of visibly aberrant anaphases. They think that temperature effects are due entirely to varying T and hence the total dose received by a cell.

Clowes & Hall (1966) tackled this problem in a different way. They used the differences in T in the different regions of root meristems and different γ-ray dose rates over 14 days to supply the variation in dose per cell cycle in *Vicia faba*. When damage, assessed as the percentage of cells with micronuclei, is plotted against dose per cell cycle a more or less linear relationship is found at 19°C, but results at 12°C do not fit this curve. This suggests that there is an effect of temperature other than that on T and this agrees with results found after acute irradiation when lowering the temperature produces greater chromosome damage in the presence of oxygen (Evans, 1962). It is often thought that this is an oxygen effect, for there is normally more oxygen available the lower the temperature and it is well established that oxygen increases sensitivity to ionizing radiations. The problem is complicated since the temperature effect may owe its existence to a smaller amount of chromosomal repair at lower temperatures rather than to an increase in primary breaks. Also we know that chronic irradiation changes the relative lengths of the phases of the mitotic cycle (Wimber, 1960, 1966). Thus in *Tradescantia* roots 30 rads per day of gamma radiation prolongs G_1 from 4 to 55 hours, S from 11 to 17 hours, G_2 from 3 to 10 hours. It may also be too much of a simplification to consider a single cell generation in isolation for presumably some of the damage accumulated during one cell cycle is passed on to the next though lineages of cells that accumulate too much damage are eliminated from the proliferating population and this leads to reorganization in the meristem.

7.7 Stimulation and Inhibition

Initiation and maintenance of cycling

It is only in meristems that cells can be usefully considered to be in cycle. When a cell stops dividing its nucleus usually stops at the G_1

phase. Lajtha (1963) considers that this ought to be called G_0 to distinguish it from the G_1 of an active cycle where protein and other syntheses continue. The G_0 phase can last a long time before the cell dies or it can pass into a real G_1 and then to S upon receiving a stimulus. The sorts of stimuli that can restart a stopped cycle are still not well understood and they are probably complex. To the auxin, indole acetic acid (IAA), has been ascribed such a role; for example in the activation of cambia in the spring or in the production of lateral root primordia. In cambia something, which is replaceable by IAA, seems to flow downwards from the bursting buds and cause the cells, which have been dormant since the previous summer, to divide to give xylem and phloem cells. The actual stimulation of the mitotic cycle is not as simple as that, however, since IAA does not have such an effect on all cells. Supplying IAA to roots of some plants causes the pericycle to proliferate and it eventually produces lateral root primordia, but it does so only on certain radii of the root and other cells of the root are not stimulated. Interactions between IAA and a host of other substances have been suggested therefore to be the stimulatory event. Much work of this kind has been done on buds and tissue cultures and from them we have acquired useful knowledge, but the nature of the trigger to the cycle still eludes us.

Other substances, such as kinins and gibberellins, have a role to play in cell division and growth. As with IAA, concentration is important and clearly the problem becomes very complex to investigate. In tobacco pith cultures both IAA and kinetin are needed for DNA synthesis and mitosis to occur at high rates over a prolonged period though IAA alone is capable of stimulating DNA synthesis and initiating divisions (Patau & Das, 1959). One of the suggestions that have been advanced for the existence of a quiescent centre to the apical meristems of roots is that the quiescent centre is the site of auxin synthesis. The argument is that the auxin would be present at high concentrations which might inhibit cycling in the quiescent centre itself but stimulate cycling at a distance where the auxin would occur at lower concentrations. Unfortunately this theory is not easily testable.

Inhibition and dormancy

Many inhibitors of the mitotic cycle are known, though little is known about what stops the cycle in nature. Naylor's (1958) investigation of this subject in the shoot apices of *Tradescantia* provides one of the few pieces of information. *Tradescantia* has strong apical dominance, i.e. lateral buds are suppressed from developing into shoots while the terminal bud is present. Naylor showed by microdensitometry that the nuclei of cells at the apices of axillary buds are held at the 2C level of DNA by the dominance of the terminal bud and that mitosis is absent. When the terminal bud is removed the DNA content of the nuclei at the tips of the lateral buds increases to the 4C value and they can then enter mitosis. Naphthalene acetic acid could replace the terminal bud in preventing DNA synthesis in the lateral buds. The situation in *Tradescantia* is more complex than this however, for whatever arrests the mitotic cycle at the apices of the lateral buds does not do so elsewhere in the buds. Moreover there appeared to be no suppression of protein synthesis in the nuclei at the apices since the nuclei reached normal volume. The DNA level at which cells are found in dormant tissues varies considerably. Setterfield (1961) found that in *Avena* embryos the coleoptiles hold their nuclei at the 2C level and so DNA synthesis is the effective arrestor of the cycle however it is blocked. But dormant embryos of *Pisum* have nuclei at the 2, 4, 8 and 16C levels though Setterfield thinks that perhaps only the 2C nuclei can continue their mitotic cycles when dormancy is over. Certainly it is true that in normal meristems we rarely see polyploid mitoses except in certain species. But probably much polyteny has been overlooked as observers do not always measure their chromosomes or determine their DNA content. As well as this there is also the possibility of somatic reduction divisions reducing the ploidy and the C-value to the 2–4 level of diploid cells and thus accounting for diploid mitoses in a previously poly-C tissue (see page 383). If cells usually stop the cycle in the G_1 condition then DNA synthesis could be regarded as the limiting factor. But some cells are able to stop their cycles in G_2 so it may be that something else is required to produce the delay. Somewhat conflicting views occur as to what happens when polyploid cells are stimulated into division. Do they first synthesize DNA as ordinary diploid cells do or do they go through mitosis without an intervening S period and so end up at the next lower degree of ploidy? Work with isotopes shows that most such cells behave like diploid cells and go through S before mitosis. But unlabelled mitoses are also found presumably reducing the level of ploidy. Stange (1965) believes that both alternatives are open to a polyploid cell, but that there is some reason to think that the lower the ploidy the more likely the cell is to enter S before mitosis perhaps because of competition between cells which need different S periods because of their different DNA content.

N*

Number of cycles

The number of cycles through which cells can pass is interesting. The usual way of expressing this leads us to semantic difficulties because a cell is no longer the same cell once it has undergone mitosis. But, to save circumlocution, let us talk of successive generations of cells as one cell passing through several mitotic cycles. The number of cycles which meristematic cells undergo is strictly limited. Erickson & Sax (1956a) have shown that in the apical 2·5 mm of *Zea* roots some 17,500 cells are produced per hour. They calculate that the initials go through an average of six cycles before stopping division and that the relative elemental rate of cell formation reaches a maximum of 0·16 per hour at 1·25 mm from the tip. Root apical meristems function for only a short time, but even the cambia of trees, which can function for hundreds of years, probably do not have cells which go on dividing continuously for the whole life of the meristem. Individual cambial initials stop dividing and are replaced in the cambial cylinder by new initials derived by anticlinal or pseudotransverse division of other initials so that multiplicative division of the cambium is not a simple exponential increase. Some kinds of cells can obviously pass through a great many generations, but there is reason to believe that normal diploid cells have a limit to the number of cycles. When the limit is reached the cell stops dividing and may die. This limit may be extended by passing through meiosis and syngamy, but clearly we cannot consider such a cell to be the same as either of the diploid cells from which the gametes were derived. Hayflick & Moorhead (1964) consider that human diploid cells *in vitro* and *in vivo* have a doubling potential of 50 ± 10 generations and that, even in cultures, cells do not exceed this limit unless they have abnormal chromosome complements. It is certainly true that the cell lines that have been used extensively are abnormal. HeLa cells, for example, were originally derived from a tumour of a human patient and they have been reproduced in vast numbers. The usual example of an indefinitely reproducing cell line given in text books is of chick heart cells, but there is reason to believe that these were not the same cells as started the clone. They may have been replaced by cells from the embryo extracts used to nourish the culture, for modern methods give a life span of only one year to similar cultures (Hayflick & Moorhead, 1964). How these views apply to clones of vegetatively reproducing plants such as *Lemna* is not known yet, but Wangermann (1965) considers that clones do not age although the individuals die. Some people also think that meristems do not age of their own accord and that the end of their activity is brought about by control from the rest of the plant.

A related problem is the total length of life of a single cell that has come to the end of its reproduction. In plants few cells live for more than one year even when the plant is perennial. Many organs of plants are ephemeral structures even in long-lived trees, but even in long-lived organs many of the cells die a short time after coming to the end of cell division. Some exceptions occur in woody plants where some of the ray cells appear to retain the properties of life for many years. It is difficult to say when a cell dies very often and probably it would be wrong to base conclusions on the appearance of ray parenchyma say 100 annual rings in from the cambium. However we do know that conifer leaves remain alive for as much as ten years without replacement of cells.

Artificial inhibition

Of the inhibitors used artificially, colchicine has already been discussed in connexion with measuring the time parameters of the cycle. Colchicine's great advantage here is that it delays the cycle at one point—metaphase—and does not affect the rate of progress up to metaphase. It does, however, have other effects on cells. It causes chromosome breakage and changes the polarity of cell expansion (see page 57). Many other spindle inhibitors are known. These can, like colchicine, lead to polyploidy by letting a nucleus return to interphase after its chromosomes have divided. Or they can lead to the formation of several small nuclei from scattered chromosomes. Other inhibitors, such as protanemonin, seem to inhibit progress from prophase, though, since prophase is the longest part of mitosis the action may not be specific (Hughes, 1952). Iodoacetate blocks entry into mitosis. 5-amino-uracil and hydroxyurea inhibit DNA synthesis. Some such agents can be used usefully to synchronize cells by accumulating the cells of a meristem at a particular stage and releasing them from the inhibition by transferring them to an agent-free medium. The difficulty of using such agents is that they usually turn out to have unsuspected side reactions. 5-amino-uracil, for instance, retards the cell cycle elsewhere than at S and this leads to complications in meristems, whose cells are never exactly alike in their cycles. The cap initials of *Zea* root meristems, for example, turn out to be hypersensitive to 5-amino-uracil probably because they have no G_1 phase and so the number of cells reaching mitosis after removal of the substance hardly reaches the normal value in this region whereas elsewhere in the meristem the partially synchronized cells have peaks of mitotic index exceeding 40 per cent (Clowes, 1965b).

Synchrony

The synchronization of mitotic cycles is an important technique in biology because of the necessity to use large numbers of cells in any biological experiment. This accounts for a lot of the interest in inhibitors of the cell cycle. As we have explained earlier, any device that changes the cycle pattern in a naturally asynchronous population leads to partial synchrony. Ionizing radiations do this by delaying the cycle differentially at different phases. Temperature shocks can be used similarly by suddenly raising or lowering the temperature for a period and then restoring it to a normal level. Fertilization, which is a trigger to the cycle of zygotes has been much used to synchronize sea-urchin and other eggs. Natural synchrony of mitosis occurs in some organisms especially when many nuclei are present in an undivided mass of protoplasm. In higher plants this sometimes occurs in the endosperm of seeds where the commonly triploid nuclei divide several times before cell wall formation sets in. Seeing this happen led to the idea of a mitotic hormone capable of diffusing throughout the cytoplast, but not able to pass quickly through walls, for as soon as walls occur the synchrony becomes lost. Like so many postulated hormones, this one has never gone beyond the hypothetical condition. Some tissues do however exhibit synchrony of the mitotic cycle even when walls separate the nuclei. Where this occurs, sometimes the phase of the synchrony differs from tissue to tissue in the same organism (Clowes, 1962; Bruce, 1965). Where synchrony does occur, Bruce considers that it does not correspond exactly with the circadian clock of the organism, but is loosely coupled to it. The cell cycle shows more variation in relation to the environment, especially to temperature, and is usually not phased by length of day whereas the phenomena of the biological clock are nearly always so. It is presumably not mere coincidence, however, that many mitotic cycles last about 24 hours.

Mitotic hormones and chalones

The idea of mitotic depressants is in much the same state as that of mitotic hormones. The idea comes from the fact that in animal bodies the rate of mitosis is balanced by cell death and if damage to a tissue occurs it leads to increased mitosis to replace the damaged cells. The different tissues of the body are independent of each other in this respect. If liver cells are damaged other liver cells divide, but cells of other organs do not. Each tissue must therefore have its own system of control of mitosis. Tissue-specific depressors of mitosis or chalones have been considered for certain tissues. In the epidermis the inhibitor is probably an unstable chalone-adrenalin complex and this may, according to Bullough & Rytomaa (1965), account for the diurnal rhythms. These workers consider that, if the chalone operates at the gene level, the operon (see page 384) must also be tissue-specific. The homeostatic mechanism affects both the number of cells in mitosis and the rate of mitosis, i.e. the length of G_1. An increase in the number of dividing cells and the rate of their multiplication in a tissue mass may be brought about by (1) a hormone affecting the rate of mitosis or (2) the introduction of new cells into the system from outside or (3) the creation of new tissue. Bullough and Rytomaa think that mitotic hormones may become tissue-specific by steric affinity for the tissue chalone. Plants present much simpler problems than animals and their dead cells are not so readily disposed of, but wounding does lead to mitotic activity in many tissues and at one time a substance, traumatic acid, was isolated from a wounded tissue and thought to be responsible for the wound response. But the theory seems to have lapsed with the discovery of other substances that affect growth and division. Torrey (1961) has demonstrated how complex some of these reactions are in plants. He showed that kinetin (6-furfurylamine purine), which stimulates many cells of both plants and animals into division, could stimulate the tetraploid endomitotic cells of a plant into mitosis, but probably inhibits the diploid cells of the same tissue. Also auxin can induce diploid cells to enter mitosis within 24 hours, but it takes more than 48 hours for it to bring tetraploid cells into mitosis.

Thus control of cell cycles, which plays a key role in morphogenesis, is a complex subject deserving much more attention.

CHAPTER 8

Differentiation

In this chapter we propose to consider how cells come to differ from each other and general ideas on some of the steps that occur in this process. Actual courses of differentiation are discussed in Chapter 2 in connexion with growth, in Chapters 4 and 5 in connexion with changes in organelles and cell walls and in Chapter 9 on specialized cells.

The problem of differentiation is this. All the cells of a plant inherit (with some exceptions) all the genes of the zygote (or of a spore if it is a haploid generation). But the cells differ from one another in the adult. How does this come about?

8.1 Genetic identity

Totipotency

First let us examine the question of genetic identity. The best evidence for this is the fact that single somatic cells can become complete new plants. This occurs in nature when a leaf epidermal cell forms plantlets as happens in some species. It also occurs in cell cultures when a single cell from a callus, originally derived perhaps from root phloem, divides and forms a cell aggregate from which a complete plant may grow. Some of these cell aggregates resemble normal embryos and are called embryoids, others produce root and shoot apices from a formless mass of cells, but both are capable of growing into complete plants like the plant from which the callus was obtained. The capacity to do this from embryoids in carrots (*Daucus carota*) decreases with the number of culture transfers effected at the free cell stage, though the vigour of growth and division is apparently unimpaired (Steward, 1966). It was once thought that, in order to found an embryoid, the cells must be completely separate and that coconut milk is necessary. Halperin (1966) has criticized these views, which are put forward to explain why zygotes and spores differ in behaviour from ordinary somatic cells. Coconut milk, which, in nature, bathes coconut embryos, was used originally in higher plant cell cultures before a completely defined nutrient solution had been discovered. It is no longer necessary. The other objection is more important and needs some investigation. It is the experience of several people growing plant cells in liquid suspensions that mitosis occurs mostly in the cell clumps and not in the single cells and Halperin says that single cells mostly die. The trouble now is that we are not sure if an embryoid is derived initially from a single cell or if it comes from a clump of cells which may already have differentiated partially in the callus or even in the original tissue. When a solid agar medium is used as in Earle & Torrey's (1965) work on cell cultures derived from *Convolvulus* callus it is possible to be sure that some of the colonies that produce buds and eventually whole plants are derived from single cells of the callus, but these cultures produce nothing like embryoids.

However, most botanists believe that plant cells retain their totipotency provided they do not lose their nuclei or die. There is controversy about this in higher animals and some zoologists hold that some kinds of cells suffer irreversible changes when they differentiate. The difficulty over animal cells arises because fully differentiated cells cannot usually be converted to other kinds of cells. The conversions that have been reported can nearly always be ascribed to the presence of undifferentiated cells in the tissue treated to bring about conversion. Even the experiments in which relatively simple animals, such as coelenterates, put through sieves to separate their cells suffer this disadvantage. Where conversions do occur, as in changing iris cells to lens cells in newts, they are due to special circumstances. The transplantation of nuclei from various regions of embryos into eggs whose own nuclei have been killed, however, shows that the nuclei are still totipotent at the time of transfer, for the egg with its new somatic diploid nucleus can grow into a normal animal. These transplantations are successful only up to certain ages in amphibians, but it is now thought that failure is due entirely to loss or damage to chromosomes and that nuclei of fully differentiated cells are totipotent except after such incidents. Transplanted nuclei that would not normally have synthesized DNA in their original cytoplasm do so in egg cytoplasm. Even mouse nuclei do this in frogs' eggs. Nuclear transplantation has not yet succeeded in higher plant cells for technical reasons, but if it were possible to put a nucleus through the wall without damaging the recipient cell and to remove or inactivate its original nucleus there is no reason to expect a result different from that in amphibians.

Another piece of information relevant to the investigation of genetic identity of somatic cells comes from the large polytene chromosomes of insects. These occur sometimes in several tissues and, where this happens, the pattern of bands on them is similar in all the tissues although the bands that puff vary with the tissue. The onset and persistence of puffing may be different too.

The interesting observation of Earle & Torrey (1965) that colonies of cells derived from filtered *Convolvulus* callus cell suspensions plated on to a solid medium can differ in their cell composition on the same medium gives rise to some doubts about totipotency. These colonies differed in their ability to form tracheids, deposit starch, store crystals, form cellular filaments and form green tissue and the differences seem not to be subject to artificial control. But there are several factors that could explain these differences without invoking loss of totipotency.

Exceptions to the inheritance of similar sets of genes in the development of plants occur because of inequalities in the inheritance of cytoplasmic genes. These lead to somatic segregation best seen in variegated plants. This subject is discussed in Chapter 10. There is not so much evidence as there is in insects for regular differences in the inheritance of nuclear genes by the elimination of whole chromosomes though, of course, accidents do happen in mitosis. In several animals there are regular differences between the soma and the germ line in the complements of chromosomes due to elimination procedures and there are other irregularities in chromosomal behaviour. The existence of B chromosomes or supernumeraries in plants makes similar irregularities possible, but it is not clear if they have any effect on the differentiation of cells.

Polyploidy

The phenomena of polyploidy and polyteny have been thought to play a role in initiating differentiation by altering the genetic complement of a cell. Polyploidy is very common among differentiated cells as may be seen by artificially inducing mitosis by applying hormones or wounding in a normally nondividing tissue. Thus the root hair-producing cells of *Hydrocharis* are always polyploid (Geitler, 1948). In leguminous plants the root cells that produce nodules are polyploid apparently before infection (Wipf & Cooper, 1940). *Spinacia* roots have regular tracts of polyploid tissue (Gentcheff & Gustafson, 1939). On *Zea* the xylem is highly polyploid (Swift, 1950; Clowes, 1959). Diploidy is usually retained in the cells that normally divide, the apical meristems, the cambium, the pericycle of roots, which normally produces the lateral roots and the cambium, and the germ line even if these have to remain quiescent for some time. Maintenance of diploidy is carried out by the exact relation between DNA synthesis and mitosis and this is really what ought to be investigated here rather than the breakdown of this relationship that results in polyploidy. Polyploid cells exhibit a reluctance to divide according to Torrey (1959), but it is not known which comes first—polyploidy or reluctance to divide. Callus cultures *in vitro* show that the medium in which the cells grow affects the predominance of diploid and tetraploid cells (Torrey, 1961) and that when roots grow out from a callus they are always made of diploid cells even when the callus contains a high proportion of polyploid cells. It looks as if some balance between auxin and kinin availability controls the ploidy of tissues, for kinetin stimulates tetraploid cells to divide rather than diploid cells and auxin brings diploid cells into division before tetraploid cells.

The evidence that we have about polyploidy in natural situations and in controlled culture conditions does not allow us to press the role of polyploidy in causing differentiation. Indeed it is not clear how multiplying the number of all genes could change the course of development. Rather it may be regarded as one of the products of differentiation. In some cases it may even be specially selected for as being an economical way of increasing the amount of gene activity by increasing the number of genes without the disruption of the cell and the expenditure of energy and material that mitosis involves in spindle formation etc. Likely examples of such a situation occur in the nutritive tissues of plants, the tapetum of anthers and the endosperm of seeds. These have to provide DNA and other substances for the rapid multiplication of essential cells. Other examples of similar functions may be secretory cells and much of this could refer to polytene cells also, though these are not so well known in plants as in animals. Obviously different tissues acquire different methods of enabling their cells to perform efficiently by holding the most appropriate nucleus-to-cytoplasm ratio. In a diploid organism the tissues that give rise to the germ cells (the shoot apical meristems) must be prevented from becoming polyploid, but it is probably wrong to think of polyploidy and polyteny as due to loss of control over DNA synthesis in cells with no mitotic future.

Some species of plants never have polyploid cells (Stange, 1965). New polyploid species (i.e. species that are polyploid in relation to other allied species) quickly evolve as diploids by mutation and the mechanism of meiosis prevents them from becoming haploid as it does in other sexually breeding species. The evolution of the dominance of the diploid generation as opposed to the haploid generation in higher plants presents another problem beyond the scope of this book.

8.2   Gene regulation

The view so far, therefore, is that there is no reason to question the genetic homogeneity of somatic nuclei in ordinary plant development and we are still left with the problem of differentiation to explain. The most popular theory about this is based upon Jacob & Monod's (1961) well-known work on β-galactosidase metabolism in *Escherichia coli*. This may be summarized briefly as it is described in most modern text books of biology and evidence for it is presented almost daily. In these bacteria there are supposed to be regulator genes making repressor (or regulator) substances. These, which may be proteins, are of two sorts (Fig. 139). (1) In the 'inducible system' they are capable of combining with inducer molecules. When they do so they are inactivated; when they are not combined they are active in repressing. (2) In the 'constitutive repressible system' the repressors are capable of combining with co-repressors. When they do so they are active as repressors; when they are not combined they are inactive. The active or activated repressors can interact with an operator gene. The operator is linked to a group of 'ordinary' structural genes in a unit called an operon. If the operator has combined with a repressor it represses the activity of all the structural genes of its operon in producing messenger RNA's and hence in synthesizing proteins. If the operator is not combined with a repressor it allows the structural genes to function. The messenger RNA is unstable and is used up in transferring information so that the operator effectively controls protein synthesis. The mode of operation of this theoretical model is essentially a feedback system since the co-repressors are usually thought of as end products of enzymic activity and the inducers the substrates of reactions mediated by the enzymes. Thus, in the constitutive repressible system when the appropriate co-repressor is present, it joins with the repressor to repress the operon, i.e. negative feedback and this must be the usual state of the operon, i.e. with the structural gene not operating. In the inducible system, if an appropriate inducer is present, it reacts with the repressor and prevents it from repressing the operon, i.e. positive feedback. In the model the complexes of both inducers and co-repressors must be able to recognize their own operator genes. Some such system of recognition must occur because variation in the level of those substances that occur in the chemical pathways of several reactions would otherwise induce enzymes for which no substrate was available.

There is a danger that, in view of the publicity given to the Jacob and Monod hypothesis and the evidence that is accumulating to support it,

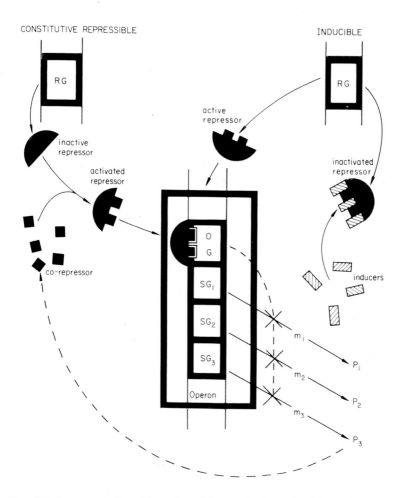

Fig. 139. A representation of the action of the constitutive repressible and inducible systems of gene regulation. The active and activated repressors produced by the regulator genes (RG) are represented as fitting into the operator gene (OG) of the operon. They then block the transcription of the structural genes (SG) of the operon in producing the messenger-RNA's (m_1, m_2, m_3) which would specify the synthesis of the protein enzymes (P_1, P_2, P_3). One of the enzymes is concerned in activating a repressor in the repressible system. In the inducible system, the inducers are represented as inactivating the repressors by preventing them from fitting the operator genes.

other possible systems for controlling the action of genes may well be ignored. Shepperd & Englesberg (1967) have put forward the suggestion that, contrary to the Jacob and Monod system in which all genes are assumed to be 'on' until they are switched 'off', there may be some genes which are off or inactive until they are switched on. The particular genes which these workers have studied are a group of four involved in some of the initial steps of breaking down the sugar, L-arabinose, in *Escherichia coli*. The two or possibly three enzymes are only produced by the genes as a response to the appearance of L-arabinose (the inducer) in the system. Three of the genes produce the three enzymes and the fourth is responsible for a regulating principle (P_1). Up to this point the mechanism is identical to that proposed by Jacob and Monod. However Shepperd and Englesberg suggest that normally in the absence of L-arabinose P_1 is inactive. When L-arabinose is presented to the bacterium, P_1 (probably a protein) is converted into an active form (P_2). The P_2 in turn reacts with an initiating region of the genes and switches on the functional genes G_1, G_2 and G_3. When the L-arabinose is used up P_2 reverts to P_1 and $G_1 - G_3$ switch off. Thus, whereas in the Jacob and Monod system a mutation occurring in the regulator system of $G_1 - G_3$ leaves all these genes switched on, in the Shepperd and Englesberg system, regardless of the amount of inducer present, such a mutation would leave all these genes permanently switched off. Shepperd and Englesberg claim that such a system of positive control seems a likely proposition not only in these particular genes, but also in other inducible enzyme systems such as those responsible for L-rhamnose metabolism.

The problem now is to see if a system similar to one of these could operate in multicellular organisms that exhibit cellular differentiation, for there seems to be no escape from the conclusion that differentiation consists of an organized use of the genetic information contained mostly in the chromosomes. The necessity for a repressive system seems even more compelling in higher organisms with a thousand times the DNA content of bacteria and we know that the enzymic activity of cells changes with development as Brown (1963) has shown mainly from assays of root tissue at different levels. We have already inferred that differentiation of cells results from differences in the enzymes specified by the genes, but all the cells have all the genes all the time. So, if this is true, there must be some mechanism for activating or suppressing some of the genes in some of the cells some of the time. We have shown that it seems likely that gene activity consists of producing a specific messenger-RNA—transcription by RNA-polymerase, and that the messenger-RNA specifies the assembly of a particular protein. It must be remembered, though, that work on *Acetabularia* and other organisms whose nuclei can be removed shows that protein synthesis can take place without DNA transcription and without RNA synthesis and can occur a long time after its induction by stored RNA. We have also shown that there is some evidence that the gene regulator in higher organisms may be a histone though how the histone chooses which genes to repress is not known. The evidence for this theory comes from Bonner and his colleagues (summarized in Bonner, 1965) who have followed the *in vitro* synthesis of pea (*Pisum*) seed globulin. They believe that DNA in pea embryo chromatin exists in two forms, one complexed with histone and one uncomplexed and that the former does not support RNA synthesis whereas the latter does. They have shown that RNA produced by chromatin of cotyledons directs a ribosomal system to produce the globulin along with other proteins, but that RNA from the buds of pea plants cannot induce globulin synthesis although other proteins are produced. They then showed that pea bud chromatin from which the protein has been removed can support the synthesis of the cotyledonary globulin. The conclusions from this are therefore that, although both buds and cotyledons have the gene for globulin production, it is operational, or derepressed, normally only in cotyledons and that it is the histone protein that represses the gene in buds.

If Bonner's theory is soundly based (and it is too early to say whether it is or not) it is a most important step forward in understanding differentiation. But it still leaves a lot of problems. Need there be a different histone to repress every gene and, if so, how are they produced? If not, how does the histone choose the 'right' gene? What decides when and where a gene shall be repressed and derepressed? We have already referred (see page 342) to the scepticism expressed by Harris about messenger-RNA. He is also sceptical about the Jacob and Monod model for genetic regulation, especially its value for higher organisms. One of Harris's most important points comes from the use of animal heterokaryons in which a cell contains more than one kind of nucleus. These heterokaryons are made by using a UV-inactivated virus to cause fusion of cells in culture and very diverse hybrid cells can be produced in this way. In one experiment (Harris, 1967) he used HeLa (human) cells containing a HeLa nucleus and a fowl erythrocyte nucleus. In the heterokaryons the erythrocyte nuclei, which are normally highly condensed and incapable of synthesizing DNA or RNA, enlarge and synthesize DNA and RNA. The enlargement, though, is not a consequence of DNA synthesis and the amount of RNA synthesized is proportional to the size of the nucleus. Thus the HeLa cytoplasm appears to 'turn on' the erythrocyte nuclei by making it open up its condensed chromatin and changes in nuclear volume may actually regulate the regions of chromatin at which RNA is made.

Now condensation of chromatin, as we have shown in Chapter 6, normally affects whole chromosomes or large pieces of chromosomes and so its control of gene activity must be very coarse, affecting huge numbers of genes at one time and, if a fine control of the Jacob and Monod type operates at all, it presumably is overruled by condensation. Moreover, the signals from the cytoplasm—the co-repressors or inducers—can hardly be very specific if human cytoplasm can successfully signal to fowl nuclei and control the state of dispersion of the chromatin and therefore the amount and type of RNA being made, but the Jacob and Monod theory requires them to be specific. It is therefore possible that precise gene regulation occurs in the cytoplasm and not in the nucleus, i.e. in 'translating' the commands of the RNA base sequence into amino acid arrangements rather than in the transcription of the DNA. This may occur in *Acetabularia* where enucleate cells can still carry out the morphogenetic sequences of stalk and cap formation using informational RNA stored in the cytoplasm. It may also occur in sea urchin (Echinoidea) and amphibian eggs where, after fertilization, protein synthesis proceeds in the absence of nuclear RNA synthesis for a time.

In the artificially produced animal heterokaryons already mentioned a general rule appears to be emerging that where one of the nuclei is synthesizing DNA or RNA all the others will do so even if they were inactive in their original cell. Hence synthesis is 'dominant' to repression.

The most likely candidates for the role of ultimately deciding when and in which cells a gene shall be repressed are the hormones. The one that has been investigated most in this connexion is ecdysone, the hormone that controls moulting in insects, for here the effect of the hormone on the genes can be watched directly by observing the puffing of the giant polytene chromosomes where only about 10 per cent of the bands puff at any one time (see page 330). A botanical system that is receiving a great deal of attention of a different sort is the effect on shoot apices of 'florigen', the hypothetical flowering hormone produced in leaves under appropriate regimes of light and dark. It is attractive to think of the hormones switching genes on or off in a switching network that leads to sequences of developmental processes, but the nature of the reactions that would be involved is unknown. Other possible mechanisms of limiting gene action involve differential effectiveness of messenger RNA and suppression of part of the ribosome complement. Although we know so little about the actual processes going on inside a plant, there has been built up in the last few years a framework of ideas about the nature of differentiation which has revolutionized the subject from being a hopeless problem only discussed by the more philosophical amongst us to being a problem broken down to more manageable theories that can be tested. Bonner's (1965) hypothesis of a switching network, in which every cell somehow senses its position in a plant and reacts in one of two ways to every aspect of differentiation (e.g. divide or not divide, lignify or not lignify), according to the position in which it finds itself, is speculation based upon the analogy of computer mechanisms. But it is speculation that could lead to a testable case because experiments with artificial environments already provide us with examples of position effects. But it should be said that the appearance of enzymes in development may differ from the induction of enzymes by the environment in adult tissues.

In plants the effects of growth substances on the initiation and differentiation of vascular tissue is the best known example of environmental effects upon cell development. Camus (1949) showed nearly twenty years ago that buds grafted on to pieces of aseptically grown roots induced vascular tissue beneath them even through cellophane and that blobs of synthetic auxin have the same effect. More recently workers in Wetmore's laboratory have used callus cultures, which consist of of parenchyma, to induce xylem and phloem at will (Wetmore & Rier, 1963; Wetmore, De Maggio & Rier, 1964). Low concentrations of sugar with high auxin concentrations favour xylem formation, high concentrations of sugar with low auxin concentrations favour phloem, while intermediate concentrations induce both xylem and phloem and a cambium in between them. Grafting of shoot apices or even of blobs of agar containing sugar and auxin on to the callus leads to the formation of nodules of vascular tissue with a circular pattern. In these nodules the xylem is on the inside and the phloem is on the outside, as it is in most normal organs, and the diameter of the circles depends upon the concentrations of the auxin.

Torrey's (1963) use of excised root cultures in which the root tip is nourished by one medium and the base by another shows that the way auxins and sugars are supplied also affects the pattern of differentiation. In particular he succeeded in achieving cambium formation in roots of *Pisum* by supplying IAA through the basal end whereas this is not normally achieved in ordinary root cultures of *Pisum*. But it is not clear whether it is the mode of supply itself that effects cambium formation or whether it is the attenuation of the supply of auxin by basal feeding that results in the change in behaviour.

8.3   Patterns of differentiation

We have so far in this chapter examined what causes one cell to differ from another on the basis of thinking that the cells are autonomous in controlling their own destinies. The degree to which one is justified in treating cells as autonomous depends upon one's outlook and purpose. The 'cell theory' as advanced by Schleiden (1801–1881) and Schwann (1810–1882) treated the cell as the independent unit of plants and animals on the grounds that all organisms were considered to be made wholly of cells and that their properties were derived from the isolated activities of the cells in an environment created by the aggregate. It is, of course, possible to be critical of the cell theory because there must be coordination between cells and there is even protoplasmic connexion between most of them in plants. But, in spite of this, cells are isolated from one another to some extent as may be seen in the existence of many kinds of chimeras where cells of differing genetic constitution exist, grow and reproduce their kind side by side though cooperating to the extent of producing a workable tissue or organ.

We have shown that there are possible mechanisms making the course of development of one cell differ from that of a genetically identical neighbouring cell. This involves some selection of the developmental pathway by regulating the expression of the genes. What decides the selection?

Firstly it should be said that the number of pathways is strictly limited. There is not a large number of different cell types even in the most complex plants and animals. Whether there could be an almost infinite range of cell types reflecting all the combinations of repressed and derepressed genes is another matter, but it might be economical to derepress the genes in related blocks. If this is what happens in multicellular organisms it reduces the number of possible courses of differentiation somewhat. But probably what happens in nature is that the number of triggering operations is much more limited.

The way in which morphogeneticists tackle the problem of selection of developmental pathways is to modify the environment of a tissue and see if it changes its differentiation. This method draws attention to differentiation, but has rarely produced any real insight into differentiation. This criticism can be applied to surgical and chemical treatments of embryonic tissues, but most such treatments are performed for purposes other than the study of differentiation. One point that does emerge from such experiments on root-tips is that it is the apex itself that plays the major part in controlling the pattern of differentiation in the root and not the already formed tissues of the older parts of the root. This is shown by Bünning's (1952) experiment in which an apex was excised, rotated about its axis and replaced on the root and by Torrey's (1955) experiments on excised roots in culture media containing auxin. On the other hand it is difficult to obtain much information about the role of natural auxin from the changes that occur in the number of xylem poles in excised root tips with differing supplies of auxin in the nutrient medium (Torrey, 1957). Auxin, among its many other supposed roles, is said to affect xylem production, but something else must occur in nature to make procambium susceptible to becoming xylem, for Jacobs (1959) has shown that fifteen times the amount of IAA needed to change a procambial cell to xylem is needed to change a parenchymatous cell to xylem.

Something should be said here about the process called 'dedifferentiation'. This occurs when a differentiated tissue changes its role and thus the appearance of its cells. But it is not a reversal of differentiation. It is always accompanied by cell division and subsequent differentiation of the new cells so formed. An example of dedifferentiation occurs in the formation of lateral roots. Here the parenchymatous cells of the pericycle and, in some species, the endodermis become meristematic at certain sites defined by the radial pattern of xylem and phloem and distance from the root tip. Before dividing, DNA is synthesized, the nuclei swell, RNA is synthesized and the cytoplasm becomes more basophilic presumably due to the increase in RNA. The pattern of cell division gives rise first to a primordium which bulges into the cortex and then to a root apex containing all the kinds of cells possessed by the mother root. Cell division thus affords a kind of rejuvenation and allows new kinds of cells to replace already differentiated ones. Stange (1965) holds that dedifferentiation proceeds more slowly the older the tissue as if the reversal of ageing becomes more difficult with age.

The problems of ageing of cells and death interests man more as his expectation of life increases, but there is very little information available. The life span of a cell varies from a few hours to perhaps less than a hundred years. Life can be prolonged only by annihilating the individual cell by division so that as soon as cells stop dividing they age. Why can a cell not go on living indefinitely? Does the formation of proteins stop? Does the DNA have a limit to the amount of RNA it can specify? Or does differentiation always end with the specification of increasing entropy? If so, what triggers the end? Or is ageing merely the chance accumulation of molecular accidents that lead to incompatible combinations of genes functioning at the same time? Whether cells can divide indefinitely is a problem we have already discussed in Chapter 7.

There are many cases where patterns of distribution of enzymes and other substances are known to precede differentiation in the same pattern. The places where axillary buds will arise show themselves by high peroxidase activity before cell division makes the site obvious (Van Fleet, 1959). Similar patterns precede the radial pattern of vascular differentiation in roots and stems (Van Fleet, 1948). The trouble with these observations is that it is difficult still to assess the significance of the chemical pattern. In most examples one cannot say whether it is the direct cause of the differentiation or whether it is merely another manifestation of some differentiation process that has preceded it.

Radially symmetrical patterns, such as those in stems and roots, exhibit the same spacing phenomena as other kinds of pattern. The number of protoxylem poles in a root fits into the size of the stele so that the poles are equidistant from each other. Where there is wide divergence in the width of roots the numbers of poles is usually, but not always, variable. Patterning of this kind may be explained by Turing's (1952) hypothesis on the chemical basis of morphogenesis. In this theoretical model a system of chemical morphogenetic substances (morphogens) interacting and diffusing through the tissue is supposed to account for morphogenesis. Turing showed that patterns, such as occur in plants and animals, may arise even from homogeneous systems of reacting substances due to instability, giving, for example, stationary waves in the amplitude of morphogen concentrations around the periphery of an apical meristem. The concept of stationary waves is important because it could explain how a pattern fits the dimensions of an organ (e.g. how a whorl has a whole number of leaves) in the same way as radio waves fit the electrical dimensions of an oscillatory circuit.

Polarity

One of the phenomena that students of differentiation have to consider is polarity. This is initiated by various stimuli in plant zygotes. In zygotes free of the parental tissue, temperature, light, auxin, oxygen and pH gradients, contact, gravity and the point of entry of the sperm have all been shown to initiate gradients of differentiation under controlled conditions as, for example, in the eggs of *Fucus* and other simple plants. Higher plants retain their zygotes within maternal tissue and it is this that decides the polarity of the embryo. In the pterido-phytes the archegonium gives an axis to the egg cell and the subsequent development of the embryo is related to it in various ways which are constant for a taxonomic group of plants. In *Selaginella* the zygote elongates parallel to the axis of the archegonium and its first division is transverse forming a cell at the outer (neck) end which becomes the suspensor tissue and an inner cell from which the shoot apex, leaves and, later, the foot and root develop. In *Isoetes* the first division is oblique to the archeogonial axis: in leptosporangiate ferns it is parallel to the axis. In *Equisetum* the shoot apex develops from the outer of the first two cells instead of the inner as in *Selaginella*. In the angiosperms, where the egg is usually only a nucleus in the cytoplasm of the embryo sac, the first division is always unequal and nearly always at right angles to the embryo sac axis. The inner of the first two cells usually produces most of the embryo proper and is provided with more RNA, more plastids and bigger mitochondria than the outer (micropylar) cell which con-tributes less to the embryo—sometimes only the suspensor and basal cell (Jensen, 1965). The polarity of the embryo, once initiated, is en-hanced by the formation of the apical meristems of the root and shoot and this occurs also in the embryoids produced in Steward's free cell cultures already mentioned (see page 380) though here the initiation of polarity is presumably the random orientation of the first mitosis that leads to a two-celled filament. Once mitosis has occurred the system is no longer homogeneous even if it started in this condition, for, as R. Brown (1958) has pointed out, the occurrence of a spindle in a cell confers for ever a polarity of its own on the daughter cells. If a cell ever starts by being completely free of polarity and no external stimulus ends its homogeneous condition, pattern could be induced by the chance reactions within it in the same way as Turing (1952) envisaged the initiation of instability in completely homogeneous cell systems to give, for example, standing waves in the amplitude of concentrations of various hypothetical morphogenetic substances.

There are many examples known of differentiation being initiated by gradients within cells or small groups of cells. The distinction between the generative cell and the vegetative cell of a pollen grain has been shown to be due to the pattern in distribution of RNA (La Cour, 1949). Similar cases of polarity occur in the formation of some root hair cells (trichoblasts) and stomatal guard cells and Stebbins (1966) has charac-terized such differentiation as having a set sequence. (1) A cytoplasmic gradient is set up in a single cell. (2) The nucleus becomes asymmetric in position. (3) Mitosis occurs normally, but the two nuclei grow to different sizes at its end. (4) The two daughter cells enter on different developmental courses, one of them, called a meristemoid, with the denser cytoplasm usually dividing more actively than the other. Some investigations have revealed differences in enzymic activity between the two poles and in one example there is known to be a difference in the amount of endoplasmic reticulum at the two poles (Avers, 1963). Experimental treatments that disrupt the cytoplasmic gradients or displace the nucleus in the gradient result in abnormal or suppressed differentiation.

Stebbins (1966) has worked extensively on the pattern of cellular differentiation in the epidermis of barley (*Hordeum*) leaves and has erected a hypothesis to explain the events he sees there. The leaf tip produces substances that promote cell elongation; the meristematic regions which include the leaf base, the apex of the shoot and the procambium of the leaf veins produce mitosis-inducing substances. In tissues that are losing their meristematic activity an asymmetrical mitosis may produce a feebly dividing daughter and an actively dividing or meristemoid cell. The meristemoids now generate mitosis-inducing substances. The meristematic cells and cells with precociously thickened walls impede the flow of the substance inducing cell elongation. This substance produces a gradient that causes all dividing cells to divide asymmetrically to produce meristemoids on the side facing the hormone flow. The kind of cell produced varies with the maturity of the cell at the time it comes under these influences and the maturity of the cell depends upon which genes are operative out of a succession of activated and repressed genes.

8.4   Crown gall

No account of differentiation in plant cells would be complete without mentioning this neoplastic disease, which is still an enigma after many years of research on it. Many dicotyledons are susceptible to the disease which is caused in nature by a bacterium, *Agrobacterium tumefaciens*. Typically a tumour or gall is produced on a stem, and some species have galls that bear abnormal buds. The bacteria produce a tumour-inducing principle (TIP) which transforms normal plant cells into tumour cells permanently in the sense that once transformation has occurred the abnormal proliferation of the tumour cells goes on independently of the bacteria. According to Braun (1962, 1963) the cells become vulnerable to transformation by irritation caused by wounding. After wounding the liquid from ruptured cells activates resting cells into division two or three days afterwards and the vulnerability to the TIP reaches its highest at 60 hours after wounding. Small, slowly growing, benign tumours are initiated at 30 hours and again at 90 hours, so tumour formation is limited to a short phase of the wound healing process, though the reason for this limitation is not known.

The tumour is a disorganized mass of small dividing cells containing some giant cells with one or more nuclei and some poorly organized nodules of vascular cells. There is a heightened rate of DNA synthesis, but this appears not to be the initial act of tumour induction though it leads to the production of polyploid or polytene nuclei. Some of the cells are always diploid though all of them behave like tumour cells and thus the tumour is similar to animal tumours in having nuclei of many kinds. The tumours may be simulated artificially by supplying auxin and kinin externally, for these substances lead to hypertrophy, hyperplasia and disorganization such as tumours possess, but such simulated tumours stop growing when the auxin and kinin supply is stopped, whereas crown gall tumours continue growth. Normal tobacco pith cells grown in culture enlarge when given auxin, but do not divide. They neither enlarge nor divide when given kinin, but, when given both kinin and auxin, they enlarge and divide. These normal cells cannot synthesize their own auxins or kinins, but transformed cells can and also they can produce all their other requirements from a medium containing minerals and sucrose. The cells from benign tumours, on the other hand, initiated at 34 hours after wounding need auxin, glutamine, myo-inositol, asparagine, cytidilic acid and guanylic acid for rapid growth. Cells from tumours intermediate between benign and fully autonomous need the first three of these substances to acquire rapid growth. Therefore tumour cells can synthesize substances that normal cells need but cannot make for themselves. The switch from normal to tumour cell involves a change in the regular metabolism to produce increased amounts of nucleic acids, proteins etc. for the enhanced rate of growth and division. And, in making the switch, the tumour cell loses its internal control over growth and division and becomes unresponsive to external control

What is it that can effect a permanent transformation of normal cells to tumour cells? It has long been known that the bacteria are not concerned because it is possible to produce a bacteria-free tumour either by killing the bacteria *in situ* or by using juice from bacteria-free tumours to induce the same kind of tumour in healthy tissue. Many attempts have been made to show that the tumour inducing principle is DNA or a virus, but it is still not known what it is. Crown gall is not unique in providing a problem of this kind. Scrapie, a disease of sheep, provides somewhat similar problems on the borderline of infection and inheritance as do episomes such as the F^+ factor in bacteria and cancer in different ways. All show that the fundamental problems of different-iation are not really understood yet.

CHAPTER 9

Specialized Cells

In this chapter we propose to consider some of the kinds of cells whose development is known from recent work especially with the electron microscope and to summarize the changes that occur in organelles during differentiation. We do not propose to produce a complete list of all the different kinds of plant cells in this chapter. To a large extent specialization in plant cells consists of specialization in walls and this has been described in Chapter 5. Variations in wall structure and chemistry undoubtedly reflect specialization in the protoplast, but in most cases all we know concerns the walls.

9.1 Meristematic cells

In a sense no cell is unspecialized. Even meristematic cells must be so organized as to make cell division possible. The fine structure of cells in division has, except for the mitotic apparatus itself and, to a lesser extent, the cell plate, been neglected until recently. The Golgi bodies, the mitochondria and the plastids are usually 'simple' in structure and the ER apparently occurs in small sheets. Nevertheless interest is developing in the study of these undifferentiated organelles because it is at this stage that much organelle duplication takes place. Some of these organelles reproduce themselves, and this implies that they have a degree of autonomy. Partial autonomy we know to be a property of plastids, probably of mitochondria and possibly even of Golgi. The organelles themselves are often unequally distributed into the two daughter cells of a division and more examples of such polarity will undoubtedly be discovered as techniques improve and such polarity may well be the basis of subsequent paths of differentiation. Attention is also being focused on meristematic cells because, as we shall see later in this chapter, the plane of division can often be predicted before mitosis begins by the distribution of certain cytoplasmic organelles (see page 441).

Srivastava & O'Brien (1966a) have studied meristematic cells in the seasonally active cambium of *Pinus strobus*. These cells demonstrate the special features possessed by meristematic cells, although the significance of all the changes from the non-meristematic to the meristematic condition as the quiescent state of winter is replaced by the intense activity of spring is not yet understood. The most striking feature of the transition from winter to spring is the conversion of numerous small vacuoles into one or two larger ones.

It has long been known that these meristematic cells were vacuolate. The electron microscope has confirmed this and has also shown that the pattern of vacuolation of meristematic cells is often characteristic of the tissue. For example, in the meristematic epidermal parenchyma of *Avena* coleoptiles the vacuoles stain deeply and are stellate, whereas the vacuoles of the meristematic cells of the sub-epidermal parenchyma stain much less densely and are more regular in outline (Wardrop & Foster, 1964). In the *Pinus* cambium, there is a general hydration and swelling of the tissue and, presumably as a result of this, the plasmalemma, which lies in folds in the winter, smooths out in the spring. A change in the appearance of the plasmalemma as growth begins has also been noticed by Wardrop & Foster (1964) in oat coleoptiles. The plastids, which, unlike the plastids of photosynthesizing cells, do not appear to contain any ribosomes, begin to accumulate starch as the season progresses. This therefore does not preclude division of the plastids. Srivastava and O'Brien suggest that the fragments of smooth ER found in winter are replaced by or perhaps are converted into rough-surfaced ER. Microtubules become more obvious in spring and summer, but smaller filaments, about 15 nm wide and usually found in bundles of two to six, disappear in summer. The microtubules of the summer cambium are found more or less parallel to the long axis in the fusiform initials, but are somewhat more irregular in the ray initials. Apart from this distribution of microtubules there seems to be very little difference at the fine structural level between the fusiform and ray initials and, for that matter, between them and the parenchymatous cells, although, as Srivastava and O'Brien admit, such differences may be quantitative and not qualitative and therefore difficult to see.

Srivastava (1966) finds a similar picture in the cambium of *Fraxinus americana*, an angiosperm. Again the ray and fusiform initials are alike; there is a reduction in the number of vacuoles during their transition from winter to summer state, but there is an increase in their size and an increase in the amount of rough-surfaced ER. The bundles of fine tubules or fibrils seen in the quiescent cambium of *Pinus* are also seen, but again are absent from the summer wood. There are, as in *Pinus*, numbers of what Srivastava calls 'coated vesicles'. These or similar structures are a common feature of other meristematic cells, and can clearly be seen after both permanganate and osmium fixation. They are present in the cap initials, the quiescent centre and in the root meristem of *Zea* (Figs. 24, 30, 51). They have also been seen by Wardrop & Foster (1964) in the meristematic cells of *Avena* coleoptiles. In *Avena*, however, the coated vesicles are present only in the young cells of the sub-epidermal parenchyma and appear to be absent from the epidermal parenchyma. Srivastava suggests that they may be outgrowths of the plasmalemma, but the role they play in plant cell metabolism is unknown.

A feature of the cells that are changing from the dormant to the meristematic state in potato (*Solanum*) tuber buds, is the multifunctional plastids, described by Marinos (1967). These plastids have already been described in the chapter on plastids, but an interesting detail is that they are closely sheathed with ER membranes, and both outer surfaces of these membranes are coated with ribosomes. This is similar to the plastids in root hair tips, but in contrast to resin-secreting cells, companion cells of phloem and secretory cells of *Pinguicula*, which will be described later in this chapter. In these, the plastids are also closely sheathed with ER membranes, but the ribosomes are on the surface only of the ER membrane facing away from the plastid (Vogel, 1960; Wooding & Northcote, 1965a, b, c; Heslop-Harrison, 1966).

It is not possible yet even to speculate on what differences in function exist between plastids sheathed in symmetrical ER and those sheathed in asymmetrical ER. However, it seems very likely that wherever one finds either of these situations the ER is serving as some sort of transport system either to or from the plastids and that the plastids are serving as mobile and specialized sites of synthesis. We shall draw attention to this situation wherever it occurs since it may well be one of the plant's methods, like the movement of lysosomes in animals, of shifting bodies of enzymes and selective transport systems into position to perform some role in differentiation.

We have suggested that no cell can be described as unspecialized, but of course, certain cells, by reason of the substances they export, the structural role they play, the physiological or reproductive function they perform or the specialized enzymes they contain, draw particular attention to themselves and these are the ones that are usually called specialized. Some of them remain alive, for example root hairs, sieve tubes and companion cells, resin secreting cells, tannin cells, stomata and symbiotic cells of leguminous roots. Some of them die, for example vessels

o

and tracheids. We cannot hope, in this chapter, to cover every type of plant cell, but we have taken certain cells which have been investigated recently and we shall try to draw attention to those aspects of their fine structure which have particular metabolic or developmental significance.

9.2 Root hairs and pollen tubes

Root hairs play an important role in the uptake of water and nutrients from the soil by increasing the surface area of the whole root system twofold or more. The root hair is a simple cell, which elongates solely by apical growth either from the surface of an otherwise unremarkable root epidermal cell or from the surface of a meristemoid called a trichoblast. As we have already seen in the description of primary wall growth, growth in the root hair is restricted to the first few microns of the extreme tip (see page 237). This restricted zone of intense growth (0·1 mm per hour) is supported by a specialized zone of cytoplasmic organization. The root hair is, moreover, one of the most striking examples of a single cell in which the whole character of the organization of the cytoplasm changes within the space of a few microns.

Pollen tubes, which also grow only at the extreme tip, have a similar strict demarcation between the growing zone and the non-growing region, but, as we shall see, the fine structure is very different. One striking feature of the tips of root hairs is the absence of vacuoles, of even the smallest dimensions. Even root cap meristematic cells, although commonly described as non-vacuolate, normally possess small vacuoles scattered throughout the cytoplasm (Fig. 23). The cytoplasm in the terminal 3–5μm of the root hair has an electron-dense matrix in which lie a large number of smooth-surfaced vesicles, some large irregularly shaped fibrous inclusions and clusters of ribosomes (Sievers, 1963 and Newcomb & Bonnet, 1965). Microtubules, which are orientated along the axis of the cell, do not approach closer than 2–3μm from the tip. No other organelles appear to occupy this part of the cell, which therefore provides a striking example of cellular polarity. Farther back, more than 5μm from the tip of the cell and corresponding roughly with the zone in which microfibrils are orientated along the axis of the cell and not at random, the cytoplasm is filled with plastids, Golgi bodies, rough surfaced ER, mitochondria and microtubules that lie parallel to the long axis of the hair itself (Newcomb & Bonnet, 1965; Bonnett & Newcomb, 1966). Many of the plastids are closely sheathed with rough-surfaced ER, but, unlike the sheathed plastids of the companion cells and some secretory cells, this ER possesses ribosomes on both surfaces of the membrane.

The Golgi bodies in the main body of the root hair appear to bud off large, smooth vesicles similar in size and structure to those seen in the tip. By analogy with Golgi bodies in other tissues, it is likely that they are making a contribution to the non-cellulose fraction of the growing cell wall. Another vesicle, which is about 85 nm thick overall and having an alveolate or chambered coat about 20 nm thick, appears to arise in the vicinity of the Golgi bodies by evagination from these large smooth vesicles. Bonnett and Newcomb suggest that proteins and carbohydrates are both marshalled in these particular Golgi bodies and are budded off in the large smooth vesicles. They also suggest that the coated vesicles, which appear to be derived secondarily from the smooth vesicles may, in fact, contain only protein and that, in this way, protein is transported to the cell surface to take part in wall synthesis. The smooth vesicles are supposed then to contain only carbohydrate on its way to the primary wall.

This is the first suggestion that Golgi bodies in plants marshall and transport protein and also that two separate but concurrent roles exist in a single Golgi body. Bruni & Porter (1965), however, have reported that Golgi bodies in rat liver cells apparently concentrate and separate two types of material. One type of material is released within large vacuoles from the Golgi bodies and is subsequently exported from the cell, while the other, also believed to be proteinaceous, is transferred from the Golgi bodies in coated vesicles for subsequent incorporation within the cell.

Although most Golgi bodies that have been studied in any detail in plant cells have been found to be concerned with supplying carbohydrate to the cell wall or cell plate, there is no reason why they should not do the same for protein. Perhaps only the relatively low level of protein metabolism compared to the carbohydrate metabolism of a plant cell prevents this function from being more conspicuous. In addition to this, Sassen (1965) believes that, in certain cases of endogenous breakdown of cell walls, the Golgi bodies may be responsible for transporting the necessary enzymes to the cell wall.

The random network of cellulose microfibrils which covers the tip of the root hair, as we have seen in Chapter 5, extends back along the sides of the outer surface of the hair. The layer of axially oriented microfibrils cover the inner surface of the wall to within about 25 μm of the tip according to Newcomb and Bonnett. Newcomb and Bonnett are confident that the images of the walls in their micrographs represent

cellulose in different orientations, although the diameter of 3·5 nm
given by them is smaller than the normal diameters of microfibrils
(8–30 nm). The discrepancy here may be due to preferential staining of
some component of the microfibril thereby reducing apparent size, since
it is unlikely that there is any other structure that these fibrils could be.

There have been suggestions that the microtubules are responsible in
some way for the orientation of the wall microfibrils. We have seen
that the microtubules in root hairs extend along the long axis of the hair
and close to the plasmalemma, to within 2–3μm of the extreme tip. The
microfibrils, however, are deposited in random array on the surface of
the wall only until a point about 25μm behind the tip is reached. Then
longitudinal deposition begins. Thus there is a region of some 20μm of the
extreme tip of the root hair in which the orientation of microfibrils is
proceeding at random under microtubules that are arranged parallel to
the axis of the cell. However, as Newcomb and Bonnett point out,
probably relatively little microfibril deposition is taking place over this
region compared with the rest of the root hair and the microtubules are
aligned parallel to a comparatively quiescent region. They put forward
other possibilities, e.g. that the microtubules are responsible for the
orientation of cytoplasmic streaming or that they may be orientating the
microfibril deposition, but, due to the speed at which the root hair is
growing, the microtubules are observed in position just behind the root
hair tip, but become functional some 12–15 minutes later and 20–25μm
further back. It also seems possible that microtubules in the very soft
tips of root hairs have a skeletal role within the cytoplasm as they have
perhaps in some animal cells. All these suggestions will be considered
when the microtubule and the synthesis of the wall as a whole is discussed later on.

Like the root hair, the pollen tube grows only at the tip, in the first
five microns. It grows even faster than the root hair. Like the root hairs,
its walls consist of cellulose embedded in a matrix of non-crystalline
polysaccharides, but it differs from the root hair in that the microfibrils
of the inner surface of the non-growing region are predominantly transverse and not axial (O'Kelly & Carr, 1954). Like the root hair, the extreme apical tip of the pollen tube is devoid of any cytoplasmic organelles or vacuoles except for large numbers of vesicles that are probably
derived from the Golgi bodies. Just behind this growing zone there is an
abundance of smooth-surfaced tubular ER, a rare phenomenon in
plants (Rosen, Gawlik, Dashek & Siegesmund, 1964 and Rosen &
Gawlik, 1966b). Covering the tip of the tube is a cap of wall material,
separated off in compartments, which appears to arise both from the

coalescence of vesicles with the cap and also with each other before they reach the boundary of the cap (Figs. 140, 141). Chemical tests demonstrate that this cap region is rich in pectins and pectin precursors as one might expect, but it also contains a considerable amount of RNA (Dashek & Rosen, 1966a). There is also some evidence that the Golgi-vesicles contain not only polysaccharides for incorporation into the wall, but also protein. The patterns of protein-incorporation are very similar to those observed by Lamport (1963). However, in this case, proline and not hydroxyproline is incorporated into the pollen tube walls. But, as Dashek and Rosen are careful to point out, there is no direct evidence yet that protein in the wall of the pollen-tube does function as a collagen-like plant protein.

Another striking difference between the pollen tube and the root hair is that, unlike the root hair which has an abundance of microtubules whose orientation is correlated with that of the microfibrils, the pollen tube appears to have no microtubules at all anywhere. This must be borne in mind when their possible role in the orientating of cellulose microfibrils is considered.

Rosen & Gawlik (1966b) have noticed that in pollen tubes growing in compatible pistils there is an early change in both morphology and nutrition. The tubes appear to become dependent for growth in length on materials secreted by the stigmatic cells of the pistil into the stylar canal. These materials appear to enter the pollen tubes via embayments in the tips of the tubes, perhaps by a process similar to pinocytosis. Pollen tubes grown in incompatible pistils and *in vitro* do not achieve this transition from the autotrophic first phase of nutrition to the heterotrophic second phase of nutrition, although the incompatibility barrier may decline after some time has elapsed from anthesis. The heterotrophic mode of nutrition of pollen tubes may well be connected with the secretion of lipids, sugars and amino acids from the stigmatic surface and intercellular spaces of the stylar canal which is described on page 422.

9.3 Sieve elements and companion cells

The quantity of published electron microscopic observations on phloem cells (mainly the sieve tube elements) probably exceeds that on any other plant tissue and, perhaps nowhere else, have changes in technique forced such complete changes in interpretation.

The basic components of the phloem are the sieve elements, several kinds of parenchyma cells, fibres and sclereids. In angiosperms the sieve

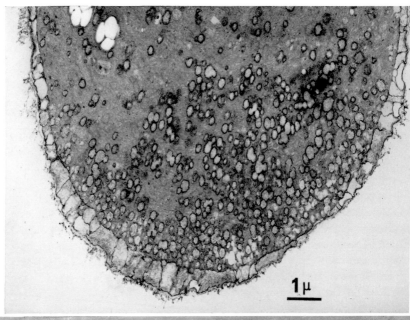

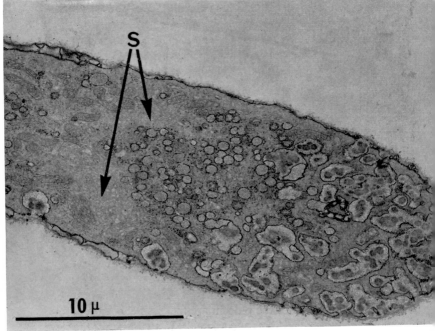

SIEVE ELEMENTS

elements are arranged end to end like vessel elements in the xylem, but the end walls do not break down as in vessels, but become modified as sieve plates. A series of connected sieve elements is called a sieve tube. In other vascular plants, the sieve elements are not joined end to end and therefore do not form sieve tubes. They are called sieve cells. In angiosperms, but not in other plants, the sieve elements usually, but not invariably, lie next to special parenchymatous cells called companion cells. These are often the sister cells of the neighbouring sieve tube element. Of the phloem cells, only the sieve tube elements and their companion cells have received much attention from electron microscopists. The fibres and sclereids are thickened and such tissues are difficult to cut with an ultramicrotome. Liese & Hoster (1966) have studied the gelatinous fibres in the phloem of some gymnosperms. These have the high proportion of cellulose to lignin characteristic of compression wood xylem (see page 287), but they are distributed symmetrically around normally growing branches and roots.

The structural peculiarities of sieve elements and companion cells that may be related to their function in the translocation of elaborated food materials have fascinated botanists since Hartig discovered sieve tubes in 1837. Sieve elements have also proved to be one of the most delicate of cells to examine, the most liable to produce confusing artefacts and one of the richest sources of dispute. Firstly, one of the most confusing artefacts, as we have already pointed out is the capacity of sieve tubes to develop deposits of callose very rapidly when injured. The speed with which this can take place has even led some workers to question whether callose occurs at all in uninjured sieve tubes (Eschrich, 1963). However Engleman (1965a) found callose present in sieve elements of *Impatiens*, when the tissue was killed by freezing only four seconds after injury. Secondly, phloem tissue fixed for the electron microscope with $KMnO_4$ or with OsO_4 alone is so severely damaged that it must be admitted that

FIG. 140. Electron micrograph of a *Lilium* pollen tube tip. A compartmented cap is formed from Golgi-derived vesicles which coalesce with each other and fuse to make the cap. This pollen tube was grown *in vitro* and is similar to pollen tubes fixed 48 hours after *self*-pollination. Compare the tip structure with that of Fig. 141. (Glut/Os/Pb/U)   Micrograph by Dr W. G. Rosen and Dr S. R. Gawlik.

FIG. 141. Electron micrograph of a *Lilium* pollen tube tip. This pollen tube was grown *in vivo* and fixed 48 hours after *cross*-pollination. Note the difference between the caps of the two pollen tubes. Note also the mass of smooth ER (S) just behind the tip which is a feature of all pollen tubes. (Glut/Os/Pb/U)
          Micrograph by Dr W. G. Rosen and Dr S. R. Gawlik.

virtually all the pictures obtained of the sieve tube after these treatments are of little value compared with those obtained when glutaraldehyde is used. As Kollmann & Schumacher (1962) and Johnson (1966) have pointed out, $KMnO_4$ alone causes a precipitate of MnO_2 to form in the sieve tube, probably by reaction with the sucrose present, and destroys virtually all the structure of the filaments that are found in the slime.

Sieve-tube elements are usually derived from a meristematic phloem cell by unequal division, so that two cells are produced, a large one, the future sieve-tube element and a small one, the companion cell (Fig. 142). The companion cell differentiates as a parenchyma-like cell, possessing a dense cytoplasm, with abundant ribosomes, no visible starch in its plastids and a large nucleus. The future sieve element, on the other hand, undergoes many modifications. The sieve elements are remarkable not only for the peculiar modifications of their protoplasts, but also for the sieve areas on the walls. The sieve areas are specialized primary pit fields and may occur singly or in a group on the end walls of the cells forming a sieve plate. In sieve cells, which are the equivalent cells in gymnosperms, but which have tapered ends, the sieve areas may be compound, scattered along the longitudinal walls. The pair of cells destined to become sieve tube element and companion cell vacuolate (Fig. 142). As it matures the sieve tube element, but not the companion cell, loses its nucleus and, in some plants, the nucleolus is extruded from the nucleus before the nucleus finally disintegrates (Esau, 1965). As the sieve tube element continues to mature, the so-called slime bodies develop and then lose their sharp outlines, become more fluid and fuse to form the slime strands present in the lumen of the mature cells. This occurs at the same time as the degeneration and disappearance of the nucleus (Fig. 142D). The resulting mixture of degenerate cytoplasmic and vacuolar contents Engleman calls 'mictoplasm' (1965b). The slime frequently collects at the sieve areas when the cell is injured and forms slime plugs. A slime plug may slow the exudation of cytoplasmic material from other elements of the damaged phloem immediately after wounding until later on when the sieve areas become plugged by callose. Thaine (1962) suggested that sieve tubes contain membrane-bounded cytoplasmic strands, which he called 'transcellular strands' but Tamule-vich & Evert (1966) believe these to be derived from the slime bodies of immature cells and to consist solely of slime. This slime is generally agreed to be made up of filaments some of which may, as the most recent work indicates, be tubular; the strands seen by transmitted light and phase microscopy are between 7·0 and 0·5μm in diameter, but these are almost certainly aggregations of the filaments or tubules which are seen under the electron microscope to be between 10 and 20 nm in diameter and probably in the undamaged state are rarely aggregated. Behnke & Dörr (1967) call these fine filaments plasmatic filaments. Large numbers of them probably traverse the whole sieve element from one sieve pore to another and pass through the pores (Fig. 143). It is interesting to note the similarity between these plasmatic filaments and the fine filaments in zones of cytoplasmic streaming (see page 248).

As the phloem continues to develop, the plasmodesmata become branched on the companion cell side of the common wall between the two cells (Fig. 142B, C). Secondary thickening of the wall begins about the same time. Golgi bodies are seen to produce numerous vesicles at this stage and, by their position close to the plasmalemma and by analogy with the xylem wall of *Acer* (see page 434), it looks as though the Golgi are contributing to this wall as well (Northcote & Wooding, 1966). The plastids of companion cells and initially also those of the sieve elements become sheathed over all or most of their surface by ER, which, as we have already seen, is coated with ribosomes only on the ER surface away from the plastid (Fig. 142B, C). This ER is also closely associated with the plasmodesmata, another hint that it has a transporting role. The plasmodesmata common to adjacent companion cells and sieve tubes have areas of electron-transparent material around the cytoplasmic ends (Fig. 142C, D). These areas are outside the plasmalemma, on the companion cell side but adjacent to sheets of ER which are closely apposed to the plasmalemma. Northcote & Wooding (1966) believe that they are callose, but the extent to which even this small amount may be a wound reaction has already been discussed. The tonoplast of the developing sieve tube lifts away from the peripheral cytoplast and later disintegrates (Kollman & Schumacher, 1964) (Fig. 142D). The plasmodesmata that will form the sieve pores, i.e. those between two sieve elements, widen within the wall along the line of the middle lamella (Fig. 142C, D). At least initially the callose, already present at the ends of these plasmodesmata, does not usually extend to this central region of the wall although there are reports that it may occasionally do so. The bowl-shaped masses of callose now formed at the ends of the plasmodesmata, shrink slightly forming a continuous lining to the pore along the site of an original plasmodesma.

By this time the nucleus, Golgi bodies and vesicles, ribosomes, tonoplast and ER have either disintegrated or completely disappeared from the cell. The mature cell is often lined with membranous structures and lamellar stacks. These may have come either from the breakdown of the nuclear envelope or the ER. The plastids generally remain, but

o*

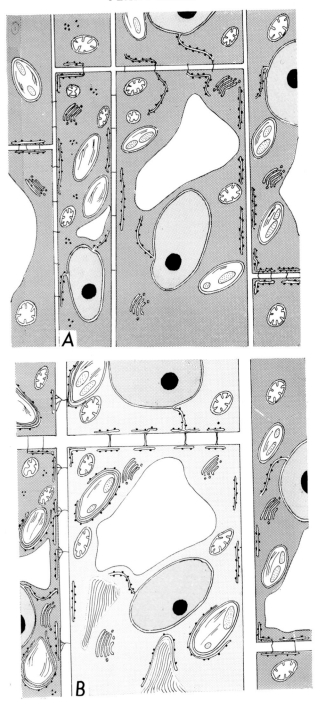

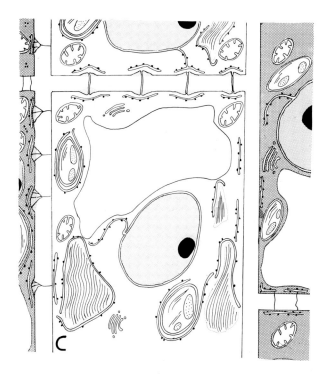

FIG. 142. Differentiation of sieve elements.

A: Unequal division in a meristematic cell produces one large cell, the future sieve element and a smaller cell, the companion cell. Numerous plasmodesmata join sieve elements to each other and to their neighbouring companion cells.

B: The cytoplasm of the young sieve elements becomes less dense. Vacuolation proceeds rapidly in the sieve elements and more slowly in the companion cells. The plastids in the sieve elements accumulate starch. Both they and the plastids of the companion cells are enveloped with sheets of ER. Profiles of ER also appear parallel to the wall, opposite both ends of the plasmodesmata joining sieve elements and, in the companion cells, opposite the branching ends of the plasmodesmata joining companion cells to sieve elements. Young slime bodies also wrapped with ER appear in the sieve elements.

C: The cytoplasm of the sieve element becomes indistinguishable from the vacuolar contents. The cell continues to vacuolate, domes of callus appear at either end of the plasmodesmata passing from one sieve element to another below the ER that lies parallel to the wall. Similar domes of callus *may* appear on the companion cell side of the plasmodesmata joining these cells to the sieve elements. The plasmodesmatal channels between the sieve elements begin to widen.

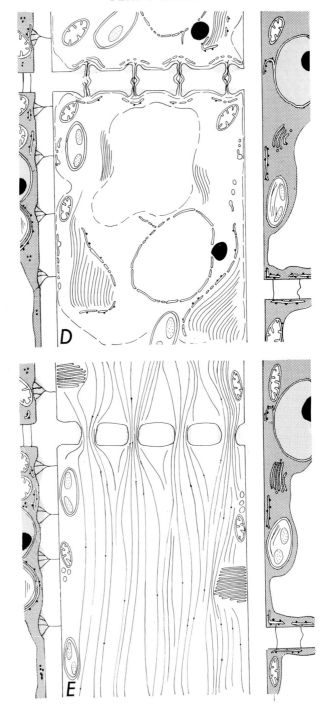

may lose all their matrix materials except starch grains, occasional lipid droplets and some ring-shaped inclusions of a possibly proteinaceous material. Falk (1964) believes that the plastids break down as the sieve element matures and that these ring-shaped inclusions become the fibrillar material of the slime bodies. However, Esau (1965) has shown that plastids in *Beta* sieve elements do not disintegrate until the sieve tube is non-functional. Now the lumen of the sieve tube is filled by a network of filaments (Fig. 142E, 143). It may also contain strands which Bouck & Cronshaw (1965) believe may be a tubular form of ER.

The most interesting feature of sieve-tube development is of course the development of the sieve-plate itself. There is general agreement that each individual pore is preceded by a plasmodesma. Plasmodesmata have rarely if ever been found in sieve tube walls except between one sieve tube and another or its companion cell, therefore either the cell type is determined at the time of cell plate formation, or unwanted plasmodesmata are occluded in subsequent secondary wall growth. Rough-surfaced ER appears to have two functions during the development of the sieve pore. Initially profiles are seen parallel to the wall, and marking out the area in the wall where callose will appear around a plasmodesma that is being converted to a sieve pore. Northcote and Wooding suggest that not only is ER directly involved in callose formation, but also that it acts as a mechanical barrier inhibiting normal wall augmentation by preventing Golgi-derived vesicles from reaching the

D: The nuclear membrane begins to break down; in some plants the nucleolus is extruded before the final disintegration takes place. The plasmodesmatal pores from one sieve element to another widen and sometimes callose forms large masses around both ends of the pore. Callose sometimes also forms on the companion cell side of the plasmodesmata joining the companion cells and sieve elements. These complex plasmodesmata have now reached their maximum degree of branching on the companion cell side, but no branching occurs on the sieve element side. The sheathing ER disappears from the surface of the plastids and the slime bodies and the latter grow and begin to fill the whole cell. The ER parallel to the cell wall opposite the sieve pores begins to disappear and the ER in the companion cells opposite the branched plasmodesmata also begins to disperse.

E: Distinction between the vacuole and cytoplasm is completely lost, a few mitochondria, plastids and fragments of ER remain pressed against the wall of the sieve element. The main body of the sieve element is completely filled with fine plasmatic filaments some of which may be grouped into bundles. The sieve pores are wide (see Fig. 143) and the plasmatic filaments run from one cell to another and throughout the length of the cell. Traces of callose may persist along the walls of the sieve pores. The companion cell retains a dense cytoplasm, sheathed plastids, numerous mitochondria and ribosomes, abundant ER and a normal nucleus.

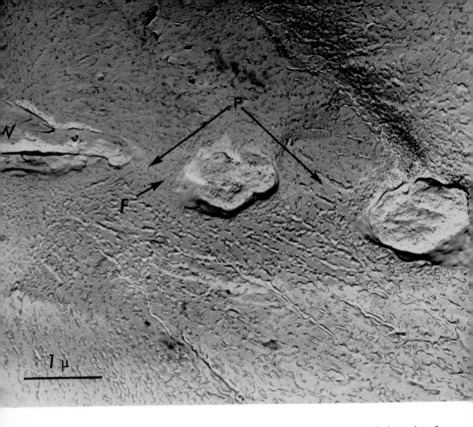

FIG. 143. Electron micrograph of a replica of a frozen and etched sieve plate from a petiole of *Nymphoides*. The pores (P) in the wall (W) of the sieve plate are larger than those usually seen in fixed and stained preparations, very little callose is present, and plasmatic filaments (F) can be seen passing through one of the pores.

Micrograph by Dr R. P. C. Johnson.

wall. They also suggest that, as the plasmodesma along the site of the sieve pore begins to swell, there is an actual removal of material along the middle lamella region, whilst at the same time the callose under the ER at the surface of the wall is also eroded away until the fully pierced sieve pore is produced. However Evert, Murmanis & Sachs (1966) were unable to find such a distribution of ER in *Cucurbita* phloem. Northcote & Wooding (1966), Evert & Derr (1964) and Eschrich (1963) all agree that much at least of the callose invariably found lining the sieve tube pore is a response to wounding. Northcote and Wooding fed the cut stems of *Acer pseudoplatanus* with tritiated glucose, and found that the incorporation of radioactive material occurs only in the callose of the sieve pore. Therefore much of the callose is formed after general wall synthesis because, in the earlier stages of sieve tube formation, there is incorporation of radioactive glucose into the sieve tube walls. Eschrich

(1963) has suggested that in the lumen of the sieve tube of *Cucurbita* the filamentous material which occupies the sieve pores is lipoprotein and Buvat (1963) and others hold that the slime bodies of *Cucurbita* contain RNA. It thus seems possible that the granular material around the slime strands is equivalent to ribosomes and, as such, may be responsible for the production of the protein that makes up the slime body. Filaments may be compressed as they pass through the sieve pore by callose which forms in the pore after wounding and, under normal conditions, they may be spaced well apart. It may well be that, were it possible to view a sieve pore at the resolution of an electron microscope without the intervention of preparative techniques, the filaments would not be aggregated but would maintain their individual 9–10 nm diameter. It is interesting that freeze-etched preparations of sieve plates show bigger pores. Companion cells, as has already been mentioned, are joined to their sieve element neighbours by very complex plasmodesmata, whereas their connexions to parenchymatous neighbours are by conventional plasmodesmata (see page 410).

The number of ribosomes found in the companion cells suggests that active protein synthesis is going on; the presence of large numbers of well developed mitochondria and sheathed plastids also suggest vigorous carbohydrate synthesis, transport and metabolism, and the presence of spherosomes may imply that the cell is capable of lipid synthesis. The companion cell is therefore, at least structurally, one of the most well and diversely equipped cells for enzymic activity of all kinds. The main facts of phloem development are summarized in Figs. 142, A-E.

The contents of the sieve tube are under a pressure of as high as 20 atmospheres. They transport mainly sucrose, at concentrations up to 30 per cent and at speeds of the order of 1 metre per hour. This activity is dependent upon the functioning of the associated companion cells and parenchyma, and may take place in both directions in the same group of sieve tubes (Canny, 1962; Peel & Weatherley, 1962). We can only speculate as to what role the companion cell plays in bringing about this massive and rapid movement of carbohydrate. The physical data tell us that the inside of the sieve tube is in rapid mass flow. This concept of mass flow applies not only to sucrose, but particles passively transported in the phloem, e.g. viruses (Esau, Cronshaw & Hoefert, 1967). It seems almost impossible that this can represent pressure flow since one assumes that, under these circumstances, the living, though tenuous, cytoplasm would be swept from the cell. How can such a mass of material flow through sieve pores which appear to be obstructed by cytoplasmic structures? The speculative but interesting idea developed by Spanner (1958) deserves further consideration. He suggests that electrokinetic forces create a rise in pressure across the sieve plate in the direction of flow.

It has generally been assumed that the 'functional' sieve tube is the enucleate and virtually organelle-free cell which contains filaments, the last stage of the developmental sequence that has just been described (Fig. 142E). All explanations of the observed behaviour of sieve tubes have been based on such a structure. However Kollmann & Schumacher (1964), Wark & Chambers (1965) and Wark (1965) conclude that the nucleate anatomically 'young' sieve tube with a complex cytoplasmic network and cytoplasmic connecting strands is the functional cell. If, as these authors suggest, one of the earlier stages is operative in translocation (and experimental evidence is accumulating to support their idea (Kollman, 1967)) it is no longer necessary to invoke the companion cell as the driving pump. This also gets round the problem of those sieve tubes with no companion cells. The companion cell, where present, via its sheathed plastid system and complex plasmodesmatal connexions may then function to regulate lateral movements of carbohydrates and other compounds in and out of the sieve tubes. But the resistance to flow which would be provided by the cytoplasm of these young sieve elements seems impossibly high when considered against the mass and speed of the substances known to be moved.

9.4 Resin-secreting cells

Wooding & Northcote (1965b) have also turned their attention to the fine structure of a secreting cell, the resin-secreting cells of the stems of *Pinus pinea*. Resin canals are found in the Pinaceae and consist of six to eight files of cells surrounding the central canal. The resin is thought to protect the tree after wounding and, in *Pinus pinea*, consists mainly of the monoterpene, limonene (Davies, Giovanelli & ap Rees, 1964). The basic structure of all terpenes, which are widespread in plants in such diverse forms as camphor, rubber, carotene and leaf surface waxes, is the isoprene group.

$$\underset{(head)}{} \quad \underset{CH_2=C-CH=CH_2}{\overset{\overset{\textstyle CH_3}{|}}{}} \quad \underset{}{(tail)}$$

these isoprene units are commonly linked head to tail, e.g.

$$CH_3-C=CH-CH-CH-CH=CH-CH_2OH \quad (geraniol)$$

which is a monoterpene. Many of the terpenes, like geraniol, are highly fragrant or aromatic oils. Many others, such as copal, rosin and limonene, which concerns us here, are resins or gums, commonly only conspicuous after injury or fungal infection. Although Golgi bodies are believed in every case to play a major role in polysaccharide secretion, they do not appear to take any direct part in the secretory system of resin-secreting cells. A very striking feature of these cells is, however, the large number of plastids which they contain in comparison with the adjacent parenchymatous cells. Moreover, whereas parenchymatous cell plastids contain a fairly complex internal membrane system, the resin cell plastids never have anything more than vestigial membrane sacs usually in close proximity to the outside of the starch grains. They are almost invariably sheathed with sheets of endoplasmic reticulum in which the ribosomes are observed only on the cytoplasmic side of the endoplasmic reticulum membranes and in which the ER is almost always a constant distance from the plastid. Moreover, in spite of the known variability of cytoplasmic organelles, such an appearance of the majority of the plastids is a constant feature of these tissues regardless of their age or position. Sheathing of this type was also noticed by Wooding & Northcote (1965c) in the companion cells of the phloem of *Acer* and by Heslop-Harrison (1966) in the cells which are thought to provide the digestive enzymes of the insectivorous plant *Pinguicula grandiflora*.

Tentatively then we can say that plant cells with material for export may have one of two distinctive features in their fine structure. They may have enhanced Golgi activity as in the sugar-secreting peripheral root cap cells, the polysaccharide sheath-secreting desmids (Drawert & Mix, 1962), the cells producing surface sugary slime of *Laminaria* (Schnepf, 1963), or the cells producing the sugary 'Fangschleim' of the leaf glands of *Drosophyllum* (Schnepf, 1966). Or they may have the very striking sheathed plastids of the tissues described above. There does not yet seem to be any physico-chemical distinction between these two groups, for although most of the sugar secreters belong to the Golgi group, Wooding & Northcote (1965c) suggest that the sheathed plastids of the companion cells of *Acer* may also be transferring carbohydrates.

9.5 Laticifers

Laticifers are cells, or groups of cells fused together, containing latex which is a liquid with solid particles in suspension which often give a milky appearance to the sap. The latex sap may be contained in these groups of cells at pressures up to 10 atmospheres. The particles are mostly terpenes, especially rubber and resin, but other substances occur in latex including proteins, tannins, sugars, and starch. The latex of some plants (*Papaver, Cannabis*) is notorious for its alkaloid content and the proteolytic enzyme, papain, is obtained from the latex of *Carica*.

Laticifers occur in many higher plants, sometimes in all parts of the plant, sometimes restricted to particular tissues especially the phloem. Laticifers in apical meristems can easily be recognized not only because of the arrangement of their constituent cells in rows in the longitudinal direction, but also by the absence of a large central vacuole. In the surrounding tissue and close to the potential laticifer, there are a few rows of cells also running longitudinally in which staining for the electron microscope reveals within their vacuoles a dark granular material whose nature and function are unknown (Sassen, 1965). The transverse walls of the young laticifers themselves are thinner than the longitudinal walls; the middle lamella is visible and plasmodesmata penetrate the wall. In the cytoplasm, most of the organelles are not apparently different from those in a meristematic cell, but two bodies, the one angular, electron transparent and bounded by a membrane and the other globular, more electron dense and also membrane-bounded can be seen. The latter are similar to organelles found in the mature laticifers. After the breakdown of the transverse wall, a rim remains around the cell. The fused cell mass may continue to expand after the wall ruptures. The normal cytoplasmic organelles disintegrate, disappear and are replaced entirely by a variety of globules. Southorn (1966) has shown that none of the latex particles are confined within anything resembling a vacuole. He believes that all the latex particles are modified cytoplasm and not vacuolar sap. There are at least three main groups of particles. Firstly there is the rubber hydrocarbon. These particles are bounded by a protective envelope of protein and phospholipid. Secondly there are bright yellow bodies about $2 \cdot 5\mu$m across, bounded by a double unit membrane and containing carotene. Thirdly there are the very numerous so-called 'lutoids'. These are spherical membrane-bounded bodies between 2 and 5μm across and contain acids, mineral salts, proteins and sugars. Thus, according to Southorn, the 'lutoids' are biologically active bodies and when the lutoids are ruptured as a result of tapping *Hevea* for its rubber they can induce clotting in the vessels so sealing off the wound.

9.6   Stomata

The functional stoma may be made up of any number of cells from two to eight, two of which, the guard cells, normally surrounded the stomatal opening and, by changes in their shape, determine its size and hence the rate of transpiration of the plant. The distortions undergone by guard cells to achieve different degrees of opening are very varied indeed. However they all depend ultimately on different patterns of thickening and sometimes lignification of the guard cells, and it is this combination of rigid and flexible parts of their walls that brings about these significant distortions (Fig. 144). Just how this differential pattern of thickening comes about is still as much a mystery as the differential thickening of xylem walls.

The mechanism which causes the changes in turgor which distort the cells is also not yet understood, nor has the study of the fine structure of these cells provided very much further information about it. The electron microscope has, however, revealed a number of interesting features of these specialized cells one of which is the existence of large cytoplasmic connexions between guard cells, both immature and mature. These were discovered by Brown & Johnson (1962) who were concerned solely with grasses. The absence of a complete wall between the guard cells of stomata was confirmed by Pickett-Heaps & Northcote (1966) in the stomata of wheat, but so far as is known it has not been confirmed outside the Gramineae. Other groups of plants have stomata of entirely different shapes.

As Fig. 144 shows, the construction of the guard cell in grasses is complicated. The nucleus is in two halves linked by a thin thread through a central tunnel in the cell only $1 \cdot 5$–$2 \cdot 5 \mu$m in diameter. In some stomata the two bulbous ends of the nucleus may separate eventually from one another. The central tunnel may contain numerous mitochondria as well as the nuclear thread. Plastids, which possess only a few lamellae and are often filled with starch, are found, along with many mitochondria, only in the bulbous ends of the guard cells. There is no evidence that chlorophyll develops in these plastids, although they can obviously synthesize starch. Neither the tunnels nor the bulbous ends of the guard cells possess any vacuoles, nor, interestingly enough, are there any plasmodesmata between the guard cells and the subsidiary cells. As Brown & Johnson (1962) state, although there are no plasmodesmata the walls between the guard and the subsidiary cells are so thin, only 100–150 nm across, that diffusion could occur rapidly, perhaps as rapidly as if plasmodesmata were present. The partial fusion of the guard cells is suggested by Pickett-Heaps & Northcote (1966) to be functionally significant, assuming walls are barriers in maintaining the two guard cells at the same osmotic pressure.

Pickett-Heaps and Northcote have concentrated upon the factors that

control the two successive asymmetrical divisions followed by one
symmetrical but incomplete division which form the normal stomatal
complex in grasses. As Fig. 144A shows, epidermal cells divide asymmetrically to form guard mother cells. The partially vacuolate cells
surrounding the guard mother cells divide asymmetrically to form the
subsidiary cells and the guard mother cell finally divides symmetrically
to form the stomatal cavity. This final division is incomplete and the
cytoplasm of the two guard cells remains in contact at their bulbous
ends. A band of microtubules appears in these dividing cells just prior
to mitosis and these show where the cell plate will join with the mother
cell wall (Fig. 86). This band is most prominent before prophase, becomes less prominent as the chromosomes start to condense and is
almost invisible by the end of prophase. In neither of these asymmetric
divisions is there any evidence of polarity of any of the cytoplasmic
particles other than the microtubules.

The symmetrical last division of the guard mother cell which gives
rise to the stomatal aperture is also characterized by a preprophase
band of microtubules this time in the strictly equatorial position. But
there are fewer microtubules than in the previous asymmetrical divisions.
Again they disappear before the completion of prophase. This particular
cell plate forms from the centre of the cell as usual by the coalescence of
vesicles. However, one or sometimes several holes are left at each end,
often opposite a stub projecting from the old transverse wall (Fig. 144F).
Pickett-Heaps and Northcote were unable to decide whether the holes
that they saw were part of a cell plate that never formed or whether they
were the result of its breakdown at a later stage. Since they were never
certain that cell plate formation was completed they favour the former

FIG. 144. Development of a stoma in a grass leaf. Two unequal cell divisions followed
by one equal but incomplete cell division give rise to the guard cells and the subsidiary cells of a stoma. In A and B unequal divisions of three cells give rise in C
to two large vacuolate cells with a nucleus displaced to one side flanking a smaller
non-vacuolate cell, the future guard mother cell (GMC). Unequal divisions in the
vacuolated cells give rise to the subsidiary cells of the stoma and finally (D–E) an
equal but incomplete division in the small non-vacuolate cell (GMC) gives rise to
the two guard cells. The position of the preprophase band of microtubules (MT)
which appears to guide the alignment of the cell plate is shown in C and D (see Fig.
86). After the division of the guard mother cell in D–E, the two nuclei partially
separate into two dumb-bell shaped bodies (F) and areas of wall thickening (TH)
are laid down. These thickenings may assist in the operation of the stoma, offering
unequal resistance to distortion and thereby allowing the expansion or contraction
of the stomatal opening. A section through F (Y–Z) is shown in G. SSC is the
substomatal cavity.

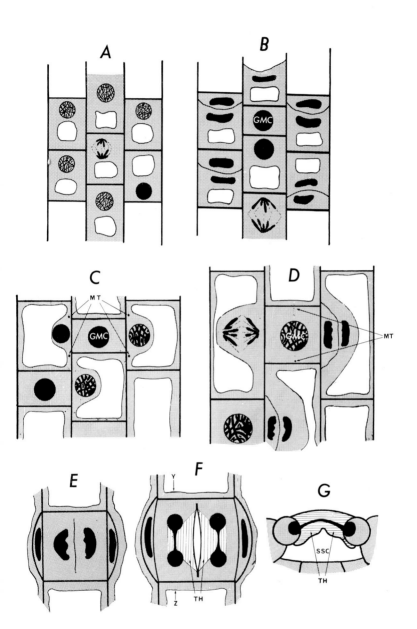

explanation. They noticed that elements of the ER frequently pass through these gaps, but there is no reason to think that the ER is in any way directly connected with the holes.

The way in which the guard mother cell somehow influences the subsidiary cells to divide in their asymmetrical fashion has been the subject of much speculation. Pickett-Heaps and Northcote suggest that this 'influence' by the guard mother cells acts by causing the band of microtubules to form in a specific position in the subsidiary mother cell. The influence of one cell upon the plane of division in another is extremely important in the understanding of patterns of differentiation. Although there is no explanation for the way in which the guard mother cell determines the position of the preprophase microtubular band, there is no doubt that it does so in some way, perhaps by the diffusion of some hormone. Similar mechanisms of control can now be looked for to account for the planes of division in other tissues such as apical meristems and procambial strands.

9.7   Secretory cells of insectivorous plants and haustoria of parasites

The secretory cells of the glands of some insectivorous plants and the haustoria of parasitic plants are amongst the few plant cells that export any quantity of protein. One might therefore expect to find the orientated closely packed sheets of rough-surfaced ER characteristic of animal pancreas and other protein exporting animal tissues (Fig. 28). This is in fact not the case; the cells of glands of, for example, *Pinguicula vulgaris* and the hyphae of *Cuscuta* are not exceptional in the amount of ER they contain, but they are remarkable for a number of other features (Vogel, 1960; Schnepf, 1966; Bonneville & Voeller, 1963). In *Pinguicula vulgaris* the cells of living glands contain large and small vacuoles in which the secretion of mucus and proteolytic enzymes is found. The extraordinarily high electron density of the vacuolar contents after they have been fixed with $KMnO_4$ or OsO_4 leads Vogel to think that at least one of the constituents of these vacuoles reduces $KMnO_4$, and he suggests that it is one of the polysaccharides that make up the mucus that does this. Around and between the vacuoles, but principally near the nucleus, there are large numbers of simple plastids. These do not seem to contain any starch, but they are, like the plastids of companion cells and resin secreting canal cells, wrapped around with ER membranes of which only the side away from the plastid surface is coated with ribosomes. Vogel was not able to come to any definite conclusions as to the mechanism of secretion in these cells nor was he able to find any sign of pores in the cuticle through which the material might pass.

Schnepf (1960), on the other hand, was able to implicate the Golgi bodies with the surface secretion from the stalked glands of *Drosophyllum lusitanicum*. Vesicles from the Golgi bodies, containing, Schnepf believes, mainly acid polysaccharides, find their way to the plasmalemma and, by a process of reverse pinocytosis similar to that we have observed in peripheral root cap cells, pass through the plasmalemma and the cell wall and accumulate on the surface of the gland. The 'Fangschleim', the sticky substance that holds insects, consists mainly of acidic polysaccharides. Since this activity of the Golgi bodies was found only in the stalked glands and since these are responsible only for trapping and not for digestion, there is no reason to think that the Golgi bodies in this tissue also secrete proteins.

Bonneville and Voeller (1963) in their study of the haustorial cells of *Cuscuta campestris* found, in the osmiophilic cells, conventional Golgi bodies and also some other as yet unidentified membranous structures. The ordinary Golgi bodies are generally distributed, but the larger and more complex bodies are apparently restricted to the hyphal cells. They bear a striking resemblance to the Golgi complexes of animal cells and of some flagellate algae. Bonneville and Voeller suggest that they may help to secrete substances that bring about the breakdown and absorption of the host cell wall, although they observe that there appears to be no localization of these bodies at the cell apex. This does not, of course, prevent them from being involved in secretion at the cell boundary since, as we have observed, the Golgi bodies, which are believed on very good evidence to be secreting material in root cap cells, in *Drosophyllum*, *Glaucocystis* and *Mesostigma* show no obvious localization within the cell. Bonneville and Voeller also note that the vesicles associated with the 'Golgi complexes' contain electron dense material scattered irregularly in a non-osmiophilic, but obviously substantial, matrix material. The plastids, although not obviously sheathed with ER as in some other protein secreting plant cells, have dense outer membranes and contain what appear to be lipid droplets and other granular material that may be phytoferritin. In this respect they are similar to the plastids seen in *Solanum* buds (see page 145; Marinos 1967).

9.8 Stigmatic surfaces

The secretions so far mentioned have usually taken place through uncutinized walls, e.g. the cap cells of roots, or the tips of pollen tubes.

There is also one well-documented instance where secretion takes place not only through the existing cellulose cell wall, but also through breaks in a cuticle as well. The epidermal cells of the stigmatic surface and the stigmatic papillae of *Petunia hybrida*, secrete large oil globules (Fig. 145). The exact mechanism whereby this takes place is not known (Konar & Linskens, 1966). Nevertheless, large oil droplets, about 1μm in diameter, pass through the cellulose cell wall and accumulate temporarily between it and cuticle above; others accumulate in the intercellular spaces. As the secretion proceeds, the cuticle becomes ruptured in many places and the oily substance flows over the surface of the stigma. A second stage of secretion starts soon after anthesis and is much more vigorous. The exudate which had accumulated in the intercellular spaces in the secretory zone just below the epidermal cells is taken in quickly into the epidermal cells. These epidermal cells become loose at maturity in *Petunia hybrida* as in a number of other plants.

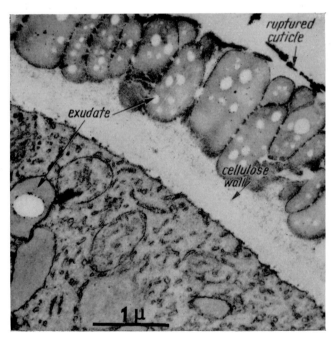

FIG. 145. Electron micrograph of the stigmatic surface of *Petunia*. A sticky exudate in the form of large vesicles accumulates in the outermost cells of the stigma, passes through the cellulose cell wall, accumulates between the wall and cuticle and finally ruptures the cuticle and forces it away in flakes. (Mn/Os/Pb)

Micrograph by Dr R. N. Konar and Prof H. F. Linskens.

We can speculate that the complex secretion in stigmas has several functions. Firstly, adhesion of the pollen grain may be helped by such a coating. Secondly, incompatibility reactions may be determined by interactions between pollen and secretion. The secretion itself may hasten the dissolution of the pollen exine and thus facilitate eruption of the pollen tube. The secretion may also serve to remove the cuticle, which could act as a barrier to pollen tube penetration. It may weaken the intercellular cement, so that it helps the tube to penetrate through the epidermis and, by providing a soluble food supply, it may nourish the pollen tube as it grows down the stigmatic tissue into the style.

9.9   Salt secretion

The secretion of salt (NaCl) from specialized cells in the leaves of several families of plants, e.g. Gramineae and Tamaricaceae is a striking phenomenon. The salt glands of the leaf surfaces of several plants have now been studied under the electron microscope (Ziegler & Luttge, 1966 and 1967; Thomson & Liu, 1967). These glands usually comprise two groups of cells. There are usually two inner, vacuolate, 'collecting' cells. With these there are usually six or more outer secretory cells which have very prominent nuclei and dense cytoplasm. A striking feature of these glands, now confirmed by the electron microscope studies, is that a cuticular layer not only covers the outer surface of the gland where this comes in contact with the environment, but also extends down the side of the gland, between the gland and the adjacent epidermal cells. Four pores penetrate this cuticle, one to each secreting cell on the surface. There is, moreover, at the base of the gland, between the collecting cells and the secretory cells of the leaf, a cross-shaped figure of cuticle whose arms extend to the cuticle cap. Thus the gland is completely surrounded by cuticle except for the few pores at the surface and four small irregularly shaped areas on the border between the collecting cells and the basal secretory cells; it is these areas that are crossed by the very large microplasmodesmata described on page 258. This cuticle-free area is generally called the transfusion zone on the assumption that it is the only area available for movement between the two groups of cells.

A feature of these secretory cells, particularly of the middle and outer ones and found most commonly on the outer wall of these, are the large numbers of protuberances of the wall which project into the cell. These protuberances are often branched and may, as is suggested by Ziegler & Lüttge in *Limonium,* be associated with plasmodesmata. They often enclose parts of the cytoplasm within their folds. Large numbers of very small vacuoles, which are usually distributed around the periphery of the cells, are found close to these protuberances. Ziegler and Lüttge, but not apparently other workers, have also noticed electron dense (after $KMnO_4$ fixation) sheaths or bands in these secretory cells, which usually lie between the non-vacuolar and vacuolar regions of the cytoplasm. These secretory cells have a much denser cytoplasm than normal, with rough-surfaced ER, Golgi bodies and numerous mitochondria as well as the sheaths or bands. The plastids are relatively empty with a few unorganized lamellae and, at least in *Tamarix*, contain very prominent osmiophilic globules. The collecting cells on the other hand are usually almost completely filled by a large vacuole; the vacuoles often have electron dense inclusions within them and the plastids, unlike those of the secreting cells, develop as normal chloroplasts like those of the mesophyll cells.

How does secretion of salt take place? Thomson and Liu speculate that the salt may be accumulated in the very prominent small vacuoles of the secretory cells. These are then assumed to drift to the periphery of the cells, fuse with the plasmalemma and release the salt into the zone between the plasmalemma and the wall. The salt is then believed to be forced along the wall and out through the cuticular pores at the top of the gland.

Some recent work by Ziegler & Lüttge (1967) in which they used both autoradiography and the electron microscope to identify silver chloride precipitate shows the pathway of secretion of salt. Their experiment leaves no doubt that the prominent plasmodesmata between the cells of the glands do act as channels for transport of the salt; one of the few experiments that does indicate unequivocally a role for the plasmo-desmata. Their evidence also seems to support the hypothesis of transport via the vacuoles put forward by Thomson and Liu in that all the small vacuoles close to the cell wall in the secretory cells contain a coarse-grained precipitate of silver chloride. Also heavily coated with silver chloride precipitate is the electron dense band of material which encircles many of the secretory cells. Ziegler and Lüttge suggest that this electron-dense band may play some role in salt secretion, but they take care to point out that their evidence does not suggest that there is any difference between the concentration of chloride in the cytoplasm of the leaf parenchyma and that in the gland cells. Their evidence suggests that sequestration of the salt takes place in the vacuoles of the secretory cells by a mechanism similar to that suggested by Thomson and Liu, but the overall picture is not yet clear.

9.10 Bacterial nodule cells

Bacteria are frequently found on the surfaces of plants (Fig. 146). The symbiotic association of nitrogen-fixing bacteria (*Rhizobium*) and the roots of leguminous plants is of immense importance to agriculture, for leguminous crops can contribute 20 g of nitrogen per square metre per season (Nutman, 1959). There appears to be a quantitative relationship between the amount of nitrogen fixed and the amount and duration of bacteroid tissue formed in the nodule. The nodules themselves are considered to be aborted lateral roots whose cells swell and whose nuclei enlarge, become polyploid and then degenerate. The cells produce a form of haemoglobin. The root stimulates the bacteria in the soil by its secretion and the bacteria produce IAA which causes the root hairs to curl. Initial infection is usually through one of the curled root hairs, but

FIG. 146. Electron micrograph of a *Zea* primary root tip. The flanks of the cap are coated with the viscous sugary mucus derived partly from the breakdown of the cap cell walls and partly from the secretion of carbohydrates by the Golgi bodies of the peripheral cells. In this mucus, just behind the root tip, are found large numbers of bacteria. (Glut/Mn)

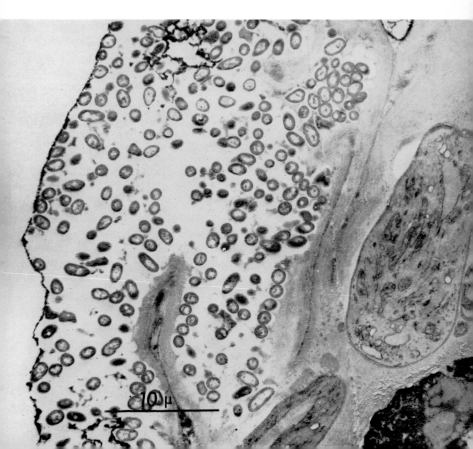

the details of penetration are not known. Once inside the root hair the bacteria form an infection thread. This thread grows and ramifies as it passes from cell to cell of the root, but only the tetraploid cells of the root are infected and the initial infection of the root appears to stimulate these tetraploid cells in the inner cortex to divide to form the nodule.

Mosse (1964) suggests that the bacterial infection of a cell develops between the paired membranes of the endoplasmic reticulum, i.e. within the enchylema. However, it is perhaps simpler to think of the initial infective penetration as an invagination of the plasmalemma to form the infection thread. A primary wall is built up as a lining to this thread and remains continuous with the primary wall of the infected cell. This lining reacts histochemically like the host cell wall; it contains cellulose and sometimes forms a thicker layer within the invagination than the original wall itself. The wall in the infection thread may be looked upon as a defence mechanism of the cell, simply a modification of the primary cell wall, and it is interesting that no sign of polyphenol accumulation, which is commonly a feature of fungus-infected cells is ever seen in cells infected by nodule bacteria. Highly pathogenic and rapidly colonizing fungi such as certain species of *Verticillium* described by Griffiths & Isaac (1966) do not trigger off host reactions. Perhaps this bacterial infection is comparable to infection by these fungi.

Bacteria that emerge from the infection thread leave behind the extended primary cell wall, but remain surrounded by a membrane (Fig. 147). They swell and may branch, but apparently never divide. They develop into the so-called bacteroids, which are such a conspicuous feature of mature infected cells (Fig. 148). This hypertrophy of the bacteroids appears to mark the point at which the nodule becomes an effective unit in nitrogen fixation.

Unchanged bacteria which remain in the infection thread may become parasitic, and their multiplication may bring about the collapse of the nodule cells. It is generally believed that the bacteroids are the site of nitrogen fixation, but the role of the membrane surrounding the bacteroid remains in doubt; it appears nevertheless to be an essential part of the symbiotic system.

9.11 Xylem vessels and tracheids

Little work has been done on the fine structure of most differentiating cells of higher plants with thick secondary walls because they are so difficult to cut. However, Wooding & Northcote (1964), Pickett-Heaps (1966), Hepler & Newcomb (1963) and Esau, Cheadle & Gill (1966a, b)

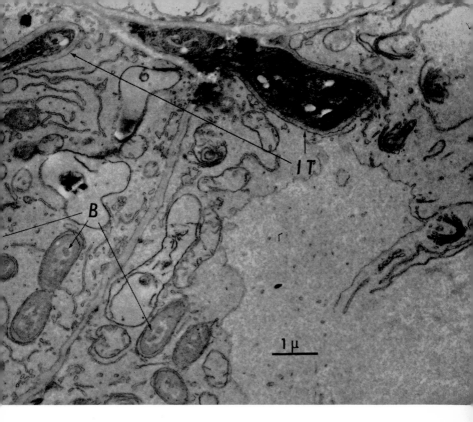

FIG. 147. Electron micrograph of an early stage in the infection of a clover (*Trifolium*) root by the symbiotic bacterium, *Rhizobium*. I.T. is part of the infection thread and B indicates bacteria already free in the cytoplasm. (Mn)

Micrograph by Dr B. Mosse.

amongst others have studied the differentiation of tracheary elements, i.e. vessels and tracheids.

The development of xylem elements has been extensively studied with the light microscope. The procambial cells from which they are formed elongate and enlarge rapidly and vacuolate leaving a thin skin of cytoplasm around the periphery of the cell, about three times as thick as the primary wall. So far none of the electron microscopical observations have been able to confirm the early findings of streams of protoplasm (see page 247) which apparently correspond with subsequent zones of deposition of annular or spiral thickenings (Wooding & Northcote, 1964 and Esau, Cheadle & Gill, 1966a). Stages of the development of the spiral thickenings in a xylem element of *Beta* and *Cucurbita* are given in Figs. 149 and 150. The dark areas arrowed in Fig. 149A are probably sites of formation of lignin. If so, lignin synthesis begins somewhat earlier in the development of the secondary wall than had hitherto been thought (Hepler & Newcomb, 1963; Esau, Cheadle & Gill, 1966a, b; Wooding & Northcote, 1964). The intense staining reaction is a feature only of permanganate-fixed preparations; after other fixatives have been used the fibrillar nature of the spiral or annular thickenings can be seen, but generally no 'lignin'. It can also be seen that both the Golgi and their vesicles increase in number in xylem elements in comparison with those of the neighbouring xylem parenchyma (Figs. 149A, 150). This proliferation is presumably associated with the enhanced wall synthesis at the site of the spiral or annular thickenings.

Thornber & Northcote (1961) have shown that, in the secondary cell walls of angiosperms and gymnosperms, more α-cellulose than hemicellulose is deposited and in angiosperms there may even be a reduction in comparison with the primary cell walls in the amount of galacturonic acid per cell. We might therefore expect, from the knowledge already gained on the source of pectin and hemicellulose substances in cells that

FIG. 148. Electron micrograph of bacteroids in a symbiotic nodule of a clover (*Trifolium*) root. The nodule has reached a later stage in development than that shown in Fig. 147. The cells containing the bacteroids also contain haemoglobin, appear pink under the light microscope and are thought to be active in fixing gaseous nitrogen. (Mn)

Micrograph by Dr B. Mosse.

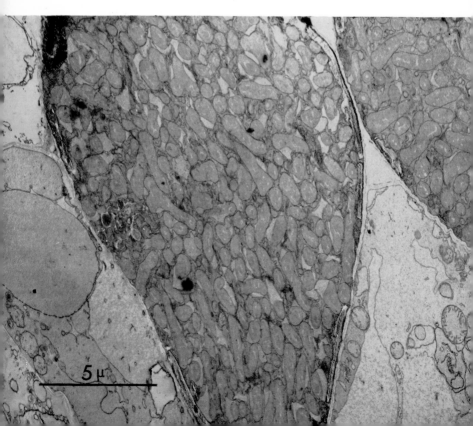

5 μ

are still expanding, that the activity of Golgi bodies would fall, as secondary cell wall formation continued. It would be very interesting to study the pattern of Golgi body activity in cells such as those of some reaction wood tissue in which microfibrillar synthesis continues to the almost total exclusion of hemicellulose and lignin formation.

Many other modifications of the cytoplasm and its inclusions can also be seen in cells differentiating in this way. Porter (1961) and Heslop-Harrison (1963) and Pickett-Heaps & Northcote (1966) noticed that the part of the wall between the spiral thickenings is lined with elements of endoplasmic reticulum. Northcote & Wooding (1966) have suggested that, in sieve tubes, the ER can act as a barrier to the deposition of wall material (but see page 240) and it seems possible that the ER in these xylem vessels may be performing the same function in selectively directing material towards the thickening areas and away from the non-thickening areas (Fig. 155). However, in other cells the ER can be found lining walls that are apparently undergoing abnormally rapid rates of thickening. This can be seen in the cortical cells of the root tip of *Vicia faba* in which elements of ER appear to line the thicker areas of the wall that face intercellular spaces, whereas the thin areas of the wall, where the cells touch, lack ER elements parallel to them or have ER elements at right angles to the wall (Fig. 95).

The microtubules in developing xylem vessels and tracheids take up the opposite distribution to that of the ER. According to Hepler & Newcomb (1964) and Wooding & Northcote (1964) the microtubules are aligned parallel to the thickenings of the wall and the cellulose microfibrils of the thickenings are parallel to the microtubules. Hepler and Newcomb report bunches of fibrils lying within the enchylema of the ER sometimes without any obvious orientation, but sometimes parallel to the bands of thickening. They were studying wounded stem segments of *Coleus blumei* which were induced, under the influence of applied indoleacetic acid, to redifferentiate into tracheary elements. In essence their findings are identical to those of Wooding and North-cote, but in addition they report these bundles of fibrils, similar in size to the microfibrils of the wall, lying within the cisternae of sheets of rough-surfaced ER. There did not seem to be any consistent relation between the bunches of fibrils and the orientation of the microfibrils in the bands of secondary thickening or of the bands themselves. Hepler and Newcomb suggest that these fibrils are incorporated into the structure of the spiral thickenings of the wall, although, since some of them were observed to be at least 1–2μm long, this preformation idea of microfibrillar synthesis is difficult to relate with the more generally held

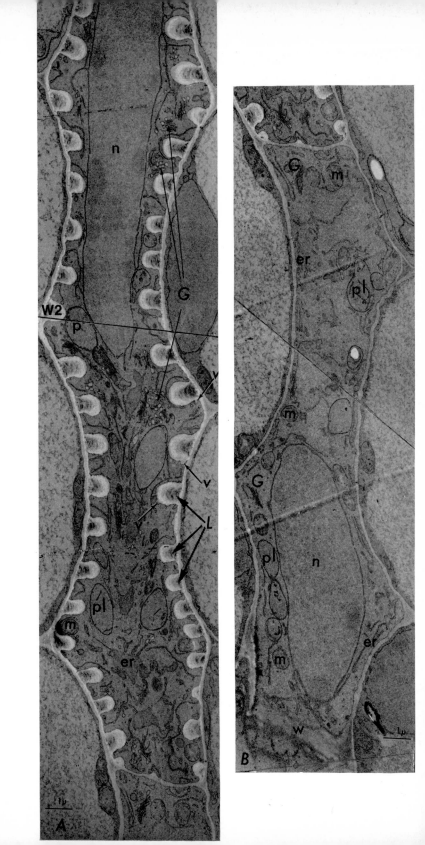

concepts of end synthesis, change of direction and interweaving of microfibrils. Nevertheless they exist and have to be explained.

Pickett-Heaps & Northcote (1966) and Pickett-Heaps (1966) in more recent work have been able to go further than the simple observation that microtubules lie parallel to the developing xylem thickenings. They have shown that the distribution of the microtubules changes during the early stages of cell wall development. Initially randomly scattered along the undifferentiated wall, the microtubules are later found between immature thickening bands and still later come to lie parallel to the thickenings themselves (Figs. 151, 152).

Pickett-Heaps has followed the incorporation into the xylem wall of derivatives of labelled glucose by high resolution autoradiography. He describes four stages in the development of a xylem vessel from the time that it is distinguishable as such, to its completion. An interpretation of these four stages with additional information from Wooding & North-cote (1964) and Cronshaw & Bouck in given in Fig. 152. Pickett-Heaps' first stage corresponds to the earliest possible identification of a xylem element; the microtubules are evenly spread along a very thin wall, and the amount of material incorporated into the walls of the young xylem is low and indistinguishable in quantity from that incorporated into neighbouring cells. Nor is there any apparent correlation between the sparse labelling of the cytoplasmic organelles of the young xylem and the labelling of the cell wall. In the second stage the beginnings of regular wall patterns appear; the microtubules are often, but not invariably, aggregated between the bands of thickening. Elements of ER generally, but again not invariably, are found orientated opposite the bands. This strikingly regular alternation of two types of organelle is shown in Fig. 152. Both at this and the first stage of development labelled carbohydrate is incorporated into the starch grains of the amyloplasts both of the young xylem cells and of the sieve tube cells. This pattern of incorporation is noticed only at these two stages. Subsequently incorporation of labelled material into the wall increases and

FIG. 149. Electron micrographs of two early stages in the differentiation of *Cucurbita* tracheary elements. The element in A adjoins the element in B; there are no signs of the banded distribution of the cytoplasm visible under the light microscope at this magnification. (A) shows the development of the secondary wall (W2) with Golgi vesicles (G, arrowed) contributing material to the thickenings (V). The Golgi bodies, at this stage, are conspicuous and are surrounded by many large vesicles. Compare their appearance in B with Fig. 151. Lignification (L) has already begun within the secondary wall. m, mitochondrion; pl, plastid; w, wall. (Mn)

Micrograph by Prof K. Esau, Dr V. I. Cheadle and Dr R. H. Gill.

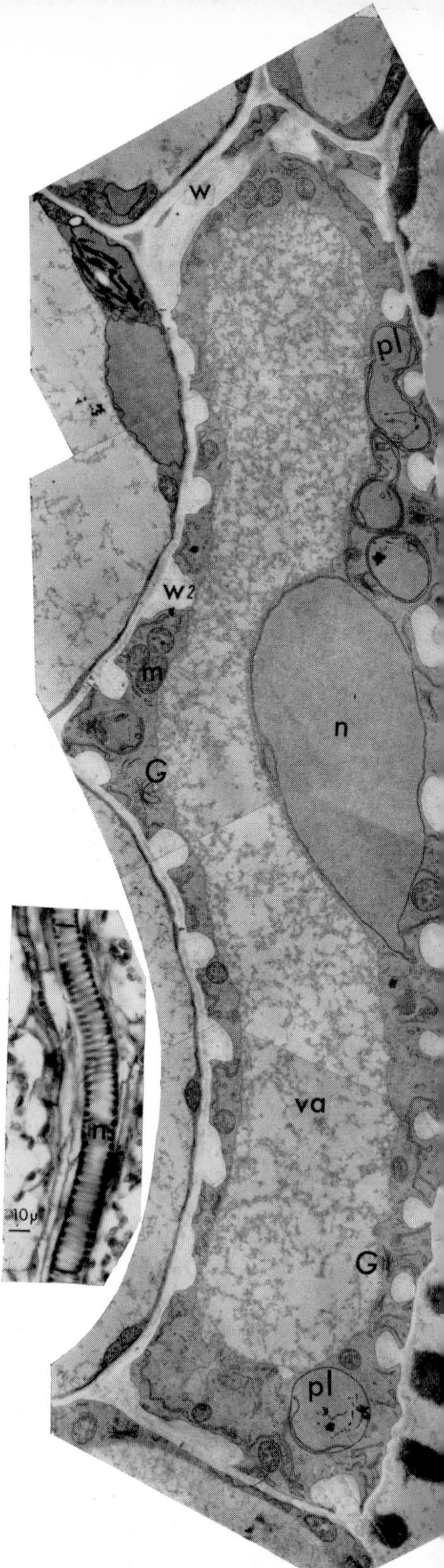

FIG. 150. Light and electron micrograph of vessel elements from a leaf of *Beta vulgaris* (sugar beet). In the electron micrograph two stages of differentiation are shown. On the right the vessel element is complete, the secondary wall is completely lignified (W2) and cytoplasm has disintegrated. On the left is a vessel member in the final stages of differentiation. The cell is almost completely vacuolate, the secondary thickenings (W2) are not yet lignified but have almost reached their full size. (Mn)

Micrograph by Prof K. Esau, Dr V. I. Cheadle and Dr R.H. Gill.

it may be that metabolic competition between areas in the cell now favours the cell wall at the expense of the plastids (Fig. 156).

During the third stage, rapid incorporation of material into specialized areas of the secondary cell wall determines the final structure of the xylem vessel. Microtubules are now to be found parallel to, above and, to a lesser extent, to the sides of the spiral or annular thickening bands (Fig. 151). Elements of the ER lie between almost all the thickening bands and almost all the labelling occurs at the 'tops' of the bands. As has already been noticed in root cap cells, a much greater degree of labelling in the carbohydrates derived from glucose $-6-{}^3$H than from

FIG. 151. Electron micrograph of a developing xylem element in *Nicotiana* callus tissue. Note the microtubules (M) orientated parallel and close to the surface of the secondary thickening.

Micrograph by Dr F. B. P. Wooding and Dr D. H. Northcote.

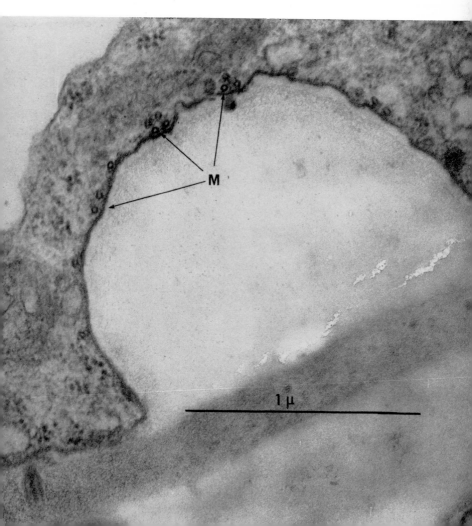

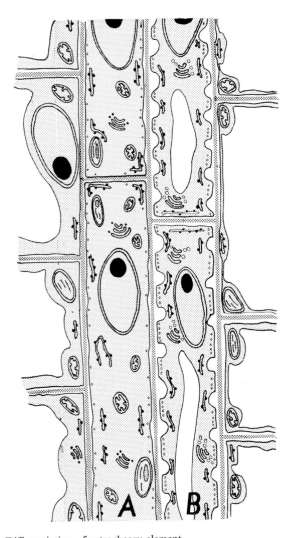

FIG. 152. Differentiation of a tracheary element.

A: The procambial cells which are to form the tracheary elements elongate and begin to vacuolate rapidly. Initially the microtubules lie parallel to the cell wall, but with no preferential distribution.

B: As vacuolation proceeds, large numbers of vesicles are budded off by the Golgi bodies, microtubules begin to concentrate between the thickened areas that now appear on the cell walls and segments of the ER are found close to the thickening areas of the wall and parallel to the transverse walls.

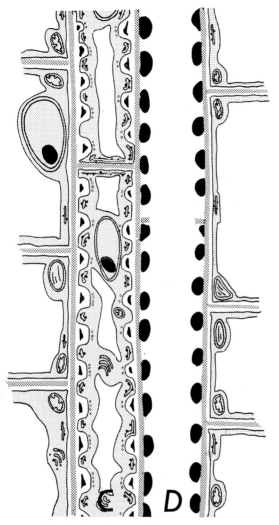

C: Lignification of the thickened areas of the wall begins well before thickening of the wall and vacuolation is complete. At this stage the microtubules are found 'over' the thickened areas and segments of ER are found between the thickenings. Golgi activity slackens at this stage.

D: Lignification of the thickened areas is completed, but the areas of lignification do not usually extend beyond the thickenings into the primary wall (see Fig. 151). The transverse walls swell, probably as a result of partial hydrolysis and break down, often leaving stumps or fragments of the wall around the edge. There may also be some breakdown of the primary wall between the thickenings, particularly where two tracheary elements lie side-by-side (see Fig. 153).

glucose —1 — ^{3}H was observed (Northcote & Pickett-Heaps, 1966). This suggests that the xylose, which forms a high percentage of secondary wall hemicellulose, is metabolized mainly via the pentose phosphate pathway (Fig. 154). The cytoplasm of the xylem cells at stage three is not heavily labelled. Only a small proportion of the Golgi bodies visible in any one section is labelled and only occasionally is label associated with Golgi vesicles. The ER that is present between the thickened zones is more consistently labelled, this time equally by both types of labelled glucose. There is no evidence that any label occurs *within* the microtubules although occasionally silver grains are found close to them.

At the fourth stage of development incorporation of labelled sugars

Fɪɢ. 153. Electron micrograph of protoxylem in a leaf bundle of *Spinacia*. This is an oblique section through the vessel. The thickening of the vessel wall (TH) is in the plane of the section. Although the transverse walls of this vessel have almost certainly broken down by this stage, the section has passed through the rim (R) of persistent material which is usually left around the edge of the hole. The primary wall (P) of the vessel has remained intact where it borders onto a parenchymatous cell, but where two vessels lie alongside, the whole primary wall has disappeared, except where it was protected by lignification, leaving behind a trace of fibrous material (F) which may be cellulose microfibrils. (Glut/Os/Pb/U)

Micrograph by Mr A. D. Greenwood.

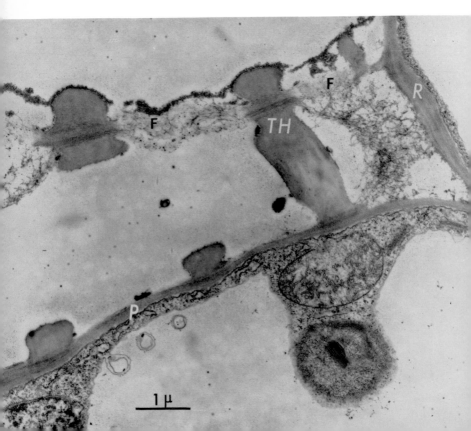

drops markedly. At the same time the cytoplasmic organelles begin to disintegrate, the end walls of the vessels break down (see page 296) and the thickened vessel becomes functional (Fig. 153).

The fact that elements of the ER, particularly those parallel to the wall, but between the thickening bands of the vessel, are found labelled with derivatives of glucose suggests that they may have some role in the synthesis and transport of material. This material must be in an insoluble form or it would be dissolved out when the autoradiographs are prepared, but the site of polymerization and the nature of the polymer are unknown (Pickett-Heaps, 1966). This is the first time that the ER has been implicated directly in wall building, but whether it synthesizes or merely transports is not yet known. The microtubules are here associated with cell walls building at rapid rates. This fact is consistent with the current hypothesis that they are concerned with the synthesis of cellulose microfibrils (see page 248), but it could also be that they are primarily concerned with the orderly direction of cell wall matrix material, e.g. pectins and hemicellulose, into the appropriate regions of the cytoplasm close to the cell wall. Pickett-Heaps suggests that the latter interpretation is the more likely since the incorporation of microfibrillar material can occur in xylem cells in the absence of microtubules after the microtubules have been destroyed or disorganized by colchicine. He also notes that their removal from the cell coincides with the appearance of grossly malformed secondary thickenings. This evidence and particularly the evidence that the future site of the cell plate is determined by a peripheral ring of microtubules (see page 418) is further evidence that they are concerned with the incorporation of matrix material and not with the synthesis of cellulose.

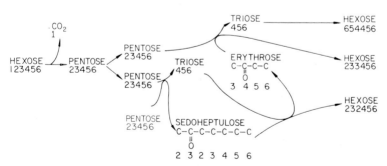

FIG. 154. The pentose phosphate pathway. One of the sequences of reactions whereby hexose is incorporated into structural polysaccharides. The C6 carbon is always retained, but the C1 carbon is lost.

Redrawn from Davies, Giovanelli and ap Rees (1964).

Many instances are recorded of mitochondria whose internal structure differentiates at the same time as the cells in which they are found
differentiate. An interesting feature of the development of a fully
differentiated vessel is that, so far as can be seen, the mitochondria do
not change at all until their final breakdown and death (Cronshaw &
Bouck, 1965).

9.12 Diversity at the organelle level

The mitochondria, the Golgi bodies, the ER with its associated ribosomes, the nuclear membrane and the recently discovered microtubules
are found in all eukaryotic cells. The fact that so many different cells
have all these in common suggests a monophyletic development of all
higher organisms. However, plants and animals differ from one another
and it may be useful to compare the cytoplasmic organelles in them and
the changes they undergo when they differentiate. A superficial similarity in the form of organelles in animals and plants may mask important differences in their function.

There is no reason to suppose that the role of mitochondria (aerobic
respiration) is different in animals and plants, although it is known that
there are small differences between the enzymes of animal and plant
mitochondria. But this is, perhaps, the only instance where one can be
sure of similarity of form and function. In contrast, the best documented
role of the Golgi bodies in plants, the formation of the non-crystalline
carbohydrate matrix of primary and secondary cell walls, has no
parallel in animals. The smooth ER of plant cells may firstly be associated with tannin accumulation, secondly with some features of the
growth of pollen tube tips through stylar tissue and thirdly with spindle
formation. There does not seem to be any link here with the steroid
secretion with which the smooth ER of animal cells is usually associated.

The rough-surfaced ER membranes of plants have always been
supposed to act in an analogous way to those of animals, i.e. protein
synthesis. However, a number of differences between the type of ER
membranes found in the two kingdoms is beginning to be noticed. In the
first place, the ER of a plant cell frequently makes contact with that of a
neighbouring cell via the plasmodesmata, a phenomenon that is not
known in animals. The ER of plant cells is frequently asymmetrical, i.e.
the ribosomes are found to coat only one surface; this is known in a
number of secretory cells and in phloem, but it is unknown in animals.
The ER of the root cap cells is known to move about when stimulated
by gravity and to concentrate in certain areas of the cell. This too has no

parallel in animal cells. The nuclear membrane of animals is almost universally coated on its outer surface with ribosomes, whereas in plants it is almost invariably smooth.

The microtubules of animals and plants are superficially similar. But it seems that they must have very different functions, for they occur in plants where the cell plate is formed centrifugally, but not in animals where it is formed centripetally. Moreover, they occur in plants near walls that are being built, whereas in animals they are believed to have some function in determining cell shape by acting as a cytoskeletal framework.

These examples indicate that the similarity of many cytoplasmic organelles of animals and plants conceal differences of function and probably also of biochemistry and adaptability. The differences have obviously come about under the influence of the very different problems that animals and plants have had to solve. Nevertheless some of the lower plants, such as the flagellate algae, have obvious affinities with some animals and further evidence of these affinities is to be found not only in the detailed structure of their cytoplasmic organelles, but possibly also in their functions. Thus the Golgi bodies of the flagellate alga, *Mesostigma*, with their associated vacuoles are much more like animal than plant Golgi bodies (Fig. 66). They are not concerned with the material of the matrix of the wall, but produce the scales which cover the outside of the organism. In this chapter we have seen that a number of processes may control the pattern of differentiation. To what extent can each cytoplasmic organelle differentiate and in what way may such differentiation contribute to the overall patterns of differentiation observed?

The differentiation of mitochondria

Very little is known about the changes that take place in the numbers of mitochondria per cell as differentiation proceeds. Such information as does exist suggests that the numbers of mitochondria in any one sequence of cells remains approximately the same per unit volume of cytoplasm as the cells grow (Fig. 53; Juniper & Clowes, 1965; Diers, 1966). It should be pointed out that these counts were made in cells that are essentially non-vacuolate and possess only a brief life span. Whether such conclusions can be extended to vacuolate cells and cells with a much longer existence remains to be seen.

A number of changes in the internal structure of mitochondria has been observed to be correlated with developmental changes in the cells.

P*

Generally speaking, as we have seen in Chapter 4, mitochondria in un-differentiated cells or cells in which metabolic activity is falling tend to have poorly developed cristae, whereas those in differentiated cells and metabolically active cells have well-developed cristae. Such patterns are not so clear cut in all cells that one is completely confident that this progressive increase in cristae with differentiation always occurs (see page 438). There is a general tendency for the cells which secrete various substances vigorously and for other active cells, such as companion cells, to contain many well-developed mitochondria. Subjective impressions of the density of cytoplasmic organelles not based on measurements can be very misleading. There does, however, seem to be some evidence that certain cells, e.g. the glandular tissue of plant nectaries are much better supplied with mitochondria in comparison with the surrounding tissue (Frey-Wyssling & Mühlethaler, 1965). Other changes in the internal structure of mitochondria such as the appearance or disappearance of electron translucent areas, commonly present in meristematic cells, are much too erratic to allow one to draw any general conclusions. Plants are unlike animals in that there are few records indicating that mitochondria concentrate in certain parts of the cell or concentrate around certain organelles. It may well be that movements and associations of mitochondria at certain phases of differentiation will become more apparent when comparative techniques with the electron microscope have improved. Jensen (1965) has, however, shown that a very striking gradient of numbers of mitochondria occurs across the synergids of *Gossypium*. The highest concentration occurs in the centre of the cell around the nucleus. A large number is found close to the filiform apparatus which is an extension of the micropylar end of the synergid wall, but relatively few are found at the other end, the chalazal end of the cell. The concentration of cristae in the mitochondria at the filiform end is much greater than that of the mitochondria at the chalazal end. This internal distinction between the mitochondria of a single cell has not previously been noticed. It may result from the intense metabolic gradient of these cells, the entry of carbohydrates through the filiform apparatus in preference to other areas of the cell wall and the utilization of the carbohydrates by those mitochondria nearest the point of entry. Mitochondria have not yet been seen to fuse in plants as they do, for example, in the spermatocytes of snails. Here, before meiosis, twenty to twenty-six mitochondria fuse in threes to form eight or nine mitochondrial rods. A similar fusion takes place in spermatogenesis of grasshoppers where fused mitochondria form a helical wrapping around the midpiece of the sperm cell. Both of these fusions appear to be reversible. It may be profitable to look for such fusion of mitochondria in certain flagellate algae where long mitochondria are sometimes found wrapped around the base of the flagellum (Fig. 58). Examples of concentrations of respiratory units may occur only in animal tissues or in the flagellates, where a highly concentrated source of energy is required for a short time. The lower respiration rate of most cells of higher plants is probably satisfied by the diffusion of energy rich compounds themselves and not by a mass movement of mitochondria.

Differentiation, redistribution and concentration of microtubules

At the centre of the problem of the growth and thickening of walls, both primary and secondary, is the control of the deposition of the skeletal and matrix materials. What cytoplasmic factors control this highly organized and coordinated deposition of carbohydrates? There seems little doubt now that at least the major proportion of matrix materials, i.e. the pectins and hemicellulose pass through and are marshalled by the Golgi bodies. This does not prove that the polymerization of the carbohydrates concerned actually takes place in the Golgi. Little evidence exists yet on the complement of enzymes of plant Golgi bodies, but experiments with isotopes suggest that the first appearance of labelled insoluble carbohydrate is in or around the Golgi bodies. The Golgi bodies also produce parts of the plasmalemma from their vesicles. Golgi-associated membrane production seems to be most striking in the algae *Mesostigma* and *Prymnesia* where vesicles up to 1 μm in diameter are formed from the cisternae of the Golgi, and despatched, with their fully developed carbohydrate surface scale, to be incorporated in the plasmalemma (see Fig. 66).

What mechanisms propel or attract these carbohydrate-filled vesicles to the area in the differentiating cell wall, to the growing cell plate, to the rapidly expanding areas of the primary cell wall or to the spiral or annular thickenings of a xylem vessel? What mechanism excludes or reduces their incorporation into the more slowly growing regions of the primary cell wall, the transverse walls of tracheids, vessels and laticifers and the regions between the thickenings of a vessel?

One kind of cytoplasmic structure does occur in almost all the regions of a plant cell in which walls are rapidly synthesized, namely the microtubules (see page 116). They are present in the form of spindle fibres at a mitotic division (Figs. 157, 84). At preprophase they form a peripheral girdle to the cell and usually mark the site where the cell plate will

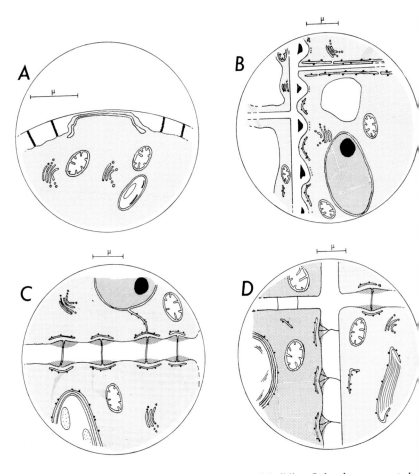

FIG. 155. The distribution of ER and uneven wall building. It has been suggested by a number of authors that the ER, where it is found lying parallel to the wall, prevents the normal deposition of wall material. That this is not always the case has been indicated in the text (see Fig. 95). However, there are several instances where this may occur. (A) Opposite the poral regions of pollen exine. (B) Between the thickenings of the longitudinal walls of tracheary elements and across their transverse walls. (C) At and around sieve pores in sieve element transverse walls. (D) Around the branched plasmodesmata on the companion cell side of a companion cell/sieve element common wall. Note that in C and D the segments of the ER lie over regions not only in which normal wall deposition is suppressed, but also in which callose deposition takes place.

Fig. 155A redrawn from Heslop-Harrison (1963).

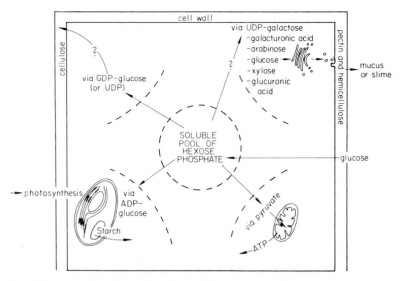

FIG. 156. Competition for carbohydrate. Within a single cell a number of organelles and enzyme systems compete at any one time for a common pool of hexose phosphate. The most important of these are the mitochondria, the Golgi bodies, the plastids and the enzymes responsible for the synthesis of cellulose.

finally join the existing cell walls; they lie in random array over primary cell walls that are undergoing rapid growth (Fig. 89) and they concentrate into parallel hoops or spirals as specialized secondary thickening gets under way in a vessel (Figs. 151, 152). Both Northcote and Esau have published micrographs showing what appear to be chains of Golgi vesicles lying close to the surface of a microtubule and very close to the forming cell plate (Fig. 84). Golgi vesicles and microtubules are also found close together in some animal cells (Slautterbach, 1963). It looks also as if the mass of microtubules, estimated at about 500 in the spindle of *Phleum* by Ledbetter & Porter (1963), attracts Golgi vesicles.

Such a coalescence of vesicles as Esau and as Northcote have seen on or close to the surfaces of the microtubules could explain why microscopic fibres, seen by interference microscopy at anaphase and telophase in endosperm cells, appear to thicken in their centres and become spindle shaped as the cell plate starts to form (Bajer & Allen, 1966). What cannot yet be explained is why the attraction, if such there is, is strongest at the equator of the spindle, and weakest at the poles. Another possibility is that the microtubules exert a general attraction and this is counterbalanced by a repulsion from the nuclear areas. A

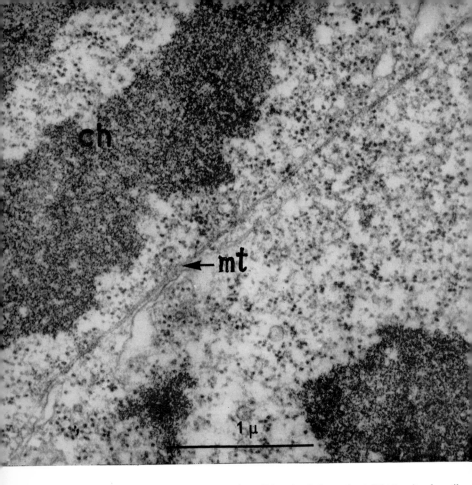

F<small>IG</small>. 157. Electron micrograph of a cell in mitosis in a wheat (*Triticum*) coleoptile cell. A spindle fibre (mt) is shown passing through a group of chromosomes (ch). Note the similarity of spindle fibres to microtubules (Figs. 38, 39, 89). (Glut/Os/ Pb/U)   Micrograph by Dr D. H. Northcote.

general repulsion of cytoplasmic particles from the nuclear region is certainly apparent at mitosis in time-lapse phase contrast cinemicrophotography. The repulsion by the two daughter nuclear areas would be weakest midway between the two nuclei; cell plates always seem to form mid-way between nuclei, although not necessarily symmetrically within the cell.

As the growing cell plate advances slowly to the existing cell wall it is preceded by a high concentration of microtubules, still aligned as they were in the spindle, around the whole of the periphery of the plate (Fig. 84). The mass of microtubules that formed the preprophase girdle has disappeared or dispersed long before the cell plate begins to form. It is still difficult to understand why such a girdle should usually appear to predict the site of junction of the cell plate with the mother wall, but usually does not either initially attract vesicles to itself or bring about other forms of wall thickening.

There seems to be no tendency for Golgi vesicles to be attracted initially to this peripheral zone; cell plate growth being entirely centrifugal. Once the cell plate is formed the microtubules are found scattered parallel to the growing cell wall, generally not less than 35 nm apart and not less than 17–20 nm from the plasmalemma (Ledbetter & Porter, 1963). In general they 'mirror' the pattern of distribution of the cellulose microfibrils in the primary cell wall and it is interesting that they are found less frequently and more randomly orientated when they are parallel to the transverse walls whose rate of growth is known to be less than that of the longitudinal walls. The fact that their distribution in the cytoplasm does, in many situations, 'mirror' the distribution of cellulose microfibrils in the primary and secondary cell walls has led some authors to suggest that they may be directly involved in the synthesis of microfibrils. This, however, would require other explanations for the role of the microtubules in mitotic cells during the phase in which only pectins and hemicellulose are being deposited. An explanation that requires fewer qualifications is that the only function of the microtubules is to deposit matrix materials in the cell. The microtubules may then occur parallel to the microfibrils because the matrix materials must be accurately placed by the microtubules between and around an existing microfibrillar structure; a shadow effect.

Attraction of a vesicle to a microtubule is obviously only an intermediate step to the incorporation of its content into an existing wall. It is significant that microtubules generally lie at a distance from the wall less than or roughly equivalent to the diameter of a Golgi vesicle. It is significant too that most, but not all, microtubules lie in regions of protoplasmic streaming or, in the spindle, of intense cytoplasmic agitation. The distance of a microtubule from the plasmalemma or of one microtubule from another in the spindle zone would be sufficiently small to allow vesicles to make contact either with the plasmalemma or with each other and the natural tendency of these bodies to coalesce would do the rest. An exception to the generalizations given above must be mentioned. Pollen tubes, which have an otherwise relatively conventional pattern of wall growth using both matrix and fibrillar materials, appear to have no microtubules at all even at the tip (see page 402).

There is some evidence from animals that the microtubules of the spindle are different, at least in some of their physical properties, from those of the cytoplasm (Slautterback, 1963). Moreover Slautterback speculates that, on the basis of size alone, the microtubules may be divided into two groups; those of the cytoplasm with sizes ranging around 27 nm and those of the spindle of 12–20 nm. He further goes on to say that the former function as elastic, skeletal bodies of the cytoplasm, whereas the latter function in the synthetic or metabolic functions of the cell. Although there is some evidence in plants for a similar bimodality of size, there seems to be little evidence for such a distinction in roles. For example, there seems to be good evidence for the assumption that both spindle and cytoplasmic microtubules are associated in some way with the building of the wall. It may well be that the skeletal functions of the microtubule have, at least as far as higher plants are concerned, long been taken over by the wall itself, leaving the microtubules the opportunity to specialize in other directions.

Differentiation of endoplasmic reticulum

The ER is the most flexible and adaptable of the more prominent cytoplasmic organelles. In no two cells is its pattern of distribution, its association with other cytoplasmic organelles, the length of the individual cisternae or the distribution of the ribosomes on its surfaces identical or even similar. Very little is known yet about what all these differences mean and it now seems likely that the ER in plant cells may have a number of roles. The ER of meristematic cells is usually fragmentary. We do not yet know how this appears in three dimensions since it is not yet known whether the ER of a single cell is completely interconnected like the lamellae of a chloroplast or whether a number of unconnected pieces obey commands to orientate in unison. The ER of meristematic cells appears to have few ribosomes on its surfaces whereas the more extensive ER of differentiating cells appear to be more heavily coated with ribosomes. In addition, Srivastava & O'Brien (1966) have noticed that the quiescent meristematic cells of *Fraxinus* cambium in winter have smooth ER whereas in spring, at the height of meristematic activity this is replaced by rough ER. According to Halperin & Jensen (1967) there is a redistribution of ribosomes that brings about a change from a high concentration of free ribosomes in meristematic cells to a high concentration of attached ribosomes in differentiating cells. However, these changes in shape and complexity do not necessarily alter in any way the concentration of ER per unit volume of cytoplasm. Where the area of ER per unit volume of cytoplasm has been measured it remains identical while the cytoplasmic volume increases fifteen-fold

(Fig. 53). Apart from the progressive concentration into longer and apparently more interconnected units the ER can be seen, as cells differentiate, to concentrate in different parts of the cell. Avers (1963) showed that in asymmetrical divisions in the epidermis of *Phleum* the basal pole possessed a greater concentration of ER. This polarity of the ER is not apparent in the symmetrical divisions in the same tissue. A similar although not so marked polarity in meristematic cells is apparent in the root cap initials of grasses in which a higher concentration of ER is found parallel to the distal transverse wall than parallel to the cap junction (Fig. 23). The ER of the synergids of *Gossypium* is concentrated towards the end with the filiform apparatus. The ER of some cells is distributed symmetrically around the cell and usually parallel to the cell wall (Fig. 30). Under the influence of gravity this symmetry may be disturbed (Fig. 32). It is also disturbed as the cells grow old (Fig. 65). In other cells the ER is found parallel to those areas of walls which are undergoing the most marked thickening and is absent from or at right angles to those areas in which thickening is restricted (Fig. 95). In other tissues, however, the ER is parallel to those areas where little or no thickening is taking place, a striking example of this may be seen in the pore regions of pollen grains (Fig. 155). In yet others the ER lies parallel to regions of the wall from which certain components are being removed, as when the pores of a sieve plate are formed. The ER is also found parallel to the regions of the wall in which multiple branched plasmodesmata are being formed (Fig. 155). In all of these situations a possible interpretation is that the orientation and concentration of the ER is involved in some way with the building up or the selective breakdown of certain of the components of the wall. This view is strengthened by the observation of Pickett-Heaps (1967) that, where cells are supplied with labelled carbohydrates, often the only organelle labelled near to the wall is the ER. It is possible that the ER in plants acts in conjunction with the Golgi bodies in building cell walls. Examples of similar cooperation have already been found in animals where radioactive label is seen to pass in sequence from the ER to the Golgi bodies and thence to the zymogen granules.

There is a good deal of indirect evidence that the ER can act as a transport system. This role is strongly suggested because it is connected with the plasmodesmata and also because it is frequently found wrapped around plastids.

The ER is also the most labile of any plant cell constituent. In response to wounding, as we have seen, it increases very rapidly in amount. It is tempting to speculate that this is because more cell wall will then need to be built. Another stimulus that increases the amount of ER in the cell is transfer from air to nitrogen. Mercer & Rathgeber (1962) found that in the nectary hairs of *Abutilon* the change in the environment completely fills the cytoplasm with ER. A similar situation seems to occur in the yeast, *Torulopsis utilis*, (Linnane, Vitols & Nowland, 1962). Under aerobic conditions these yeasts contain normal mitochondria and a normal respiratory system. Under anaerobic conditions they contain no mitochondria and no cytochrome system. However, the cells now contain an extensive membrane system which is similar to ER although it has not yet been proved to be identical to it. This membrane system does contain two primary dehydrogenases of the terminal respiratory chain, which, in the aerobic cells are located in the mitochondria. In both the higher plant and in the yeasts it may well be that under these extraordinary conditions some of the functions of the mitochondria are transferred to the ER. We can speculate even further and suggest that under these conditions there is, in fact, a transfer of the respiratory system to membranous structures, approaching the system known in bacteria in which the respiratory enzymes are believed to be located on extensions of the plasmalemma just within the cell wall. The flexibility of such membrane systems and their adaptability to extraordinary and, we suppose, ordinary problems of differentiations is further emphasized by Linnane *et al.* (1962). They suggest that, when anaerobically grown colonies of *T. utilis* are transferred back to air, the membranes appear to line up, fuse, and infold to form primitive forms of mitochondria.

Although no evidence has yet, to our knowledge, been presented from higher plants, it is perhaps dangerous to think of any cytoplasmic organelle as fixed and immutable in its function.

Differentiation of Golgi bodies

The Golgi bodies, like the mitochondria, in many tissues respond to the demands made upon them by increasing in size and increasing the number of and size of the vesicles that are budded off from the periphery. Because Golgi bodies are often concerned with building cell walls, we may expect to find that the least differentiated and the least active of the Golgi are in those cells that are building the least wall. The cells of the quiescent centre of root tips are dividing very slowly indeed (in *Zea* once every 200 hours). That wall synthesis is continuing slowly can be assumed because the walls of the cells of the quiescent centre are slightly thicker than those of the meristematic cells surrounding them (Clowes &

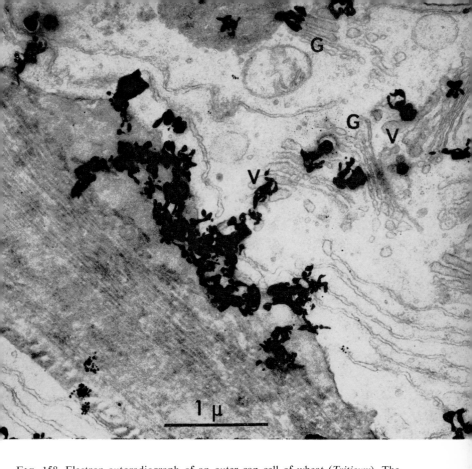

FIG. 158. Electron autoradiograph of an outer cap cell of wheat (*Triticum*). The excised root was exposed to D-[6 − ³H] glucose for 30 min. The distribution of the silver grains (black) over the Golgi bodies (G), the Golgi vesicles (V) and the material accumulated between the plasmalemma and the cell wall traces the path of the glucose. After 30 min exposure very little activity has yet reached the wall itself. After longer exposures radioactivity appears in the wall itself and subsequently in the mucus surrounding the root tip. Compare with Fig. 63 and 65. (Mn)

Micrograph by Dr D. H. Northcote and
Dr J. D. Pickett-Heaps.

Juniper, 1964). The Golgi of these cells are small (about 0·5μm across), the individual cisternae are closely pressed together and very few vesicles indeed are found at the periphery of the cisternae (Fig. 51). The hypertrophied Golgi bodies of the peripheral cap cells of the root are at the other extreme of differentiation. These Golgi may lie only a few cells distant from the Golgi of the quiescent centre, yet the cisternae have six or seven times the area and the vesicles that they seem to produce are more numerous and much larger than those of the Golgi of the quiescent centre (Figs. 63, 158). It is thought that this vigorous activity occurs because large quantities of carbohydrate are released from the amyloplasts. This carbohydrate is available to the Golgi because there is a lack of competition for it by other enzyme systems, which, in these semi-moribund cells, have slowed down or ceased to function (Fig. 156; Juniper & Roberts, 1966). There is little evidence in plants that Golgi bodies concentrate in differentiating cells in certain parts of the cell, as we have seen with other cytoplasmic organelles, although it is possible that, at anaphase and telophase, the spindle poles cause some displacement of the Golgi from the ends of the cell. This displacement would bring the Golgi closer to the regions of the cell plate where their products are at this time being rapidly incorporated. Jensen (1965a) has, however, shown that Golgi can vary in their appearance not only from one cell to another, but also along the length of a single cell. The Golgi of the filiform end of the synergid cells (see page 440) consist of three or four cisternae with few, if any, vesicles associated with them. The Golgi of the central region have six or seven cisternae. These are shorter than those of the filiform end and are associated with a moderate number of vesicles. The individual cisternae range in thickness from about 85 nm on one side down to about 25 nm on the other and the thinnest of them appears frequently to make contact with the ER. Around the periphery of the cell is a third type of Golgi, about the same size ($0\cdot5\mu$m) as those of the central part of the cell, but its cisternae are not so obviously graduated in size and not obviously associated with the ER. These Golgi produce many vesicles which increase in size and electron density as they move away from the cisternae. Jensen suggests that these Golgi may help to synthesize cell wall. It is not known what the other two types of Golgi do, but their appearance, their association with different organelles and the different sorts of vesicles they produce suggest that the Golgi in the synergid cells may have more than one role to play. The haustorial cells of *Cuscuta* have two types of Golgi; the one large, associated with vacuoles like an animal Golgi and the other small with no vacuoles and more like the usual plant Golgi (Bonneville & Voeller, 1963). No distinction in the roles of these two structures has yet been attempted. It is also possible that any single type of Golgi in some specialized cell may produce two or more different sorts of vesicle. Such a situation is not uncommon in animal cells and there are now suggestions that it may happen just at the growing point in root hair tips (see page 401). There are also indications that one side of a single Golgi body in certain specialized cells may have a different function from the other (see page 181 and Pickett-Heaps, 1967). Unlike the Golgi (and the mitochondria) of animals, plant Golgi cannot fuse into a single large functional mass.

Recent observations are tending to link together the roles of the Golgi, the ER and the microtubules. Although physical connexions between these structures are infrequent there is growing evidence both from direct observation and from autoradiography that, in many aspects of differentiation, they co-operate in the common task of wall building. It is no longer useful to study any one of these structures without appreciating or understanding its effect on other cytoplasmic organelles within the cell.

Differentiation of plastids

The plastids have no homologues in the animal cell, but certain of the roles they play in plants have parallels in similar structures in animals. One such structure which is immediately obvious is the retinal rod of the eye which is similar to the photosynthetic mechanism of the chloroplast. It is also now realized that plastids can do more than photosynthesize or store starch and pigments. They may, in certain specialized cells, be responsible for the synthesis or accumulation of phenolic substances or phytoferritin. They are believed to increase in numbers in resin cells and to be associated with the synthesis or accumulation of precursors of the resin (see page 415). In all these instances it is reasonable to speculate that the plastid/ER complex provides a site for the rapid synthesis or accumulation of materials and a rapid means to transport them within the cell. It is no longer sufficient to think of the leucoplasts as organelles into which metabolites are deposited for long periods of time, but rather one must think of them, as of the Golgi, as mobile, membrane-bounded centres of metabolism which have a range of enzymes at their disposal and which can be moved into position wherever they are wanted. The old statolith theory of the perception of gravity has been revived and this suggests that the amyloplasts even in their relatively inert state may have a role to play (Audus, 1962). It seems possible that, although not directly concerned themselves, in the perception of gravity, plastids may help to create gradients of growth-controlling substances. They may do this either by influencing the behaviour of certain membranes on to which they sediment, or they may disturb the distribution of other cytoplasmic organelles by sedimenting on to them and set up gradients in this way. Somewhat better understood now are the many changes which individual plastids undergo when certain cells ripen, such as those of fruits. Little of the bio-chemistry of the changes from say a chloroplast to a chromoplast or amyloplast to chromoplast is known, nor is much known of the mechanisms which control them, but a good deal is now known of the changes of structure that are involved and this may, we hope, stimulate work on the chemistry.

CHAPTER 10

Cell Heredity

10.1 Transmission of information

All cells are derived from other cells and in this chapter we shall discuss some aspects of the transmission of information from one cell to its daughters. We are not concerned especially with inheritance from one individual plant to another—the subject of genetics—except in as far as it gives us information about cell inheritance. Nor are we especially concerned here with the activities of chromosomes, for we have discussed these briefly in earlier chapters. In sexually breeding organisms the problems of inheritance are complicated by the necessity for meiosis and the mixing of cell organelles at fertilization. In such organisms there is a stage, often meiosis or gamete production, when the cell is as it were, cleaned up, leaving parts of the cell to be made afresh, wholly perhaps at the beginning, on the instructions of the chromosomes. The happenings already described in the egg cell of *Pteridium* are examples of some extraordinary process going on that does not occur between one generation of somatic cells and the next. Similarly meiosis removes some of the properties of cells acquired during the somatic life of a plant. The effect of vernalization is an example of something acquired by all the cells of a plant from the seedling stage onwards, but not transmitted to the next generation via sexual reproduction. However, as we have seen, some parts of the cell outside the chromosomes have a certain amount of autonomy, being able to duplicate themselves and having continuity from one generation of cells to another and, in some cases, from one generation of individuals to another, for it is clear that a zygote inherits more than the nuclei of the gametes that fuse to form it.

For some time the possibility of extrachromosomal inheritance was neglected because of the success of cytology and breeding experiments in demonstrating the role of the chromosomes in deciding the structure and behaviour of cells. It was not until exceptions to Mendelian laws became known that cytoplasmic inheritance was recognized. Attempts to explain the appearance and breeding behaviour of variegated plants by Correns and Baur at the beginning of the century provided the first real indication that cytoplasmic organelles, in this case plastids, were inherited independently of the nucleus. We now know that it is not possible properly to separate chromosomal inheritance from non-chromosomal inheritance, for the cell is an integrated whole with the nucleus and cytoplasm interacting in many ways. Nevertheless it is safe to say that most of the characters of a plant are decided mainly by the chromosomes. Estimates of the amount that is decided by cytoplasmic factors have been made at between 5 and 20 per cent, but these figures depend heavily on how much is recognized as genetical by the existence of mutants.

Extrachromosomal inheritance occurs because parts of the cytoplasm are passed on to daughter cells and these parts are self-duplicating. Chromosomes are duplicated very precisely so that each daughter cell shares all the genes of the mother. This precision is missing from cytoplasmic inheritance except perhaps in the centrioles of which there are only two to a cell if there are any at all. Inheritance of other particles is frequently very obviously unequal though some cytoplasm is necessary for all cells as the chromosomes cannot exist by themselves. Although there is cytological evidence for some aspects of extra-chromosomal inheritance, most evidence comes from breeding which shows anomalies of transmission of the factors of inheritance. The term 'plasmagene' was given by Darlington to those factors occurring in the cytoplasm.

The bodies that bear the plasmagenes must be able to replicate themselves either by growth and fission or by producing a particle capable of forming a similar body itself. Of the three kinds of cytoplasmic organelles which are known to fulfil this condition, the plastids and mitochondria probably reproduce by fission though commonly at an early stage of development rather than at maturity. The third organelle, the centriole, appears sometimes to reproduce by giving rise to a minute particle which becomes another centriole. It is possible that other organelles behave in this way and that they produce master molecules invisible in life and unrecognized under the electron microscope.

The bodies bearing plasmagenes must also be distributed to the daughter cells. To some extent we may distinguish here between bodies that are distributed to daughter cells in somatic reproduction and bodies that are distributed to the next generation of individual plants.

Jinks (1964) divided organelles that exhibit genetic continuity from cell to cell into fibre producers and controllers of metabolism. The fibre producers are the centrioles, which form the asters at mitosis in animal, but apparently not in plant cells, and the blepharoplasts or kinetosomes, which form the basal granules of flagella and cilia. Centrioles and blepharoplasts are, as we have shown, related though it is not clear in what way. The controllers of metabolism include the plastids and mitochondria. It is possible that other organelles will later be found to exhibit genetic continuity. We have shown for example that there are at least two postulated methods of dividing the Golgi bodies, but there is no proof that they are inherited from one cell to another let alone between one plant and another.

For geneticists the most important evidence for extra-chromosomal inheritance comes from inequalities in reciprocal crosses and the departure from Mendelian rules in the appearance of the F_1 and subsequent offspring. Generally it makes no difference to the transmission of a character whether it comes from the mother or the father. The only common exceptions to this rule are sex-linked genes and these are rare in higher plants because sex is not often genetically determined. There are some uncommon exceptions caused by preferential segregation at meiosis in those organisms where only one of the four products of meiosis becomes a female gamete. When all these have been eliminated matriclinal inheritance can be ascribed to the cytoplasm, but, since the female usually provides the environment for the zygote nucleus, it may favour the female characters. When this happens, however, the effect is transient and can be eliminated over a few generations. Other examples of non-Mendelian segregation that are due to chromosomal genes occur because of mitotic recombination, gene conversion, paramutation, Dauermodifikation and aneuploidy and so some caution must be exercised in using the criterion as proof of extranuclear heredity. Various other phenomena, notably apomixis and systemic viral infections have also to be eliminated.

In ordinary Mendelian inheritance the F_1 generation usually resembles one of the parents. Selfing the F_1's then results in segregation into some individuals resembling one of the original parents and some resembling the other. The proportions of the two types depends upon the number of genes involved. Extrachromosomal inheritance, on the other hand, may exhibit a variety of phenotypes in the F_1. A cross between a white *Pelargonium* and a green one results in some offspring being white, some green and some variegated. In this example a white *Pelargonium* means one in which the germ line is white and such a plant would usually be a chimera with some green tissue. It should also be noted that plants other than *Pelargoniums* and certain others would have had all their F_1 offspring of the same appearance because the male parent normally makes no contribution to the chloroplasts of the zygote. A cross between white and green parents of such a species would then result in an F_1 resembling the offspring of a Mendelian cross with ordinary dominance. But the reciprocal crosses would differ and the F_2 generation from selfed plants would not show segregation.

A possible explanation of the phenomena ascribed to non-chromosomal inheritance is that they reflect the occurrence of different cytoplasmic states that change the expression of ordinary chromosomal genes. This hypothesis has been eliminated by the analysis of the behaviour of streptomycin-induced mutants of *Chlamydomonas* by Sager & Ramanis (1963).

The extranuclear complement of hereditary particles can be changed by mutations just as nuclear genes mutate. The complement can also be altered by invasion from outside. This can happen as a result of infection or by the special methods that are available to filamentous fungi. We have commented elsewhere on the view that plastids and mitochondria are, in evolutionary origin, separate organisms or quasi-organisms taken in by cells and conferring on them an enormous increase in metabolic efficiency by allowing the separation of chemical reactions into compartments. Virus infection of cells is especially interesting to biologists because viruses exhibit the properties of life only when they are exploiting the cell in which they are living and a lot has been learnt about the fundamental aspects of genetics from using phages. Non-Mendelian inheritance involving DNA or RNA as in plastids and mitochondria must always raise the possibility of viral infection. Extranuclear genes mutate at a rate that appears to be higher than that of conventional genes (Hagemann, 1959). Acridine dyes, for example, can convert normal yeast to 'petite' in all cells treated. Petite is a non-lethal condition exhibiting slow growth caused by affecting the mitochondria. It is possible to see this mutation because yeast has an alternative, anaerobic, respiratory pathway. Similarly the other frequently seen extranuclear mutation from green to white plastids—shows itself either because the cell with mutant plastids is able to go over to another, holozoic, method of nutrition as in *Euglena* or because tracts of white plastid-containing cells can be supported by normal cells in a chimera. Other mutations in organelles may be lethal and therefore overlooked.

Another major feature of inheritance of cytoplasmic particles is sorting out, the process by which the organelles are distributed to the progeny of a cell with both mutant and non-mutant organelles. In this process there exist stages with similar 'mixed' cells and later stages with cells containing only the mutant organelles or only the normal ones. The later stages have the cells arranged in a fine mosaic pattern which becomes coarser as the cells proliferate until whole organs or tissues may consist entirely of mutant or non-mutant cells. Nothing like this occurs in nuclear inheritance, but it is not always easy to distinguish between plants exhibiting sorting out and plants showing patterns of structure, physiology or infection.

We shall deal in greater detail with the inheritance of plastids because much of the work here concerns higher plants and it still raises many problems for future research. Mitochondria also concern higher plants, but most of the work on their inheritance comes from yeast and *Neurospora*.

10.2 Inheritance of plastids

Self-replication

We have seen in Chapter 4 that there is some evidence that plastids are self-replicating and that, among multicellular organisms, green plants provide the best evidence there is for non-chromosomal inheritance. In multicellular animals the search for non-chromosomal inheritance has not been nearly so rewarding. Some zoologists believe that the cell surface is self-replicating, but it is not nearly so easy to demonstrate this as the inheritance of plastids or even of plant cell walls whose continuity is shown most elegantly in the green alga, *Oedogonium*.

The evidence for self-replication of plastids is not so convincing as to be beyond doubt, however, in higher plants. It rests largely on the obvious division of chloroplasts in those algae with a small number of plastids per cell. In the higher plants, as we have seen, belief in the division of proplastids and of mature chloroplasts is based largely upon the appearance of the organelles not upon any observation of fission and we have no direct information about independence and self-replication in the very early stages. We have been hindered here in not knowing for certain if we could properly distinguish mitochondria from plastids at the early stages of development before the cristae or lamellae appear. That the number of plastids increases is obvious enough, but we cannot yet be sure that this comes about solely by the replication of other plastids. However, the evidence of inheritance makes this a good hypothesis.

In some unicellular algae, if the chloroplasts of one cell disappear, as happens, for example, when *Euglena* is treated with streptomycin, its progeny will lack chloroplasts for ever. Moreover the use of ultra-violet microbeams on *Euglena* has shown that only when the cytoplasm is irradiated is there an irreversible bleaching of the chloroplasts. When the nucleus is irradiated this does not occur. (Gibor & Granick, 1964). The bleached chloroplasts multiply over several generations of the *Euglena* as tiny plastids and so growth and multiplication is presumably controlled by the plastids' own DNA and not that of the nucleus. In such plants it looks, therefore, as if chloroplasts cannot arise from any other part of the cell and that the control of plastid inheritance is in the plastids themselves, or, at any rate, in the cytoplasm, and not in the nucleus. But the plants where this has been demonstrated normally lack proplastids and so the argument cannot be properly extended to higher plants. It is worth stressing that in *Euglena* and similar unicellular green organisms continuity of plastids between one generation and another is by the fission of mature plastids whereas in higher plants, where a sexual stage intervenes between generations, continuity is through proplastids and fission of mature plastids occurs only in vegetative tissue if at all. The best information about plastid replication comes from plastid inheritance.

Inheritance

As we have shown in Chapter 4, quite a lot of plastid mutations are known especially, of course, those that affect the colour of the plant. It was early discovered that many of these mutations are inherited in a non-Mendelian fashion. The obvious supposition is that the egg cell provides a large volume of cytoplasm whereas the sperm cell provides none. The young embryo will therefore inherit all its plastids from its mother. Until recently it has not been possible to check this visually because the organs concerned with sexual reproduction do not usually contain plastids big enough to see under the light microscope. In some plants chloroplasts are carried over from the male to the egg cell, but degenerate in the female cytoplasm. This occurs in *Spirogyra* and in some other algae and in *Pinus* (Granick, 1961). In some other plants the plastids are eliminated in the male gametes before fertilization. Post-zygotic and pre-zygotic reduction of male plastids result in matriclinal inheritance. The same result is achieved by having very small male gametes. Bell, Frey-Wyssling & Mühlethaler (1966) have stressed that the usual evidence for maternal inheritance does not necessarily mean that a cytoplasmic factor in the egg is involved. We have already referred to the work of these authors on the fern, *Pteridium*, in Chapter 4. The evidence that Bell and his colleagues considers to be important here is that the plastids and mitochondria in the egg of *Pteridium* appear to degenerate and disappear prior to fertilization. When this happens nuclear evaginations arise and produce a membrane system in the cytoplasm which somehow produces plastids and mitochondria. It is this last point which gives rise to controversy because other workers in this field have failed to find any evidence for creation of plastids in this way. Now it may be that *Pteridium* is peculiar, but even here many hold that the electron micrographs published by Bell *et al.* are not convincing. Let us evade this issue for the moment and assume that Bell's theory is right. The important point is that the generation of plastids either from the nuclear envelope or by some other means begins before fertilization and may end before the sperm nucleus becomes genetically active in the egg cytoplasm. Henceforth the plastids may be autonomous. Therefore the inheritance of plastids can be maternal even though the cytoplasm is not involved directly. Bell *et al.* believe that this may be true also in flowering plants and so it had become important to investigate plastid initiation from the nucleus more thoroughly. The evidence that we have presented in Chapter 4 is most unfavourable to Bell's theory, but too little is known yet to condemn it even if the nuclear evagination theory proves to be wrong.

Diers (1966) working on the liverwort, *Sphaerocarpus*, has found that the nuclear envelope evaginates, but could see no sign that the evaginating membranes give rise to plastids or mitochondria. Similarly there is no degeneration or elimination of plastids or mitochondria as there is in *Pteridium*. The egg cell of *Sphaerocarpus* grows from about $3,000\mu m^3$ to $10,000\mu m^3$ during maturation and in doing so the plastids multiply four-fold, from 40–65 to 160–270, and the mitochondria similarly, from 250–400 to 1,000–1,600. The nuclear volume also increases four-fold in this time and goes on growing for a while after the plastid and mitochondrial numbers decrease slightly in the final stage of maturity.

Kirk holds that the degeneration described by Bell and his colleagues may be only an internal reorganization in preparation for rapid cell division after fertilization and thus a kind of dedifferentiation whose significance is different from that ascribed to it originally (Kirk & Tilney-Bassett, 1967).

Exceptions to the general rule of matriclinal inheritance of chloroplasts are known, notably in *Pelargonium* and *Oenothera*. In these plants the proplastids from the male parent are transferred to the zygote by the pollen tube rather than from any cytoplasm attached to the sperm nuclei. A proportion of the progeny of such crosses does not resemble plants in which there is matriclinal inheritance. Plastids derived from both parents occur in them and are believed often to partition themselves between the cells of the young plant so that some tracts of tissue carry the maternal plastids and some tracts the paternal plastids. This segregation is visible if one of the sorts of plastids is a colour mutant and some variegated plants, originating in this way, later become quite stable because of the behaviour of the apical meristem in maintaining discrete germ layers (Clowes, 1961a). Similar variegated plants can also arise from a somatic mutation. In *Pelargonium* some 30 per cent of the progeny of a cross between a white female and a green male are variegated. In a reciprocal cross some 70 per cent of the progeny possess white plastids and some of these have no green plastids.

Mixed cells

An essential feature of this hypothesis is that there should be, at some stage, cells that contain two kinds of plastids and some controversy arises from evidence presented for the existence of such 'mixed' cells. Several workers have demonstrated that there are cells with plastids of two or more forms, but these have been mature plastids as by the very nature of the investigation they have to be. There are two objections to the use of mature plastids here. Firstly what the hypothesis requires is that there should be mixed cells in the meristems or embryos whose cells have only proplastids. Secondly one kind of plastid could be a degenerate form or developmental stage of the other in a mature cell. Wettstein (1961) believes that cells with mixed proplastids have never been seen and, of course, it is not likely that we should recognize them, for the amount of structure visible in a proplastid is too small. We have already seen that the precursors of chloroplasts and amyloplasts are indistinguishable. So, although the mixed cell evidence does not support as well as could be desired the hypothesis of the genetic independence of the plastids, the absence of supporting evidence is not a fatal blow. One of the best investigations of mixed cells is that of Hagemann (1960) on *Antirrhinum*. In a strain of this plant, pale plastids can be recognized by their smaller size and abnormal grana as well as by their colour. In young leaves the mixed cells contain the two kinds of plastids in any ratio and the frequencies of the ratios are binomially distributed, but in older leaves, pale plastids degenerate and mixed cells are hard to find. For this and other reasons mixed cells must be looked for in young tissue and, of course, it is in such tissues that confusion is likely to arise between truly mixed cells and cells with plastids at different stages of development. Mixed cells have also been seen in investigations with the electron microscope. An interesting example occurs in *Arabidopsis thaliana* homozygous for the nuclear gene, albomaculans (Röbbelen, 1966). The leaves of this strain are variegated and the variegation is inherited only from the female parent and so the nuclear gene presumably acts as an inducer of plastid mutations. The mutated white plastids can reproduce themselves independently of the nuclear gene for at least four generations of plants. Mixed cells occur at the boundary between white and green areas of the leaves. In wholly white cells the plastids contain few vesicles and osmiophilic globules. In the mixed cells the mutated plastids, however, contain prolamellar bodies (see page 131) and even thylakoids while the unmutated plastids show some reduction in the lamellar system. Röbbelen interprets this as indicating an interaction between mutated and normal plastids when in the same cell. Such interactions are also known between different cells (see page 158).

Mixed cells have been reported in the alga, *Spirogyra* where one of the spiral, ribbon-shaped chloroplasts has pyrenoids and another lacks them. Both sorts replicate prior to cell division (Gibor & Granick, 1964) and, as there is no difficulty about these being in different developmental stages, they provide good evidence for some degree of independence from the nucleus.

In spite of this evidence for mixed cells there are examples of extra-chromosomally inherited variegation where mixed cells have not been found. In fact, it was the rarity of mixed cells that led Correns to suppose that the plastids themselves do not contain the factors of inheritance, but that some other cytoplasmic entity was responsible.

Plastid mutation

Plastid defects have been found in every species that has been adequately investigated. Mutational blocks are known for every step in the formation of chloroplasts and these can be used in genetics just like the biochemical mutants of the fungus, *Neurospora*. For instance, we know that supplying aspartic acid will overcome the albina-7 mutant and leucine will overcome the xantha-23 mutant in *Hordeum* (Wettstein, 1961; see also Walles, 1963). The final form of the plastid is of course, not necessarily that at which the block is applied. In spite of this wealth of data the mechanisms of plastid inheritance are still, to a large extent, obscure. Some ordinary nuclear genes are known to control plastid development (Darlington & Mather, 1949) and the nucleus has an overall control over the development of plastids just as it does over everything else in the cell. In the example of Mendelian inheritance of plastids given by Darlington and Mather the plants (*Primula sinensis* homozygous for the mutant) are so pale that they die. The heterozygotes are yellower than the normal and survive. But probably most gene mutations known to affect plastids are normal recessives. Tilney-Bassett believes that the white areas of some variegated *Arabidopsis* plants are caused by the somatic loss of a chromosome fragment (Kirk & Tilney-Bassett, 1967).

It is the fact that the plastids are self-replicating that leads to complications in their genetics. Obviously there must then be a balance between the importance of the nucleus and the cytoplasm in determining what will happen to the plastids. A plastid character derived from a nuclear mutation may thereafter be inherited independently of the nucleus. Thus Arnason & Walker (1949) have shown that a gene-induced mutation to white plastids in *Hordeum* is irreversible even when the plastids are returned to a cell with the gene for green plastids. Not only the nucleus and plastids themselves may be concerned, but other parts of the cytoplasm must affect plastid development and may be more important in determining development than the plastids themselves in some plants. Even in plants in which somatic segregation of plastids appears to occur there is often no conclusive proof that the genetic factors causing the aberration are in the plastids and not somewhere else in the cytoplasm. Other characters are known to be inherited in a non-Mendelian fashion presumably in some other cytoplasmic particle. Tests have, however, been possible in plants where the genetic background is well known, as in *Oenothera*. In this genus a nucleus of a particular genetic composition behaves differently in different cytoplasmic situations and the results of certain crosses can be explained only if it is assumed that plastids are carried over to the egg cell by the pollen tube in a proportion of individuals. The presence of these plastids from the male parent can be tested for by further crosses with the hybrids. Although it is possible to devise alternative explanations, the simplest is that, in these cases, the plastids are themselves independent of other cytoplasmic factors. This view has led to the plastogene hypothesis that the plastids carry genes whose reproduction determines the similarity of the daughter plastids to the parent. The recent discovery of DNA in plastids naturally has made this view more attractive and there is, as we have seen (see page 128), increasing evidence for the genetic role of the plastid DNA. As originally developed by Imai (1937) the plastogene hypothesis supposed that there was only one gene per plastid because, although cells with two kinds of plastids exist, hybrid plastids of mixed constitution had not been found. Our lack of understanding of plastid structure makes this a naïve reason for the one to one relationship, but nevertheless, as the simplest view, we may use it as a useful basis for tests.

In considering the possibility of hybrid plastids it is interesting to note that Arnason, Harrington & Friesen (1964) also suppose that the heterozygous condition for a nuclear gene may lead to the mutation of fewer plastids compared with the homozygous condition rather than to the production of plastids of intermediate structure.

Breeding behaviour in most plants does not provide us with sufficient information about the location of the factors of inheritance and it is easy enough to imagine conditions in the cytoplasm affecting the development of the plastids, for this is presumably how some mineral deficiencies lead to chlorotic tissue. The results with *Oenothera* come nearest to providing a proof of the plastogene hypothesis, but the proof is not rigorous. Renner (1934, 1936, 1937) showed that, in the cross between *O. hookeri* female and *O. muricata* male, the plastids are mostly yellow, whereas, in the reciprocal cross, the plastids are mostly green. In progeny derived from this reciprocal cross there are yellow sectors, which were shown to be due to plastids derived from the *O. hookeri* male. These plastids, however, turn green when placed by breeding in cells with a pure *O. hookeri* nucleus. In cells with a hybrid nucleus they stay yellow, but can always revert to green in the presence of a pure *O. hookeri* nucleus. An interesting side light on mutation is provided by one of the *Oenothera* crosses in which the offspring were weak and yellow. When these plants were selfed for four generations the progeny became healthy and green. Presumably either the plastids or the nucleus changed. Introducing new chromosomes of the same Renner (nuclear) complex as the original weak yellow plant by sexual reproduction produces weak, yellow plants again. So here it was the nucleus that changed originally and the chloroplasts remained stable (Weier & Stocking, 1952). The opposite result is common enough —the breakdown of the plastids in the presence of an incompatible genome (Schötz & Senser, 1964).

Sorting out

Sorting out of plastids occurs when a zygote inherits plastids of two different kinds or when a plastid mutation occurs in a cell of a meristem or embryo. In discussing mixed cells we have pointed out that the direct

Q

evidence is rather thin (see page 460). Nevertheless the sorting out that can easily be observed in colour mutants has to be explained on the basis of mixed cells at some stage. Crossing between flowers of *Pelargonium zonale* on green shoots and flowers on white shoots produces a crop of seedlings some of which are wholly green, some wholly white and some variegated. It is the variegated plants that are most instructive for these should contain both green and white plastids in the same cell at some early stage, but in later stages the cells contain either green or white plastids, not both. Some of the seedlings are sectorial chimeras having, for example, one green leaf and one white leaf or half a leaf green and the other half white. Other seedlings are periclinal chimeras having some layers of the plant green and others white (Fig. 159). The most distinctive type of periclinal chimera is the white-over-green where the leaf margins are white and the centres green (Fig. 159A). Other seedlings have irregular green and white areas. Of these variegated seedlings only the periclinal chimeras are at all stable and the others and also some periclinal chimeras usually revert during further growth of the shoot to produce, wholly green shoots or periclinal chimeras (Fig. 159B, 160). The stability of the periclinal chimeras is due to the discreteness of the cell layers in the apical meristems and there are some plants where special behaviour in the apex results in a sectoring of one of the layers thus producing stable mericlinal chimeras (Fig. 161; Thielke, 1954; Clowes, 1961a).

The genetical problem is how the originally mixed cells produce the definite segregation of tissues into green and white areas so soon. The number of proplastids in a cell is of the order of fifty. If they partition themselves at random between the daughter cells at every mitosis it will take a lot of divisions before a wholly white or wholly green cell could be expected. In a theoretical model with random mixing of plastids and random separation at cell division the number of divisions required to produce over 99 per cent complete sorting out is about five times the number of plastids in a cell if cell division halves the number exactly and growth doubles the number exactly at each generation (Kirk & Tilney-Bassett, 1967). Yet segregation appears from the pattern of colour to occur quite quickly and mixed cells are often hard to find except at the seedling stage. The statistical problem is not as acute as it seems at first sight, for there is no reason to assume that the plastids are randomly mixed in the first place. It may well be that in a zygote the maternal and paternal plastids tend to keep to their own group because of their origin and the same may be true of a somatic cell in which a mutation arises in a single plastid out of the cell's full complement of fifty. This would make sorting out quicker and account for the apparent rarity of mixed cells. The random assortment of chromosomes at meiosis is brought about by movements of the chromosomes and there is no evidence that plastids are mixed even by cyclosis to produce a similar result. Other reasons for the rarity of mixed cells in mature plants are the breakdown of some kinds of mutant plastids such as we have seen in *Antirrhinum* and the delayed greening of mutant plastids of the virescens type. In plants that exhibit purely maternal inheritance of plastids presumably any male plastids that come over with the pollen tube are eliminated in the female cytoplasm. In plants that exhibit inheritance from both parents we do not know what

FIG. 159. Periclinal chimeras of *Pelargonium* in which cells with white plastids remain separate from cells with green plastids because of the discreteness of the layers of cells in the shoot apex. (A) Cultivar 'Flower of Spring' with green centres and white margins to the leaves due to the second layer at the apex of the shoot being genetically white and inner layers being genetically green. (B) Cultivar 'Freak of Nature' with some leaves white with green margins due to the genetically green epidermis proliferating at the margin to produce green mesophyll. In the centre of the leaf the epidermis does not produce enough chlorophyll to mask the underlying white tissues. There are also some wholly white and wholly green leaves produced by a breakdown in the stability of the layers of cells in the shoot apices.

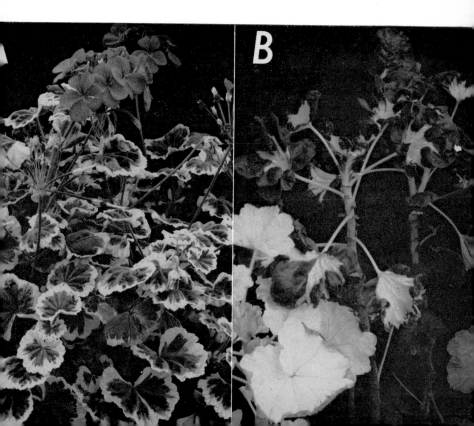

proportion of each sort of plastid survive. Similarly we do not know whether two sorts of plastid multiply at the same rate though, where sorting out appears, the rates cannot be very different.

Another possibility that must be considered is that the plastids may move independently of each other. In a mixed cell it is possible that green plastids move towards the light and the white plastids do not. This would also speed up sorting out. Nevertheless it is not impossible that random assortment can lead to the observed rates of sorting out into wholly white and wholly green cells especially if the number of plastids per cell is small.

Plastid interaction

Another point that is relevant here is the effect that plastids have on one another. The bleaching effect that white cells seem sometimes to exert on genetically green cells has already been mentioned on page 158. An interesting phenomenon of the same kind has also been reported by Stubbe (1958) in which plastids of one kind cause plastids of a second kind to change to a third type. This occurs in *Oenothera albive-lutina*, a true breeding hybrid of *O. suaveolens* and *O. lamarckiana*. In the plants studied, chlorophyll-deficient (yellow-green), mutant plastids from *O. suaveolens* were present in the same individuals as pale *O. lamarckiana* plastids. But, in these plants, cells with an unexpected, green type of plastid also appeared. Stubbe's analysis shows that these green plastids are really *lamarckiana* plastids that have become green instead of pale, and they have done so under the influence of the yellow-green *suaveolens* plastids. In fact, only in cells above or below cells with green-yellow plastids do the *lamarckiana* plastids become green. In cells to the side (looking at a cross-section of a leaf) of those with yellow-green plastids the *lamarckiana* plastids behave normally and become pale unless there is *suaveolens* tissue below or above them. The chemistry of these three types of plastids is not yet known, but the phenomenon could be a kind of intercellular complementation in which the *suaveolens* plastids provide something that is deficient in the *lamarckiana* plastids and thus turn them into normal green plastids. It is interesting that the possible complementing factors moves vertically and not sideways, for the same is true of the 'bleaching' effects reported by Thielke (1955) in *Hemerocallis* mericlinal chimeras. In view of this kind of action it is also possible that a white plastid could exert an influence on the development of what would otherwise be green plastids within the same cell and vice versa. This is just one of the

FIG. 160. A leaf of *Sedum rubrotinctum* which has regenerated new leaves. The original big leaf is a periclinal chimera having white cells and green cells, but the new leaves are either wholly white, or wholly green or sectored white and green.

possibilities that makes plastid inheritance so intricate and maybe accounts for the difficulty in deciding whether the factors for inheritance reside within the plastids themselves or in some other part of the cytoplasm. If one plastid exerts an influence on another it behaves like an infective agent. It has even been suggested that cytoplasmically inherited variegation is indeed caused by parasitic agents. In fact, there are, as we have shown, enough similarities between plastids and bacteria or blue-green algae to have led some biologists to speculate on the possibility that photosynthetic plants are symbiotic associations like those of certain protozoans and algae in evolutionary origin. The same could also be said of mitochondria and bacteria or ribosomes and viruses.

If intracellular effects of one plastid on another do occur it puts a different complexion on the problems of sorting out and inheritance. Workers in this field have distinguished between plastome and plasmone mutations (e.g. Wettstein, 1961). In plastome mutations what is changed is the plastids themselves; in plasmone mutations it is the cytoplasm outside the plastids that is changed and influences the development of plastids. The mutant factor is inherited in a non-Mendelian way in both, but, if there is no somatic segregation of the factor causing the defect, the mutation is considered to be outside the plastids because the cells are uniform in showing the defect. This kind of inheritance has been proposed for *Humulus japonicus* (Wettstein, 1961). The difference between plastone and plasmone rests in the discreteness of the genes therefore and this can be tested only by how they segregate. Obviously, if the hereditary effect observed is modified by whatever causes the bleaching or complementation phenomena, plastone cannot be properly distinguished from plasmone.

At present then, in thinking of plastid inheritance, we have to consider whether the plastids themselves are genetic particles inherited from the mother or from both parents, whether there is interaction between different kinds of plastids or between plastids and nucleus, whether something else in the cytoplasm determines the development of plastids and whether this is an all-or-nothing phenomenon or has an effect which is variable in respect of the proportion of plastids affected or the degree to which all are affected.

Plastid DNA

The strong possibility that plastids are to some extent autonomous, self-replicating structures has promoted the search for nucleic acids in them. Until recently the evidence for DNA was negative or equivocal. Where DNA was found in chloroplast samples there was always the possibility that the samples were contaminated by nuclear fragments or that the plants were infected with bacteria or viruses. The evidence from feeding tritiated thymidine was also equivocal (see page 126). But recently there has been a considerable body of evidence from refined experimental techniques that favours the view that plastids do contain DNA and that it is different from nuclear DNA (see page 128). In the alga, *Acetabularia*, where the nucleus can be removed easily, Gibor & Granick (1964) report 0·2 μg of DNA per mg of chloroplast protein. This comes to 1×10^{-16} g of DNA per plastid. Determinations of DNA in higher plant chloroplasts give values of $10^{-15} - 10^{-14}$ g per plastid. 10^{-15} g contains nearly two million nucleotides. A single strand of DNA (if all the DNA in a plastid consists of one double strand) therefore contains one million bases. If there are three bases to a codon as in nuclei, the DNA could then code for about 300,000 amino acids, enough for say 1,500 different protein molecules or genes. There is the possibility that a plastid contains more than one DNA area (see page 146) i.e. that it is 'polyploid'. If this is true the number of genes derived above should be divided by the ploidy, but even so the number is substantial and enough to perform all that we know goes on in plastids.

The plastids of some species of plants have Feulgen-positive regions that disappear after DNA-ase treatment. This is true of *Chlamydomonas* and these regions also show the fluorescence after acridine orange treatment that is characteristic of DNA (Ris & Plaut, 1962). Electron micrographs of these regions reveal fibrils in them. These fibrils have the appearance and reactions of DNA fibrils such as has been found in bacteria and blue-green algae. Such fibres have now also been found in the chloroplasts of higher plants where the amount of DNA may be too small to give a positive Feulgen reaction. It is tempting to assume that these DNA fibrils provide the genetic system of the chloroplasts determining the proteins synthesized and perhaps controlling division. Some weight is given to this view by the experiment already mentioned in which *Euglena* cells were irradiated with microbeams of ultra-violet

FIG. 161. *Tradescantia geniculata*, a mericlinal chimera with white and green stripes due to the segregation of white and green cells into sectors by the unusual method of cell division in the shoot apices.

radiation. The plastids mutated even when the nucleus was shielded from the beam and the mutated plastids multiplied and stayed mutant even in the presence of the presumably normal nucleus of the cell and its progeny. The genetic material of the plastids must therefore have replicated.

Does the same kind of regulation of gene activity occur in plastids as in nuclei? If, as appears likely, both nuclear and plastid genes control plastid behaviour, do both structural and regulator genes exist in both organelles? If plastids are really blue-green algal cells that have been enslaved by a host cell, could structural genes affecting plastid behaviour migrate to the nucleus or have they evolved since capture?

Another problem about plastid genetics concerns the different kinds of plastids. Some kinds of plastids can always change into other kinds according to the age of the cell or environmental conditions. This is true of chloroplasts which can turn into chromoplasts, and amyloplasts, which can turn into chloroplasts. This is merely an ordinary problem of differentiation. But some kinds of plastids such as those of the roots of most plants do not do this. They remain colourless even in light. Are these genetically different from chloroplasts or is it merely that the right conditions for conversion do not or cannot occur? The same kind of problem also crops up in connexion with centrioles and blepharoplasts.

10.3   Inheritance of mitochondria

We know much less about the inheritance of mitochondria than we do about plastids because mitochondria lack the conspicuous characters of plastids. But there is now enough convincing evidence in the literature on microbial genetics to show a situation similar to that in plastids. Both nuclear and cytoplasmically determined mutants affecting the mitochondria and hence the respiration and growth of the organism have been found and worked on in yeast and *Neurospora*. About the origin of mitochondria we have the same controversy as we have for plastids. There are advocates of *de novo* synthesis, origin from other membrane systems and the division or fragmentation of existing mitochondria. There is no good proof of *de novo* synthesis, but this is, of course, the most difficult of the three to find. Schjeide, McCandless & Munn (1964) hold that the mitochondria in embryonic tissues of the hen could be derived by vesicle complexes originating in the nucleus, passing into the cytoplasm and there assisting or directing the elaboration of the mitochondria *de novo*. Certainly we cannot rule out the possibility of *de novo* synthesis at this stage. Origin from other membrane systems has been discussed in Chapter 4. All the evidence in favour is circumstantial so far and some people think that this method may occur only in special cells such as egg cells. Some of the other membrane systems of cells have part of the enzyme array of mitochondria and it is not difficult to imagine that a transformation could occur. Division of mitochondria, like division of plastids, has been observed, but only in a few organisms. The dumb-bell-shaped organelles seen so often in sections are, as we have seen, not sufficient proof that division does occur. Apart from those algae with single mitochondria, the best evidence for division is probably that of Luck (1963a, b) for *Neurospora* and of Parsons (1965) for *Tetrahymena* already described in Chapter 4 and the division hypothesis is still the simplest and the most attractive though it may not be the only method of mitochondrial production.

Thus we see that although the evidence for the independence of the mitochondrial complement or chondriome is not as good as it is for the independence of the plastidom because of the scarcity of genetical information, there is nothing to suggest that the chondriome is different from the plastidom. Both mitochondria and plastids contain their own DNA and RNA and so they have a possible mechanism for autoreplication (though we do not know that they use their nucleic acids for this purpose). They are capable of independent protein synthesis and RNA synthesis and it is assumed that the mitochondrial DNA is involved in this. An experiment by Diacumakos, Garnjobst & Tatum (1965) supports independent inheritance. They used microinjection techniques to introduce various cell fractions from mutant strains of *Neurospora* into other mutants with complementary chemical requirements. Nuclear fractions and DNA had no effect when introduced in this way, but mitochondria did. Mitochondria from an abnormal, inositol-less strain cause big changes in growth rate, morphology, reproduction and cytochrome spectrum of the receiving hyphae. This is evidence for transmission of a replicating or transforming substance and Diacumakos *et al.* think there are grounds for believing that it is the mitochondria themselves that are concerned. Maternal inheritance of cytochrome defects in *Neurospora* has already been mentioned (see page 176) but it is even more difficult than it is with plastids to prove that it is the mitochondria that are inherited.

We depend heavily on work on yeast and *Neurospora* for our views on the transmission of mitochondria. This is because mutant cells of these fungi can be isolated and scored whereas this has not been possible
Q*

in higher plants. The slow-growing or 'petite' strains of yeast have been particularly valuable. Slow growth results in a cell forming only small colonies compared with the wild type and is due to the absence of enzymes of the normal respiratory pathway. The analysis of experiments on breeding yeasts is complex and would require much explanation that would be out of place in a book dealing mainly with higher plant cells and short reviews of the subject are given by Jinks (1964) and Wilkie (1964a). The outcome of the experiments is that respiratory mutants are inherited cytoplasmically and that the genetic unit is probably nucleic acid in the mitochondria themselves.

An experiment which has enhanced the theory of the genetic role of mitochondria is that of Tuppy & Wildner (1965) on a petite strain of the yeast, *Saccharomyces cerevisiae*, originally obtained by acriflavin treatment and worked on extensively by Ephrussi. These petite cells fail to respire because they have acquired an irreversible, hereditary alteration of the structure and behaviour of their mitochondria with complete loss of the cytochrome oxidase activity. Tuppy and Wildner prepared their petite yeast cells by treating them with the digestive juices of a snail. This is a standard technique in yeast genetics for breaking down the cell wall. The treated cells were mixed with mitochondria from a normal, respiring yeast and a proportion of them acquired the ability to respire and form normal colonies. This was held to indicate that they had incorporated the normal mitochondria which must therefore be considered to be transmissible carriers of cytoplasmic genes. But other explanations of this experiment are possible.

Yotsuyanagi (1962) has shown that, in a cytoplasmic mutant of yeast with characteristically modified mitochondria, the visible change in the organelles is due to the mutation itself and not to the physiological changes in respiration also caused by the mutation. Humm & Humm (1966) have shown that in brain and liver cells there may be two different compounds in the mitochondrial RNA, one coded by the nuclear DNA and one coded by the mitochondrial DNA itself. They demonstrated that mitochondrial DNA did not hybridize with nuclear DNA and so it is likely that mitochondrial DNA is unique and unrelated to nuclear DNA. Wilkie (1964b) thinks that mitochondrial DNA, which is circular (Fig. 162) and which he regards as single-stranded, may have a distinctive base composition and that nuclear genes may act as repressors of mitochondrial genes in the same way that gene repressors work in bacteria. But this last is speculation so far based on assuming that mitochondrial DNA plays a genetic role. The evidence

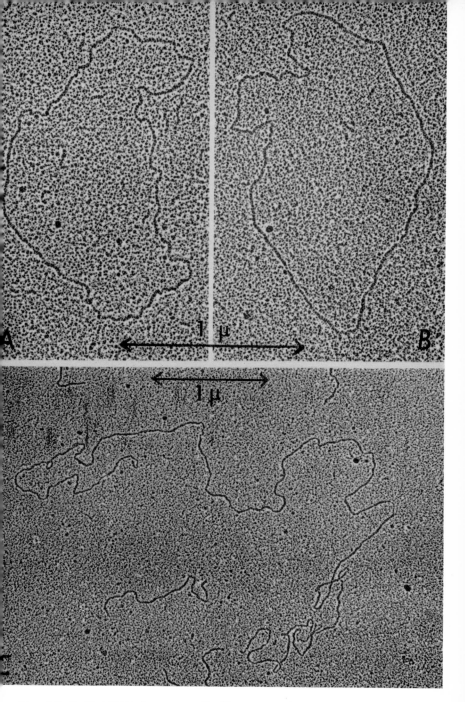

FIG. 162. Purified DNA from mouse fibroblasts rotary shadowed with platinum-iridium. A and B from mitochondria showing circular nature; C from nuclei showing linear nature.   Micrograph by Dr M. M. K. Nass.

here is reasonably good however. There are examples that suggest strongly that both mitochondria and plastids can change as a result of extra-nuclear mutations and we know that these cytoplasmic mutations can be brought about by ultra-violet light, which is strongly absorbed by nucleic acids, and by those dyes that react with nucleic acids. (These acridine dyes do not affect nuclear DNA unless activated by light and the effects on mitochondria are probably due to inhibition of reproduction rather than to mutation.) We also know now that both mitochondrial and plastid DNA have a base composition different from nuclear DNA (Rabinowitz, Sinclair, De Salle, Haselkorn & Swift, 1965; Tewari & Wildman, 1966). We may reasonably expect therefore that a genetic role for mitochondrial DNA will be found.

10.4 Inheritance of centrioles and blepharoplasts

We may deal with this subject briefly because it hardly concerns higher plants. Centrioles (Fig. 163) replicate either by fission or by producing a minute particle which grows to be another centriole. There is normally a pair in each animal cell, one orientated at right angles to the other, and reproduction is tied closely to division of the cell, the decision to reproduce being taken apparently at the end of the previous mitosis. So far as is known they never arise *de novo*. Some animals apparently always obtain their centrioles from the male gamete, the egg centriole either being non-functional or else suppressed by the sperm centriole unless, for some reason, this is missing.

Blepharoplasts or kinetosomes also always arise from pre-existing organelles and crosses between mutants with unusual ciliar patterns show that they are inherited independently of the nucleus probably as blepharoplasts. They can persist and multiply for a long time without forming flagella or cilia in those animals that have flagella or cilia in only part of their life cycles. But what happens in those plants with flagellate sperms is not known, though some workers expect that centrioles will eventually be found even in ordinary plant cells.

The relationship between centrioles and blepharoplasts is puzzling. In ciliates there seems to be little evidence for thinking that the two organelles are in any way related genetically, but in flagellates and, as we have shown, in ferns, the centrioles produce blepharoplasts some-times in large numbers as well as new centrioles. In such cells, if the centrioles are lacking due to misdivision or some other accident neither asters nor flagella are formed.

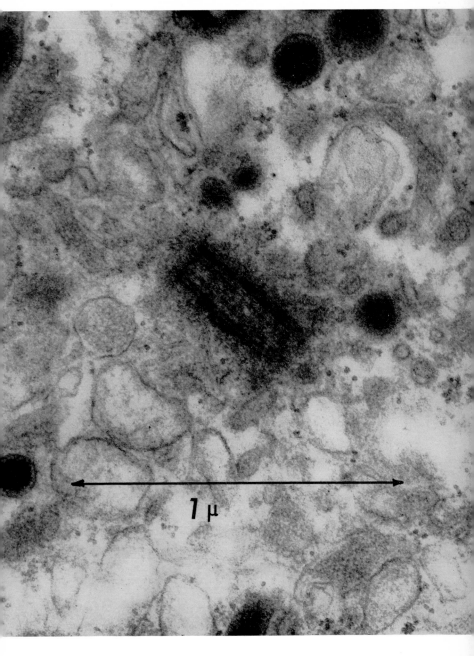

1 μ

F<small>IG</small>. 163. A centriole in a thyroid follicle cell of a mouse. (Glut/Os/Pb/U)

Micrograph by Dr S. Bradbury.

10.5   Inheritance of other cell parts

Clearly plastids, mitochondria, centrioles and blepharoplasts are not the only parts of cells to be passed on from a cell to its daughters though they are the only cytoplasmic organelles proved to be self-replicating. Cell walls are examples of parts that are partly inherited and partly new in each cell generation. The newly formed cross wall, which divides a cell after mitosis, is made *de novo*, but the side and end walls usually are based on the mother cell wall which then grows by intercalation. The number of generations through which a wall has existed may be estimated by its thickness in many meristems. There are a few exceptions to the rule that a cell wall is partly new and partly old. One of these occurs in *Oedogonium*, a filamentous alga. Here a cell that divides produces one daughter whose walls are almost wholly those of the mother and one daughter whose walls are almost wholly new. Similarly the 'fission' yeasts, which appear to divide in two instead of 'budding', really produce a completely new wall for one of the daughters while the old wall is used for the sister cell.

Glossary

A   Adenine in a base sequence in which G = guanine, T = thymine, C = cytosine
U = uracil.

acentric   Having no centromere. Refers to a fragment of a chromosome.

acronematic   Of a flagellum; bearing no hairs.

actinomycin-D   Inhibitor of DNA-dependent RNA synthesis.

acute   Of irradiation; given over a short time.

adenine   One of the purine bases of DNA and RNA.

ADP   Adenosine diphosphate.

aerenchyma   Tissue containing conspicuous air spaces between the cells.

aleurone grain   A cytoplasmic granule containing storage protein. Found mainly
in seeds.

α–cellulose   An arbitrary fraction of the cell wall, which remains after delignification and extraction of pectins and hemicelluloses. The final extraction is carried
out with 17·5 per cent NaOH. The fraction consists mainly but not entirely
of, *β* 1-4 linked glucose (cellulose).

α–link, in which the successive molecules of a polymer e.g. glucose in starch are all
orientated in the same plane.

amino acid   The units of protein molecules of general structure:

$$\begin{array}{ccc} H & R & O \\ | & | & \diagup\diagup \\ H-N-C-C & & \\ | & | & \diagdown \\ H & H & O \end{array}$$

amino acid activating enzyme   Enzyme concerned with the formation of the amino
acid—AMP—enzyme complex before its attachment to transfer—RNA.

amoeboid

(1)   Shaped like an amoeba, of irregular outline.

(2)   Moving like an amoeba by pseudopodia.

Confusion often arises if it is not clear which is meant.

AMP   Adenosine monophosphate.

amyloplast   A plastid filled with starch grains.

anaphase   The stage of mitosis or meiosis at which the chromosomes move from
the equator to the poles of the spindle.

aneuploid   Having differing numbers of each chromosome in a cell, e.g. having
5 of one chromosome and 4 of all the rest.

anisotropic   Having optical properties, etc. that are different along different axes,
thus giving birefringence.

'annulate' lamellae   Stacks of lamellae, arranged like the cisternae of a Golgi body
often found close to the surface of the nuclear membrane.

anthesis   The stage during which plants are in flower.

antibody   A substance formed in response to the presence of another substance.

antipodal cell   One of three cells in the embryo sac which lie at the end away from
the micropyle.

apical cell   The single initial cell in the apical meristems of some lower plants.

apical meristem   The region of dividing cells at the tips of roots and shoots.

apomixis   Reproduction which appears to be sexual but lacks fertilization and sometimes also meiosis.

arabinan   A sugar polymer made up entirely of arabinose units.

archegonium   The organ that contains the egg in bryophytes, pteridophytes and some seed plants. It is characterized by having a neck down which sperms swim to fertilize the egg.

ascites tumour   Transplantable tumour cells of animals made to grow as suspensions of free cells within the peritoneal cavity. Some of the malignant cells may also be cultured *in vitro*.

aster   The star-like structure found at the spindle poles of animal (but not plant) cells.

ATP   Adenosine triphosphate. A high-energy phosphate used as a source of energy, when it gives up one phosphate group to become ADP.

autonomy   Of organelles; independent of other organelles in multiplication. No organelle is completely autonomous.

autoradiograph   A device for indicating the location of radioactive substances. A photographic emulsion is placed over the specimen containing radioactive atoms. The radiation reacts with the silver halides of the emulsion to produce silver grains (blackening) after development. In cytology the emulsion is usually kept in contact with the specimen on a slide and both specimen and emulsion are seen together under a microscope.

autotrophic   Able to nourish itself independently.

auxin   A hormone affecting growth.

Avogadro's number   The number of molecules in a gram-molecule, $= 6 \times 10^{23}$.

backcross   Cross between a hybrid and one of the parents or an individual of similar genetical constitution.

bacteroid   A bacterial cell of abnormal form.

Balbiani ring   A large puff.

Barr body   A heterochromatic blob from one of the X chromosomes (or from more than one in polysomics). In man and some other animals this occurs much more frequently in females and can be used to determine genetic sex.

basal body   The organelle at the base of a flagellum, = basal granule = kinetosome.

basophilic, basiphilic   Having strong affinity for basic dyes.

benign   Not malignant.

β–link   In which the successive molecules of a polymer, e.g. glucose in cellulose, are rotated through 180° with respect to one another.

β–particle   The electron emitted from the nucleus of atoms of certain radioactive elements.

binomial distribution   A frequency distribution obtained by use of the binomial expansion of $(p + q)^n$ to give the probabilities of 0, 1, 2, 3 . . . . . . n successes in n trials where p is the probability of success of an event in a single trial and q is the probability of failure.

biological clock   The endogenous rhythm of organisms,

birefringence   Double refraction. An anisotropic substance causes a beam of light passing through it to emerge as two plane-polarized beams and has two refractive indices.

birefringence, form Double refraction due to heterodiametric molecules or particles being in a regular array.

birefringence of flow Birefringence caused by alignment of rods in a flowing medium.

bleaching The effect of cells with mutant, chlorophyll-deficient plastids on other cells nearby in causing genetically green plastids to become chlorophyll-deficient.

blepharoplast An organelle concerned with the formation of flagella.

Brownian motion The motion seen in small particles and due to the unequal impact of molecules of the surrounding fluid in different directions.

bulliform cell A large epidermal cell often occurring in rows along the length of grass leaves. Changes in turgor of these cells are said to be responsible for rolling and unrolling the leaves.

C The unit of DNA content of a single nucleus. 1 C is the amount in a haploid nucleus (before DNA replication) in any species.

callose An amorphous polymer of β, 1–3 linked glucose.

callus Parenchyma that develops after injury to a plant. Often used in tissue culture.

Calvin cycle The method of carbohydrate generation in photosynthesis.

cambium The sheet of meristematic tissue between the xylem and phloem. Its cells divide tangentially to produce more xylem and phloem. Also applied to the similar meristem that produces the outer bark.

cancer A disease in which cells proliferate beyond the normal control of the body.

carotene An orange pigment found in plastids.

Casparian strip A band occurring in the radial and transverse walls of endodermal cells. Thought to consist of lignin or suberin and to play some role in the control of water movement between stele and cortex.

catenary The curve formed by a flexible cord held at two ends.

cell plate The first visible sign of a wall in a dividing cell.

centriole Organelle concerned with the formation of spindle poles in animal cells and in those plant cells that bear flagella. Usually a pair in one cell near the nuclear membrane.

centromere The part of a chromatid to which the spindle fibre is attached in mitosis.

centrosome, = centriole or sometimes a part of the centriole.

chalaza The base of an ovule; the end opposite the micropyle.

chase A period spent by cells in the absence of a radioactive substrate after a pulse-labelling period.

chalone A natural depressor of mitosis specific to a tissue.

chelation The formation of a complex between (here) an organic compound and a metallic ion.

chiasma The crossing over of two chromatids seen between homologous chromosomes in prophase of meiosis.

chimera A plant or animal having cells of differing genetic constitution.

chitin A nitrogen-containing polysaccharide forming the skeleton of arthropods and some fungi.

chloroplast A plastid containing chlorophyll.

chondriome All the mitochondria of a single cell. Sometimes all the mitochondria and plastids.

chondriosome, = mitochondrion (sometimes used especially for plants).

chromatid A chromosome divides longitudinally into two chromatids which separate to different daughter nuclei at mitosis.

chromatin The complex of DNA and protein in chromosomes. The substance in nuclei with affinity for basic dyes.

chromocentre Heterochromatic segments of chromosomes or agglomerations of these in interphase nuclei.

chromomere Bead-like granules seen along chromosomes in prophase of meiosis, and forming bands in polytene chromosomes.

chromoplast A plastid containing a pigment. Sometimes excluding chlorophyll and hence different from chloroplast.

chronic Of irradiation; continuous or lasting a long time.

crown gall A neoplastic disease of plants caused by *Agrobacterium tumefaciens.*

circadian About one day. Of a rhythm, one lasting about 24 hours.

cisterna An enclosed space.

cistron A mutational unit of a chromosome.

cnidocyst Ejectile organelles in certain dinoflagellates. Similar to nematocysts.

codon The unit that specifies one amino acid in protein synthesis. Believed to be a triplet of nucleotides.

colchicine An alkaloid obtained from *Colchicum.* Used as a mitotic poison and disorganizer of microtubules.

coleoptile The tubular leaf-like sheath that covers the developing foliage leaves of grass embryos and seedlings.

collagen A structural material of animals, a major component of skin, tendon and bone formed of fibrous proteins about 280 nm in length and 1·4 nm in diameter. Contains the rare amino-acid, hydroxyproline.

collenchyma A tissue made of living cells whose walls are thickened with cellulose, usually unevenly, before the end of cell extension.

companion cell A parenchymatous cell associated with a sieve tube element.

complementarity Of nucleic acids, having a sequence of bases that is the complement in one molecule of that in another. See p. 334.

complementary cells The cells produced from the outer side of the phellogen in lenticels. They become rounded and loose unlike the other derivatives of the phellogen.

conservative replication Replication that leaves the original atoms of the parent particle intact. If labelled the label remains in one particle irrespective of the number of replicas produced. (See Fig. 131.)

co-repressor A substance able to combine with a repressor to activate it to repress the structural genes of an operon.

cork cell Dead suberized cells usually produced by a phellogen.

cortex
  (1) The tissue of a stem or root lying between the epidermis and the stele or vascular tissue.
  (2) The outer region of the cytoplasm of a cell.

co-valent bond The union of two atoms by the sharing of a pair of electrons.

crassulae Thickened bars of the primary wall lying between pits in the tracheids of conifers.

cristae (*cristae mitochondriales*)   The invaginations of the inner membrane of the mitochondrial envelope.

crossing over   The exchange of homologous segments between sister chromatids.

cross-linked   Having chemical bonds in three dimensions.

Curie   The amount of any radioactive substance in which there are $3\cdot7 \times 10^{10}$ disintegrations per second.

cuticle   A thin varnish-like layer usually found on walls in contact with air.

cutin   A polyester compound, a polymer of long-chain hydroxy fatty acids, one of the components of the cuticle.

cyclosis   Streaming of cytoplasm.

cystolith   Outgrowths of a cell wall impregnated with calcium carbonate.

cytochromes   Iron-containing compounds concerned with electron transfer in respiration.

cytomictic channels   Holes in walls joining the protoplasm of two living cells.

cytoplasm   All the protoplasm of a cell except for the nucleus. (Sometimes also excludes other organelles and sometimes includes all organelles.)

cytoplast, = protoplast.

cytosine   A pyrimidine base in DNA and RNA.

cytosome   A cytoplasmic organelle with single bounding membrane.

Dauermodifikation   A mutation produced by a change in the environment and persisting over several generations, but finally disappearing.

dedifferentiation   A process that brings about a change in an already differentiated cell.

degenerate   Of a code, having more than one code symbol for a single idea.

deletion   A region of a chromosome that is lacking.

density gradient   A gradient of density arranged in a medium so that particles of different densities settle at different rates in the medium during centrifugation.

depth of field   Distance between two planes in an object where the image is reasonably sharp (defined by arbitrary acceptance of confusion). Sometimes called depth of focus.

desmid   A group of unicellular green algae in the Conjugatae.

diakinesis   The end of prophase of meiosis just before the nuclear membrane breaks down.

diastase   An enzyme able to convert starch to sugar.

dictyosome   The Golgi apparatus or the individual Golgi bodies.

dimer   A molecule of two similar halves.

diploid   Containing a double set of chromosomes.

diplotene   The stage of prophase of meiosis at which the paired and divided chromosomes begin to separate.

Diptera   A group of two-winged flies.

DNA   Deoxyribose nucleic acid.

dodecahedron   A solid figure with 12 faces. There are two regular dodecahedra, one with rhombic figures and one with pentagonal faces.

DPN = *NAD*

DPNH = *NADH$_2$*

E. coli   *Escherichia coli*, a bacterium of the intestinal flora.

ectodesmata   Thread-like structures not cytoplasmic in origin and having a strong reducing capacity found in the outer epidermal walls of leaves.

ectoplasm   Outer part of cytoplasm. Sometimes also defined by other properties.

ectoplast = plasmalemma.

elaioplast   A plastid containing fat.

elasticity   The tendency to return to the original size and shape after deformation.

embryoid   A clump of cells in culture having the approximate shape of a plant embryo.

embryo sac   The female gamete-bearing generation in flowering plants.

enchylema   The contents of the endoplasmic reticulum between the membranes.

endodermis   The innermost layer of the cortex sometimes having a special wall structure in its cells, e.g. a Casparian strip, and sometimes having starch grains.

endomitosis   Duplication of chromosomes that occurs without the nucleus going through the visible stages of mitosis.

endoplasm   Inner part of cytoplasm. Sometimes also defined by other properties.

endoplasmic reticulum   The system of double membranes that permeates the cytoplasm forming tubes or flat sacs.

endosperm   The nutritive tissue of seeds formed from the proliferation of cells derived from the fusion of embryo sac nuclei usually with one male gamete in angiosperms. Often triploid.

entropy   A measure of the extent to which the total energy of a system is not available.

enucleate   Lacking a nucleus. To remove a nucleus.

enzyme   A protein that behaves as a catalyst.

epidermis   The outer layer of cells in primary tissues.

episome   A genetic particle which can exist and replicate in a cell either independently or integrated with the cell's genome.

ER   Endoplasmic recticulum.

ergastoplasm   Basophilic regions of cytoplasm or cytoplasm rich in ER coated with ribosomes.

ergosome = polysome.

erythrocyte   A red blood cell.

etiolation   The condition of plants grown in poor or no light where stems are elongated more than normal and leaves are poorly developed.

euchromatin   The parts of chromosomes that show the normal cycle of stainability—strong affinity for dyes during mitosis and poor affinity during interphase.

exine   Outer layer of pollen grain walls.

exponential growth   Growth according to the law,

$$n = n_0 e^{\lambda t}$$

where n is the number (or size) at time t;
n_0 is the original number
λ is a constant
e is the base of natural logarithms.

eye-spot   An organelle with a red pigment thought to be concerned in the perception of light in motile cells. May be a chromoplast or part of a chloroplast.

Fangschleim   The sticky substance that traps insects in certain insectivorous plants.

feed-back Reference of information from one part of a system to another, enabling some control to be exerted. Term derived from radio circuits.

ferritin A crystallizable protein containing up to 25% of iron present as particles of a ferric hydroxideferric phosphate complex bound to the protein.

Feulgen A chemical procedure for showing DNA in which hydrolysis by HCl enables an aldehyde group from the deoxyribose to restore a quinoid group to decolourized fuchsin which turns magenta.

fibre An elongated sclerenchymatous cell with tapered ends.

filiform apparatus An extension inwards of the wall of a synergid at the micropylar end in some plant embryos.

Flimmergeissel Flagellum bearing lateral hairs.

floridean pit The protoplasmic connexion between cells of the Florideae, a group of red algae.

florigen The hypothetical hormone that induces flowering after being produced in leaves under appropriate regimes of light and dark.

flavonoids (or anthoxanthins). A group of compounds possessing a C_6—C_3—C_6 (diarylpropane) unit.

Most of these are yellow or orange pigments commonly occurring in woody tissues and they also form the farina on the surface of the leaves of Primulaceae.

fluorescence Absorption of light (or other radiation) of one wavelength and emission at a longer wavelength.

freeze-drying Drying by sublimation of ice.

freeze-etching Technique in which a frozen specimen is splintered, its surface etched by sublimation and replicated to give a preparation for electron microscopy.

fructosan A sugar polymer made up entirely of fructose units.

fusiform Shaped like a spindle, with tapering ends.

fusiform initials The cambial cells that produce the longitudinal elements of xylem and phloem as opposed to the ray initials.

G_1 The part of the mitotic cycle between the end of mitosis and the onset of DNA synthesis. Also the duration of this phase.

G_2 The part of the mitotic cycle after the end of DNA synthesis and before the onset of mitosis. Also the duration of this phase.

g The acceleration due to gravity = 981 cm. per second per second.

gall An outgrowth of a plant caused by bacteria, fungi or animals.

gamete Cells that are capable of fusing in sexual reproduction.

gel A solid (jelly-like) colloidal solution.

generative nucleus In pollen, the smaller of the two cells in the mature grain. The one that gives rise to the male gametes.

GDP Guanosine diphosphate.

gelatinous Of fibres or layers of walls, having a glistening, jelly-like appearance.

germ line The tissue from which gametes are derived.

gibberellin A class of growth promoting substances. Originally found in plants attacked by the parasitic fungus, *Gibberella fujikuroi*, but now known to be produced also by higher plants.

G layer = gelatinous layer.

glucosan A sugar polymer, e.g. cellulose or starch, made up entirely of glucose units. Where two different sugars contribute to a polymer it is known as a glucomannan or arabino-xylan, etc.

glycolysis The series of steps by which sugars are converted to pyruvic acid.

Golgi Cytoplasmic organelles made of piles of flattened sacs. Named after the discoverer, C. Golgi (1844–1926).

granum Pile of lamellae in chloroplasts of higher plants. Seen as granules under the light microscope. Contain all or most of the chlorophyll.

guanine A purine base in DNA and RNA.

guard cells The two cells that regulate the size of a stoma.

gum A sticky plant exudate.

haploid Containing a single set of chromosomes.

haptonema A flagellum with a swollen tip.

haustorium An outgrowth of stem, root or hyphae of parasitic plants adapted to
HeLa cells food from a host plant.

    draw A line of human cancer cells in culture. The name is derived from the name of the person whose tumour started the clone.

heterochromatin Segments of chromosomes with a staining cycle different from euchromatin.

heterocyclic compounds Organic compounds having rings in which atoms other than carbon occur.

E.g.

heterogeneous linkages Polymers held together by bonds of more than one kind, e.g. cellulose, in which the glucose is held together by covalent and hydrogen bonds.

heterokaryon A cell (or undivided mass of protoplasm) having nuclei of different genetical constitution.

heteropycnotic Staining more heavily or less heavily than the euchromatin of a chromosome.

heterotrophic Dependent upon other organisms for its nourishment.

heterozygous Derived from fusion of gametes dissimilar in respect of a gene or genes.

histochemistry Reactions carried out to reveal the chemistry of tissues.

histogenesis The formation of tissues.

histone Proteins containing more than the usual fraction of basic amino acids and associated with DNA in chromosomes.

holozoic   Feeding like an animal.

homeostasis   Maintenance of an equilibrium or form.

homologous chromosomes   Chromosomes that pair at meiosis and have genes for the same characters.

hormone   A substance produced in cells and having some effect at low concentration on the normal activity of some other cells at a distance from the site of production.

hyaloplasm   Part of cytoplasm in which no substructure has yet been seen. The cytoplasmic matrix.

hybridization   Of nucleic acids, the property of extracted molecules to fuse with other molecules of DNA or RNA if they have complementary base sequences. Denotes affinity.

hydrogen bond   An atom of hydrogen which acts as a bond between two other atoms.

hydrolysis   Breaking a molecule into two parts by the addition of a water molecule.

hydroxyproline   A rare amino acid found only in collagen and in the protein of higher plant cell walls.

hyperplasia   An abnormal increase in the number of cells.

hypertrophy   An abnormal enlargement of a cell or tissue. If of a tissue, then usually due to increased size of cells rather than number.

IAA   β–indole acetic acid.

idioblast   A cell that differs conspicuously from other cells in the same tissue.

incompatibility reaction
   (1)   A reaction that prevents or slows the growth through the stigma or style of a pollen tube of the incorrect genotype.
   (2)   In fungi a reaction that prevents the normal fusion of gametangia of incorrect genotype.

inducer
   (1)   A substance capable of combining with a repressor and inactivating it.
   (2)   A substance that promotes the production of an enzyme.

infection-thread   The nitrogen-fixing bacteria, *Rhizobium leguminosarum*, enter root hairs of leguminous plants and multiply to form a thread-like colony which ramifies and infects other cells of the root.

initial
   (1)   The cells that initiate the formation of tissues in meristems. One of the daughters of an initial is always meristematic.
   (2)   The precursors of certain organelles, especially very small proplastids.

interference microscopy   Technique involving the conversion of differences of phase into differences of colour or intensity by interference.

interphase   The part of the mitotic cycle when the chromosomes are not easily visible, i.e. when mitosis is not taking place.

intrusive growth   The growth of a cell which pushes its way between other cells.

intussusception   The insertion of new building units into an existing and expanding structure.

inversion   The part of a chromosome in which the genes are in inverse order compared with the normal. Arises by fragmentation and reunion.

isotropic   Having similar properties when viewed in any direction.

karyotype A nucleus of a particular sort as defined by the number and kind of chromosomes it possesses.

kinetoplast In trypanosomes, a body composed of a blepharoplast with another organelle.

kinetin 6-furfurylamine purine. One of the kinins.

kinetosome = blepharoplast.

kinin A class of substances that promote cell division and growth in plant cells. Some occur in nature.

kinoplasm The part of the cytoplasm that moves in streaming. Term used when it is thought that the outer part of the cytoplasm is static. Sometimes = endoplasm.

Krebs cycle The cycle whereby pyruvic acid is broken down to CO_2 and water in aerobic respiration with the production of ATP.

lampbrush chromosomes The long chromosomes of the oocytes of amphibians which have large loops emerging along their length.

Langmuir trough method A technique for electron microscopy in which a protein solution is used to spread a specimen out to reveal its internal structure.

latex A liquid, often milky, that exudes from the cut surfaces of certain plants. Produced in special cells or fused cell masses called laticifers. The latex can be a suspension or emulsion of many different substances including rubber, proteins, resins or oils.

laticifer A cell or group of cells containing latex.

leptotene Early prophase of meiosis before the chromosomes pair or divide.

leucoplast A plastid without pigment.

leukemia A disease in which the white blood cells proliferate beyond the normal control of the body.

lignin A polymer of derivatives of phenyl-propane found in walls.

lipid A fatty substance.

lithocyst A cell containing a cystolith.

logarithmic phase of growth The steady state during which growth proceeds with time in geometrical progression according to the law

$$n = n_0 e^{\lambda t}$$

where n is the number (or size) at time, t,

   n_0 is the original number,

   λ is a constant,

   e is the base of natural logarithms.

lomasome Organelle in the periphery of plant cytoplasm possibly concerned with wall synthesis.

lutoids Spherical membrane-bounded bodies 2–5μm in diameter found in laticifers.

lysis Breakdown of cells especially by enzymes.

lysosome A cytoplasmic organelle containing hydrolytic enzymes.

M The part of the mitotic cycle occupied by mitosis. Also the duration of mitosis.

macrofibril A fasciated group of several microfibrils sometimes found in fibres or in certain layers of the normal secondary cell wall.

macrophage A large phagocyte or leucocyte.

mastigoneme Hair on a flagellum.

matrix The ground substance as opposed to the skeleton of a structure.

meiosis The process whereby the diploid number of chromosomes is halved by having the nucleus divide twice but the chromosomes only once.

mercerization A textile process which increases the lustre of cotton yarns and fabrics. The cellulose is treated with concentrated NaOH, causing a swelling of the fibres and, if the material is kept under tension, causes the fibres to become transparent.

mericlinal chimera A periclinal chimera in which only a sector of one of the layers in the shoot apex is of different genetic constitution from the rest of the apex. Cf. sectorial.

meristem A tissue of dividing cells.

meristemoid A cell that divides more actively than its neighbours.

mesophyll The parenchyma between the upper and lower epidermises of leaves.

mesophytic Of a plant; living in temperate conditions especially in respect of water supply.

mesosome Region of the protoplast of some bacteria with the function of mitochondria. Analogous organelles also develop from the membranes of yeast mitochondria under certain conditions.

messenger RNA The RNA produced in nuclei and bearing the instructions of the DNA for protein synthesis in the cytoplasm.

metachronal The rhythm shown by cilia in which one cilium bends immediately after its neighbour.

metaphase The stage of mitosis and meiosis at which the chromosomes lie on the equator of the spindle.

micelle A term proposed by Nägeli for elongated crystalline sub-light microscopic particles. Now often used as a synonym for elementary fibril, the pure crystalline cellulose sub-unit of the microfibril about 3–4 nm in diameter.

microbody = cytosome.

microfibril Thin cellulose threads 8×30 nm in diameter and up to 5 μm long, comprising several micelles or elementary fibrils and forming the skeleton of higher plant walls.

micronucleus

    (1) A nucleus formed from only part of the chromosome complement of a cell, often from only a fragment of a chromosome.

    (2) The small nucleus of certain protozoans that also have a large nucleus.

micropyle The hole left at the apex of an ovule by the failure to fuse of the integuments after they have grown up from the base over the nucellus.

microsome Formerly = spherosome. A centrifuged fraction containing ribosomes and broken fragments of ER.

microspore The spore of a vascular plant that gives rise to the male gametophyte, e.g. a pollen grain at the uninucleate stage.

microtubule A small tube about 22 nm wide, of an unknown length and in plants made up of thirteen protein sub-units in a circle. They are found close to the cell wall and to the nucleus and are believed to be identical in size and structure to spindle fibres.

middle lamella The first formed portion of the cell wall. Said to consist mainly of pectin with no cellulose.

mitochondrion A cytoplasmic organelle concerned with respiration.

mitosis The process of nuclear division in which a half of each chromosome goes to both daughter nuclei.

mitotic cycle The whole cycle through which dividing cells pass. Includes interphase as well as mitosis.

mixed cell A cell with genetically diverse plastids.

monomers The subunits from which polymers are made.

monostromatic One cell thick.

morphogen A substance produced in an organism and affecting its development.

morphogenesis Development of form.

m–RNA Messenger–RNA.

multiplicative The type of division in a cambium in which the number of dividing cells is increased, thus increasing the rate of production of xylem and phloem cells.

mucilage A basically carbohydrate substance in plants, hard when dry, swelling and slimy when moist.

mutation An inheritable change not due to the assortment of genes.

myelin figures Protrusions in the form of small bent or coiled tubes formed when fatty acids come in contact with water. Their resemblance to the lipid forming the medullary sheath of nerve fibres has led to the confusing name.

myofibrils Contractile fibres of muscle.

myxomycete Slime molds, organisms with a fungus-like stage and a plasmodial stage.

NAD Nicotinamide adenine dinucleotide; = DPN = Co-enzyme I.

$NADH_2$ Reduced NAD, = DPNH, = reduced co-enzyme I.

NADP NAD phosphate, = TPN, = Co-enzyme II.

$NADPH_2$ Reduced NADP, = TPNH, = reduced co-enzyme II.

nectary A gland secreting nectar, a sugary liquid, often in or near insect-pollinated flowers.

negative staining Electron dense material is not incorporated into the specimen, but provides a dense background of non-crystalline material which can be displaced by the biological structure.

neoplastic Of a tissue, newly formed especially on an already developed organ.

Newtonian fluid A fluid in which viscosity remains constant when pressure is varied when flowing through a tube. Fluids containing long fibre-like molecules are non-Newtonian in that viscosity decreases with increasing pressure as the molecules become orientated and freer to move in relation to each other.

Newton's colour scale A scale of interference colours giving the path difference between the two interfering light beams, e.g. red of the 1st order indicates a path difference of 550 nm.

non-disjunction Failure to separate of paired chromosomes at meiosis.

nucleolus Nuclear organelle.

nucleoplasm
   (1) The contents of the nucleus excluding the chromosomes and nucleolus.
   (2) The region of the cell in bacteria and blue-green algae that contains the equivalent of a nucleus.

nucleoside The combination of a sugar with a purine or pyrimidine base.

nucleotide The monomer of nucleic acids consisting of a sugar, a phosphate group and either a purine or a pyrimidine base.

numerical aperture Of a lens, the value $n \sin \phi$ where n is the refractive index of the medium between specimen and lens and ϕ is half the angle of the cone of light entering the lens.

ontogeny Development of an individual or its organs or organelles.

oocyte The mother cell which, by meiosis, gives rise to the female gamete. Used of animals.

operator gene A gene that controls the functioning of other genes near it on the same chromosome.

operon A set of genes controlled by one operator gene.

osmiophilic Having a strong attraction for osmium.

osteoclast A cell that attacks bone or cartilage.

oxysome Particle attached to the cristae of mitochondria.

pachytene The stage in the prophase of meiosis when homologous chromosomes pair closely.

Palade granules = ribosomes.

palisade The elongated cells of leaf mesophyll. Their long axis is perpendicular to the leaf surface and in most species they occur just below the upper epidermis.

panicoid Belonging to one of the main subdivisions of the Gramineae.

para-crystalline Of a substance in which only some of the atoms or molecules are arranged in a definite pattern.

paramutation A permanent alteration in the expression of a gene brought about by a temporary association with certain other genes. First described for the R locus of *Zea* by R.A. Brink.

parenchyma Living plant cells with thin cellulose walls. (In wood anatomy also includes dead cells and cells with other kinds of walls with a characteristic position in the wood.)

periclinal chimera A chimera in which the various layers of a shoot apex are of different genetic constitution.

pericycle The outer part of the stele lying between the phloem and the cortex. Occurs in roots, but not commonly in stems.

periderm The protective tissue of organs whose epidermis is replaced after growth in thickness. Formed from the cork cambium (phellogen) which produces phellem (cork) cells to the outside and phelloderm to the inside.

perinuclear space The space between the 2 unit membranes forming the nuclear envelope.

peroxidase. An enzyme that enables a reaction with hydrogen peroxide to take place.

petiole The stalk of a leaf.

petite A non-lethal condition in yeasts where the colonies exhibit slow growth. Can be due to a nuclear or mitochondrial mutation which affects the respiratory chemical pathway in mitochondria. Is non-lethal because yeast has an alternative type of respiration.

phaeoplasts The chloroplasts of brown algae containing brown pigments as well as chlorophylls.

phage = bacteriophage A virus which infects bacteria.

phagocyte A white blood cell able to ingest solid particles.

phase microscopy Technique involving the conversion of phase differences at the image into amplitude differences to make visible transparent objects.

phellogen Cork cambium.

phloem The tissue that conducts organic solutions in vascular plants. Consists of sieve elements, parenchyma and sclerenchyma.

phosphorylase   The enzymes inducing phosphorylation.

phosphorylation   The addition of phosphate to a compound.

photoinduction   Induction (e.g. of flowering) by a particular regime of light and dark.

photolysis of water   Cleavage of water molecules by light to give molecular oxygen and hydrogen which is used to reduce carbon dioxide and to produce new water molecules in photosynthesis.

photon   Quantum of light energy.

photosynthesis   The synthesis of carbohydrates from CO_2 and water in the presence of light and a pigment which acts as an energy transformer.

phototropic movement   Movement of part of a plant in relation to the direction from which light comes.

phragmoplast   A modified region of the equatorial plane of the spindle after the chromosomes have moved to the poles and within which the cell plate begins to form.

phragmosome

> (1) Term formerly used for cytosome.
> (2) The region of cytoplasm in which a phragmoplast forms. Originally used only for the cytoplasm that suspends a nucleus in a vacuole.

phylogeny   Evolutionary history of a group of organisms or of an organ or organelle.

phytoferritin   A protein containing iron found in small granules in some plastids.

pinocytosis   Intake of water or solids by invagination of the plasmalemma.

pit   A thin area in the cell wall of plants.

pit-field   Thin areas in primary cell walls penetrated by numerous plasmodesmata.

plasmagene   A cytoplasmic gene.

plasmalemma   The membrane on the outside of the cytoplasm.

plasma membrane = plasmalemma.

plasmodesma   A fine protoplasmic connexion between plant cells in the cell wall.

plasmodium   A multinucleate mass of protoplasm often formed by fusion of protoplasts.

plasmolysis   The removal of water from a cell by a hypertonic solution.

plasmone   Pertaining to the cytoplasm and not to the plastids.

plastid   A cytoplasmic organelle. There are several kinds, all having some onto-genetic relation to each other.

plastidom   The collection of plastids in one cell.

plastogene   A gene in a plastid determining the character of the progeny of the plastid.

plastone   Pertaining to the plastids.

pleuronematic   Of a flagellum, bearing hairs.

ploidy   The number of complete sets of chromosomes in a cell.

polarized light   Light whose plane of vibration is confined to a single plane (plane polarized).

polar nuclei   The two nuclei of an embryo sac that fuse together and with a male nucleus to form the triploid endosperm of flowering plants.

polycentric   Having many centromeres.

polymer   A molecule consisting of a large number of one or a few kinds of molecules joined together.

polymerisation   The chemical union of monomers such as glucose or nucleotides to form cellulose and nucleic acid.

Homopolymer   — of the same sub-units.
Heteropolymer   — of two or more different sub-units.

polyphenol   Polymers of phenols.

polyploid   Having more than two sets of chromosomes in a nucleus.

polysomaty   Polyploidy in somatic cells.

polysome   A group of ribosomes thought to be concerned with protein synthesis as a group.

polysomic   Having more than two of some but (usually) not all of the chromosomes of a set.

polytene

(1)   A chromosome becomes polytene by replicating itself many times without the threads separating. It thus becomes wider and longer.
(2)   The state of a nucleus with polytene chromosomes.

polyuronides   Polymers of galacturonic and/or glucuronic acids.

primary meristem mantle   The part of the shoot apical meristem of certain plants that causes growth in thickness of the shoot by continuing divisions under the bases of the leaf primordia.

primary tissue   Tissue produced from an apical meristem up to the time at which elongation ends.

primary wall   The part of the cell wall formed up to the end of extension of the cell.

primordium   An organ at its earliest stages of development.

procambium   The tissue that gives rise to the primary vascular tissue in an apical meristem.

prolamellar body   Part of a chloroplast that occurs under certain circumstances in development. Consists of a three-dimensional lattice of tubules.

prophase   The first part of mitosis and meiosis up to the breakdown of the nuclear membrane. In meiosis it is subdivided into leptotene, zygotene, pachytene, diplotene and diakinesis.

proplastid   The precursor of plastids in most, but not all, plants.

protamines   The special nuclear protein of fish sperm.

proteinoplast   A plastid containing storage protein.

proteoplast   A plastid containing storage protein.

proton   The positively charged nucleus of the hydrogen atom.

protopectin   A general term for all insoluble pectic substances. It may be pectinic acids linked to cellulose by covalent bonds or chains of pectinic acids linked to each other.

protoplasm   The living substance of a cell.

protoplast   The living contents of a cell.

pseudotransverse division   The oblique division of cambial initials in gymnosperms and most angiosperms which results in an increase in the number of initials (multiplicative).

puff   The swelling that occurs at certain times at specific places along the length of giant chromosomes. Considered by some to be due to genes producing m–RNA.

pulse labelling   Labelling of cells with radioactive substances for a short time in order to follow the fate of the labelled substance in the cell in the absence of further supplies of the substance.

pyrenoid   The part of a chloroplast thought to be concerned with starch synthesis in certain lower plants.

quantasome   Particles on chloroplast membranes.

quiescent centre   The region of a root apical meristem at the pole of the stele and cortex where rates of mitosis are much lower than in surrounding cells.

R   Roentgen.

rad   Unit of absorbed dose of ionizing radiations. = 100 ergs per gram. The energy absorbed by water (or tissue) = 93·2 ergs/g for 1 Roentgen.

radian   There are 2π radians in $360°$.

raphides   Needle-shaped crystals in a bundle.

rays   Vertical sheets of usually thin-walled cells that run radially in secondary xylem and phloem.

ray initials   The cambial cells that produce the rays in secondary xylem and phloem.

reaction wood   Abnormal wood produced in tissues under tension or compression.

regulator gene   A gene that controls the activity of some other gene, especially an operator gene.

relative elemental rate

$$\frac{\delta\,(\delta x/\delta t)}{\delta x}$$

The rate of increase of x per unit of x.

repeating period of a crystal   The distance between the centres of the complete unit of a crystal and the next. In cellulose the unit, because of the β link, is cellobiose, not glucose, and the repeating period is 1·03 nm.

repressor   A substance produced by a regulator gene and able with or without a co-repressor to repress the structural genes of an operon.

resin   Plant resins are highly polymerized organic acids and terpenes. They are usually amorphous vitreous solids insoluble in water, but soluble in organic solvents.

Synthetic resins are also polymers, but of a wide variety of organic compounds, usually insoluble in water and some are soluble in no known solvent.

resin canal   A duct containing resin. Formed schizogenously and common in the wood of some plants.

resolution   The distance between two points which can just be seen as separate. A measure of the quality of a lens equal to

$$\frac{1\cdot2\lambda}{2n\sin\phi}$$

where λ is the wavelength of the radiation used, n is the refractive index of the medium between specimen and lens, and ϕ is half the angle of the cone of light entering the lens.

ribosome   Particles containing RNA concerned with protein synthesis. Occur within cytoplasm, nucleus and other organelles.

RNA   Ribonucleic acid.

RNA–polymerase   The enzyme that catalyses RNA formation using DNA as a template.

Roentgen or Röntgen   Unit of X– or gamma-radiation that produces electrons in 1 cc. of dry air at NTP enough to produce ions carrying 1 ESU of charge of either sign or $1\cdot61 \times 10^{12}$ ion pairs per gram of air at NTP.

root cap The conical mass of parenchyma at the tip of a root covering the apical meristem.

root hair Extensions of epidermal cells of roots. Increases the surface area of the root and therefore concerned with water uptake.

rough surfaced ER ER with ribosomes on it.

rubber A polymerization product of isoprene, resin-like substances, nitrogeneous substances and carbohydrates. Sulphur, added in the vulcanization process, gives rubber its special properties by forming within it large numbers of S–S links.

S (1) The part of the mitotic cycle during which DNA is synthesized. Also the duration of this phase.
(2) Svedberg unit.

s Sedimentation coefficient. The rate at which a particle sediments in a field of 1 dyne (in water at 20°C). The ratio of the velocity attained by a particle and the acceleration given to it. A sedimentation constant of $1 \times 10^{-13}/\text{sec.} = 1$ Svedberg.

S_1, S_2 *and* S_3 The constant layers of the secondary cell wall differing from one another in the angle at which the microfibrils are deposited. S_1 is the outer and first formed layer.

schizogenous Formed by the separation of cells as opposed to the breakdown of cells (lysigenous). Used of intercellular spaces and canals.

sclerenchyma Tissue consisting of cells with lignified walls.

secondary tissue Tissue produced after the end of elongation notably by the cambium and other secondary meristems.

secondary wall The part of the cell wall formed after the end of cell extension.

secondary thickening meristem The meristem in certain monocotyledons that adds to the width of stems away from the apices.

sectorial chimera A chimera in which one whole sector of a shoot apex is of different genetic constitution from the rest of the apex. Cf. mericlinal.

semi-conservative replication Replication in which each of the products of division contains some material from the parent and some new material, but where the parental material is not spread evenly all over the progeny. (See Fig. 131).

sex chromosome A chromosome whose presence or absence helps to determine the sex of an individual.

sieve area The specialized primary pit fields of sieve cells and sieve tube elements bearing characteristic pores.

sieve cell The conducting cells of the phloem of lower vascular plants.

sieve elements The conducting cells of phloem bearing sieve areas.

sieve plate A special region of the wall of a sieve element bearing one or more sieve areas.

sieve tube A series of cells forming the conducting elements of the phloem of angiosperms.

slime body A viscous mass of very finely filamentous material, very variable in size and shape and of an unknown ontogeny or constitution; found in the middle and late stages of sieve element differentiation.

smooth surfaced ER ER without ribosomes.

sol A colloidal suspension of solid particles in a liquid.

soma   The part of an organism not concerned with the formation of a new generation by sexual reproduction.

sonic rupture   Breaking by sound waves.

spermatocyte   Cell giving rise to sperm cells by meiosis.

spherosome   Cytoplasmic organelles with high fat content and bounded by a single unit membrane.

spindle   The part of a cell that organizes the separation of the chromatids to the two daughter nuclei in mitosis and meiosis.

spindle fibres.
    (1)   Tubular structures similar to microtubules in the mitotic spindle.
    (2)   Fibres seen in the spindle under the light microscope. Relationship to (1) uncertain.

spore   A single cell that reproduces a plant. In higher plants, the product of meiosis; in lower plants produced by meiosis or by mitosis.

sporocyte   Spore mother cell. In higher plants it is diploid and divides meiotically to produce haploid spores.

sporophyte   The spore-bearing generation. In seed plants and pteridophytes this is the main generation and it has twice the chromosome number of the gametophytic generation.

sporopollenin   Resistant cell wall compound found in the exine of pollen.

statocyte   A cell that contains statoliths.

statolith   A granule that moves in the cell under the influence of gravity, possibly responsible for the perception of gravity.

stele   The part of a plant organ containing the vascular tissues and associated tissues. Forms a central cylinder in roots and stems.

stigma   Region of the pistil adapted to receive and retain pollen.

stoma   An opening in the epidermis of a plant sometimes including the two guard cells which surround it.

storied cambium   Cambium in which the ends of the cells occur at the same level because multiplicative division is radial. Occurs in certain dicotyledons only.

streptomycin   Antibiotic derived from *Streptomyces griseus*.

stroma   Ground substance of a plastid or other similar organelle.

stromacentre   Region of the stroma of a plastid consisting of an aggregation of fibrils.

structural gene   An 'ordinary' gene, i.e. one not concerned with controlling other genes.

substrate-limited   An enzymic reaction in which the speed of the reaction is limited by the small quantity present or by the slow supply of the substrate.

suspensor   In embryo of seed plant, the filamentous base of the embryo at the root pole, connecting the main part of the embryo to a basal cell.

Svedberg unit   Unit of sedimentation; proportional to the rate of sedimentation in a centrifugal field. Related to molecular weight and shape. $= 1 \times 10^{-13}$ cm/sec/ unit of centrifugal force.

symbiosis   The condition in which two animals, two plants or an animal and a plant live in mutually beneficial partnership.

symplastic growth   Growth in which adjacent cells expand conformably with no slipping in relation to each other.

synapsis   Chromosome pairing during prophase of meiosis.

synergid   One of two cells lying near the egg cell in the embryo sac.

syngamy Fusion of gametes in sexual reproduction.

T The duration of a complete mitotic cycle.

tannin An amorphous polymer of phenol derivatives such as flavan-3-ol, flavan-3, 4-ol, and gallic acids. Imparts the bitter taste to some fruits, tea and beer.

tapetum A nutritive tissue of anthers surrounding the cells that form the pollen grains.

telophase The end of mitosis when daughter nuclei are formed.

terpene Unsaturated hydrocarbons, $C_{10}H_{16}$, derived from isoprene.

tertiary wall The last of the layers of the normal secondary wall to be formed $= S_3$.

tetrakaidecahedron A solid figure with 14 faces. The orthic tetrakaidecahedron has 8 hexagonal faces and 6 square faces and is also called the truncated octahedron.

thixotropic Having the property of becoming liquid when disturbed mechanically and becoming solid on standing.

thylakoid The lamellae within a chloroplast including both those of the grana and those between the grana (stroma lamellae).

thymidine The nucleoside containing thymine and deoxyribose.

thymine A pyrimidine base found in DNA but not RNA.

time-lapse cinephotography Cinephotography in which a longer than usual time is allowed to elapse between successive frames.

tonoplast The membrane surrounding a vacuole in a cell.

trabecula
(1) A rod of cell wall material crossing the lumen of some cells.
(2) Extension of the wall of mature companion cell whose ontogeny and function is unknown.

tracheary element A conducting cell of the xylem, either a tracheid or a vessel element.

tracheid A water-conducting cell of the xylem in which the end walls do not break down.

transcription The process by which genetic information in DNA is transferred to RNA.

transfer–RNA The type of RNA that combines selectively with amino acid—adenylate enzyme complexes so that the amino acid is transferred to the t–RNA which transfers it to a ribosome for incorporation into a protein. = Soluble or s–RNA.

translation The process by which genetic information in m–RNA is used to arrange the amino acids in a protein molecule.

trichoblast The special epidermal cells of roots that produce root hairs.

trichocyst Ejectile organelles in certain dinoflagellates and ciliates. Smaller than cnidocysts.

tritiated Labelled with tritium.

tritium The radioactive isotope of hydrogen, H^3.

t–RNA Transfer–RNA.

tumour A swelling, especially one occurring in an organ late in its development.

tylosis The part of a parenchymatous cell that bulges through a pit into an adjacent vessel. It may block the lumen of the vessel.

ubisch bodies Irregularly shaped bodies with staining reactions similar to the exine of pollen grains found firstly in the tapetal cells and later discharged into the fluid within the microsporangium.

R

ultra-violet Electromagnetic radiation of wavelength less than 390 nm, the lower limit of the visible spectrum.

undulipodia Collective name for cilia and flagella.

unit membrane The unit of all the membrane systems of a cell. Appears as two dark lines separated by a pale line. Occurs singly in the tonoplast and plasmalemma and around certain organelles and doubly in the ER, nuclear, plastid and mitochondrial envelopes.

units of length We use subunits of the metre in steps of one thousand. (See preface).

1m	m	
10^{-3}m	mm	millimetre
10^{-6}m	μm	micron
10^{-9}m	nm	nanometre
		(= 10 Angström units)
		(= 1 millimicron mμ.)
10m^{-12}	pm	picometre
		(= 1 micromicron $\mu\mu$.)

uracil A pyrimidine base found in RNA but not DNA.

uridine The nucleoside containing uracil and ribose.

vacuole A watery solution separated from the cytoplasm by a membrane.

variegated Of the normally green parts of a plant, having some areas green and others white or some other colour.

vascular tissue Xylem and phloem. The conducting tissues of a plant.

vegetative nucleus In pollen, the larger of the two cells of the mature grain.

vessel A series of lignified xylem cells arranged end to end like drain pipes and with the end walls perforated to form a tube. Found in most flowering plants, but only rarely in other vascular plants.

viscosity Internal friction in a fluid due to cohesion of particles or molecules.

warty structure A superficial deposit of irregular lumps sometimes found covering the S_3 layer of secondary walls.

X_1, X_2 The first and second mitoses after an experimental treatment such as irradiation.

X chromosome A sex chromosome. In dioecious diploids, the sex chromosomes two of which occur in the homozygous sex. In dioecious haploids, the sex chromosome of the female.

xerophytic Of a plant, living in dry conditions or in conditions with a similar physiological effect.

X-ray Electromagnetic radiation of wavelength 1pm − 5 nm.

xylem The water conducting tissue of a plant consisting of vessels and/or tracheids, parenchyma and sclerenchyma. Also serves a structural function. = wood.

zygote The cell resulting from the fusion of two gametes.

zygotene The stage of prophase of meiosis at which the chromosomes of homologous pairs come together.

zymogen A precursor of an enzyme.

Literature Cited

ALBERSHEIM P. & KILLIAS U. (1963) Histochemical localization at the electron microscope level. *Amer. J. Bot.*, **50**, 732–745.

ALFERT M. & SWIFT H. (1953) Nuclear DNA constancy: a critical evaluation of some exceptions reported by Lison and Pasteels. *Exp. Cell Res.*, **5**, 455–460.

ALLISON A.C. & PATON G.R. (1965) Chromosome damage in human diploid cells following activation of lysosomal enzymes. *Nature, Lond.*, **207**, 1170–1173.

AMELUNXEN F. & GRONAU G. (1966) Über die Polarität der Dictyosomen von *Acorus calamus*. *Z. Pflanzenphys.*, **55**, 327–336.

AMELUNXEN F., MORGENROTH K. & PICKSAK T. (1967) Untersuchungen an der Epidermis mit dem Stereoscan-Elektronenmikroskop. *Z. Pflanzenphysiol.* Bd. **57**, 79–95.

ARNASON T.J., HARRINGTON J.B. & FRIESEN L.A. (1946) Inheritance of variegation in barley. *Canad. J. Res.*, **C24**, 145–157.

ARNASON T.J. & WALKER G.W.R. (1949) An irreversible gene-induced plastid mutation. *Canad. J. Res.*, **C27**, 172–178.

ARRIGONI O. & ROSSI G. (1963) I lomasomi: Loro probabili rapporti con la crescita per distensione della parcte cellulare. *Giorn. Bot. Ital.*, **70**, 476–481.

ASHBY E. (1950b) Leaf morphology and physiological age. *Science Progress*, **152**, 678–685.

AUDUS L.J. (1962) The mechanism of the perception of gravity by plants. *Symp. Soc. exp. Biol.*, **16**, 196–226.

AVERS C.J. & KING E.E. (1960) Histochemical evidence of intracellular enzymatic heterogenicity of plant mitochondria. *Amer. J. Bot.*, **47**, 220–225.

AVERS C.J. (1963) Fine structure studies of *Phleum* root meristem cells. II Mitotic asymmetry and cellular differentiation. *Amer. J. Bot.*, **50**, 140–148.

AVERY G.S., Jr. (1933) Structure and development of the tobacco leaf. *Amer. J. Bot.*, **20**, 565–592.

BACH M.K. & JOHNSON H.G. (1966) Polysomes on a nuclear membrane fraction as intermediates in the transfer of ribonucleic acid from the nucleus to the cytoplasm. *Nature, Lond.*, **209**, 893–895.

BADENHUIZEN N.P. (1963) Formation and distribution of amylose and amylopectin in the starch granule. *Nature, Lond.*, **197**, 464–467.

BADENHUIZEN N.P. (1964) A note on green amyloplasts. *Revista de Biologia*, **4**, 113–120.

BAILEY I.W. (1957) Need for a broadened outlook in cell wall terminologies. *Phytomorphology*, **7**, 136–138.

BAIN J.M. (1961) Some morphological, anatomical, and physiological changes in the pear fruit (*Pyrus communis* var. Williams Bon Chretien) during development and following harvest. *Aust. J. Bot.*, **9**, 99–123.

BAINTON D.F. & FARQUHAR M.G. (1966) Origin of granules in polymorphonuclear leukocytes. *J. Cell Biol.*, **28**, 277–301.

BAJER A. (1961) A note on the behaviour of spindle fibres at mitosis. *Chromosoma*, **12**, 64–71.

BAJER A. (1965) Ciné micrographic analysis of cell plate formation in endosperm. *Exp. Cell Res.*, **37**, 376–398.

BAJER A. & ALLEN R.D. (1966) Role of phragmoplast filaments in cell plate formation. *J. Cell Sci.*, **1**, 455–462.

BAKER E.A. & MARTIN J.T. (1963) Cutin of plant cuticles. *Nature, Lond.*, **199**, 1268–1270.

BAKER J.R. (1957) The Golgi controversy. *Symp. Soc. exp. Biol.*, **10**, 1–10.

BAKER P.F., NORTHCOTE D.H. & PETERS R. (1962) Structure and enzyme activity. *Nature, London.*, **195**, 661–662.

BAMBER R.K. (1961) Staining reaction of the pit membrane of wood cells. *Nature, Lond.*, **191**, 409–410.

BANNAN M.W. (1950) The frequency of anticlinal divisions in fusiform cambial initials of *Chamaecyparis*. *Amer. J. Bot.*, **37**, 511–519.

BANNAN M.W. (1960) Ontogenetic trends in conifer cambium with respect to frequency of anticlinal division and cell length. *Canad. J. Bot.*, **38**, 795–802.

BARBER H.N. & CALLAN H.G. (1943) The effects of cold and colchicine on mitosis in the newt. *Proc. roy. Soc. B.*, **131**, 258–271.

BARBER R., JOSEPH S. & MEEK G.A. (1960) The origin and fate of the nuclear membranes in meiosis. *Proc. roy. Soc. B.*, **152**, 353–366.

BARGHOORN E.S. (1964) Evolution of cambium in geologic time. In 'The Formation of Wood in Forest Trees'. Ed M. H. Zimmerman, 3–13.

BARTELS F. (1964) Plastidenzählungen bei *Epilobium hirsutum*. *Planta*, **60**, 434–452.

BARTON R. (1964) Electron microscope studies on the uptake of ferritin by plant roots. *Exp. Cell Res.*, **36**, 432–434.

BARTON R. (1965) An unusual organelle in the peripheral cytoplasm of *Chara* cells. *Nature, Lond.*, **205**, 201.

BASERGA R. (1963) Mitotic cycle of ascites tumour cells. *Archs. Path.*, **75**, 156–161.

BATTAGLIA E. (1947) Richerche cariologiche e embriologiche sul genere Rudbeckia XI Semigamia in *Rudbeckia speciosa*. *Nuovo Giornole Bot. Ital.*, N.S. **54**, 531–559.

BAYLEY S.T. (1964) Physical studies on ribosomes from pea seedlings. *J. Mol. Biol.*, **8**, 231–238.

BECKER G., ALBERSHEIM P. & HUI P. (1963) Synthesis of extra-cellular polysaccharide by suspensions of *Acer pseudoplatanus* cambium cells. *Plant Physiol. Suppl.*, **38**, LVIII.

BEDNAR T.W. & JUNIPER B.E. (1964) Microfibrillar structure in the fungal portions of the lichen *Xanthoria parietina* (L.) TH.Fr. *Exp. Cell Res.*, **36**, 680–693.

BEER M. & SETTERFIELD G. (1958) Fine structure in thickened primary walls of collenchyma cells of celery petioles. *Amer. J. Bot.*, **45**, 571–580.

BEERMANN W. (1961) Ein Balbiani-ring als Locus einer Speicheldrüsenmutation. *Chromosoma*, **12**, 1–25.

BEHNKE H.D. (1966) Cell structures in relation to translocation phenomena in plants. in 'Viruses of Plants'. Ed. A. B. R. Beemster and J. Dijksta, 28–43.

BEHNKE H.D. & DÖRR I. (1967) Zur Herkunft und Struktur der Plasmafilamente in Assimilatleitbahnen. *Planta*, **74**, 18–44.

BELL P.R., FREY-WYSSLING A. & MÜHLETHALER, K. (1966) Evidence for the discontinuity of plastids in the sexual reproduction of a plant. *J. Ultrastr. Res.*, **15**, 108–121.

BELL P.R. & MÜHLETHALER, K. (1964a) Evidence for the presence of deoxyribonucleic acid in the organelles of the egg cells of *Pteridium aquilinum. J. Mol. Biol.*,
8, 853–862.

BELL P.R. & MÜHLETHALER K. (1964b) The degeneration and reappearance of
mitochondria in the egg cells of a plant. *J. Cell Biol.*, **20**, 235–248.

BEN-HAYYIM G. & OHAD I. (1965) Synthesis of cellulose by *Acetobacter xylinum.
J. Cell Biol.*, **25**, 191–207.

BENNETT C.W. (1944) Dodder transmission of plant viruses. *Phytopathology*, **34**,
905–932.

BENNET-CLARK T.A. (1965) Salt accumulation and mode of action of auxin. in
'Chemistry and Mode of Action of Plant Growth Substances'. Ed. R. L. Wain
and F. Wightman, 284–291.

BENNET-CLARK T.A. (1959) Water relations of cells. *Plant Physiol.*, **2**, 105–191.

BENSON A.A. (1964) Plant membrane lipids. *Ann. Rev. Pl. Physiol.*, **15**, 1–16.

BERGONIÉ J. & TRIBONDEAU L. (1906) Interpretation de quelques résultats de la
radiothérapie et essai de fixation d'une technique rationelle. *C.R. Acad. Sci.*,
Paris, **143**, 983–985.

BERLOWITZ L. & BIRNSTIEL M.L. (1967) Histones of the wildtype and the anucleolate
mutant of *Xenopus laevis. Science*, **156**, 78–80.

BERNIER G. & JENSEN W.A. (1966) Pattern of DNA synthesis in the meristematic
cells of *Sinapis. Histochemie*, **6**, 85–92.

BISSON C.V., VANSELL C.H. & DYE W.B. (1940) Investigations on the physical and
chemical properties of beeswax. *U.S. Dept. of Agr. Tech. Bull.*, **716**, 1–23.

BOARDMAN N.K. & ANDERSON J.M. (1964) Studies on the greening of dark-grown
bean plants. *Aust. J. Biol. Sci.*, **17**, 86–92.

BÖHMER, H. (1958) Untersuchungen über das Wachstum und den Feinbau der
Zellwände in der *Avena* Koleoptile. *Planta*, **50**, 461–497.

BOND V.P. (1959) Sensitivity of different cells in the same organism. in 'Radio-
biology at the Intra-Cellular Level'. Ed. Hennessy *et al*, 55–63.

BONNER, J. (1936) Zum Mechanismus der Zellstreckung auf Grund der Micellarlehre.
Pringsh. Jahrb. wiss. Bot., **82**, 377–410.

BONNER J. (1959) Protein synthesis and the control of plant processes. *Amer. J. Bot.*,
46, 58–62.

BONNER J. (1965) 'The Molecular Biology of Development'. Oxford, Clarendon
Press.

BONNETT H.T. & NEWCOMB E.H. (1966) Coated vesicles and other cytoplasmic
components of growing root hairs of radish. *Protoplasma*, **62**, 59–75.

BONNEVILLE M.A. & VOELLER B.R. (1963) A new cytoplasmic component of plant
cells. *J. Cell Biol.*, **18**, 703–708.

BOPP-HASSENKAMP G. (1958) Lichtmikroskopische und electronenoptische Untersuchungen über den Aufban pflanzlicher Chromosomen in Pachytän der Meiosis.
Protoplasma, **50**, 243–268.

BOSTOCK C.J., DONACHIE W.D., MASTERS M. & MITCHISON J.M. (1966) Synthesis
of enzymes and DNA in synchronous cultures of *Schizosaccharomyces pombe.
Nature, Lond.*, **210**, 808–810.

BOUCK G.B. (1962) Chromatophore development, pits and other fine structure in
the red alga, *Lomentaria baileyana J. Cell Biol.*, **12**, 553–569.

BOUCK G.B. (1963) An examination of the effect of ultracentrifugation on the
organelles in living root tip cells. *Amer. J. Bot.*, **50**, 1046–1054.

R*

BOUCK G.B. & CRONSHAW J. (1965) The fine structure of differentiating sieve tube elements. *J. Cell Biol.*, **25**, 79–95.

BOVÉ J. & ROACKE I.D. (1959) Amino acid-activating enzymes in isolated chloroplasts from spinach leaves. *Arch. Biochem. Biophys.*, **85**, 521–531.

BOWES B.G. (1965) The origin and development of vacuoles in *Glechoma hederacea*. *La Cellule*, **65**, 359–364.

BRADFUTE O.E., CHAPMAN-ANDRESEN C. & JENSEN W.A. (1964) Concerning morphological evidence for pinocytosis in higher plants. *Exp. Cell Res.*, **36**, 207–210.

BRADLEY D.E. (1965) Replica and shadowing techniques. in 'Techniques for Electron Microscopy' (2nd Ed.). Ed. D. Kay, 96–152.

BRADLEY D.E. (1965) Observations on the mastigonemes of two Chrysophyceae using negative staining. *Quart. J. roy. Micro. Soc.*, **106**, 327–331.

BRADLEY D.E. (1966) The ultrastructure of the flagella of three chrysomonads with particular reference to the mastigonemes. *Exp. Cell Res.*, **41**, 162–173.

BRAKKE M.K. (1951) Density gradient centrifugation: a new separation technique. *J. Amer. Chem. Soc.*, **73**, 1847–1848.

BRANDT P.W. & PAPPAS G.D. (1962) An electron microscopic study of pinocytosis in ameba. II The cytoplasmic uptake phase. *J. Cell Biol.*, **15**, 55–71.

BRANTON D. (1966) Fracture faces of frozen membranes. *Proc. nat. Acad. Sci., Wash.*, **55**, 1048–1056.

BRANTON D. & MOOR H. (1964) Fine structure in freeze-etched *Allium cepa* root tips. *J. Ultrastr. Res.*, **11**, 401–411.

BRAUN A.C. (1962) Tumor inception and development in the crown gall disease. *Ann. Rev. Pl. Physiol.*, **13**, 533–558.

BRAUN A.C. (1963) Biochemical changes of a heritable type that result in cellular autonomy. in 'The General Physiology of Cell Specialization'. Ed. Mazia & Tyler, 73–79.

BRAWERMAN G. (1962) A specific species of ribosomes associated with the chloroplasts of *Euglena gracilis*. *Biochem. Biophys. Acta*, **61**, 313–315.

BRIERLEY G. & GREEN D.E. (1965) Compartmentation of the mitochondrion. *Proc. nat. Acad. Sci., Wash.*, **53**, 73–79.

BROWN D.D. & GURDON J.B. (1964) Absence of ribosomal RNA synthesis in the anucleolate mutant of *Xenopus laevis*. *Proc. nat. Acad. Sci., Wash.*, **51**, 139–146.

BROWN R. (1951) The effects of temperature on the durations of the different stages of cell divisions in the root tip. *J. exp. Bot.*, **2**, 96–110.

BROWN R. (1958) Cellular basis for the induction of morphological structures. *Nature, Lond.*, **181**, 1546–1547.

BROWN R. (1960) The plant cell and its inclusions. in 'Plant Physiology'. Ed. F. C. Steward, Ia, 3–129.

BROWN R. (1963) Cellular differentiations in the root. *Symp. Soc. exp. Biol.*, **17**, 1–17.

BROWN R. & BROADBENT D. (1950) The development of cells in the growing zones of the root. *J. exp. Bot.*, **1**, 249–263.

BROWN R., REITH W.S. & ROBINSON E. (1952) The mechanism of plant cell growth. *Symp. Soc. exp. Biol.*, **6**, 329–347.

BROWN R. & RICKLESS P. (1949) A new method for the study of cell division and cell extension with some preliminary observations on the effect of temperature and nutrients. *Proc. roy. Soc. B.*, **136**, 110–125.

BROWN R. & ROBINSON E. (1955) Cellular differentiation and the development of enzyme proteins in plants. in 'Biological Specificity and Growth'. Ed. E. G. Butler, 93–118.

BROWN S.A. (1964) Lignin and tannin biosynthesis. in 'Biochemistry of Phenolic Compounds'. Ed. J.B. Harborne., 361–398.

BROWN S.W. (1966) Heterochromatin. *Science*, **151**, 417–425.

BROWN W.V. & EMERY W.H.P. (1957) Persistent nucleoli and grass systematics. *Amer. J. Bot.*, **44**, 585–590.

BROWN W.V. & JOHNSON S.C. (1962) The fine structure of the grass guard cell. *Amer. J. Bot.*, **49**, 110–115.

BRUCE V.G. (1965) Cell division rhythms and the circadian clock. in 'Circadian Clocks'. Ed. Aschoff, Amsterdam, 123–138.

BRUNI C. & PORTER K.R. (1965) The fine structure of the parenchymal cell of normal rat liver. I. General observations. *Amer. J. Pathol.*, **46**, 691–755.

BULLOUGH W.S. & RYTÖMAA, T. (1965) Mitotic homeostasis. *Nature, Lond.*, **205**, 573–578.

BÜNNING E. (1957) Polarität und inäquale Teilung des pflanzlichen Protoplasten. *Protoplasmotologia*, **8**, 9a.

BURTON P.R. (1966) Substructure of certain cytoplasmic microtubules: An electron microscopic study. *Science*, **154**, 903–905.

BUTT V.S. (1959) The distribution of ascorbic oxidase during growth. *Proc. IX Intern. Congr. Bot. Montreal*, Abstracts—**2**, 53–54.

BUTTROSE M.S. (1963) Ultrastructure of the developing wheat endosperm. *Aust. J. Biol. Sci.*, **16**, 305–317.

BUVAT R. (1957) Formations de golgi dans les cellules radiculaires d'*Allium cepa*. *C.R. Acad. Sci., Paris*, **244**, 1401–1403.

BUVAT R. (1963) Electron microscopy of plant protoplasm. *Int. Rev. Cytol.*, **14**, 41–155.

BUVAT R. & LANCE A. (1958) Évolution des infrastructures de mitochondries au cours de la différenciation cellulaire. *C.R. Acad. Sci., Paris*, **247**, 1130–1132.

CADMAN C.H. (1960) Inhibition of plant virus infections by tannins. in 'Phenolics in Plants in Health and Disease'. Ed. J. B. Pridham, 101–105.

CALLAN H.C. & TOMLIN S.G. (1950) Experimental studies on amphibian oocyte nuclei. *Proc. roy. Soc.*, *B*, **137**, 367–378.

CAMUS G. (1949) Recherches sur la rôle des bourgeons dans les phénomènes de morphogénèse. *Rev. Cytol., Paris*, **11**, 1–199.

CANNY M.J. (1962) The mechanism of translocation. *Ann. Bot.*, **26**, 603–617.

CAPORALI L. (1959) Recherches sur les infrastructures des cellules radiculaires de *Lens culinaris* et particulièrement sur l'évolutions des leucoplastes. *Ann. Sci. nat. Botanique*, **11** sér **20**, 215–247.

CARLQUIST, S. (1956) On the occurrence of intercellular pectic warts in *Compositae*. *Amer. J. Bot.*, **43**, 425–429.

CHAMBERLAIN C.J. (1937) 'Gymmosperms. Structure and Evolution', Chicago, Illinois, 125.

CHANCE B. & PARSON D.F. (1963) Cytochrome function in relation to inner membrane structure of mitochondria. *Science*, **142**, 1176–1180.

CHAYEN, J. (1960) The localization of deoxyribose nucleic acid in cells of the root meristem of *Vicia faba*. *Exp. Cell Res.*, **20**, 150–171.

CHAYEN J. & DENBY E. (1960) The distribution of deoxyribonucleic acid in homogenates of plant roots. *Exp. Cell Res.*, **20**, 182–192.

CHEN P.L. (1964) The membrane system of *Streptonmyces cinnamonensis*. *Amer. J. Bot.*, **51**, 125–132.

CHIPCHASE M.I.H., & BIRNSTIEL M.L. (1963) On the nature of nucleolar RNA. *Proc. nat. Acad. Sci., Wash.*, **50**, 1101–1106.

CHOUINARD L.A. (1966) Nucleolonema and pars amorpha in root meristematic cells of *Vicia faba*. *Canad. J. Bot.*, **44**, 403–411.

CHRISPEELS M.J., VATTER A.E. & HANSON J.B. (1966) Morphological development of mitochondria during cell elongation in the roots of *Zea mays* seedlings. *J. roy. Micro. Soc.*, **85**, 29–44.

CLELAND R. (1963) Independence of effects of auxin on cell wall methylation and elongation. *Plant Physiol.*, **38**, 12–18.

CLOWES F.A.L. (1956) Nucleic acids in root apical meristems of *Zea*. *New Phytol.*, **55**, 29–34.

CLOWES F.A.L. (1959) Apical meristems of roots. *Biol. Rev.*, **34**, 501–529.

CLOWES F.A.L. (1961a) 'Apical Meristems'. Oxford, Blackwell Scientific Publications.

CLOWES F.A.L. (1961b) Duration of the mitotic cycle in a meristem. *J. exp. Bot.*, **12**, 283–293.

CLOWES F.A.L. (1962) Rates of mitosis in a partially synchronous meristem. *New Phytol.*, **61**, 111–118.

CLOWES F.A.L. (1963) Micronuclei in irradiated meristems. *Radiat. Bot.*, **3**, 223–229.

CLOWES F.A.L. (1964) Micronuclei and radiosensitivity in the root meristem of *Vicia faba*. *Ann. Bot., Lond. N.S.*, **28**, 345–350.

CLOWES F.A.L. (1965a) The duration of the G_1 phase of the mitotic cycle and its relation to radiosensitivity. *New Pyhtol.*, **64**, 355–359.

CLOWES F.A.L. (1965b) Synchronization in a meristem by 5-amino-uracil. *J. exp. Bot.*, **16**, 581–586.

CLOWES F.A.L. (1967) Synthesis of DNA during mitosis. *J. exp. Bot.* (In press).

CLOWES F.A.L. & HALL E.J. (1962) The quiescent centre in root meristems of *Vicia faba* and its behaviour after acute X-irradiation and chronic gamma irradiation. *Radiat. Bot.*, **3**, 45–53.

CLOWES F.A.L. & HALL E.J. (1966) Meristems under continuous irradiation. *Ann. Bot., Lond. N.S.*, **30**, 243–251.

CLOWES F.A.L. & JUNIPER B.E. (1964) The fine structure of the quiescent centre and neighbouring tissues in root meristems. *J. exp. Bot.*, **15**, 622–630.

CLOWES F.A.L. & STEWART H.E. (1967) Recovery from dormancy in roots. *New Phytol.*, **66**, 115–123.

COCKING E.C. (1966a) An electron microscopic study of the initial stages of infection of isolated tomato fruit protoplasts by tobacco mosaic virus. *Planta*, **68**, 206–214.

COCKING E.C. (1966b) Electron microscopic studies on isolated protoplasts. *Z. Naturf.*, **21b**, 581–584.

COCKING E.C. & GREGORY D.W. (1963) Organized protoplasmic units of the plant cell. I Their occurrence, origin and structure. *J. exp. Bot.*, **14**, 504–511.

COLVIN J.R. (1965) The morphology of synthetic polymer films as a guide for interpreting microfibrillar orientation in plant cell walls. *Canad. J. Bot.*, **43**, 1478–1479.

CORBETT N.H. (1965) Micro-morphological studies on the degradation of lignified cell walls by ascomycetes and fungi imperfecti. *J. Inst. Wood Sci.*, **14**, 18–29.

COTÉ W.A. & DAY A.C. (1963) Vestured pits-fine structure and apparent relationships with warts. *Tappi*, **45**, 906–910.

CRAWLEY J.C.W. (1965) A cytoplasmic organelle associated with the cell walls of *Chara* and *Nitella*. *Nature, Lond.*, **205**, 200–201.

CRICK F.H.C. (1966) The genetic code III. *Sci. American*, **215/4**, 55–62.

CRONSHAW J. (1960) The fine structure of the pits of *Eucalyptus regnans* (F. Muell.) and their relation to the movement of liquids into the wood. *Aust. J. Bot.*, **8**, 51–57.

CRONSHAW J. (1965) The organization of cytoplasmic components during the phase of cell wall thickening in differentiating cambial derivatives of *Acer rubrum*. *Canad. J. Bot.*, **43**, 1401–1407.

CRONSHAW J. (1967) Tracheid differentiation in tobacco pith cultures. *Planta*, **72**, 78–90.

CRONSHAW J. & BOUCK G.B. (1965) The fine structure of differentiating xylem elements. *J. Cell Biol.*, **24**, 415–431.

CRONSHAW J. & WARDROP A.B. (1964) The organization of cytoplasm in differentiating xylem. *Aust. J. Bot.*, **12**, 15–23.

CUNNINGHAM W.P., MORRÉ D.J. & MOLLENHAUER H.H. (1966) Structure of isolated plant Golgi apparatus revealed by negative staining. *J. Cell Biol.*, **28**, 169–179.

DAEMS W.T. & WISSE E. (1966) Shape and attachment of the cristae mitochondriales in mouse hepatic cell mitochondria. *J. Ultrastr. Res.*, **16**, 123–140.

DAINTY J. (1963) Water relations of plant cells. in 'Advances in Botanical Research'. Ed. Preston, 279–326.

D'AMATO F. & AVANZI S. (1965) DNA content, DNA synthesis and mitosis in the root apical cell of *Marsilea strigosa*. *Caryologia*, **18**, 383–394.

DARLINGTON C.D. (1947) Nucleic acid and the chromosomes. *S.E.B. Symp. I*, 252–269.

DARLINGTON C.D. (1958) 'Evolution of Genetic Systems'. Edinburgh, Oliver & Boyd.

DARLINGTON C.D. (1965) 'Cytology'. Churchill, London.

DARLINGTON C.D. & HAQUE A. (1966) Organization of DNA synthesis in rye chromosomes. in 'Chromosomes Today'. Ed. Darlington & Lewis, 102–107.

DARLINGTON C.D. & LA COUR L. (1940) Nucleic acid starvation of chromosomes in *Trillium*. *J. Genet.*, **40**, 185–212.

DARLINGTON C.D. & MATHER K. (1949) 'The Elements of Genetics', London, MacMillan.

DARLINGTON C.D. & VOSA C.G. (1963) Bias in the internal coiling direction of chromosomes. *Chromosoma*, **13**, 609–622.

DASHEK W.V. & ROSEN W.G. (1966a) Electron microscopical localization of chemical components in the growth zone of lily pollen tubes. *Protoplasma*, **61**, 192–204.

DAUWALDER M., KEPHART J.E. & WHALEY W.G. (1966). Phosphatases and the Golgi apparatus in differentiating cells. *J. Cell Biol.*, **31**, No. 2. Abstracts of 6th Ann. Meeting Amer. Soc. Cell Biol., No. 49.

DAVIDSON D. (1958) The irradiation of dividing cells: Changes in sensitivity to X-rays during mitosis. *Ann. Bot., Lond. N.S.*, **22**, 183–195.

DAVIES D.D., GIOVANELLI J. & ap REES T. (1964) 'Plant Biochemistry'. Blackwell Scientific Publications, Oxford

DE DUVE C. (1963) Structure and functions of Lysosomes. *Funktionelle und Morphologische Organisation der Zelle Berlin, Göttingen, Heidelberg Springer-Verlag*, 209–218.

DE DUVE C. & WATTIAUX R. (1966) Functions of lysosomes. *Ann. Rev. Physiol.*, **28**, 435–492.

DEFENDI V. & MANSON L.A. (1961) Studies on the relationship of DNA synthesis time to proliferation time in cultured mammalian cells. *Path. Biol., Paris*, **9**, 525–528.

DERMEN H. (1945) The mechanism of colchicine-induced cytohistological changes in cranberry. *Amer. J. Bot.*, **32**, 387–394.

DIACUMAKOS E.G., GARNJOBST L. & TATUM E.L. (1965) A cytoplasmic character in *Neurospora crassa*. The role of nuclei and mitochondria. *J. Cell Biol.*, **26**, 427–443.

DIBOLL A.G. & LARSON D.A. (1966) An electron microscope study of the mature megagametophyte in *Zea mays*. *Amer. J. Bot.*, **53**, 391–402.

DIERS L. (1966) On the plastids, mitochondria, and other cell constituents during oogenesis of a plant. *J. Cell Biol.*, **28**, 527–543.

DIERS L. & SCHÖTZ F. (1965) Über den Feinbau pflanzlicher Mitochondrien. *Z. Pflanzenphysiol.*, **53**, 334–343.

DINGLE A.D. & FULTON C. (1966) Development of the flagellar apparatus of *Naegleria*. *J. Cell Biol.*, **31**, 43–54.

DODD J.D. (1948) On the shapes of cells in the cambial zone of *Pinus sylvestris*. *Amer. J. Bot.*, **35**, 666–682.

DRAWERT H. & MIX M. (1962) Zur Funktion des Golgi-Apparates in der Pflanzenzelle. *Planta*, **58**, 448–542.

DRIESSCHE V. (1966) Circadian rhythms in *Acetabularia*. *Exp. Cell Res.*, **42**, 18–30.

DRUM R.W. (1966) Electron microscopy of paired Golgi structures in the diatom *Pinnularia nobilis*. *J. Ultrastr. Res.*, **15**, 100–107.

DUFFY R.M. (1951) Comparative cellular configurations in the meristematic and mature cortical cells of the primary root of tomato. *Amer. J. Bot.*, **38**, 393–408.

EARLE E.D. & TORREY J.G. (1965) Morphogenesis in cell colonies grown from *Convolvulus* cell suspensions plated on synthetic media. *Amer. J. Bot.*, **52**, 891–899.

ECHLIN P. (1965) An apparent helical arrangement of ribosomes in developing pollen mother cells of *Ipomea purpurea*. *J. Cell Biol.*, **24**, 150–153.

EDELMAN M., COWAN C.A., EPSTEIN H.T. & SCHIFF J.A. (1964) Studies of chloroplast development in *Euglena* VIII chloroplast-associated DNA. *Proc. nat. Acad. Sci., Wash.*, **52**, 1214–1219.

EILAM Y. & KLEIN S. (1962) The effect of light intensity and sucrose feeding on the fine structure in chloroplasts and on the chlorophyll content of etiolated leaves. *J. Cell Biol.*, **14**, 169–182.

EISENSTADT J.M. & BRAWERMAN G. (1964) The protein-synthesizing systems from the cytoplasm and the chloroplasts of *Euglena* gracilis. *J. Mol. Biol.*, **10**, 392–402.

ENGLEMAN E.M. (1965a) Sieve element of *Impatiens sultanii*. I Wound reaction. *Ann. Bot., Lond. N.S.*, **29**, 83–100.

ENGLEMAN E.M. (1965b) Sieve element of *Impatiens sultanii*. II Developmental aspects. *Ann. Bot., Lond. N.S.*, **29**, 103–118.

ERICKSON R.O. & SAX K.B. (1956a) Rates of cell division and cell elongation in the growth of the primary root of *Zea mays*. *Proc. Amer. phil. Soc.*, **100**, 499–514.

ERICKSON R.O. & SAX K.B. (1956b) Elemental growth rate of the primary root of *Zea mays*. *Proc. Amer. phil. Soc.*, **100**, 487–498.

ESAU K. (1948a) Some anatomical aspects of plant virus disease problems. *Bot. Rev.*, **14**, 413–449.

ESAU K. (1948b) Anatomic effects of Pierce's disease and Phony Peach. *Hilgardia*, **18**, 423–482.

ESAU K. (1953) 'Plant Anatomy'. John Wiley & Sons Inc. New York., Chapman & Hall Ltd., London.

ESAU K. (1963) Ultrastructure of differentiated cells in higher plants. *Amer. J. Bot.*, **50**, 495–506.

ESAU K. (1965a) Fixation images of sieve element plastids in *Beta*. *Proc. nat. Acad. Sci., Wash.*, **54**, 429–437.

ESAU K. (1965b) 'Vascular Differentiation in Plants'. Holt, Rinehart & Winston, New York, Chicago, San Francisco, Toronto, London, Fig. 4–5, p. 66.

ESAU K. (1966) Explorations of the food conducting system in plants. *Amer. Scientist*, **54**, 141–157.

ESAU K., CHEADLE V.I. & GILL R.H. (1966a) Cytology of differentiating tracheary elements. I. Organelles and membrane systems. *Amer. J. Bot.*, **53**, 756–764.

ESAU K., CHEADLE V.I. & GILL R.H. (1966b) Cytology of differentiating tracheary elements. II Structures associated with cell surfaces. *Amer. J. Bot.*, **53**, 765–771.

ESAU K. CHEADLE V.I. & RISLEY E.B. (1962) Development of sieve plate pores. *Bot. Gaz.*, **123**, 233–243.

ESAU K., CRONSHAW J. & HOEFERT L.L. (1967) Relation of beet yellows virus to the phloem and to movements in the sieve tube. *J. Cell Biol.*, **32**, 71–87.

ESAU K. & GILL R.H. (1965) Observations on cytokinesis. *Planta*, **67**, 168–181.

ESAU K. & HEWITT W.B. (1940) Structure of end walls in differentiating vessels. *Hilgardia*, **13**, 229–244.

ESCHRICH W. (1963) Beziehung zwischen dem Auftreten von Callose und der Feinstruktur des primären Phloems bei *Cucurbita ficifolia*. *Planta*, **59**, 243–261.

ESCHRICH, W. (1963) Der Phloemsaft von *Cucurbita ficifolia*. *Planta*, **60**, 216–224.

EVANS H.J. (1962) Chromosome aberrations induced by ionizing radiations. *Int. Rev. Cytol.*, **13**, 221–321.

EVANS H.J., NEARY G.J. & TONKINSON S.M. (1957) The use of colchicine as an indicator of mitotic rate in broad bean root meristems. *J. Genet.*, **55**, 487–502.

EVANS H.J. & POND V. (1964) The influence of the centromere on chromosome fragment frequency under chronic irradiation. *Portugal Acta. Biol.*, **A8**, 125–146.

EVANS H.J. & SAVAGE J.R.K. (1959) The effect of temperature on mitosis and on the action of colchicine in root meristem cells of *Vicia faba*. *Exp. Cell Res.*, **18**, 51–61.

EVANS H.J. & SPARROW A.H. (1961) Nuclear factors affecting Radiosensitivity. II Dependence on nuclear and chromosome structure and organization. *Brookhaven Symp. Biol.*, **14**, 101–127.

EVERT R.F. & DERR W.F. (1964a) Callose substance in sieve elements. *Amer. J. Bot.*, **51**, 552–559.

EVERT R.F. & DERR W.F. (1964b) Slime substance and strands in sieve elements. *Amer. J. Bot.*, **51**, 875–880.

EVERT R.F. & MURMANIS L. (1965) Ultrastructure of the secondary phloem of *Tilia americana. Amer. J. Bot.*, **52**, 95–106.

EVERT R.F., MURMANIS L. & SACHS I.B. (1966) Another view of the ultrastructure of *Cucurbita* phloem. *Ann. Bot., Lond. N.S.*, **30**, 563–585.

FALK H. (1961) Spiralige Anordnung von Ribosomen in Pflanzenzellen. *Protoplasma*, **54**, 594–597.

FALK H. (1964) Zur Herkunft des Siebröhrenschleimer vei *Tetragona expansa* Murr. *Planta*, **60**, 558–567.

FAWCETT D. (1961) Cilia and flagella. in 'The Cell'. Ed. Brachet and Mirsky, 217–297.

FEENEY P.P. (1966) The loss of palatibility and nutritive value of leaves of *Quercus* sp. to the winter moth *Operophtera brumata*. *Phytochemistry* (in the press).

FERNÁNDEZ-MORÁN H., ODA T., BLAIR P.V. & GREEN D.E. (1964) A macromolecular repeating unit of mitochondrial structure and function. *J. Cell Biol.*, **22**, 63–100.

FESSLER J.H. & FESSLER L.I. (1966) Electron microscope visualization of the polysaccharide hyaluronic acid. *Proc. nat. Acad. Sci., Wash.*, **56**, 141–147.

FRANKE W. (1961) Ectodesmata and foliar absorption. *Amer. J. Bot.*, **48**, 683–691.

FRANKE W. (1964a) The nature and function of ectodesmata. Abstracts of the *Proc. Xth Bot. Congr. Edin.*, No. **471**.

FRANKE W. (1964b) Role of guard cells in foliar absorption. *Nature, Lond.*, **202**, 1236–1237.

FRANKE W.W. (1966) Isolated nuclear membranes. *J. Cell Biol.*, **31**, 619–623.

FRANKE W. (1967) Mechanisms of foliar penetration of solutions. *Annu. Rev. Pl. Physiol.*, **18**, 281–300.

FREDERIC J. (1952) Recherches cytologiques sur le chondriome normal ou soumis à l'expérimentation dans des cellules vivantes cultivées *in vitro*. *Arch. Biol.*, **69**, 167–341.

FREESE E. (1958) The arrangement of DNA in the chromosome. *Cold Spr. Harb. Symp. quant. Biol.*, **23**, 13–18.

FREIFELDER D. & KLEINSCHMIDT A.K. (1965) Single strand breaks in Duplex DNA of coliphage T7 as demonstrated by electron microscopy. *J. Mol. Biol.*, **14**, 271–278.

FREY-WYSSLING A. (1964) Ultrastructural cell organelles. *Proc. Xth Internat. Bot. Congr.*, 57–68.

FREY-WYSSLING A., BOSSHARD H.H. & MÜHLETHALER K. (1956) Die submikroskopische Entwicklung der Hoftüpfel. *Planta*, **47**, 115–126.

FREY-WYSSLING A., GRIESHABER E. & MÜHLETHALER K. (1963) Origin of spherosomes in plant cells. *J. Ultrastr. Res.*, **8**, 506–516.

FREY-WYSSLING A. & KREUTZER E. (1958) Die submikroskopische Entwicklung der Chromoplasten in den Blüten von *Ranunculus repens*. *Planta*, **51**, 104–114.

FREY-WYSSLING A., LOPEZ-SAEZ J.F. & MÜHLETHALER K. (1964) Formation and development of the cell plate. *J. Ultrastr. Res.*, **10**, 422–431.

FREY-WYSSLING A. & MÜHLETHALER K. (1965) 'Ultrastructural Plant Cytology'. Amsterdam, Elsevier.

FREY-WYSSLING A. & MÜLLER H.R. (1957) Differentiation of plasmodesmata and sieve plates. *J. Ultrastr. Res.*, **1**, 38–48.

FREY-WYSSLING A. & STECHER. (1951) Das Flächenwachstum der pflanzlichen Zellwände. *Experientia*, **7**, 420–421.

GAFF D.E., CHAMBERS T.C. & MARKUS K. (1964) Studies of extrafascicular movements of water in the leaf. *Aust. J. Biol. Sci.*, **17**, 581–586.

GAHAN P.B. & MAPLE A.J. (1966) The behaviour of lysosome-like particles during cell differentiation. *J. Exp. Bot.*, **17**, 151–155.

GALL J.G. (1966) Microtubule fine structure. *J. Cell Biol.*, **31**, 639–643.

GANTT E. & ARNOTT H.J. (1963) Chloroplast division in the gametophyte of the fern *Matteuccia struthiopteris*. *J. Cell Biol.*, **19**, 446–448.

GATES R.R. (1911) Pollen formation in *Oenothera gigas*. *Ann. Bot.*, **25**, 909–940.

LITERATURE CITED 507

GAULDEN M.E. (1956) DNA synthesis and X-ray effects at different mitotic stages in grasshopper neuroblasts. *Genetics*, **41**, 645.

GEITLER L. (1948) Notizen zur endomitolischen Polyploidisierung in Trichocyten und Elaiosomen sowie über Kernstructuren bei *Gagea lutea*. *Chromosoma*, **3**, 271–281.

GELFANT S. (1962) Initiation of mitosis in relation to the cell division cycle. *Exp. Cell Res.*, **26**, 395–403.

GELFANT S. (1963a) Patterns of epidermal cell division. *Exp. Cell Res.*, **32**, 521–528.

GELFANT S. (1963b) A new theory on the mechanism of cell division. *Symp. Internat. Soc. Cell Biol.*, **2**, 229–259.

GENTCHEFF G. & GUSTAFSON A. (1939) The double chromosome reproduction in *Spinacia* and its causes. I & II. *Hereditas*, **25**, 349–358.

GIBBS S.P. (1962) Nuclear envelope-chloroplast relationships. *J. Cell Biol.*, **14**, 433–444.

GIBOR A. & GRANICK S. (1964) Plastids and mitochondria: inheritable systems. *Science*, **145**, 890–897.

GIFFORD E.M. & STEWART K.D. (1965) Ultrastructure of vegetative and reproductive apices of *Chenopodium album*. *Science*, **149**, 75–77.

GINZBURG B.Z. (1958) Evidence for a protein component in the middle lamella of plant tissue: a visible site for indolyl acetic acid action. *Nature, Lond.*, **181**, 398–400.

GINZBURG B.Z. (1961) Evidence for a protein gel structure cross-linked by metal cations in the intercellular cement of plant tissue. *J. exp. Bot.*, **12**, 85–107.

GLAUERT A.M. (1965a) The fixation and embedding of biological specimens. in 'Techniques for Electron Microscopy'. Ed. D. H. Kay. 2nd Edn., Chap. VII.

GLAUERT A.M. (1965b) Section staining, cytology, autoradiography and immunochemistry for biological specimens. in 'Techniques for Electron Microscopy'. Ed. D. H. Kay. 2nd Edn., 254–310.

GLAUERT A.M. (1966) Moiré patterns in electron micrographs of a bacterial membrane. *J. Cell Sci.*, **1**, 425–428.

GOLDSTEIN L. (1958) Localization of nucleus-specific protein as shown by transplantation experiments in *Amoeba proteus*. *Exp. Cell Res.*, **15**, 635–637.

GOODCHILD D.J. & BERGERSEN F.J. (1966) Electron microscopy of the infection and subsequent development of soybean nodule cells. *J. Bact.*, **92**, 204–213.

GOODWIN R.H. & AVERS C.J. (1956) Studies on roots. III An analysis of root growth in *Phleum pratense* using photomicrographic records. *Amer. J. Bot.*, **43**, 479–487.

GRAHAM C.F. (1966a) The effect of cell size and DNA content on the cellular regulation of DNA synthesis in haploid and diploid embryos. *Exp. Cell Res.*, **43**, 13–19.

GRAHAM C.F. (1966b) The regulation of DNA synthesis and mitosis in multinucleate frog eggs. *J. Cell Sci.*, **1**, 363–374.

GRANICK S. (1961) The chloroplasts: inheritance, structure, and function. in 'The Cell'. Ed. Brachet & Mirsky, 489–602.

GRAY L.H. & SCHOLES M.E. (1951) The effect of ionizing radiations on the broad bean root. Part VIII Growth rate studies and histological analysis. *Brit. J. Radiol. N.S.*, **24**, 82–92; 176–180; 228–236; 285–291; 348–352.

GREEN D.E. (1964) The mitochondrion. *Sci. Amer.*, Vol. **210**, No. 1, 63–74.

GREEN D.E. & FLEISCHER S. (1963) The role of lipids in mitochrondrial electron transfer and oxidative phosphorylation. *Biochim. Biophys. Acta*, **70**, 554–582.

GREEN J.C. & JENNINGS D.H. (1967) A physical and chemical investigation of the scales produced by the Golgi apparatus within and found on the surface of the cells of *Crysochromulina chiton* Parke et Manton. *J. exp. Bot.*, **18**, 359–370.

GREEN P.B. (1962) Mechanism for plant cellular morphogenesis. *Science*, **138**, 1404–1405.

GREEN P.B. (1963) Cell walls and the geometry of plant growth. in 'Meristems and Differentiation', Brookhaven Symposia in Biology No. **16**, 203–217.

GREEN P.B. (1965a) Pathways of cellular morphogenesis. *J. Cell Biol.*, **27**, 343–363.

GREEN P.B. (1965b) Anion-exchange resin spheres as marking material for wet cell surfaces. *Exp. Cell Res.*, **40**, 195–196.

GREENAWALT J.W. & HALL D.O. (1964) Structural studies on the biogenesis of mitochondria in *Neurospora crassa*. *J. Cell Biol.*, **23**, 38A.

GREENWOOD A.D., LEECH R.M. & WILLIAMS J.P. (1963) The osmiophilic globules of chloroplasts. I Osmiophilic globules as a normal component of chloroplasts and their isolation and composition in *Vicia faba*. *Biochim. Biophys. Acta*, **78**, 148–162.

GRELL K. & SCHWALBACH G. (1965) Elektronenmikroskopische Untersuchungen an der Chromosomen der Dinoflagellaten. *Chromosoma* (Berlin), **17**, 230–245.

GRIFFITHS H.J. & AUDUS L.J. (1964) Oganelle distribution in the statocyte cells of the root-tip of *Vicia faba* in relation to geotropic stimulation. *New Phytol.*, **63**, 319–333.

GRIFFITHS D.A. & ISAAC I. (1966) Host/parasite relationships between tomato and pathogenic isolates of *Verticillium*. *Ann. Appl. Biol.*, **58**, 259–272.

GRUN P. (1963) Ultrastructure of plant plasma and vacuolar membranes. *J. Ultrastr. Res.*, **9**, 198–208.

GRÜNEBERG H. (1967) Gene action in the mammalian X-chromosome. *Genet. Res.*, **9**, 343–357.

GUÉNIN H-A. (1965) Observations sur la structure submicroscopique du complexe axial dans les chromosomes méiotiques chez *Gryllus campestris* et *G. bimaculatus*. *J. Microscopie*, **4**, 749–758.

GUNNING B.E.S. (1965a) The fine structure of chloroplast stroma following aldehyde osmium-tetroxide fixation. *J. Cell. Biol.*, **24**, 79–93.

GUNNING B.E.S. (1965b) The greening process in plastids. I The structure of the prolamellar body. *Protoplasma*, **60**, 111–130.

GURDON J.B. & GRAHAM C.F. (1967) Nuclear changes during cell differentiation. *Sci. Prog. Oxf.*, **55**, 259–277.

HAGEMANN R. (1959) 'Plasmatische Vererbung'. Wittenberg (A Ziemsen Verlag).

HAGEMANN R. (1960) Das Vorkommen von Mischzellen bei einer gaterslebener Herkunft des *Status albomaculatus* von *Antirrhinum majus* L. *Die Kulturpflanze*, **8**, 168–184.

HALDAR D., FREEMAN K. & WORK T.S. (1966) Biogenesis of mitochondria. *Nature, Lond.*, **211**, 9–12.

HALPERIN W. (1966) Single cells, coconut milk and embryogenesis *in vitro*. *Science*, **153**, 1287–1288.

HALPERIN W. & JENSEN W.A. (1967) Ultrastructural changes during growth and embryogenesis in carrot cell cultures. *J. Ultrastr. Res.*, **18**, 428–443.

HALL D.M. (1967) The ultrastructure of wax deposits on plant leaf surfaces. II Cuticular pores and wax formation. *J. Ultrastr. Res.*, **17**, 34–44.

HANCOCK R. & RYSER H.J–P. (1967) Histones in prophase and their possible role in nuclear membrane breakdown. *Nature, London.*, **213**, 701–702.

HAQUE A. (1963) Differential labelling of *Trillium* chromosomes by H₃-thymidine at low temperature. *Heredity*, **18**, 129–133.

HARRIS H. (1965) The ribonucleic acids in the nucleus and cytoplasm of animal cells. *Endeavour*, **24**, 50–56.

HARRIS H. (1967) The reactivation of the red cell nucleus. *J. Cell Sci.*, **2**, 23–32.

HASITSCHKA-JENSCHKE G. (1959) Vergleichende Karyologische Untersuchungen an Antipoden. *Chromosoma (Berlin)*, **10**, 229–267.

HAWKER L.E. (1965) Fine structure of fungi as revealed by electron microscopy. *Biol. Rev.*, **40**, 52–92.

HAWKER L.E., GOODAY M.A. & BRACKER C.E. (1966) Plasmodesmata in fungal cell walls. *Nature, Lond.*, **212**, 635 only.

HAYASHI T. (1964) Role of the cortical gel layer in cytoplasmic streaming. in 'Primitive Motile Systems'. Ed. Allen & Kamiya, 19–29.

HAYFLICK L. & MOORHEAD P.S. (1964) The limited *in vitro* lifetime of human diploid cell strains. *Symp. Internat. Soc. Cell Biol.*, **3**, 155–173.

HEINRICH G. (1966) Die Feinstruktur der Proteinoplasten von *Helleborus corsicus*. *Protoplasma*, **61**, 157–163.

HEJNOWICZ Z. (1961) Anticlinal divisions, intrusive growth, and loss of fusiform initials in nonstoried cambium. *Acta Soc. Bot. Poloniae*, **30**, 730–747.

HEJNOWICZ Z. (1964) Orientation of the partition in pseudotransverse division in cambia of some conifers. *Canad. J. Bot.*, **42**, 1685–1691.

HENDY R.J. (1966) Resemblance of lomasomes of *Pythium debaryanum* to structures recently described in *Chara* and *Nitella*. *Nature, Lond.*, **209**, 1258–1259.

HEPLER P.K. & NEWCOMB E.H. (1963) The fine structure of young tracheary xylem elements arising by redifferentiation of parenchyma in wounded *Coleus* stem. *J. Exp. Bot.*, **14**, 496–503.

HEPLER P.K. & NEWCOMB E.H. (1964) Microtubules and fibrils in the cytoplasm of *Coleus* cells undergoing secondary wall deposition. *J. Cell Biol.*, **20**, 529–534.

HESLOP-HARRISON J. (1962) Origin of exine, *Nature, Lond.*, **195**, 1069–1071.

HESLOP-HARRISON J. (1963a) An ultrastructural study of pollen wall ontogeny in *Silene pendula*. *Grana Pal.*, **4**, 7–24.

HESLOP-HARRISON J. (1963b) Ultrastructural aspects of differentiation in sporogenous tissue. *Soc. Exp. Biol. Symp.*, **17**, 315–340.

HESLOP-HARRISON J. (1963c) Structure and morphogenesis of lamellar systems in grana-containing chloroplasts. *Planta*, **60**, 243–260.

HESLOP-HARRISON J. (1964) Cell walls, cell membranes and protoplasmic connexions during meiosis and pollen development. in 'Pollen Physiology and Fertilization'. Ed. H. F. Linskens.

HESLOP-HARRISON J. (1966a) Cytoplasmic continuities during spore formation in flowering plants. *Endeavour*, **25**, 65–72.

HESLOP-HARRISON J. (1966b) Cytoplasmic connexions between angiosperm meiocytes. *Ann. Bot., Lond. N.S.*, **30**, 221–230.

HICKS R.M. (1965) The fine structure of the transitional epithelium of rat ureter. *J. Cell Biol.*, **26**, 25–48.

HINEGARDNER R.T., RAO B. & FELDMAN D.E. (1964) The DNA synthetic period during early development of the sea urchin egg. *Exp. Cell Res.*, **36**, 53–61.

HODGE A.J., McLEAN J.D. & MERCER F.V. (1956) A possible mechanism for the morphogenesis of lamellar systems in plant cells. *J. Biophysic. Biochem. Cytol.*, **2**, 597–608.

HOFFMAN H. & GRIGG C.W. (1958) An electron microscopic study of mitochondria formation. *Exp. Cell Res.*, **15**, 118–131.

HOFFMAN J.G. (1949) Theory of the mitotic index and its application to tissue growth measurement. *Bull. Math. Biophys.*, **11**, 139–144.

HOLLEMAN J. (1967) Direct incorporation of hydroxyproline into protein of sycamore cells incubated at growth-inhibitory levels of hydroxyproline. *Proc. nat. Acad. Sci., Wash.*, **57**, 50–53.

HOLLIDAY R. (1964) A mechanism for gene conversion in fungi. *Genet. Res.*, **5**, 282–304.

HOLT S.J. & HICKS R.M. (1961) The localization of acid phosphatase in rat liver cells as revealed by combined cytochemical staining and electron microscopy. *J. Biophysic. Biochem. Cytol.*, **11**, 47–66.

HONDA S.I., HONGLADAROM T. & WILDMAN S.G. (1964) Characteristic movements of organelles in streaming cytoplasm of plant cells. in 'Primitive Motile Systems in Cell Biology'. Ed. Allen & Kamiya, 485–502.

HORNE R.W. (1965) Negative staining methods. in 'Techniques for Electron Microscopy'. Ed. D. H. Kay. 2nd Edn., 328–355.

HORNE R. W. & BRENNER, S. (1958) A negative staining technique for high resolution of viruses. *Proc. IVth Int. Conf. Electron Microscopy, Berlin*, **Vol. II**, 625–627.

HORTON R.F. & OSBORNE D.J. (1967) Senescence, abscission and cellulase activity in *Phaseolus vulgaris*. *Nature, Lond.*, **214**, 1086–1088.

HÖSTER H.R. & LIESE, W. (1966) Über das Vorkommen von Reaktionsgewebe in Wurzeln und Asten der Dikotyledonen. *Holzforschung*, **20**, 80–90.

HOWARD A. & DEWEY D.L. (1960) Variation in the period preceding deoxyribonucleic acid synthesis in bean root cells. in 'The Cell Nucleus', London, Butterworth, 155–162.

HOWARD A. & DEWEY D.L. (1961) Non-uniformity of labelling rate during DNA synthesis. *Exp. Cell Res.*, **24**, 623–624.

HOWARD A. & PELC S.R. (1951a) Synthesis of deoxyribose nucleic acid and nuclear incorporation of 35S as shown by autoradiographs. in 'Isotopes in Biochemistry' (CIBA), 138–148.

HOWARD A. & PELC S.R. (1951b) Synthesis of nucleoprotein in bean root cells. *Nature, Lond.*, **167**, 599–600.

HOWARD A. & PELC S.R. (1951c) Nuclear incorporation of P^{32} as demonstrated by autoradiographs. *Exp. Cell Res.*, **2**, 178.

HOWARD A. & PELC S.R. (1953) Synthesis of deoxyribonucleic acid in normal and irradiated cells and its relation to chromosome breakage. *Heredity*, **6**, 261–273. (Supplement).

HUGHES A. (1952) 'The Mitotic Cycle', London, Butterworths.

HUME M. (1913) Connecting threads in graft hybrids. *New Phytol.*, **12**, 216–220.

HUMM D.G. & HUMM J.H. (1966) Hybridization of mitochondrial RNA with mitochondrial and nuclear DNA in agar. *Proc. nat. Acad. Sci., Wash.*, **55**, 114–119.

HUXLEY H.E. & ZUBAY G. (1960) Electron microscope observations on the structure of microsomal particles from *Escherichia coli*. *J. Mol. Biol.*, **2**, 10–18.

HYDE B.B. (1965) Ultrastructure in chromatin. *Progr. Biophys. molec. Biol.*, **15**, 131–148.

HYDE B.B. (1967) Changes in nucleolar ultrastructure associated with differentiation in the root tip. *J. Ultrastr. Res.*, **18**, 25–54.

IMAI Y. (1937) Is the variegation of *Humulus japonica* due to defect cytoplasm? *Z. indukt. Abstamm.–u Vererblehre*, **73**, 598–600.

INOUÉ S. (1964) Organization and function of the mitotic spindle. in 'Primitive Motile Systems in Cell Biology'. Ed. Allen & Kamiya, 549–598.

ITERSON G. van. (1937) A few observations on the hairs of the stamens of *Tradescantia virginica*. *Protoplasma*, **27**, 190–211.

JACOB F. & MONOD J. (1961) Genetic regulatory mechanisms in the synthesis of proteins. *J. Mol. Biol.*, **3**, 318–356.

JACOB J. (1966) Intranucleolar deoxyribonucleic acid components in insect cells as revealed by electron microscopy. *Nature, Lond.*, **211**, 36–38.

JACOBS W.P. (1959) What substance normally controls a given biological process? I Formation of some rules. *Devel. Biol.*, **1**, 527–533.

JENSEN W.A. (1964) Observations on the fusion of nuclei in plants. *J. Cell Biol.*, **23**, 669–672.

JENSEN W.A. (1965a) The ultrastructure and histochemistry of the synergids of cotton. *Amer. J. Bot.*, **52**, 238–256.

JENSEN W.A. (1965b) The ultrastructure and composition of the egg and central cell of cotton. *Amer. J. Bot.*, **52**, 781–797.

JINKS J.L. (1964) 'Extrachromosomal Inheritance'. Prentice-Hall, Englewood Cliffs, New Jersey.

JOHNSON R.P.C. (1966) Potassium permanganate fixation and the electron microscopy of sieve tube contents. *Planta*, **68**, 36–43.

JONES K.W. (1965) The role of the nucleolus in the formation of ribosomes. *J. Ultrastr. Res.*, **13**, 257–262.

JUNIPER B.E. (1960) Growth development and the effect of the environment on the ultrastructure of plant surfaces. *J. Linn. Soc. (Bot.)*, **56**, 413–419.

JUNIPER B.E. (1963) Origin of plasmodesmata between sister cells of the root tips of barley and maize. *J. roy. Micro. Soc.*, **82**, 123–126.

JUNIPER B.E. & BRADLEY D.E. (1958) The carbon replica technique in the study of the ultrastructure of plant surfaces. *J. Ultrastr. Res.*, **2**, 16–27.

JUNIPER B.E. & CLOWES F.A.L. (1965) Cytoplasmic organelles and cell growth in root caps. *Nature, Lond.*, **208**, 864–865.

JUNIPER B.E., GROVES S., LANDAU-SCHACHAR B. & AUDUS L.J. (1966) Root cap and the perception of gravity. *Nature, Lond.*, **209**, 93–94.

JUNIPER B.E. & ROBERTS R.M. (1966) Polysaccharide synthesis and the fine structure of root cap cells. *J. roy. Micro. Soc.*, **85**, 63–72.

KAMIYA N. (1960) Physics and chemistry of protoplasmic streaming. *Annu. Rev. Pl. Physiol.*, **11**, 323–340.

KASSANIS B., TINSLEY T.W. & QUAK F. (1958) The inoculation of tobacco callus tissue with tobacco mosaic virus. *Ann. Appl. Biol.*, **46**, 11–19.

KAVANAU J.L. (1963) Structure and functions of biological membranes. *Nature, Lond.*, **198**, 525–530.

KEEBLE F., NELSON M.G. & SNOW R. (1929) The integration of plant behaviour. I Separate geotropic stimulations of tip and stump in roots. *Proc. roy. Soc.*, **B 105**, 493–498.

KERTESZ Z.I. (1951) 'The Pectic Substances'. Interscience, New York & London.

KEY J.L. & INGLE J. (1964) Requirement for the synthesis of DNA-like RNA for growth of excised plant tissue. *Proc. nat. Acad. Sci., Wash.*, **52**, 1382–1388.

KIRK J.T.O. (1963) The deoxyribonucleic acid of broad bean chloroplasts. *Biochim. Biophys. Acta*, **76**, 417–424.

512   PLANT CELLS

KIRK J.T.O. (1964) DNA-dependent RNA synthesis in chloroplast preparations. *Biochem. Biophys. Res. Comm.*, **14**, 393–397.

KIRK J.T.O. & TILNEY-BASSETT R.A.E. (1967) 'The Plastids'. London, Freeman.

KLEIN S. (1960) The effect of low temperature on the development of the lamellar system in chloroplasts. *J. Biophys. Biochem. Cytol.*, **8**, 529–538.

KLEIN S. & GINZBURG B.Z. (1960) An electron microscope investigation into the effect of EDTA on plant cell walls. *J. Biophys. Biochem. Cytol.*, **7**, 335–338.

KLEINSCHMIDT A.K., LANG D., JACHERTS D. & ZAHN R.K. (1961) Darstellung und Längenmessung des gesamten Desoxyribonucleinsäure Inhaltes von T_2-Bakteriophagen. *Biochim. Biophys. Acta*, **61**, 857–864.

KOEHLER J.K. (1962) The nuclear envelope of *Saccharomyces cerevisiae. J. Ultrastr. Res.*, **6**, 432–436.

KOLLMANN R. (1967) Autoradiographischer Nachweis der Assimilat Transportbahn in sekundären Phloem von *Metasequoia glyptostroboides. Z. Pflanzenphysiologie*, **56**, 401–409.

KOLLMAN R. & SCHUMACHER W. (1961) Über die Feinstruktur des Phloems von *Metasequoia glyptostroboides* und seine jahreszeitliche Veränderung. I Mitteilung das Ruhephloem. *Planta*, **57**, 583–607.

KOLLMAN R. & SCHUMACHER W. (1962) Feinstruktur des Phloems von *Metasequoia glyptostroboides. Planta*, **58**, 366–386.

KOLLMANN R. & SCHUMACHER W. (1962) Über die Feinstruktur des Phloems von *Metasequoia glyptostroboides* und sein jahreszeitlichen Veränderung. III Mitteilung die Reaktivierung der Phloemzellen im Frühjahr. *Planta*, **59**, 195–221.

KOLLMANN R. & SCHUMACHER W. (1964) Über die Feinstruktur des Phloems von *Metasequoia glyptostroboides* und seine jahreszeitlichen Veränderung. v. *Planta*, **63**, 155–190.

KONAR R.N. & LINSKENS H.F. (1966) The morphology and anatomy of the stigma of *Petunia hybrida. Planta*, **71**, 356–371.

KRULL R. (1960) Untersuchungen über den Bau und die Entwicklung der Plasmaodesmen im Rindenparenchym von *Viscum album. Planta*, **55**, 598–629.

KÜNTZEL H. & NOLL H. (1967) Mitochondrial and cytoplasmic polysomes from *Neurospora crassa. Nature. Lond.*, **215**, 1340–1345.

LA COUR L.F. (1949) Nuclear differentiation in the pollen grain. *Heredity*, **3**, 319.

LA COUR L.F. (1966) The internal structure of nucleoli. in 'Chromosomes Today'. Ed. Darlington & Lewis, 150–160.

LA COUR L.F. & PELC S.R. (1958) Effect of colchicine on the utilization of labelled thymidine during chromosome reproduction. *Nature, Lond.*, **182**, 506–508.

LAFONTAINE J.G. & CHOUINARD L.A. (1963) A correlated light and electron microscope study of the nucleolar material during mitosis in *Vicia faba. J. Cell Biol.*, **17**, 167–201.

LAJTHA L.G. (1961) The effect of ionizing radiations and tumourchemotherapeutic agents on the bone marrow. *Progr. Biophys.*, **11**, 79–109.

LAJTHA L.G. (1963) On the concept of the cell cycle. *J. cell. comp. Physiol.*, **62**, Suppl. 1, 143–145.

LAMPORT D.T.A. (1965) The protein component of primary cell walls. in 'Advances in Botanical Research'. Vol. II. Ed. R.D. Preston, 151–213.

LAMPORT D.T.A. & NORTHCOTE D.H. (1960a) The use of tissue cultures for the study of plant cell walls. *Biochem. J.*, **76**, 52.

LAMPORT D.T.A. & NORTHCOTE D.H. (1960b) Hydroxyproline in primary cell walls of higher plants. *Nature, Lond.*, **188**, 665–666.

LARSON D.A. (1963) Cytoplasmic dimorphism within pollen grains. *Nature, Lond.*, **200**, 911–912.

LARSON D.A. (1964) Further electron microscopic studies of exine structure and stratification. *Grana Palynologica*, **5**, 265–276.

LARSON D.A. (1965) Fine structural changes in the cytoplasm of germinating pollen. *Amer. J. Bot.*, **52**, 139–154.

LEADBEATER B. & DODGE J.D. (1967) Fine structure of the dinoflagellate transverse flagellum. *Nature, Lond.*, **213**, 421–422.

LEDBETTER M.C. (1965) The fine structure of the cytoplasm in relation to the plant cell wall. *Agric. Food Chem.*, **13**, 405–407.

LEDBETTER M.C. & PORTER K.R. (1963) A 'microtubule' in plant cell fine structure. *J. Cell Biol.*, **19**, 239–250.

LEDBETTER M.C. & PORTER K.R. (1964) Morphology of microtubules in plant cells. *Science*, **144**, 872–874.

LEHNINGER A.L. (1964) 'The Mitochondrion'. Benjamin, New York & Amsterdam.

LEWIS F.T. (1943) A geometric accounting for diverse shapes of 14-hedral cells: The transition from dodecahedra to tetrakaidecahedra. *Amer. J. Bot.*, **30**, 74–81.

LEWIS K.R. & JOHN B. (1963) 'Chromosome Marker'. Churchill, London.

LIESE W. (1963) Tertiary wall and the warty layer in wood cells. *J. Polymer. Sci.*, **2**, 213–229.

LIESE W. & HÖSTER H-R. (1966) Gelatinöse Bastfasern im Phloem einiger Gymnospermen. *Planta*, **69**, 338–346.

LIESE W. & LEDBETTER M.C. (1963) Occurrence of a warty layer in vascular cells of plants. *Nature, Lond.*, **197**, 201–202.

LIMA-DE-FARIA A. (1956) The role of the Kinetochore in chromosome organization. *Hereditas*, **42**, 83–160.

LIMA-DE-FARIA A. (1962) Progress in tritium autoradiography. *Progr. Biophys.*, **12**, 282–317.

LIMA-DE-FARIA A. & MOSES M.J. (1965) Labelling of *Zea mays* chloroplasts with H^3-thymidine. *Hereditas*, **52**, 367–378.

LINDEGREN C.C. (1962) Origin of the endoplasmic reticulum. *Nature*, **195**, 1225–1227.

LINNANE A.W., VITOLS E. & NOWLAND P.G. (1962) Studies on the origin of yeast mitochondria. *J. Cell Biol.*, **13**, 345–350.

LIVINGSTON L.G. (1935) The nature and distribution of plasmodesmata in the tobacco plant. *Amer. J. Bot.*, **22**, 75–87.

LIVINGSTON L.G. (1964) The nature of plasmodesmata in normal (living) plant tissue. *Amer. J. Bot.*, **51**, 950–957.

LOENING U.E. & INGLE J. (1967) Diversity of RNA components in green plant tissues. *Nature, Lond.*, **215**, 363–367.

LOPEZ-SAEZ J.F. & GIMENEZ-MARTIN G. & RISUENO M.C. (1966) Fine structure of the plasmodesm. *Protoplasma*, **61**, 81–84.

LONGO C. & ARRIGONI O. (1964) Functional properties of isolated plant mitochondria. *Exp. Cell Res.*, **35**, 572–579.

LUCK D.J.L. (1963a) Formation of mitochondria in *Neurospora crassa*. *J. Cell Biol.*, **16**, 483–499.

LUCK D.J.L. (1963b) Genesis of mitochondria in *Neurospora crassa*. *Proc. nat. Acad. Sci., Wash.*, **49**, 233–239.

Lucy J.A. & Glauert A.M. (1964) A micellar model for the lipids of membranes. *Proc. Soc. Gen. Microbiol.*, **2-3.**

Lyndon R.F. (1963) Changes in the nucleus during cellular development in the pea seedling. *J. exp. Bot.*, **14,** 419–430.

McCready R.M., McComb E.A. & Jansen E.F. (1955) The action of tomato and avocado polygalacturonase. *Food Res.*, **20,** 186–191.

Machattie L.A., Berns K.I. & Thomas C.A. (1965) Electron microscopy of DNA from *Hemophilus influenzae*. *J. Mol. Biol.*, **11,** 648–649.

Maclachlan S. & Zalik S. (1963) Plastid structure, chlorophyll concentration, and free amino acid composition of a chlorophyll mutant of barley. *Canad. J. Bot.*, **41,** 1053–1062.

McLeish J. (1964) Deoxyribonucleic acid in plant nucleoli. *Nature, Lond.*, **204,** 36–39.

Mahlberg P.G. (1964) Rates of organelle movement in streaming cytoplasm of plant tissue culture cells. in 'Primitive Motile Systems'. Ed. Allen & Kamiya, 43–68.

Majumdar G.P. & Preston R.D. (1941) The fine structure of collenchyma cells in *Heracleum sphondylium* L. *Proc. roy. Soc. B.*, **130,** 201–217.

Maksymowych R. (1959) Quantitative analysis of leaf development in *Xanthium pensylvanicum*. *Amer. J. Bot.*, **46,** 635–644.

Maltzahn K. von & Mühlethaler K. (1962) Observations on division of mitochondria in dedifferentiating cells of *Splachnum ampullaceum*. *Experientia*, **18,** 315–316.

Maly R. & Wild A. (1956) Ein cytologischer Beitrag zur Entmischungstheorie verschiedener Plastidensarten. *Z. indukt. Abstamn -u Vererblehre*, **87,** 493–496.

Manley R.S.J. (1964) Fine structure of native cellulose microfibrils. *Nature, Lond.*, **204,** 1155–1157.

Manton I. (1957) Observations with the electron microscope on the cell structure of the antheridium and spermatozoid of *Sphagnum*. *J. Exp. Bot.*, **8,** 382–400.

Manton I. (1959a) Electron microscopical observations on a very small flagellate: the problem of *Chromulina pusila*. *J. mar. Biol. Ass. U.K.*, **38,** 319–333.

Manton I. (1959b) Observations on the microanatomy of the spermatozoid of the bracken fern *Pteridium aquilinum*. *J. Biophys. Biochem. Cytol.*, **6,** 413–418.

Manton I. (1960) On a reticular derivative from Golgi bodies in the meristem of *Anthoceros*. *J. Biophys. Biochem. Cytol.*, **8,** 221–231.

Manton I. (1961a) Plant cell structure. in 'Contemporary Botanical Thought'. Ed. MacLeod & Cobley.

Manton I. (1961b) Some problems of mitochondrial growth. *J. exp. Bot.*, **12,** 421–429.

Manton I. (1961c) Observations on phragmosomes. *J. exp. Bot.*, **12,** 108–113.

Manton I. (1962) Observations on stellate vacuoles in the meristem of *Anthoceros*. *J. exp. Bot.*, **13,** 161–167.

Manton I. (1964) Observations with the electron microscope on the division cycle in the flagellate *Prymnesium parvum* Carter. *J. roy. Micro. Soc.*, **83,** 317–325.

Manton I. (1966) Observations on scale production in *Prymnesium parvum*. *J. Cell Sci.*, **1,** 375–380.

Manton I. & Ettl H. (1965) Observations on the fine structure of *Mesostigma viride*. *J. Linn. Soc. (Bot.)*, **59,** 175–184.

MANTON I. & PARK M. (1965) Observations on the fine structure of two species of *Platymonas* with special reference to flagellar scales and the mode of origin of the theca. *J. mar. Biol. Ass. U.K.*, **45**, 743–754.

MANTON I. & STOSCH H.A. von. (1966) Observations on the fine structure of the male gamete of the marine centric diatom *Lithodesmium undulatum*. *J. roy. Micro. Soc.*, **85**, 119–134.

MARKHAM R., FREY S. & HILLS G.J. (1963) Methods for the enhancement of image detail and accentuation of structure in electron microscopy. *Virology*, **20**, 88–102.

MARINOS N.G. (1962) Studies on submicroscopic aspects of mineral deficiencies. I. Calcium deficiency in the shoot apex of barley. *Amer. J. Bot.*, **49**, 834–841.

MARINOS N.G. (1963) Vacuolation in plant cells. *J. Ultrastr. Res.*, **9**, 177–185.

MARINOS N.G. (1967) Multifunctional plastids in the meristematic region of potat tuber buds. *J. Ultrastr. Res.*, **17**, 91–113.

MATCHETT W.H. & NANCE J.F. (1962) Cell wall breakdown and growth in pea seedling stems. *Amer. J. Bot.*, **49**, 311–322.

MATZKE E.B. (1950) In the twinkling of an eye. *Bull. Torrey bot. Cl.*, **77**, 222–227.

MAZLIAK P. (1963) Thèses presentées à la Faculté des Sciences de l'Université de Paris. I. La cire cuticulaire des pommes (*Pirus malus*). II. Propositions données par la Faculté.

MENKE W. (1960a) Weitere Untersuchungen zur Entwicklung der Plastiden von *Oenothera hookeri*. *Z. Naturf.*, **15b**, 479–482.

MENKE W. (1960b) Das allgemeine Bauprinzip des Lamellarsystems der Chloroplasten. *Experientia (Basel)*, **16**, 537–538.

MERCER F.V. & RATHGEBER N. (1962) Nectar secretion and cell membranes. *Vth Inter. Congr. Elec. Mic. Philadelphia*, **2**, WW-11.

MEYER M. (1938) Die submikroskopische Structur der kutinisierter Zellmembranen. *Protoplasma*, **29**, 552–586.

MILLER A., KARLSON U. & BOARDMAN N.K. (1966) Electron microscopy of ribosomes isolated from tobacco leaves. *J. Mol. Biol.*, **17**, 487–489.

MIRSKY A.E. & OSAWA S. (1961) The interphase nucleus. in 'The Cell'. Ed. Brachet & Mirsky, **2**, 677–770.

MITCHISON J.M. (1966) Some functions of the nucleus. *Int. Rev. Cytol.*, **19**, 97–110.

MITTERMAYER C., BRAUN R. & RUSCH H.P. (1965) The effect of actinomycin D on the timing of mitosis in *Physarum Polycephalum*. *Exp. Cell Res.*, **38**, 33–41.

MIZUKAMI I. & GALL J. (1966) Centriole replication. II. Sperm formation in the fern, *Marsilea* and the cycad, *Zamia*. *J. Cell Biol.*, **29**, 97–111.

MOLLENHAUER H.H. & LARSON D.A. (1966) Developmental changes in raphideforming cells of *Vanilla planifolia* and *Monstera deliciosa*. *J. Ultrastr. Res.*, **16**, 55–70.

MOLLENHAUER H.H. & MORRÉ D.J. (1966) Golgi apparatus and plant secretion. *Annu. Rev. Pl. Physiol.*, **17**, 27–46.

MOLLENHAUER H.H., MORRÉ D.J. & KELLEY A.G. (1966) The widespread occurrence of plant cytosomes resembling animal microbodies. *Protoplasma*, **62**, 44–52.

MOLLENHAUER H.H. & WHALEY W.G. (1963) An observation on the functioning of the Golgi apparatus. *J. Cell Biol.*, **17**, 222–225.

MOLLENHAUER H.H., WHALEY W.G. & LEECH J.H. (1961) A function of the Golgi apparatus in outer rootcap cells. *J. Ultrastr. Res.*, **5**, 193–200.

MOOR H. & MÜHLETHALER K. (1963) Fine structure in frozen-etched yeast cells. *J. Cell Biol.*, **17**, 609–628.

516 PLANT CELLS

MOOR H., MÜHLETHALER K., WALDNER H. & FREY-WYSSLING A. (1961) A new freezing ultramicrotome. *J. Biophys. Biochem. Cytol.*, **10**, 1–13.

MORTON R.K. & RAISON J.K. (1963) A complete intracellular unit for incorporation of amino acid into storage utilizing adenosine triphosphate generated from phytate. *Nature. Lond.*, **200**, 429–433.

MOSS G.I. & HESLOP-HARRISON J. (1967) A cytochemical study of DNA, RNA, and protein in the developing maize anther II. *Ann. Bot., Lond. N.S.*, **31**, 555–572.

MOSSE B. (1964) Electron microscope studies of nodule development in some clover species. *J. Gen. Microbiol.*, **36**, 49–66.

MOTA M. (1963) Electron microscope study of the relationship between the nucleus and mitochondria in *Chlorophytum capense*. *Cytologia*, **28**, 409–416.

MOULÉ Y. (1964) Endoplasmic reticulum and microsomes of rat liver. in 'Cellular Membranes in Development'. Ed. Locke, New York & London, Academic Press. 97–131.

MUCKENTHALER F.A. & MAHOWALD A.P. (1966) DNA synthesis in the ooplasm of *Drosophila melanogaster*. *J. Cell Biol.*, **28**, 199–208.

MÜHLETHALER K. (1950a) The structure of plant slimes. *Exp. Cell Res.*, **1**, 341–350.

MÜHLETHALER K. (1950b) Elektronenmikroskopische Untersuchungen über den Feinbau und das Wachstum der Zellmembranen in Mais –und Haterkoleoptilen. *Ber. Schweiz. bot. Ges.*, **60**, 614–628.

MÜHLETHALER K. (1961) Plant cell walls. in 'The Cell'. Ed. Brachet & Mirsky, **2**, 86–134.

MÜHLETHALER K. & FREY-WYSSLING A. (1959) Entwicklung und Struktur der Proplastiden. *J. Biophys. Biochem. Cytol.*, **6**, 507–512.

MÜHLETHALER K., MOOR H. & SZARKOWSKI J.W. (1965) The ultra-structure of the chloroplast lamellae. *Planta*, **67**, 305–323.

MURAKAMI S. (1963) Ribosomes in spinach chloroplasts. *Exp. Cell Res.*, **32**, 398–400.

NADAKAVUKAREN M.J. (1964) Fine structure of negatively stained plant mitochondria. *J. Cell Biol.*, **23**, 193–195.

NAGAI R. & REBHUN L.I. (1966) Cytoplasmic microfilaments in streaming *Nitella* cells. *J. Ultrastr. Res.*, **14**, 571–589.

NASS M.M.K., NASS S. & AFZELIUS B.A. (1965) The general occurrence of mitochondrial DNA. *Exp. Cell Res.*, **37**, 516–539

NASS M.M.K. (1966) The circularity of mitochondrial DNA. *Proc. nat. Acad. Sci.*, *Wash.*, **56**, 1215–1222.

NAYLOR J.M. (1958) Control of nuclear processes by auxin in axillary buds of *Tradescantia paludosa*. *Canad. J. Bot.*, **36**, 221–232.

NEARY G.J., EVANS H.J. & TONKINSON S.M. (1959) A quantitative determination of the mitotic delay induced by Gamma radiation in broad bean root meristems. *J. Genet.*, **56**, 363–394.

NEGBI M., BALDEV B. & LANG A. (1964) Studies on the orientation of the mitotic spindle in the shoot apex of *Hyoscyamus niger* and other rosette plants. *Israel J. Bot.*, **13**, 134–153.

NĚMEC B. (1901) Über die Wahrnehmung des Schwerkraftreizes bei den Pflanzen. *Jb. wiss. Bot.*, **36**, 80–178.

NEWCOMB E.H. (1963) Cytoplasm—cell wall relationships. *Annu. Rev. Pl. Physiol.*, **14**, 43–64.

NEWCOMB E.H. (1967) Fine structure of protein-storing plastids in bean root tips. *J. Cell Biol.*, **33**, 143–163.

NEWCOMB E.H. & BONNETT H.T. (1965) Cytoplasmic microtubule and wall microfibril orientation in root hairs of radish. *J. Cell Biol.*, **27**, 575–589.

NIEUWDORP P.J. & BUYS M.C. (1964) Electron microscopic structure of the epithelial cells of the scutellum of barley. II. Cytology of the cells during germination. *Act. Bot. Neerlandica*, **13**, 559–565.

NITSAN J. & LANG A. (1966) DNA synthesis in the elongating non-dividing cells of the lentil epicotyl and its promotion by gibberellin. *Plant Physiol.*, **41**, 965–970.

NOLL H. (1967) Characterization of macromolecules by constant velocity sedimentation. *Nature. Lond.* **215**, 360–363.

NOODEN L.D. & THIMANN K.V. (1963) Evidence for a requirement for protein synthesis for auxin-induced cell enlargement. *Proc. nat. Acad. Sci., Wash.*, **50**, 194–200.

NORRIS R.E. (1966) Unarmoured marine dinoflagellates. *Endeavour*, **25**, 124–128.

NORTHCOTE D.H. (1963) The biology and chemistry of the cell walls of higher plants, algae and fungi, *International Review of Cytology*, **14**, 223–265.

NORTHCOTE D.H. & PICKETT-HEAPS J.D. (1966) A function of the Golgi apparatus in polysaccharide synthesis and transport in the root-cap cells of wheat. *Biochem. J.*, **98**, 159–167.

NORTHCOTE D.H. & WOODING F.B.P. (1966) Development of sieve tubes in *Acer pseudoplatanus. Proc. roy. Soc. B.*, **163**, 524–537.

NOUGARÈDE A. & PILET P-E. (1964) Infrastructure des cellules du scutellum du *Triticum vulgare* au cours des premières phases de la germination. *C.R. Acad. Sci., Paris*, **258**, 2641–2644.

NOVIKOFF A.B. (1961) Lysosomes and related particles. in 'The Cell'. Ed. Brachet & Mirsky, New York & London, Academic Press, **2**, 423–488.

NUTMAN P.S. (1959) Sources of incompatibility affecting nitrogen fixation in legume symbiosis. Symposia of the Society for Experimental Biology, **13**. 'Utilization of nitrogen and its compounds by plants', 42–58.

OATLEY C.W. & SMITH K.C.A. (1955) The scanning electron microscope and its fields of application. *Brit. J. Appl. Physiol.*, **6**, 391–399.

O'BRIEN T.P. & THIMANN K.V. (1966) Intracellular fibres in oat coleoptile cells and their possible significance in cytoplasmic streaming. *Proc. nat. Acad. Sci., Wash.*, **56**, 888–894.

O'BRIEN T.P. & THIMANN K.V. (1967) Observations on the fine structure of the oat coleoptile. III. Some aspects of the vascular system. *Protoplasma*, **63**, 443–478.

O'BRIEN T.W. & KALF G.F. (1967) Ribosomes from rat liver mitochondria. I. Isolation procedure and contamination. II. Partial characterization. *J. Biol. Chem.*, **242**, 2172–2185.

O'KELLEY J.C. & CARR P.H. (1954) An electron micrographic study of the cell walls of elongating cotton fibers, root hairs and pollen tubes. *Amer. J. Bot.*, **41**, 261–264.

ÖPIK H. (1965) The form of nuclei in the storage cells of the cotyledons of germinating seeds of *Phaseolus vulgaris. Exp. Cell Res.*, **38**, 517–522.

ÖPIK H. (1966) Changes in cell fine structure in the cotyledons of *Phaseolus vulgaris* during germination. *J. exp. Bot.*, **17**, 427–439.

ORDIN L., CLELAND R. & BONNER J. (1955) Influence of auxin on cell wall metabolism. *Proc. nat. Acad. Sci., Wash.*, **41**, 1023–1029.

PAGE D.H. & SARGENT J.W. (1965) Ultrathin sections of softwood tracheids and paper. *Nature, Lond.*, **207**, 217–218.

PAINTER T.S. (1964) Fundamental chromosome structure. *Proc. nat. Acad. Sci., Wash.*, **51**, 1282–1285.

PAINTER T.S. & BIESELE J.J. (1966) Endomitosis and polyribosome formation. *Proc. nat. Acad. Sci., Wash.*, **56**, 1920–1925.

PAOLILLO D.J. jr. (1962) The plastids of *Isoetes howellii. Amer. J. Bot.*, **49**, 590–598.

PARK R.B. (1965) Subsctructure of chloroplast lamellae. *J. Cell Biol.*, **27**, 151–161.

PARK R.B. & PON N.G. (1961) Correlation of structure with function in *Spinacia oleracea* chloroplasts. *J. Mol. Biol.*, **3**, 1–10.

PARSONS J.A. (1965) Mitochondrial incorporation of tritiated thymidine in *Tetrahymena pyriformis. J. Cell Biol.*, **25**, 641–646.

PASTEELS J. & LISON L. (1950) Recherches histophotométriques sur la teneur en acide désoxyribosenucléique au cours de mitoses somatiques. *Arch. Biol.*, (*Liege*), **61**, 445–474.

PATAU K. & DAS N.K. (1959) Induced cell reproduction in differentiated tissue. *Proc. IXth Internat. Bot. Congress*, **2A**, 27–28.

PEACHEY L.D. (1964) Electron microscope observations on the accumulation of divalent cations in intramitochondrial granules. *J. Cell Biol.*, **20**, 95–111.

PEACOCK W.J. (1963) Chromosome duplication and structure as determined by autoradiography. *Proc. nat. Acad. Sci., Wash.*, **49**, 793–801.

PEASE D.C. (1963) The ultrastructure of flagellar fibrils. *J. Cell Biol.*, **18**, 313–326.

PEEL A.J. & WEATHERLEY P.E. (1962) Studies in sieve-tube exudation through aphid mouth-parts: the effects of light and girdling. *Ann. Bot., Lond. N.S.*, **26**, 633–646.

PELC S.R. & LA COUR L.F. (1959) Some aspects of replication in chromosomes. in 'The Cell Nucleus', 232–239.

PELC S.R. & LA COUR L.F. (1959) The incorporation of H³ thymidine in newly differentiated nuclei of roots of *Vicia faba*. Experientia, **15**, 131–133.

PEREZ DEL CERRO M.I. (1961) The action of ribonuclease on root tip cells, an electron microscope study. *Exp. Cell Res.*, **24**, 580–584.

PERNER E. (1965) Elektronen mikroskopische Untersuchungen an Zellen von Embryonen im Zustand völliger Samenruhe. I. Die zelluläre Strukturordnung in der Radicula lufttrockner Samen von *Pisum sativum*. Planta, **65**, 334–357.

PERRY R.P. (1966) Nucleolus: structure and function. *Science*, **153**, 214–219.

PEVELING E. (1961) Elektronenmikroskopische Untersuchungen an Zellkernen von *Cucumis sativus*. Planta, **56**, 530–554.

PICKEN L.E.R. (1960) 'The Organization of Cells and Other Organisms'. Oxford, Clarendon Press.

PICKETT-HEAPS J.D. (1967a) Further observations on the Golgi apparatus and its functions in cells of the wheat seedling. *J. Ultrastr. Res.*, **18**, 287–303.

PICKETT-HEAPS J.D. (1967b) The effects of colchicine on the ultrastructure of dividing plant cells, xylem wall differentiation and distribution of microtubules. *Devel. Biol.*, **15**, 206–236.

PICKETT-HEAPS J.D. & NORTHCOTE D.H. (1966a) Relationship of cellular organelles to the formation and development of the plant cell wall. *J. exp. Bot.*, **17**, 20–26.

PICKETT-HEAPS J.D. & NORTHCOTE D.H. (1966b) Cell division in the formation of the stomatal complex of the young leaves of wheat. *J. Cell Sci.*, **1**, 121–128.

PICKETT-HEAPS J.D. & NORTHCOTE D.H. (1966c) Organization of microtubules and endoplasmic reticulum during mitosis and cytokinesis in wheat meristems. *J. Cell Sci.*, **1**, 109–120.

PORTER K.R. (1961) The endoplasmic reticulum: some current interpretations of its forms and functions. in 'Biological Structure and Function'. Ed. Goodwin & Lindberg, New York & London, Academic Press, 127–155.

PORTER K.R. & CAULFIELD J.B. (1958) The formation of the cell plate during cytokinesis in *Allium cepa* L. *Proc. IVth Internat. Conf. Electron Microscopy, Berlin*, Vol. II, 503–509.

PORTER K.R. & MACHADO R.D. (1960) Studies on the endoplasmic reticulum. IV. Its form and distribution during mitosis in cells of onion root tip. *J. Biophys. Biochem. Cytol.*, 7, 167–180.

PRESTON R.D. (1948) The fine structure of the wall of the conifer tracheid. III. Dimensional relationships in the central layer of the secondary wall. *Biochim. Biophys. Acta*, 2, 370–383.

PRESTON R.D. (1961) Cellulose-protein complexes in plant cell walls. in 'Macromolecular Complexes'. Ed. Edds, New York, Ronald Press, 229–253.

PRESTON R.D. (1964) Structural plant polysaccharides. *Endeavour*, 23, 153–159.

PRESTON R.D. (1965–1966) Physical approaches to some botanical problems. *The Advancement of Science*, 22, 1–15.

PRESTON R.D. & KUYPER B. (1951) Electron microscopic investigations of the walls of green algae. *J. exp. Bot.*, 2, 247–256.

PRIESTLEY J.H. (1930) Studies in the physiology of cambial activity. II. The concept of sliding growth. *New Phytol.*, 29, 96.

QUASTLER H. & SHERMAN F.G. (1959) Cell population kinetics in the intestinal epithelium of the mouse. *Exp. Cell Res.*, 17, 420–438.

RABINOWITZ M., SINCLAIR J., DE SALLE L., HASELKORN R. & SWIFT H. (1965) Isolation of deoxyribonucleic acid from mitochondria of chick embryo. *Proc. nat. Acad. Sci., Wash.*, 53, 1126–1133.

RADLEY J.M. (1965) Deoxyribonucleic acid content of basal cells of mouse epidermis. *Nature, Lond.*, 205, 594.

RAE P.M.M. (1966) Whole mount electron microscopy of *Drosophila* salivary chromosomes. *Nature, Lond.*, 212, 139–142.

RAJAN K.T. (1966) Lysosomes and gout. *Nature, Lond.*, 210, 959–960.

RASCH E., SWIFT H. & KLEIN R.M. (1959) Nucleoprotein changes in plant tumor growth. *J. Biophys. Biochem. Cytol.*, 6, 11–34.

RAYNS D.G., SIMPSON F.O. & BERTAUD W.S. (1967) Transverse tubule apertures in mammalian myocardial cells: surface array. *Science*, 156, 656–657.

READ J. (1959) 'Radiation Biology of *Vicia faba* in Relation to the General Problem'. Oxford, Blackwell Scientific Publications.

RENNER O. (1934) Die Pflanzlichen Plastiden als selbständige Elemente der genetischen Konstitution. *Ber. Sächs. Akad. Wiss. nat. Klasse*, 86, 241–266.

RENNER O. (1936) Zur Kenntnis der nichtmendelnden Buntheit der Laubblätter. *Flora*, 130, 218–290.

RENNER O. (1937) Zur Kenntnis der Plastiden-und Plasma-vererbung. *Cytologia Jubilee*, Vol. 2, 644–653.

RICH A. (1963) Polyribosomes. *Sci. Amer.*, 209, 44–53.

RIS H. (1962) Interpretation of ultrastructure in the cell nucleus. *Symp. Internat. Soc. Cell Biol.*, 1, 69–88.

RIS H. (1963) Ultrastructure of the cell nucleus. in 'Funktionelle und Morphologische Organisation der Zelle'. Springer-Verlag, 3–14.

S

RIS H. & PLAUT W. (1962) Ultrastructure of DNA-containing areas in the chloroplasts of *Chlamydomonas*. *J. Cell Biol.*, **13**, 383–391.

RIS H. & SINGH R.N. (1961) Electron microscope studies on blue-green algae. *J. Biophys. Biochem. Cytol.*, **9**, 63–80.

ROBARDS A. W. (1968) Desmotubule—a plasmodesmetal substructure. *Nature*, **218**, 784.

ROBBELEN G. (1966) Chloroplastendifferenzierung nach geninduzierter Plastommutation bei *Arabidopsis thaliana*. *Z. Pflanzenphys.*, **55**, 387–403.

ROBERTSON J.D. (1962) The membrane of the living cell. *Sci. Amer.*, **206** (4), 64–72.

ROBERTSON J.D. (1964) Unit membranes: a review with recent new studies of experimental alterations and a new subunit structure in synaptic membranes. in 'Cellular Membranes in Development'. Ed. Locke, 1–96.

ROBINSON E. & BROWN R. (1953) Cytoplasmic particles in bean root cells. *Nature, Lond.*, **171**, 313.

ROELOFSEN P.A. (1954) On the softening of fruits of *Mespilus germanica*. *Acta Bot. Neerlandica*, **3**, 154–160.

ROELOFSEN P.A. (1965) Ultrastructure of the wall in growing cells, and its relation to the direction of growth. in 'Advances in Botanical Research'. Ed. R.D. Preston. New York & London, Academic Press, **2**, 69–149.

ROELOFSEN P.A. & HOUWINK A.L. (1953) Architecture and growth of the primary cell wall in some plant hairs and in *Phycomyces* sporangiophore. *Acta Bot. Neerlandica*, **2**, 218–225.

ROSEN W.G. & GAWLIK S.R. (1966a) Fine structure of lily pollen tubes following various fixation and staining procedures. *Protoplasma*, **61**, 181–191.

ROSEN W.G. & GAWLIK S.R. (1966b) Relation of lily pollen tube fine structure to pistil compatibility and mode of nutrition. *Proc. VIth Internat. Congr. Electron Microscopy, Kyoto*, 313–314.

ROSEN W.G., GAWLIK S.R., DASHEK W.V. & SIEGESMUND K.A. (1964) Fine structure and cytochemistry of *Lilium* pollen tubes. *Amer. J. Bot.*, **51**, 61–71.

ROTH L.E. & DANIELS E.W. (1962) Electron microscopic studies of mitosis in amebae. II. The giant ameba *Pelomyxa carolinensis*. *J. Cell Biol.*, **12**, 57–78.

ROTH T.F. (1966) Changes in the synaptinemal complex during meiotic prophase in mosquito oocytes. *Protoplasma*, **61**, 346–386.

ROWLEY J.R., MÜHLETHALER K. & FREY-WYSSLING A. (1959) A route for the transfer of materials through the pollen grain wall. *J. Biophys. Biochem. Cytol.*, **6**, 537–538.

ROWLEY J.R. & SOUTHWORTH D. (1967) Deposition of sporopollenin on lamellae of unit membrane dimensions. *Nature, Lond.*, **213**, 703–704.

RUCH F. & HENGARTNER H. (1960) Quantitative Bestimmung der Ligninverteilung in der pflanzlichen Zellwand. *Beih. Zeitschriften. Schweiz. Forstrer.*, **30**, 75–90.

SABATINI D.D., BENSCH K. & BARRNETT R.J. (1963) The preservation of cellular ultrastructure and enzymatic activity by aldehyde fixation. *J. Cell Biol.*, **17**, 19–58.

SACHS I.B. (1963) Torus of the bordered-pit membrane in conifers. *Nature, Lond.*, **198**, 906–907.

SACHSENMAIER W. & RUSCH H.P. (1964) The effect of 5-fluoro-2-deoxyuridine on synchronous mitosis in *Physarum polycephalum*. *Exp. Cell Res.*, **36**, 124–133.

SAGER R. (1959) The architecture of the chloroplast in relation to its photosynthetic activities. *Brookhaven Symp. Biol.*, **11**, 101–117.

SAGER R. & RAMANIS Z. (1963) The particulate nature of nonchromosomal genes in *Chlamydomonas. Proc. nat. Acad. Sci., Wash.,* **50,** 260–268.

SALPETER M.M. & BACHMANN L. (1964) Autoradiography with the electron microscope. *J. Cell Biol.,* **22,** 469–477.

SAMPSON M., CLARKSON D. & DAVIES D.D. (1965) DNA synthesis in aluminium treated roots of barley. *Science,* **148,** 1476–1477.

SAMPSON M. & DAVIES D.D. (1966) Synthesis of a metabolically labile DNA in the maturing root cells of *Vicia faba. Exp. Cell Res.,* **43,** 669–673.

SASSEN M.M.A. (1964) Growth and breakdown of cell walls. *Proc. IIIrd Europ. Reg. Conf. Electron Microscopy, Prague,* 147.

SASSEN M.M.A. (1965) Breakdown of the plant cell wall during the cell fusion process. *Acta Bot. Neerlandica,* **14,** 165–196.

SATINA S. (1959) Chimeras. in 'Blakeslee: The Genus *Datura*'. Ed. Avery, Satina & Rietsema, New York, Ronald Press, 132–151.

SAX K. & SWANSON C.P. (1941) Differential sensitivity of cells to X-rays. *Amer. J. Bot.,* **28,** 52–59.

SCHARFF M.D. & ROBBINS E. (1966) Polyribosome disaggregation during metaphase. *Science,* **151,** 992–995.

SCHJEIDE O.A., McCANDLESS R.G. & MUNN R.J. (1964) Mitochondrial morphogenesis. *Nature, Lond.,* **203,** 158–160.

SCHMID R. (1965) The fine structure of pits in hardwoods. in 'Cellular Ultrastructure of Woody Plants'. Ed. Coté, 291–304.

SCHMID R. & LIESE W. (1964) Über die mikromorphologischen Veränderung der Zellwandstrukturen von Buchen-und Fichtenholz beim Abbau durch *Polyporus versicolor* (L.) Fr. *Archiv. Mikrobiol.,* **47,** 260–276.

SCHNEPF E. (1960) Zur Feinstruktur der Drüsen von *Drosophyllum lusitanicum. Planta,* **54,** 641–674.

SCHNEPF E. (1961) Licht-und elektronmikroskopische Beobachtungen an Insektivoren - Drüsen über die Sekretion des Fangschleimes. *Flora,* **151,** 73–87.

SCHNEPF E. (1961) Quantitative Zusammenhänge zwischen der Sekretion des Fangschleimes und den Golgi Strukturen bei *Drosophyllum lusitanicum. Z. Naturf.,* **16B,** 605–610.

SCHNEPF E. (1966) Feinbau und Funktion pflanzlicher Drüsen. *Umschau. Wiss. Technik.,* **16,** 522–527.

SCHNEPF E. & KOCH W. (1966a) Über die Entstehung der pulsierenden Vacuolen von *Vacuolaria virescens* (Chloromonadophycae) aus dem Golgi-Apparat. *Archiv. Mikrobiol.,* **54,** 229–236.

SCHNEPF E. & KOCH W. (1966b) Golgi-Apparat und Wasserausscheidung bei *Glaucocystis. Z. Pflanzerphysiol.,* **55,** 97–109.

SCHOETZ F. (1956) The process of photosynthesis in various varieties of plumed oenotheres. *Photogr. u. Forsch.,* **7,** 12–16.

SCHOETZ F. (1965) Zur Frage der Vermehrung der Thylakoidschichten in den Chloroplasten. *Planta,* **64,** 376–380.

SCHOETZ F. & SENSER F. (1964) Untersuchungen über die Chloroplastenenlwicklung bei *Oenothera.* III. Der Pictirubata-Typ. *Planta,* **63,** 191–212.

SCHRÖDER K.H. (1962) Mikroskopische Untersuchungen über die Vermehrung der Plastiden im Scheitelmeristem und in den Blättern von *Oenothera albilaeta. Z. Bot.,* **50,** 348–367.

SCHUSTER F.L. (1965) A deoxyribose nucleic acid component in mitochondria of *Didymium nigripes*, a slime mold. *Exp. Cell Res.*, **39**, 329–345.

SCHWEIGER H.G. & SCHWEIGER E. (1965) The role of the nucleus in a cytoplasmic diurnal rhythm. in 'Circadian Clocks'. Ed. Aschoff, Amsterdam, North-Holland, 195–197.

SCOTT D. & EVANS H.J. (1964) Influence of the nucleolus on DNA synthesis and mitosis in *Vicia faba*. *Exp. Cell Res.*, **36**, 145–159.

SCOTT D. & EVANS H.J. (1964) On the non-requirement for deoxyribonucleic acid synthesis in the production of chromosome aberrations by 8-ethoxycaffeine. *Mutation Res.*, **1**, 146–156.

SETTERFIELD G. (1961) Structure and composition of plant cell organelles in relation to growth and development. *Canad. J. Bot.*, **39**, 469–489.

SETTERFIELD G. & BAILEY S.T. (1957) Studies on the mechanism of deposition and extension of primary cell walls. *Canad. J. Bot.*, **35**, 435–444.

SETTERFIELD G. & BAILEY S.T. (1958) Deposition of wall material in thickened primary walls of elongating plant cells. *Exp. Cell Res.*, **14**, 622–625.

SHAW G. & YEADON A. (1966) Chemical studies on the constitution of some pollen and spore membranes. *J. Chem. Soc.*, **1**, 16–22.

SHEPHARD D.C. (1965) Chloroplast multiplication and growth in the unicellular alga *Acetabularia mediterranea*. *Exp. Cell Res.*, **37**, 93–110.

SHEPPERD D.E. & ENGLESBERG E. (1967) Further evidence for positive control of the L-arabinose system by gene *ara*C. *J. Mol. Biol.*, **25**, 443–454.

SIEVERS A. (1963) Beteiligung des Golgi-Apparates bei der Bildung der Zellwand von Wurzelhaaren. *Protoplasma*, **56**, 188–192.

SIMMEL E.B. & KARNOFSKY D.A. (1961) Observations on the uptake of tritiated thymidine in the pronuclei of fertilized sand dollar embryos. *J. Biophys. Biochem. Cytol.*, **10**, 59–65.

SIMON E.W. & CHAPMAN J.A. (1961) The development of mitochondria in *Arum spadix*. *J. exp. Bot.*, **12**, 414–420.

SINGH M. & HILDEBRANDT A.C. (1966) Movements of TMV inclusion bodies within tobacco callus cells. *Virology*, **30**, 134–142.

SINNOTT E.W. (1939) The cell-organ relation in plant organization. *Growth (Suppl.)*, *Symp.*, **3**, 77.

SINNOTT E.W. (1944) Cell polarity and the development of form in cucurbit fruits. *Amer. J. Bot.*, **31**, 388–391.

SINNOTT E.W. & BLOCH R. (1941) Division of vacuolate plant cells. *Amer. J. Bot.*, **28**, 225–232.

SINNOTT E.W. & BLOCH R. (1945) The cytoplasmic basis of intercellular patterns in vascular differentiation, *Amer. J. Bot.*, **32**, 151–156.

SISKEN J.E. (1959) The synthesis of nucleic acids and proteins in the nuclei of *Tradescantia* root tips. *Exp. Cell Res.*, **16**, 602–614.

SJÖSTRAND F.S. (1963) A new repeat structural element of mitochondrial and certain cytoplasmic membranes. *Nature, Lond.*, **199**, 1262–1264.

SJÖSTRAND F.S., CEDERGREN E.A. & KARLSSON U. (1964) Myelin-like figures formed from mitochondrial material. *Nature, Lond.*, **202**, 1075–1079.

SLAUTTERBACH D.B. (1963) Cytoplasmic microtubules. *J. Cell Biol.*, **18**, 367–388.

SNOAD B. (1955) Somatic instability of chromosome number in *Hymenocallis calathinum*. *Heredity*, **9**, 129–134.

SOMA K. & BALL E. (1963) Studies of the surface growth of the short apex of *Lupinus albus*. *Brookhaven Symp. Biol.*, **16**, 13–45.

SOROKIN H.P. & SOROKIN S. (1966) The spherosomes of *Campanula persicifolia*. *Protoplasma*, **62**, 216–236.

SOUTHORN W. A. (1966) Electron microscope studies on the latex of *Hevea brasiliensis*. *VIth Internat. Congr. for Electron Microscopy, Kyoto*, 385–386.

SPANNER D.C. (1958) The translocation of sugar in sieve tubes. *J. exp. Bot.*, **9**, 332–342.

SPARROW A.H. (1951) Radiation sensitivity of cells during mitotic and meiotic cyles with emphasis on possible cytochemical changes. *Ann. N.Y. Acad. Sci.*, **51**, 1508–1540.

SPARROW A.H. & Evans H.J. (1961) Nuclear factors affecting radiosensitivity. I. The influence of nuclear size and structure, chromosome complement, and DNA content. *Brookhaven Symp. Biol.*, **14**, 76–100.

SRIVASTAVA L.M. (1966) On the fine structure of the cambium of *Fraxinus americana*. *J. Cell Biol.*, **31**, 79–93.

SRIVASTAVA L.M. & O'BRIEN T.P. (1966a) On the ultrastructure of cambium and its vascular derivatives. I. Cambium of *Pinus strobus* L. *Protoplasma*, **61**, 257–276.

SRIVASTAVA L.M. & O'BRIEN T.P. (1966b) On the ultrastructure of cambium and its vascular derivatives. II. Secondary phloem of *Pinus strobus* L. *Protoplasma*, **61**, 277–293.

STANGE L. (1965) Plant cell differentiation. *Annu. Rev. Pl. Physiol.*, **16**, 119–140.

STEBBINS G.L. (1966) Polarity gradients and the development of cell patterns. in 'Trends in Plant Morphogenesis'. Ed. Cutter, 115–139.

STEFFENSEN D.M. & SHERIDAN W.F. (1965) Incorporation of H^3-thymidine into chloroplast DNA of marine algae. *J. Cell Biol.*, **25**, 619–626.

STEFFEN K. & WALTER F. (1958) Die Chromoplasten von *Solanum capsicasrtum* und ihre Genese. *Planta*, **50**, 640–670.

STEVENS B.J. & SWIFT H. (1966) RNA transport from nucleus to cytoplasm in *Chironomus* salivary glands. *J. Cell Biol.*, **31**, 55–77.

STEWARD F.C. (1966) Physiological aspects of organization. in 'Trends in Plant Morphogenesis'. Ed. Cutter.

STOECKENIUS W. (1963) Some observations on negatively stained mitochondria. *J. Cell Biol.*, **17**, 443–454.

STOCKING C.R. & GIFFORD E.M. (Jr.) (1959) Incorporation of thymidine into chloroplasts of *Spirogyra*. *Biochem. Biophys. Res. Commun.*, **1**, 159–164.

STRUGGER S. (1957a) Der elektron mikroskopische Nachweis von Plasmodesmen mit Hilfe der Uranylimprägnierung an Wurzelmeristemen. *Protoplasma*, **48**, 231–236.

STRUGGER S. (1957b) Elektronenmikroskopische Beobachtungen an den Plasmodesmen des Urmeristems der Wurzelspitze von *Allium cepa*. *Protoplasma*, **48**, 365–367.

STUBBE W. (1958) Dreifarbenpanaschierung bei *Oenothera*. II. Wechselwirkungen zwischen Geweben mit zwei erblich verschiedenen Plastidensorten. *Z.–u Vererblehre*, **89**, 189–203.

STUTZ E. & NOLL H. (1967) Characterization of cytoplasmic and chloroplast polysomes in plants: Evidence for three classes of ribosomal RNA in nature. *Proc. nat. Acad. Sci., Wash.*, **57**, 774–781.

SWIFT H. (1950) The constancy of desoxyribose nucleic acid in plant nuclei. *Proc. nat. Acad. Sci., Wash.*, **36**, 643–654.

TAMULEVICH S.R. & EVERT R.F. (1966) Aspects of sieve element ultrastructure in *Primula obconica. Planta*, **69**, 319–337.

TAYLOR J.H. (1957) The time and mode of duplication of chromosomes. *Amer. Nat.*, **91**, 209–221.

TAYLOR J.H. (1958) The mode of chromosome duplication in *Crepis capillaris. Exp. Cell Res.*, **15**, 350–357.

TAYLOR J.H. (1961) The growth of the nucleus. in '*Handbuch der Pflanzenphysiologie*'. Ed. Ruhland, **14**, 227–236.

TAYLOR J.H. & McMASTER R.D. (1954) Autoradiographic and microphotometric studies of desoxyribose nucleic acid during microgametogenesis in *Lilium longiflorum. Chromosoma*, **6**, 489–521.

TAYLOR J.H., WOODS P.S. & HUGHES W.L. (1957) The organization and duplication of chromosomes as revealed by autoradiographic studies using tritium-labelled thymidine. *Proc. nat. Acad. Sci.*, **43**, 122–127.

TAYLOR M.M. & STORCK R. (1964) Uniqueness of bacterial ribosomes. *Proc. nat. Acad. Sci.* **52**, 958–965.

TEWARI K.K. & WILDMAN S.G. (1966) Chloroplast DNA from tobacco leaves. *Science*, **153**, 1269–1271.

THAINE R. (1962) A translocation hypothesis based on the structure of plant cytoplasm. *J. exp. Bot.*, **13**, 152–160.

THAINE R. (1964) The protoplasmic streaming theory of phloem transport. *J. exp. Bot.*, **15**, 470–484.

THAINE R. (1965) Surface associations between particles and the endoplasmic reticulum in protoplasmic streaming. *New Phytol.*, **64**, 118–130.

THIELKE C. (1954) Die histologische Struktur des Sprossvegetationskegels einiger Commelinaceen unter Berücksichtigung panaschierter Formen. *Planta*, **44**, 18–74.

THIELKE C. (1955) Die Struktur des Vegetationskegels einer sektorial panaschierten *Hemerocallis fulva. Ber. dtsch. bot. Ges.*, **68**, 233–238.

THIMANN K.V. & CURRY G.M. (1961) Phototropism. in 'Light and Life'. Ed. McElroy & Glass, Baltimore, Johns Hopkins Press, 646–672.

THOMPSON D.W. (1942) 'On Growth and Form'. Cambridge University Press.

THOMPSON E.W. & PRESTON R.D. (1967) Proteins in the cell walls of some green algae. *Nature, Lond.*, **213**, 684–685.

THOMSON W.W. & LIU L.L. (1967) Ultrastructural features of the salt gland of *Tamarix aphylla. Planta*, **73**, 201–220.

THOMSON W.W., WEIER T.E. & DREVER H. (1964) Electron microscopic studies on chloroplasts from phosphorus deficient plants. *Amer. J. Bot.*, **51**, 933–938.

THOMSON W.W. (1966) Ultrastructural development of chromoplasts in Valencia oranges. *Bot. Gaz.*, **127**, 133–139.

THORNBER J.P. & NORTHCOTE D.H. (1961) Changes in the chemical composition of a cambial cell during its differentiation into xylem and phloem tissue in trees. *Biochem. J.*, **81**, 449–455.

TILNEY-BASSETT R.A.E. (1963) The structure of periclinal chimeras. I. The analysis of periclinal chimeras. *Heredity*, **18**, 265–285.

TORREY J.G. (1955) On the determination of vascular patterns during tissue differentiation in excised pea roots. *Amer. J. Bot.*, **42**, 183–198.

TORREY J.G. (1957) Auxin control of vascular pattern formation in regenerating pea root meristems grown *in vitro*. *Amer. J. Bot.*, **44**, 859–870.

TORREY J.G. (1959) 'Experimental Modification of Development in the Root Cell, *Organism and Milieu*.' Ed. D. Rudnik, 189–222.

TORREY J.G. (1961) Kinetin as trigger for mitosis in mature endomitotic plant cells. *Exp. Cell Res.*, **23**, 281–299.

TORREY J.G. (1963) Cellular patterns in developing roots. *Symp. Soc. exp. Biol.*, **17**, 285–314.

TORREY J.G. & REINERT J. (1961) Suspension cultures of higher plant cells in synthetic media. *Plant Physiol.*, **36**, 483–491.

TS'O, P.O.P. (1962) The ribosomes—ribonucleoprotein particles. *Annu. Rev. Pl. Physiol.*, **13**, 45–80.

TUPPER-CAREY R.M. & PRIESTLEY J.H. (1923) The composition of the cell wall at the apical meristem of stem and root. *Proc. roy. Soc. B.*, **95**, 109–131.

TUPPY H. & WILDNER G. (1965) Cytoplasmic transformation: mitochondria of wild-type baker's yeast restoring respiratory capacity in the respiratory deficient 'petite' mutant. *Biochem. Biophys. Res. Comm.*, **20**, 733–738.

TURING A.M. (1952) The chemical basis of morphogenesis. *Phil. Trans. B.*, **237**, 37–72.

UEDA R. & WADA M. (1964) Structure and development of the plastids in leaf epidermis. *Sci. Rep. Tokyo Kyoiku Diagaku*, **10**, 95–110.

VAN FLEET D.S. (1948) Cortical patterns and gradients in vascular plants. *Amer. J. Bot.*, **35**, 219.

VAN FLEET D.S. (1959) Analysis of the histochemical localization of peroxidase related to the differentiation of plant tissues. *Canad. J. Bot.*, **37**, 449–458.

VAN'T HOF J. (1965) Cell population kinetics of excised roots of *Pisum sativum*. *J. Cell Biol.*, **27**, 179–189.

VAN'T HOF J. (1966) Comparative cell population kinetics of tritiated thymidine-labeled diploid and colchicine-induced tetraploid cells in the same tissue of *Pisum. Exp. Cell Res.*, **41**, 274–288.

VAN'T HOF J. & SPARROW A.H. (1963) The effect of mitotic cycle duration on chromosome breakage in meristematic cells of *Pisum sativum*. *Proc. nat. Acad. Sci.*, **50**, 855–860.

VAN'T HOF J. & SPARROW A.H. (1965) Radiation effects on the growth rate and cell population kinetics of actively growing and dormant roots of *Tradescantia paludosa*. *J. Cell Biol.*, **26**, 187–199.

VAN'T HOF J. & YING H-K. (1964) Simultaneous marking of cells in two different segments of the mitotic cycle. *Nature, Lond.*, **202**, 981–983.

VIRGIN H.I., KAHN A. & WETTSTEIN D. von. (1963) The physiology of chlorophyll formation in relation to structural changes in chloroplasts. *Photochem. Photobiol.*, **2**, 83–91.

VOGEL A. (1960) Zur Feinstruktur der Drüsen von *Pinguicula*. *Beih. Z. Schweiz. Forst.*, **30**.

WADDINGTON C.H. (1963) Ultrastructure aspects of cellular differentiation. *Symp. Soc. exp. Biol.*, **17**, 85–97.

WALEK-CZERNECKA A. & KWIATKOWSKA M. (1961) Elajoplasty slazowatych (Elaioplastes chez les Malvacees) (+ French summary). *Acta Soc. Bot. Polon.*, **30**, 345–365.

WALKER D.G. & SEILIGMAN A.M. (1963) The use of formalin fixation in the cytochemical demonstration of succinic and DPN- and TPN-dependent dehydrogenases in mitochondria. *J. Cell Biol.*, **16**, 455–469.

WALLES B. (1963) Macromolecular physiology of plastids. IV. On amino acid requirements of lethal chloroplast mutants in barley. *Hereditas*, **50**, 317–344.

WANGERMANN E. (1965) Longevity and ageing in plants and plant organs. in 'Encyclopaedia of Plant Physiology'. Ed. Ruhland, **15/2**, 1025–1057.

WARDROP A.B. (1955) The mechanism of surface growth in parenchyma of *Avena* coleoptiles. *Amer. J. Bot.*, **3**, 137–148.

WARDROP A.B. (1959) Cell wall organization in higher plants. *Nature, Lond.*, **184**, 996–997.

WARDROP A.B. (1964) Structure and formation of cell wall in xylem. in 'The Formation of Wood in Forest Trees'. Ed. M.H. Zimmerman, New York & London, Academic Press, 87–134.

WARDROP A.B. & BLAND D.E. (1959) The process of lignification in woody plants. *Proc. IVth Internat. Congr. Biochem.*, *Vienna*, 92–116.

WARDROP A.B. & CRONSHAW J. (1958) Changes in cell wall organization resulting from surface growth in parenchyma of oat coleoptiles. *Aust. J. Bot.*, **6**, 89–95.

WARDROP A.B. & DADSWELL H.E. (1950) The nature of reaction wood. II. The cell wall organization of compression wood tracheids. *Aust. J. Sci. Res. B.*, **3**, 1–13.

WARDROP A.B. & DADSWELL H.E. (1955) The nature of reaction wood. IV. Variations in cell wall organization of tension wood fibres. *Aust. J. Bot.*, **3**, 177–189.

WARDROP A.B. & DAVIES G.W. (1962) Wart structure of gymnosperm tracheids. *Nature, Lond.*, **194**, 497–498.

WARDROP A.B. & FOSTER R.C. (1964) A cytological study of the oat coleoptile. *Aust. J. Bot.*, **12**, 135–141.

WARDROP A.B., INGLE H.D. & DAVIES G.W. (1963) Nature of vestured pits in angiosperms. *Nature, Lond.*, **197**, 202–203.

WARK M.C. (1965) Fine structure of the phloem of *Pisum sativum*. II. The companion cell and phloem parenchyma. *Aust. J. Bot.*, **13**, 185–193.

WARK M.C. & CHAMBERS T.C. (1965) Fine structure of the phloem of *Pisum sativum*. I. The sieve element ontogeny. *Aust. J. Bot.*, **13**, 171–183.

WARNER J.R., KNOPF P.M., & RICH A. (1963) A multiple ribosomal structure in protein synthesis. *Proc. nat. Acad. Sci., Wash.*, **49**, 122–129.

WATSON J.D. (1963) Involvement of RNA in the synthesis of proteins. *Science*, **140**, 17–26.

WEHRMEYER W. (1964) Über Membranbildungsprozesse in Chloroplasten. *Planta*, **63**, 13–30.

WEIER T.E., BISALPUTRA T. & HARRISON A. (1966) Subunits in chloroplast membranes of *Scenedesmus quadricauda*. *J. Ultrastr. Res.*, **15**, 38–56.

WEIER T.E., ENGELBRECHT A.H.P., HARRISON A. & RISLEY E.B. (1965) Subunits in the membranes of chloroplasts of *Phaseolus vulgaris*, *Pisum sativum*, and *Aspidistra* sp. *J. Ultrastr. Res.*, **13**, 92–111.

WEIER T.E. & STOCKING C.R. (1952) The chloroplast: structure, inheritance, and enzymology. II. *Bot. Rev.*, **18**, 14–75.

WEILING F. (1965) Zur Feinstruktur der Plasmodesmen und Plasmakanäle bei Pollenmutterzellen. *Planta*, **64**, 97–118.

WEINTRAUB M. & RAGETLI H.W.J. (1964) An electron microscope study of tobacco mosaic virus lesions in *Nicotiana glutinosa*. *J. Cell Biol.*, **23**, 499–509.

WETMORE R.H., DeMAGGIO A.E. & RIER J.P. (1964) Contemporary outlook on the differentiation of vascular tissues. *Phytomorph.*, **14**, 203–217.

WETMORE R.H. & RIER J.P. (1963) Experimental induction of vascular tissues in callus of angiosperms. *Amer. J. Bot.*, **50**, 418–430.

WETTSTEIN D. VON. (1961) Nuclear and cytoplasmic factors in development of chloroplast structure and function. *Canad. J. Bot.*, **39**, 1537–1545.

WEURMAN C. (1953) Pectinase inhibitors in pears. *Acta Bot. Neerlandica*, **2**, 107–121.

WEURMAN C. (1954) Pectase in Doyenne Boussoch pears and changes in the quantity of the enzyme during development. *Acta Bot. Neerlandica*, **3**, 100–107.

WHALEY W.G., DAUWALDER M. & KEPHART J.E. (1966) The Golgi apparatus and an early stage in cell plate formation. *J. Ultrastr. Res.* **15** 169–180.

WHALEY W.G., KEPHART J.E. & MOLLENHAUER H.H. (1964) The dynamics of cytoplasmic membranes during development. in 'Cellular Membranes in Development'. Ed. Locke, 135–173.

WHALEY W.G., MERICLE L.W. & HEIMSCH C. (1952) The wall of the meristematic cell. *Amer. J. Bot.*, **39**, 20–26.

WHALEY W.G. & MOLLENHAUER H.H. (1963) The Golgi apparatus and cell plate formation—a postulate. *J. Cell Biol.*, **17**, 216–221.

WHALEY W.G., MOLLENHAUER H.H. & KEPHART J.E. (1962) Developmental changes in cytoplasmic organelles. *Vth Internat. Congr. Electron Microscopy*, **2**, W12.

WHALEY W.G., MOLLENHAUER H.H. & LEECH J.H. (1960a) The ultra-structure of the meristematic cell. *Amer. J. Bot.*, **47**, 401–449.

WHALEY W.G., MOLLENHAUER H.H. & LEECH J.H. (1960b) Some observations on the nuclear envelope. *J. Biophys. Biochem. Cytol.*, **8**, 233–245.

WHEELER G.E. (1955) The effects of cell division on three-dimensional cell shape in *Aloe barbadensis*. *Amer. J. Bot.*, **42**, 855–865.

WHEELER G.E. (1962a) Polygonal aspects of cell faces. I. Pentagons and hexagons as prevailing types. *Amer. J. Bot.*, **49**, 246–252.

WHEELER G.E. (1962b) Polygonal aspects of cell faces. II. Quadrilaterals as the prevailing type. *Amer. J. Bot.*, **49**, 355–362.

WHITE D.J.B. (1965) The anatomy of reaction tissue in plants. in 'Viewpoints in Biology', Vol. 4. Ed. J.D. Carthy & C.L. Duddington, 54–79.

WIENER J., SPIRO D. & LOEWENSTEIN W.B. (1965) Ultrastructure and permeability of nuclear membranes. *J. Cell Biol.*, **27**, 107–117.

WILDON D.C. & MERCER F.V. (1963) The ultrastructure of the vegetative cell of blue-green algae. *Aust. J. Biol. Sci.*, **16**, 585–596.

WILKIE D. (1964a) 'The Cytoplasm in Heredity'. London, Methuen.

WILKIE D. (1964b) Aspects of the chemistry and inheritance of mitochondria. *Sci. Progr.*, **52**, 459–465.

WILLIAMS R.C. & WYCKOFF R.W.G. (1946) Applications of metallic shadow-casting to microscopy. *J. appl. Phys.*, **17**, 23–33.

WIMBER D.E. (1961) A synchronous replication of deoxyribonucleic acid in root tip chromosomes of *Tradescantia paludosa*. *Exp. Cell Res.*, **23**, 402–407.

WIMBER D.E. (1966a) Duration of the nuclear cycle in *Tradescantia* root tips at three temperatures as measured with H^3-thymidine. *Amer. J. Bot.*, **53**, 21–24.

WIMBER D.E. (1966b) Prolongation of the cell cycle in *Tradescantia* root tips by continuous gamma irradiation. *Exp. Cell Res.*, **42**, 296–301.

WIMBER D.E. & QUASTLER H. (1963) A ^{14}C and ^3H– thymidine double labeling technique in the study of cell proliferation in *Tradescantia* root tips. *Exp. Cell Res.*, **30**, 8–22.

S*

WIPF L. & COOPER D.C. (1940) Somatic doubling of chromosomes and nodular infections in certain leguminosae. *Amer. J. Bot.*, **27**, 821–824.

WOHLFARTH-BOTTERMANN K.E. (1964) Cell structures and their significance for ameboid movement. *Int. Rev. Cytol.*, **16**, 61–131.

WOLFE S.L. & HEWITT G.M. (1966) The strandedness of meiotic chromosome from *Oncopeltus. J. Cell Biol.*, **31**, 31–42.

WOODARD J., RASCH E. & SWIFT H. (1961) Nucleic acid and protein metabolism during the mitotic cycle in *Vicia faba. J. Biophys. Biochem. Cytol.*, **9**, 445–462.

WOODING F.B.P. & NORTHCOTE D.H. (1964) The development of the secondary wall of the xylem in *Acer pseudoplatanus. J. Cell Biol.*, **23**, 237–337.

WOODING F.B.P. & NORTHCOTE D.H. (1965a) Association of the endoplasmic reticulum and the plastids in *Acer* and *Pinus. Amer. J. Bot.*, **52**, 526–531.

WOODING F.B.P. & NORTHCOTE D.H. (1965b) The fine structure of the mature resin canal cells of *Pinus pinea. J. Ultrastr. Res.*, **13**, 233–244.

WOODING F.B.P. & NORTHCOTE D.H. (1965c) The fine structure and development of the companion cell of the phloem of *Acer pseudoplatanus. J. Cell Biol.*, **24**, 117–128.

YAMAMOTO T. (1963) On the thickness of the unit membrane. *J. Cell Biol.*, **17**, 413–422.

YASUZUMI G. & TSUBO I. (1966) The fine structure of nuclei as revealed by electron microscopy. III. Adenosine triphosphatase activity in the pores of nuclear envelope of mouse choroid plexus epithelial cells. *Exp. Cell Res.*, **43**, 281–292.

YOO B.Y. & BAYLEY S.T. (1967) The structure of pores in isolated pea nuclei. *J. Ultrastr. Res.*, **18**, 651–660.

YOTSUYANAGI Y. (1962) Études sur le chondriome de la levure. *J. Ultrastr. Res.*, **7**, 141–158.

YOTSUYANAGI Y. (1966) Un mode de différenciation de la membrane mitochondriale evoquant le mesosome bacterien. *C.R. Acad. Sci., Paris*, **262**, 1348–1351.

YOTSUYANAGI Y. & GUERRIER C. (1965) Mise en évidence par les techniques cytochimiques et la microscopie électronique d'acide désoxyribonucléique dans les mitochondries et les proplastes d'*Allium cepa. C.R. Acad. Sci., Paris*, **260**, 2344–2347.

ZIEGLER H. & LUTTGE U. (1966) Die Salzdrüsen von *Limonium vulgare*. I. Mitteilung die Feinstruktur. *Planta*, **70**, 193–206.

ZIEGLER H. & LUTTGE U. (1967) Die Salzdrüsen von *Limonium vulgare*. II. Mitteilung die Lokalisierung des Chlorids. *Planta*, **74**, 1–17.

ZIEGLER H. & RUCK I. (1967) Untersuchungen über die Feinstruktur des Phloems. III. Die 'Trompetenzellen' von Laminaria-Arten. *Planta*, **73**, 62–73.

Index

544   INDEX

Sugar 82, 277
Supernumerary chromosome 321-322, 325, 339
Surface area—volume ratio 42, 43, 47, 61
Surfaces of plants 275-280
Surface tension 47, 48, 51
Svedberg 35, 36, 494
Swanson C.P. 369
Swift H. 171, 316, 353, 358, 364, 382, 474
Symplastic growth 65, 66, 494
Synapsis 334, 494
Synchronous mitosis 350-351, 354, 359, 377-378
Synergid 308, 313, 440, 494
Szarkowski J.W. 77, 138

Tamarix 258, 424
Tamulevich S.R. 406
Tannin 82, 203, 213-214, 266, 399, 495
Tapetum 280-284, 310, 321, 383, 495
Tatum E.L. 471
Taylor J.H. 336, 338, 339, 361, 362, 364
Taylor M.M. 110
Tea 214
Tension wood 287-290
Terpene 99, 414, 495
Tertiray wall 285, 495
Tetrahymena 174, 175
Tetrakaidecahedron 51, 52, 53, 54, 55, 495
Tewari K.K. 126, 474
Thaine R. 72, 88, 96, 102, 406
Thielke C. 158, 464, 466
Thimann K.V. 65, 150, 231, 248, 295, 297
Thomas C.A. 24
Thompson D.W. 48, 50, 255
Thompson J. 371
Thomson W.W. 143, 144, 258, 423
Thornber J.P. 252, 428
Thylakoid 132, 134, 135, 137, 138, 145, 153, 155, 158, 461, 495
Thymidine 31, 126, 127, 128, 174, 175, 309, 314, 315, 336, 495
Thymine 112, 113, 495
Tilney-Bassett R.A.E. 150, 155, 157, 160, 459, 462, 464
Timber 212, 287, 288
Tinsley T.W. 267
Tomlin S.G. 303
Tonkinson S.M. 349, 370
Tonoplast 78, 82-88, 407-411, 495

Torrey J.G. 320, 379, 381, 382, 383, 389, 391
Torulopsis 167, 448
Torus 270, 273
Totipotency 380-382
Trabecula 285, 495
Tracheid 7, 45, 46, 65, 288, 426-438, 495
Tradescantia 234, 241, 247, 300, 309, 310, 327, 329, 339, 358, 360-361, 370, 373-375, 469
Transcription 112, 341-346, 365, 385-387, 388, 495
Transfer-RNA 113, 114, 130, 341, 344, 495
Translation 388, 495
Tree 39, 124, 287
Trianea 247
Tribondeau L. 371
Trichoblast 51, 63, 172, 318, 320, 393, 400, 495
Trichocyst 122, 202, 495
Trifolium 427, 428
Trillium 310, 322, 324
Trisomic 321
Triticum 79, 86, 91, 101, 108, 183, 222, 263
Tritium 30, 31, 444, 449, 495
Triturus 24, 119, 120
Trypanosome 310
Ts'o P.O.P. 108, 109, 111, 112
Tsubo I. 305
Tswett 32
Tulipa 213
Tumour inducing principle 394-395
Tupper-Carey R.M. 253
Tuppy H. 472
Turgor 60, 228, 275
Turing A.M. 45, 392, 393
Tylosis 274, 495

Ubisch body 281-284, 495
U.D.P.G. 142
Ueda R. 124
Ultra-violet 2, 8, 25, 171, 474, 496
Undulipodium 195, 496
Unit membrane 74-78, 83, 88, 91, 138, 162, 283, 496
Uracil 113, 115, 496
Ursolic acid 279

Vacuolaria 190
Vacuole 42, 44, 69, 82-88, 89, 142, 145, 191, 200, 398, 400, 417, 450, 496

Valonia 233
Van Fleet D.S. 392
Vansel C.H. 279
Van't Hof J. 350, 360, 363, 366, 370, 372
Variegation 464, 496
Vascular tissue 55, 496
Vatter A.E. 171
Vernalization 453
Vessel 67, 193, 274, 293, 296, 426-438, 441, 496
Vestures 273, 274
Vicia 61, 84, 85, 100, 104, 106, 128, 132, 136, 149, 191, 239, 240, 244, 264, 300, 309, 310, 313, 314, 315, 340, 345, 353, 358, 360-261, 364, 366, 369, 372-377, 429
Virgin H.I. 155
Virus 8, 10, 15, 16, 17, 24, 27, 35, 36, 42, 47, 80, 114, 130, 171, 176, 266-267, 387, 455-456, 467
Viscosity 70, 71, 82, 496
Viscum 262
Vitamin A. 193
Vitis 262, 266
Vitols E. 167, 448
Voeller B.R. 93, 186, 420, 421, 450
Vogel A. 399, 420
Vosa C.G. 327, 329

Wada M. 124
Waddington C.H. 300, 303
Waldner 21
Walek-Czernecka A. 145
Walker D.G. 164
Walker G.W.R. 462
Wall of cell 42, 69, 70, 95, 99, 203-297, 476
Wall, breakdown of 293-297, 412, 418, 421, 422, 435, 437
Walles B. 461
Wall extension 252-256
Walter F. 143
Wangermann E. 376
Wardrop A.B. 140, 161, 181, 233, 237, 239, 274, 285, 288, 290, 291, 398, 399
Wark M.C. 264, 285, 414
Warner J.R. 114
Warty layer 273, 274, 285, 286, 496
Watson J.D. 111
Wattiaux R. 193
Wax 203, 210, 214, 277, 279
Weatherley P.E. 413

Wehrmeyer W. 134, 137
Weier T.E. 138, 139, 144, 170, 463
Weight of cell 43
Weiling F. 274
Weintraub M. 130
Wetmore R.H. 389
Wettability 279
Wettstein D. von 155, 158, 160, 460, 461, 467, 468
Weurman C. 295
Whaley W.G. 78, 85, 88, 89, 90, 102, 183, 187, 192, 224, 225, 303, 305
Wheeler G.E. 54
White D.J.B. 287
Wiener J. 303
Wild A. 125
Wildman S.G. 71, 126, 674
Wildner G. 472
Wildon D.C. 139
Wilkie D. 472
Williams J.P. 132
Williams R.C. 10
Wimber D.E. 339, 358, 359, 373
Wipf L. 382
Wisse E. 163
Wohlfarth-Bottermann K.E. 72, 248
Wolfe S.L. 331, 333, 335
Wood 67
Woodard J. 364
Wooding F.B.P. 13, 90, 93, 99, 130, 177, 187, 190, 216, 217, 262, 277, 291, 293, 399, 407, 412, 414, 415, 426, 427, 428, 429, 431, 433
Woods P.S. 336
Work T.S. 176
Wounding 64, 216, 379, 394, 407, 412, 415, 447
Wyckoff R.W.G. 10

Xanthium 40
Xanthophyll 125, 155
Xanthoria 243, 249
Xenopus 314, 343, 363
Xerophyte 276, 496
X-ray 2, 496
X-ray diffraction 37-38
Xylan 284
Xylose 436
Xylem 41, 193, 382, 389, 426, 438, 496

Yamamoto T. 75
Yasuzumi G. 305
Yeadon A. 217